CORNERSTONE COURSE
FOURTH EDITION

Compiled by
WILLIAM CALLARMAN

University of Central Florida
College of Business Administration

McGraw-Hill Primis
Custom Publishing

Boston   Burr Ridge, IL   Dubuque, IA   Madison, WI   New York   San Francisco
St. Louis   Bangkok   Bogotá   Caracas   Lisbon   London   Madrid   Mexico City   Milan
New Delhi   Paris   Seoul   Singapore   Sydney   Taipei   Toronto

McGraw-Hill Higher Education

A Division of The **McGraw-Hill** Companies

CORNERSTONE COURSE

This book contains selected material from the following sources:

Behavior in Organizations: An Experimental Approach, Seventh Edition by A.B. (Rami) Shani and James B. Lau.
   Copyright © 2000, 1996, 1992, 1988, 1984, 1989, 1978, 1975 by The McGraw-Hill Companies, Inc.

Human Relations in Organizations: Applications and Skill-Building, Fifth Edition by Robert N. Lussier.
   Copyright © 2002, 1999 by The McGraw-Hill Companies, Inc.

Communicating in Business and Professional Settings, Fourth Edition by Michael S. Hanna and Gerald L. Wilson.
   Copyright ©1998, 1991, 1988, 1984 by The McGraw-Hill Companies, Inc.

Operations Management, Seventh Edition by William J. Stevenson. Copyright © 2002, 1998, 1995, 1992, 1988, 1985 by The McGraw-Hill Companies, Inc.

Organizational Behavior and Management, Sixth Edition by John M. Ivancevich and Michael T. Matteson.
   Copyright © 2002, 1999, 1996, 1993, 1990, 1987 by The McGraw-Hill Companies, Inc.

Management and Organizational Behavior, Third Edition by Curtis W. Cook, Phillip L. Hunsaker, Robert E. Coffey. Copyright © 2001, 1997, 1994 by The McGraw-Hill Companies, Inc.

Organizational Behavior, Fifth Edition by Robert Kreitner and Angelo Kinicki. Copyright © 2001, 1998, 1995, 1992, 1989 by The McGraw-Hill Companies, Inc.

Organizational Behavior by Steven L. McShane and Mary Ann Von Glinow. Copyright © 2000 by The McGraw-Hill Companies, Inc.

Business Communication: Building Critical Skills, by Kitty O. Locker and Stephen Kyo Kaczmarek.
   Copyright © 2001 by The McGraw-Hill Companies, Inc.

All reproduced with permission of the publisher.

1 2 3 4 5 6 7 8 9 0 QPD   QPD   0 9 8 7 6 5 4 3 2

ISBN 0-07-284729-8

Editor: Lynn Nordbrock
Production Editor: Lynn Nagel
Cover Photo: Richard Spencer
Manuscript Design: Jane Pope
Cover Design: Maggie Lytle
Printer/Binder: Quebecor World

Preface

PREFACE

In 1991, the UCF College of Business Administration faculty established a goal to deliver the best undergraduate business education in Florida. Since then, our faculty and staff have been hard at work building the nucleus of that education - a new curriculum.

We call it Business Education 2010 (BE2010).

BE 2010 is centered around four competencies identified through extensive research, consultation, lengthy discussions, and debates. This process led to:

1. the redesign of the core curriculum within the College of Business Administration and

2. the design of this new course - *The Cornerstone Course* - introducing those competencies.

The competencies of teamwork, communication, creative thinking, and adapting to change are the elements of *The Cornerstone Course* and are introduced in this textbook. The curriculum revision and this course are pioneering efforts - no other such course and integrated program of studies exists in collegiate business education today.

BE 2010 is a major breakthrough in competency-based business education, combining the four competencies with the concept of partnerships with representatives from the business community who have provided considerable input into the course in terms of time, effort, and materials. These partners may come into the classroom to address the application of the competencies in their organizations. Executives from companies such as *Darden Restaurants, AT & T, Disney World, Lockheed-Martin, Marriott, and IBAX*, have joined in the presentation of the competencies of teamwork, communication, creative thinking, and adapting to change respectively.

As a UCF Business student....

You will *learn* about these competencies in this course, *The Cornerstone Course* - taken during your first semester in the College. This course combines lectures by some of our very finest classroom teachers with learning exercises where you will be able to apply the new competencies and skills to real business problems. It also features the presentations by the corporate executives who have agreed to help us strengthen your educational experience from the outset.

You will then *apply* the competencies in other core curriculum courses including Quantitative Tools I and II, Management, Finance, Marketing, Legal and Ethics, Quality Management, and International Business.

You will *refine* your competencies in your major field - Accounting, Economics, Finance, Management, General Business, Hospitality Management, or Marketing.

You will *use* your competencies during formal internships with major corporations - our "placement service without walls."

And just before graduation, you will *demonstrate* those competencies in the Capstone Course, where the focus is bringing your competencies together, thinking strategically, and fine tuning your skills for success in the real world.

The identification of those four overall competencies was based on input from four College of Business Administration constituency groups - faculty, students, alumni, and business leaders. The following specific skills associated with each competency were also identified:

TEAMWORK...

College of Business Administration graduates must have an ability to:
- function effectively as a team member and understand group dynamics
- see the "big picture" in terms of the organization
- behave ethically and understand the concept of social responsibility
- serve as an effective team leader who provides vision and inspiration for the team

COMMUNICATION...

College of Business Administration graduates must have an ability to:

- communicate well orally
- communicate well in writing
- make clear and persuasive presentations
- negotiate effectively
- listen to the ideas and opinions of others

CREATIVE THINKING...

College of Business Administration graduates must have an ability to:

- solve problems and make decisions
- recognize and respond to opportunities
- think critically and analytically
- assume an integrative perspective with regard to the organization

ADAPTING TO CHANGE...

College of Business Administration graduates must have an ability to:

- recognize and adapt to change in a proactive manner
- manage for quality and continuous improvement
- understand the global environment
- respond to the changing needs of customers and clients
- capitalize on opportunities for life long learning
- manage resources effectively and efficiently with an appreciation for both short-term and long-term bottom-line results

This textbook, then, is designed to introduce the four competencies, present the specific skills associated with each competency, and lay the cornerstone upon which the competencies may be built.

As demonstrated by this sixth edition of the textbook, we believe in practicing the competency of adapting to change. The process of building a textbook is an ongoing process - we believe in continuous improvement.

NEW FEATURES OF THE SIXTH EDITION

1. One new chapter has been added to strengthen the competencies:

    · Communication Applications: Meetings - to provide understanding of how meetings can best be managed for effective communication.

2. New, updated chapters have been selected to ensure that students are receiving the "best" material available to get an up-to-date view of the competencies. Only two chapters remain from the previous edition. Eight of the new chapters were selected from material published in 2001. Six of the new chapters will appear in text books with 2002 publication dates.

3. The Cornerstone Course Web site is up and running to support faculty and students through the course in both the lecture and the labs.

4. An improved format of the book utilizing two colors to enhance readership.

Each of these changes has been made to ensure that The Cornerstone Course continues to provide all with a quality, practical approach to understanding and applying the four competencies.

ACKNOWLEDGMENTS

During the course of six editions, many individuals have been instrumental in the evolution of this book and I am extremely grateful to all. Special thanks go to the custom publishing unit of McGraw-Hill for all of their efforts in ensuring the success of this project, the students of *The Cornerstone Course* who are in no way reticent to provide input for continuous improvement, and to the various deans under whom I have served throughout this course.

Most important, though, to the success of *The Cornerstone Course* and this text are five lab instructors who keep me straight and provide significant insight into the overall project: Anke Arnaud, Lynn Becker, Leslie Connell, Bonnie McKay, and Linda Putchinski. Without their continued, long-standing, outstanding effort, this would not have been nearly as easy as it was. Thank you.

William G. Callarman
Orlando, Florida

Table of Contents

Part 1

Introduction to Teamwork

In the workplace, a new recognition and appreciation of individuals and groups is emerging. Effective organizations must pull together their human resources to forge a strong, viable organizational culture that emphasizes teamwork. In recent years, teamwork has become increasingly important to quality and effectiveness of organizations. With downsizing, rightsizing, and reengineering, organizations are changing dramatically. The pyramidal organization is giving way to the much reduced "pancake," with the elimination of numerous levels of structure. Organizations are redesigning relationships by creating work teams composed of teammates and coaches.

Teams are becoming an increasingly important organizational asset. Accordingly, managers are concerned with creating effective teams that make real contributions to the continuing success of the total organization. Effective organizations must help people understand how to work together and eliminate the barriers that separate functions within the organizations.

To create more effective teams, individuals must learn several key behaviors. First, they have to learn trust. Lack of trust is an obstacle to flexibility and information flow. Involvement is another key behavior for team effectiveness. Each team member's participation counts because these individuals are dependent upon each other, regardless of where they fit in the organization's hierarchy. Teams that are effective place emphasis on others' strengths, not weaknesses. Therefore, individuals must look for ways to cooperate, rather than compete, with each other. Team members must become good listeners and be willing to involve others in the decision-making process. They also must be both good leaders and good followers. Finally, everyone must be accountable and take personal responsibility for completing the team's tasks.

Individuals must learn to pull together in a team and focus on common goals. Therefore, Part 1 focuses attention on understanding teams and teamwork and the elements that are necessary for effective teams. This part begins with with Chapter 1 focusing on an understanding of building groups into teams. As teams develop and grow individuals exert power – power that comes from who they are and the position they hold in an organization. Accompanying that power is political activity. Power and politics then become an important element of teams that must be understood and managed if teams are going to be effective. Chapter 2 explores power and politics As teams work together, conflict will naturally arise. The impact of conflict and how to manage that conflict is an important element of successful teams and is presented in Chapter 3. Effective teams must have both effective leaders and followers. Leadership and followership are examined in Chapter 4.

Chapter 1

Teams and Teamwork

SOURCE: Robert Kreitner and Angelo Kinicki, *Organizational Behavior*, 5th ed., Chapter 13, © McGraw-Hill, 2001, 1998, 1995, 1992, 1989.

Learning Objectives

When you finish studying the material in this chapter, you should be able to:

- Explain how a work group becomes a team.

- Identify and describe the four types of work teams.

- Explain the ecological model of work team effectiveness.

- Discuss why teams fail.

- List at least three things managers can do to build trust.

- Distinguish two types of group cohesiveness, and summarize cohesiveness research findings.

- Define quality circles, virtual teams, and self-managed teams.

- Discuss what must be done to set the stage for self-managed teams.

- Describe high-performance teams.

---

www.monsanto.com

St. Louis—At Monsanto Co. headquarters here, Frederick Perlak and Kevin Holloway are "box buddies." They work in adjoining cubicles, share a secretary and spend hours keeping each other posted about what's happening with the company's global cotton team, which they oversee as co-directors.

"Often I'll lean over from my cubicle and say, 'Kevin, did you get this mail message? Have you discussed this? What did you guys decide on this?' " Dr. Perlak says. Adds Mr. Holloway, "It's not unusual we'll call each other at home or spend time together after hours."

Monsanto's three-year-old buddy system, known internally as "two in the box," pairs a scientist with a marketing or financial specialist in dozens of critical management positions. In the company's giant agricultural sector, for instance, 30 pairs of box buddies lead most of the crop and geographic teams. In the cotton division, the 45-year-old Dr. Perlak is a noted geneticist who has spent years researching bug-resistant crops, while Mr. Holloway, also 45, has a background in marketing, business and human resources.

Monsanto is betting this unusual structure will help it transform itself from a chemical conglomerate into a life-sciences powerhouse. By joining its commercial and research-and-development sides at the head, the company is seeking a jump-start in developing break-through genetic technologies and bringing them to market before competitors.

Chairman and CEO Robert B. Shapiro, the champion of two in the box, believes that any competitive edge Monsanto gains over its biotech rivals derives from just how effectively the R&D and commercial staffs work together. "We want to be creative, and we want to be fast," he says.

The fortunes of the paired individuals rise and fall together: Box buddies earn the same pay and benefits, including bonuses.

As co-equals, Messrs. Perlak and Holloway together make the key marketing and business decisions on global cotton matters. Twenty-seven associates report to them. "I'm never going to be a financial analyst or an MBA, and Kevin's most likely not ever going to be a molecular biologist. But our diversity of experience really makes us more effective because we can look at problems from very different perspectives," says Dr. Perlak, sitting next to his box buddy. The men are wearing identical dark-green sweaters with "Global Cotton Team" emblazoned on them.

"We're two people doing one job, not doing the same job, so we try not to step over each other," he adds. For instance, they try not to attend the same meetings, so Mr. Holloway may attend a marketing presentation while Dr. Perlak takes in a discussion about teaming up with a seed company. They then compare notes and decide which key decisions they must make jointly. . . .

In between meetings, they huddle for updates and align on positions to take in meetings that affect the cotton business. At day's end, they huddle again to share ideas, counsel each other and respond to electronic mail.

If either man is unavailable when a critical issue arises, the other makes the decision. "We don't want to hamper ourselves in the marketplace by not being able to make quick decisions," says Mr. Holloway. "It's not paralysis through analysis here." That was especially important last year, when Dr. Perlak spent about three months out of town testifying in three court cases for Monsanto. While they communicated by phone or e-mail, Mr. Holloway still had to take the lead on several important matters.

When they disagree, the weight falls on whoever has the expertise. . . .

Mr. Shapiro expresses some surprise at how well two in the box is working, noting that most box buddies "are strong personalities with powerful track records and, in many cases, with pretty large and not unreasonable ambitions." One concern, he says: "To what extent will the system be really collaborative, and to what extent will rivalry develop?"[1]

For Discussion

What is the likelihood of other big companies adopting this two-in-the-box approach to teamwork? Explain.

Teams and *teamwork* are popular terms in management circles these days. Cynics might dismiss teamwork as just another management fad or quick-fix gimmick. But a closer look reveals a more profound and durable trend. For instance, former English professor Martin Jack Rosenblum finds fulfillment in Harley-Davidson's motorcycle operations where teamwork is a central feature:

> What Rosenblum found at Harley was camaraderie, teamwork, and the sense of accomplishment that made him feel like a contributor to his microcosm. Says Rosenblum, a bearded long-hair who likes to wear snakeskin boots and cowboy shirts to his job as the archivist at Harley's Milwaukee headquarters: "For the first time in my life I feel like I'm part of a community. Harley is the university I've always been looking for."
>
> When Rosenblum was a professor at the University of Wisconsin, he hated all the politics and backstabbing and despaired at all the ineffectual intellectual banter. It was, he says, diametrically opposed to effective teamwork. During those years in the 1980s, he developed an ulcer that nearly killed him. But once he found a more open, goal-oriented environment at Harley, his life improved.[2]

The team approach to managing organizations is having diverse and substantial impacts on organizations and individuals. Teams promise to be a cornerstone of progressive management for the foreseeable future. According to management expert Peter Drucker, tomorrow's organizations will be flatter, information based, and organized around teams.[3] This means virtually all employees will need to polish their team skills. Southwest Airlines, a company that credits a strong team spirit for its success, puts team skills above all else. Case in point:

> Southwest rejected a top pilot from another airline who did stunt work for movie studios because he was rude to a receptionist. Southwest believes that technical skills are easier to acquire than a teamwork and service attitude.[4]

Fortunately, the trend toward teams has a receptive audience today. Both women and younger employees, according to recent studies, thrive in team-oriented organizations.[5]

Examples of the trend toward teams and teamwork abound. Consider this global sampling from the business press:

- *Siemens, the $63-billion-a-year German manufacturing company:* ". . . a new generation of managers is fostering cooperation across the company: They are setting up teams to develop products and attack new markets. They are trying hiking expeditions and weekend workshops to spur ideas and new work methods."[6]

- *Motorola's walkie-talkie plants in Penang, Malaysia, and Plantation, Florida:* "The goal, pursued by Motorola worldwide, is to get employees at all levels to forget narrow job titles and work together in teams to identify and act on problems that hinder quality and productivity. . . . New applicants are screened on the basis of their attitude toward 'teamwork.' "[7]

- *Fiat's new auto plant in Melfi, Italy:* "Fiat slashed the layers between plant managers and workers and spent $64 million training its 7,000 workers and engineers to work in small teams. Now, the 31 independent teams—with 15 to 100 workers apiece—oversee car-assembly tasks from start to finish."[8]

Table 1–1 The Evolution of a Team

A work group becomes a team when
1. *Leadership* becomes a shared activity.
2. *Accountability* shifts from strictly individual to both individual and collective.
3. The group develops its own *purpose* or mission.
4. *Problem solving* becomes a way of life, not a part-time activity.
5. *Effectiveness* is measured by the group's collective outcomes and products.

SOURCE: Condensed and adapted from J R Katzenbach and D K Smith, *The Wisdom of Teams: Creating the High-Performance Organization* (New York: HarperBusiness, 1999), p 214.

- *Ford Motor Company's product-development Web site:* "The Web brings 4,500 Ford engineers from labs in the United States, Germany, and England together in cyberspace to collaborate on projects. The idea is to break down the barriers between regional operations so basic auto components are designed once and used everywhere."[9]

All of these huge global companies have staked their future competitiveness on teams and teamwork.

Emphasis in this chapter is on tapping the full and promising potential of work groups. We will (1) identify different types of work teams, (2) introduce a model of team effectiveness, (3) discuss keys to effective teamwork— such as trust, (4) explore applications of the team concept, and (5) review team-building techniques.

WORK TEAMS: TYPES, EFFECTIVENESS, AND STUMBLING BLOCKS

Jon R. Katzenbach and Douglas K. Smith, management consultants at McKinsey & Company, say it is a mistake to use the terms *group* and *team* interchangeably. After studying many different kinds of teams—from athletic to corporate to military—they concluded that successful teams tend to take on a life of their own. Katzenbach and Smith define a **team** as "a small number of people with complementary skills who are committed to a common purpose, performance goals, and approach for which they hold themselves mutually accountable."[10] Relative to Tuckman's theory of group development —forming, storming, norming, performing, and adjourning— teams are task groups that have matured to the *performing* stage (but not slipped into decay). Because of conflicts over power and authority and unstable interpersonal relations, many work groups never qualify as a real team.[11] Katzenbach and Smith clarified the distinction this way: "The essence of a team is common commitment. Without it, groups perform as individuals; with it, they become a powerful unit of collective performance."[12] (See Table 1–1.)

When Katzenbach and Smith refer to "a small number of people" in their definition, they mean between 2 and 25 team members. They found effective teams to typically have fewer than 10 members. This conclusion was echoed in a survey of 400 workplace team members in the United States and Canada: "The average North American team consists of 10 members. Eight is the most common size."[13]

Table 1–2 Four General Types of Work Teams and Their Outputs

Types and Examples	Degree of Technical Specialization	Degree of Coordination with Other Work Units	Work Cycles	Typical Outputs
Advice Committees Review panels, boards Quality circles Employee involvement groups Advisory councils	Low	Low	Work cycles can be brief or long; one cycle can be team life span.	Decisions Selections Suggestions Proposals Recommendations
Production Assembly teams Manufacturing crews Mining teams Flight attendant crews Data processing groups Maintenance crews	Low	High	Work cycles typically repeated or continuous process; cycles often briefer than team life span.	Food, chemicals Components Assemblies Retail sales Customer service Equipment repairs
Project Research groups Planning teams Architect teams Engineering teams Development teams Task forces	High	Low (for traditional units) or High (for cross-functional units)	Work cycles typically differ for each new project; one cycle can be team life span.	Plans, designs Investigations Presentations Prototypes Reports, findings
Action Sports team Entertainment groups Expeditions Negotiating teams Surgery teams Cockpit crews Military platoons and squads	High	High	Brief performance events, often repeated under new conditions, requiring extended training and/or preparation.	Combat missions Expeditions Contracts, lawsuits Concerts Surgical operations Competitive events

SOURCE: Excerpted and adapted from E Sundstrom, K P De Meuse, and D Futrell, "Work Teams," *American Psychologist*, February 1990, p 125.

A General Typology of Work Teams

Work teams are created for various purposes and thus face different challenges. Managers can deal more effectively with those challenges when they understand how teams differ. A helpful way of sorting things out is to consider a typology of work teams developed by Eric Sundstrom and his colleagues.[14] Four general types of work teams listed in Table 1–2 are (1) advice, (2) production, (3) project, and (4) action. Each of these labels identifies a basic *purpose*. For instance, advice teams generally make recommendations for managerial decisions. Less commonly do they actually make final decisions. In contrast, production and action teams carry out management's decisions.

Four key variables in Table 1–2 deal with technical specialization, coordination, work cycles, and outputs. Technical specialization is low when the team draws upon members' general experience and problem-solving ability. It is high when team members are required to apply technical skills acquired through higher education and/or extensive training. The degree of coordination with other work units is determined by the team's relative independence (low coordination) or interdependence (high coordination). Work cycles are the amount of time teams need to discharge their missions. The various outputs listed in Table 1–2 are intended to illustrate real-life impacts. A closer look at each type of work team is in order.[15]

Advice Teams

As their name implies, advice teams are created to broaden the information base for managerial decisions. Quality circles, discussed later, are a prime example because they facilitate suggestions for quality improvement from volunteer production or service workers. Advice teams tend to have a low degree of technical specialization. Coordination also is low because advice teams work pretty much on their own. Ad hoc committees (e.g., the annual picnic committee) have shorter life cycles than standing committees (e.g., the grievance committee).

Production Teams

This second type of team is responsible for performing day-to-day operations. Minimal training for routine tasks accounts for the low degree of technical specialization. But coordination typically is high because work flows from one team to another. For example, railroad maintenance crews require fresh information about needed repairs from train crews.

Project Teams

Projects require creative problem solving, often involving the application of specialized knowledge. For example, Boeing's new 777 jumbo jet was designed by project teams consisting of engineering, manufacturing, marketing, finance, and customer service specialists. State-of-the-art computer modeling programs allowed the teams to assemble three-dimensional computer models of the new aircraft. Design and assembly problems were ironed out in project team meetings before production workers started cutting any metal for the first 777. Boeing's 777 design teams required a high degree of coordination among organizational subunits because they were cross functional.[16] A pharmaceutical research team of biochemists, on the other hand, would interact less with other work units because it is relatively self-contained.

Action Teams

This last type of team is best exemplified by a baseball team. High specialization is combined with high coordination. Nine highly trained athletes play specialized defensive positions. But good defensive play is not enough because effective hitting is necessary. Moreover, coordination between the manager, base runners, base coaches, and the bull pen needs to be precise. So it is with airline cockpit crews, hospital surgery teams, mountain-climbing expeditions, rock music groups, labor contract negotiating teams, and police SWAT teams, among others. A unique challenge for action teams is to exhibit peak performance on demand.[17]

This four-way typology of work teams is dynamic and changing, not static. Some teams evolve from one type to another. Other teams represent a combination of types. For example, consider the work of a team at General Foods: "The company launched a line of ready-to-eat desserts by setting up a team of nine people with the freedom to operate like entrepreneurs starting their own business. The team even had to oversee construction of a factory with the technology required to manufacture their product."[18] This particular team was a combination advice-project-action team. In short, the General Foods team did everything but manufacture the end product themselves (that was done by production teams).

Work Team Effectiveness:
An Ecological Model

The effectiveness of athletic teams is a straightforward matter of wins and losses. Things become more complicated, however, when the focus shifts to work teams in today's organizations.[19] Figure 1–1 lists two effectiveness criteria for work teams: performance and viability. According to Sundstrom and his colleagues: "*Performance* means acceptability of output to customers within or outside the organization who receive team products, services, information, decisions, or performance events (such as presentations or competitions)."[20] While the foregoing relates to satisfying the needs and expectations of outsiders such as clients, customers, and fans, another team-effectiveness criterion arises. Namely, **team viability,** defined as team member satisfaction and continued willingness to contribute. Are the team members better or worse off for having contributed to the team effort? A work team is not truly effective if it gets the job done but self-destructs in the process or burns everyone out.

Figure 1–1 is an *ecological* model because it portrays work teams within their organizational environment. In keeping with the true meaning of the word *ecology*—the study of interactions between organisms and their environments—this model emphasizes that work teams need an organizational life-support system. Six critical organizational context variables are listed in Figure 1–1. Work teams have a much greater chance of being effective if they are nurtured and facilitated by the organization. The team's purpose needs to be in concert with the organization's strategy. Similarly, team participation and autonomy require an organizational culture that values those processes. Team members also need appropriate technological tools and training. Teamwork needs to be reinforced by the organizational reward system. Such is not the case when pay and bonuses are tied solely to individual output.

Figure 1–1   An Ecological Model of Work Team Effectiveness

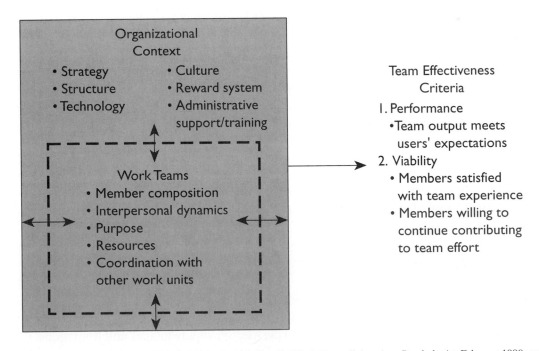

SOURCE: Adapted in part from E Sundstrom, K P De Meuse, and D Futrell, "Work Teams," *American Psychologist,* February 1990, pp 120–33.

Table 1–3	Characteristics of an Effective Team
1. Clear purpose	The vision, mission, goal, or task of the team has been defined and is now accepted by everyone. There is an action plan.
2. Informality	The climate tends to be informal, comfortable, and relaxed. There are no obvious tensions or signs of boredom.
3. Participation	There is much discussion, and everyone is encouraged to participate.
4. Listening	The members use effective listening techniques such as questioning, paraphrasing, and summarizing to get out ideas.
5. Civilized disagreement	There is disagreement, but the team is comfortable with this and shows no signs of avoiding, smoothing over, or suppressing conflict.
6. Consensus decisions	For important decisions, the goal is substantial but not necessarily unanimous agreement through open discussion of everyone's ideas, avoidance of formal voting, or easy compromises.
7. Open communication	Team members feel free to express their feelings on the tasks as well as on the group's operation. There are few hidden agendas. Communication takes place outside of meetings.
8. Clear roles and work assignments	There are clear expectations about the roles played by each team member. When action is taken, clear assignments are made, accepted, and carried out. Work is fairly distributed among team members.
9. Shared leadership	While the team has a formal leader, leadership functions shift from time to time depending on the circumstances, the needs of the group, and the skills of the members. The formal leader models the appropriate behavior and helps establish positive norms.
10. External relations	The team spends time developing key outside relationships, mobilizing resources, and building credibility with important players in other parts of the organization.
11. Style diversity	The team has a broad spectrum of team-player types including members who emphasize attention to task, goal setting, focus on process, and questions about how the team is functioning.
12. Self-assessment	Periodically, the team stops to examine how well it is functioning and what may be interfering with its effectiveness.

SOURCE: G M Parker, *Team Players and Teamwork: The New Competitive Business Strategy* (San Francisco: Jossey-Bass, 1990), Table 2, p 33. Copyright © 1990 by Jossey-Bass Inc., Publishers. Reprinted by permission of John Wiley &Sons, Inc.

Regarding the internal processes of work teams, five important factors are listed in Figure 1–1. Table 1–3 contains an expanded list of characteristics of effective teams that can be useful for evaluating task teams both in school and on the job.[21]

Why Do Work Teams Fail?

Advocates of the team approach to management paint a very optimistic and bright picture. Yet there is a dark side to teams.[22] While exact statistics are not available, they can and often do fail. Anyone contemplating the use of team structures in the workplace needs a balanced perspective of advantages and limitations. One dissenting opinion comes from Gerald A Kraines, head of a major management consulting company, who "denounces trends toward employee empowerment and work teams."[23] In a recent exchange with *The Wall Street Journal*, Kraines offered this unconventional view:

Q: Isn't hierarchy a dirty word these days?

A: This is the greatest disservice that business schools and the business media have perpetrated on the public. They say hierarchies stifle initiative, creativity, and job fulfillment. They say work groups should form and dissolve flexibly, and without regard to accountability.

The assumption is that employees would be so relieved to be freed from their chains of enslavement that they will act very responsibly and creatively. But they have been so discouraged, beaten, and demoralized that they essentially give up. Then the CEO says, "Poof, you're empowered." What people say, under their breath, is, "I haven't been empowered, I've been poofed."[24]

Team advocates may find these words harsh, but they challenge us to reject the myth that teams can magically replace traditional authority and accountability links. If teams are to be effective, both management and team members must make a concerted effort to think and do things differently.

Common Management Mistakes with Teams

The main threats to team effectiveness, according to the center of Figure 1–2, are *unrealistic expectations* leading to *frustration*. Frustration, in turn, encourages people to abandon teams. Both managers and team members can be victimized by unrealistic expectations.[25]

Figure 1–2   **Why Work Teams Fail**

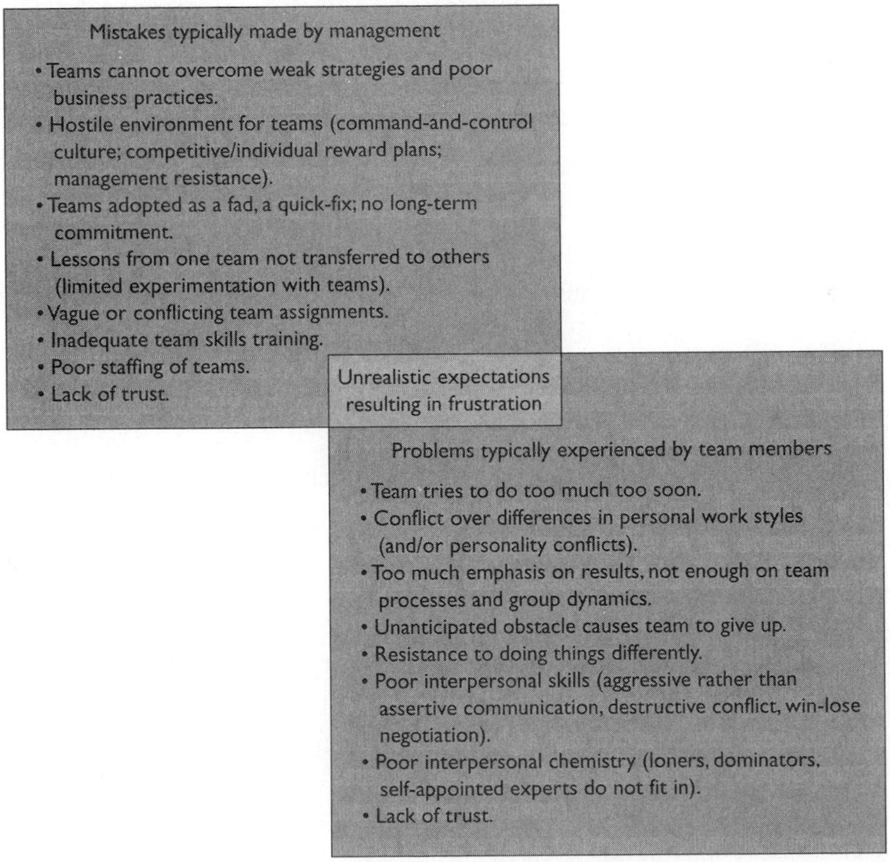

Mistakes typically made by management

- Teams cannot overcome weak strategies and poor business practices.
- Hostile environment for teams (command-and-control culture; competitive/individual reward plans; management resistance).
- Teams adopted as a fad, a quick-fix; no long-term commitment.
- Lessons from one team not transferred to others (limited experimentation with teams).
- Vague or conflicting team assignments.
- Inadequate team skills training.
- Poor staffing of teams.
- Lack of trust.

Unrealistic expectations resulting in frustration

Problems typically experienced by team members

- Team tries to do too much too soon.
- Conflict over differences in personal work styles (and/or personality conflicts).
- Too much emphasis on results, not enough on team processes and group dynamics.
- Unanticipated obstacle causes team to give up.
- Resistance to doing things differently.
- Poor interpersonal skills (aggressive rather than assertive communication, destructive conflict, win-lose negotiation).
- Poor interpersonal chemistry (loners, dominators, self-appointed experts do not fit in).
- Lack of trust.

SOURCES: Adapted from discussion in S R Rayner, "Team Traps: What They Are, How to Avoid Them," *National Productivity Review,* Summer 1996, pp 101–15; L Holpp and R Phillips, "When Is a Team Its Own Worst Enemy?" *Training,* September 1995, pp 71–82; and B Richardson, "Why Work Teams Flop—and What Can Be Done About It," *National Productivity Review,* Winter 1994/95, pp 9–13.

On the left side of Figure 1–2 is a list of common management mistakes. These mistakes generally involve doing a poor job of creating a supportive environment for teams and teamwork. Reward plans that encourage individuals to compete with one another erode teamwork. As mentioned earlier, teams need a good organizational life-support system.

Problems for Team Members

The lower-right portion of Figure 1–2 lists common problems for team members. Contrary to critics' Theory X contention about employees lacking the motivation and creativity for real teamwork, it is common for teams to take on too much too quickly and to drive themselves too hard for fast results. Important group dynamics and team skills get lost in the rush for results. Consequently, team members' expectations need to be given a reality check by management and team members themselves. Also, teams need to be counseled against quitting when they run into an unanticipated obstacle. Failure is part of the learning process with teams, as it is elsewhere in life. Comprehensive training in interpersonal skills can prevent many common teamwork problems.

Additional insights lie ahead as we turn our attention to cooperation, trust, and cohesiveness.

EFFECTIVE TEAMWORK THROUGH COOPERATION, TRUST, AND COHESIVENESS

As competitive pressures intensify, experts say organizational success increasingly will depend on teamwork rather than individual stars. If this emphasis on teamwork has a familiar ring, it is because sports champions generally say they owe their success to it. For example, teamwork is paramount to Mike Krzyzewski, coach of the two-time National Champion Duke University men's basketball team. Here's a brief exchange during a recent recruiting talk by "Coach K:"

> What makes your heart beat, a young man asks.
>
> "I love interacting with people," Krzyzewski replies. "I love molding a team, getting them to be as one."[26]

Whether in the athletic arena or the world of business, three components of teamwork receiving the greatest attention are cooperation, trust, and cohesiveness. Let us explore the contributions each can make to effective teamwork.

Cooperation

Individuals are said to be cooperating when their efforts are systematically *integrated* to achieve a collective objective. The greater the integration, the greater the degree of cooperation.

Cooperation versus Competition

A widely held assumption among American managers is that "competition brings out the best in people." From an economic standpoint, business survival depends on staying ahead of the competition. But from an interpersonal standpoint, critics contend competition has been overemphasized, primarily at the expense of cooperation.[27] According to Alfie Kohn, a strong advocate of greater emphasis on cooperation in our classrooms, offices, and factories,

> My review of the evidence has convinced me that there are two . . . important reasons for competition's failure. First, success often depends on sharing resources efficiently, and this is nearly impossible when people have to work against one another. Cooperation takes advantage of all the skills represented in a group as well as the mysterious process by which that group becomes more than the sum of its parts. By contrast, competition makes people suspicious and hostile toward one another and actively discourages this process. . . .

> Second, competition generally does not promote excellence because trying to do well and trying to beat others simply are two different things. Consider a child in class, waving his arm wildly to attract the teacher's attention, crying, "Oooh! Oooh! Pick me!" When he is finally recognized, he seems befuddled. "Um, what was the question again?" he finally asks. His mind is focused on beating his classmates, not on the subject matter.[28]

Research Support for Cooperation

After conducting a meta-analysis of 122 studies encompassing a wide variety of subjects and settings, one team of researchers concluded that

1. Cooperation is superior to competition in promoting achievement and productivity.

2. Cooperation is superior to individualistic efforts in promoting achievement and productivity.

3. Cooperation without intergroup competition promotes higher achievement and productivity than cooperation with intergroup competition.[29]

Given the size and diversity of the research base, these findings strongly endorse cooperation in modern organizations. Cooperation can be encouraged by reward systems that reinforce teamwork, along with individual achievement.

Another study involving 84 male US Air Force trainees uncovered an encouraging link between cooperation and favorable race relations. After observing the subjects interact in three-man teams during a management game, the researchers concluded: "[Helpful] teammates, both black and white, attract greater respect and liking than do teammates who have not helped. This is particularly true when the helping occurs voluntarily."[30] These findings suggest that managers can enhance equal employment opportunity and diversity programs by encouraging *voluntary* helping behavior in interracial work teams. Accordingly, it is reasonable to conclude that voluntary helping behavior could build cooperation in mixed-gender teams and groups as well.

A more recent study involving 72 health care professionals in a US Veterans Affairs Medical Center found a negative correlation between cooperation and team size. In other words, cooperation diminished as the health care team became larger.[31] Managers thus need to restrict the size of work teams if they desire to facilitate cooperation.

Trust

These have not been good times for trust in the corporate world. Years of mergers, downsizings, layoffs, bloated executive bonuses, and broken promises have left many employees justly cynical about trusting management. After conducting a series of annual workplace surveys, one management consultant recently concluded: "Trust in corporate America is at a low point."[32] Clearly, managers need to take constructive action to close what *Fortune* magazine has called "the trust gap."[33] General Electric's Jack Welch framed the challenge this way:

> Trust is enormously powerful in a corporation. People won't do their best unless they believe they'll be treated fairly—that there's no cronyism and everybody has a real shot. The only way I know to create that kind of trust is by laying out your values and then walking the talk. You've got to do what you say you'll do, consistently, over time.[34]

One encouraging sign: Interest in the topic of trust has blossomed recently in the management literature.[35]

In this section, we examine the concept of trust and introduce six practical guidelines for building trust.

A Cognitive Leap

Trust is defined as reciprocal faith in others' intentions and behavior.[36] Experts on the subject explain the reciprocal (give-and-take) aspect of trust as follows:

> When we see others acting in ways that imply that they trust us, we become more disposed to reciprocate by trusting in them more. Conversely, we come to distrust those whose actions appear to violate our trust or to distrust us.[37]

In short, we tend to give what we get: trust begets trust; distrust begets distrust.

A newer model of organizational trust includes a personality trait called **propensity to trust.** The developers of the model explain:

> Propensity might be thought of as the *general willingness to trust others.* Propensity will influence how much trust one has for a trustee prior to data on that particular party being available. People with different developmental experiences, personality types, and cultural backgrounds vary in their propensity to trust. . . . An example of an extreme case of this is what is commonly called blind trust. Some individuals can be observed to repeatedly trust in situations that most people would agree do not warrant trust. Conversely, others are unwilling to trust in most situations, regardless of circumstances that would support doing so.[38]

What is your propensity to trust? How did you develop that personality trait? (See the trust questionnaire in the Personal Awareness and Growth Exercise at the end of this chapter.)

Trust involves "a cognitive 'leap' beyond the expectations that reason and experience alone would warrant"[39] (see Figure 1–3). For example, suppose a member of a newly formed class project team works hard, based on the assumption that her teammates also are working hard. That assumption, on which her trust is based, is a cognitive leap that goes beyond her actual experience with her teammates. When you trust someone, you have *faith* in their good intentions. The act of trusting someone, however, carries with it the inherent risk of betrayal.[40] Progressive managers believe that the benefits of interpersonal trust far outweigh any risks of betrayed trust. For example, Michael Powell, who founded the chain of bookstores bearing his name more than 25 years ago, built his business around the principles of open-book management, empowerment, and trust. Powell's propensity to trust was sorely tested when one of his employees stole more than $60,000 in a used book purchasing scheme. After putting in some accounting safeguards, Powell's propensity to trust remains intact. He observed:

> The incident was a watershed for me and my staff, dispelling any naïveté we may have had about crime. We realized that not only *can* theft happen; it *will* happen. At the same time, dealing with the matter forced us to revisit our basic values and managerial philosophies. We believe that the modern demands of business call for an empowered and fully flexible staff, and we know that such a staff will often have to handle valuable commodities and money. We also believe that most people are not going to abuse our trust if they are put in a position with a reasonable amount of review and responsibility.[41]

How to Build Trust

Management professor/consultant Fernando Bartolomé offers the following six guidelines for building and maintaining trust:

1. *Communication.* Keep team members and employees informed by explaining policies and decisions and providing accurate feedback. Be candid about one's own problems and limitations. Tell the truth.[42]

2. *Support.* Be available and approachable. Provide help, advice, coaching, and support for team members' ideas.

3. *Respect.* Delegation, in the form of real decision-making authority, is the most important expression of managerial respect. Actively listening to the ideas of others is a close second. (Empowerment is not possible without trust.)[43]

4. *Fairness.* Be quick to give credit and recognition to those who deserve it. Make sure all performance appraisals and evaluations are objective and impartial.[44]

5. *Predictability.* As mentioned previously, be consistent and predictable in your daily affairs. Keep both expressed and implied promises.

6. *Competence.* Enhance your credibility by demonstrating good business sense, technical ability, and professionalism.[45]

Trust needs to be earned; it cannot be demanded.

Figure 1–3   Interpersonal Trust Involves a Cognitive Leap

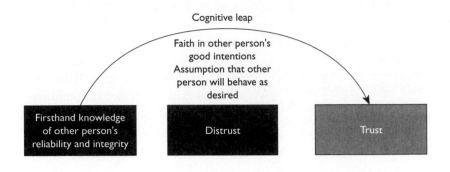

Cohesiveness

Cohesiveness is a process whereby "a sense of 'we-ness' emerges to transcend individual differences and motives."[46] Members of a cohesive group stick together. They are reluctant to leave the group. Cohesive group members stick together for one or both of the following reasons: (1) because they enjoy each others' company or (2) because they need each other to accomplish a common goal. Accordingly, two types of group cohesiveness, identified by sociologists, are socio-emotional cohesiveness and instrumental cohesiveness.[47]

Socio-Emotional and Instrumental Cohesiveness

Socio-emotional cohesiveness is a sense of togetherness that develops when individuals derive emotional satisfaction from group participation. Most general discussions of group cohesiveness are limited to this type. However, from the standpoint of getting things accomplished in task groups and teams, we cannot afford to ignore instrumental cohesiveness. **Instrumental cohesiveness** is a sense of togetherness that develops when group members are mutually dependent on one another because they believe they could not achieve the group's goal by acting separately. A feeling of "we-ness" is *instrumental* in achieving the common goal. Team advocates generally assume both types of cohesiveness are essential to productive teamwork. But is this really true?

Lessons from Group Cohesiveness Research

What is the connection between group cohesiveness and performance? A landmark meta-analysis of 49 studies involving 8,702 subjects provided these insights:

- There is a small, but statistically significant cohesiveness → performance effect.

- The cohesiveness → performance effect was stronger for smaller and real groups (as opposed to contrived groups in laboratory studies).

- The cohesiveness → performance effect becomes stronger as one moves from nonmilitary real groups to military groups to sports teams.

- Commitment to the task at hand (meaning the individual sees the performance standards as legitimate) has the most powerful impact on the cohesiveness → performance linkage.

- The *performance* → *cohesiveness* linkage is stronger than the cohesiveness → performance linkage. Thus, success tends to bind group or team members together rather than closely knit groups being more successful.

• Contrary to the popular view, cohesiveness is not "a 'lubricant' that minimizes friction due to the human 'grit' in the system."[48]

• All this evidence led the researchers to this practical conclusion: "Efforts to enhance group performance by fostering interpersonal attraction or 'pumping up' group pride are not likely to be effective."[49]

A second meta-analysis found no significant relationship between cohesiveness and the quality of group decisions. However, support was found for Janis' contention that *groupthink* tends to afflict cohesive in-groups with strong leadership. Groups whose members liked each other a great deal tended to make poorer quality decisions.[50]

Getting Some Positive Impact from Group Cohesiveness

Research tells us that group cohesiveness is no "secret weapon" in the quest for improved group or team performance. The trick is to keep task groups small, make sure performance standards and goals are clear and accepted, achieve some early successes, and follow the tips in Table 1–4. A good example is Westinghouse's highly automated military radar electronics plant in College Station, Texas. Compared with their counterparts at a traditional factory in Baltimore, each of the Texas plant's 500 employees produces eight times more, at half the per-unit cost:

> The key, says Westinghouse, is not the robots but the people. Employees work in teams of 8 to 12. Members devise their own solutions to problems. Teams measure daily how each person's performance compares with that of other members and how the team's performance compares with the plant's. Joseph L Johnson, 28, a robotics technician, says that is a big change from a previous hourly factory job where he cared only about "picking up my paycheck." Here, peer pressure "makes sure you get the job done."[51]

Self-selected work teams (in which people pick their own teammates) and off-the-job social events can stimulate socio-emotional cohesiveness.[52] The fostering of socio-emotional cohesiveness needs to be balanced with instrumental cohesiveness. The latter can be encouraged by making sure everyone in the group recognizes and appreciates each member's vital contribution to the group goal. While balancing the two types of cohesiveness, managers need to remember that groupthink theory and research cautions against too much cohesiveness.

TEAMS IN ACTION: QUALITY CIRCLES, VIRTUAL TEAMS, AND SELF-MANAGED TEAMS

All sorts of interesting approaches to teams and teamwork can be found in the workplace today. A great deal of experimentation is taking place as organizations struggle to be more flexible and responsive. New information technologies also have spurred experimentation with team formats. This section profiles three different approaches to teams: quality circles, virtual teams, and self-managed teams. We have selected these particular types of teams for three reasons: (1) They have recognizable labels. (2) They have at least some research evidence. (3) They range from low to mixed to high degrees of empowerment.

Table 1–4 Steps Managers Can Take to Enhance the Two Types of Group Cohesiveness

Socio-Emotional Cohesiveness
Keep the group relatively small.
Strive for a favorable public image to increase the status and prestige of belonging.
Encourage interaction and cooperation.
Emphasize members' common characteristics and interests.
Point out environmental threats (e.g., competitors' achievements) to rally the group.

Instrumental Cohesiveness
Regularly update and clarify the group's goal(s).
Give every group member a vital "piece of the action."
Channel each group member's special talents toward the common goal(s).
Recognize and equitably reinforce every member's contributions.
Frequently remind group members they need each other to get the job done.

As indicated in Table 1–5, the three types of teams are distinct, but not totally unique. Overlaps exist. For instance, computer-networked virtual teams may or may not have volunteer members and may or may not be self-managed. Another point of overlap involves the fifth variable in Table 1–5: relationship to organization structure. Quality circles are called *parallel* structures because they exist outside normal channels of authority and communication.[53] Self-managed teams, on the other hand, are *integrated* into the basic organizational structure. Virtual teams vary in this regard, although they tend to be parallel because they are made up of functional specialists (engineers, accountants, marketers, etc.) who team up on temporary projects. Keeping these basic distinctions in mind, let us explore quality circles, virtual teams, and self-managed teams.

Quality Circles

Quality circles are small groups of people from the same work area who voluntarily get together to identify, analyze, and recommend solutions for problems related to quality, productivity, and cost reduction. Some prefer the term *quality control circles*. With an ideal size of 10 to 12 members, they typically meet for about 60 to 90 minutes on a regular basis. Some companies allow meetings during work hours, others encourage quality circles to meet after work on employees' time. Once a week or twice a month are common schedules. Management facilitates the quality circle program through skills training and listening to periodic presentations of recommendations. Monetary rewards for suggestions tend to be the exception rather than the rule. Intrinsic motivation, derived from learning new skills and meaningful participation, is the primary payoff for quality circle volunteers.

The Quality Circle Movement

American quality control experts helped introduce the basic idea of quality circles to Japanese industry soon after World War II. The idea eventually returned to the United States and reached fad proportions during the 1970s and 1980s. Proponents made zealous claims about how quality circles were the key to higher productivity, lower costs, employee development, and improved job attitudes. At its zenith during the mid-1980s, the quality circle movement claimed millions of employee participants around the world.[54] Hundreds of US companies and government agencies adopted the idea under a variety of labels.[55] Dramatic growth of quality circles in the United States was attributed to (1) a desire to replicate Japan's industrial success, (2) America's penchant for business fads, and (3) the relative ease of installing quality circles without restructuring the organization.[56] All too often, however, early enthusiasm gave way to disappointment, apathy, and abandonment.[57]

Table 1–5 Basic Distinctions among Quality Circles, Virtual Teams, and Self-Managed Teams

	Quality Circles	Virtual Teams	Self-Managed Teams
Type of team	Advice	Advice or project (usually project)	Production, project, or action
Type of empowerment	Consultation	Consultation, participation, or delegation	Delegation
Members	Production/service personnel	Managers and technical specialists	Production/service, technical specialists
Basis of membership	Voluntary	Assigned (some voluntary)	Assigned
Relationship to organization structure	Parallel	Parallel or integrated	Integrated
Amount of face-to-face communication	Strictly face to face	Periodic to none	Varies, depending on use of information technology

But quality circles, if properly administered and supported by management, can be much more than a management fad seemingly past its prime. According to USC researchers Edward E Lawler and Susan A Mohrman, "quality circles can be an important first step toward organizational effectiveness through employee involvement."[58]

Insights from Field Research on Quality Circles

There is a body of objective field research on quality circles. Still, much of what we know comes from testimonials and case histories from managers and consultants who have a vested interest in demonstrating the technique's success. Although documented failures are scarce, one expert concluded that quality circles have failure rates of more than 60%.[59] Poor implementation is probably more at fault than the quality circle concept itself.[60]

To date, field research on quality circles has been inconclusive. Lack of standardized variables is the main problem, as it typically is when comparing the results of field studies.[61] Team participation programs of all sizes and shapes have been called quality circles. Here's what we have learned to date. A case study of military and civilian personnel at a US Air Force base found a positive relationship between quality circle participation and desire to continue working for the organization. The observed effect on job performance was slight. A longitudinal study spanning 24 months revealed that quality circles had only a marginal impact on employee attitudes but had a positive impact on productivity. In a more recent study, utility company employees who participated in quality circles received significantly better job performance ratings and were promoted more frequently than nonparticipants. This suggests that quality circles live up to their billing as a good employee development technique.[62]

Overall, quality circles are a promising participative management tool, *if they are carefully implemented and supported by all levels of management.*

Virtual Teams

Virtual teams are a product of modern times. They take their name from *virtual reality* computer simulations, where "it's almost like the real thing." Thanks to evolving information technologies such as the Internet, E-mail, videoconferencing, groupware, and fax machines, you can be a member of a work team without really being there.[63] Traditional team meetings are location specific. Team members are either physically present or absent. Virtual teams, in contrast, convene electronically with members reporting in from different locations, different organizations, and even different time zones (see the International OB 1-1).

Because virtual teams are so new, there is no consensual definition. Our working definition of a **virtual team** is a physically dispersed task group that conducts its business through modern information technology.[64] Advocates say virtual teams are very flexible and efficient because they are driven by information and skills, not by time and location. People with needed information and/or skills can be team members, regardless of where or when they actually do their work. On the negative side, lack of face-to-face interaction can weaken trust, communication, and accountability.

Research Insights

As one might expect with a new and ill-defined area, research evidence to date is a bit spotty. Here is what we have learned so far from recent studies of computer-mediated groups:

- Virtual groups formed over the Internet follow a group development process similar to that for face-to face groups.[65]
- Internet chat rooms create more work and yield poorer decisions than face-to-face meetings and telephone conferences.[66]
- Successful use of groupware (software that facilitates interaction among virtual group members) requires training and hands-on experience.[67]
- Inspirational leadership has a positive impact on creativity in electronic brainstorming groups.[68]

Practical Considerations

Virtual teams may be in fashion, but they are not a cure-all. In fact, they may be a giant step backward for those not well versed in modern information technology. Managers who rely on virtual teams agree on one point: *Meaningful face-to-face contact, especially during early phases of the group development process, is absolutely essential.* Virtual group members need "faces" in their minds to go with names and electronic messages (see the OB in Action Case Study at the end of this chapter). Additionally, virtual teams cannot succeed without some old-fashioned factors such as top-management support, hands-on training, a clear mission and specific objectives, effective leadership, and schedules and deadlines.[69]

Self-Managed Teams

Have you ever thought you could do a better job than your boss? Well, if the trend toward self-managed work teams continues to grow as predicted, you just may get your chance. Entrepreneurs and artisans often boast of not having a supervisor. The same generally cannot be said for employees working in organizational offices and factories. But things are changing. In fact, an estimated half of the employees at *Fortune* 500 companies are working on teams.[70] A growing share of those teams are self-managing, as exemplified by the following situations:

At a General Mills cereal plant in Lodi, California, teams . . . schedule, operate, and maintain machinery so effectively that the factory runs with no managers present during the night shift.[71]

[Teams of United Steel Worker's Union members] run Inland Steel Industries Inc. and Nippon Steel Corp.'s $1.1 billion joint venture in New Carlisle, Indiana—with no foremen. Workers share profits and production bonuses, and all make the same pay—about $50,000.[72]

www.shellglobalsolutions.com

International OB 1-1

A Virtual Shell Game for the Seven-Time-Zone Team

About the time the sun starts to go down in the Netherlands, Russ Conser's workday kicks into high gear. As a member of a team responsible for evaluating business opportunities for Shell Technology Ventures, a subsidiary of the oil giant Royal Dutch/Shell, Conser has been helping set up an office near The Hague. Thus far, much of his work has focused on hiring staff and figuring out the logistics of how to get the work done.

What often complicates Conser's day isn't so much the challenges that go along with opening a new office, it's keeping up with his team members—about half of whom are seven time zones away in Houston.

Conser and his colleagues rely heavily on E-mail and videoconferences to communicate with one another. But getting the right message to the right people on both sides of the Atlantic hasn't been easy. "We routinely find out we're miscommunicating, that we forgot to inform a person in the loop, that some people had different expectations as to what's going to happen," he says.

The time difference adds another wrinkle. "We have about a three-hour window each day when we can interact in real time," he explains. Consequently, phone conversations often extend into the night, when the Houston staff is at the office. Other times, the team members in the Netherlands have to wait until the sun comes up in Houston to get information they need. "When they get back to us, we've lost another day on the calendar," says Conser, who has been in the Netherlands since August.

Conser isn't alone in his struggle to communicate with colleagues an ocean away. Rather, he is part of a growing community of people who work as members of "virtual" teams, separated by time, distance, culture and organizational boundaries.

SOURCE: K Kiser, "Working on World Time," *Training*, March 1999, pp 29–30. Reprinted with permission from the March 1999 issue of Training magazine. Copyright © 1999, Lakewood Publications, Minneapolis, MN. All rights reserved. Not for resale.

At Texas Instruments' electronics factory near Kuala Lumpur, Malaysia, quality circles have evolved into a system made up almost entirely of self-managing teams:

> Daily administration, explains A. Subramaniam, [the factory's] . . . training manager, involves teams taking on routine activities formerly performed by supervisors. "Now," he says, "they are expected to take care of the daily operations like marking attendance, setup, control of material usage, quality control, monitoring cycle time, safety, and line audits." . . .
>
> Low Say Sun, training and development administrator, adds, "They [team members] are expected in daily management to detect abnormality and take corrective action as well as make improvements in their work area using problem-solving techniques and quality control tools. It will be just like running a business company. Of course," he adds, "there will be facilitators or managers whom they can turn to for help. In other words, there will be somebody to take care of the team. Training will be provided to enable them to manage their operation and process well."[73]

General Mills has found that, when it comes to management, less can mean more. At the Lodi plant, some of the self-managed teams have set higher production goals for themselves than those formerly set by management. Self-managed teamwork does have its price tag, however. "Training alone costs $70,000 per worker"[74] at the New Carlisle steel plant. Each team member at Texas Instruments' Malaysian facility undergoes 50 hours of intensive training in everything from quality control tools to problem solving to team building and communication.

This section explores self-managed teams by looking at their past, present, and future.

What Are Self-Managed Teams?

Something much more complex is involved than this apparently simple label suggests. The term *self-managed* does not mean simply turning workers loose to do their own thing. Indeed, as we will see, an organization embracing self-managed teams should be prepared to undergo revolutionary changes in management philosophy, structure, staffing and training practices, and reward systems. Moreover, the traditional notions of managerial authority and control are turned on their heads. Not surprisingly, many managers strongly resist giving up the reins of power to people they view as subordinates. They see self-managed teams as a threat to their job security.[75] Texas Instruments has constructively dealt with this problem at its Malaysian factory by making former production supervisors part of the all-important training function.

Self-managed teams are defined as groups of workers who are given administrative oversight for their task domains. Administrative oversight involves delegated activities such as planning, scheduling, monitoring, and staffing. These are chores normally performed by managers. In short, employees in these unique work groups act as their own supervisor.[76] Self-managed teams are variously referred to as semiautonomous work groups, autonomous work groups, and superteams. A common feature of self-managed teams, particularly among those above the shop-floor or clerical level, is **cross-functionalism.**[77] In other words, specialists from different areas are put on the same team. Amgen, a rapidly growing biotechnology company in Thousand Oaks, California, is literally run by cross-functional, self-managed teams:

> There are two types: product development teams, known as PDTs, which are concerned with everything that relates to bringing a new product to market, and task forces, which do everything else. The members of both come from all areas of the company, including marketing and finance as well as the lab bench. The groups range from five or six employees up to 80 and usually report directly to senior management. In a reversal of the normal process, department heads called facilitators don't run teams; they work for them, making sure they have the equipment and money they need. Teams may meet weekly, monthly, or whenever the members see fit.[78]

Among companies with self-managed teams, the most commonly delegated tasks are work scheduling and dealing directly with outside customers (see Table 1–6). The least common team chores are hiring and firing. Most of today's self-managed teams remain bunched at the shop-floor level in factory settings. Experts predict growth of the practice in the managerial ranks and in service operations.[79]

Historical and Conceptual Roots of Self-Managed Teams

Self-managed teams are an outgrowth of a blend of behavioral science and management practice.[80] Group dynamics research of variables such as cohesiveness initially paved the way. A later stimulus was the socio-technical systems approach in which first British, and then American researchers, tried to harmonize social and technical factors. Their goal was to simultaneously increase productivity and employees' quality of work life. More recently, the idea of self-managed teams has gotten a strong boost from job design and participative management advocates. According to their model, internal motivation, satisfaction, and performance can be enhanced through five core job characteristics. Of those five core factors, increased *autonomy* is a major benefit for members of self-managed teams. Three types of autonomy are method, scheduling, and criteria autonomy (see the OB Exercise). Members of self-managed teams score high on group autonomy. Autonomy empowers those who are ready and able to handle added responsibility. How did you score? Finally, the social learning theory of self-management has helped strengthen the case for self-managed teams.

The net result of this confluence is the continuum in Figure 1–4. The traditional clear-cut distinction between manager and managed is being blurred as nonmanagerial employees are delegated greater authority and granted increased autonomy. Importantly, self-managed teams do not eliminate the need for all managerial control (see the upper right-hand corner of Figure 1–4). Semiautonomous work teams represent a balance between managerial and group control.[81]

Table 1–6 Survey Evidence: What Self-Managing Teams Manage

Percentage of Companies Saying Their Self-Managing Teams Perform These Traditional Management Functions by Themselves.

Schedule work assignments	67%
Work with outside customers	67
Conduct training	59
Set production goals/quotas	56
Work with suppliers/vendors	44
Purchase equipment/services	43
Develop budgets	39
Do performance appraisals	36
Hire co-workers	33
Fire co-workers	14

SOURCE: Adapted from "1996 Industry Report: What Self-Managing Teams Manage," *Training,* October 1996, p 69.

OB Exercise   Measuring Work Group Autonomy

Instructions
Think of your current (or past) job and work groups. Characterize the group's situation by circling one number on the following scale for each statement. Add your responses for a total score:

Strongly   Strongly
Disagree   Agree
1 —— 2 —— 3 —— 4 —— 5 —— 6 —— 7

Work Method Autonomy
1. My work group decides how to get the job done.   _____
2. My work group determines what procedures to use.   _____
3. My work group is free to choose its own methods when carrying out its work.   _____

Work Scheduling Autonomy
4. My work group controls the scheduling of its work.   _____
5. My work group determines how its work is sequenced.   _____
6. My work group decides when to do certain activities.   _____

Work Criteria Autonomy10
7. My work group is allowed to modify the normal way it is evaluated so some
   of our activities are emphasized and some deemphasized.   _____
8. My work group is able to modify its objectives (what it is supposed to accomplish).   _____
9. My work group has some control over what it is supposed to accomplish.   _____

Total score   _____

Norms
 9–26 = Low autonomy
27–45 = Moderate autonomy
46–63 = High autonomy

SOURCE: Adapted from an individual autonomy scale in J A Breaugh, "The Work Autonomy Scales: Additional Validity Evidence," *Human Relations,* November 1989, pp 1033–56.

Figure 1–4   The Evolution of Self-Managed Work Teams

Traditional   Semiautonomous   Self-Managed
Work Groups   Work Groups   Teams

Managerial control of group's
structure, staffing, and
task procedures
                                          Group control of its own
                                          structure, staffing, and
                                          task procedures

Are Self-Managed Teams Effective? Research Evidence

As with quality circles and virtual teams, much of what we know about self-managed teams comes from testimonials and case studies. Fortunately, a body of higher quality field research is slowly developing. A review of three meta-analyses covering 70 individual studies concluded that self-managed teams had

- A positive impact on productivity.

- A positive impact on specific attitudes relating to self-management (e.g., responsibility and control).

- No significant impact on general attitudes (e.g., job satisfaction and organizational commitment).

- No significant impact on absenteeism or turnover.[82]

Although encouraging, these results do not qualify as a sweeping endorsement of self-managed teams. Nonetheless, experts say the trend toward self-managed work teams will continue upward in North America because of a strong cultural bias in favor of direct participation. Managers need to be prepared for the resulting shift in organizational administration.

Setting the Stage for Self-Managed Teams

Experience shows that it is better to build a new production or service facility around self-managed teams than to attempt to convert an existing one. The former approach involves so-called "green field sites." General Foods, for example, pioneered the use of autonomous work teams in the United States in 1971 by literally building its Topeka, Kansas, Gravy Train pet food plant around them.[83] Green field sites give management the advantage of selecting appropriate technology and carefully screening job applicants likely to be good team players.

But the fact is, most organizations are not afforded green field opportunities. They must settle for introducing self-managed teams into an existing organization structure.[84]

Making the Transition to Self-Managed Teams

Extensive *management training and socialization* are required to deeply embed Theory Y and participative management values into the organization's culture. This new logic necessarily has to start with top management and filter down. Otherwise, resistance among middle- and lower-level managers will block the transition to teams.[85] Some turnover can be expected among managers who refuse to adjust to broader empowerment. Both *technical and organizational redesign* are necessary. Self-managed teams may require special technology. Volvo's team-based auto assembly plant, for example, relies on portable assembly platforms rather than traditional assembly lines. Structural redesign of the organization must take place because self-managed teams are an integral part of the organization, not patched onto it as in the case of quality circles. For example, in one of Texas Instruments' computer chip factories a hierarchy of teams operates within the traditional structure. Four levels of teams are responsible for different domains. Reporting to the steering team that deals with strategic issues are quality-improvement, corrective-action, and effectiveness teams. TI's quality-improvement and corrective-action teams are cross-functional teams made up of middle managers and functional specialists such as accountants and engineers. Production workers make up the effectiveness teams. The corrective-action teams are unique because they are formed to deal with short-term problems and are disbanded when a solution is found. All the other teams are long-term assignments.[86]

In turn, *personnel, goal setting, and reward systems* need to be adapted to encourage teamwork. Staffing decisions may shift from management to team members who hire their own co-workers. A recent study of 60 self-managing teams involving 540 employees suggests how goal setting should be reoriented. Teams with highly *cooperative* goals functioned more smoothly and had better results than teams with competitive goals.[87] Accordingly, individual bonuses must give way to team bonuses. *Supervisory development workshops* are needed to teach managers to be facilitators rather than order givers.[88] Finally, extensive *team training* is required to help team members learn more about technical details, the business as a whole, and how to be team players. This is where team building enters the picture.

TEAM BUILDING

Team building is a catch-all term for a whole host of techniques aimed at improving the internal functioning of work groups. Whether conducted by company trainers or outside consultants, team-building workshops strive for greater cooperation, better communication, and less dysfunctional conflict. Experiential learning techniques such as interpersonal trust exercises, conflict-handling role play sessions, and interactive games are common. For example, Germany's Opel uses Lego blocks to teach its auto workers the tight teamwork necessary for just-in-time production.[89] In the mountains of British Columbia, Canada, DowElanco employees try to overcome fear and build trust as they help each other negotiate a difficult tree-top rope course.[90] Meanwhile, in the United States, the Target department store chain has its salesclerks learn cooperation and teamwork with this exercise: "employees linked in a human chain must each wriggle through two Hula-Hoops moving in opposite directions, without breaking the chain or letting the hoops touch the ground."[91] And in Prescott, Arizona, trainees at Motorola's Advanced Leadership Academy polish their teamwork skills by trying to make music with an odd assortment of percussion instruments.[92]

Rote memorization and lecture/discussion are discouraged by teambuilding experts who prefer this sort of *active* versus passive learning. Greater emphasis is placed on *how* work groups get the job done than on the job itself.

Complete coverage of the many team-building techniques would require a separate book. Consequently, the scope of our current discussion is limited to the goal of team building and the day-to-day development of self-management skills. This foundation is intended to give you a basis for selecting appropriate team-building techniques from the many you are likely to encounter in the years ahead.[93]

The Goal of Team Building: High-Performance Teams

Team building allows team members to wrestle with simulated or real-life problems. Outcomes are then analyzed by the group to determine what group processes need improvement. Learning stems from recognizing and addressing faulty group dynamics. Perhaps one subgroup withheld key information from another, thereby hampering group progress. With cross-cultural teams becoming commonplace in today's global economy, team building is more important than ever[94] (see the International OB 1-2).

A nationwide survey of team members from many organizations, by Wilson Learning Corporation, provides a useful model or benchmark of what we should expect of teams. The researchers' question was simply: "What is a high-performance team?"[95] The respondents were asked to describe their peak experiences in work teams. Analysis of the survey results yielded the following eight attributes of high-performance teams:

1. *Participative leadership.* Creating an interdependency by empowering, freeing up, and serving others.
2. *Shared responsibility.* Establishing an environment in which all team members feel as responsible as the manager for the performance of the work unit.

International OB 1-2

www.onepine.demon.co.uk/people.htm

The Wild World of Cross-Cultural Team Building

Brussels—Anyone can talk about cultural differences. Fons Trompenaars tries to make his students feel them.

To do that, the Dutch leader of workshops on "multicultural" management teaches his students (mostly executives) to play a game invented by one of his colleagues, L. J. P. Brug. The object: building towers made of paper.

Mr. Trompenaars, a 39-year-old former Royal Dutch/Shell executive, divides a group of several dozen Swedish managers into two groups. Four are designated as "international experts" in building paper towers. Everyone else becomes a native of a make-believe village called Derdia.

"Your culture loves towers but doesn't know how to build them," Mr. Trompenaars tells the Derdians. "It's a bit like the British car industry."

The experts are sent out of the room to learn to make paper towers and prepare to pass that skill on to Derdia. Meanwhile, Mr. Trompenaars initiates the Swedes into the strange customs of Derdia.

Derdians' greetings involve kissing one another on the shoulder. Holding out a hand to someone means "Please go away." If they disagree, Derdians say "Yes!" and nod their heads vigorously.

What's more, Derdian women have a taboo against using paper or scissors in the presence of men, while men would never use a pencil or a ruler in front of women.

The Swedes, reserved a moment ago, throw themselves into the task of acting like Derdians. They merrily tap one another, kiss shoulders and bray "Yessss!"

Soon, two "experts" are allowed back into the room for a brief study of Derdian culture. The Derdians flock to the experts and gleefully kiss their shoulders. The experts turn red. They seem lost already.

"Would you please sit?" asks Hans Olav Friberg, a young "expert" who, back home in Sweden, works for a company that makes flooring.

"Yessss!" the Derdians say in a chorus. But they don't sit down.

"Who is in charge here?" Mr. Friberg inquires. "Yessss!" the Derdians reply.

Mr. Friberg leaves the room to confer with his fellow experts. "They didn't understand us," he tells them. But fellow expert Hakan Kalmermo isn't about to be deterred by strange habits. He is taking charge. As he briskly practices making a paper tower, Mr. Kalmermo says firmly to the other experts: "The target is to have them produce one tower."

The four experts carry paper and other supplies to the adjoining room, now known as Derdia. They begin to explain the process to the Derdians very slowly, as if speaking to small children. When one of the Derdians shows he understands the workings of a scissors, Mr. Kalmermo exclaims: "Good boy!"

Although Mr. Kalmermo works hard at making himself clear, the Derdians' customs and taboos obstruct progress. The men won't use rulers as long as women are around but don't explain this behavior to the experts. The answer to every question seems to be "yes." At the end of 30 minutes, no tower has been completed.

The game is over; now comes the self-criticism. "They treated us like idiots," protests one of the Derdians.

The lessons are clear, but Mr. Trompenaars drives them home: If you don't figure out basics of a foreign culture, you won't get much accomplished. And if your biases lead you to think of foreign ways as childish, the foreigners may well respond by acting childish.

Still, Mr. Kalmermo, the take-charge expert, thinks his team was on the right track. "If we'd had another hour," he says, "I think we would have had 15 towers built."

SOURCE: B Hagerty, "Learning to Turn the Other Shoulder," *The Wall Street Journal*, June 14, 1993, pp B1, B3. Reprinted by permission of *The Wall Street Journal*, © 1993 Dow Jones & Company, Inc. All Rights Reserved Worldwide.

---

3. *Aligned on purpose.* Having a sense of common purpose about why the team exists and the function it serves.

4. *High communication.* Creating a climate of trust and open, honest communication.

5. *Future focused.* Seeing change as an opportunity for growth.

6. *Focused on task.* Keeping meetings focused on results.

7. *Creative talents.* Applying individual talents and creativity.

8. *Rapid response.* Identifying and acting on opportunities.[96]

These eight attributes effectively combine many of today's most progressive ideas on management,[97] among them being participation, empowerment, service ethic, individual responsibility and development, self-management, trust, active listening, and envisioning. But patience and diligence are required. According to a manager familiar with work teams, "high-performance teams may take three to five years to build."[98] Let us keep this inspiring model of high-performance teams in mind as we conclude our discussion of team building.

Developing Team Members' Self-Management Skills

A promising dimension of team building has emerged in recent years. It is an extension of the behavioral self-management approach. Proponents call it **self-management leadership,** defined as the process of leading others to lead themselves. An underlying assumption is that self-managed teams likely will fail if team members are not expressly taught to engage in self-management behaviors. This makes sense because it is unreasonable to expect employees who are accustomed to being managed and led to suddenly manage and lead themselves. Transition training is required, as discussed in the prior section. A key transition to self-management involves *current managers* engaging in self-management leadership behaviors. This is team building in the fullest meaning of the term.

Six self-management leadership behaviors were isolated in a field study of a manufacturing company organized around self-managed teams. The observed behaviors were:

1. *Encourages self-reinforcement* (e.g., getting team members to praise each other for good work and results).

2. *Encourages self-observation/evaluation* (e.g., teaching team members to judge how well they are doing).

3. *Encourages self-expectation* (e.g., encouraging team members to expect high performance from themselves and the team).

4. *Encourages self-goal-setting* (e.g., having the team set its own performance goals).

5. *Encourages rehearsal* (e.g., getting team members to think about and practice new tasks).

6. *Encourages self-criticism* (e.g., encouraging team members to be critical of their own poor performance).[99]

According to the researchers, Charles Manz and Henry Sims, this type of leadership is a dramatic departure from traditional practices such as giving orders and/or making sure everyone gets along. Empowerment, not domination, is the overriding goal.

SUMMARY OF KEY CONCEPTS

1. *Explain how a work group becomes a team.* A team is a mature group where leadership is shared, accountability is both individual and collective, the members have developed their own purpose, problem solving is a way of life, and effectiveness is measured by collective outcomes.

2. *Identify and describe the four types of work teams.* Four general types of work teams are advice, production, project, and action teams. Each type has its characteristic degrees of specialization and coordination, work cycle, and outputs.

3. *Explain the ecological model of work team effectiveness.* According to the ecological model, two effectiveness criteria for work teams are performance and viability. The performance criterion is met if the group satisfies its clients/customers. A work group is viable if its members are satisfied and continue contributing. An ecological perspective is appropriate because work groups require an organizational life-support system. For instance, group participation is enhanced by an organizational culture that values employee empowerment.

4. *Discuss why teams fail.* Teams fail because unrealistic expectations cause frustration and failure. Common management mistakes include weak strategies, creating a hostile environment for teams, faddish use of teams, not learning from team experience, vague team assignments, poor team staffing, inadequate training, and lack of trust. Team members typically try too much too soon, experience conflict over differing work styles and personalities, ignore important group dynamics, resist change, exhibit poor interpersonal skills and chemistry, and display a lack of trust.

5. *List at least three things managers can do to build trust.* Six recommended ways to build trust are through communication, support, respect (especially delegation), fairness, predictability, and competence.

6. *Distinguish two types of group cohesiveness, and summarize cohesiveness research findings.* Cohesive groups have a shared sense of togetherness or a "we" feeling. Socio-emotional cohesiveness involves emotional satisfaction. Instrumental cohesiveness involves goal-directed togetherness. There is a small but significant relationship between cohesiveness and performance. The effect is stronger for smaller groups. Commitment to task among group members strengthens the cohesiveness → performance linkage. Success can build group cohesiveness. Cohesiveness is not a cure-all for group problems. Too much cohesiveness can lead to groupthink.

7. *Define quality circles, virtual teams, and self-managed teams.* Quality circles are small groups of volunteers who meet regularly to solve quality-related problems in their work area. Virtual teams are physically dispersed work groups that conduct their business via modern information technologies such as the Internet, E-mail, and videoconferences. Self-managed teams are work groups that perform their own administrative chores such as planning, scheduling, and staffing.

8. *Discuss what must be done to set the stage for self-managed teams.* Management must embed a new Theory Y logic in the organization's culture. Technology and the organization need to be redesigned to accommodate self-managed teams. Personnel changes, goals, and reward systems that reinforce cooperation and teamwork are necessary. Supervisory training helps managers learn to be facilitators rather than traditional order givers. Team members need lots of training and team building to make them cooperative team players.

9. *Describe high-performance teams.* Eight attributes of high-performance teams are (*a*) participative leadership, (*b*) shared responsibility, (*c*) aligned on purpose, (*d*) high communication, (*e*) future focused for growth, (*f*) focused on task, (*g*) creative talents applied, and (*h*) rapid response.

DISCUSSION QUESTIONS

1. Do you agree or disagree with Drucker's vision of more team-oriented organizations? Explain your assumptions and reasoning.

2. Which of the factors listed in Table 1–1 is most crucial to a successful team? Explain.

3. Why bother taking an ecological perspective of work team effectiveness?

4. In your personal friendships, how do you come to trust someone? How fragile is that trust? Explain.

5. Why is delegation so important to building organizational trust?

6. Why should a group leader strive for both socio-emotional and instrumental cohesiveness?

7. Are virtual teams likely to be just a passing fad? Why or why not?

8. Would you like to work on a self-managed team? Explain.

9. How would you respond to a manager who said, "Why should I teach my people to manage themselves and work myself out of a job?"

10. Have you ever been a member of a high-performing team? If so, explain the circumstances and success factors.

INTERNET EXERCISE

www.briefings.com
www.akgroup.com

As covered in this chapter, teams are the organizational unit of choice today. Auto companies have design and production teams. Hospitals have patient care teams. Team policing is practiced by many law enforcement agencies. Airlines have ground crew teams. Current and future managers (indeed, all employees) need to know as much as possible about teams and teamwork. The purpose of this exercise is to continue building your knowledge of workplace teams and to assess your readiness for Internet-age teamwork.

Instructive Updates on Teams and Teamwork
Start with the home page of Briefings Publishing Group (www.briefings.com), and select the navigation tab "Team Management." At the "Team Management Briefings" page, click on topics from the latest issue that seem relevant and interesting. Next, select relevant categories in the TMB archives menu for helpful advice and tips. This is quick reading intended for busy managers.

A Free Virtual Team Readiness Questionnaire
Virtual teams, where members attempt to complete projects despite being geographically dispersed, will grow more common as advanced computer networks and communication technologies becomes even more sophisticated. Are you (and your organization) ready to work in this sort of electronically connected team environment? You can find out, thanks to the Web site of The Applied Knowledge Group, a consulting company. Call up their home page (www.akgroup.com), and select "Assessment Tool" from the main menu. (Note: Our use of this questionnaire is for instructional purposes only and does not constitute an endorsement of any products that may or may not suit your needs. There is no obligation to buy anything.) Complete the single organizational question (for your current or past employer), complete the next 25 individual questions, and then click on the "Score Test" button. You will be given a virtual team readiness score and a brief interpretation. A personal copy of the questionnaire and results can be printed, if you desire.

Questions

1. If you consulted the Team Management Briefings, what useful ideas, advice, or tips did you pick up?

2. What are your main concerns about today's rush to adopt team-based organizations?

3. How did you score on the Virtual Team Readiness questionnaire? Did you score higher or lower than you might have expected? What are the practical implications of your score?

4. Regarding the first response category on the questionnaire, is your target organization an appropriate place for virtual teams? Explain.

OB IN ACTION CASE STUDY

With the Stakes High, A Lucent Duo Conquers Distance and Culture[100]

Imagine designing the most complex product in your company's history. You need 500 engineers for the job. They will assemble the world's most delicate hardware and write more than a million lines of code. In communicating, the margin for error is minuscule.

Now, scatter those 500 engineers over 13 time zones. Over three continents. Over five states in the United States alone. The Germans schedule to perfection. The Americans work on the fly. In Massachusetts, they go to work early. In New Jersey, they stay late.

Now you have some idea of what Bill Klinger and Frank Polito have been through in the past 18 months. As top software-development managers in Lucent Technologies' Bell Labs division, they played critical roles in creating a new fiber-optic phone switch called the Bandwidth Manager, which sells for about $1 million, the kind of global product behind the company's surging earnings. The high-stakes development was Lucent's most complex undertaking by far since its spin-off from AT&T in 1996.

Managing such a far-flung staff ("distributed development," it's called) is possible only because of technology. But as the two Lucent leaders painfully learned, distance still magnifies differences, even in a high-tech age. "You lose informal interaction—going to lunch, the water cooler," Mr. Klinger says. "You can never discount how many issues get solved that way."

The product grew as a hybrid of exotic, widely dispersed technologies: "light-wave" science from Lucent's Merrimack Valley plant, north of Boston, where Mr. Polito works; "cross-connect" products here in New Jersey, where Mr. Klinger works; timing devices from the Netherlands; and optics from Germany.

Development also demanded multiple locations because Lucent wanted a core model as a platform for special versions for foreign and other niche markets. Involving overseas engineers in the flagship product would speed the later development of spinoffs and impress foreign customers.

And rushing to market meant tapping software talent wherever it was available—ultimately at Lucent facilities in Colorado, Illinois, North Carolina, and India. "The scary thing, scary but exciting, was that no one had really pulled this off on this scale before," says Mr. Polito.

Communication technology was the easy part. Lashing together big computers in different cities assured everyone was working on the same up-to-date software version. New project data from one city were instantly available on Web pages everywhere else. Test engineers in India could tweak prototypes in New Jersey. The project never went to sleep.

Technology, however, couldn't conquer cultural problems, especially acute between Messrs. Klinger's and Polito's respective staffs in New Jersey and Massachusetts. Each had its own programming traditions and product histories. Such basic words as "test" could mean different things. A programming chore requiring days in one context might take weeks in another. Differing work schedules and physical distance made each location suspect the other of slacking off. "We had such clashes," says Mr. Klinger.

Personality tests revealed deep geographic differences. Supervisors from the sleek, glass-covered New Jersey office, principally a research facility abounding in academics, scored as "thinking" people who used cause-and-effect analysis. Those from the old, brick facility in Massachusetts, mainly a manufacturing plant, scored as "feeling" types who based decisions on subjective, human values. Sheer awareness of the differences ("Now I know why you get on my nerves!") began to create common ground.

Amid much cynicism, the two directors hauled their technical managers into team exercises—working in small groups to scale a 14-foot wall and solve puzzles. It's corny, but such methods can accelerate trust-building when time is short and the stakes are high. At one point Mr. Klinger asked managers to show up with the product manuals from their previous projects—then, in a ritualistic break from technical parochialism, instructed everyone to tear the covers to pieces.

More than anything else, it was sheer physical presence—face time—that began solidifying the group. Dozens of managers began meeting fortnightly in rotating cities, socializing as much time as their technical discussions permitted. (How better to grow familiar than over hot dogs, beer, and nine innings with the minor league Durham Bulls?) Foreign locations found the direct interaction especially valuable. "Going into the other culture is the only way to understand it," says Sigrid Hauenstein, a Lucent executive in Nuremberg, Germany. "If you don't have a common understanding, it's much more expensive to correct it later."

Eventually the project found its pace. People began wearing beepers to eliminate time wasted on voice-mail tag. Conference calls at varying levels kept everyone in the loop. Staffers posted their photos in the project's Web directory. Many created personal pages. "It's the ultimate democracy of the Web," Mr. Klinger says.

The product is now shipping—on schedule, within budget, and with more technical versatility than Lucent expected. Distributed development "paid off in spades," says Gerry Butters, Lucent optical-networking chief.

Even as it helps build the infrastructure of a digitally connected planet, Lucent is rediscovering the importance of face-to-face interaction. All the bandwidth in the world can convey only a fraction of what we are.

Questions for Discussion

1. Could the 500 Lucent engineers who worked on the Bandwidth Manager project be called a *team?* Why or why not? Could Bill Klinger and Frank Polito be called a team? Explain.

2. What role, if any, did trust play in this case?

3. What lessons about managing virtual teams does this case teach us?

4. Which of the eight attributes of high-performance teams are evident in this case?

5. Based on what you have read, what was the overriding key to success in this case?

PERSONAL AWARENESS AND GROWTH EXERCISE

How Trusting Are You?

Objectives

1. To introduce you to different dimensions of interpersonal trust.

2. To measure your trust in another person.

3. To discuss the managerial implications of your propensity to trust.

Introduction

The trend toward more open and empowered organizations where teamwork and self-management are vital requires heightened interpersonal trust. Customers need to be able to trust organizations producing the goods and services they buy, managers need to trust nonmanagers to carry out the organization's mission, and team members need to trust each other in order to get the job done. As with any other interpersonal skill, we need to be able to measure and improve our ability to trust others. This exercise is a step in that direction.

Instructions[101]

Think of a specific individual who currently plays an important role in your life (e.g., current or future spouse, friend, supervisor, co-worker, team member, etc.), and rate his or her trustworthiness for each statement according to the following scale. Total your responses, and compare your score with the arbitrary norms provided.

Strongly   **Strongly**
Disagree   **Agree**
1   ----   2   ----   3   ----   4   ----   5   ----   6   ----   7   ----   8   ----   9   ----   10

Overall Trust   *Score*

1. I can expect this person to play fair.   _____
2. I can confide in this person and know she/he desires to listen.   _____
3. I can expect this person to tell me the truth.   _____
4. This person takes time to listen to my problems and worries.   _____

Emotional Trust

5. This person would never intentionally misrepresent my point of view to other people.   _____
6. I can confide in this person and know that he/she will not discuss it with others.   _____
7. This person responds constructively and caringly to my problems.   _____

Reliableness

8. If this person promised to do me a favor, she/he would carry out that promise.   _____
9. If I had an appointment with this person, I could count on him/her showing up.   _____
10. I could lend this person money and count on getting it back as soon as possible.   _____
11. I do not need a backup plan because I know this person will come through for me.   _____

Total score   _____

Trustworthiness Scale

77–110 = High (Trust is a precious thing.)
45–76   = Moderate (Be careful; get a rearview mirror.)
11–44   = Low (Lock up your valuables!)

Questions for Discussion

1. Which particular items in this trust questionnaire are most central to your idea of trust? Why?

2. Does your score accurately depict the degree to which you trust (or distrust) the target person?

3. Why do you trust (or distrust) this individual?

4. If you trust this person to a high degree, how hard was it to build that trust? Explain. What would destroy that trust?

5. Based on your responses to this questionnaire, how would you rate your "propensity to trust"? Low? Moderate? High?

6. What are the managerial implications of your propensity to trust?

GROUP EXERCISE

Student Team Development Project

Objectives

1. To help you better understand the components of teamwork.

2. To give you a practical diagnostic tool to assess the need for team building.

3. To give you a chance to evaluate and develop an actual group/team.

Introduction

Student teams are very common in today's college classrooms. They are an important part of the move toward cooperative and experiential learning. In other words, learning by doing. Group dynamics and teamwork are best learned by doing. Unfortunately, many classroom teams wallow in ambiguity, conflict, and ineffectiveness. This team development questionnaire can play an important role in the life cycle of your classroom team or group. All members of your team can complete this evaluation at one or more of the following critical points in your team's life cycle: (1) when the team reaches a crisis point and threatens to break up, (2) about halfway through the life of the team, and (3) at the end of the team's life cycle. Discussion of the results by all team members can enhance the group's learning experience.

Instructions[102]

Either at the prompting of your instructor or by group consensus, decide at what point in your team's life cycle this exercise should be completed. *Tip:* Have each team member write their responses to the 10 items on a sheet of paper with no names attached. This will permit the calculation of a group mean score for each item and for all 10 items. Attention should then turn to the discussion questions provided to help any team development problems surface and to point the way toward solutions.

(An alternative to these instructions is to evaluate a team or work group you are associated with in your current job. You may also draw from a group experience in a past job.)

1. To what extent do I feel a real part of the team?

5	4	3	2	1
Completely a part all the time.	A part most of the time.	On the edge— sometimes in, sometimes out.	Generally outside except for one or two short periods.	On the outside, not really a part of the team.

2. How safe is it in this team to be at ease, relaxed, and myself?

5	4	3	2	1
I feel perfectly safe to be myself; they won't hold mistakes against me.	I feel most people would accept me if I were completely myself, but there are some I am not sure about.	Generally one has to be careful what one says or does in this team.	I am quite fearful about being completely myself in this team.	I am not a fool; I would never be myself in this team.

3. To what extent do I feel "under wraps," that is, have private thoughts, unspoken reservations, or unexpressed feelings and opinions that I have not felt comfortable bringing out into the open?

1	2	3	4	5
Almost completely under wraps.	Under wraps many times.	Slightly more free and expressive than under wraps.	Quite free and expressive much of the time.	Almost completely free and expressive.

4. How effective are we, in our team, in getting out and using the ideas, opinions, and information of all team members in making decisions?

1	2	3	4	5
We don't really encourage everyone to share their ideas, opinions, and information with the team in making decisions.	Only the ideas, opinions, and information of a few members are really known and used in making decisions.	Sometimes we hear the views of most members before making decisions, and sometimes we disregard most members.	A few are sometimes hesitant about sharing their opinions, but we generally have good participation in making decisions.	Everyone feels his or her ideas, opinions, and information are given a fair hearing before decisions are made.

5. To what extent are the goals the team is working toward understood, and to what extent do they have meaning for you?

5	4	3	2	1
I feel extremely good about the goals of our team.	I feel fairly good, but some things are not too clear or meaningful.	A few things we are doing are clear and meaningful.	Much of the activity is not clear or meaningful to me.	I really do not understand or feel involved in the goals of the team.

6. How well does the team work at its tasks?

1	2	3	4	5
Coasts, loafs, makes no progress.	Makes a little progress, but most members loaf.	Progress is slow; spurts of effective work.	Above average in progress and pace of work.	Works well; achieves definite progress.

7. Our planning and the way we operate as a team are largely influenced by:

1	2	3	4	5
One or two team members.	A clique.	Shifts from one person or clique to another.	Shared by most of the members, but some are left out.	Shared by all members of the team.

8. What is the level of responsibility for work in our team?

5	4	3	2	1
Each person assumes personal responsibility for getting work done.	A majority of the members assume responsibility for getting work done.	About half assume responsibility; about half do not.	Only a few assume responsibility for getting work done.	Nobody (except perhaps one) really assumes responsibility for getting work done.

9. How are differences or conflicts handled in our team?

1	2	3	4	5
Differences or conflicts are denied, suppressed, or avoided at all costs.	Differences or conflicts are recognized but remain mostly unresolved.	Differences or conflicts are recognized, and some attempts are made to work them through by some members, often outside the team meetings.	Differences and conflicts are recognized, and some attempts are made to deal with them in our team.	Differences and conflicts are recognized, and the team usually is working them through satisfactorily.

10. How do people relate to the team leader, chairperson, or "boss"?

1	2	3	4	5
The leader dominates the team, and people are often fearful or passive.	The leader tends to control the team, although people generally agree with the leader's direction.	There is some give and take between the leader and the team members.	Team members relate easily to the leader and usually are able to influence leader decisions.	Team members respect the leader, but they work together as a unified team, with everyone participating and no one dominant.

Total score = _____

Questions for Discussion

1. Have any of the items on the questionnaire helped you better understand why your team has had problems? What problems?

2. Based on Table 1–1, are you part of a group or team? Explain.

3. How do your responses to the items compare with the average responses from your group? What insights does this information provide?

4. If you are part way through your team's life cycle, what steps does your team need to take to become more effective?

5. If this is the end of your team's life cycle, what should your team have done differently?

6. What lasting lessons about teamwork have you learned from this exercise?

NOTES

1. Excerpted from T D Schellhardt, "Monsanto Bets on 'Box Buddies,'" *The Wall Street Journal,* February 23, 1999, pp B1–B10.

2. B Dumaine, "Why Do We Work?" *Fortune,* December 26, 1994, p 202.

3. See P F Drucker, "The Coming of the New Organization," *Harvard Business Review,* January–February 1988, pp 45–53.

4. J Pfeffer and J F Veiga, "Putting People First for Organizational Success," *Academy of Management Executive,* May 1999, p 41.

5. See N Enbar, "What Do Women Want? Ask 'Em," *Business Week,* March 29, 1999, p 8; and M Hickins, "Duh! Gen Xers Are Cool with Teamwork," *Management Review,* March 1999, p 7.

6. K Lowry Miller, "Siemens Shapes Up," *Business Week,* May 1, 1995, p 52.

7. P Engardio and G DeGeorge, "Importing Enthusiasm," *Business Week,* 1994 Special Issue: 21st Century Capitalism, p 122.

8. J Rossant, "The Man Who's Driving Fiat Like a Ferrari," *Business Week,* January 23, 1995, p 82.

9. S Hamm and M Stepanek, "From Reengineering to E-Engineering," *Business Week* E.BIZ, March 22, 1999, pp EB15,EB18.

10. J R Katzenbach, and D K Smith, *The Wisdom of Teams: Creating the High-Performance Organization* (New York: HarperBusiness, 1999), p 45.

11. See L G Bolman and T E Deal, "What Makes a Team Work?" *Organizational Dynamics,* Autumn 1992, pp 34–44.

12. J R Katzenbach and D K Smith, "The Discipline of Teams," *Harvard Business Review,* March–April 1993, p 112.

13. "A Team's-Eye View of Teams," *Training,* November 1995, p 16.

14. See E Sundstrom, K P DeMeuse, and D Futrell, "Work Teams," *American Psychologist,* February 1990, pp 120–33.

15. For an alternative typology of teams, see S G Cohen, "New Approaches to Teams and Teamwork," in *Organizing for the Future: The New Logic for Managing Complex Organizations,* eds J R Galbraith, E E Lawler III and Associates (San Francisco: Jossey-Bass, 1993), ch. 8, pp 194–226.

16. For a good update, see A Reinhardt and S Browder, "Boeing," *Business Week,* September 30, 1996, pp 119–25. Also see G Van der Vegt, B Emans, and E Van de Vliert, "Effects of Interdependencies in Project Teams," *The Journal of Social Psychology,* April 1999, pp 202–14.

17 Descriptions of action teams can be found in D Field, "Air and Ground Crews Team to Turn around Flights," *USA Today,* March 17, 1998, p 10E; and K S Peterson, "Minding the Patient: Teams Listen to Hearts, Minds," *USA Today,* November 9, 1998, p 6D. Also see A B Drexler and R Forrester, "Interdependence: The Crux of Teamwork," *HRMagazine,* September 1998, pp 52–62.

18 P King, "What Makes Teamwork Work?" *Psychology Today,* December 1989, p 16.

19 An instructive overview of group effectiveness models can be found in P S Goodman, E Ravlin, and M Schminke, "Understanding Groups in Organizations," in *Research in Organizational Behavior,* eds L L Cummings and B M Staw (Greenwich, CT: JAI Press, 1987), vol. 9, pp 121–73. Also see D Dunphy and B Bryant, "Teams: Panaceas or Prescriptions for Improved Performance?" *Human Relations,* May 1996, pp 677–99; and G A Neuman and J Wright, "Team Effectiveness: Beyond kills and Cognitive Ability," *Journal of Applied Psychology,* June 1999, pp 376–89.

20 Sundstrom, De Meuse, and Futrell, "Work Teams," p 122.

21 Other team criteria are discussed in N R Anderson and M A West, "Measuring Climate for Work Group Innovation: Development and Validation of the Team Climate Inventory," *Journal of Organizational Behavior,* May 1998, pp 235–58; and M J Stevens and M A Campion, "Staffing Work Teams: Development and Validation of a Selection Test for Teamwork Settings," *Journal of Management,* no 2, 1999, pp 207–28.

22 For example, see S R Rayner, "Team Traps: What They Are, How to Avoid Them," *National Productivity Review,* Summer 1996, pp 101–15; P W Mulvey, J F Veiga, and P M Elsass, "When Teammates Raise a White Flag," *Academy of Management Executive,* February 1996, pp 40–49; L Holpp and R Phillips, "When Is a Team Its Own Worst Enemy?" *Training,* September 1995, pp 71–82; B Richardson, "Why Work Teams Flop—and What Can Be Done about It," *National Productivity Review,* Winter 1994/95, pp 9–13; and B Dumaine, "The Trouble with Teams," *Fortune,* September 5, 1994, pp 86–92.

23 H Lancaster, "Those Rotten Things You Say about Work May Be True After All," *The Wall Street Journal,* February 20, 1996, p B1.

24 Ibid.

25 Team problems are revealed in L Holpp, "The Betrayal of the American Work Team," *Training,* May 1996, pp 38–42; S Wetlaufer, "The Team That Wasn't," *Harvard Business Review,* November–December 1994, pp 22–38; "More Trouble with Teams," *Training,* October 1996, p 21; and E Neuborne, "Companies Save, But Workers Pay," *USA Today,* February 25, 1997, pp 1B–2B.

26 J Lieber, "Coach Seeks to Ring in 3rd Title," *USA Today,* March 11, 1999, p 2C.

27 See J T Delaney, "Workplace Cooperation: Current Problems, New Approaches," *Journal of Labor Research,* Winter 1996, pp 45–61; H Mintzberg, D Dougherty, J Jorgensen, and F Westley, "Some Surprising Things about Collaboration—Knowing How People Connect Makes It Work Better," *Organizational Dynamics,* Spring 1996, pp 60–71; R Crow, "Institutionalized Competition and Its Effects on Teamwork," *Journal for Quality and Participation,* June 1995, pp 46–54; K G Smith, S J Carroll, and S J Ashford, "Intra- and Interorganizational Cooperation: Toward a Research Agenda," *Academy of Management Journal,* February 1995, pp 7–23; M E Haskins, J Liedtka, and J Rosenblum, "Beyond Teams: Toward an Ethic of Collaboration," *Organizational Dynamics,* Spring 1998, pp 34–50; and C C Chen, X P Chen, and J R Meindl, "How Can Cooperation Be Fostered? The Cultural Effects of Individualism-Collectivism," *Academy of Management Review,* April 1998, pp 285–304.

28 A Kohn, "How to Succeed without Even Vying," *Psychology Today,* September 1986, pp 27–28. Sports psychologists discuss "cooperative competition" in S Sleek, "Competition: Who's the Real Opponent?" *APA Monitor,* July 1996, p 8.

29 D W Johnson, G Maruyama, R Johnson, D Nelson, and L Skon, "Effects of Cooperative, Competitive, and Individualistic Goal Structures on Achievement: A Meta-Analysis," *Psychological Bulletin,* January 1981, pp 56–57. An alternative interpretation of the foregoing study that emphasizes the influence of situational factors can be found in J L Cotton and M S Cook, "Meta-Analysis and the Effects of Various Reward Systems: Some Different Conclusions from Johnson et al.," *Psychological Bulletin,* July 1982, pp 176–83. Also see A E Ortiz, D W Johnson, and R T Johnson, "The Effect of Positive Goal and Resource Interdependence on Individual Performance," *The Journal of Social Psychology,* April 1996, pp 243–49; and S L Gaertner, J F Dovidio, M C Rust, J A Nier, B S Banker, C M Ward, G R Mottola, and M Houlette, "Reducing Intergroup Bias: Elements of Intergroup Cooperation," *Journal of Personality and Social Psychology,* March 1999, pp 388–402.

30 S W Cook and M Pelfrey, "Reactions to Being Helped in Cooperating Interracial Groups: A Context Effect," *Journal of Personality and Social Psychology,* November 1985, p 1243. Also see W E Watson, L Johnson, and D Merritt, "Team Orientation, Self-Orientation, and Diversity in Task Groups," *Group & Organization Management,* June 1998, pp 161–88.

31 See A J Stahelski and R A Tsukuda, "Predictors of Cooperation in Health Care Teams," *Small Group Research,* May 1990, pp 220–33. Also see K Aquino and A Reed II, "A Social Dilemma Perspective on Cooperative Behavior in Organizations," *Group & Organization Management,* December 1998, pp 390–413.

32 J C McCune, "That Elusive Thing Called TRUST," *Management Review,* July–August 1998, p 11.

33 See A Farnham, "The Trust Gap," *Fortune,* December 4, 1989, pp 56–78. Also see B Ettorre, "The Trust Factor," *Management Review,* July 1996, p 19.

34 "Jack Welch's Lessons for Success," *Fortune,* January 25, 1993, p 92.

35 For instance, see C Lee, "Trust Me," *Training,* January 1997, pp 28–37; the entire July 1998 issue of *Academy of Management Review* (9 articles); and A Parkhe, "Understanding Trust in International Alliances," *Journal of World Business,* Fall 1998, pp 219–40.

36 Also see D M Rousseau, S B Sitkin, R S Burt, and C Camerer, "Not So Different After All: A Cross-Discipline View of Trust," *Academy of Management Review,* July 1998, pp 393–404; and A C Wicks, S L Berman, and T M Jones, "The Structure of Optimal Trust: Moral and Strategic Implications," *Academy of Management Review,* January 1999, pp 99–116.

37 J D Lewis and A Weigert, "Trust as a Social Reality," *Social Forces,* June 1985, p 971. Trust is examined as an *indirect* factor in K T Dirks, "The Effects of Interpersonal Trust on Work Group Performance," *Journal of Applied Psychology,* June 1999, pp 445–55.

38 R C Mayer, J H Davis, and F D Schoorman, "An Integrative Model of Organizational Trust," *Academy of Management Review,* July 1995, p 715.

39 Lewis and Weigert, "Trust as a Social Reality," p 970. Also see S G Goto, "To Trust or Not to Trust: Situational and Dispositional Determinants," *Social Behavior and Personality,* no. 2, 1996, pp 119–32; T Tyler, P Degoey, and H Smith, "Understanding Why the Justice of Group Procedures Matters: A Test of the Psychological Dynamics of the Group-Value Model," *Journal of Personality and Social Psychology,* May 1996, pp 913–30; S C Currall and T A Judge, "Measuring Trust between Organizational Boundary Role Persons," *Organizational Behavior and Human Decision Processes,* November 1995, pp 151–70; L T Hosmer, "Trust: The Connecting Link between Organizational Theory and Philosophical Ethics," *Academy of Management Review,* April 1995, pp 379–403; and D J McAllister, "Affect- and Cognition-Based Trust as Foundations for Interpersonal Cooperation in Organizations," *Academy of Management Journal,* February 1995, pp 24–59.

40   For an interesting trust exercise, see G Thompson and P F Pearce, "The Team-Trust Game," *Training & Development Journal,* May 1992, pp 42–43.

41   M Powell, "Betrayal," *Inc.,* April 1996, p 24. For related research and reading, see T E Becker, "Integrity in Organizations: Beyond Honesty and Conscientiousness," *Academy of Management Review,* January 1998, pp 154–61; K van den Bos, H A M Wilke, and E A Lind, "When Do We Need Procedural Fairness? The Role of Trust in Authority," *Journal of Personality and Social Psychology,* December 1998, pp 1449–58; and O Harari, "The TRUST Factor," *Management Review,* January 1999, pp 28–31.

42   For interesting new theory and research on telling lies, see B M DePaulo, D A Kashy, S E Kirkendol, M M Wyer, and J A Epstein, "Lying in Everyday Life," *Journal of Personality and Social Psychology,* May 1996, pp 979–95; and D A Kashy and B M DePaulo, "Who Lies?" *Journal of Personality and Social Psychology,* May 1996, pp 1037–51.

43   For support, see G M Spreitzer and A K Mishra, "Giving Up Control without Losing Control: Trust and Its Substitutes' Effects on Managers' Involving Employees in Decision Making," *Group & Organization Management,* June 1999, pp 155–87.

44   For more on fairness, see K Seiders and L L Berry, "Service Fairness: What It Is and Why It Matters," *Academy of Management Executive,* May 1998, pp 8–20.

45   Adapted from F Bartolomé, "Nobody Trusts the Boss Completely—Now What?" *Harvard Business Review,* March–April 1989, pp 135–42. Also see P Chattopadhyay, "Beyond Direct and Symmetrical Effects: The Influence of Demographic Dissimilarity on Organizational Citizenship Behavior," *Academy of Management Journal,* June 1999, pp 273–87.

46   W Foster Owen, "Metaphor Analysis of Cohesiveness in Small Discussion Groups," *Small Group Behavior,* August 1985, p 416. Also see J Keyton and J Springston, "Redefining Cohesiveness in Groups," *Small Group Research,* May 1990, pp 234–54.

47   This distinction is based on discussion in A Tziner, "Differential Effects of Group Cohesiveness Types: A Clarifying Overview," *Social Behavior and Personality,* no. 2, 1982, pp 227–39.

48   B Mullen and C Copper, "The Relation between Group Cohesiveness and Performance: An Integration," *Psychological Bulletin,* March 1994, p 224.

49   Ibid. Additional research evidence is reported in T Kozakaï, S Moscovici, and B Personnaz, "Contrary Effects of Group Cohesiveness in Minority Influence: Intergroup Categorization of the Source and Levels of Influence," *European Journal of Social Psychology,* November–December 1994, pp 713–18; and J Henderson, A E Bourgeois, A LeUnes, and M C Meyers, "Group Cohesiveness, Mood Disturbance, and Stress in Female Basketball Players," *Small Group Research,* April 1998, pp 212–25.

50   Based on B Mullen, T Anthony, E Salas, and J E Driskell, "Group Cohesiveness and Quality of Decision Making: An Integration of Tests of the Groupthink Hypothesis," *Small Group Research,* May 1994, pp 189–204.

51   G L Miles, "The Plant of Tomorrow Is in Texas Today," *Business Week,* July 28, 1986, p 76.

52   See, for example, P Jin, "Work Motivation and Productivity in Voluntarily Formed Work Teams: A Field Study in China," *Organizational Behavior and Human Decision Processes,* 1993, pp 133–55. The related topic of commitment is discussed in B Fehr, "Laypeople's Conceptions of Commitment," *Journal of Personality and Social Psychology,* January 1999, pp 90–103.

53   Based on discussion in E E Lawler III and S A Mohrman, "Quality Circles: After the Honeymoon," *Organizational Dynamics,* Spring 1987, pp 42–54.

54   For a report on 8,000 quality circles in Mexico, see R Carvajal, "Its Own Reward," *Business Mexico,* Special edition 1996, pp 26–28.

55   The historical development of quality circles is discussed by C Stohl, "Bridging the Parallel Organization: A Study of Quality Circle Effectiveness," in *Organizational Communication,* ed M L McLaughlin (Beverly Hills, CA: Sage Publications, 1987), pp 416–30; T Li-Ping Tang, P Smith Tollison, and H D Whiteside, "The Effect of Quality Circle Initiation on Motivation to Attend Quality Circle Meetings and on Task Performance," *Personnel Psychology,* Winter 1987, pp 799–814; and N Kano, "A Perspective on Quality Activities in American Firms," *California Management Review,* Spring 1993, pp 12–31. Also see the discussion of quality circles in J B Keys, L T Denton, and T R Miller, "The Japanese Management Theory Jungle—Revisited," *Journal of Management,* Summer 1994, pp 373–402.

56   Based on discussion in K Buch and R Spangler, "The Effects of Quality Circles on Performance and Promotions," *Human Relations,* June 1990, pp 573–82.

57   See G R Ferris and J A Wagner III, "Quality Circles in the United States: A Conceptual Reevaluation," *The Journal of Applied Behavioral Science,* no. 2, 1985, pp 155–67.

58   Lawler and Mohrman, "Quality Circles: After the Honeymoon," p 43. Also see E E Lawler III, "Total Quality Management and Employee Involvement: Are They Compatible?" *Academy of Management Executive,* February 1994, pp 68–76.

59   See M L Marks, "The Question of Quality Circles," *Psychology Today,* March 1986, pp 36–38, 42, 44, 46.

60   See A K Naj, "Some Manufacturers Drop Effort to Adopt Japanese Techniques," *The Wall Street Journal,* May 7, 1993, p A1.

61   See E E Adam, Jr, "Quality Circle Performance," *Journal of Management,* March 1991, pp 25–39.

62   See R P Steel and R F Lloyd, "Cognitive, Affective, and Behavioral Outcomes of Participation in Quality Circles: Conceptual and Empirical Findings," *The Journal of Applied Behavioral Science,* no. 1, 1988, pp 1–17; M L Marks, P H Mirvis, E J Hackett, and J F Grady, Jr, "Employee Participation in a Quality Circle Program: Impact on Quality of Work Life, Productivity, and Absenteeism," *Journal of Applied Psychology,* February 1986, pp 61–69; and Buch and Spangler, "The Effects of Quality Circles on Performance and Promotions." Additional research is reported in T Li-Ping Tang, P Smith Tollison, and H D Whiteside, "Differences between Active and Inactive Quality Circles in Attendance and Performance," *Public Personnel Management,* Winter 1993, pp 579–90; and C Doucouliagos, "Worker Participation and Productivity in Labor-Managed and Participatory Capitalist Firms: A Meta-Analysis," *Industrial and Labor Relations Review,* October 1995, pp 58–77.

63   See K Kiser, "Tools for Teaming," *Training,* March 1999, pp 32–33.

64   See A M Townsend, S M DeMarie, and A R Hendrickson, "Virtual Teams: Technology and the Workplace of the Future," *Academy of Management Executive,* August 1998, pp 17–29.

65   Based on P Bordia, N DiFonzo, and A Chang, "Rumor as Group Problem Solving: Development Patterns in Informal Computer-Mediated Groups," *Small Group Research,* February 1999, pp 8–28.

66   See K A Graetz, E S Boyle, C E Kimble, P Thompson, and J L Garloch, "Information Sharing in Face-to-Face, Teleconferencing, and Electronic Chat Groups," *Small Group Research,* December 1998, pp 714–43.

67   Based on F Niederman and R J Volkema, "The Effects of Facilitator Characteristics on Meeting Preparation, Set Up, and Implementation," *Small Group Research,* June 1999, pp 330–60.

68   Based on J J Sosik, B J Avolio, and S S Kahai, "Inspiring Group Creativity: Comparing Anonymous and Identified Electronic Brainstorming," *Small Group Research,* February 1998, pp 3–31. For practical advice on brainstorming, see C Caggiano, "The Right Way to Brainstorm," *Inc.,* July 1999, p 94.

69   For practical tips, see K Kiser, "Building a Virtual Team," *Training,* March 1999, p 34.

70   Data from C Joinson, "Teams at Work," *HRMagazine,* May 1999, pp 30–36.

71   B Dumaine, "Who Needs a Boss?" *Fortune,* May 7, 1990, p 52.

72   S Baker and T Buell, Jr, "Buddy-Buddy at the Steel Smelter," *Business Week,* April 5, 1993, p 27.

73   A B Cheney, H P Sims, Jr, and C C Manz, "Teams and TQM," *Business Horizons,* September–October 1994, pp 22–23.

74   Baker and Buell, "Buddy-Buddy at the Steel Smelter."

75   See M Moravec, O J Johannessen, and T A Hjelmas, "The Well-Managed SMT," *Management Review,* June 1998, pp 56–58; and "Case Study in C-Sharp Minor," *Training,* October 1998, p 21.

76   For example, see M Selz, "Testing Self-Managed Teams, Entrepreneur Hopes to Lose Job," *The Wall Street Journal,* January 11, 1994, pp B1–B2. Also see "Even in Self-Managed Teams There Has to Be a Leader," *Supervisory Management,* December 1994, pp 7–8.

77   See D R Denison, S L Hart, and J A Kahn, "From Chimneys to Cross-Functional Teams: Developing and Validating a Diagnostic Model," *Academy of Management Journal,* August 1996, pp 1005–23. Cross-functional teams are discussed in D Lei, J W Slocum, and R A Pitts, "Designing Organizations for Competitive Advantage: The Power of Unlearning and Learning," *Organizational Dynamics,* Winter 1999, pp 24–38.

78   A Erdman, "How to Keep that Family Feeling," *Fortune,* April 6, 1992, p 95.

79   See P S Goodman, R Devadas, and T L Griffith Hughson, "Groups and Productivity: Analyzing the Effectiveness of Self-Managing Teams," in *Productivity in Organizations,* eds J P Campbell, R J Campbell and Associates (San Francisco: Jossey-Bass, 1988), pp 295–327.

80   Good background discussions can be found in work cited in note 73 and in C Lee, "Beyond Teamwork," *Training,* June 1990, pp 25–32. Also see S G Cohen, G E Ledford, Jr, and G M Spreitzer, "A Predictive Model of Self-Managing Work Team Effectiveness," *Human Relations,* May 1996, pp 643–76.

81   For an instructive continuum of work team autonomy, see R D Banker, J M Field, R G Schroeder, and K K Sinha, "Impact of Work Teams on Manufacturing Performance: A Longitudinal Field Study," *Academy of Management Journal,* August 1996, pp 867–90.

82   Drawn from Goodman, Devadas, and Hughson, "Groups and Productivity: Analyzing the Effectiveness of Self-Managing Teams." Also see E F Rogers, W Metlay, I T Kaplan, and T Shapiro, "Self-Managing Work Teams: Do They Really Work?" *Human Resource Planning,* no. 2, 1995, pp 53–57; and V U Druskat and S B Wolff, "Effects and Timing of Developmental Peer Appraisals in Self-Managing Work Groups," *Journal of Applied Psychology,* February 1999, pp 58–74.

83   See R E Walton, "Work Innovations at Topeka: After Six Years," *The Journal of Applied Behavioral Science,* 1977, pp 422–33.

84   For useful tips, see L Holpp, "Five Ways to Sink Self-Managed Teams," *Training,* September 1993, pp 38–42.

85   See B Dumaine, "The New Non-Manager Managers," *Fortune,* February 22, 1993, pp 80–84. Also see "Easing the Fear of Self-Directed Teams," *Training,* August 1993, pp 14, 55–56.

86   See Dumaine, "Who Needs a Boss?" pp 55, 58; and J Hillkirk, "Self-Directed Work Teams Give TI Lift," *USA Today,* December 20, 1993, p 8B. A good contingency model for empowering teams is presented in R C Liden, S J Wayne, and L Bradway, "Connections Make the Difference," *HRMagazine,* February 1996, pp 73–79.

87   Data from S Alper, D Tjosvold, and K S Law, "Interdependence and Controversy in Group Decision Making: Antecedents to Effective Self-Managing Teams," *Organizational Behavior and Human Decision Processes,* April 1998, pp 33–52.

88   For an instructive case study on this topic, see C C Manz, D E Keating, and A Donnellon, "Preparing for an Organizational Change to Employee Self-Management: The Managerial Transition," *Organizational Dynamics,* Autumn 1990, pp 15–26. Also see B L Kirkman and B Rosen, "Beyond Self-Management: Antecedents and Consequences of Team Empowerment," *Academy of Management Journal,* February 1999, pp 58–74.

89   Based on K Lowry Miller, "GM's German Lessons," *Business Week,* December 20, 1993, pp 67–68.

90   See J T Buckley, "Getting into Outdoors Builds Corporate Buddies," *USA Today,* August 19, 1996, pp 1A–2A; and J T Taylor, "Participants Learn the Ropes of Team Building," *USA Today,* August 19, 1996, p 7B. For more on outdoor experiential learning, see H Campbell, "Adventures in Teamland," *Personnel Journal,* May 1996, pp 56–62; E Brown, "War Games to Make You Better at Business," *Fortune,* September 28, 1998, pp 291–96; and M Hickins, "A Day at the Races," *Management Review,* May 1999, pp 56–61.

91   R Henkoff, "Companies that Train Best," *Fortune,* March 22, 1993, p 73.

92   See M J McCarthy, "A Management Rage: Beating the Drums for the Company," *The Wall Street Journal,* August 13, 1996, pp A1, A6.

93   An excellent resource is W G Dyer, *Team Building: Current Issues and New Alternatives,* 3rd ed (Reading, MA: Addison-Wesley, 1995). Also see G L Stewart, C C Manz, and H P Sims, Jr, *Team Work and Group Dynamics* (New York: Wiley, 1999).

94 See A B Hollingshead, "Group and Individual Training: Impact of Practice on Performance," *Small Group Research,* April 1998, pp 254–80; and L McDermott, B Waite, and N Brawley, "Putting Together a World-Class Team," *Training & Development,* January 1999, pp 47–51.

95 S Bucholz and T Roth, *Creating the High-Performance Team* (New York: John Wiley & Sons, 1987), p xi.

96 Ibid., p 14. Also see S A Wheelan, D Murphy, E Tsumura, and S F Kline, "Member Perceptions of Internal Group Dynamics and Productivity," *Small Group Research,* June 1998, pp 371–93; M F R Kets De Vries, "High-Performance Teams: Lessons from the Pygmies," *Organizational Dynamics,* Winter 1999, pp 66–77; G Buzaglo and S A Wheelan, "Facilitating Work Team Effectiveness: Case Studies from Central America," *Small Group Research,* February 1999, pp 108–29; K Maani and C Benton, "Rapid Team Learning: Lessons from Team New Zealand America's Cup Campaign," *Organizational Dynamics,* Spring 1999, pp 48–62; J Lipman-Blumen and H J Leavitt, "Hot Groups 'With Attitude': A New Organizational State of Mind," *Organizational Dynamics,* Spring 1999, pp 63–73; and M J Waller, "The Timing of Adaptive Group Responses to Nonroutine Events," *Academy of Management Journal,* April 1999, pp 127–37.

97 See S Caminiti, "What Team Leaders Need to Know," *Fortune,* February 20, 1995, pp 93–100; K Labich, "Elite Teams Get the Job Done," *Fortune,* February 19, 1996, pp 90–99; and E Hart, "Top Teams," *Management Review,* February 1996, pp 43–47.

98 P King, "What Makes Teamwork Work?" *Psychology Today,* December 1989, p 17. A critical view of teams is presented in C Casey, " 'Come, Join Our Family': Discipline and Integration in Corporate Organizational Culture," *Human Relations,* February 1999, pp 155–78.

99 Adapted from C C Manz and H P Sims, Jr, "Leading Workers to Lead Themselves: The External Leadership of Self-Managing Work Teams," *Administrative Science Quarterly,* March 1987, pp 106–29. Also see C C Manz, "Beyond Self-Managing Work Teams: Toward Self-Leading Teams in the Workplace," in *Research in Organizational Change and Development,* vol. 4, eds R W Woodman and W A Pasmore (Greenwich, CT: JAI Press, 1990), pp 273–99; C C Manz, "Self-Leading Work Teams: Moving Beyond Self-Management Myths," *Human Relations,* no. 11, 1992, pp 1119–40; C C Manz, *Mastering Self-Leadership: Empowering Yourself for Personal Excellence* (Englewood Cliffs, NJ: Prentice-Hall, 1992); M Uhl-Bien and G B Graen, "Individual Self-Management: Analysis of 'Professional' Self-Managing Activities in Functional and Cross-Functional Work Teams," *Academy of Management Journal,* June 1998, pp 340–50; G E Prussia, J S Anderson, and C C Manz, "Self-Leadership and Performance Outcomes: The Mediating Influence of Self-Efficacy," *Journal of Organizational Behavior,* September 1998, pp 523–38; and P Troiano, "Nice Guys Finish First," *Management Review,* December 1998, p 8.

100 T Petzinger Jr, "With the Stakes High, a Lucent Duo Conquers Distance and Culture," *The Wall Street Journal,* April 23, 1999, p B1.

101 Questionnaire items adapted from C Johnson-George and W C Swap, "Measurement of Specific Interpersonal Trust: Construction and Validation of a Scale to Assess Trust in a Specific Other," *Journal of Personality and Social Psychology,* December 1982, pp 1306–17; and D J McAllister, "Affect- and Cognition-Based Trust as Foundations for Interpersonal Cooperation in Organizations," *Academy of Management Journal,* February 1995, pp 24–59.

102 Ten questionnaire items excerpted from W G Dyer, *Team Building: Current Issues and New Alternatives,* 3rd ed (Reading, MA: Addison-Wesley, 1995), pp 96–99.

Chapter 2

Power and Politics

SOURCE: Robert N. Lussier, *Human Relations in Organizations, Applications and Skill Building*, 5th ed., Chapter 9, McGraw-Hill, 2002, 1999, 1996, 1995, 1990.

Learning Objectives

After completing this chapter, you should be able to:

- Describe seven bases of power.

- List techniques to increase your power bases.

- Discuss the necessity of political behavior and how to use ethical politics to help you achieve our objectives.

- State the Human Relations Guide to Ethical Decision Making.

- Identify techniques to develop effective human relations with superiors, subordinates, peers, and members of other departments.

- State how power, politics, and ethics affect behavior, human relations, and performance.

- Define the following key terms:

coercive power	**information power**	**reciprocity**
connection power	**legitimate power**	**referent power**
ethical politics	**open-door policy**	**reward power**
ethics	**politics**	**Type I ethics**
expert power	**power**	**Type II ethics**
		unethical politics

Bob and Sally are at the water fountain talking.

BOB: "I'm sorry the Peterson account was not assigned to you. You deserved it. Roger's claim of being more qualified to handle the job is not true. I'm really surprised that our boss, Ted, believed Roger's claim."

SALLY: "I agree. Nobody likes Roger because he always has to get his own way. I can't stand the way Roger puts down coworkers and members of other departments to force them to give him his own way. Roger has pulled the old emergency routine so many times now that purchasing and maintenance ignore his requests. This hurts our department."

BOB: "You're right. Roger only thinks of himself; he never considers other people or what's best for the company. I've overheard Ted telling him he has to be a team player if he wants to get ahead."

SALLY: "The way he tries to beat everyone out all the time is sickening. He'll do anything to get ahead. But the way he behaves, he will never climb the corporate ladder."

Besides good work, what does it take to get ahead in an organization? To climb the corporate ladder, you will have to gain power and utilize ethical political skills with your superiors, subordinates, peers, and members of other departments.

POWER

To be effective in an organization, you must understand how power is used.[1] In this section, we discuss the importance of power in organizations, bases of power and how to increase your power, and how power affects behavior, human relations, and performance. Begin by completing Self-Assessment Exercise 2–1, Power Base, to determine your preferred use of power.

Self-Assessment Exercise 2–1
Power Base

When you want to get something and need others' consent or help, which approach do you use more often? Think of recent specific situation(s) in which you tried to get something. If you cannot develop your own example, assume you and a coworker both want the same job assignment for the day. How would you get it? Rank all seven approaches below from 1, the first approach you would most commonly use, to 7, the last approach you would most commonly use. Be honest.

_____ I did/would somehow use a form of coercive power—pressure, blackmail, force, threat, retaliation, and so forth—to get what I want.

_____ I did/would use the influential connection power I have. I'd refer to my friend, or actually have the person tell the person with authority to do it (like your boss).

_____ I did/would use reward power by offering the coworker something of value to him or her as part of the process, or in return for compliance.

_____ I did/would convince the coworker to give me what I want by making a legitimate request (like referring to your seniority over the coworker).

_____ I did/would convince the coworker using referent power—relying on our relationship. Others comply because they like me, or are my friends.

_____ I did/would convince my coworker to give me what I want with information power. The facts support the reason why he or she should do what I want. I have information my coworker needs.

_____ I did/would convince my coworker to give me what I wanted by making him or her realize that I have the skill and knowledge. Since I'm the expert, it should be done my way.

Your selection rank (1–7) prioritizes your preferred use of power. Each power base is a key term and will be explained in this chapter.

Organizational Power

Some people view power as the ability to make people do what they want them to do, or the ability to do something to people or for people. These definitions may be true, but they tend to give power a manipulative, negative connotation, as does the old adage "Power corrupts and absolute power corrupts absolutely." Within an organization, power should be viewed in a positive sense.[2] Without power, managers could not achieve organizational objectives.[3] Employees are not influenced without a reason, and the reason is often related to the power a manager wields over them. People do not actually have to use power to influence others. Often it is the perception of power, rather than the actual power, that influences employees.[4] Leadership and power go hand in hand. For our purposes, **power** *is a person's ability to influence another person's behavior.*

Power generally begins at the top of an organization and works its way down the hierarchy.[5] The buzzword for giving more power to employees is empowerment.[6] Empowerment enables employees to participate in management.[7] With the trend toward larger global business, power is an important topic.[8]

Bases of Power and How to Increase Your Power

Amital Etzioni differentiated two sources of power—position power and personal power, which are commonly used today.[9] Position power is derived from top-level management and is delegated down the chain of command. Personal power is derived from the follower, rather than delegated by management. Everyone has personal power to varying degrees.[10] Personal power is largely due to one's personality. Leaders with personal power get it from followers because they meet their needs.

John French and Bertram Raven[11] proposed five bases of power—coercive, legitimate, expert, reward, and referent—which are commonly used today.[12] Below, we will examine bases of power[13] and how to increase each. You do not have to take power away from others to increase your power base. Generally, power is given to those who get results. High-level performers are given increased power as they take on more responsibility.

Coercive Power

The use of **coercive power** *involves threats and/or punishment to influence compliance.* Out of fear that noncompliance will lead to reprimands, probation, suspension, or dismissal, employees often do as the supervisor or coworker requests. Other examples of coercive power include verbal abuse, humiliation, and ostracism. In the opening case, when Roger puts coworkers and members of other departments down to force them to give him his own way, he is using coercive power.

Coercive power is appropriate to use in maintaining discipline when enforcing rules. When an employee is not willing to do as the manager requests, he or she may use coercive power to gain compliance. However, it is advisable to keep the use of coercive power to a minimum because it hurts human relations and often productivity as well.[14]

Increasing Coercive Power: To have strong coercive position power, you need to have a management job that enables you to gain and maintain the ability to hire, discipline, and fire your employees. However, some people can pressure others to do what they want without management authority.

Connection Power

Connection power *is based on the user's relationship with influential people.* It relies on the use of contacts or friends who can influence the person you are dealing with. The right connections can give you the perception of having power, and they can actually give you power. If people know you are friendly with people in power, they are more apt to do as you request. The case at the end of the chapter illustrates how people use networking connection power to get ahead.

Increasing Connection Power: To increase your connection power, expand your network of contacts with important managers who have power.[15] Join the "in crowd," and the "right" clubs. Sports like golf may help you meet influential people. When you want something, identify the people who can help you attain it, make alliances, and win them over to your side. Get people to know your name. Get all the publicity you can. Have your accomplishments known by the people in power; send them notices.

Reward Power

Reward power *is based on the user's ability to influence others with something of value to them.* In a management position, use positive reinforcement with incentives such as praise, recognition, pay raises, and promotions to ensure compliance. With peers you can exchange favors as a reward, or give something of value to the other party.

When appropriate, let people know what's in it for them. If you have something attractive to others, use it. For example, when Professor Smith is recruiting a student aide, he tells candidates that if they are selected and do a good job, he will recommend them for an MBA fellowship at Suffolk University, where he has connection power. As a result he gets good, qualified help for minimum wages, while helping both his student aide and his alma mater. Professor Smith meets the goal of human relations by creating a win-win situation for himself, the student, and the university.

Increasing Reward Power: Get a management position and gain and maintain control over resources. Have the power to evaluate your employees' performance and determine their raises and promotions. Find out what others value, and try to reward them in that way.[16] Using praise can help increase your power. Employees who feel they are appreciated rather than being used will give the manager more power.

Legitimate Power

Legitimate power *is based on the user's position power,* which is given by the organization. Employees tend to feel that they ought to do what the supervisor says within the scope of the job. For example, the supervisor asks an employee to take out the trash. The employee does not want to do it, but thinks, "The boss made a legitimate request and I ought to do it," and takes it out. If the employee was hesitant to take out the trash, the supervisor could refer to his or her position power as well.

The use of legitimate power is appropriate when asking people to do something that is within the scope of their job. Most day-to-day interactions are based on legitimate power.[17]

Increasing Legitimate Power: Let people know the power you possess, and work at gaining people's perception that you do have power. Remember—people's perception that you have power gives you power.

Referent Power

You may use **referent power**, *which is based on the user's personal power.* The person relies on personality and the relationship with employees to gain compliance. For example, say, "Will you please do it for me?" not "This is an order." Identification stems primarily from the employee's attractiveness to the person using power and is manifested in personal feelings of "liking." Since Roger is not well liked in the organization, he has weak referent power.

The use of referent power is particularly appropriate for people with weak, or no, position power.[18] Roger has no position power, so he should increase his referent power.

Increasing Referent Power: To gain referent power, develop your relationship with others; stand up for them. Using the nine guidelines for effective human relations can help you win referent power. Remember that your boss's success depends upon you. Gain his or her confidence in order to get more power; work at your relationship with the boss.

Information Power

Information power *is based on the user's information being desired by others.* Managers rely on the other person's need for the information they possess.[19] However, with central computer networks, individual managers have less power.[20] The information is usually related to the job, but not always. Some secretaries have more information than the managers they work for.

Increasing Information Power: Have information flow through you. Know what is going on in the organization. Provide service and information to other departments. Serve on committees; it gives you both information and a chance to increase connection power, and attend seminars and other meetings.

Expert Power

Expert power *is based on the user's skill and knowledge.* Being an expert makes other people dependent upon you.[21] The fewer the people who possess the skill or knowledge, the more power the individual who possesses it has.[22] People often respect an expert.[23] For example, because there are so few people possessing the ability to become top athletes, they command multimillion dollar contracts.

Expert power is essential to people who have to work with people from other departments and organizations. They have no direct position power to use, so being seen as an expert gives credibility and power. Roger, rather than Sally, got the Peterson account because he convinced Ted of his expertise.

Increasing Expert Power: To become an expert, take all the training and educational programs your organization provides. Stay away from routine tasks, in favor of more complex, hard-to-evaluate tasks. Project a positive image.

Remember to use the appropriate type of power in a given situation. Figure 2–1 matches the two sources of power and the seven bases of power with the four situational communication styles. As shown, coercive, reward, and legitimate power come from position power, while referent, information, and expert power come from personal power.

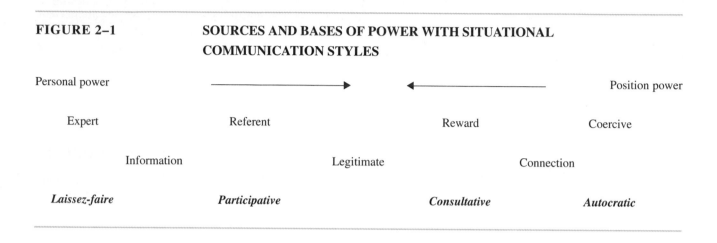

FIGURE 2–1   **SOURCES AND BASES OF POWER WITH SITUATIONAL COMMUNICATION STYLES**

Personal power ——————————→   ←—————————— Position power

| Expert | Referent | Reward | Coercive |

| Information | Legitimate | Connection |

Laissez-faire   *Participative*   *Consultative*   *Autocratic*

WORK APPLICATIONS

1. Of the many suggestions for increasing your power bases, which two are your highest priority for using on the job? Explain.

APPLICATION SITUATIONS

Using Power AS 2–1
Identify the appropriate power to use in each situation.
  A. Coercive   C.   Reward or legitimate   E. Information or expert
  B. Connection   D.   Referent

_____ 1.   Carl is one of the best workers you supervise. He needs little direction, but he has slowed down his production level. You know he has a personal problem, but the work needs to get done.

_____ 2.   You want a new personal computer to help you do a better job.

_____ 3.   José, one of your best workers, wants a promotion. He has asked you to help prepare him for when the opportunity comes.

_____ 4.   Your worst employee has ignored one of your directives again.

_____ 5.   Wonder, who needs some direction and encouragement to maintain production, is not working to standard today. Wonder claims to be ill, as she does occasionally.

How Power Affects Behavior, Human Relations, and Performance

In an organizational setting, your boss has a direct influence over your behavior.[24] For example, Ted's boss asked him to do a special report for the department, which he did. Ted was influenced to do something he would not have done otherwise. As you know, not everyone does what the manager wants them to. Some employees behave in direct defiance of management. But in either case, managers in power influence employee behavior. Our coworkers also influence our behavior, though you may not be as willing to behave as they request as you are for your boss. Employees often behave differently with their coworkers than they do with their boss. Coworkers tend to have personal friendship relations, while superior and subordinate often have a professional relationship. Many managers do not socialize with employees because it may interfere with the power they have with them.

Some people want and seek power, while others wouldn't take it if you offered it to them. Motivation is the reason for this, which includes a person's need for power, and determined your own need for power. Do you want power? Do you plan to follow the suggestions in the book to increase your power base?

WORK APPLICATIONS

2. Give two examples, preferably from an organization you work(ed) in, of people using power. Identify the power base and describe the behavior and how it affected human relations and performance.

ORGANIZATIONAL POLITICS

You will learn the nature of politics and how to develop political skills. Begin by determining your use of political behavior by completing Self-Assessment Exercise 2–2.

Self-Assessment Exercise 2–2
Political Behavior

Select the response that best describes your actual or planned use of the following behavior on the job. Place the number 1–5 on the line before each statement.

(5) Usually	(4) Frequently	(3) Occasionally	(2) Seldom	(1) Rarely

_____ 1. I get along with everyone, even those recognized as difficult. I avoid or delay giving my opinion on controversial issues.

_____ 2. I try to make people feel important and compliment them.

_____ 3. I compromise when working with others and avoid telling people they are wrong; instead, I suggest alternatives that may be more effective.

_____ 4. I try to get to know the managers and what is going on in as many of the other departments as possible.

_____ 5. I take on the same interests as those in power (watch or play sports, join the same clubs, etc.).

_____ 6. I purposely seek contacts and network with higher-level managers so they will know who I am by name and face.

_____ 7. I seek recognition and visibility for my accomplishments.

_____ 8. I form alliances with others to increase my ability to get what I want.

_____ 9. I do favors for others and use their favors in return.

_____ 10. I say I will do things when I am not sure I can deliver; if I cannot meet the obligation, I explain why it was out of my control.

To determine your political behavior add the 10 numbers you selected as your answers. The number will range from 10 to 50. The higher your score, the more political behavior you use. Place your score here _____ and on the continuum below.

Nonpolitical   10 - - - - - - - 20 - - - - - - - - 30 - - - - - - - 40 - - - - - - - 50   Political

The Nature of Organizational Politics

Politics is critical to your career success.[25] You cannot keep out of politics and be successful.[26] Politics is a fact of organizational life.[27] In our economy, money is the medium of exchange; in an organization, politics is the medium of exchange. Managers are, and must be, political beings in order to meet their objectives.[28] **Politics** *is the process of gaining and using power*. As you can see from the definition, power and politics go hand in hand.

Managers cannot meet their objectives without the help of other people[29] and departments over which they have no authority or position power. For example, Tony, a production department supervisor, needs materials and supplies to make the product, but he must rely on the purchasing department to acquire them. If Tony does not have a good working relationship with purchasing, he may not get the materials when he needs them.

Using **reciprocity** *involves creating obligations and debts, developing alliances, and using them to accomplish objectives*. When people do something for you, you incur an obligation that they may expect to be repaid. When you do something for people, you create a debt that you may be able to collect at a later date when you need a favor.[30] Over a period of time, when the trade-off results in both parties getting something they want, an alliance usually develops to gain group power in attaining mutually desirable benefits.[31] You should work at developing a network of alliances that you can call on for help in meeting your objectives.[32] When the trade-off of help with alliances creates a win-win situation for all members of the alliances and the organization, the goal of human relations is met.[33]

Like power, politics often has a negative connotation due to people who abuse political power.[34] Mahatma Gandhi called politics without principle a sin. However, ethical politics helps the organization by meeting the goal of human relations without negative consequences.[35] Few areas of corporate life are more universally despised than politics, yet few have more impact on a manager's career.[36] The amount and importance of politics varies from organization to organization. In the global context, political skills are even more important.[37]

As you can see, organizational politics is an integral part of everyday corporate life. You should develop your political behavior to take advantage of political realities that can help you and the organization and to avoid being hurt by politics.[38] Developing political skills is the next topic.

WORK APPLICATIONS

3. Give an example of reciprocity, preferably from an organization you work(ed) for. Explain the trade-off.

Developing Political Skills

Yes, you can be good at politics without being a jerk.[39] If you want to progress, you should develop your political skills. Human relations skills are critical to political success in organizations. Following the nine human relations guidelines can help you develop political skills. More specifically, review the 10 statements in Self-Assessment Exercise 2–2 and consciously increase your use of these behaviors, especially any that had a low frequency of use. However, use number 10, saying you will do something when you are not sure you can, sparingly and don't use the word "promise." You don't want to be viewed as a person who doesn't keep his or her word. Developing trust is very important.[40] And being honest builds trust.[41]

Use reciprocity. When you want something, determine who else will benefit and create alliance power to help you, the other party(s), and the organization to benefit.[42] Ongoing alliances are also known as political coalitions.[43] Networking is a form of politics.[44]

Successfully implementing these behaviors results in increased political skills. However, if you don't agree with one of the political behaviors, don't use it. You may not need to use all of the political behaviors to be successful. Learn what it takes in the diverse organization where you work.

WORK APPLICATIONS

4. Of the 10 political behaviors in Self-Assessment Exercise 2–2, which two need the most effort on your part? Which two need the least? Explain your answers.

BUSINESS ETHICS AND ETIQUETTE

Ethical behavior is a popular topic.[45] Organizations seek employees with integrity.[46] Are all power and political behavior ethical? What is the relationship between ethics and politics? In this section, we discuss Type I and Type II ethics, ethical and unethical politics, and a simple guide to ethical decisions. First complete Self-Assessment Exercise 2-3.

Self-Assessment Exercise 2–3
Ethical Behavior

Below are 15 statements. Identify the frequency of which you do, have done, or would do these things in the future when employed full time. Place the numbers 4, 3, 2, or 1 on the line before each statement.

(4) Regularly	(3) Occasionally	(2) Seldom	(1) Never

_____ 1. I come to work late and get paid for it.

_____ 2. I leave work early and get paid for it.

_____ 3. I take long breaks/lunches and get paid for it.

_____ 4. I call in sick to get a day off, when I'm not sick.

_____ 5. I use the company phone to make personal long distance calls.

_____ 6. I do personal work while on company time.

_____ 7. I use the company copier for personal use.

_____ 8. I mail personal things through the company mail.

_____ 9. I take home company supplies or merchandise.

_____ 10. I give company supplies or merchandise to friends, or allow them to take them without saying anything.

_____ 11. I put in for reimbursement for meals and travel or other expenses that I did not actually eat or make.

_____ 12. I use the company car for personal business.

_____ 13. I take my spouse/friend out to eat and charge it to the company expense account.

_____ 14. I take my spouse/friend on business trips and charge the expense to the company.

_____ 15. I accept gifts from customers/suppliers in exchange for giving them business.

Total your score. It will be between 15 and 60. Place it here _____ and an X on the continuum below that represents your score.

Ethical   15 - - - 20 - - - 25 - - - 30 - - - 35 - - - 40 - - - 45 - - - 50 - - - 55 - - - 60   Unethical

All of these items are considered unethical behavior by most organizations. However, many of these actions happen regularly in organizations. If many employees do them, does that make it all right for you to do them too?

There has been increased emphasis on business ethics and the need to use power in a socially responsible manner.[47] Companies are being judged on their ethics and social responsibility.[48] In addition, there is a daily radio audience offering advice on ethics and moral responsibility.[49] Some experts distinguish between moral behavior and ethical behavior. Morals refers to absolute worldwide standards of right and wrong behavior, such as "Thou shalt not commit murder." Ethical behavior, on the other hand, reflects established customs and mores that may vary throughout the world and that are subject to change from time to time. For our purpose we combine the two: **ethics** *is the moral standard of right and wrong behavior.* Mahatma Gandhi called business without morality a sin.

Right behavior is considered ethical behavior, while wrong behavior is considered unethical behavior. In the business world, the difference between right and wrong behavior is not always clear. Many unethical behaviors are illegal, but not all. In the diversified global workplace, people have different values, which leads to behaviors that some people view as ethical while others do not. Ethics is also considered to be relative. In one situation, people may feel certain behavior is ethical while the same behavior in a different situation is unethical. For example, giving someone a gift is legal, but giving a gift as a condition of attaining business (a bribe) is illegal. A gift versus a bribe is not always clear.

In your daily life, you face decisions in which you can make ethical or unethical choices. You make your choices based on your past learning from parents, teachers, friends, coworkers, and so forth. Our combined past experiences make up what many refer to as our *conscience,* which helps us to choose right from wrong.

Type I and Type II Ethics

Behavior known as **Type I ethics** *refers to behavior that is considered wrong by authorities, yet not accepted by others as unethical.* The number of people who do not accept authorities' decisions on wrong behavior affects people's decision to behave in unethical ways. In Self-Assessment Exercise 2–3, these behaviors are considered unethical by most organizations, yet many employees do not agree and perform these behaviors. Generally, the more people disagree with specific behavior as being unethical, the more people will perform the behavior. People tend to rationalize, "Everyone does it; it's okay to do it." People also tend to exaggerate the numbers. Often the number "everyone" is actually a small percentage of the population. Employee theft costs stores $10 billion annually.[50]

A person who knowingly conducts unethical behavior because he or she does not agree with authority's view on ethical behavior is guilty of Type I ethics. For example, the company rules say there shall be no smoking in a specific area, yet the employee does not believe smoking is dangerous and smokes anyway.

Another behavior, **Type II ethics,** *refers to behavior that is considered wrong by authorities and the individual, yet conducted anyway.* A person who agrees that the behavior is unethical yet conducts the behavior anyway is guilty of Type II ethics. To continue the smoking example above, the employee knows smoking is not allowed and agrees that it is dangerous, yet smokes anyway.

Why are managers unethical? Some of the many reasons include to gain power, money, advancement, recognition, and anger at the system.

WORK APPLICATIONS

5. Give an example of Type I and Type II ethics behavior, preferably from an organization you work(ed) for.

APPLICATION SITUATIONS

Type I and Type II Ethics AS 2–2

Identify each statement as:
A. Type I ethics   B. Type II ethics

_____ 6.   Bill just let another toy go as acceptable quality, when it's not. He agrees that it's wrong to do this, so why does he?

_____ 7.   Carla told me it's okay to take home company pens and things; everyone does it.

_____ 8.   Wayne is spreading stories about coworkers again. Why doesn't he agree that this is unethical?

_____ 9.   Danielle is making copies of directions to the party she is having. I told her it was wrong, and she agreed with me, but she did it anyway.

_____ 10. Mike just left work early again. He says he is underpaid, so it's okay.

Ethical and Unethical Politics

Politics can be helpful or harmful to an organization depending upon the behavior. We classify political behavior into two categories: ethical and unethical. **Ethical politics** *includes behavior that benefits both the individual and the organization.* Ethical politics creates a win-win situation, meeting the goal of human relations. On the other hand, **unethical politics** *includes behavior that benefits the individual and hurts the organization.* Unethical politics creates a win-lose situation; unethical politics also includes management behavior that helps the organization, but hurts the individual. Behavior that helps the individual but does not hurt the organization is also considered ethical. The term *organization* includes people because if employees are hurt, so is the organization. When dealing with people outside the firm, use the stakeholders approach to ethics.[51] Creating a win-win situation for all relevant parties, it increases firm financial performance.[52]

The 10 political behavior statements in Self-Assessment Exercise 2–2 are generally ethical. Another example of ethical political behavior includes Tom, the computer manager, who wants a new computer. He talks to several of the powerful managers and sells them on the benefits to them. They form an alliance and attain the funds to purchase the computer. Tom benefits because he now manages a new and more powerful computer. He also looks good in the eyes of the other managers who will also benefit through the use of the new computer. Overall, the organization's performance increases.

Examples of unethical behavior that hurt the organization include the following: (1) Karl, a production manager, wants to be promoted to the general manager's position. To increase his chances, he spreads untrue gossip about his main competitor. (2) There is a vacant office, which is large and well furnished. Sam, a sales manager who spends most of his time on the road, sees the office as prestigious, so he requests it, even though he knows that Cindy, a public relations manager, wants it and will get better use from it. Sam speaks to his friends in high-level management positions and he gets the office. (3) A person lies on his or her resume.[53] (4) A manager asks the secretary (or other employee) to lie.[54]

Ethical political behavior pay?[55] Good business and good ethics are synonymous; ethics is at the heart and center of business, and profits and ethics are intrinsically related.[56] At first, one may be richly rewarded for knifing people in the back, but retaliation follows, trust is lost, and productivity declines. This is illustrated in the opening case. Roger uses unethical politics in hopes of getting ahead. But according to his peers, he will not climb the corporate ladder. It is difficult to get ahead when people don't like you and you make a lot of enemies. Unethical behavior and stress appear to be linked. Exercising good human relations skills is exercising good ethics.

WORK APPLICATIONS

6. Give an example of ethical and unethical politics, preferably from an organization you work(ed) for. Describe the behavior and consequences for all parties involved.

Codes of Ethics

A good code of ethics establishes guidelines that clearly describe ethical and unethical behavior.[57] Most organizations consider ethics codes to be important,[58] and many have developed codes of ethics.[59] Figure 2–2 is an example of a code of ethics as it relates to its employees.[60]

To be ethically successful, organizations must audit the ethical behavior of its employees[61] and confront and discipline employees who are unethical.[62] Top managers need to lead by ethical example,[63] they need to be honest with employees,[64] and they need to build trust.[65] Does ethics education lead to successful work ethics? Yes, to some extent it has a positive effect, but other factors also influence ethics,[66] such as a person's basic values and ethical beliefs before, during, and after the ethics education.

APPLICATION SITUATIONS

Ethical and Unethical Politics AS 2–3

Identify each statement as:

A. Ethical politics   B. Unethical politics

_____ 11.   Pete goes around telling everyone about any little mistake his peer Sue makes.

_____ 12.   Tony is taking tennis lessons so he can challenge his boss.

_____ 13.   Carol delivers her daily exhibits at 10:00 each day because she knows she will run into Ms. Big Power on the way.

_____ 14.   Carlos goes around asking about what is happening in other departments during his work time.

_____ 15.   Frank sent a copy of his department's performance record to three high-level managers to whom he does not report.

FIGURE 2–2   CODE OF ETHICS*

- We will treat our employees fairly with regard to wages, benefits, and working conditions.
- We will never violate the legal or moral rights of employees in any way.
- We will never employ children in our facilities, nor will we do business with any company that makes use of child labor.
- We are committed to an ongoing program of monitoring all our facilities and those of companies with whom we do business.

*Excerpts from the Philips-VanHeusen statement of Corporate Responsibility.

Do Ethics Programs Work?

We've just stated how to make ethics programs effective. However, are ethics programs working? Like many ethical situations, there is no clear right or wrong answer.

On the positive side, American businesses are investing in formal ethics programs. A recent survey of large U.S. corporations found that 78% of responding companies had codes of ethics, 51% had telephone lines for reporting ethical concerns, and 30% had offices for dealing with ethics and legal compliance. Corporate ethics officers now have their own professional association—the Ethics Officers Association—with more than 300 major corporations represented.[67]

On the negative side, misrepresentation by tobacco executives about the addictive properties of nicotine, misstatements of earning by Phar-Mor, Inc., and allegations against hospital executives for misrepresenting Medicare claims can only add to concerns about unethical behavior.[68] A recent study stated that ethics programs are not stopping employee misconduct. More than 75% of respondents said they had observed violation of the law or company standards in the previous last 12 months, and 61% thought management wouldn't administer impartial discipline. People are not reporting unethical behavior, known as *whistle blowing,* because they are not encouraged to do so,[69] or there is no reinforcement motivation.

Can Ethics Programs be Improved?

Have you observed unethical behavior at college and work? Did you report it? Why or why not? If managers really encourage reporting ethics violations, positively reinforce the whistle-blowers and negatively reinforce the violators, will people report ethics violations? Will business ethics improve?

A Human Relations Guide to Ethical Decisions

When making decisions try to meet the goal of human relations by creating a win-win situation for all parties. Some of the stakeholder relevant parties include peers, your boss, subordinates, other department members, the organization, and people/organizations outside the organization you work for as well. The stakeholder will often change from situation to situation. The higher up in the organization, the more relevant parties there are to deal with. For example, if you are not a manager, you will not have any subordinates to deal with. *If, after making a decision, you are proud to tell all these relevant parties your decision, the decision is probably ethical. If you are embarrassed to tell others your decision, or you keep rationalizing the decision, it may not be ethical.*

A second simple guide is the golden rule: "Do unto others as you want them to do unto you." Or, "Don't do anything to anyone that you would not want them to do to you." A third guide is the Rotary International four-way test: (1) Is it the truth? (2) Is it fair to all concerned? (3) Will it build goodwill and better friendship? (4) Will it be beneficial to all concerned?

The rest of this chapter will focus on how to use ethical politics with your boss, subordinates, peers and members of other departments.

WORK APPLICATIONS

7. Give an example, preferably from an organization you work(ed) for, of an individual creating a win-win situation for all parties involved. Identify all parties involved and how they won. Use Figure 2–3, Human Relations Guide to Ethical Decision Making, to help you answer the question.

FIGURE 2–3   **Human Relations Guide to Ethical Decision Making**

If you are proud to tell all relevant parties your decision, it is probably ethical.

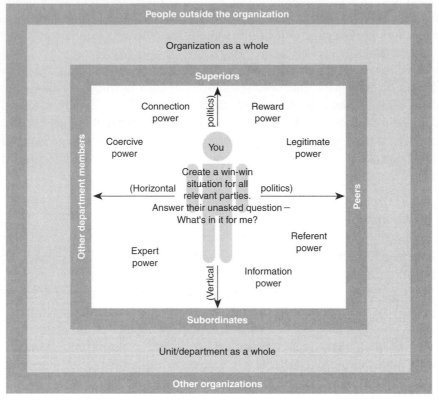

If you are embarrassed to tell all the relevant parties your decision or keep rationalizing, it is probably unethical.

Etiquette

Etiquette is the socially accepted standard of right and wrong behavior. It includes manners beyond simply saying please and thank you. Notice the similarity in our definition of ethics and etiquette. Etiquette is very important to your career success.[70] However, unlike with ethics, organizations don't usually have codes or any formal training in etiquette.

Many organizations weigh etiquette during the job interview as part of the selection criteria. In fact, some managers will take the job candidate out to eat and observe etiquette, including table manners. Candidates with poor etiquette are not offered the job. You may be thinking that it is unfair to judge job candidates by their etiquette, and you may be right. However, the reality of the business world is that firms do not want employees representing their organization who do not project a favorable image for the organization. Recall that customers, suppliers, and everyone the organization comes into contact with judge the organization based on individual behavior. Organizations do not want employees who will embarrass them.

Organizations assume that people are taught etiquette at home or that it is learned through experience or observation. However, this is not always the case. Etiquette skills can be improved.[71] If you haven't been concerned with business etiquette, start now. We'll give you some tips to improve now.

Job Interview Etiquette

The career service department at your college may offer job interview training. Take advantage of its services. Here are some dos and don'ts of job interviewing.

· Do research the organization before the interview so that you can talk intelligently about it. For example, what products/services does it offer? How many employees and locations does it have? What is the company's financial status, such as revenues and net profit last year? What are its strategic plans? Much of this information can be found in the company annual report.

· Do go to the job interview properly dressed.

· Do be sure to get there a little early. Allow plenty of time for traffic and parking. If you are more than 10 minutes early, you can relax and wait before going to the receptionist.

· Do bring extra copies of your resume and other material you may need in a briefcase or nice folder.

· Do get the last name and proper pronunciation of the person who will be interviewing you and greet the interviewer by last name. For example, "How do you do, Mr. Smith?"

· Don't call the interviewer by first name unless told to do so by the interviewer.

· Do firmly shake hands and make eye contact if the interviewer extends his or her hand to you, but don't make the first move.

· Do state the interviewer's name a few times during the job interview. For example, "That is a good question, Mr. Smith."

· Don't sit down until the interviewer invites you to sit, and wait for the interviewer to sit first.

· Do be careful of your nonverbal communication. Don't sit back and slouch. Sit up straight leaning a bit forward in the seat and maintain adequate eye contact to show your interest. You may cross your legs, but crossed arms are a sign of defensiveness or being closed.

· Do not be the first one to bring up salary and benefits. If asked what you expect for a salary, give a range below and above the actual figure you expect. Part of your research prior to the interview should be to find out the salary range for the job you are interviewing for.

· Do take a little time to think about your answers. Talk clearly and loud enough while watching your vocabulary to include proper English; avoid street talk or jargon.

· Do thank the interviewer for his or her time at the close of the interview. If the interviewer does not tell you how long it will take to make a decision, ask when you can expect an answer.

· Do send a short followup written thank-you for the interview letter with another copy of your resume the same day or the next, if you want the job. Include any other information in the letter that you thought about after the interview and state that you look forward to the selection decision by XXX (state the date given by the interviewer).

· Do call back if you do not hear whether you got the job by the decision date given by the interviewer.

Table Manners

Let's give a few simple tips in case you are taken out to eat during the job interview. If you get the job and take others out to eat, you are the interviewer role even if it's not a job interview. Many of the tips also apply to eating with others during your lunch breaks.

· Don't go out to eat starving and letting the interviewer realize that you are by pigging out.

· Do follow the lead of the interviewer; don't take charge.

· Do let the interviewer sit first.

- Do place your napkin on your lap after the interviewer does and repeat other behavior. For example, if there are dip and crackers, the interviewer will not double-dip bitten crackers, so you don't either.

- If the server asks if you want a drink, do wait for the interviewer to respond. Don't ask for alcohol if you are underage, even if you have a fake id; you don't want the interviewer to know this.

- Don't order alcohol unless asked if you want a drink by the interviewer. If asked, ask the interviewer if he or she will be having a drink. If the interviewer says yes, have one; if no, don't have a drink. However, don't have a drink if you will feel its effects. You want to be in top form for the interview questions and discussion, and you want to maintain your proper etiquette.

- Do expect to order an appetizer, main course, and dessert. However, you don't have to order them all, especially if the interviewer does not. For example, if the interviewer asks if you would like an appetizer/ dessert, ask the interviewer if he or she is having one. If the server asks, wait for the interviewer lead.

- Don't begin to eat any serving until everyone at the table is served and the interviewer starts.

- Do try to eat at the same pace as the interviewer so that you are not done eating each serving too much faster or slower than the interviewer.

- Don't talk with food in your mouth. Take small bites to help avoid this problem.

- Don't take the last of anything that you are sharing. It is also polite to leave a little food on your plate, even if you are still hungry.

- Do start using the silverware from the outside in. Again, follow the interviewer's lead when in doubt.

- Do not offer to pay part or all of the bill. The general rule is whoever invites the other out to eat pays the bill, unless otherwise agreed before going to eat.

- Do thank the interviewer for the meal. Also, be polite (say please and thank you) to the server.

Telephone Etiquette

After you get the job, you may use the telephone as part of your job. These tips assume you are not a telephone operator, a position which should get proper training.

Etiquette when you call others:

- Do have a written outline/plan of the topics you want to discuss. Do write notes on the plan sheet as you talk. Don't use a small piece of scrap paper; a notebook works well to keep track of your calls.

- Do leave a "brief" message if the person does not answer. Do state (1) your name, (2) the reason for the call and message, (3) the telephone number to call back, and (4) the best time for the return call. Do speak loud and clear enough and speak slowly, especially when leaving your number. Don't use voice mail for bad news, sensitive/confidential information, and complicated information and instructions. Do control your emotions; don't leave emotional messages that can be played back for the entertainment of others or against you in any way, such as a complaint against you to a boss.

- Do ask if the person has time to talk. If he or she is busy, set up a time to call back.

- Do call the person back if you get disconnected; it's the caller's responsibility to call back.

- Don't eat while on the phone.

- Don't talk to others while you or they are on the phone.

- Do be the first to hang up, and do hang up gently.

Etiquette when others call you:

- Do try to answer the phone within three rings.

- Do say hello followed by your name (not a nickname) and department or organization.

- If people are calling you at a bad time, and did not ask if you have time to talk, do tell them you do not have time to talk now. Do give them a time when you will call them back, and be sure to call back on time.

- If you have to put people on hold for more than a minute, such as if you have to look up information, do offer to call them back.

- Don't take multiple calls at one time keeping people on hold. Do let the voice mail take a message and call back the person waiting.

- Do keep paper (telephone notebook) and pencil ready. Do write down the person's name immediately when you don't know them and call them by name during the conversation as you jot down notes.

- Don't give out personal information about others over the phone.

- Do be the last one to hang up.

- Do leave a "brief" message on your voice mail for callers. Do include: (1) your name, (2) your organization, (3) invite the caller to leave a message, and (4) suggest a good time to call. Do remember to send calls directly into your voice mail when you are not in, so people don't have to wait to leave their message.

- Do call people back within 24 hours.

Etiquette for pagers and cellular phones:

- Don't interrupt others with your messages. Do use a vibrating pager rather than audio. But even with a vibrating pager, don't interrupt meetings and other activities that are not true emergencies.

- Don't disrupt others with your cellular phone conversations, such as talking in meeting and public places (walking down the street, in a theater, restaurant, or classroom). Do leave to a private place.

- Do be extra careful when talking on the phone while driving for your own safety and that of others, as many accidents are phone related.

E-mail Etiquette

- Do use e-mail for short messages, two-page max. Do get to the point quickly and clearly; don't ramble.

- Do use attachments for sending long messages, three or more pages. However, do send the attachment so that it is readable to the receiver.

- Do use the spelling and grammar checkers. People place more value on what you say when it is said correctly.

- Do avoid Internet and other jargon that others may not know.

- Don't say anything in an e-mail that you don't want others to know about. It is possible for organizations to read your e-mail, even the ones you delete can be read by some systems.

- Don't send emotional messages, for the same reasons as leaving phone messages.

- Do avoid junk e-mail. Don't send needless messages. Don't "cc:" (carbon copy) people who don't need to know your message.

Meeting etiquette

If you are running a meeting, follow the guidelines in Chapter 10 on managing meeting skills. Below is etiquette for attendees of meetings.

- Do arrive on time.

- Do come to the meeting properly prepared. Do any reading and assignments before the meeting.

- If you are late, do apologize. But do not give a reason for being late. Excuses only take up meeting time and are often not believed anyway.

- Don't be a problem member.

Hoteling etiquette

Hoteling is the sharing of workspace and equipment, such as desks, computers, phones, fax machines, copiers, eating areas, refrigerators, coffee machines, water coolers, and so on.

- Do follow the general golden rule—do unto others as you would have them do to you.

- Do clean up after yourself and make sure the equipment is ready for the next person to use when you are done, even if you find the area cluttered or dirty, the machine without paper, the coffee pot without coffee, etc. Do assertively confront others who do not clean up or make ready the equipment.

- Do pay your fair share of any expenses, such as coffee or water money, splitting the bill for lunch, chipping in for employee presents, and so on. Don't take other people's food and drinks without permission. And if they give it to you, return the favor.

- Do respect others privacy. Don't read anything on anyone's desk, computer screen, messages, or fax. It's like opening and reading their mail, which is a don't.

- Don't monopolize shared workspace and equipment; share it equitably.

WORK APPLICATIONS

8.   Give a job example of when someone behaved with improper etiquette.

VERTICAL POLITICS

Vertical politics are relations with superiors and subordinates. Your superiors are persons in the organization who are on a higher level than you. Your subordinates are persons who are on a lower level than you. Your boss and the employees you supervise and who report to you are the most important persons with whom to develop effective relations.[72]

Relations with Your Boss

Your relationship with your boss will affect your job satisfaction and can mean the difference between success or failure on the job. Not getting along with your boss can make life miserable for you. Needless to say, you should work at developing a good working relationship with your boss.[73]

Analyze your boss's style and, if necessary, change your style to match it. For example, if your boss is very businesslike and you are very informal and talkative, be businesslike when you are with your boss. Remember, people generally like people who behave like themselves.

Knowing your boss can lead to better human relations between the two of you. It is helpful to know your boss's primary responsibility, what your boss regards as good performance, how your performance will be evaluated, and what your boss expects of you.

Common Expectations of Bosses

Your boss will most likely expect loyalty, cooperation, initiative, information, and openness to criticism.

Loyalty: Executives value loyalty most in subordinates.[74] You will be expected to carry out the organization's standing plans and any special orders with the proper attitude. You should not talk negatively about your boss behind his or her back,[75] even if others are doing so. Regardless of how careful you are, or how trustworthy the other person is, gossip always seems to get back to the boss. When it does, it can seriously hurt your relationship. Your boss may never forget it or forgive you for doing it. The benefits, if any, don't outweigh the cost of not being loyal. In fact, you should never talk negatively about anyone; it can only get you into trouble. The old adage "If you can't say anything good about someone, don't say anything at all" is a good one to follow. Continuing to listen to, and especially agreeing with, negative statements only encourages others to continue this behavior. The discussion between Bob and Sally is an example of negative talk about others. If people are talking negatively about others, encourage them to stop in a nice way, change the subject, or leave them. For example, "Complaining about Roger really doesn't change anything. Why don't we talk about the things we can change like . . ." "Did you/anyone see the movie/game on TV last night?"

Cooperation: Your boss expects you to be cooperative with him or her and with everyone you must work with. If you cannot get along with others, you can be an embarrassment to your boss. And bosses don't like to be embarrassed. Roger is not cooperative; his boss Ted has told him that if he wants to get ahead he will have to be a team player.

Initiative: Your boss will expect you to know your responsibility and authority and to act without having to be told to do so. If there is a problem, the boss may expect you to solve it, rather than bring it to him or her to solve. If it is appropriate to include the boss in solving a problem, at least analyze the situation and have a recommended solution to present to him or her.

Information: Your boss expects you to keep him or her informed about what your objectives are and how you are progressing. If there are problems, your boss expects you to tell him or her about them.[76] You should not cover up your mistakes, your employees' mistakes, or your boss's mistakes. You can cause your boss the embarrassment of looking stupid by finding out from others what's going on in his or her department. Bosses don't like to be surprised.

Openness to Criticism: We all make mistakes; part of your boss's job is to help you avoid repeating them. When your boss criticizes you, try not to become defensive and argumentative. Remember that criticism is a means of improving your skills; be open to it even though it may hurt. Don't take it personally.

If you use the nine guidelines to effective human relations, get to know your boss, and meet his or her expectations, you should develop a good relationship. If you meet your boss's expectations, he or she will most likely be willing to help you meet your needs. Meeting your boss's expectations can help you meet the goal of human relations by creating a win-win situation for both of you.

If you don't get along with your boss, your chances of promotion may be hurt, and you could be transferred to a dead-end job.[77] Also, be careful about going over his or her head (to your boss's boss) because you may be viewed as a betrayer of loyalty and as unethical.[78] Or going to complain about your boss can create more problems for you than solutions.[79]

WORK APPLICATIONS

9. Of the five common expectations of bosses, which is your strongest area? Your weakest area? Explain your answers.

Relations with Subordinates

If the goal of human relations is to satisfy employee needs while achieving organizational objectives, why are poor human relations common? One reason is the fact that the manager must consider the work to be accomplished as ultimately more important than the needs and desires of those doing the work, including the manager's own needs. Managers get so busy getting the job done that they forget about the needs of the employees doing the work. Employees tend to start a job enthusiastically, but the manager does not take the time to develop the human relations necessary to maintain that enthusiasm. As a manager, you must take the time to develop effective human relations.[80]

Developing Manager-Employee Relations

In developing manager-employee relations, one should follow the nine guidelines to human relations. Perfect human relations probably don't exist. The manager should strive for harmonious relations where differences of opinion are encouraged and settled in a peaceful manner. Morale should be kept at high levels, but don't try to please all of the people all of the time. As a manager, you may face resentment from an employee who resents you for what you are (the manager), rather than for who you are. Others may not like you for any number of reasons. A manager can have good human relations without being well liked personally or being popular.

Friendship

The relationship between manager and employee cannot be one of "real" friendship. The nature of supervision excludes true friendship because the manager must evaluate the employee's performance; true friends don't evaluate or judge each other in any formal way. The manager must also give employees directions; friends don't order each other around. The manager must also get the employee to change; friends usually don't seriously try to change each other.

Trying to be friends may cause problems for you, the employee, and the department. Will your friend try to take advantage of your friendship to get special favors? Will you be able to treat your friend like the other members of the department? The other employees may say you play favorites. They may resent your friend(s) and ostracize him or her. Your friendship could adversely affect department morale.

Managers not being true friends to employees does not mean that they should not be friendly. If the manager takes an "I'm the boss" attitude, employees may resent him or her and morale problems could result. As in most cases, there are exceptions to the rule. Some managers are friends with employees and are still very effective managers.

WORK APPLICATIONS

10. Assume you are hired for or promoted to a management position. Will you develop a relationship with your employees based on friendship? Describe the relationship you plan to develop.

The Open-Door Policy

The **open-door policy** *is the practice of being available to employees.* Your management ability is directly proportional to the amount of time your door is open, both literally and figuratively. For effective human relations, you must be available to employees to give them the help they need, when they need it. If employees view the manager as too busy or not willing to help them, poor human relations and low morale can result. Wal-Mart credits part of its success to its open-door policy. An open-door policy does not mean that you must stop everything whenever an employee wants to see you. For nonemergencies the employee should make an appointment. You should prioritize spending time with an employee, along with other responsibilities. Managers are also using an open e-mail policy.

WORK APPLICATIONS

11. Does your present or past boss use the open-door policy? Explain.

Following the above guidelines should help you develop effective human relations with your subordinates. Use your power wisely to meet the goal of human relations. Remember, as a manager your success depends upon your subordinates.[81] If you want employees to meet your expectations, create a win-win situation. Help your subordinates meet their needs while attaining the high performance that will make you a success. When you ask subordinates to do something, answer their unasked question, "What's in it for me?" The Professor Smith–student aide example under reward power is a superior subordinate win-win situation example.

HORIZONTAL POLITICS

Horizontal politics are your relations with your peers and members of other departments. Your peers are the people who are on the same level in the organizational hierarchy as you. Your direct peers also report to your boss. You will learn how to develop effective horizontal politics.

Relations with Peers

To be successful you must cooperate, compete with, and sometimes even criticize your peers.

Cooperating with Peers

Your success as an employee is linked to other employees in the organization.[82] If you are cooperative and help them, they should have a positive attitude toward you and be willing to help you meet your objectives. If you don't cooperate with your peers, your boss will know it.

Competing with Peers

Even though you are cooperative with your peers, you are still in competition with them. Your boss will compare you to them when evaluating your performance, giving raises, and granting promotions. Like a great athlete, you must learn to be a team player and help your peers to be successful, but at the same time you have to look good as well.

Criticizing Peers

Do not go looking for faults in your peers. But if your peers do something they shouldn't, you owe it to them to try to correct the situation or prevent it from recurring in the future. Tactfully and sincerely telling a peer of a shortcoming is often appreciated. Sometimes peers are not aware of the situation. But there are people who don't appreciate criticism or unsolicited advice.

Do not go to the boss unless it is a serious offense, such as disregarding safety rules that endanger the welfare of employees. Unless your own safety is in danger, tell the boss only after discussing it with the peer and warning him or her of the consequences of continuing the behavior. Do not cover for a peer in trouble—you will only make things worse for everyone involved. And don't expect or ask others to cover for you.

Roger violates peer relations. He always has to get his own way. Roger is uncooperative, too competitive, and criticizes coworkers and members of other departments to force them to give him his own way.

WORK APPLICATIONS

12. Give an example, preferably from an organization you work(ed) for, of a situation in which you had good human relations with your peers. Describe how you cooperated, competed, and/or criticized your peers.

Relations with Members of Other Departments

You will most likely need the help of other departments.[83] You will need personnel to hire new employees, accounting to approve budgets, purchasing to get materials and supplies, maintenance to keep the department's equipment running efficiently, quality control to help maintain the quality of the product, payroll to okay overtime pay, and so forth.

Some of these departments have procedures you should follow. Develop good human relations through being cooperative and following the guidelines set by the organization.[84] It is also advisable to develop good relations with people in other organizations.[85]

Roger's "pulling the old emergency routine" so many times has resulted in purchasing and maintenance ignoring him. This is an embarrassment for Ted and the department, and it is hurting performance.

Following the guidelines in the text should help you to develop effective human relations with others. Make your peers and members of other departments your friends and allies.[86] Use your power wisely to meet the goal of human relations. Your success depends upon others. When you want something, remember to use effective horizontal politics to create a win-win situation for all involved. Answer people's unasked question, "What's in it for me?" Tom, the computer manager in the example under ethical politics, used horizontal politics to get the new computer.

WORK APPLICATIONS

13. Give an example, preferably from an organization you work(ed) for, of a situation in which you had good human relations with members of other departments. Describe how your relations affected your performance, the other departments, and the organization as a whole.

APPLICATION SITUATIONS

Relations with Others AS 2–4
Identify the other party being mentioned in each statement.
   A.   Subordinate   C.   Peers
   B.   Superior   D.   Other departments

_____   16.   "As a supervisor, I report to a middle manager named Kim."

_____   17.   "The guys in sales are always trying to rush us to ship the product."

_____   18.   "Willy is reluctant to accept the task I delegated to him."

_____   19.   "That's the owner of the company."

_____   20.   "The supervisors are getting together for lunch. Will you join us?"

How Politics and Ethics Affect Behavior, Human Relations, and Performance

People who are politically inclined tend to use different behavior than those who do not use politics. In reviewing the 10 statements in Self-Assessment Exercise 2–2, Political Behavior, you can see the difference in behavior between political people and nonpolitical people.

People who are ethical behave differently than those who are not ethical. Roger behaves differently than Bob and Sally. Think about the highly ethical and unethical people you have worked with. How does their behavior differ?

Generally, people who use ethical politics have good human relations, while those who use unethical political behavior tend to have poor human relations. People who are ethical and unethical deal with people differently. People using unethical politics tend to lie, cheat, and break the rules. In time people recognize unethical people and distrust them. Bob and Sally don't have effective human relations with Roger because of his political behavior. The purchasing and maintenance department members ignore Roger's request because of his behavior, while Bob and Sally have good relations with these departments. Roger is not meeting Ted's expectations because of his political behavior.

Human relations affect performance.[87] Generally, people who use ethical politics are more productive in the long run than people who use unethical politics.[88] People who use unethical politics may get short-run performance results, but in the long run, performance will be lower. Roger's use of emergencies may have worked for a while, but the purchasing and maintenance departments now ignore his emergency requests. As a result of Roger's behavior, his performance, his peers' performance, his boss Ted's performance, other departments' performance, and the performance of the organization as a whole are affected negatively.

Unethical behavior can get you fired, which will stop your performance within an organization completely, and can also result in your going to prison.

See Figure 2–3 for an illustration that puts the concepts of power, politics, and ethics together. You start in the center with the goal of human relations to create a win-win situation through horizontal politics with your peers and people in other departments and through vertical politics with your superiors and subordinates. You also use appropriate power with your politics.

REVIEW

Select one or more methods: (1) fill in the missing key terms from memory; (2) match the key terms, from the end of the review, with their definitions below; and/or (3) copy the key terms in order from the key terms at the beginning of the chapter.

In addition to having good performance, if you want to climb the corporate ladder, you will have to gain power and utilize ethical political skills with your superiors, subordinates, peers, and members of other departments.

_____ is a person's ability to influence another person's behavior. Generally, the higher the organizational level, the more power one has. The two sources of power are position power and personal power, while the seven bases of power include: _____, based on threats and/or punishment to influence compliance; _____, based on the user's relationship with influential people; _____, based on the user's ability to influence others with something of value to them; _____, based on the user's position power; _____, based on the user's personal power; _____, based on the user's information being desired by others; and _____, based on the user's skill and knowledge. The use of power affects behavior, human relations, and performance. The power used should be appropriate for the situation.

_____, the process of gaining and using power, is an important part of meeting organizational objectives. _____ involves creating obligations and debts, developing alliances, and using them to accomplish objectives.

_____ is the moral standard of right and wrong behavior. _____ refers to behavior that is considered wrong by authorities, yet not accepted by others as unethical; while _____ refers to behavior that is considered wrong by authorities and the individual, yet conducted anyway. _____ includes behavior that benefits both the individual and the organization, while _____ includes behavior that benefits the individual and hurts the organization. The human relations guide to ethical decisions seeks to meet the goal of human relations by creating a win-win situation for all parties including superiors, subordinates, peers, members of other departments, and people and organizations outside the organization. If you are proud to tell all relevant parties your decision, that decision is probably ethical; if you are embarrassed to tell or if you rationalize, it is probably unethical behavior.

Relations with your superiors and subordinates, vertical politics, are important to career success. Get to know your boss and his or her expectations. Common expectations of bosses include loyalty, cooperation, initiative, information, and openness to criticism. With your employees develop a professional relationship, rather than friendship, and use the _____, the practice of being available to employees.

Relations with peers and other departments, horizontal politics, are also important to career success. Learn to cooperate and compete with your peers and criticize them when necessary. Be cooperative and follow company guidelines in working with other departments.

In general, ethical politics have a positive effect on behavior, human relations, and performance in the long run. In the short run, unethical behavior may increase performance, but in the long run, it tends to have a negative effect on behavior, human relations, and performance.

KEY TERMS

coercive power
connection power
ethical politics
ethics
expert power

information power
legitimate power
open-door policy
politics
power

reciprocity
referent power
reward power
Type I ethics
Type II ethics
unethical politics

CASE

Carlton Petersburg is a tenured professor of leadership at a small teaching college in the Midwest. The Department of Leadership (DL) has nine faculty members; it is one of 10 departments in the School of Arts and Sciences (SAS). The leadership department chair is Tina Joel, who is in her first year as chair. Six faculty members, including Carlton, have been in the department for longer than Tina. She likes to have policies so that faculty members have guides for their behavior. On the college-wide level, there is no policy about the job of graduate assistants. Tina asked the Dean of the SAS what the policy was. The Ddean stated that there is not policy, and he had spoken to the V.P. for Academic Affairs. The V.P. and the Dean suggested letting the individual departments develop their own policy regarding what graduate assistants can and cannot do. So Tina put use of graduate assistants on the department-meeting agenda.

During the DL meeting, Tina asked for members' views on what graduate assistants should and should not be allowed to do. Tina was hoping that the department would come to a consensus on a policy. Carlton Petersburg was the only faculty member who was using graduate assistants to grade exams. All but one of the other faculty members spoke out against the use of graduate assistants grading exams. Other faculty members believed it is the job of the professor to grade the exams. Carlton made a few statements in hopes of not having to correct his own exams. Carlton stated that his exams were objective, thus there being a correct answer, it was not necessary for him to personally correct the exams. He also pointed out that across the campus, and across the country, other faculty members are using graduate assistants to teach entire courses and to correct subjective papers and exams. Carlton stated that he did not think it would be fair to tell him that he could not use graduate assistants to grade objective exams when others could do so. He also stated that the department did not need to have a policy, and requested that the department not set a policy. However, Tina stated that she wanted a policy. He held a single minority view during the meeting. However, after the meeting, one other member, Fred Robbinson, of the department, who said nothing during the meeting, told Carlton that he agreed that it was not fair to deny him the use of a graduate assistant.

There was no department consensus, as Tina hoped there would be. Tina said that she would draft a department policy, which would be discussed at a future DI meeting. The next day, Carlton sent a memo to department members asking if it was ethical and legal to deny him the use of the same resources as others across the campus. He also stated that if the department set a policy stating that he could no longer use graduate assistants to correct objective exams, he would appeal the policy decision to the Dean, V.P. and President.

Go to the Internet

This case actually did happen. However, the names have been changed for confidentiality. Thus, you cannot go to the college website where the case really happened. Therefore, go to your own college website and get information about your college that you did not know.

Support your answer to the following questions with specific information from the case and text, or information you get from other source.

1. What source of power does Tina have, and what type of power is she using during the meeting?

2. (a) What source of power does Carlton have, and (b) what type of power is he using during the meeting? (c) Is the memo a wise political move for Carlton? What may be gained and lost by sending it?

3. What would you do if you were Tina? (a) Would you talk to the dean letting him know that Carlton said he would appeal the policy decision? (b) Which political behavior would the discussion be? (c) Would you draft a policy directly stating that graduate assistants cannot be used to grade objective exams? (d) Would your answer to c be influenced by your answer to a?

4. If you were Carlton, (a) knowing you had no verbal supporters during the meeting, would you have continued to defend your position or agree to stop using a graduate assistant? (b) What do you think of Carlton sending the memo? (c) As a tenured full professor, Carlton is secure in his job. Would your answer change if you/ Carlton had not received tenure or promotion to the top rank?

5. If you were Carlton, and Tina drafted a policy and department members agreed with it, what would you do? (a) Would you appeal the decision to the dean? (b) Again, would your answer change if you/Carlton had not received tenure or promotion to the top rank?

6. If you were the Dean of SAS, knowing that the v.p. does not want to set a college-wide policy, and Carlton appealed to you, what would you do? Would you develop a school-wide policy for SAS?

7. At what level (college wide, by schools, or by departments within each school) should a graduate-assistant policy be set?

8. (a) Should Fred Robbinson have spoken up in defense of Carlton during the meeting? (b) If you were Fred, would you have taken Carlton's side against the other seven members? (c) Would your answer change if you were and were not friends with Carlton, and if you were and were not a tenured full professor?

9. What is the role of perception and attitudes and values in this case?

10. What type of communications were used in this case? What was the major barrier to communications?

11. Which motivation theory was Carlton using to defend his position to use graduate assistance?

12. Which situational supervisory leadership style was Tina using to set the policy?

13. Which conflict management style did Tina and Carlton use in setting the policy? Which conflict management style would you have used if you were in Carlton's situation?

OBJECTIVE CASE

Politicking

Karen Whitmore is going to be promoted in two months. She will be replaced by her subordinate Jim Green or Lisa Fesco. Both Jim and Lisa know they are competing for the promotion. Their years of experience and quality and quantity of work are about the same. Below is some of the political behavior each used to help them get the promotion.

Lisa has been going to night classes and company training programs in management to prepare herself for the promotion. Lisa is very upbeat; she goes out of her way to be nice to people and compliment them. She gets along well with everyone. Knowing that Karen was an officer in a local businesswomen's networking organization, Lisa joined the club six months ago and now serves on a committee. At work Lisa talks regularly to Karen about the women's organization. Lisa makes an effort to know what is going on in the organization. One thing Karen doesn't like about Lisa is the fact that when she points out Lisa's errors, she always has an answer for everything.

Jim is good at sports and has been playing golf and tennis with upper-level managers for over a year now. In the department, especially with Karen, Jim refers to conversations with managers all the time. When Jim does something for someone, they can expect to do a favor in return. Jim really wants this promotion, but he fears that with more women being promoted to management positions, Lisa will get the job just because she is a woman. To increase his chances of getting the job, Jim stayed late and made a few changes—errors—in the report Lisa was working on. Jim sees nothing wrong with making the changes to get ahead. When Lisa passed in the report, without checking prior work, Karen found the errors. The one thing Karen doesn't like about Jim is the fact that, on occasion, she has to tell him what to do before he acts.

Answer the following questions. Then in the space between the questions, state why you selected that answer. (Note: Meetings between Lisa and Jim, Karen and Jim or all three may be role-played in class.)

_____ 1. We know that Karen has _____ power.
　　　　　　　a. position　　　　　b. personal

_____ 2. To be promoted Lisa is stressing _____ power. Refer to the opening statement about Lisa.
　　　　　　　a. coercive　　　　c. reward　　　　　e. referent　　　　　g. expert
　　　　　　　b. connection　　d. legitimate　　　f. information

_____ 3. To be promoted Jim is stressing _____ power. Refer to the opening statement about Jim.
　　　　　　　a. coercive　　　　c. reward　　　　　e. referent　　　　　g. expert
　　　　　　　b. connection　　d. legitimate　　　f. information

_____ 4. _____ appears to use reciprocity the most.
　　　　　　　a. Lisa　　　　　　b. Jim

_____ 5. Lisa _____ conducted unethical political behavior.
　　　　　　　a. has　　　　　　　b. has not

_____ 6. Jim _____ conducted unethical political behavior.
　　　　　　　a. has　　　　　　　b. has not

_____ 7. Jim has committed _____ behavior in changing the report.
　　　　　　　a. Type I　　　　　b. Type II

_____ 8. Who was not affected by Jim changing the report?
　　　　　　　a. supervisors　　　c. peers　　　　　　e. other departments
　　　　　　　b. subordinates　　d. Karen's department　f. the organization

_____ 9. Lisa does not meet Karen's expectation of
      a. loyalty   c. initiative   e. openness to criticism
      b. cooperation   d. information

_____ 10. Jim does not meet Karen's expectation of
      a. loyalty   c. initiative   e. openness to criticism
      b. cooperation   d. information

11. In Lisa's situation, she suspects Jim made the changes in the report but she has no proof. What would you do?

12. In Karen's situation, she suspects Jim made the changes in the report, but she has no proof. What would you do?

MG WEBZINE

Go to the MG website (*www.mgeneral.com*) and read *Fiscal Fairy Tale # 7: The Three Pugs* (your instructor may ask you to print a copy and bring it to class). Answer these questions (your instructor may ask you to type them and bring them to class):

Questions Relating to the Tale Only

1. As stated at the end of the tale, in 50 words or so, what is your response to this tale? You may send it to MG.

2. Have you, or anyone you know, been sold something you did not need, more than you needed, or something that you could not afford to buy?

3. Do you generally trust salespeople?

4. Does it pay to be unethical?

Questions Relating the Tale to the Chapter Concepts

5. What base of power did Wick Wolf use to sell the three houses to the pugs?

6. Based on which power base did the three pugs go to Wick Wolf to buy a house?

7. Which characters in the tale used ethical and unethical behavior?

8. Is Wick Wolf on the Type I or Type II ethics?

VIDEO CASE 2

ETHICS: ARTHUR ANDERSON

This video presents separate short cases.

Vignette 1: The High-Bid Dilemma

A purchasing agent and his assistant are reviewing bids from seven companies. They disagree on who to give the contract to. Place yourself in the role of the assistant.

Critical Thinking Questions:

1. Is there a conflict of interest in this case?
2. From the purchasing manager's view, is this Type I or II ethical behavior.
3. Should you, as the assistant, agree with the purchasing agent and give the business to Spin Cast or disagree and object to giving the business to Spin Cast?
4. Would you, as the assistant, be proud to tell all relevant parties your decision or would you be embarrassed? Would you be rationalizing your decision?
5. If you, as the assistant, disagree with your boss, should you go to your boss' boss and explain the situation and/or should you report this biding process to outside sources (whistleblowing)?
6. Should you, as the assistant, go to the Spin Cast party?

Vignette 5: Creative Expense Reporting

Jim, a salesperson, asks a colleague Ken for information on expenses. Jim tells Ken of his creative expense reporting to claim entertainment expenses. Place yourself in both roles.

Critical Thinking Questions:

1. From Jim's view, is this Type I or II ethical behavior.
2. Should Jim have told Ken about his creative expense reporting?
3. Should Ken have told Jim that adding money to lunch and dinner to pay for entertainment is wrong and suggest that he not pad the expense report? Should Ken say to Jim that he will report this creative expense reporting to the boss, if he does it?
4. Would you, as Jim, be proud to tell all relevant parties your decision or would you be embarrassed? Would you be rationalizing your decision?
5. If you, as Ken, disagree with Jim's behavior, should you go to your boss and explain the situation and/or should you report this to outside sources (whistle-blowing)?

IN-CLASS SKILL-BUILDING EXERCISE

Who Has the Power? SB 2–1

Note:	This exercise is designed for permanent groups that have worked together at least twice.
Objective:	To better understand power and how people gain power.
SCANS:	The SCANS competencies of resources, interpersonal skill, information, and systems and the foundations of basic, thinking, and personal qualities are developed through this exercise.
Preparation:	You should have read and understood the text chapter.
Experience:	Your group will discuss power within the group.

Procedure 1 (5–10 minutes)

Permanent teams get together and decide which member has the most power at this time (greatest ability to influence group members' behavior). Power can change with time. Before discussion, all members select the member they believe has the most power. You may select yourself. Write the most powerful person's name here _____. After everyone has made their selection, each member should state who was selected and explain why. Record the names of those selected below.

Come to an agreement on the one person with the most power. Write the group's choice here.

Was there a struggle for power?

Why is this person the most powerful in the group? To help you answer this question, as a group, answer the following questions about your most powerful person.

Procedure 2 (7–12 minutes)

1. Which of the nine human relations guidelines does he or she follow: (1) be optimistic, (2) be positive, (3) be genuinely interested in other people, (4) smile and develop a sense of humor, (5) call people by name, (6) listen to people, (7) help others, (8) think before you act, and (9) create win-win situations.

2. How does this person project a positive image? What type of image does his or her appearance project? What nonverbal communication does this person project that sends a positive image? What behavior does this person use that gains him or her power?

3. The primary source of this person's power is: (position/personal).

4. The primary base for this person's power in the group is: (coercive, connection, reward, legitimate, referent, information, expert).

5. This person uses which of the following political behaviors (gets along with everyone, makes people feel important and compliments them, compromises and avoids telling people they are wrong)?

6. This person uses (ethical/unethical) politics.

7. This person (cooperates with, competes with, criticizes) group members.

    Overall, why is this person the most powerful? (Agree and write the reason below.)

    Share the feeling you experienced doing this exercise. How did you feel about not being, or being, selected as the most powerful group member? Who wanted power and who didn't? Is it wrong or bad to want and seek power?

Optional:
1. A spokesperson from each group tells the class which member was selected the most powerful, and the overall reason why the person is the most powerful.

2. A spokesperson from each group does not tell the class which member was selected the most powerful, but does state the overall reason why the person is the most powerful.

Conclusion: The instructor leads a class discussion and/or makes concluding remarks.

Application: (2–4 minutes) What did I learn from this exercise? How will I use this knowledge in the future?

Sharing: Volunteers give their answers to the application section.

PREPARATION FOR SKILL-BUILDING EXERCISE

Ethics SB 2–2

For each of the following statements, place an "O" on the line if you observed someone doing this behavior. Also place an "R" on the line if you reported this behavior within the organization.

(O) Observed   (R) Reported

_____ 1.   Coming to work late and getting paid for it.

_____ 2.   Leaving work early and getting paid for it.

_____ 3.   Taking long breaks/lunches and getting paid for it.

_____ 4.   Calling in sick to get a day off, when not sick.

_____ 5.   Using the company phone to make personal long distance calls.

_____ 6.   Doing personal work while on company time.

_____ 7.   Using the company copier for personal use.

_____ 8.   Mailing personal things through the company mail.

_____ 9.   Taking home company supplies or merchandise.

_____ 10.   Giving company supplies or merchandise to friends or allowing them to take them without saying anything.

_____ 11.   Putting in for reimbursement for meals and travel or other expenses that weren't actually eaten or taken.

_____ 12.   Using the company car for personal business.

_____ 13.   Taking spouse/friends out to eat and charging it to the company expense account.

_____ 14.   Taking spouse/friend on business trips and charging the expense to the company.

_____ 15.   Accepting gifts from customers/suppliers in exchange for giving them business.

_____ 16.   A student cheating on homework assignments.

_____ 17.   A student passing off someone else's term paper as his or her own work.

_____ 18.   A student cheating on an exam.

_____ 19.   For items 1–15, select the three which you consider the most severe unethical behavior. Who is harmed and who benefits by these unethical behaviors?

_____ 20.   For items 16–18, who is harmed and who benefits from these unethical behaviors?

_____ 21.   If you observed unethical behavior but didn't report it, why didn't you report the behavior? Also, if you did report the behavior, why did you report it? What was the result?

IN-CLASS SKILL-BUILDING EXERCISE

Ethics   SB 2–2

Objective: To better understand ethics and whistle-blowing.

SCANS: The SCANS competencies of resources, interpersonal skills, information, and systems and the foundations of basic, thinking, and personal qualities are developed through this exercise.

Preparation: You should have answered the questions in the preparation.

Experience: You will share your answers to the preparation questions.

Procedure 1 (5–30 minutes)

Option A: Break into groups of five or six and share your answers to the preparation questions.

Option B: The instructor leads a discussion in which students share their answers to the preparation questions. (The instructor may begin by going over the 18 statements and have students who have observed the behavior raise their hand.) Then the instructor will have them raise their hand if they reported the behavior.

Conclusion: The instructor may lead a class discussion and/or make concluding remarks.

Application (2–4 minutes): What did I learn from this exercise? How will I use this knowledge in the future?

Sharing: Volunteers give their answers to the application section.

VIDEO EXERCISE

Bases of Power VE 2–1

Objectives: To better understand the seven bases of power and when to use each.

SCANS: The SCANS competencies of resources, interpersonal skills, information, and systems and the foundations of basic, thinking, and personal qualities are developed through this exercise.

Preparation: You should understand the seven bases of power.

Procedure (10–20 minutes)

The instructor shows video module 10, Power. As you view each of the seven scenes, identify the power base being used by the manager.

Scene 1. _____	A.	coercive power
Scene 2. _____	B.	connection power
Scene 3. _____	C.	reward power
Scene 4. _____	D.	legitimate power
Scene 5. _____	E.	referent power
Scene 6. _____	F.	information power
Scene 7. _____	G.	expert power

After viewing each of the seven scenes, identify/match the power base used by the manager by placing the letter of the power base on the scene line.

Option A: View all seven scenes and identify the power base used by the manager. After viewing all seven scenes, discuss and/or have the instructor give the correct answers.

Option B: After each scene the class discusses the power base used by the manager. The instructor states the correct answer after each of the seven scenes.

Procedure (2–5 minutes)

Select the one power base you would use to get the employee to take the letter to the mail room. Which other power bases are also appropriate? Which power bases would you not use (are not appropriate) for this situation? Next to each power base listed above, write the letter 'A' for appropriate or 'N' for not appropriate.
Discussion:

Option A: In groups of four to six, answer the questions below.

Option B: As a class, answer the questions below.

　　　1. Which power bases are not appropriate to use in this situation?

　　　2. Which power bases are appropriate to use in this situation?

　　　3. Is there one base of power most appropriate in this situation?

Conclusion: The instructor may make concluding remarks.

Application (2–4 minutes): What did I learn from this exercise? How will I use this knowledge in the future?

Sharing: Volunteers give their answers to the application section.

NOTES

1. C.W. Moom and A.A. Lado, "MNC-Host Government Bargaining Power Relationship: A Critique and Extension Within the Resource-Based View," *Journal of Management 26, No. 1* (January 2000), p. 85.

2. "Criterion: Arming Management With the Power of Information," *Dallas Business Journal 23, No. 39* (May 19, 2000), p. 18c.

3. T. Gautschi, "Don't Confuse Authority, Power, and Politics," *Design News 52, No. 9* (May5, 1997), pp.202-3.

4. M. A. Carpenter and B.R. Golden, "Perceived Managerial Discretion: A Study of Cause and Effect," *Strategic Management Journal 18, No. 3* (March 1997), pp. 187-206.

5. D.E. Conlon and D. P. Sullivan, "Examining the Actions of Organizations in Conflict: Evidence from the Delaware Court of Chancery," *Academy of Management Journal 42, No. 3* (1999), pp.319-29.

6. A. Bird. "The Ten Commandmanets of Super Community Banking," *The Bankers Magazine 180, No. I* (january-February 1997), pp. 12-9.

7   H.P. Guzda, "The Business Employee Empowerment: Democracy and Ideologyin the Workplace," *Monthly Labor Review 123*, No.2 (February 2000), p.49.

8. Pascarelle, *"Thinking Globally,"* pp. 58-60.

9. G.P. Zachary, "Workplace, The New Search for Meaning in 'Meaningless' Work," *The Wall Street Journal*, January 9,1997, p. 81.

10. M.A. Carpenter and B.R. Golden , "Perceived Managerial Direction : A Case Sudy and Effect," *Strategic Management Journal* 18, No. 3 (March 1997), pp.187-206.

11. J. French and B. Raven, "A Comparative Analysis of Power and Preference," in J.T. Tedeschi, ed., *Prospectives on Social Power* (Hawthorne, N.Y.: Adline Publishing, 1974).

12. S.S.K. Lam, "Social Power for Compliance of Middle Managers and Front-Line Workers with Quality Improvement Policies," *Journal of Managment Development* 15. No. 9 (September 1996), pp.13-7.

13. D.E. Colon and D.P. Sullivan, "Examing the Actions of Organizations in Conflict," Evidence from the Delaware Court of Chancery," *Academy of Management Journal 42. No. 3* (1999). pp.319-29.

14. C.S. Katsikeas, M.M.H. Goode, and E. Katsikea. "Sources of Power in International Marketing Channels," *Journal of Marketing Management 16,* No. 1-3 (January 2000), p. 185.

15. "Managing your Career" or "You Can Be Good At Office Policies Without Being A Jerk," *The Wall Street Journal*, March 18,1997, p. A1.

16. C.S. Katsikeas, M.M.H. Goodeand E. Kastsikea. "Sources of Power International Marketing Channels ," *Journal of Marketing Management 16,* No. 1-3 (Januaury 2000), p.185.

17. Ibid.

18. H.P. Guzda, "The Business of Employee Empowerment: Democracy and Ideology in the Workplace," *Monthly Labor Review 123*, Iss. 2 (February 2000), p. 49.

19. "Criterion: Arming Management With the Power of Information," *Dallas Business Journal 23,* No. 39 (May 19,2000), p. 18c.

20. M. Schrage, "Net Computers Hinge or Corporate Politics," *Computerworld 30,* No. 50 (December 9,1996), p. 37.

21. M.I. Reed, "Expert Power and Control in Late Modernity: An Emperial Review and Theoretics Synthesis (Special Issue: Change as an Underlying Theme in Professional Service Organizations)," *Orgazational Studies 17,* No. 4 (Fall 1996), pp. 273-97.

22. C.W. Moon and A.A. Lado. "MNC.Host Government Bargaining Power Relationship: A Critique and Extension Within the Resource Based View." *Journal of Management 26 ,* No.1 (January 2000), p. 85.

23. C. Oswick and D. Grant. "Personal Management in the Public Sector : Power, Roles and Relationships," *Personnel Review 25,* No. 2 (February 1996). pp. 4-18.

24. Pascarella, "Thinking Globally," pp.58-60.

25. M.A. Reed-Woodward. "Campaigning for Office," *Black Enterprise 30.* No. 9 (2000), p. 68.

26. G.R. Ferris, D.D. Frink, M.C.Galang, J. Zhou, K.M. Kacmar and J.L. Howard,"Perceptions of Organizational Politics: Prediction, Stress-Related Implications, and Outcomes," *Human Relations 49*, No.2 (February 1996), pp.233-66.

27. M.Schrage, "Net Computers Hinge on Corporate Politics," *Computerworld 30,* No, 50 (December 9,1996). p. 37.

28. T.Gautschi, "Don't Confuse Authority, Power, and Politics," *Design News 52.* No. 9 (May,5, 1997), pp. 202-3.

29. R.G. Cook and D.R. Fox, "Resources, Frequency, and Methods." *Business and Society 39*, No.1 (March 2000), pp.94-113.

30. J.M. Brett, D.L. Shapiro, and A.L.Lytle. "Breaking the Bonds of Reciprocity in Negotiations,"*Academy of Management Journal 41*, No. 4 (1998), pp.410-24.

31. J, Steininger, "When Personalities Collide, Look for the 'Catbird Seat,'" *The Business Journal-Milwaukee 14,* No. 18 (January 31,1997), p. 10.

32. Managing Your Career, "You Can Be good at Office Politics Without Being A Jerk," *The Wall Street Journal*, March 18, 1997, p. 81.

33. R.T. Sparrowe and R.C. Liden. "Process and Structure in Leader-Member Exchange." *Academy of Management Exchange 22*, No. 2 (April 1997), p. 10.

34. M. Valle and P.M. Perrewe. "Do Politics Relate to Political Behavior? Test of an Implicit Assumption and Expanded Model ," *Human Relations 53*, No. 3 (March 2000), p. 359.

35. T. Gautschi, "Don't Confuse Authority, Power, and Politics." *Design News 52*, No. 9 (May 5, 1997), pp. 202-3.

36. Managing Your Career. "You Can Be good At Office Politics Without Being A Jerk." *The Wall Street Journal*. March18, 1997. p. B1.

37. M.I. Reed, "Expert Power and Control in Late Modernity:An Empirical Review and Theoretical Synthesis (Special Issue: Change as an Underlying Theme in Professional Service Organizations)." *Organizational Studies 17*. No. 4 (Fall 1996). pp. 573-97.

38. Ibid.

39. Managing your Career. You Can Be Good at office Politics Without Being A Jerk," *The Wall Street Journal*, March 18,1997, p.B1.

40. E.J. Walsh, "Leadership in an Age of Distrust." *Industry Week 246*, No. 13 (July 7,1997), pp.78-83.

41. N. Fitzgerald. "Real Investment," *CA Magazine 101*. No. 1088 (1997), pp.58-60.

42. J. Steininger, "When Personalities Collide, Look for the'Catbird Seat,'" *The Business Journal-Milwaukee* 14, No. 18 (January 31, 1997), p.10.

43. J.T. Polzer, E.A. Mannix, and M.A, Neale, "Interest Alignment and Coalitions in Multiparty Negotiation." *Academy of Management Journal 41*. No. I (1998), pp.42-54.

44. "Finding A Niche In Networking." *Women in Business 49*, No. 1 (January-February 1997), p. 6.

45. D.J. Brass, K.D. Butterfield, and B.C. Skaggs, "Relationships and Unethical Behavior: A Social Network Perspective," *Academy of Management Review 12*, No. 1 (1998) pp. 14-31.

46. T.B. Becker, "Integrity in Organizations: Beyond Honesty and Conscientiousness." *Academy Management Review 23*, No.1. pp. 154-61.

47. J.Vidal. "The Real Politics of Power (Growing Power of Large Corporations; Excerpt from McLibel: Burger Culture on Trial; Society)," *The Guardian* (April30,1997). pp.54-55.

48. R.Barrett, "Liberating the Corporate Soul," *HR Focus 74*, No. 4 (April 1997), pp.15-16.

49. J.M. Schrof, "No Whining! (Profile of Talk Show Host Laura Schlessinger)," *US News and World Report 123*, No. 2 (July 14,1997), pp.48-53.

50. Business Bulletin, "A Special Background Report on Trends in Industry and Finance, "*The Wall Street Journal*, April 17, 1997, p. B1.

51. S.G.Scott and V.R. Lane, "A Stakeholder Approach to Organizational Identity," *Academy of Management Review 25*, No. 1 (2000) pp.488-506.

53. "Liars Index," *The Wall Street Journal*, February 1, 2000. p. A1.

54. "Lying For The Boss," *The Wall Street Journal*, November 30,1999, p. A1.

55. J.F. Harison and R.E. Freeman, "Stakeholders, Social Responsibility, and Performance: Empirical Evidence and Theoretical Perspectives," *Academy of Management Journal 42*, No. 5 (1999). pp. 479-85.

56. S Berman, A.C. Wicks, S. Kotha, T.M. Jones, "Does Stakeholder Orientation Matter? The Relationship Between Stakeholder Management and Firm Financial Performance," *Academy of Management Journal 42*, No.5. pp. 488-506.

57. L.A. Gjertsen. "Future of Insurance Relies on Ethics (How Insurance Companies Can Encourage Ethical Behavior in Employees)" *National Underwriter Property & Casualty-Risk & Benefits Management 101*, No. 24 (Jume16,1997), pp. 9-10.

58. "Most Companies Consider Ethics Codes Important But Few Back Them Up" *The Wall Street Journal*, May 14, 1996, p.A1.

59. G.R. Weaver, L.K. Trevino, and P.L. Cochran, "Corporate Ethics Programs as Control Systems; Influences of Executive Commitment and Enviornmental Factors," *Academy of Management Journal 42*, No. 1 (1999). pp.41-57.

60. W. Bounds , "Critics Confront CEO Dedicated to Human Rights," *The Wall Street Journal*, February 24, 1997, p. B1.

61. B. Heller, "Growing Pains: APOR to Explore Ethics, Standardization (Association for Pharmacoeconomics and Outcomes Research Major Objectives for 1997)," *Drug Topics 141*. No. 10 (May 19,1197), p.47.

62. D. Lemoert, "Holding Accountable the Powers That Be: Protecting Our Integirty and the Public We Serve." *Public Administration Review 57*, No. 4 (July-August 1997). pp.11-4.

63. S.L. Robinson and A.M. O'Leary-Kelly, "Monkey See, Monkey Do: The Influence of Work Groups on the Antisocial Behavior of Employees," *Academy of Management Journal 41*. No. 6, (1998), pp.658-72.

64. D. Carnegie, "Human Relations Skills Provide Entrepreneurial Breadth," *Training 34*, No. 4 (1997), p.53.

65. "How Do You Rate as a CyberManager," *The Wall Street Journal*, May 28, 1996, p. B1.

66. D.C. Menzel, "Teaching Values and Ethics in Public Administration: Are We Making A Difference?" *Public Administration Review 57*, No. 3 (May-June 1997). pp.224-30.

67. G.R. Weaver, L.K. Trevino, and P.L. Cochran, "Corporate Ethics Programs as Control Systems: Influences of Executive Commitment and Enviornmental Factors," *Academy of Management Journal 42*, No.3 (1999), pp.41-57.

68. A. Tenbrunsel, " Misrepresentation and Expectations of Misrepresentation in an Ethical Dilemma: The Role of Incentives and Temptation," *Academy of Management Journal 41*, No. 3 (1998), pp.330-39.

69. P.S. Ridge, "Ethics Programs Aren't Stemming Employee Misconduct, a Study Indicates," *The Wall Street Journal*. May 11, 2000, p.A1.

70. R.A. Baron and G.D. Markman, "Beyond Social Capital: How Social Skills Can Enhance Entrepreneurs' Success," *Academy of Management Executive 14*, No. 1 (2000). p. 106-8.

71. Ibid.

72. Lancaster, Managing Your Career, "Start Listening," *The Wall Street Journal*, p. B1.

73. M. Lynn, "How to Manage Your Boss," *Management Today* (January 2000), p.66.

74 "Blind Devotion Wanted?" *The Wall Street Journal*, July 22, 1997, p. A1.

75. M. Lynn, "How to Manage Your Boss," *Management Today* (January 2000), pp. 66.

76. Ibid.

77. Managing Your Career, "You Can Be Good At Office Politics Without Being A Jerk," *The Wall Street Journal*, March 18, 1997, p. B1.

78. H. Lancaster, Managing Your Career, "Pick Your Fights Before Going Over Your Boss' Head," *The Wall Street Journal*, June 17,1997, p. B1.

79. M. Lynn, "How To Manage Your Boss," *Management Today*, January 2000, pp. 66.

80. C.S. Grizzard Sr., "Family Values At Work," *Fund Raising Management 27,* No. 8 (October 1996), p. 48.

81. M. Lynn, "How To Manage Your Boss," *Management Today*, January 2000, pp. 66.

82. Lancaster, "Managing Your Career, Start Listening," *The Wall Street Journal*, p. B1

83. D.L. Swanson, "Toward an Integrative Theory of Business and Society: A Research Strategy for Corporate Social Performance," *Academy of Management Review 24. No. 3* (1999), pp.506-21.

84. T. O'Toole and B. Donaldson, "Relationship Governance Structures and Performance," *Journal of Marketing Management 16, No. 4* (May 2000), p. 327.

85. Managing Your Career, "You Can Be Good at Office Politics Without Being a Jerk," *The Wall Street Journal*, March 18, 1997. p.B1.

86. Lancaster, Managing Your Career, "Start Listening," *The Wall Street Journal*, p. B1.

87. T. O'Toole and B. Donaldson. "Relationship Governance Structures and Performance," *Journal of Marketing Management 16, No. 4* (May 2000). p. 327.

88. B. Kotey and G.G. Meredith, "Relationships Among Owner/Manager Personal Values, Business Strategies and Enterprise Performance," *Journal of Small Business Management 35, No. 2* (April 1997), pp. 37-65.

Chapter 3

Conflict Management

SOURCE: Robert N. Lussier, *Human Relations in Organizations, Applications and Skill Building*, 5th ed., Chapter 8, McGraw-Hill, 2002, 1999, 1996, 1995, 1990.

Learning Objectives

After completing this chapter, you should be able to:

- Describe the three ego states of transactional analysis.

- Explain the three types of transactions.

- Identify the differences among passive, aggressive, and assertive behavior.

- List the four steps of assertive behavior.

- Explain when a conflict exists.

- State when and how to use five conflict management styles.

- List the steps of initiating, responding to, and mediating conflict resolutions.

- Define the following key terms:

accommodating conflict style	**forcing conflict style**
assertiveness	**initiating conflict resolution steps**
avoiding conflict style	**mediating conflict resolution steps**
collaborating conflict style	**responding to conflict resolution steps**
compromising conflict style	**transactional analysis**
conflict	**types of transactions**
ego states	**XYZ model**

Larry and Helen work together doing the same job at Harvey's Department Store. They share a special calculator because it is expensive and it is only used for part of their job. The calculator is generally kept in one's possession until the other person requests it. Recently, the amount of time each has to use the calculator has increased.

When Larry wants the calculator, he says, "I need the calculator now" (in a bold, intimidating voice), and Helen gives it to him, even when she is using it. When Helen needs the calculator, she says, "I don't like to bother you, but I need the calculator." If Larry is using it, he tells Helen that he will give it to her when he is finished with it, and Helen says, "OK." Helen doesn't think this arrangement is fair and is getting upset with Larry. But she hasn't said anything to Larry yet. Larry comes over to Helen's desk and this discussion takes place:

LARRY: I need the calculator right now.

HELEN: I'm sick and tired of your pushing me around. Go back to your desk, and I'll bring it to you when I'm good and ready.

LARRY: What's wrong with you? You've never acted like this before.

Helen: Just take the calculator and go back to your desk and leave me alone.

LARRY: (Says nothing; just takes the calculator and leaves.)

HELEN: (Watches Larry walk back to his desk with the calculator, feels a bit guilty, and thinks to herself) Why do I let little annoyances build up until I explode and end up yelling at people? It's rather childish behavior to let people walk all over me, then to reverse and be tough and rude. I wish I could stand up for my rights in a positive way without hurting my relations.

> Can this be done? It can, and you will learn how in this chapter.
>
> The major theme of this chapter is the development of interpersonal dynamic skills. This chapter focuses on dealing with your emotions and those of others in an effective way. When you interact with people, you respond (transactional analysis): You can let people push you around or you can stand up for your rights (assertiveness). When you are in disagreement with others (conflict), you can decide to ignore, or resolve, your differences. Being able to transact with people on the appropriate level, assertively stand up for your rights, and resolve your conflicts without hurting human relations will improve your effectiveness in organizations and in your personal life. The discussion of interpersonal development skills begins with transactional analysis.

TRANSACTIONAL ANALYSIS

Transactional analysis (TA) provides useful models for leadership styles.[1] Eric Berne developed transactional analysis,[2] and it has been applied[3] and written about ever since.[4] TA has been used with organizational development,[5] and to improve quality of work life.[6] Recently TA has been used to help multinational corporations prepare managers to operate effectively within other cultures[7]. TA is being used within relationship marketing to develop good human relations with customers.[8]

Transactional analysis *is a method of understanding behavior in interpersonal dynamics.* When you talk to someone about anything, you are involved in interpersonal dynamics, and a series of transactions take place. An organization is a product of the process of its human relations.[9]

Organizations have trained their employees in TA to improve their ability to handle difficult personal situations. A few of these companies include Pan American World Airways, the United Telephone Company of Texas and Pitney Bowes. Studying TA can help you to better understand people's behavior, and how to deal with emotions in a more positive way.

Below are three ego states, types of transactions, and life positions and stroking. Keep in mind that people are diverse and you will encounter a variety of ego states.

Ego States

According to Berne, we all have three major ego states that affect our behavior or the way we transact. The three **ego states** *are the parent, child, and adult.* We change ego states throughout the day, and even during a single discussion a series of transactions can take place between different ego states. Your parent, child, and adult ego states interact with other people's parent, child, and adult ego states. Understanding the ego state of the person you are interacting with can help you to understand his or her behavior and how to transact in an effective way.

Parent Ego State

When the parent ego state is in control, people behave from one of two perspectives:

1. Critical parent. When you behave and respond with evaluative responses that are critical, judgmental, opinionated, demanding, disapproving, disciplining, and so on, you are in the critical parent ego state. People in the critical parent ego state use a lot of do's and don'ts. Managers using the autocratic style tend to be in the critical parent ego state because they use high task/directive behavior.
2. Sympathetic parent. On the other hand, you can also be a different type of parent. When you behave and respond with reassuring responses that are protecting, permitting, consoling, caring, nurturing, and so on, you are in the sympathetic parent ego state. Managers using the consultative and participative styles tend to be in the sympathetic parent state because they are using high supportive/relationship behavior.

Child Ego State

When the child ego state is in control, people behave from one of two perspectives:

1. Natural child. When you behave and respond with probing responses that show curiosity, intimacy, fun, joyfulness, fantasy, impulsiveness, and so on, you are in the natural child ego state. Successful managers do not tend to continuously operate from the natural child ego state.
2. Adapted child. When you behave and respond with confronting responses that express rebelliousness, pouting, anger, fear, anxiety, inadequacy, procrastination, blaming others, and so on, you are in the adapted child ego state. Managers should avoid behaving from the adapted child ego state because this type of behavior often leads to the employee becoming emotional and behaving in a similar manner. When managers are transacting with an employee in this ego state, they should not react with similar behavior, but should be in the adult ego state.

Adult Ego State

When the adult ego state is in control, people behave in a thinking, rational, calculating, factual, unemotional manner. The adult gathers information, reasons things out, estimates probabilities, and makes decisions with cool and calm behavior. When communicating in the adult ego state, you avoid becoming the victim of the other person by controlling your response to the situation.

Generally, the most effective behavior, human relations, and performance come from the adult ego state.[10] When interacting with others, you should be aware of their ego state. Are they acting like a parent, child, or adult? Identifying their ego state will help you understand why they are behaving the way they are and help you to determine which ego state you should use during the interaction. For example, if the person is acting like an adult, you most likely should, too. If the person is acting like a child, it may be appropriate for you to act like a parent rather than an adult. And there are times when it is appropriate to act out of the child ego state and have a good time.

Types of Transactions

Within ego states there are three different **types of transactions**: *complementary, crossed, and ulterior.*

Complementary Transactions

A complementary transaction occurs when the sender of the message gets the intended response from the receiver. For example, an employee makes a mistake and, wanting some sympathy, apologizes to the boss. Employee—"I just dropped the thing when I was almost done. Now I have to do it all over again." Supervisor—"It happens to all of us; don't worry about it." This complementary transaction is illustrated below.

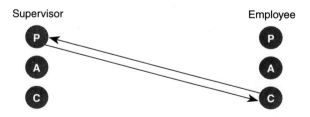

Another example of a complementary transaction is a supervisor who wants a job done and delegates it, expecting the employee to do it. The supervisor behaves on an adult-to-adult level. Supervisor—"Please get this order ready for me by two o'clock." Employee—"I'll have it done before two o'clock, no problem."

Generally, complementary transactions result in more effective communication with fewer hurt feelings and arguments. In other words, they help human relations and performance. Exceptions are if an employee uses an adapted child or critical parent ego state and the supervisor does, too. These complementary transactions can lead to problems.

WORK APPLICATIONS

1. Give an example of a complementary transaction you experienced. Be sure to identify the ego states involved.

Crossed Transactions

Crossed transactions occur when the sender of a message does not get the expected response from the receiver. Returning to our first example: Employee—"I just dropped the thing when I was almost done. Now I have to do it all over again." Supervisor—"You are so clumsy." This crossed transaction is illustrated below.

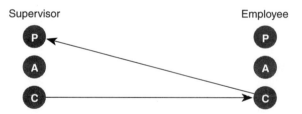

From our second example: Supervisor—"Please get this order ready for me by two o'clock." Employee— "Why do I have to do it? Why don't you do it yourself? I'm busy." This crossed transaction is an adult-adapted-to-child response.

Generally, crossed transactions result in surprise, disappointment, and hurt feelings for the sender of the message. The unexpected response often gets the person emotional, which often results in his or her changing to the adapted child ego state, which causes the communication to deteriorate further. Crossed transactions often end in arguments and hurt human relations.

Crossed transactions can be helpful when the negative parent or child ego response is crossed with an adult response. This crossover may result in the preferred adult-to-adult conversation.

WORK APPLICATIONS

2. Give an example of a crossed transaction you experienced. Be sure to identify the ego states involved.

Ulterior Transactions

Ulterior, or hidden, transactions occur when the words seem to be coming from one ego state, but in reality the words or behaviors are coming from another. For example, after a training program, one of the participants came up to a consultant asking advice on an adult ego state. When the consultant gave advice, the participant twice had quick responses as to why the advice would not work (child rather than adult behavior). The consultant realized that what the participant actually wanted was sympathetic understanding for his situation, not advice. The consultant stopped making suggestions and listened actively, using reflective responses. The consultant changed from the adult to the sympathetic parent ego state in order to have a complementary transaction.

Sometimes people don't know what they want or how to ask for it in a direct way, so they use ulterior transactions. When possible, it is best to avoid ulterior transactions because they tend to waste time. Avoid making people search for your hidden meaning. Plan your message before you send it. When receiving messages look for ulterior transactions and turn them into complementary transactions, as stated above.

WORK APPLICATIONS

3. Give an example of an ulterior transaction you experienced. Be sure to identify the ego states involved.

APPLICATION SITUATIONS

Transactional Analysis AS 3–1
Identify each transaction as being:
A. Complementary   B. Crossed   C. Ulterior

_____ 1.   "Would you help me move this package over there?" "Sure thing."

_____ 2.   "Will you serve on my committee?" "Yes, I think the experience will be helpful to me" (thinking—I want to get to know you, goodlooking).

_____ 3.   "Will you help me fill out this report?" "You have done several of them. Do it on your own, then I will check it for you."

_____ 4.   "How much will you pay me to do the job?" "$10.00." "What! You're either joking or trying to take advantage of me."

_____ 5.   "You're lying." "No, I'm not! You're the one who is lying."

Life Positions and Stroking

Life Positions

Attitudes affect your behavior and human relations. Within the transactional analysis framework, you have attitudes toward yourself and toward others. Positive attitudes are described as OK, and negative attitudes are described as not OK. The four life positions are illustrated in Figure 3–1.

FIGURE 3–1   **LIFE POSITIONS**

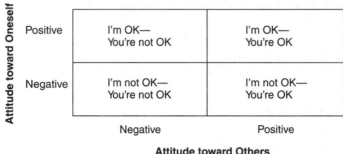

The most desirable life position is shown in the upper right-hand box: "I'm OK—You're OK." With a positive attitude toward yourself and others, you have a greater chance for having adult-to-adult ego state communication. You can change your attitudes and you should, if they are not positive, to create win-win situations. People with a positive self-concept tend to have positive attitudes.

Stroking

Stroking is any behavior that implies recognition of another's presence. Strokes can be positive and make people feel good about themselves, or they can be negative and hurt people in some way.

We all want praise and recognition. Giving praise (positive strokes) is a powerful motivation technique that is easy to use and costs nothing. We should all give positive strokes and avoid giving negative strokes.

Through work and effort, you can learn to control your emotional behavior and transact on an adult-to-adult level in most situations. Skill-Building Exercise 3–1 presents 10 situations in which you are required to identify the ego states being used to help you communicate on an adult-to-adult level.

In the opening case, Larry was behaving out of the critical parent ego state. He showed disapproval of Helen by asking, "What's wrong with you? You never acted like this before." Helen responded to Larry's request for the calculator from the adapted child ego state. Helen was rebellious and showed her anger by saying, "I'm sick and tired of your pushing me around. Go back to your desk and I'll bring it to you when I'm good and ready." They had a crossed transaction because Larry opened in his usual manner, but was surprised when Helen did not respond in her typical manner. Larry was in the I'm OK—You're not OK life position; while Helen was in the I'm not OK—You're not OK life position. Both used negative strokes.

WORK APPLICATIONS

4. Identify your present/past boss' life position and use of stroking.

ASSERTIVENESS

Arnold Lazarus popularized what is known as assertiveness[11] and others have adapted his work.[12] Hundreds of organizations have trained their employees to be assertive[13] including Trans World Airlines Inc., HSBC, Mazda Cars, Ford Motor Co., and the U.S. government. Walt Disney Productions trains all of its managers in assertiveness. Through assertiveness training, people learn how to deal with anxiety-producing situations in productive ways. Participants learn to express feelings, ask for favors, give and receive compliments, request behavior changes, and refuse unreasonable requests. Trainees learn to ask for what they want in a direct, straightforward, deliberate, and honest way that conveys self-confidence without being obnoxious or abusive. When people stand up for their rights without violating the rights of others, they are using assertive behavior.

The term **assertiveness** *is the process of expressing thoughts and feelings while asking for what one wants in an appropriate way.* You need to present your message without falling into stereotypical "too pushy" (aggressive) or "not tough enough" (nonassertive-passive) traps. Assertiveness is becoming more global. For example, the employees in Thailand are becoming more assertive[14] and the Japanese include more strategies of assertiveness.[15]

Being assertive is generally the most productive behavior. However, there are situations in which passive or aggressive behavior is appropriate. These situations are discussed in the section on conflict resolution. Next we discuss passive, aggressive, passive-aggressive, and assertive behavior, and how to be assertive with a diversity of people.

Passive Behavior

Passive or nonassertive behavior comes primarily through the obedient child or supportive parent ego state. Passive people are in an "I'm not OK" life position. Passive behavior is an avoidance of behavior or an accommodation of the other party's wishes without standing up for one's own rights. It involves self-denial and sacrifice.

Nonverbal communication of the passive person includes downcast eyes, soft voice, helpless gestures, and slouched posture. Passive people tend to deny the importance of things. They rationalize things—"It doesn't matter to me"—and take an "it's not my responsibility, let someone else do it" attitude. Passive people are often internally distressed and in pain. Becoming assertive decreases stress.[16]

When people know someone is passive, they tend to take advantage of the person. They make unreasonable requests, knowing the person cannot say no, and refuse to meet the passive person's rare mild request. When the passive person does speak, others tend not to listen and tend to interrupt. In fact, men freely interrupt women and dismiss women's ideas—and many women tolerate this![17]

Passive people often have a poor self-concept and are unhappy. Passivity is often based on fear: fear of failure, fear of rejection, fear of displeasing others, fear of retaliation, fear of hurting others, fear of being hurt, fear of getting into trouble, and so on. Some women are passive due to a lifetime of conditioning in which they were taught to serve others and to give way to men. Many men are also passive; you may know some.

Continued passive behavior is usually unproductive for both the individual and the organization. If you are continuously passive, determine what really is important, and stand up for your rights in an assertive way.

Aggressive Behavior

Aggressive behavior comes primarily through the adapted child and the critical parent ego state. Aggressive people are demanding, tough, rude, and pushy. They insist on getting their own way and use force to gain control. They are very competitive, hate to lose to the point of cheating, and tend to violate the rights of others to get what they want.[18]

Nonverbal communication used by aggressive people includes glaring and frowning to convey coldness. Aggressive people tend to speak loudly and quickly with threatening gestures and an intimidating posture.

When faced with aggressive behavior, the other party often retaliates with aggressive behavior (fight back) or withdraws and gives in (flight). People often avoid contact with the aggressive person or prepare themselves for a fight when transacting.[19]

Aggressive people seem to be self-confident, but their behavior is more often the result of a poor self-concept. They are in an "I'm not OK" life position, but consistently try to prove they are OK by beating and controlling others. They must win to prove their self-worth, and because they violate others' rights, they are often unhappy and feel guilty. They seem to have a complaint about everything. Some women become aggressive because they feel it is behavior necessary to compete in the business world. No one should feel as though he or she has to be aggressive to be taken seriously; assertiveness is more effective.

Continuous use of aggressive behavior is usually destructive to the individual and the organization.[20] If you are continually aggressive, work at becoming more sensitive to the needs of others. Learn to replace aggressive behavior with assertive behavior.

Violence in the Workplace

Violence is clearly aggressive behavior at the extreme level. Violence in the workplace has become the number-one security concern.[21] Human resources managers have reported increased violence,[22] stating it can happen anywhere.[23] Women commit nearly a quarter of all threats or attacks.[24] Aggression is increasing personal injury, property damages, stress, absenteeism, and turnover while decreasing morale and productivity, all of which affect the bottom-line profits of the firm.[25]

People tend to copy, or model, others' behavior.[26] For example, children who have been abused (emotionally and/or physically) are more likely, as parents, to abuse their children. If employees see others being violent, and nothing is done about it, they are more apt to also use violent behavior at work. From the manager's perspective, it is very important to take quick disciplinary action against employees who are violent at work. Otherwise, aggression will spread in the organization and it will be more difficult to stop.[27] Managers especially need to avoid using aggression at work because employees more readily copy managers' behavior than other employees.[28] This practice of copying violent behavior is one of the reasons why social-conscious groups complain about too much violence on television and in the movies. Women's groups are especially concerned about men abusing women. Some groups and individuals claim that television and movie producers are a cause of increased violence in society.

Passive-Aggressive Behavior

Passive-aggressive behavior is displayed in three major ways:
1. The person uses both types of behavior sporadically. For example, a manager may be very aggressive with subordinates, yet passive with superiors.[29] Or the person may be passive one day or moment and aggressive the next. This type of person is difficult to work with because no one knows what to expect.

2. The person uses passive behavior during the situation, then shortly after uses aggressive behavior. For example, an employee may agree to do something, then leave and slam the door or yell at the next person he or she sees.

3. The person uses passive behavior, but inside is building up hostility. After the repeated behavior happens often enough, the passive person becomes aggressive.[30] Too often the person who was attacked really doesn't understand the full situation and blames everything on the exploder, rather than examining his or her self-behavior, and changing. The person who becomes aggressive often feels guilty. The end result is usually hurt human relations and no change in the situation. For example, during a meeting, Carl interrupted June three times when she was speaking. June said nothing each time, but was building up hostility. The fourth time Carl interrupted June, she attacked him by yelling at him for being so inconsiderate of her. He simply said, "What's wrong with you?" It would have been better for June to assertively tell Carl not to interrupt her the first time he did it.

If you use passive-aggressive behavior, try to learn to be assertive on a consistent basis and you will be easier to work with, and you will get the results you want more often.

WORK APPLICATIONS

5.   Recall an example of when you used/observed passive-aggressive behavior. How did it affect human relations?

Assertive Behavior

Assertive behavior comes through the adult ego state, with an "I'm OK—You're OK" life position. As stated earlier, the assertive person expresses feelings, thoughts, and asks for things without aggressive behavior. The person stands up for his or her rights without violating the rights of others.

The nonverbal communication of the assertive person includes positive facial expressions like smiling and eye contact, pleasant voice qualities, firm gestures, and erect posture.

People who use assertive behavior tend to have a positive self-concept. They are not threatened by others, and they do not let others control their behavior. When others are out of the adult ego state, people using assertive behavior continue to transact in an adult ego state. Assertive people project a positive image of being confident, friendly, and honest. Using assertive behavior wins the respect of others. Use it on a consistent basis.

Being Assertive

Assertive behavior is generally the most effective method of getting what you want while not taking advantage of others. Being assertive can create a win-win situation. To better understand the differences among passive, aggressive, and assertive behavior, see Figure 3–2. The phrases can be thought of as do's and don'ts. Do make assertive phrases and don't make passive and aggressive phrases. But remember, there are times when passive and aggressive behavior are appropriate. You will learn when later in this chapter.

Below is an example that puts it all together. When a person who is talking is interrupted, he or she could behave:

1.   Passively. The person would say and do nothing.

2.   Aggressively. The person could say, "I'm talking; mind your manners and wait your turn," in a loud voice, while pointing to the interrupter.

3.   Assertively. The person could say, "Excuse me; I haven't finished making my point," with a smile and in a friendly but firm voice.

The passive behavior will most likely lead to the person being cut off and not listened to on a regular basis. The aggressive behavior will most likely lead to hurt human relations and could lead to an argument, while the assertive response will most likely lead to the interrupted person getting to finish now and in the future, without hurting human relations.

We will further explain how to be assertive in the next section. In-Class Skill-Building Exercise 3–2 requires you to identify passive, aggressive, and assertive behavior in 10 different situations. With the trend toward increased use of teamwork, organizations are focusing on how to be assertive within teams to improve human relations and performance.[31]

In the opening case introduction, before the conversation took place, Helen used passive behavior, while Larry used aggressive behavior. During the confrontation Helen used aggressive behavior, but when Larry responded with aggressive behavior, she returned to passive behavior, giving him the calculator.

FIGURE 3-2   **PASSIVE, ASSERTIVE, AND AGGRESSIVE PHRASES**

Passive Phrases

Passive speakers use self-limiting qualifying expressions without stating their position/needs.

- I don't know/care (when I do).
- It doesn't matter (when it does).
- Either one/way is fine with me (when I have a preference).
- I'm sorry (when I don't mean it).
- It's just my opinion . . .
- I don't want to bother you, but . . .
- It's not really important, but . . .

Assertive Phrases

Assertive speakers state their position/needs without violating the rights of others.

- I don't understand . . .
- I need/want/prefer . . .
- I would like . . .
- No, I won't be able to . . .
- I'd prefer that you don't tell me these jokes anymore.
- My opinion is . . .
- I need some of your time to . . .
- I thought that you would like to know . . .

Aggressive Phrases

Aggressive speakers state their position/needs while violating the rights of others using "you-messages" and absolutes.

- You don't need/want . . .
- Your opinion is wrong.
- You don't know what you're talking about.
- You're doing it wrong.
- That won't work!
- You have to . . .
- You need to know . . .

WORK APPLICATIONS

6. Recall an actual conflict you faced. Identify a passive, aggressive, and assertive response to the situation.

Assertiveness Steps

Below are the four assertive steps that Helen, in the opening case, could have used. These steps are summarized in Figure 3–3.

FIGURE 3–3   **ASSERTIVENESS STEPS**

Step 1. Set an objective.
Step 2. Determine how to create a win-win situation.
Step 3. Develop an assertive phrase(s).
Step 4. Implement your plan persistently.

Step 1. Set an Objective: Specify what you want to accomplish. Helen's objective could have been "to tell Larry that I will give him the calculator after I'm finished with it."

Step 2. Determine How to Create a Win-Win Situation: Assess the situation in terms of meeting your needs and the other person's needs. Larry's needs are already being met by Helen's giving him the calculator any time he wants it. Presently, there is a win-lose situation. Helen needs to be assertive to meet her own needs to get her work done as well as Larry's. Equitably sharing the use of the calculator will create a win-win situation. The present system of giving it to each other when done may work fine if Helen finishes using it before giving it to Larry.

Step 3. Develop an Assertive Phrase(s): Before confronting Larry, Helen could have developed a statement like "I'm using it now, and I'll give it to you as soon as I'm finished with it."

Step 4. Implement Your Plan Persistently: Helen could have used the above statement. If Larry continued to use aggressive behavior to get the calculator, Helen could persistently repeat the phrase again until it sinks in, and Larry leaves without it. It is not necessary, but Helen could explain why she feels the situation is not fair and that she will continue to give the calculator to Larry when she is done with it.

APPLICATION SITUATIONS

Assertiveness AS 3–2

Identify each response to a supervisor's request for the employee to make a personal purchase for him on company time:
A. Passive   B. Aggressive   C. Assertive

_____ 6. I'm not doing that, and I'll report you to the union if you ask again.

_____ 7. Is that a part of my job description?

_____ 8. I'll get on it just as soon as I finish this.

_____ 9. You know I'm not going to do a stupid thing like that. Do your own shopping.

_____ 10. Your request is unreasonable because it is not part of my job. I will not do it because we could both get in trouble.

CONFLICT MANAGEMENT STYLES

We begin by defining conflict and stating why managing conflict skills are important. We also discuss reasons for conflicts and five conflict management styles.

A **conflict** *exists whenever two or more parties are in disagreement.* Conflict is an inherent element of any organization.[32] It cannot be avoided because individual basic traits, ideas, and beliefs are always clashing.[33] Personality conflicts will always exist,[34] and a conflict-free environment is essentially nonexistent.[35] Conflict can be detrimental to productivity.[36] However, conflict and competition can breed creativity,[37] and trying to completely eliminate it from the workplace may cause harm to the organization.[38]

Reasons for Conflict and Avoiding Conflicts

All human relations rely on unwritten, implicit expectations by each party. Often, we are not aware of our expectations until they have not been met. Communications problems or conflicts arise for three primary reasons: (1) We fail to make our expectations known to other parties; (2) We fail to find out the expectations of other parties; (3) We assume that the other parties have the same expectations that we have.

In any relationship, to avoid conflict, share information and assertively discuss expectations early, before the conflict escalates. Unfortunately, avoiding is easier said than done. As stated, we don't always know our expectations until they are not met, and they change over time. At this point we are in conflict. However, making expectations clear early can help resolve conflicts before they escalate.

In the opening case, Larry expected Helen to give him the calculator when he wants it, which he made explicit to Helen. Larry failed to find out Helen's expectations (probably did not care), and may have assumed that she did not mind giving him the calculator whenever he wanted it. Helen's expectation was that Larry would share the calculator, and she found out his expectations were not the same as hers. However, she did not assertively tell Larry this early. Thus, they are in conflict and need to talk about their expectations. Also, there are times when the other party is not being reasonable, like Larry, making conflict more common and more difficult to resolve. Helen is going to need to be assertive with Larry.

People often think of conflict as fighting and view it as disruptive. Conflict, however, can be beneficial.[39] The question today is not whether conflict is good or bad but rather how to manage conflict to benefit the organization.[40] A balance of conflict is essential to all organizations.[41] Too little or too much conflict is usually a sign of management's unwillingness or inability to adapt to a diversified environment. Challenging present methods and presenting innovative change causes conflict, but can lead to improved performance.[42]

Constructive conflict skills are one of the most important skills you can acquire.[43] How well you handle conflict affects your job satisfaction and success.

WORK APPLICATIONS

7. Describe a conflict you observed in an organization, preferably an organization with which you are/were associated. Classify the conflict by the people involved and the reasons for the conflict.

Before examining the five conflict management styles, complete Self-Assessment Exercise 3–1 to determine your preferred style.

Self-Assessment Exercise 3–1
Determining Your Preferred Conflict Management Style

Below are four situations. Rank all five alternative actions from 1, the first approach you would use (most desirable), to 5, the last approach you would use (least desirable). Don't try to pick a best answer. Select the alternative that best describes what you would actually do in the situation based on your past experiences.

1. You are the general manager of a manufacturing plant. The purchasing department has found a source of material at a lower cost than the one being used. However, the production manager says the current material is superior, and he doesn't want to change. The quality control manager says that both will pass inspection with similar results. You would:

   _____ a. Do nothing; let the purchasing and production managers work it out between themselves.

   _____ b. Suggest having the purchasing manager find an alternative material that is cheaper but acceptable to the production manager.

   _____ c. Have the purchasing and production managers compromise.

   _____ d. Decide who is right and make the other comply.

   _____ e. Get the purchasing and production managers together and work out an agreement acceptable to both parties.

2. You are a professor at a college. You have started a consulting organization and have the title of director of consulting services, which the dean has approved. You run it through the business department, using other faculty and yourself to consult. It has been going well. Randy, the director of continuing education, says that your consulting services should come under his department and not be a separate department. You would:

   _____ a. Suggest that some services be under continuing education, but that others, like your consulting service, remain with you in the business department.

   _____ b. Do what you can to stop the move; you go to the dean and request that the consulting services stay under your direction in the business department, as the dean OK'd originally.

   _____ c. Do nothing. The dean will surely see through this "power grab" and turn Randy down.

   _____ d. Go and talk to Randy. Try to come up with an agreement you are both satisfied with.

   _____ e. Go along with Randy's request. It's not worth fighting about; you can still consult.

3. You are a branch manager for a bank. One of your colleagues cut you off twice during a managers' meeting which just ended. You would:

   _____ a. Do nothing; it's no big deal.

   _____ b. Discuss it in a friendly manner, but try to get the colleague to stop this behavior.

   _____ c. Don't do or say anything because it might hurt your relations, even if you're a little upset about it.

   _____ d. Forcefully tell the colleague that you put up with being cut off, but will not tolerate it in the future.

   _____ e. Tell the colleague that you will listen without interrupting if he or she does the same for you.

4. You are the human resources/personnel manager. You have decided to have visitors sign in and wear guest passes. However, only about half of the employees sign their guests in before taking them to their offices to do business. You would:

   _____ a. Go talk to the general manager about why employees are not signing in visitors.

   _____ b. Try to find a method that will please most employees.

   _____ c. Go to the general manager and request that he require employees to follow your procedures. If the general manager says to do it, employees will.

   _____ d. Do not require visitors to sign in; only require them to wear guest passes.

   _____ e. Let employees do things the way they want to.

To determine your preferred conflict management style, place your numbers 1–5 on the lines below.

Situation 1			Situation 2		
_____	a.	Forcing	_____	a.	Compromising
_____	b.	Avoiding	_____	b.	Forcing
_____	c.	Accommodating	_____	c.	Avoiding
_____	d.	Compromising	_____	d.	Collaborating
_____	e.	Collaborating	_____	e.	Accommodating

Situation 3			Situation 4		
_____	a.	Avoiding	_____	a.	Collaborating
_____	b.	Collaborating	_____	b.	Accommodating
_____	c.	Accommodating	_____	c.	Forcing
_____	d.	Forcing	_____	d.	Compromising
_____	e.	Compromising	_____	e.	Avoiding

Now place your ranking numbers 1–5 that correspond to the styles from the four situations in order; then add the four numbers.

Situation 1	Situation 2	Situation 3	Situation 4		
_____ A.	_____ B.	_____ D.	_____ C.	= _____	total, Forcing style
_____ B.	_____ C.	_____ A.	_____ E.	= _____	total, Avoiding style
_____ C.	_____ E.	_____ C.	_____ B.	= _____	total, Accommodating style
_____ D.	_____ A.	_____ E.	_____ D.	= _____	total, Compromising style
_____ E.	_____ D.	_____ B.	_____ A.	= _____	total, Collaborating style

The total with the lowest score is your preferred conflict management style. There is no one best conflict style in all situations. Like situational supervision and communications, the best style depends upon the situation. The more even the totals are, the more flexible you are at changing conflict management styles. Very high and very low totals indicate less flexibility. It is also helpful to identify others' preferred styles in order to plan how to resolve conflicts with them.

The five conflict management styles—forcing, avoiding, accommodating, compromising, and collaborating—will be presented next. See Figure 3–4 for an overview of the five styles.

Forcing Conflict Style

The **forcing conflict style** *user attempts to resolve the conflict by using aggressive behavior.* The forcer uses the critical parent or adapted child ego state with aggressive behavior. The forcing approach uses an uncooperative, autocratic attempt to satisfy one's own needs at the expense of others, if necessary. A win-lose situation is created. Forcers use authority, threaten, intimidate[44] and call for majority rule when they know they will win. For example, a manager tells an employee "if you don't do it now, you're fired!"

Advantages and Disadvantages of the Forcing Style

The advantage of the forcing style is that better organizational decisions will be made (assuming the forcer is correct) rather than less effective compromised decisions. The disadvantage is that overuse of this style leads to hostility and resentment toward its user.[45]

FIGURE 3–4   **MANAGEMENT CONFLICT STYLES**

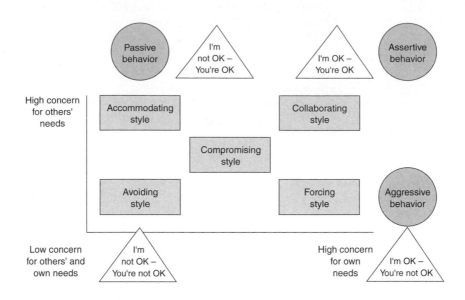

Appropriate Use of the Forcing Style

The forcing style is appropriate to use when (1) the conflict is about personal differences (particularly values that are hard to change); (2) maintaining close, supportive relationships is not critical; and (3) conflict resolution is urgent.

Avoiding Conflict Style

The **avoiding conflict style** *user attempts to passively ignore the conflict rather than resolve it.* The avoider uses the obedient child or sympathetic parent ego state, with passive behavior. Its user is unassertive and uncooperative, and wants to avoid or postpone confrontation. A lose-lose situation is created because the conflict is not resolved. People avoid the conflict by refusing to take a stance, physically leaving it, or escaping the conflict by mentally leaving the conflict.

Advantages and Disadvantages of the Avoiding Conflict Style

The advantage of the avoiding style is that it may maintain relationships that would be hurt through conflict resolution. The disadvantage of this style is the fact that conflicts do not get resolved. An overuse of this style leads to conflict within the individual. People tend to walk all over the avoider. Supervisors use this style when they allow employees to break rules without confronting them. Avoiding problems usually does not make them go away; the problems usually get worse.

Appropriate Use of the Avoiding Conflict Style

The avoiding style is appropriate to use when (1) one's stake in the issue is not high; (2) confrontation will damage a critical working relationship; and (3) a time constraint necessitates avoidance. Some people use the avoiding style out of fear that they will handle the confrontation poorly, making the situation worse rather than better. After studying this chapter and following its guidelines, you should be able to handle confrontations effectively.

Accommodating Conflict Style

The **accommodating conflict style** *user attempts to resolve the conflict by passively giving in to the other party.* The user is in the obedient child or sympathetic parent ego state, using passive behavior. The accommodating approach is unassertive and cooperative. It attempts to satisfy the other party while neglecting one's own needs. A win-lose situation is created, with the other party being the winner.

Advantages and Disadvantages of the Accommodating Conflict Style
The advantage of the accommodating style is that relationships are maintained. The disadvantage is that giving in to the other party may be counterproductive. The accommodated person may have a better solution. An overuse of this style leads to people taking advantage of the accommodator, and the relationship the accommodator tries to maintain is often lost.

Appropriate Use of the Accommodating Conflict Style
The accommodating style is appropriate when: (1) maintaining the relationship outweighs all other considerations; (2) the changes agreed to are not important to the accommodator, but are to the other party; and (3) the time to resolve the conflict is limited. This is often the only style one can use with an autocratic boss.

Compromising Conflict Style

The **compromising conflict style** *user attempts to resolve the conflict through assertive give-and-take concessions.* Its user is in the adult ego state, using assertive behavior. It attempts to meet one's need for harmonious relationships. An I-win-part–I-lose-part situation is created through compromise, making the compromising style intermediate in assertiveness and cooperation. It is used in negotiations.[46]

Advantages and Disadvantages of the Compromising Conflict Style
The advantage of the compromise style is that the conflict is resolved quickly and relationships are maintained. The disadvantage is that the compromise often leads to counterproductive results (suboptimum decisions). An overuse of this style leads to people playing games such as asking for twice as much as they need in order to get what they want. It is commonly used during management and labor collective bargaining.[47]

Appropriate Use of the Compromising Conflict Style
The compromise style is appropriate to use when (1) the issues are complex and critical, and there is no simple and clear solution; (2) all parties have a strong interest in different solutions; and (3) time is short.

Collaborating Conflict Style

The **collaborating conflict style** *user assertively attempts to jointly resolve the conflict with the best solution agreeable to all parties.* It is also called the problem-solving style. Its user is in the adult ego state, using assertive behavior. The collaborating approach is assertive and cooperative. The collaborator attempts to fully address the concerns of all. The focus is on finding the best solution to the problem that is satisfactory to all parties. Unlike the forcer, the collaborator is willing to change if a better solution is presented. This is the only style that creates a win-win situation.

Advantages and Disadvantages of the Collaborating Style
The advantage of the collaborating style is that it tends to lead to the best solution to the conflict using assertive behavior. One great disadvantage is that the time and effort it takes to resolve the conflict is usually greater and longer than the other styles.

Appropriate Use of the Collaborating Conflict Style

The collaborating style is appropriate when (1) maintaining relationships is important; (2) time is available; and (3) it is a peer conflict. To be successful, one must confront conflict. The collaborating conflict style is generally considered to be the best style because it confronts the conflict assertively, rather than passively ignoring it or aggressively fighting one's way through it.

The situational perspective states that there is no one best style for resolving all conflicts. A person's preferred style tends to meet his or her needs. Some people enjoy forcing, while others prefer to avoid conflict, and so forth. Success lies in one's ability to use the appropriate style to meet the situation. Of the five styles, the most difficult to implement successfully (and probably the most underutilized when appropriate) is the collaborative style. Therefore, the collaborative style is the only one that will be given detailed coverage in the next section of this chapter.

In the opening case, Larry consistently used the forcing conflict resolution style, while Helen began using the accommodating style, changed to the forcing style, and returned to the accommodating style. To create a true win-win situation for all parties, Helen could have used the collaborating conflict management style.

WORK APPLICATIONS

8.   Give an example of a conflict situation you face/faced and identify and explain the appropriate conflict management style to use.

APPLICATION SITUATIONS

Selecting Conflict Management Styles AS 3–3

Identify the most appropriate conflict management style as:
A. Forcing   C.   Compromising   E. Collaborating
B. Avoiding   D.   Accommodating

_____ 11.   You are in a class that uses small groups for the entire semester. Under normal class conditions the most appropriate style is:

_____ 12.   You have joined a committee in order to meet people. Your interest in its function itself is low. While serving on the committee, you make a recommendation that is opposed by another member. You realize that you have the better idea. The other party is using a forcing style.

_____ 13.   You are the supervisor of a production department. An important order is behind schedule. Two of your employees are in conflict, as usual, over how to meet the deadline.

_____ 14.   You are on a committee that has to select a new computer. The four alternatives will all do the job. It's the brand, price, and service that people disagree on.

_____ 15.   You are a sales manager. One of your competent salespersons is trying to close a big sale. The two of you are discussing the next sales call she will make. You disagree on strategy.

_____ 16.   You are on your way to an important meeting. You're late. As you turn a corner, at the end of the shop you see one of your employees goofing off instead of working.

_____ 17.   You have a department crisis. Your boss calls you up and tells you, in a stern voice, to get up here right away.

	18.	You are in a special one-hour budget meeting with your boss and fellow supervisors. You have to finalize the total budget for each department.
	19.	You and a fellow supervisor are working on a report. You disagree on the format to use.
	20.	You're over budget for labor this month. It's slow today so you asked a part-time employee to go home early. He tells you he doesn't want to go because he needs the money.

RESOLVING CONFLICTS WITH THE COLLABORATING CONFLICT STYLE

When a conflict exists, determine the appropriate style to use. Collaboration is not always appropriate in supervisor-employee conflicts. However, it is generally the appropriate style for conflict between colleagues and peers.

The objective of this section is to develop your ability to assertively confront (or be confronted by) people you are in conflict with, in a manner that resolves the conflict without damaging interpersonal relationships. This section examines the roles of initiator, responder, and mediator in conflict resolution.

Initiating Conflict Resolution

An initiator is a person who confronts another person(s) about a conflict. The initiator's attitude will have a major effect on the outcome of the confrontation. We tend to get what we are looking for. If you go into a confrontation expecting to argue and fight, you probably will. If you expect a successful resolution, you will probably get it.

To resolve conflicts, you should develop a plan of action.[48] When initiating a conflict resolution using the collaborating style, the **initiating conflict resolution steps** *are: step 1, plan to maintain ownership of the problem using the XYZ model; step 2, implement your plan persistently; step 3, make an agreement for change.*

Step 1. Plan to Maintain Ownership of the Problem Using the XYZ Model
Part of the reason confronters are not successful at resolving conflict is that they wait too long before confronting the other party, and they do it in an emotional state without planning (passive-aggressive behavior). People end up saying things they don't mean because they haven't given thought to what it is they want to say and accomplish through confrontation. You should realize that when you are upset and frustrated, the problem is yours, not the other party's. For example, you don't smoke and someone visits you who does smoke. The smoke bothers you, not the smoker. It's your problem. Open the confrontation with a request for the respondent to help you solve your problem. This approach reduces defensiveness and establishes an atmosphere of problem solving.

Know what you want to accomplish, your expectations, and say it ahead of time. Be descriptive, not evaluative. Avoid trying to determine who is to blame.[49] Both parties are usually partly to blame. Fixing blame only gets people defensive, which is counterproductive to conflict resolution. Keep the opening statement short. The longer the statement, the longer it will take to resolve the conflict. People get defensive when kept waiting for their turn to talk. Use the XYZ model.[50] The **XYZ model** *describes a problem in terms of behavior, consequences, and feelings:* When you do X (behavior), Y (consequences) happens, and I feel Z (feelings). For example, when you smoke in my room (behavior), I have trouble breathing and become nauseous (consequence), and I feel uncomfortable and irritated (feeling). Vary the sequence and start with a feeling or consequence to fit the situation and to provide variety.

Timing is also important. Don't confront people when they are involved in something else. If the other party is busy, set an appointment to discuss the conflict. In addition, don't confront a person on several unrelated issues at once.

WORK APPLICATIONS

9.   Use the XYZ model to describe a conflict problem you face/faced.

Step 2. Implement Your Plan Persistently

After making your short, planned XYZ statement, let the other party respond. If the confronted party acknowledges the problem and says he or she will change, you may have succeeded. Often people do not realize there is a conflict and when approached properly are willing to change. However, if the other party does not understand or avoids acknowledgment of the problem, persist. You cannot resolve a conflict if the other party will not even acknowledge its existence. Repeat your planned statement several times, and/or explain it in different terms, until you get an acknowledgment or realize it's hopeless. But don't give up too easily, and be sure to listen to the other party and watch nonverbal clues.[51]

When the other party acknowledges the problem, but is not responsive to resolving it, appeal to common goals. Make the other party realize the benefits to him or her and the organization as well.

Step 3. Make an Agreement for Change

Try to come to an agreement of specific action you will both take to resolve the conflict.[52] Remember that you are collaborating, not forcing. If possible, get a commitment statement describing the change.

Below is an example conflict resolution:

PAM: Hi, Bill! Got a few minutes to talk?

BILL: Sure, what's up?

PAM: Something's been bothering me lately, and I wanted you to know about it. When you come to class without doing your homework [behavior], I get irritated [feeling], and our group has to wait for you to read the material, or make a decision without your input [consequences].

BILL: Hey, I'm busy!

PAM: Do you think the rest of the group isn't?

BILL: No.

PAM: Are grades important to you?

BILL: Yeah, if I don't get good grades I can't play on the football team.

PAM: You get a grade for doing your homework, and we all get the same group grade. Your input helps us all to get a better grade.

BILL: You're right; sometimes I forget about that. Well, sometimes I don't do it because I don't understand the assignment.

PAM: I'll tell you what; when you don't understand it call me, or come over, and I'll explain it. You know my number and address.

BILL: I'd appreciate that.

PAM: So you agree to do your homework before class, and I agree to help you when you need it.

BILL: OK, I'll do it from now on.

Responding to Conflict Resolution

A responder is a person confronted by an initiator. Here's how to handle the role of the responder to a conflict.

Most initiators do not follow the model above. Therefore, the responder must take responsibility for successful conflict resolution by following the conflict resolution model. The **responding to conflict resolution steps** *are: step 1, listen to and paraphrase the problem using the XYZ model; step 2, agree with some aspect of the complaint; step 3, ask for, and/or give, alternative solutions; step 4, make an agreement for change.* These steps are also presented in Figure 3-5.

Mediating Conflict Resolution

Frequently, conflicting employees cannot resolve their dispute. In these cases, the manager should mediate to help them resolve their differences.[53]

Before bringing the conflicting parties together, the manager should decide whether to start with a joint meeting or conduct individual meetings. If one employee comes to complain, but has not confronted the other party, or if there is a serious discrepancy in employee perceptions, the manager should meet one-on-one with each party before bringing them together. On the other hand, when both parties have a similar awareness of the problem and motivation to solve it, the manager can begin with a joint meeting when all parties are calm. The manager should be a mediator, not a judge. Make employees realize it's their problem, not yours, and that they are responsible for solving it.[54] Get the employees to resolve the conflict,[55] if possible. Remain impartial, unless one party is violating company policies. Don't belittle the parties in conflict. Don't make parent comments like "I'm disappointed in you two; you're acting like babies."

When bringing conflicting parties together, follow the mediating conflict model. The **mediating conflict resolution steps** *are: step 1, have each party state his or her complaint using the XYZ model; step 2, agree on the problem(s); step 3, develop alternative solutions; step 4, make an agreement for change and follow up.* These steps also appear in Figure 3-5.

FIGURE 3–5

CONFLICT RESOLUTION

Initiating Conflict Resolution

Step 1. Plan to maintain ownership of the problem using the XYZ model.
Step 2. Implement your plan persistently.
Step 3. Make an agreement for change.

Responding to Conflict Resolution

Step 1. Listen to and paraphrase the problem using the XYZ model.
Step 2. Agree with some aspect of the complaint.
Step 3. Ask for, and/or give, alternative solutions.
Step 4. Make an agreement for change.

Mediating Conflict Resolution

Step 1. Have each party state his or her complaint using the XYZ model.
Step 2. Agree on the problem(s).
Step 3. Develop alternative solutions.
Step 4. Make an agreement for change and follow up.

In the assertiveness section, there was an example of how Helen could have been assertive with Larry in the opening case. In addition to being assertive with Larry, Helen could have used the collaborating conflict style to resolve the calculator problem. Helen could have suggested to Larry that the two of them go to the boss and ask for another calculator so that they could each have their own. A second calculator could create a win-win situation for all parties. Helen and Larry would both win because they would not have to wait for the calculator. The department would win because productivity would increase; there would be less time wasted getting and waiting for the calculator. The organization wins because the department performs efficiently. Obtaining a second calculator is a good conflict resolution. However, the department/organization may not have the money in the budget to buy a new calculator, or the idle time may actually be cheaper. If this is the case, Helen can be assertive and keep the calculator until she is finished—this is a win-win situation; or they could work out some other collaborative agreement, such as each having the calculator during specific hours. If Larry is not willing to collaborate, their boss will have to mediate the conflict resolution.

WORK APPLICATIONS

10. Describe an actual situation in which the initiating, responding, and/or mediating conflict resolution model would be appropriate.

INTERPERSONAL DYNAMICS

Interpersonal dynamics are the behavior used during our human relations,[56] and interpersonal dynamics grow increasing complex as more people interact.[57] TA, assertiveness, and conflict management are all interpersonal skills that can help you develop good human relations. Let's discuss how these three skills fit together to create interpersonal dynamic skills, and how they affect behavior, human relations, and performance.

Putting It All Together

To see the relationship between TA, assertiveness, and conflict management, see Figure 3–6. Notice that the first two columns come from conflict management, the third is from assertiveness, the fourth and fifth come from TA, and the last column relates to the goal of human relations. The last column shows the order of priority of which interpersonal behavior to use to meet the goal of human relations. However, remember that this is general advice. As stated in the chapter, at times other behavior is appropriate. In the majority of your human relations, you should strive to have a high concern for meeting your needs while meeting the needs of others. You should use an assertive, adult, collaborating style to create a win-win situation for all parties.

How Interpersonal Dynamics Affect Behavior, Human Relations, and Performance

In reviewing Figure 3–6, you should see that people using the passive, accommodating-avoiding conflict styles behave the opposite of the people who use the aggressive, forcing conflict style. Assertive people use the collaborative conflict style, and their behavior is between the other two extremes.

You should also understand that people using the passive, accommodating-avoiding conflict styles tend to have opposite human relations than people using the aggressive, forcing conflict style. The passive person tends to shy away from making friends and being actively involved, while the aggressive person tries to take over and is offensive to the group. Assertive people use the collaborating style and tend to be friendly and outgoing as they work to create win-win situations for all parties. Generally, people that are passive don't get their needs met; they get walked over by the aggressive people. Aggressive people are disliked because they violate the rights of others. Assertive people tend to have the best human relations.

FIGURE 3–6   **INTERPERSONAL DYNAMICS STYLES**

Concern for Meeting Needs	Conflict Styles Used to Meet Needs	Type of Behavior Used to Meet Needs	TA Ego State Behavior Comes from	TA Life Position	Situation Created/ Priority to Meet Goal of Human Relations
High concern for meeting others' needs Low concern for meeting own needs	→ Accommodating		Supportive parent	I'm OK– You're not OK or I'm not OK– You're not OK	→ Lose–Win 3*
Low concern for meeting own and others' needs	→ Avoiding	Passive	Natural child	I'm not OK– You're not OK or I'm not OK– You're OK	→ Lose–Lose 5
High concern for meeting own and others' needs	→ Collaborating				Win–Win 1
Moderate concern for meeting own and others' needs	→ Compromising	Assertive → Adult		I'm OK– You're OK	Win–part Lose–part 2
High concern for meeting own needs Low concern for meeting others' needs	→ Forcing	→ Aggressive	Adapted child or Critical parent	I'm OK– You're not OK	→ Win–Lose 3*

*The win-lose and lose-win situations are equal in priority to the group/organization because both an individual and the group/organization lose. The individual's loss is more important to the loser than to the group.

No clear relationship exists between individual performance and the interpersonal dynamic style used. Many passive people work well alone, and so do aggressive people. Aggressive people are sometimes more productive than passive people because they can take advantage of passive people. This happened in the opening case. When it comes to group/organizational performance, the assertive person is generally the most responsible for the group effort because passive people may have great ideas on how to do a good group job, but they don't say how. Aggressive people only look out for themselves. If someone offers a different idea than theirs, they are not willing to collaborate for the good of all. The assertive group member collaboratively shares ideas but is willing to change to a better alternative to create a win-win situation for all.

By following the guidelines in this chapter, you can develop assertive collaborating skills.

REVIEW

Select one or more methods: (1) fill in the missing key terms from memory; (2) match the key terms from the end of the review with their definitions below; and/or (3) copy the key terms in order from the key terms at the beginning of the chapter.

_____ is a method of understanding behavior in interpersonal dynamics. The three _____ are the parent, child, and adult. The parent includes the critical parent and sympathetic parent, while the child ego state includes the natural and adapted child. The three _____ are complementary, crossed, and ulterior. Complementary adult-to-adult discussions are generally more productive in organizations. There are four life positions, and giving positive strokes is desirable.

Passive behavior is an avoidance of behavior or an accommodation of the other party's wishes without standing up for one's rights. Aggressive behavior is the forcing of one's will on others without regard for their rights. Passive-aggressive behavior is the use of both types of behavior. _____ is the process of expressing thoughts and feelings while asking for what one wants in an appropriate way. Generally, assertive behavior is most productive; however, there are situations in which passive and aggressive behavior is appropriate.

The steps in being assertive are: step 1, set an objective; step 2, determine how to create a win-win situation; step 3, develop an assertive phrase(s); step 4, implement your plan persistently.

_____ exists whenever two or more parties are in disagreement. Conflict management skills are important to interpersonal relations.

There are two methods of classifying types of conflict: (1) constructive and destructive, and (2) by the people involved—conflict within the individual, interpersonal conflict, conflict between an individual and a group, intragroup conflict, and conflict between organizations. These sources of conflict include personal differences, information, different objectives, and environmental factors. The conflict management styles are:

The _____ user attempts to resolve the conflict by using aggressive behavior. The _____ user attempts to passively ignore the conflict rather than resolve it. The _____ user attempts to resolve the conflict by passively giving in to the other party. The _____ user attempts to resolve the conflict through assertive give-and-take concessions. The _____ user assertively attempts to jointly resolve the conflict with the best solution agreeable to all parties. Each style has its advantages and disadvantages, and each is appropriate in certain situations.

The _____ are: step 1, plan to maintain ownership of the problem using the XYZ model; step 2, implement your plan persistently; step 3, make an agreement for change. The _____ describes a problem in terms of behavior, consequences, and feelings. The _____ are: step 1, listen to and paraphrase the problem using the XYZ model; step 2, agree with some aspect of the complaint; step 3, ask for, and/or give, alternative solutions; step 4, make an agreement for change. The _____ are: step 1, have each party state his or her complaint using the XYZ model; step 2, agree on the problem(s); step 3, develop alternative solutions; step 4, make an agreement for change and follow up.

Interpersonal dynamics are the behavior used during our human relations. People who are passive and aggressive use opposite behavior, while assertive people behave between these two extremes. Generally, the people who use assertive behavior, from the adult ego state, have a high concern for meeting their own needs and the needs of others. They tend to use the collaborate conflict style and use the most appropriate behavior, which contributes to creating a win-win situation. Figure 3–6, Interpersonal Dynamics Styles, summarizes TA, assertiveness, and conflict management; return to it as a review.

KEY TERMS

accommodating conflict style	forcing conflict style
assertiveness	initiating conflict resolution steps
avoiding conflict style	mediating conflict resolution steps
collaborating conflict style	responding to conflict resolution steps
compromising conflict style	transactional analysis
conflict	types of transactions
ego states	XYZ model

CASE

Andrea Cunningham started her own public relations (PR) firm in Santa Clara, California. Andrea believed that any PR firm could package and disseminate information. Her mission gave Cunningham a competitive advantage keeping clients apprised of how they were perceived by the market. To live the mission, Cunningham keeps tabs on the financial community, the press, consultants, customers, and even employees within the firm. High-quality employees are critical to PR success because the client must have extreme confidence in the PR people in charge of their account because they often times have to give the client bad news based on the data they gather. Client turnover is high at most PR agencies, and employee job-hopping is also common as PR representatives search for higher pay and new challenges.

Cunningham acquired some of Silicon Valley's best clients including Borland International and Aldus Corporation software makers and Hewlett-Packard and Motorola. Andrea's Cunningham Communication revenues grew to over $3 million annually with 24 employees. However, Andrea made a common entrepreneurial error. She tried to make all the decisions herself without delegating authority. As a result, managers were constantly fighting, morale was very low, turnover of both clients and employees was very high, and Andrea faced the threat of losing money for the first time since she started the business.

Faced with problems, Andrea knew changes were needed. Her first attempt was to assign clients to individual teams and to give bonuses based on profitability. Unfortunately, internal competition became fierce. Turf wars developed, employees refused to share information, and there was no cooperation between teams. Andrea realized that teams were a good idea, but the team system needed to be changed.

Andrea came to the realization that she had to delegate authority if she was going to have a turnaround. Andrea decided to develop a goal-driven system with a cooperative management program called input teams. Andrea set annual objectives for each team that developed the necessary plans and budgets to achieve the objectives. Every employee was a member of at least one team that meet for five hours per week. Andrea also realized that her human resource practices had to support the Cunningham mission and new management system. Working with her human resource manager and others they developed the following program.

To attract and retain employees, called associates, they developed a career path system. A career path is a sequence of job assignments that leads to more responsibility with raises and promotions. The career path system was designed to develop associates to a level of competence that inspired the confidence of clients. New associates were oriented to the organizational culture, which is called the Cunningham Culture. They are taught about the input teams and develop team skills, the various departments, and develop time-management skills. New associates attend Cunningham Communications Inc. University for a formal three-day training session.

The compensation system was also changed. All associates receive a set pay for the year and a bonus based on meeting objectives. Each associate determines his or her responsibilities, objectives, and pay. Andrea says that associates rarely request compensation that they are not worth. Frequent advisory sessions give associates feedback from their bosses on how well they are meeting expectations. On occasion when associates fall short of their objectives, compensation has been withheld without complaint. To increase compensation, associates have to generate more revenue.

Some of Andrea's productive senior employees complained about the new system. They did not want to be included with a team. However, Andrea stayed firm in keeping the system, even when senior people started to quit. Within six months of implementing the above changes, all but three members of the senior staff voluntarily terminated employment at Cunningham. Andrea was sad to see them go, but felt they were not right for the new management system. On the positive side, the company became profitable and continues to grow; the number of associates went from 24 to 59 under the new system.

Go to the Internet: For more information on Andrea Cunningham and Cunningham Communications, Inc. to update the information provided in this case, do a name search on the Internet and visit *www.ccipr.com.*

Support your answer to the following questions with specific information from the case and text, or other information you get from the web or other source.

1. How is assertiveness illustrated in this case?

2. Identify at least two conflict situations at Cunningham.

3. Which conflict management style did Andrea use with the senior staff?

4. Did Andrea Cunningham effectively resolve the two conflicts you identified in Question 2?

5. What are the learning organization issues in this case?

6. What happened to job satisfaction through the change to teams?

7. What is the role of organizational structure and communications in this case?

8. Which two motivation techniques did Andrea primarily use in the new teams?

9. Which situational supervision style did Andrea use in this case in developing the team system and team objectives? Which situational supervision style did she use on an individual basis?

OBJECTIVE CASE 3

Bill and Saul's Conflict

The following conversation takes place over the telephone between Bill, the salesperson, and Saul, the production manager. (Note: This conversation can be role-played in class.)

BILL: Listen, Saul, I just got an order for 1,000 units and promised delivery in two days. You'll get them out on time, won't you?

SAUL: Bill, you know the normal delivery time is five days.

BILL: I know, but I had to say two days to get the order, so fill it.

SAUL: We don't have the capability to do it. You should have checked with me before taking the order. The best I can do is four days.

BILL: What are you—my mother, or the production manager?

SAUL: I cannot have 1,000 units ready in two days. We have other orders that need to be filled before yours. Four days is the best I can do on short notice.

BILL: Come on, Saul, you cannot do this to me, I want to keep this account. It can mean a lot of business.

SAUL: I know, Bill; you've told me this on three other orders you had.

BILL: But this is a big one. Don't you care about sales?

SAUL: Yes, I do, but I cannot produce the product as fast as you sales reps are selling it lately.

BILL: If I don't meet my sales quota, are you going to take the blame?

SAUL: Bill, we are going in circles here. I'm sorry, but I cannot fill your request. The order will be ready in five days.

BILL: I was hoping you would be reasonable. But you've forced me to go to Mr. Carlson. You know he'll be telling you to fill my order. Why don't you just do it and save time and aggravation?

SAUL: I'll wait to hear from Mr. Carlson. In the meantime, have a good day, Bill.

Answer the following questions. Then state why you selected that answer.

_____ 1. Bill was transacting from the _____ ego state.

        a. critical parent   c. adult   e. adapted child
        b. sympathetic parent   d. natural child

_____ 2. Saul was transacting from the _____ ego state.

        a. critical parent   c. adult   e. adapted child
        b. sympathetic parent   d. natural child

_____ 3. The telephone discussion was a(n) _____ transaction.

        a. complementary   b. crossed   c. ulterior

_____ 4. Bill's life position seems to be:

        a. I'm OK—You're not OK   c. I'm not OK—You're not OK
        b. I'm OK—You're OK   d. I'm not OK—You're OK

_____ 5. Bill's behavior was:

     a. passive   b. aggressive   c. assertive

_____ 6. Saul's behavior was:

     a. passive   b. aggressive   c. assertive

_____ 7. Bill and Saul have an _____ conflict.

     a. individual   c. individual/group
     b. interpersonal   d. intragroup

_____ 8. Their source of conflict is:

     a. personal differences   c. objectives
     b. information   d. environment

_____ 9. Bill used the _____ conflict style.

     a. forcing   c. accommodating   e. collaborating
     b. avoiding   d. compromising

_____ 10. Saul used the _____ conflict style.

     a. forcing   c. accommodating   e. collaborating
     b. avoiding   d. compromising

11. What would you have done if you were Bill?

12. Assume you are Mr. Carlson, the boss. What would you do if Bill called?

INTERNET EXERCISES

The objective of this Internet exercise is to assess your use of assertiveness as low to high.

1. Go to the Body-Mind QueenDom website homepage—*www.queendom.com*

2. Click "Tests" and scroll down to the Career/Jobs tests section and Click "Assertiveness" and take the test by clicking your selections then click score to get your score and interpretation (your instructor may ask you to make a copy of it to bring to class).

3. Questions: (1) What was your score? (2) Do you have a low, moderate, or high assertiveness? (3) What can you do to improve your assertiveness? (Your instructor may ask you to type and print your answer and bring them to class.)

The objective of this exercise is to learn more about conflict by using a supersite. A supersite is a website with links to other websites. Essentially, you go to one site that links/directs you to another website. Thus, for this exercise, you will actually visit two websites.

1. Go to the Work911 website homepage—*www.work911.com*

2. Scroll down to find a list of articles under the heading "Community and Conflict Related" and Click "view" for the one you want to read. You will be taken to another website where you read the article (your instructor may require you to make a copy of it).

3. Questions: (1) What is the name of the website you went to? (2) Who is the author and what is the title of the article you read. (3) What is the basic message of the article you read? (4) How can you use this information to help resolve conflicts in your personal and professional life? (Your instructor may require you to type and print your answers.)

The objective of this exercise is to learn more about a concept of your choice.

1. Go to the MG homepage—*www.mgeneral.com*

2. Click "Search (Site Map)."

3. Click the "Concept" button/circle to use the concept search mode then type in a concept from this or another chapter that you want to learn more about.

4. Click the resource you want to learn more about (your instructor may require you to print it).

5. Questions: (1) Who is the author and what is the title and year of the resource? (2) What are the primary concept ideas? (3) How can you use these ideas in your personal and professional life? (Your instructor may require you to type and print your answers.)

PREPARATION FOR SKILL-BUILDING EXERCISE

Transactional Analysis SB 3–1

Below are 10 situations. For each situation:

1. Identify the sender's communication ego state as:

>CP Critical Parent
>SP Sympathetic Parent
>NC Natural Child
>AC Adapted Child
>A Adult

2. Place the letters CP, SP, NC, AC, or A on the S _____ to the left of each numbered situation.

3. Identify each of the five alternative receiver's ego states as in instruction 1 above. Place the letters CP, SP, NC, AC, or A on the R _____.

4. Select the best alternative to achieve effective communication and human relations. Circle the letter a, b, c, d, or e.

S _____ 1. Ted delegates a task, saying, "It's not much fun, but someone has to do it. Will you please do it for me?" Sue, the delegatee, says:

a. "A good boss wouldn't make me do it." R _____
b. "I'm always willing to help you out, Ted." R _____
c. "I'm not cleaning that up." R _____
d. "You're not being serious, are you?" R _____
e. "I'll get right on it." R _____

S _____ 2. Helen, a customer, brought a dress to the cleaners and later she picked it up, paid, and went home. At home she opened the package and found that the dress was not clean. Helen returned to the cleaners and said, "What's wrong with this place? Don't you know how to clean a dress?" The cleaning person, Saul, responds:

a. "It's not my fault. I didn't clean it personally." R _____
b. "I'm sorry this happened. We'll do it again right now." R _____
c. "I can understand your disappointment. Were you planning on wearing it today? What can I do to make this up to you?" R _____
d. "These are stains caused by your carelessness, not ours." R _____
e. "Gee whiz, this is the first time this has happened." R _____

S _____ 3. In an office, Bill drops a tray of papers on the floor. Mary, the manager, comes over and says, "This happens once in awhile to all of us. Let me help you pick them up." Bill responds:

a. "Guess I slipped, ha ha ha." R _____
b. "This wouldn't have happened if people didn't stack the papers so high." R _____
c. "It's not my fault; I'm not picking up the papers." R _____
d. "Thanks for helping me pick them up, Mary." R _____
e. "It will not take long to pick them up." R _____

S _____ 4. Karl and Kelly were talking about the merit raise given in their branch of the bank. Karl says: "I heard you did not get a merit raise." Kelly responds:

a. "It's true; how much did you get?" R _____
b. "I really don't need a raise anyway." R _____
c. "The branch manager is unfair." R _____
d. "The branch manager didn't give me a raise because he is prejudiced. The men got bigger raises than the women." R _____
e. "It's nice of you to show your concern. Is there anything I can do to help you out?" R _____

S _____ 5. Beckie, the store manager, says to an employee: "Ed, there is no gum on the counter; please restock it." Ed responds:

    a. "Why do I always get stuck doing it?"   R _____

    b. "I'd be glad to do it. I know how important it is to keep the shelves stocked for our customers."   R _____

    c. "I'll do it just as soon as I finish this row."   R _____

    d. "I'll do it if I can have a free pack."   R _____

    e. "Why don't we buy bigger boxes so I don't have to do it so often?"   R _____

S _____ 6. Carol, the manager, asked Tim, an employee, to file some forms. Awhile later Carol returned and asked Tim why he hadn't filed the forms. Tim said: "Oh, oh! I forgot about it." Carol responds:

    a. "I've told you before; write things down so you don't forget to do them."   R _____

    b. "It's OK. I know you're busy and will do it when you can."   R _____

    c. "Please do it now."   R _____

    d. "What's wrong with you?"   R _____

    e. "You daydreaming or what?"   R _____

S _____ 7. Joan just finished making a budget presentation to the controller, Wayne. He says: "This budget is padded." Joan responds:

    a. "I'm sorry you feel that way. What is a fair budget amount?"   R _____

    b. (laughing) "I don't pad any more than the others."   R _____

    c. "You don't know what you're talking about. It's not padded."   R _____

    d. "What items do you believe are padded?"   R _____

    e. "You can't expect me to run my department without some padding for emergencies, can you?"   R _____

S _____ 8. Jill, a computer repair technician, says to the customer: "What did you do to this computer to make it malfunction like this?" The customer responds:

    a. "Can you fix it?"   R _____

    b. "I take good care of this machine. You better fix it fast."   R _____

    c. "I'm sorry to upset you. Are you having a rough day?"   R _____

    d. "I'm going to tell your boss what you just said."   R _____

    e. "I threw it down the stairs, ha ha."   R _____

S _____ 9. Pete is waiting for his friend, Will, whom he hasn't seen for some time. When Will arrives, Pete says, "It's good to see you," and gives Will a hug, spinning him around. Will responds:

    a. "Don't hug me on the street; people can see us."   R _____

    b. "I'm not late; you got here early."   R _____

    c. "Sorry I'm late. Is there anything I can do to make it up to you? Just name it."   R _____

    d. "Let's go party, party, party."   R _____

    e. "Sorry I'm late; I got held up in traffic."   R _____

S _____ 10. Sally gives her secretary, Mike, a note saying: "Please, type this when you get a chance." About an hour later, Sally returns from a meeting and asks: "Mike, is the letter I gave you done yet?" Mike responds:

    a. "If you wanted it done by 11, why didn't you say so?"   R _____

    b. "I'm working on it now. It will be done in about 10 minutes."   R _____

    c. "You said to do it when I got a chance. I've been too busy doing more important things."   R _____

    d. "Sure thing, boss lady, I'll get right on it."   R _____

    e. "I'm sorry, I didn't realize how important it was. Can I type it right now and get it to you in about 15 minutes?"   R _____

IN-CLASS SKILL-BUILDING EXERCISE

Transactional Analysis SB 3–1

Objective: To improve your ability to use transactional analysis.

SCANS: The SCANS competencies of resources, interpersonal skills, and information and the foundations of basic, thinking, and personal qualities are developed through this exercise.

Preparation: You should have completed the preparation (10 situations) for this exercise.

Procedure

Select one option.

1. The instructor goes over the recommended answers to the 10 situations.

2. The instructor asks students for their answers to the situations, followed by giving the recommended answers.

3. Break into groups of two or three and together follow the three-step approach for two to three situations at a time, followed by the instructor going over the recommended answers. Discuss the possible consequences of each alternative response in the situation. Would it help or hurt human relations and performance? How?

Conclusion: The instructor leads a class discussion and/or makes concluding remarks.

Application: What have I learned from this experience? How will I use this knowledge in the future?

Sharing: Volunteers give their answers to the application section.

PREPARATION FOR SKILL-BUILDING EXERCISE

Assertiveness SB 3–2

In this exercise are 10 situations with 5 alternative statements or actions. Identify each as assertive (A), aggressive (G), or passive (P). Place the letter A, G, or P on the line before each of the five alternatives. Circle the letter (a–e) of the response that is the most appropriate in the situation.

1.   In class, you are in small groups discussing this exercise; however, two of the members are talking about personal matters instead. You are interested in this exercise.

   _____ a. "Don't you want to learn anything in this class?"

   _____ b. Forget the exercise, join the conversation.

   _____ c. "This is a valuable exercise. I'd really appreciate your input."

   _____ d. "This exercise is boring, isn't it?"

   _____ e. "Stop discussing personal matters, or leave the class!"

2.   You and your roommate do not smoke. Smoke really bothers you. However, your roommate has friends over who smoke in your room regularly.

   _____ a. Throw them out of your room.

_____ b. Purposely cough repeatedly saying, "I cannot breathe."

_____ c. Ask your roommate to have his guests refrain from smoking, or meet at a different place.

_____ d. Complain to your favorite professor.

_____ e. Do and say nothing.

3. Your boss has repeatedly asked you to go get coffee for the members of the department. It is not part of your job responsibility.

        _____ a. "It is not part of my job. Why don't we set up a rotating schedule so that everyone has a turn?"

        _____ b. "Go get it yourself."

        _____ c. Continue to get the coffee.

        _____ d. File a complaint with personnel/union.

        _____ e. "Why don't we skip coffee today?"

4. You are riding in a car with a friend. You are nervous because your friend is speeding, changing lanes frequently, and passing in no-passing zones.

        _____ a. "Are you trying to kill me?"

        _____ b. "What did you think of Professor Lussier's class today?"

        _____ c. "Please slow down and stay in one lane."

        _____ d. Try not to look where you are going.

        _____ e. "Stop driving like this or let me out right here."

5. You are in a department meeting that is deciding on the new budget. However, some of the members are going off on tangents and wasting time. Your boss hasn't said anything about it.

        _____ a. Don't say anything. After all, it's your boss's meeting.

        _____ b. "So far we agree on XYZ, and we still need to decide on ABC. Does anyone have any ideas on these line items?"

        _____ c. "Let's stop wasting time and stay on the subject."

        _____ d. "Let's just vote so we can get out of here."

        _____ e. "Excuse me, I have to go to the bathroom."

6. One of your coworkers repeatedly tries to get you to do his or her work with all kinds of excuses.

        _____ a. Do the work.

        _____ b. "I have no intention of doing your work, so please stop asking me to do it."

        _____ c. "Buzz off. Do it yourself, freeloader."

        _____ d. "I'd like to do it for you, but I'm tied up right now."

        _____ e. "Get away from me and don't bother me again."

7. You bought a watch. It doesn't work so you return to the store with the receipt. The salesclerk says you cannot exchange it.

        _____ a. Insist on the exchange. Talk to the person's boss and his or her boss if necessary.

        _____ b. Leave with the watch.

        _____ c. Drop the watch on the counter and pick up a new watch and walk out.

        _____ d. Come back when a different salesclerk is there.

        _____ e. Create a scene, yell, and get other customers on your side. Disrupt business until you get the new watch.

8. You are about to leave work and go to see your child/friend perform in a play. Your boss comes to you and asks you to stay late to do a report she needs in the morning.

        _____ a. "Sorry, I'm on my way to see a play."

        _____ b. "I'd be happy to stay and do it."

        _____ c. "Are you sure I cannot do it tomorrow?"

        _____ d. "I'm on way to see a play. Can I take it home and do it later tonight?"

        _____ e. "Why should I get stuck here? Why don't you do it yourself?"

9.   You believe that cheating is wrong. Your roommate just asked you if he or she could copy the homework you spent hours preparing.

_____ a. "Here you go."

_____ b. "I don't help cheaters."

_____ c. "OK, if you don't copy it word for word."

_____ d. "I'd like to help you. You're my friend, but in good conscience I cannot let you copy my homework."

_____ e. "You go out and have a good time, then you expect me to be a fool and get you off the hook? No way."

10.   Some people you know stop by your dorm room. One of them pulls out some drugs, takes some, and passes it along. You don't take drugs.

_____ a. "I don't approve of taking drugs. You can get me into trouble. Please put them away or leave."

_____ b. Grab them and get rid of them.

_____ c. Take some drugs because you don't want to look bad.

_____ d. Pass them along without taking any.

_____ e. "Are you trying to kill yourselves? Get out of here with that stuff."

IN-CLASS SKILL-BUILDING EXERCISE

Assertiveness SB 3–2

Objective: To improve your ability to be assertive.

SCANS: The SCANS competencies of resources, and interpersonal skills, and information and the foundations of basic, thinking, and personal qualities are developed through this exercise.

Preparation: You should have completed the preparation (10 situations) for this exercise.

Procedure

Select one option.

1. The instructor goes over the recommended answers to the 10 situations.

2. The instructor asks students for their answers to the situations, followed by giving the recommended answers.

3. Break into groups of two or three and together follow the three-step approach for 2–3 situations at a time, followed by the instructor going over the recommended answers. Discuss the possible consequences of each alternative response in the situation. Would it help or hurt human relations and performance? How?

Conclusion: The instructor leads a class discussion and/or makes concluding remarks.

Application: What have I learned from this experience? How will I use this knowledge in the future?

Sharing: Volunteers give their answers to the application section.

PREPARATION FOR SKILL-BUILDING EXERCISE

Initiating Conflict Resolution SB 3–3

During class you will be given the opportunity to role-play a conflict you face, or have faced, in order to develop your conflict skills. Fill in the information below and also record your answers on a separate sheet of paper. Other party(ies) (You may use fictitious names) _____ Define the situation:

1. List pertinent information about the other party (e.g., relationship with you, knowledge of the situation, age, background).

2. State what you wish to accomplish (objective) as a result of the conflict confrontation/discussion.

3. Identify the other party's possible reaction to your confrontation (resistance to change: intensity, source, focus).

How will you overcome this resistance to change?

Using the three steps in initiating conflict resolution, write out your plan to initiate the conflict resolution. Write your plan on a separate sheet of paper and bring it to class.

For In-Class Use SB 3–3

Feedback for _____

Try to have positive improvement comments for each step in initiating conflict resolution. Remember to be DESCRIPTIVE and SPECIFIC, and for all improvements have an alternative positive behavior (APB) (i.e., if you would have said/done. . . , it would have improved the conflict resolution by. . .).

Positive Improvement

Step 1. Did the initiator maintain ownership of the problem?

Did he or she have and implement a well-thought-out XYZ plan?

Step 2. Did he or she persist until the confrontee acknowledged the problem?

Step 3. Did the initiator get the confrontee to agree to a change/solution?

IN-CLASS SKILL-BUILDING EXERCISE

Initiating Conflict Resolution SB 3–3

Objective: To experience and develop skills in resolving a conflict.

SCANS: The SCANS competencies of information and especially interpersonal skills and the foundations of basic, and especially thinking through problems, and personal qualities are developed through this exercise.

Preparation: You should have completed the questionnaire in the preparation for this exercise.

Experience: You will initiate, respond to, and observe a conflict role play, and then evaluate the effectiveness of its resolution.

Procedure 1 (2–3 minutes)

Break into as many groups of three as possible. If there are any people not in a triad, make one or two groups of two. Each member selects the number 1, 2, or 3. Number 1 will be the first to initiate a conflict role play, then 2, followed by 3.

Procedure 2 (8–15 minutes)

1. Initiator number 1 gives his or her information from the preparation to number 2 (the responder) to read. Once number 2 understands, role-play (see number 2 below). Number 3 is the observer.
2. Role-play the conflict resolution. Number 3, the observer, writes his or her observations on the feedback sheet.
3. Integration. When the role play is over, the observer leads a discussion on the effectiveness of the conflict resolution. All three should discuss the effectiveness. Number 3 is not a lecturer. Do not go on until told to do so.

Procedure 3 (8–15 minutes)

Same as procedure 2, only number 2 is now the initiator, number 3 is the responder, and number 1 is the observer.

Procedure 4 (8–15 minutes)

Same as procedure 2, only number 3 is the initiator, number 1 is the responder, and number 2 is the observer.

Conclusion: The instructor leads a class discussion and/or makes concluding remarks.

Application (2–4 minutes): What did I learn from this experience? How will I use this knowledge in the future?

Sharing: Volunteers give their answers to the application section.

NOTES

1. Julie Hay, "Creating Community: The Task of Leadership," *Leadership & Organizational Development*, Vol. 14, Iss. 7, 1993, pp. 12–17.

2. Eric Berne, *Transactional Analysis in Psychotherapy* (New York: Grove Press, 1961).

3. Eric Berne, *Games People Play* (New York: Grove Press, 1964).

4. N. Nykodym, L.D. Freedman, J.L. Simonetti, W.R. Nielson, and K. Battles, "Mentoring: Using Transactional Analysis to help Organizational Members Use Their Energy in More Productive Ways," *Transactional Analysis Journal 25, No. 2* (1995), p. 170.

5. N. Nykodym, W.R. Nielson, and J.C. Christen, "Can Organization Development Use Transactional Analysis?" *Transactional Analysis Journal 15, No. 4* (October 1985), p.278.

6. N. Nykodym, C.O. Longenecker, and W.N. Ruud, "Improving Quality of Work Life with Transactional Analysis as an Intervention Change Strategy,:" *Applied Psychology: An International Review 40, No. 4* (1991), pp.395-404.

7. H. Park and K. Harrison, "Enhancing Managerial Cross-Cultural Awareness and Sensitivity: Transactional Analysis Revisited," *Journal of Management Development, Vol. 12, Iss. 3,* 1993, pp. 20–29.

8. R. Bennett, "Relationship Formation and Governance in Consumer Markets: Transactional Analysis Versus the Behaviorist Approach," *Journal of Marketing Management 12, No. 5* (July 1996). pp.417-35.

9. L. Weinberg. "Seeing through Organization: Exploring the Constitutive Quality of Social Relations," *Administration & Society 28*, No. 2 (1996), pp. 177-90.

10. H. Park and K. Harrison, "Enhancing Managerial Cross-Cultural Awareness and Sensitivity: Transactional Analysis Revisted," *Journal of Management Development 12, No. 3*, 1993, pp.20-29.

11. A. Lazarus. He first published a paper in the late 1960's "On Assertive Behavior: A Brief Note," *Behavior Therapy 4* (October 1973), pp. 697-99.

12. K. Aquino, S.L. Grover, M. Bradford, and D.C. Allen. "The Effects of Negative Affectivity, Hierarchival Status and Self-Determination on Workplace Victimization." *Academy of Management Journal 42, No. 2* (1999), pp. 260-72.

13. A. Chaudhurl. "The New Boy Network," *The Guardian*, May 26, 1999. p T6-7.

14. G. Fairclough. "Feeling Squeezed: Thailand's Economic Woes Fuel Worker Unrest," *Far Eastern Economic Review 160, No. 2* (January 9, 1997), p.8.

15. A. Rao and K. Hashimoto. "Intercultural Influences: A Study of the Japanese Expatriate Managers in Canada." *Journal of International Business Studies 27, No. 3* (Fall 1996), pp. 443-66.

16. B. Dossey. "Help Your Patient Break Free from Anxiety." *Nursing 26, No. 10* (1996). pp. 52-54.

17. B.J. Tepper. "Consequences of Abusive Supervision," *Academy of Management Journal 43, No. 2* (2000). pp. 178-90.

18. D.P. Skarlicki, R.F. Folger, and P.Tesluk. "Personality as a Moderator in the Relationship Between Fairness and Retaliation." Academy of Management Journal 41, No. 6, (1998). pp. 658-72.

19. S.L. Robinson and A.M. O'Leary-Kelly. "Monkey See, Monkey Do: The Influence of Work Groups on the Antisocial Behavior of Employees." *Academy of Management Journal 41, No. 6.* (1998). pp. 658-72.

20. B.J. Tepper. "Consequences of Abusive Supervision." *Academy of Management Journal 43, No. 2* (2000), pp. 178-90.

21. "Workplace Violence." *The Wall Street Journal,* April 4, 2000. p. A1.

22. A.G. Podolak, "Is Workplace Violence in Need of Refocusing?" *Security Management 44, No. 6* (June 2000), pp. 152-53.

23. C. Garvey. "Looking for Chinks in the Armor." *HR Magazine 45, No. 6* (June 2000), pp. 161-62.

24. "Put Up Your Dukes." *Wall Street Journal*, August 13, 1996, p. A1.

25. L. Goulet. "Modeling Aggression in the Workplace: The Role of Role Models." *Academy of Management Executive 11, No. 2* (February 1997), pp. 84-5.

26. S.L. Robinson and A.M. O'Leary-Kelly. "Monkey See, Monkey Do: The Influence of Work Groups on the Antisocial Behavior of Employees." *Academy of Management Journal 41, No. 6* (1998), pp. 658-72.

27. L. Goulet. "Modeling Aggression in the Workplace: The Role of Role Models." *Academy of Management Executive 11, No. 2* (February 1997), pp. 84-5.

28. B.J. Tepper. "Consequences of Abusive Supervision." *Academy of Management Journal 43, No. 2* (2000), pp. 178-90.

29. Ibid.

30. D.P. Skarlicki, R.F. Folger, and P. Tesluk. "Personality as a Moderator in the Reltaionship Between Fairness and Retaliation." *Academy of Management Journal 42, No. 1* (1999), pp. 100-8.

31. K.A. Smith-Jentsch, E. Salas and D.P. Baker. "Training Team Performance-Related Assertivenesss." *Personal Psychology 49, No. 4* (Winter 1996), pp. 909-56.

32. J.M. Brett, D.L. Shapiro, and A.L. Lytle. "Breaking the Bonds of Reciprocity in Negotiations." *Academy of Management Journal 41*, No. 4 (1998), pp. 410-24.

33. G. Labianca, D.J. Brass and B. Gray. "Social Networks and Perceptions of Intergroup Conflict: The Role of Negative Relationships and Third Parties." *Academy of Management Journal 41, No. 1* (1998). pp. 55-67.

34. J. Steininger. "When Personalities Collide, Look for the Catbird Seat." *The Business Journal —Milwaukee 14, No. 18* (January 31, 1997), p. 10.

35. T. Pollock, "A Personal File of Stimulating Ideas, Little Known Facts and Daily Problems," *Supervision 58, No. 2* (February 1997), pp. 24-7.

36. J.M. Brett, D.L. Shapiro, and A.L. Lytle. "Breaking the Bonds of Reciprocity in Negotiations." *Academy of Management Journal 41, No. 4* (1998), pp. 410-24.

37. T.L. Simons and R.S. Peterson, "Task Conflict and Relationship Conflict in Top Management Teams: The Pivotal Role of Intragroup Trust." *Journal of Applied Psychology 85, No. 1* (2000), pp. 102-11.

38. S. Berglas. "Boom! There's Nothing Wrong with You or Your Business That a Little Conflict Wouldn't Cure." *Inc. 19 No. 6* (May 1997), pp.56-58.

39. E.J. Van Slyke. "Facilitating Productive Conflict." *HR Focus 74, No. 4* (April 1997), pp. 17-8.

40. D. Lynch. "Unresolved Conflicts Affect the Bottom Line." *HR Magazine 42, No. 5* (May 1997), pp. 49-50.

41. T.L. Simons and R.S. Peterson. "Task Conflict and Relationship Conflict in Top Management Teams: The Pivotal Role of Intragroup Trust." *Journal of Applied Psychology 85, No. 1* (2000) pp.102-11.

42. J.F. Brett, G.B. Northcraft, and R.B. Pinkley. "Stairways to Heaven: An Interlocking Self-Regulation Model of Negotiation." *Academy of Management Review 24, No. 3* (1999), pp. 435-51.

43. T. Pollock. "A Personal File of Stimulating Ideas, Little Known Facts and Daily Problems," *Supervision 58, No. 2* (February 1997) pp. 24-7.

44. B.J. Tepper. "Consequences of Abusive Supervision." *Academy of Management Journal 43, No. 2* (2000), pp. 178-90.

45. Ibid.

46. J.T. Polzer, E.A. Mannix, and M.A. Neale. "Interest Alignment and Coalitions in Multiparty Negotiation." *Academy of Management Journal 41 No. 1* (1998), pp. 42-54.

47. J.F. Brett, G.B. Northcraft, and R.B. Pinkley. "Stairways to Heaven: An Interlocking Self-Regulation Model of Negotiation." *Academy of Manangement Review 24, No. 3* (1999), pp. 435-51.

48. A.E. Schwartz, "How to Handle Conflict." *The CPA Journal 67, No. 4* (April 1997), pp. 72-73.

49. D. Lynch. "Unresolved Conflicts Affect the Bottom Line." *HR Magazine 42, No. 5* (May 1997), pp. 49-50.

50. T. Gordon. *Parent Effectiveness Training* (New York: Wyden 1970).

51. T. Pollock. "A Personal File of Stimulating Ideas, Little Known Facts and Daily Problems." *Supervision 58, No. 2* (February 1997), pp. 24-7.

52. A.E. Schwartz. "How to Handle Conflict." *The CPA Journal 67, No. 4* (April 1997), pp. 72-3.

53. D.E. Conlon and D.P. Sullivan. "Examining the Actions of Organizations in Conflict: Evidence from the Delaware Court of Chancery." *Academy of Management Journal 42, No. 3* (1999), pp. 319-29.

54. T. Gunderson. "It's Not My Problem." *Restaurant Hospitality 81, No. 5* (May 1997), p. 46.

55. E.J. Van Slyke. "Facilitating Productive Conflict." *HR Focus 74, No. 4* (April 1997), pp. 17-8.

56. L. Weinberg. "Seeing through Organization: Exploring the Constitutive Quality of Social Relations." *Administrative & Society 28, No. 2* (1996), pp. 177-90.

57. J.T. Polzer, E.A. Mannix, and M.A. Neale. "Interest Alignment and Coalitions in Multiparty Negotiations." *Academy of Management Journal 41, No. 1* (1998), pp. 42-54.

Chapter 4

Leadership

SOURCE: Robert Kreitner and Angelo Kinicki, *Organizational Behavior*, 5th ed., Chapter 17, © McGraw-Hill, 2001, 1998, 1995, 1992, 1989.

Learning Objectives

When you finish studying the material in this chapter, you should be able to:

- Define the term leadership, and explain the difference between leading versus managing.
- Review trait theory research, and discuss the idea of one best style of leadership, using the Ohio tate studies and the Leadership Grid® as points of reference.
- Explain, according to Fiedler's contingency model, how leadership style interacts with situational control.
- Discuss House's path–goal theory, and Hersey and Blanchard's situational leadership theory.
- Define and differentiate transactional and charismatic leadership.
- Explain how charismatic leadership transforms followers and work groups.
- Summarize the managerial implications of charismatic leadership.
- Explain the leader–member exchange model of leadership.
- Describe the substitutes for leadership, and explain how they substitute for, neutralize, or enhance the effects of leadership.
- Describe servant-leadership and superleadership.

---

http://www.womenswire.com/work/management.htm

Catherine Hapka is executive vice president, markets US West Communications, and oversees a $6.8 billion telecommunications business. Her leadership style is represented by her favorite saying and secret to success. Her favorite saying is "winning begets winning," and her secret is "make your own luck through hard work and perseverance."

Amid washed-out white shirts and nonconfrontational neckties, Catherine Hapka is wearing a searingly red jacket, one that puts the blaze back in blazer. She's at US West's Minneapolis office conducting a meeting—an "event" in her lexicon—to discuss how the company can win back market share in the local long-distance telephone business. Hapka is known around the company as a master motivator, a trait she credits for her success. Today her stated goal is to "raise the temperature in the room."

Hapka kicks off by exhorting her charges: "We need to retake Pork Chop Hill." A half-dozen executives proceed to lay out their battle plans. Hapka listens intently, tapping her pen, rocking back and forth, literally vibrating with energy. She makes frequent interjections. "What's the headline," she demands when confronted with insufficiently digested data. At another point, she simply urges: "Speed, speed, speed, speed!" She wraps up the meeting with a rousing, "I smell victory already."

Equal parts intensity and acumen, Hapka is charged with supercharging US West Communications, which provides phone service to 25 million customers in 14 states. Marketing, sales, customer service, and new-venture development are all her bailiwick. "My job is to get us ready for brutal competition," she explains. "No one believes a Baby Bell can be a lean, mean machine." But Hapka seems to relish the challenge and states with a grin: "I love to do things that people say can't be done."

Hapka learned this aggressive style early in her career. Her first job after graduating from the University of Minnesota was as a financial management trainee with GE in Syracuse, New York. Driving to work each day, Hapka passed a brand new Schlitz brewery in nearby Baldwinsville. "It looked like more fun," she says. So she signed on as a supervisor, overseeing 40 union workers through two shifts a day. In this gritty environment, Hapka began to evolve her management philosophy, what she terms "existential leadership." In essence: Try to involve workers in big ideas that matter to the survival of the company rather than small processes. Within the brewery, the big idea was ever-increasing productivity. End-of-shift beer blasts proved a potent incentive. Says Hapka: "I learned to be more of a coach and less of a supervisor." . . . Her existential approach means finding the big ideas that will motivate unionized phone workers in one breath, entrepreneurs in the next. The process, she says, leaves her feeling like "Jekyll and Hyde."

As for her future, "My goal is to be the CEO of a major corporation. Period." After a pause to let that sink in, she continues: "Ambition is good for the people who hire me, good for the people who follow me. I don't know why people are so worried about talking about ambition. It's what drives this country."[1]

For Discussion

Would you like to work for Catherine Hapka? Explain.

Someone once observed that a leader is a person who finds out which way the parade is going, jumps in front of it, and yells "Follow me!" The plain fact is that this approach to leadership has little chance of working in today's rapidly changing world. Admired leaders, such as civil rights activist Martin Luther King, John Kennedy, and Microsoft's Bill Gates, led people in bold new directions. They envisioned how things could be improved, rallied followers, and refused to accept failure. In short, successful leaders are those individuals who can step into a difficult situation and make a noticeable difference. But how much of a difference can leaders make in modern organizations?

OB researchers have discovered that leaders can make a difference. One study, for example, tracked the relationship between net profit and leadership in 167 companies from 13 industries. It also covered a time span of 20 years. Higher net profits were earned by companies with effective leaders.[2] A more recent study examined the relationship between leadership and performance within major-league baseball teams. The sample consisted of all managers who directed a major-league baseball team during any season from 1945 to 1965. The researchers then tracked the performance of their teams up to the year the manager retired. Using a sophisticated measure of managerial effectiveness, results demonstrated that effective managers won more games with player performance held constant than did less effective managers.[3] Leadership makes a difference!

After formally defining the term *leadership,* this chapter focuses on the following areas: (1) trait and behavioral approaches to leadership, (2) alternative situational theories of leadership, (3) charismatic leadership, and (4) additional perspectives on leadership. Because there are many different leadership theories within each of these areas, it is impossible to discuss them all. This chapter is based on reviewing those theories with the most research support.

WHAT DOES LEADERSHIP INVOLVE?

Because the topic of leadership has fascinated people for centuries, definitions abound. This section presents a definition of leadership and highlights the similarities and differences between leading versus managing.

What Is Leadership?

Disagreement about the definition of leadership stems from the fact that it involves a complex interaction among the leader, the followers, and the situation. For example, some researchers define leadership in terms of personality and physical traits, while others believe leadership is represented by a set of prescribed behaviors. In contrast, other researchers believe that leadership is a temporary role that can be filled by anyone. There is a common thread, however, among the different definitions of leadership. The common thread is social influence.

As the term is used in this chapter, **leadership** is defined as "a social influence process in which the leader seeks the voluntary participation of subordinates in an effort to reach organizational goals."[4] Tom Peters and Nancy Austin, authors of the best-seller, *A Passion for Excellence,* describe leadership in broader terms:

> Leadership means vision, cheerleading, enthusiasm, love, trust, verve, passion, obsession, consistency, the use of symbols, paying attention as illustrated by the content of one's calendar, out-and-out drama (and the management thereof), creating heroes at all levels, coaching, effectively wandering around, and numerous other things. Leadership must be present at all levels of the organization. It depends on a million little things done with obsession, consistency, and care, but all of those million little things add up to nothing if the trust, vision, and basic belief are not there.[5]

As you can see from this definition, leadership clearly entails more than wielding power and exercising authority and is exhibited on different levels. At the individual level, for example, leadership involves mentoring, coaching, inspiring, and motivating. Leaders build teams, create cohesion, and resolve conflicts at the group level. Finally, leaders build culture and create change at the organizational level.[6]

Figure 4–1   **A Conceptual Framework for Understanding Leadership**

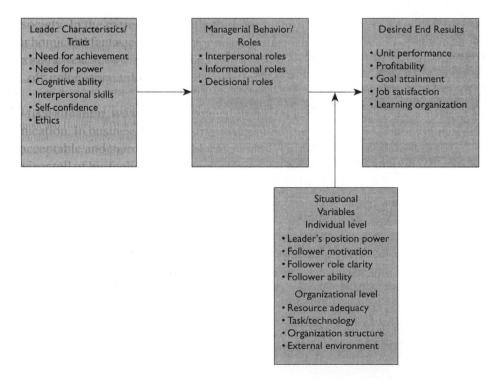

SOURCE: Adapted in part from G Yukl, "Managerial Leadership: A Review of Theory and Research," *Journal of Management,* June 1989, p 274.

Table 4–1   **Differences between Leaders and Managers**

Leaders	Managers
Innovate	Administer
Develop	Maintain
Inspire	Control
Long-term view	Short-term view
Ask what and why	Ask how and when
Originate	Initiate
Challenge the status quo	Accept the status quo
Do the right things	Do things right

SOURCE: Distinctions were taken from W G Bennis, *On Becoming a Leader* (Reading, MA: Addison-Wesley, 1989).

Figure 4–1 provides a conceptual framework for understanding leadership. It was created by integrating components of the different theories and models discussed in this chapter. Figure 4–1 indicates that certain leader characteristics/traits are the foundation of effective leadership. In turn, these characteristics affect an individual's ability to carry out various managerial behaviors/roles. Effective leadership also depends on various situational variables. These variables are important components of the contingency leadership theories discussed later in this chapter. Finally, leadership is results oriented.

Leading versus Managing

It is important to appreciate the difference between leadership and management to fully understand what leadership is all about. Bernard Bass, a leadership expert, concluded that "leaders manage and managers lead, but the two activities are not synonymous."[7] Bass tells us that although leadership and management overlap, each entails a unique set of activities or functions. Broadly speaking, managers typically perform functions associated with planning, investigating, organizing, and control, and leaders deal with the interpersonal aspects of a manager's job. Leaders inspire others, provide emotional support, and try to get employees to rally around a common goal. Leaders also play a key role in creating a vision and strategic plan for an organization. Managers, in turn, are charged with implementing the vision and strategic plan. Table 4–1 summarizes the key differences found between leaders and managers.[8]

The distinction between leaders and managers is more than a semantic issue for four reasons:

1. It is important from a hiring standpoint. Because leaders and managers perform a subset of unique functions, it is important to recruit and select people who have the required intellectual abilities, experience, and job-relevant knowledge to perform their jobs.[9]

2. Differences may affect group effectiveness. Work group performance can be increased by staffing a productive mix of leaders and managers.

3. Successful organizational change is highly dependent upon effective leadership throughout an organization. Senior executives cannot create change on their own. According to organizational change expert John Kotter, successful organizational transformation is 70% to 90% leadership and 10% to 30% management.[10]

4. Distinctions between leading and managing highlight the point that leadership is not restricted to people in particular positions or roles. Anyone from the bottom to the top of an organization can be a leader. Many an informal leader have contributed to organizational effectiveness. Consider the behavior exhibited by Skip Tobey, an employee at America West Airlines.

> "I'm not just an aircraft cleaner," the 36-year-old Phoenix native said. "That's my title, but that's not the end of my job."
>
> Tobey said he looks for ways to help passengers, lending a hand to young families maneuvering strollers through narrow aircraft aisles and assisting elderly travelers.
>
> "My satisfaction is tied into quality, helping the passengers," he said. "No matter what it takes, if it means going to the furthest extreme, I'll do it."[11]

Skip's behavior is not only inspirational, but it supports leadership expert Warren Bennis's conclusion about leaders and managers. Bennis characterized managers as people who do things right and leaders as individuals who do the "right" things. Skip Tobey is clearly doing the "right" things to help America West provide excellent customer service.

TRAIT AND BEHAVIORAL THEORIES OF LEADERSHIP

This section examines the two earliest approaches used to explain leadership. Trait theories focused on identifying the personal traits that differentiated leaders from followers. Behavioral theorists examined leadership from a different perspective. They tried to uncover the different kinds of leader behaviors that resulted in higher work group performance. Both approaches to leadership can teach current and future managers valuable lessons about leading.

Trait Theory

At the turn of the 20th century, the prevailing belief was that leaders were born, not made. Selected people were thought to possess inborn traits that made them successful leaders. A **leader trait** is a physical or personality characteristic that can be used to differentiate leaders from followers.

Before World War II, hundreds of studies were conducted to pinpoint the traits of successful leaders. Dozens of leadership traits were identified. During the postwar period, however, enthusiasm was replaced by widespread criticism. Studies conducted by Ralph Stogdill in 1948 and by Richard Mann in 1959, which sought to summarize the impact of traits on leadership, caused the trait approach to fall into disfavor.

Stogdill's and Mann's Findings

Based on his review, Stogdill concluded that five traits tended to differentiate leaders from average followers: (1) intelligence, (2) dominance, (3) self-confidence, (4) level of energy and activity, and (5) task-relevant knowledge.[12] Consider the leadership traits that Jack Welch, chief executive officer of General Electric, indicated that he is looking for in his replacement during an interview with *Fortune*.

> "Vision. Courage. The four E's: energy, ability to energize others, the edge to make tough decisions, and execution, which is key because you can't just decide but have got to follow up in 19 ways. Judgment. The self-confidence to hire always someone who's better than you. Are they growing things? Do they add new insights to the businesses they run? Do they like to nurture small businesses?"
>
> And one more: an insatiable appetite for accomplishment. Too many CEOs, Welch once said, believe that the high point comes the day they land the job. Not Welch, who says, "I'm 63 and finally getting smart."[13]

Although Welch is looking for some of the same traits identified by Ralph Stogdill, research revealed that these five traits did not accurately predict which individuals became leaders in organizations. People with these traits often remained followers.

Mann's review was similarly disappointing for the trait theorists. Among the seven categories of personality traits he examined, Mann found intelligence was the best predictor of leadership. However, Mann warned that all observed positive relationships between traits and leadership were weak (correlations averaged about 0.15).[14]

Together, Stogdill's and Mann's findings dealt a near deathblow to the trait approach. But now, decades later, leadership traits are once again receiving serious research attention.

Contemporary Trait Research

Two OB researchers concluded in 1983 that past trait data may have been incorrectly analyzed. By applying modern statistical techniques to an old database, they demonstrated that the majority of a leader's behavior could be attributed to stable underlying traits.[15] Unfortunately, their methodology did not single out specific traits.

A 1986 meta-analysis by Robert Lord and his associates remedied this shortcoming. Based on a reanalysis of Mann's data and subsequent studies, Lord concluded that people have leadership *prototypes* that affect our perceptions of who is and who is not an effective leader. Your **leadership prototype** is a mental representation of the traits and behaviors that you believe are possessed by leaders. We thus tend to perceive that someone is a leader when he or she exhibits traits or behaviors that are consistent with our prototypes.[16] Lord's research demonstrated that people are perceived as being leaders when they exhibit the traits associated with intelligence, masculinity, and dominance. A more recent study of 200 undergraduate and graduate students also confirmed the idea that leadership prototypes influence leadership perceptions. Results revealed that perceptions of an individual as a leader were affected by that person's sex—males were perceived to be leaders more than females— and behavioral flexibility. People who were more behaviorally flexible were perceived as more leaderlike.[17]

Another pair of leadership researchers attempted to identify key leadership traits by asking the following open-ended question to more than 20,000 people around the world: "What values (personal traits or characteristics) do you look for and admire in your superiors?" The top four traits included honesty, forward-looking, inspiring, and competent.[18] The researchers concluded that these four traits constitute a leader's credibility. This research suggests that people want their leaders to be credible and to have a sense of direction.

Gender and Leadership

The increase of women in the workforce has generated much interest in understanding the similarities and differences in female and male leaders. Important issues concern whether women and men (1) assume varying leadership roles within work groups, (2) use different leadership styles, (3) are relatively more or less effective in leadership roles, and (4) whether there are situational differences that produce gender differences in leadership effectiveness. Three meta-analyses were conducted to summarize research pertaining to these issues.

The first meta-analysis demonstrated that men and women differed in the type of leadership roles they assumed within work groups. Men were seen as displaying more overall leadership and task leadership. In contrast, women were perceived as displaying more social leadership.[19] Results from the second meta-analysis revealed that leadership styles varied by gender. Women used a more democratic or participative style than men. Men employed a more autocratic and directive style than women.[20] Finally, a recent meta-analysis of more than 75 studies uncovered three key findings: (1) Female and male leaders were rated as equally effective. This is a very positive outcome because it suggests that despite barriers and possible negative stereotypes toward female leaders, female and male leaders were equally effective. (2) Men were rated as more effective leaders than women when their roles were defined in more masculine terms, and women were more effective than men in roles defined in less masculine terms. (3) Gender differences in leadership effectiveness were associated with the percentage of male leaders and male subordinates. Specifically, male leaders were seen as more effective than females when there was a greater percentage of male leaders and male subordinates. Interestingly, a similar positive bias in leadership effectiveness was not found for women.[21]

Trait Theory in Perspective

We can no longer afford to ignore the implications of leadership traits. Traits play a central role in how we perceive leaders. It is important to determine the traits embodied in people's schemata (or mental pictures) for leaders. If those traits are inappropriate (i.e., foster discriminatory selection and invalid performance appraisals), they need to be corrected through training and development. Consider the stereotypes associated with who gets selected for corporate assignments overseas.

> While women represent about half of the global workforce, surveys indicate they count for less than 12% of the expatriate population. Why? Because many male managers still believe women aren't interested in overseas jobs or won't be effective at them. The managers cite dual-career complications, gender prejudice in many countries, and the risk of sexual harassment. That's hogwash, according to researchers at Loyola University (Chicago). Their recent survey of 261 female expats and their supervisors concluded that women are just as interested as men in foreign assignments and just as effective once there. In fact, contends Linda Stroh, one of the researchers, the traits considered crucial for success overseas—knowing when to be passive, being a team player, soliciting a variety of perspectives—are more often associated with women's management styles than men's.[22]

www.amcham.ru

International OB — Russian Leadership Traits in Three Eras

Leadership Trait	Traditional Russian Society (1400s to 1917)	The Red Executive (1917 to 1991)	The Market-Oriented Manager (1991 to Present)
Leadership Motivation			
Power	Powerful autocrats	Centralized leadership stifled grass-roots democracy	Shared power and ownership
Responsibility	Centralization of responsibility	Micromanagers and macropuppets	Delegation and strategic decision making
Drive			
Achievement motivation	Don't rock the boat	Frustrated pawns	The sky's the limit
Ambition	Equal poverty for all	Service to party and collective good	Overcoming the sin of being a winner
Initiative	Look both ways	Meticulous rule following and behind-the-scenes finessing	Let's do business
Energy	Concentrated spasms of labor	"8-hour day," 8 to 8, firefighting	8-day week, chasing opportunities
Tenacity	Life is a struggle	Struggling to accomplish the routine	Struggling to accomplish the new
Honesty and Integrity			
Dual ethical standard	Deception in dealings, fealty in friendship	Two sets of books, personal integrity	Wild capitalism, personal trust
Using connections (*blat*)	Currying favor with landowners	Greasing the wheels of the state	Greasing palms, but learning to do business straight
Self-Confidence	From helplessness to bravado	From inferior quality to "big is beautiful"	From cynicism to overpromising

SOURCE: S M Puffer, "Understanding the Bear: A Portrait of Russian Business Leaders," *Academy of Management Executive*, February 1994, p 42. Used with permission.

It appears that managers should be careful to avoid using gender-based stereotypes when making overseas assignments. Moreover, organizations may find it beneficial to consider selected leadership traits when choosing among candidates for leadership positions. Gender should not be used as one of these traits. Consider, for example, the qualities that Colin Powell, former chairman of the Joint Chiefs of Staff and White House national security advisor, believes that effective leaders need to have in the 21st century:

> Leadership will always require people who have a vision of where they wish to take "the led." Leadership will always require people who are able to organize the effort of [others] to accomplish the objectives that flow from the vision. And leadership will always put a demand on leaders to pick the right people. . . .
>
> Leadership also requires motivating people. And that means pushing the vision down to every level of the organization.
>
> What will make things different in the 21st century, however, is that the world is going through a transformation . . . At the same time, the world is being fundamentally reshaped by the information and technology revolution, which is supplanting the industrial revolution. . . . The leaders of this new industrial-information era have to be able to use these tools and understand the power of information and technology—and how that gives them new opportunities.[23]

In contrast to these traits, the International OB, outlines the relevant leadership traits of Russian leaders from the 1400s to the present time. As you can see, Russian organizations need to nurture and develop a similar but different set of leadership traits.

Behavioral Styles Theory

This phase of leadership research began during World War II as part of an effort to develop better military leaders. It was an outgrowth of two events: the seeming inability of trait theory to explain leadership effectiveness and the human relations movement, an outgrowth of the Hawthorne Studies. The thrust of early behavioral leadership theory was to focus on leader behavior, instead of on personality traits. It was believed that leader behavior directly affected work group effectiveness. This led researchers to identify patterns of behavior (called leadership styles) that enabled leaders to effectively influence others.

The Ohio State Studies

Researchers at Ohio State University began by generating a list of behaviors exhibited by leaders. At one point, the list contained 1,800 statements that described nine categories of leader behavior. Ultimately, the Ohio State researchers concluded there were only two independent dimensions of leader behavior: consideration and initiating structure. **Consideration** involves leader behavior associated with creating mutual respect or trust and focuses on a concern for group members' needs and desires. **Initiating structure** is leader behavior that organizes and defines what group members should be doing to maximize output. These two dimensions of leader behavior were oriented at right angles to yield four behavioral styles of leadership (see Figure 4–2).

Ethics at Work

The following situation involved Paul Orfalea, founder and chairman of Kinko's, and one of his employees:

About 20 years ago, I had a manager working for me who lied and was quick to fire people. Nobody liked this guy. He was real bad. Then the bookkeeper caught him stealing. I was too weak to deal with the situation, and I just let it go on. When I finally confronted him, he gave me some excuse about his father having a heart attack. The stress had driven him to steal, he said. I really should have fired him and sent him to jail. But I was gutless, and I felt sorry for him. In those days we had three or four workers at every store, and my job was to get all those people to like one another. I tried to get people out of their stores to talk with one another.

SOURCE: Excerpted from P Orfalea, "My Biggest Mistake," *Inc.,* March 1999 p 88.

You Decide . . .

Was Mr Orfalea being too considerate by not firing the employee? What is the effect of letting the behavior of stealing go unpunished?

For an interpretation of this issue, visit our Web site **www.mhhe.com/kreitner**

Figure 4–2   **Four Leadership Styles Derived from the Ohio State Studies**

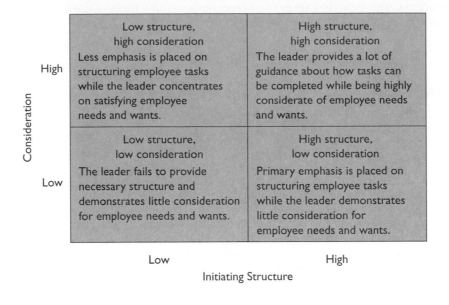

Figure 4–3   **The Leadership Grid®**

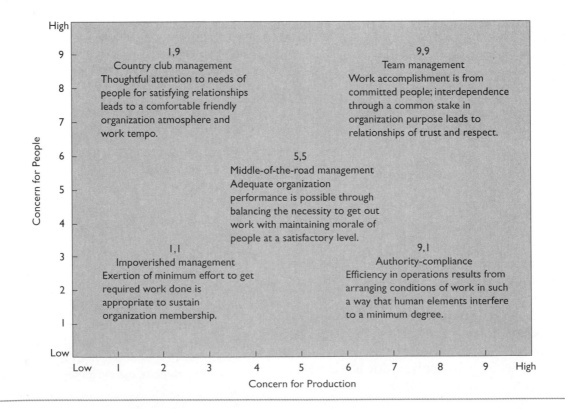

It initially was hypothesized that a high-structure, high-consideration style would be the one best style of leadership. Through the years, the effectiveness of the high-high style has been tested many times. Overall, results have been mixed. Researchers thus concluded that there is not one best style of leadership.[24] Rather, it is argued that effectiveness of a given leadership style depends on situational factors.

University of Michigan Studies

As in the Ohio State studies, this research sought to identify behavioral differences between effective and ineffective leaders. Researchers identified two different styles of leadership: one was employee centered, the other was job centered. These behavioral styles parallel the consideration and initiating-structure styles identified by the Ohio State group. In summarizing the results from these studies, one management expert concluded that effective leaders (1) tend to have supportive or employee-centered relationships with employees, (2) use group rather than individual methods of supervision, and (3) set high performance goals.[25]

Blake and Mouton's Managerial/Leadership Grid®

Perhaps the most widely known behavioral styles model of leadership is the Managerial Grid.® Behavioral scientists Robert Blake and Jane Srygley Mouton developed and trademarked the grid. They use it to demonstrate that there *is* one best style of leadership. Blake and Mouton's Managerial Grid® (renamed the **Leadership Grid**® in 1991) is a matrix formed by the intersection of two dimensions of leader behavior (see Figure 4–3). On the horizontal axis is "concern for production." "Concern for people" is on the vertical axis. Blake and Mouton point out that "the variables of the Managerial Grid® are *attitudinal and conceptual,* with *behavior* descriptions derived from and connected with the thinking that lies behind action."[26] In other words, concern for production and concern for people involve attitudes and patterns of thinking, as well as specific behaviors. By scaling each axis of the grid from 1 to 9, Blake and Mouton were able to plot five leadership styles. Because it emphasizes teamwork and interdependence, the 9,9 style is considered by Blake and Mouton to be the best, regardless of the situation.

In support of the 9,9 style, Blake and Mouton cite the results of a study in which 100 experienced managers were asked to select the best way of handling 12 managerial situations. Between 72% and 90% of the managers selected the 9,9 style for each of the 12 situations.[27] Moreover, Blake and Mouton report, "The 9,9, orientation . . . leads to productivity, satisfaction, creativity, and health."[28] Critics point out that Blake and Mouton's research may be self-serving. At issue is the grid's extensive use as a training and consulting tool for diagnosing and correcting organizational problems.

Behavioral Styles Theory in Perspective

By emphasizing leader *behavior,* something that is learned, the behavioral style approach makes it clear that leaders are made, not born. This is the opposite of the trait theorists' traditional assumption. Given what we know about behavior shaping and model-based training, leader *behaviors* can be systematically improved and developed. Consider, for example, how Steve Sitek, director of performance development and training at Ernst and Young's Finance, Technology, and Administration Division, is striving to grow and develop leadership talent within the organization:

> Sitek oversees a senior development program that helps executives gain feedback on how they measure up against 11 critical leadership characteristics. Internal studies have shown a direct correlation between executive performance and the 11 characteristics, which include being innovative, excited, persuasive, and strategic. In one-on-one encounters with superiors, managers discuss their assessments to identify characteristics that need strengthening and are charged with structuring their own development plans. . . . Managers are encouraged to work on the characteristics they need to grow incrementally over a multi-year period. Sitek produces specific training geared to each characteristic. "I have a training program for each one," he says. "For example, the No. 1 development gap that we discovered was the characteristic of persuasiveness. I offer a one-day program on this characteristic.[29]

Behavioral styles research also revealed that there is no one best style of leadership. The effectiveness of a particular leadership style depends on the situation at hand. For instance, employees prefer structure over consideration when faced with role ambiguity.[30] Finally, research also reveals that it is important to consider the difference between how frequently and how effectively managers exhibit various leader behaviors. For example, a manager might ineffectively display a lot of considerate leader behaviors. Such a style is likely to frustrate employees and possibly result in lowered job satisfaction and performance. Because the frequency of exhibiting leadership behaviors is secondary in importance to effectiveness, managers are encouraged to concentrate on improving the effective execution of their leader behaviors.[31] At this time we would like you to complete the OB

OB EXERCISE 4-1   ASSESSING TEACHER LEADERSHIP STYLE, CLASS SATISFACTION, AND STUDENT ROLE CLARITY

Instructions

A team of researchers converted a set of leadership measures for application in the classroom. For each of the items shown here, use the following rating scale to circle the answer that best represents your feelings. Next, use the scoring key to compute scores for your teacher's leadership style and your class satisfaction and role clarity.

1 = Strongly disagree
2 = Disagree
3 = Neither agree nor disagree
4 = Agree
5 = Strongly agree

1.	My instructor behaves in a manner which is thoughtful of my personal needs.	1 — 2 — 3 — 4 — 5
2.	My instructor maintains a friendly working relationship with me.	1 — 2 — 3 — 4 — 5
3.	My instructor looks out for my personal welfare.	1 — 2 — 3 — 4 — 5
4.	My instructor gives clear explanations of what is expected of me.	1 — 2 — 3 — 4 — 5
5.	My instructor tells me the performance goals for the class.	1 — 2 — 3 — 4 — 5
6.	My instructor explains the level of performance that is expected of me.	1 — 2 — 3 — 4 — 5
7.	I am satisfied with the variety of class assignments.	1 — 2 — 3 — 4 — 5
8.	I am satisfied with the way my instructor handles the students.	1 — 2 — 3 — 4 — 5
9.	I am satisfied with the spirit of cooperation among my fellow students.	1 — 2 — 3 — 4 — 5
10.	I know exactly what my responsibilities are.	1 — 2 — 3 — 4 — 5
11.	I am given clear explanations of what has to be done.	1 — 2 — 3 — 4 — 5

Scoring Key

Teacher consideration (1, 2, 3)   _____
Teacher initiating structure (4, 5, 6)   _____
Class satisfaction (7, 8, 9)   _____
Role clarity (10, 11)   _____

Arbitrary Norms

Low consideration = 3–8
High consideration = 9–15
Low structure   = 3–8
High structure   = 9–15
Low satisfaction   = 3–8
High satisfaction = 9–15
Low role clarity   = 2–5
High role clarity = 6–10

Exercise 4-1. The exercise gives you the opportunity to test the behavioral styles theory by assessing your teacher's leadership style and your associated class satisfaction and role clarity. Are you satisfied with this class? If yes, the behavioral styles approach is supported if your teacher displayed both high consideration and initiating structure. In contrast, the behavioral style approach is not supported if you are satisfied with this class and your teacher exhibits something other than the standard high-high style. Do your results support the proposition that there is one best style of leadership? Are your results consistent with past research that showed leadership behavior depends on the situation at hand? The answer is yes if you prefer initiating structure over consideration when faced with high role ambiguity. The answer also is yes if you prefer consideration over structure when role ambiguity is low. We now turn our attention to discussing alternative situational theories of leadership.

SITUATIONAL THEORIES

Situational leadership theories grew out of an attempt to explain the inconsistent findings about traits and styles. **Situational theories** propose that the effectiveness of a particular style of leader behavior depends on the situation. As situations change, different styles become appropriate. This directly challenges the idea of one best style of leadership. Let us closely examine three alternative situational theories of leadership that reject the notion of one best leadership style.

Fiedler's Contingency Model

Fred Fiedler, an OB scholar, developed a situational model of leadership. It is the oldest and one of the most widely known models of leadership. Fiedler's model is based on the following assumption:

> The performance of a leader depends on two interrelated factors: (1) the degree to which the situation gives the leader control and influence—that is, the likelihood that [the leader] can successfully accomplish the job; and (2) the leader's basic motivation—that is, whether [the leader's] self-esteem depends primarily on accomplishing the task or on having close supportive relations with others.[32]

With respect to a leader's basic motivation, Fiedler believes that leaders are either task motivated or relationship motivated. These basic motivations are similar to initiating structure/concern for production and consideration/concern for people. Consider the basic leadership motivation possessed by Cynthia Danaher, general manager of Hewlett-Packard's Medical Products Group:

> Once a manager is in charge of thousands of employees, the ability to set direction and delegate is more vital than team-building and coaching, she believes. . . . When Ms. Danaher changed her top management team and restructured the Medical Products Group, moving out of slow-growth businesses to focus on more-profitable clinical equipment, she had to relinquish her need for approval. "Change is painful, and someone has to be the bad guy," she says. Suddenly employees she considered friends avoided her and told her she was ruining the group. "I didn't use to be able to tolerate that, and I'd try to explain over and over why change had to occur," she says. Over time, she has learned to simply "charge ahead," accepting that not everyone will follow and that some won't survive.[33]

Danaher clearly has used a task motivation to create organizational change within Hewlett-Packard.

Fiedler's theory also is based on the premise that leaders have one dominant leadership style that is resistant to change. He suggests that leaders must learn to manipulate or influence the leadership situation in order to create a "match" between their leadership style and the amount of control within the situation at hand. After discussing the components of situational control and the leadership matching process, we review relevant research and managerial implications.[34]

Figure 4–4   Representation of Fiedler's Contingency Model

Situational Control	High Control Situations			Moderate Control Situations			Low Control Situations	
Leader–member relations	Good	Good	Good	Good	Poor	Poor	Poor	Poor
Task structure	High	High	Low	Low	High	High	Low	Low
Position power	Strong	Weak	Strong	Weak	Strong	Weak	Strong	Weak
Situation	I	II	III	IV	V	VI	VII	VIII
Optimal Leadership Style	Task-Motivated Leadership			Relationship-Motivated Leadership			Task-Motivated Leadership	

SOURCE: Adapted from F E Fiedler, "Situational Control and a Dynamic Theory of Leadership," in *Managerial Control and Organizational Democracy*, eds B King, S Streufert, and F E Fiedler (New York: John Wiley & Sons, 1978), p 114.

Situational Control

Situational control refers to the amount of control and influence the leader has in her or his immediate work environment. Situational control ranges from high to low. High control implies that the leader's decisions will produce predictable results because the leader has the ability to influence work outcomes. Low control implies that the leader's decisions may not influence work outcomes because the leader has very little influence. There are three dimensions of situational control: leader–member relations, task structure, and position power. These dimensions vary independently, forming eight combinations of situational control (see Figure 4–4).

The three dimensions of situational control are defined as follows:

- **Leader–member relations** reflect the extent to which the leader has the support, loyalty, and trust of the work group. This dimension is the most important component of situational control. Good leader–member relations suggest that the leader can depend on the group, thus ensuring that the work group will try to meet the leader's goals and objectives.

- **Task structure** is concerned with the amount of structure contained within tasks performed by the work group. For example, a managerial job contains less structure than that of a bank teller. Because structured tasks have guidelines for how the job should be completed, the leader has more control and influence over employees performing such tasks. This dimension is the second most important component of situational control.

- **Position power** refers to the degree to which the leader has formal power to reward, punish, or otherwise obtain compliance from employees.[35]

Linking Leadership Motivation and Situational Control

Fiedler's complete contingency model is presented in Figure 4–4. The last row under the Situational Control column shows that there are eight different leadership situations. Each situation represents a unique combination of leader–member relations, task structure, and position power. Situations I, II, and III represent high control situations. Figure 4–4 shows that task-motivated leaders are hypothesized to be most effective in situations of high control. Under conditions of moderate control (situations IV, V, and VI), relationship-motivated leaders are expected to be more effective. Finally, the results orientation of task-motivated leaders is predicted to be more effective under conditions of low control (situations VII and VIII).

Research and Managerial Implications

The overall accuracy of Fiedler's contingency model was tested through a meta-analysis of 35 studies containing 137 leader style–performance relations. According to the researchers' findings, (1) the contingency theory was correctly induced from studies on which it was based; (2) for laboratory studies testing the model, the theory was supported for all leadership situations except situation II; and (3) for field studies testing the model, three of the eight situations (IV, V, and VII) produced completely supportive results, while partial support was obtained for situations I, II, III, VI, and VIII. A more recent meta-analysis of data obtained from 1,282 groups also provided mixed support for the contingency model.[36] These findings suggest that Fiedler's model needs theoretical refinement.[37]

The major contribution of Fiedler's model is that it prompted others to examine the contingency nature of leadership. This research, in turn, reinforced the notion that there is no one best style of leadership. Leaders are advised to alter their task and relationship orientation to fit the demands of the situation at hand.

Path–Goal Theory

Path–goal theory is based on the expectancy theory of motivation. Expectancy theory proposes that motivation to exert effort increases as one's effort→performance→outcome expectations improve. Path–goal theory focuses on how leaders influence followers' expectations.

Robert House originated the path–goal theory of leadership. He proposed a model that describes how expectancy perceptions are influenced by the contingent relationships among four leadership styles and various employee attitudes and behaviors (see Figure 4–5).[38] According to the path–goal model, leader behavior is acceptable when employees view it as a source of satisfaction or as paving the way to future satisfaction. In addition, leader behavior is motivational to the extent it (1) reduces roadblocks that interfere with goal accomplishment, (2) provides the guidance and support needed by employees, and (3) ties meaningful rewards to goal accomplishment. Because the model deals with pathways to goals and rewards, it is called the path–goal theory of leadership. House sees the leader's main job as helping employees stay on the right paths to challenging goals and valued rewards.

Leadership Styles

House believes leaders can exhibit more than one leadership style. This contrasts with Fiedler, who proposes that leaders have one dominant style. The four leadership styles identified by House are as follows:

- *Directive leadership.* Providing guidance to employees about what should be done and how to do it, scheduling work, and maintaining standards of performance.

- *Supportive leadership.* Showing concern for the well-being and needs of employees, being friendly and approachable, and treating workers as equals.

- *Participative leadership.* Consulting with employees and seriously considering their ideas when making decisions.

- *Achievement-oriented leadership.* Encouraging employees to perform at their highest level by setting challenging goals, emphasizing excellence, and demonstrating confidence in employee abilities.[39]

Figure 4–5   **A General Representation of House's Path–Goal Theory**

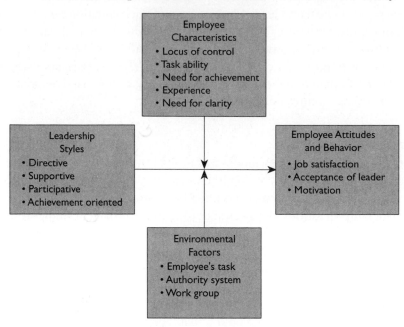

Research evidence supports the idea that leaders exhibit more than one leadership style.[40] Descriptions of business leaders reinforce these findings. For example, PepsiCo's CEO, Roger Enrico, uses multiple leadership styles to influence others:

> "Roger is at once one of the warmest and most personable people, and so cold," says a former PepsiCo executive. "His strength is his ability to charm you and get you on his side, and also dispassionately evaluate a business and fix it. He never gets sucked into the culture, the history of a business. So he's not afraid to cut the fat, storm ahead, reorganize, shut the factory, kill the product line. He's agile and he's cunning."
>
> He challenges everything and assumes nothing. For example, when Enrico took charge at PepsiCo's Frito-Lay division five years ago, the numbers looked fine. But Enrico smelled something rotten at the food company. Profits were rising, it turned out, because management was pumping up prices on Doritos and other snacks. Frito was scrimping on product quality. Enrico slashed costs, firing 1,700 workers and sweeping out management.[41]

Contingency Factors

Contingency factors are situational variables that cause one style of leadership to be more effective than another. In this context, these variables affect expectancy or path–goal perceptions. This model has two groups of contingency variables (see Figure 4–5). They are employee characteristics and environmental factors. Five important employee characteristics are locus of control, task ability, need for achievement, experience, and need for clarity. Three relevant environmental factors are (1) the employee's task, (2) the authority system, and (3) the work group. All these factors have the potential for hindering or motivating employees.

Research has focused on determining whether the various contingency factors influence the effectiveness of different leadership styles. A recent summary of this research revealed that only 138 of 562 (25%) contingency relationships tested confirmed the theory. Although these results were greater than chance, they provided limited support for the moderating relationships predicted within path–goal theory. On the positive side, however, the *task characteristics* of autonomy, variety, and significance and the *employee characteristics* of ability, experience, training and knowledge, professional orientation, indifference to organizational rewards, and need for independence obtained results that were semiconsistent with the theory.[42]

Figure 4–6   **Situational Leadership Model**

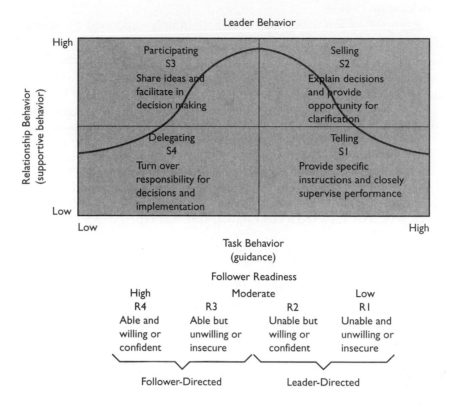

SOURCE: Reprinted with permission from Dr. Paul Hersey (1984). *The Management of Organizational Behavior: Utilizing Human Resources,* The Center for Leadership Studies, Escondido.

Managerial Implications

There are two important managerial implications. First, leaders possess and use more than one style of leadership. Managers thus should not be hesitant to try new behaviors when the situation calls for them. Second, a small set of task and employee characteristics are relevant contingency factors. Managers are encouraged to modify their leadership style to fit these various task and employee characteristics. For example, supportive and achievement leadership are more likely to be satisfying when employees have a lot of ability and experience.

Hersey and Blanchard's Situational Leadership Theory

Situational leadership theory (SLT) was developed by management writers Paul Hersey and Kenneth Blanchard.[43] According to the theory, effective leader behavior depends on the readiness level of a leader's followers. **Readiness** is defined as the extent to which a follower possesses the ability and willingness to complete a task. Willingness is a combination of confidence, commitment, and motivation.

The SLT model is summarized in Figure 4–6. The appropriate leadership style is found by cross referencing follower readiness, which varies from low to high, with one of four leadership styles. The four leadership styles represent combinations of task and relationship-oriented leader behaviors (S1 to S4). Leaders are encouraged to use a "telling style" for followers with low readiness. This style combines high task-oriented leader behaviors, such as providing instructions, with low relationship-oriented behaviors, such as close supervision (see Figure 4–6). As follower readiness increases, leaders are advised to gradually move from a telling, to a selling, to a participating, and, ultimately, to a delegating style. In the most recent description of this model, the four leadership styles depicted in Figure 4–6 are referred to as telling or directing (S1), persuading or coaching (S2), participating or supporting (S3), and delegating (S4).[44]

Although SLT is widely used as a training tool, it is not strongly supported by scientific research. For instance, leadership effectiveness was not attributable to the predicted interaction between follower readiness and leadership style in a study of 459 salespeople.[45] Moreover, a study of 303 teachers indicated that SLT was accurate only for employees with low readiness. This finding is consistent with a survey of 57 chief nurse executives in California. These executives did not delegate in accordance with SLT.[46] Finally, researchers have concluded that the self-assessment instrument used to measure leadership style and follower readiness is inaccurate and should be used with caution.[47] In summary, managers should exercise discretion when using prescriptions from SLT.

FROM TRANSACTIONAL TO CHARISMATIC LEADERSHIP

New perspectives of leadership theory have emerged in the past 15 years, variously referred to as "charismatic," "heroic," "transformational," or "visionary" leadership.[48] These competing but related perspectives have created confusion among researchers and practicing managers. Fortunately, Robert House and Boas Shamir have given us a practical, integrated theory. It is referred to as *charismatic leadership.*

This section begins by highlighting the differences between transactional and charismatic leadership. We then discuss a model of the charismatic leadership process and its research and management implications.

What Is the Difference between Transactional and Charismatic Leadership?

Most of the models and theories previously discussed in this chapter represent transactional leadership. **Transactional leadership** focuses on the interpersonal transactions between managers and employees. Leaders are seen as engaging in behaviors that maintain a quality interaction between themselves and followers. The two underlying characteristics of transactional leadership are that (1) leaders use contingent rewards to motivate employees and (2) leaders exert corrective action only when subordinates fail to obtain performance goals.

In contrast, **charismatic leadership** emphasizes "symbolic leader behavior, visionary and inspirational messages, nonverbal communication, appeal to ideological values, intellectual stimulation of followers by the leader, display of confidence in self and followers, and leader expectations for follower self-sacrifice and for performance beyond the call of duty."[49] Charismatic leadership can produce significant organizational change and results because it "transforms" employees to pursue organizational goals in lieu of self-interests. Ken Chenault, chief operating officer of American Express Company, is a good example of a charismatic leader. Consider what others have to say about his leadership style:

> An elegant, quietly charismatic man of even temper and unrelenting drive, Chenault tends to inspire his admirers to extravagant praise. "Ken radiates such a depth of belief that people would do anything for him," says Rochelle Lazarus, chairman and CEO of Ogilvy & Mather Worldwide Inc., AmEx's lead advertising agency. "He is a true leader," adds Amy DiGeso, a former AmEx executive who is chief executive of Mary Kay Inc.: "I can say unequivocally that I admire Ken more than anyone else I've ever worked with. I think he will be our generation's Jack Welch." . . . A former management consultant himself, Chenault is said to be as hard-driving and pragmatic as his boss [Harvey Golub]. Unlike Golub, though, he has always been able to engage the emotions of his colleagues as well as their intellects. "Harvey is a brilliant man, but Ken has the hearts and minds of the people at the TRS [Travel Related Services] company," says Thomas O Ryder, a longtime AmEx exec who recently became CEO of Reader's Digest Assn.[50]

Let us now examine how charismatic leadership transforms followers.

Figure 4–7 A Charismatic Model of Leadership

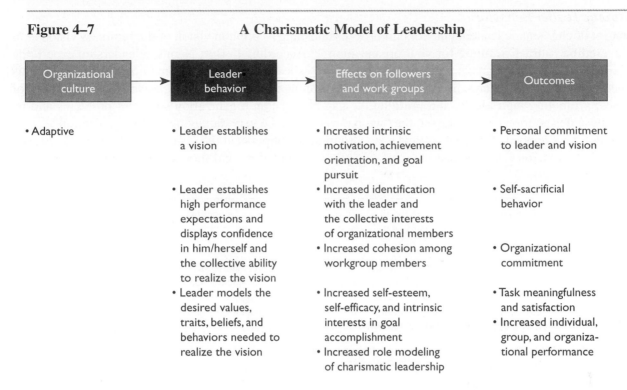

SOURCE: Based in part on D A Waldman and F J Yammarino, "CEO Charismatic Leadership: Levels-of-Management and Levels-of-Analysis Effects," *Academy of Management Review,* April 1999, pp 266–85; and B Shamir, R J House, and M B Arthur, "The Motivational Effects of Charismatic Leadership: A Self-Concept Based Theory," *Organization Science,* November 1993, pp 577–94.

How Does Charismatic Leadership Transform Followers?

Charismatic leaders transform followers by creating changes in their goals, values, needs, beliefs, and aspirations. They accomplish this transformation by appealing to followers' self-concepts—namely, their values and personal identity. Figure 4–7 presents a model of how charismatic leadership accomplishes this transformation process.

Figure 4–7 shows that organizational culture is a key precursor of charismatic leadership. Organizations with adaptive cultures anticipate and adapt to environmental changes and focus on leadership that emphasizes the importance of service to customers, stockholders, and employees. This type of management orientation involves the use of charismatic leadership.

Charismatic leaders first engage in three key sets of leader behavior. If done effectively, these behaviors positively affect individual followers and their work groups. These positive effects, in turn, influence a variety of outcomes. Before discussing the model of charismatic leadership in more detail, it is important to note two general conclusions about charismatic leadership.[51] First, the two-headed arrow between organizational culture and leader behavior in Figure 4–7 reveals that individuals with charismatic behavioral tendencies are able to influence culture. This implies that charismatic leadership reinforces the core values of an adaptive culture and helps to change dysfunctional aspects of an organization's culture that develop over time. Second, charismatic leadership has effects on multiple levels within an organization. For example, Figure 4–7 shows that charismatic leadership can positively influence individual outcomes (e.g., motivation), group outcomes (e.g., group cohesion), and organizational outcomes (e.g., financial performance). You can see that the potential for positive benefits from charismatic leadership is quite widespread.

Charismatic Leader Behavior

The first set of charismatic leader behaviors involves establishing a common vision of the future. A vision is "a realistic, credible, attractive future for your organization."[52] According to Burt Nanus, a leadership expert, the "right" vision unleashes human potential because it serves as a beacon of hope and common purpose. It does this by attracting commitment, energizing workers, creating meaning in employees' lives, establishing a standard of excellence, promoting high ideals, and bridging the gap between an organization's present problems and its future goals and aspirations.[53] In contrast, the "wrong" vision can be very damaging to an organization.

Consider what happened to Coastal Physician Group Inc. as it pursued the vision of its founder Dr. Steven Scott. Dr. Scott's vision was to create networks of physician practices and then sell the network services to health care providers:

> Today, his dream of a physician-led revolution has turned into a nightmare. Major clients and top executives have fled. Coastal is abandoning many of its businesses, selling clinics and trying to resuscitate its original activity, staffing hospitals. . . .
>
> Dr Scott himself, a 48-year-old workaholic obstetrician turned entrepreneur, sits in his fenced-in two-story brick home here, cooling his heels and sipping iced tea. In May, his hand-picked board ousted him as chief executive officer and put him on "sabbatical." The CEO who made a practice of calling subordinates at home at night is now barred, by motion of the board, from speaking to Coastal's employees. He also can't enter its offices, even though he owns the building. . . .
>
> Current management describes him as an arrogant boss who ruined Coastal through a series of missteps and can't bear to let go.[54]

As you can see, Coastal Physician Group's vision produced disastrous results. This highlights the fact that charismatic leaders do more than simply establish a vision. They also must gain input from others in developing an effective implementation plan. For example, Johnson & Johnson obtained input about its vision and implementation plan by surveying all of its 80,000 employees.[55]

The second set of leader behaviors involves two key components:

1. Charismatic leaders set high performance expectations and standards because they know challenging, attainable goals lead to greater productivity.

2. Charismatic leaders need to publicly express confidence in the followers' ability to meet high performance expectations. This is essential because employees are more likely to pursue difficult goals when they believe they can accomplish what is being asked of them.

The third and final set of leader behaviors involves being a role model. Through their actions, charismatic leaders model the desired values, traits, beliefs, and behaviors needed to realize the vision.

Motivational Mechanisms Underlying the Positive Effects of Charismatic Leadership

Charismatic leadership positively affects employee motivation (see Figure 4–7). One way in which this occurs is by increasing the intrinsic value of an employee's effort and goals. Leaders do this by emphasizing the symbolic value of effort; that is, charismatic leaders convey the message that effort reflects important organizational values and collective interests. Followers come to learn that their level of effort represents a moral statement. For example, high effort represents commitment to the organization's vision and values, whereas low effort reflects a lack of commitment.

Charismatic leadership also increases employees' effort $\rightarrow$ performance expectancies by positively contributing to followers' self-esteem and self-efficacy. Leaders also increase the intrinsic value of goal accomplishment by explaining the organization's vision and goals in terms of the personal values they represent. This helps employees to personally connect with the organization's vision. Charismatic leaders further increase the meaningfulness of actions aimed toward goal accomplishment by showing how goals move the organization toward its positive vision, which then gives followers a sense of "growth and development," both of which are important contributors to a positive self-concept.

Research and Managerial Implications

The charismatic model of leadership presented in Figure 4–7 was partially supported by previous research. A study of 50 field companies in the Israel Defense Forces revealed that charismatic leader behavior was positively related to followers' identification with and trust in the leader, motivation, self-sacrifice, identification with the work group, and attachment to the work group.[56] A meta-analysis of 54 studies further indicated that charismatic leaders were viewed as more effective leaders by both supervisors and followers and had followers who exerted more effort and reported higher levels of job satisfaction than noncharismatic leaders.[57] Other studies showed that charismatic leadership was positively associated with followers' individual performance, job satisfaction, and satisfaction with the leader.[58] At the organizational level, a second meta-analysis demonstrated that charismatic leadership was positively correlated with organizational measures of effectiveness.[59] Two additional studies demonstrated that both charismatic and transactional leadership were positively associated with a variety of important employee outcomes.[60] Finally, a study of 31 presidents of the United States indicated that charisma significantly predicted presidential performance.[61]

These results underscore four important managerial implications. First, the best leaders are not just charismatic, they are both transactional and charismatic. Leaders should attempt these two types of leadership while avoiding a "laissez-faire" or "wait-and-see" style. Laissez-faire leadership is the most ineffective leadership style.[62]

Second, charismatic leadership is not applicable in all organizational situations. According to a team of experts, charismatic leadership is most likely to be effective when

1. The situation offers opportunities for "moral" involvement.

2. Performance goals cannot be easily established and measured.

3. Extrinsic rewards cannot be clearly linked to individual performance.

4. There are few situational cues or constraints to guide behavior.

5. Exceptional effort, behavior, sacrifices, and performance are required of both leaders and followers.[63]

Third, employees at any level in an organization can be trained to be more transactional and charismatic.[64] This reinforces the organizational value of developing and rolling out a combination of transactional and charismatic leadership training for all employees. Fourth, charismatic leaders can be ethical or unethical. Whereas ethical charismatic leaders enable employees to enhance their self-concepts, unethical ones select or produce obedient, dependent, and compliant followers.[65] Top management can create and maintain ethical charismatic leadership by

1. Creating and enforcing a clearly stated code of ethics.

2. Recruiting, selecting, and promoting people with high morals and standards.

3. Developing performance expectations around the treatment of employees—these expectations can then be assessed in the performance appraisal process.

4. Training employees to value diversity.

5. Identifying, rewarding, and publicly praising employees who exemplify high moral conduct.[66]

ADDITIONAL PERSPECTIVES ON LEADERSHIP

This section examines four additional approaches to leadership: leader–member exchange theory, substitutes for leadership, servant leadership, and superleadership. We spend more time discussing leader–member exchange theory and substitutes for leadership because they have been more thoroughly investigated.

Figure 4–8   **A Role-Making Model of Leadership**

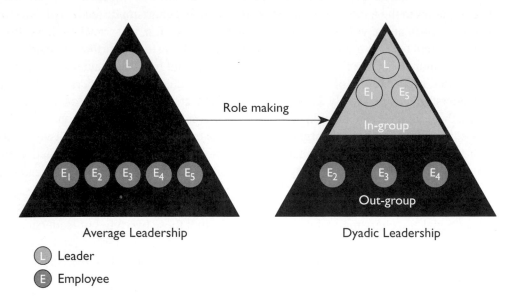

SOURCE: Adapted from F Dansereau, Jr., G Graen, and W J Haga, "A Vertical Dyad Linkage Approach to Leadership within Formal Organizations," *Organizational Behavior and Human Performance,* February 1975, p 72.

The Leader–Member Exchange (LMX) Model of Leadership

The leader–member exchange model of leadership revolves around the development of dyadic relationships between managers and their direct reports. This model is quite different from those previously discussed in that it focuses on the quality of relationships between managers and subordinates as opposed to the behaviors or traits of either leaders or followers. It also is different in that it does not assume that leader behavior is characterized by a stable or average leadership style as does the Leadership Grid® and Fiedler's contingency theory. In other words, these models assume a leader treats all subordinates in about the same way. This traditional approach to leadership is shown in the left side of Figure 4–8. In this case, the leader (designated by the circled L) is thought to exhibit a similar pattern of behavior toward all employees (E_1 to E_5). In contrast, the LMX model is based on the assumption that leaders develop unique one-to-one relationships with each of the people reporting to them. Behavioral scientists call this sort of relationship a *vertical dyad.* The forming of vertical dyads is said to be a naturally occurring process, resulting from the leader's attempt to delegate and assign work roles. As a result of this process, two distinct types of leader–member exchange relationships are expected to evolve.[67]

One type of leader–member exchange is called the **in-group exchange.** In this relationship, leaders and followers develop a partnership characterized by reciprocal influence, mutual trust, respect and liking, and a sense of common fates. Figure 4–8 shows that E_1 and E_5 are members of the leader's in-group. In the second type of exchange, referred to as an **out-group exchange,** leaders are characterized as overseers who fail to create a sense of mutual trust, respect, or common fate.[68] E_2, E_3, and E_4 are members of the out-group on the right side of Figure 4–8.

Research Findings

If the leader–member exchange model is correct, there should be a significant relationship between the type of leader–member exchange and job-related outcomes. Research supports this prediction. For example, a positive leader–member exchange was positively associated with job satisfaction, job performance, goal commitment, organizational citizenship behaviors, and satisfaction with leadership.[69] Positive leader–member exchange also was correlated with greater safety communication, safety commitment, and a reduction in the number of accidents at work.[70] The type of leader–member exchange was found to predict not only turnover among nurses and computer analysts, but also career outcomes, such as promotability, salary level, and receipt of bonuses over a seven-year period.[71] Finally, studies also have identified a variety of variables that influence the quality of an LMX. For example, LMX was related to personality similarity and demographic similarity.[72] Further, the quality of an LMX was positively related with the extent to which leaders and followers like each other, the leaders' positive expectations of their subordinates, and employees' impression management techniques.[73] The quality of an LMX also was negatively associated with the number of employees reporting to a manager and the work load.[74]

Managerial Implications

There are three important implications associated with the LMX model of leadership. First, leaders are encouraged to establish high-performance expectations for all of their direct reports because setting high-performance standards fosters high-quality LMXs. Second, because personality and demographic similarity between leaders and followers is associated with higher LMXs, managers need to be careful that they don't create a homogeneous work environment in the spirit of having positive relationships with their direct reports. Diversity clearly documented that there are many positive benefits of having a diverse workforce. The third implication pertains to those of us who find ourselves in a poor LMX. Before providing advice about what to do in this situation, we would like you to assess the quality of your current leader–member exchange. The OB Exercise 4-2, contains a measure of leader–member exchange that segments an LMX into four subdimensions: mutual affection, loyalty, contribution to work activities, and professional respect.[75]

What is the overall quality of your LMX? Do you agree with this assessment? Which subdimensions are high and low? If your overall LMX and associated subdimensions are all high, you should be in a very good situation with respect to the relationship between you and your manager. Having a low LMX overall score or a low dimensional score, however, reveals that part of the relationship with your manager may need improvement. OB researcher Robert Vecchio offers the following tips to both followers and leaders for improving the quality of leader–member exchanges:

1. New employees should offer their loyalty, support, and cooperativeness to their manager.

2. If you are an out-group member, either accept the situation, try to become an in-group member by being cooperative and loyal, or quit.

3. Managers should consciously try to expand their in-groups.

4. Managers need to give employees ample opportunity to prove themselves.[76]

Substitutes for Leadership

Virtually all leadership theories assume that some sort of formal leadership is necessary, whatever the circumstances. But this basic assumption is questioned by this model of leadership. Specifically, some OB scholars propose that there are a variety of situational variables that can substitute for, neutralize, or enhance the effects of leadership. These situational variables are referred to as **substitutes for leadership.**[77] Substitutes for leadership can thus increase or diminish a leader's ability to influence the work group. For example, leader behavior that initiates structure would tend to be resisted by independent-minded employees with high ability and vast experience. Consequently, such employees would be guided more by their own initiative than by managerial directives.

Kerr and Jermier's Substitutes for Leadership Model

According to Steven Kerr and John Jermier, the OB researchers who developed this model, the key to improving leadership effectiveness is to identify the situational characteristics that can either substitute for, neutralize, or improve the impact of a leader's behavior. Table 4–2 lists the various substitutes for leadership. Characteristics

Table 4–2

Substitutes for Leadership

Characteristic	Relationship-Oriented or Considerate Leader Behavior Is Unnecessary	Task-Oriented or Initiating Structure Leader Behavior Is Unnecessary
Of the Subordinate		
1. Ability, experience, training, knowledge		X
2. Need for independence	X	X
3. "Professional" orientation	X	X
4. Indifference toward organizational rewards	X	X
Of the Task		
5. Unambiguous and routine		X
6. Methodologically invariant		X
7. Provides its own feedback concerning accomplishment		X
8. Intrinsically satisfying	X	
Of the Organization		
9. Formalization (explicit plans, goals, and areas of responsibility)		X
10. Inflexibility (rigid, unbending rules and procedures)		X
11. Highly specified and active advisory and staff functions		X
12. Closely knit, cohesive work groups	X	X
13. Organizational rewards not within the leader's control	X	X
14. Spatial distance between superior and subordinates	X	X

SOURCE: Adapted from S Kerr and J M Jermier, "Substitutes for Leadership: Their Meaning and Measurement," *Organizational Behavior and Human Performance,* December 1978, pp 375–403.

of the subordinate, the task, and the organization can act as substitutes for traditional hierarchical leadership. Further, different characteristics are predicted to negate different types of leader behavior. For example, tasks that provide feedback concerning accomplishment, such as taking a test, tend to negate task-oriented but not relationship-oriented leader behavior (see Table 4–2). Although the list in Table 4–2 is not all-inclusive, it shows that there are more substitutes for task-oriented leadership than for relationship-oriented leadership.

Research and Managerial Implications

Two different approaches have been used to test this model. The first is based on the idea that substitutes for leadership are contingency variables that moderate the relationship between leader behavior and employee attitudes and behavior.[78] A recent summary of this research revealed that only 318 of 3,741 (9%) contingency relationships tested supported the model.[79] This demonstrates that substitutes for leadership do not moderate the

OB EXERCISE 4-2   ASSESSING YOUR LEADER–MEMBER EXCHANGE

Instructions

For each of the items shown below, use the following scale to circle the answer that best represents how you feel about the relationship between you and your current manager/supervisor. If you are not currently working, complete the survey by thinking about a previous manager. Remember, there are no right or wrong answers. After circling a response for each of the 12 items, use the scoring key to compute scores for the subdimensions within your leader–member exchange.

1 = Strongly disagree
2 = Disagree
3 = Neither agree nor disagree
4 = Agree
5 = Strongly agree

1. I like my supervisor very much as a person.	1 — 2 — 3 — 4 — 5
2. My supervisor is the kind of person one would like to have as a friend.	1 — 2 — 3 — 4 — 5
3. My supervisor is a lot of fun to work with.	1 — 2 — 3 — 4 — 5
4. My supervisor defends my work actions to a superior, even without complete knowledge of the issue in question.	1 — 2 — 3 — 4 — 5
5. My supervisor would come to my defense if I were "attacked" by others.	1 — 2 — 3 — 4 — 5
6. My supervisor would defend me to others in the organization if I made an honest mistake.	1 — 2 — 3 — 4 — 5
7. I do work for my supervisor that goes beyond what is specified in my job description.	1 — 2 — 3 — 4 — 5
8. I am willing to apply extra efforts, beyond those normally required, to meet my supervisor's work goals.	1 — 2 — 3 — 4 — 5
9. I do not mind working my hardest for my supervisor.	1 — 2 — 3 — 4 — 5
10. I am impressed with my supervisor's knowledge of his/her job.	1 — 2 — 3 — 4 — 5
11. I respect my supervisor's knowledge of and competence on the job.	1 — 2 — 3 — 4 — 5
12. I admire my supervisor's professional skills.	1 — 2 — 3 — 4 — 5

Scoring Key

Mutual affection (add items 1–3)   _____
Loyalty (add items 4–6)   _____
Contribution to work activities (add items 7–9)   _____
Professional respect (add items 10–12)   _____
Overall score (add all 12 items)   _____

Arbitrary Norms

Low mutual affection = 3–9
High mutual affection = 10–15
Low loyalty = 3–9
High loyalty = 10–15
Low contribution to work activities = 3–9
High contribution to work activities = 10–15
Low professional respect = 3–9
High professional respect = 10–15
Low overall leader–member exchange = 12–38
High overall leader–member exchange = 39–60

SOURCE: Survey items were taken from R C Liden and J M Maslyn, "Multidimensionality of Leader–Member Exchange: An Empirical Assessment through Scale Development," *Journal of Management,* 1998, p 56.

effect of a leader's behavior as suggested by Steve Kerr and John Jermier. The second approach to test the substitutes model examined whether substitutes for leadership have a direct effect on employee attitudes and behaviors. A recent meta-analysis of 36 different samples revealed that the combination of substitute variables and leader behaviors significantly explained a variety of employee attitudes and behaviors. Interestingly, the substitutes for leadership were more important than leader behaviors in accounting for employee attitudes and behaviors.[80]

The key implication is that managers should be attentive to the substitutes listed in Table 4–2 because they directly influence employee attitudes and performance. Managers can positively influence the substitutes through employee selection, job design, work group assignments, and the design of organizational processes and systems.[81]

Servant-Leadership

Servant-leadership is more a philosophy of managing than a testable theory. The term *servant-leadership* was coined by Robert Greenleaf in 1970. Greenleaf believes that great leaders act as servants, putting the needs of others, including employees, customers, and community, as their first priority. **Servant-leadership** focuses on increased service to others rather than to oneself.[82] According to Jim Stuart, co-founder of the leadership circle in Tampa, Florida, "Leadership derives naturally from a commitment to service. You know that you're practicing servant-leadership if your followers become wiser, healthier, more autonomous—and more likely to become

---

Table 4–3   **Characteristics of the Servant-Leader**

Servant-Leadership Characteristics	Description
1. Listening	Servant-leaders focus on listening to identify and clarify the needs and desires of a group.
2. Empathy	Servant-leaders try to empathize with others' feelings and emotions. An individual's good intentions are assumed even when he or she performs poorly.
3. Healing	Servant-leaders strive to make themselves and others whole in the face of failure or suffering.
4. Awareness	Servant-leaders are very self-aware of their strengths and limitations.
5. Persuasion	Servant-leaders rely more on persuasion than positional authority when making decisions and trying to influence others.
6. Conceptualization	Servant leaders take the time and effort to develop broader based conceptual thinking. Servant-leaders seek an appropriate balance between a short-term, day-to-day focus and a long-term, conceptual orientation.
7. Foresight	Servant-leaders have the ability to foresee future outcomes associated with a current course of action or situation.
8. Stewardship	Servant-leaders assume that they are stewards of the people and resources they manage.
9. Commitment to the growth of people	Servant-leaders are committed to people beyond their immediate work role. They commit to fostering an environment that encourages personal, professional, and spiritual growth.
10. Building community	Servant-leaders strive to create a sense of community both within and outside the work organization.

SOURCE: These characteristics and descriptions were derived from L C Spears, "Introduction: Servant-Leadership and the Greenleaf Legacy," in *Reflections on Leadership: How Robert K Greenleaf's Theory of Servant-Leadership Influenced Today's Top Management Thinkers,* ed L C Spears (New York: John Wiley & Sons, 1995), pp 1–14.

---

servant-leaders themselves."[83] Servant-leadership is not a quick-fix approach to leadership. Rather, it is a long-term, transformational approach to life and work. Table 4–3 presents 10 characteristics possessed by servant-leaders. One can hardly go wrong by trying to adopt these characteristics.

Superleadership

A **superleader** is someone who leads others to lead themselves. Superleadership is equally relevant within teams as well as any general leadership situation. Superleaders empower followers by acting as a teacher and coach rather than as a dictator and autocrat. The need for this form of leadership is underscored by a survey of 1,046 Americans. Results demonstrated that only 38% of the respondents ever had an effective coach or mentor.[84]

Productive thinking is the cornerstone of superleadership. Specifically, managers are encouraged to teach followers how to engage in productive thinking.[85] This is expected to increase employees feelings of personal control and intrinsic motivation. Superleadership has the potential to free up a manager's time because employees are encouraged to manage themselves. Future research is needed to test the validity of recommendations derived from this new approach to leadership.

SUMMARY OF KEY CONCEPTS

1. *Define the term* leadership, *and explain the difference between leading versus managing.* Leadership is defined as a social influence process in which the leader tries to obtain the voluntary participation of employees in an effort to reach organizational objectives. Leadership entails more than having authority and power. Although leadership and management overlap, each entails a unique set of activities or functions. Managers typically perform functions associated with planning, investigating, organizing, and control, and leaders deal with the interpersonal aspects of a manager's job. Table 4–1 summarizes the differences between leading and managing.

2. *Review trait theory research, and discuss the idea of one best style of leadership, using the Ohio State studies and the Leadership Grid® as points of reference.* Historical leadership research did not support the notion that effective leaders possessed unique traits from followers. However, teams of researchers reanalyzed this historical data with modern-day statistical procedures. Results revealed that individuals tend to be perceived as leaders when they possess one or more of the following traits: intelligence, dominance, and masculinity. A recent study further demonstrated that employees value credible leaders. Credible leaders are honest, forward-looking, inspiring, and competent. Research also examined the relationship between gender and leadership. Results demonstrated that (*a*) men and women differed in the type of leadership roles they assume, (*b*) leadership styles varied by gender, and (*c*) gender differences in ratings of leadership effectiveness were associated with the percentage of male leaders and male subordinates. The Ohio State studies revealed that there were two key independent dimensions of leadership behavior: consideration and initiating structure. Authors of the Leadership Grid® proposed that leaders should adopt a style that demonstrates high concern for production and people. Research did not support the premise that there is one best style of leadership.

3. *Explain, according to Fiedler's contingency model, how leadership style interacts with situational control.* Fiedler believes leader effectiveness depends on an appropriate match between leadership style and situational control. Leaders are either task motivated or relationship motivated. Situation control is composed of leader–member relations, task structure, and position power. Task-motivated leaders are effective under situations of both high and low control. Relationship-motivated leaders are more effective when they have moderate situational control.

4. *Discuss House's path–goal theory and Hersey and Blanchard's situational leadership theory.* According to path–goal theory, leaders alternately can exhibit directive, supportive, participative, or achievement-oriented styles of leadership. The effectiveness of these styles depends on various employee characteristics and environmental factors. Path–goal theory has received limited support from research. There are two important managerial implications: (*a*) leaders possess and use more than one style of leadership, and (*b*) managers are advised to modify their leadership style to fit a small subset of task and employee characteristics. According to situational leadership theory (SLT), effective leader behavior depends on the readiness level of a leader's followers. As follower readiness increases, leaders are advised to gradually move from a telling to a selling to a participating and, finally, to a delegating style. Research does not support SLT.

5. *Define and differentiate transactional and charismatic leadership.* There is an important difference between transactional and charismatic leadership. Transactional leaders focus on the interpersonal transactions between managers and employees. Charismatic leaders motivate employees to pursue organizational goals above their own self-interests. Both forms of leadership are important for organizational success.

6. *Explain how charismatic leadership transforms followers and work groups.* Organizational culture is a key precursor of charismatic leadership, which is composed of three sets of leader behavior. These leader behaviors, in turn, positively affect followers' and work groups' goals, values, beliefs, aspirations, and motivation. These positive effects are then associated with a host of preferred outcomes.

7. *Summarize the managerial implications of charismatic leadership.* There are four managerial implications: (*a*) The best leaders are both transactional and charismatic. (*b*) Charismatic leadership is not applicable in all organizational situations. (*c*) Employees at any level in an organization can be trained to be more transactional and charismatic. (*d*) Top management needs to promote and reinforce ethical charismatic leadership because charismatic leaders can be ethical or unethical.

8. *Explain the leader–member exchange model of leadership.* This model revolves around the development of dyadic relationships between managers and their direct reports. These leader–member exchanges qualify as either in-group or out-group relationships. Research supports this model of leadership.

9. *Describe the substitutes for leadership, and explain how they substitute for, neutralize, or enhance the effects of leadership.* There are 14 substitutes for leadership (see Table 4–2) that can substitute for, neutralize, or enhance the effects of leadership. These substitutes contain characteristics of the subordinates, the task, and the organization. Research shows that substitutes directly influence employee attitudes and performance.

10. *Describe servant-leadership and superleadership.* Servant-leadership is more a philosophy than a testable theory. It is based on the premise that great leaders act as servants, putting the needs of others, including employees, customers, and community, as their first priority. A superleader is someone who leads others to lead themselves. Superleaders empower followers by acting as a teacher and coach rather than as a dictator and autocrat.

DISCUSSION QUESTIONS

1. Is everyone cut out to be a leader? Explain.

2. Has your college education helped you develop any of the traits that characterize leaders?

3. Should organizations change anything in response to research pertaining to gender and leadership? If yes, describe your recommendations.

4. What leadership traits and behavioral styles are possessed by the president of the United States?

5. Does it make more sense to change a person's leadership style or the situation? How would Fred Fiedler and Robert House answer this question?

6. Describe how a college professor might use House's path–goal theory to clarify student's path–goal perceptions.

7. Identify three charismatic leaders, and describe their leadership traits and behavioral styles.

8. Have you ever worked for a charismatic leader? Describe how he or she transformed followers.

9. Have you ever been a member of an in-group or out-group? For either situation, describe the pattern of interaction between you and your manager.

10. In your view, which leadership theory has the greatest practical application? Why?

INTERNET EXERCISE

---

www.leader-values.com

The topic of leadership has been important since the dawn of time. History is filled with examples of great leaders such as Mohandas Gandhi, Martin Luther King, and Bill Gates. These leaders likely possessed some of the leadership traits discussed in this chapter, and they probably used a situational approach to lead their followers. The purpose of this exercise is for you to evaluate the leadership styles of an historical figure.

Go to the Internet home page for Leadership Values (**www.leader-values.com**), and select the subheading "4 E's" on the left side of the screen. This section provides an overview of leadership and suggests four essential traits/behaviors that are exhibited by leaders: to envision, enable, empower, and energize. After reading this material, go back to the home page, and select the subheading "Historical Leaders" from the list on the left-hand side of the page. Next, choose one of the leaders from the list of historical figures, and read the description about his or her leadership style. You may want to print all of the material you read thus far from this web page to help you answer the following questions.

Questions
1. Describe the 4 E's of leadership.

2. To what extent do the 4 E's overlap with the theories and models of leadership discussed in this chapter?

3. Using any of the theories or models discussed in this chapter, how would you describe the leadership style of the historical figure you investigated?

4. Was this leader successful in using the 4 E's of leadership? Describe how he/she used the 4 E's.

OB IN ACTION CASE STUDY[86]

---

www.maytag.com

Lloyd Ward Becomes CEO of Maytag
The journey began on a narrow country road in southern Michigan. There, in a 20-foot-by-20-foot house with no running water, lived the Ward family: mother, father, three sons, and two daughters. In the rare moments during the 1950s and 1960s that Rubert Ward wasn't working—at his day job as postman, his night job as movie house

janitor, or his Sunday job as Baptist preacher—he liked to gather his boys and talk about "Ward & Sons." It was the imaginary auto-repair shop that he dreamed about one day running with them.

In reality, he had no training as a mechanic, but he had made himself an expert by checking out manuals from the library, in the same way he later figured out how to remedy the house's sagging roof and install plumbing. "He would take on things he had no clue about, and he would get a book, and he would learn," says the middle Ward child, Lloyd.

Rubert Ward never got to start Ward & Sons. He died of a heart attack in 1967, at 47. But from his tiny house, with its tight quarters and big dreams, would emerge one of the most driven men in America today: a star college basketball player who studied to become an engineer, an engineer who transformed himself into an inspirational speaker and one of the country's most respected marketers, and a marketer who next month will become only the second African American ever to lead a large US company.

He is Lloyd David Ward, a singular study in ambition, smarts, and resilience. When he assumes the top job at Maytag Corp. on Aug. 12, Ward, 50, will have made a longer journey than any other executive in Corporate America. Some chieftains, such as Lee A Iacocca, have escaped poverty to find their way to the corner office. A few African American executives, such as American Express Co. CEO-in-waiting Kenneth Chenault, have overcome the racism that still plagues the workplace. The country's first black CEO of a major corporation, Fannie Mae's Franklin D Raines, is one of them, but his impressive rise from poverty in Seattle to head of the government-sponsored company has taken place more in the political arena of Washington, DC than in the corporate world.

No one, in fact, has defeated the pincer of poverty and prejudice as Lloyd Ward has. And he has done it at some of the world's best-known companies, from Procter & Gamble to Ford to PepsiCo. Working with Maytag CEO Leonard A Hadley, Ward over the last three years has reinvented the staid appliance company, helping to triple its stock price. A master motivator who listens as well as he speaks, Ward has convinced Maytag veterans that change was both necessary and possible. Colleagues laud his ability to challenge people's beliefs without criticizing them personally, to seize on nuggets of common ground, and then to exploit them. "He is a good thinker," says PepsiCo Inc. CEO Roger A Enrico, "but he is an exceptional leader."

His energy, however, is also the cause of one of Ward's few weaknesses as a manager: impatience. It led to his rash decision to quit P&G in the 1970s when he did not get a transfer he wanted. And it has at times created friction between him and Hadley.

Sincere. Ward's engaging ways seem always on display. He greets people with a firm handshake, pulling himself closer to them, putting a palm on the back of their elbow, and quickly asking questions about their own life, even when he has never before met them. "Were you born here?" "What's your husband's name?" "How long have you worked here?" . . .

But Corporate America's newest star is hardly a stranger to challenges. "My whole life I've been faced with 'No,' " he says. Indeed, his success against all odds demonstrates to what extent bigotry continues to be a part of the American experience. Every step of the way, from a college roommate who wanted nothing to do with Ward to a resident of Maytag's hometown who told Ward his "kind" wasn't wanted there, he has encountered indignities and obstacles that every African American knows and few whites can fathom. . . .

It would have been difficult for anyone to see his way to the corner office from the street where Ward grew up. It was in Romulus, [Michigan], then a rural town about 20 miles west of Detroit and now the site of the sprawling Detroit Metro Airport. His neighborhood was little more than a stretch of gravel, pockmarked by tiny square houses. The Wards and their five children squeezed their lives into three small rooms. The three boys lived in one, with a bunk bed that nearly scraped the ceiling. The girls slept in another, and the parents bedded down on a fold-out couch in a living room full of secondhand furniture covered with dropcloths.

Despite the hardships, the Ward household was a happy place. "It's hard to imagine," Lloyd says now, "but when I think back, it was a wonderful childhood because we were so close." . . .

Finishing high school in 1969, Ward won a college basketball scholarship to Michigan State University. Ward knew how to use it: He wanted to become a doctor. . . .

Other barriers awaited him at Michigan State as well. When the basketball team's academic adviser saw Ward's courses in organic chemistry and calculus, the adviser told him to switch to easier classes such as health and "introductory basketball." Jordan [his teammate] remembers a coach telling Ward: "We're paying you to be a basketball player." Ward balked. So the adviser called the registrar's office and switched his courses himself. But Ward walked over to the office and changed them right back.

Good grades and a strong record on the court proved the coaches wrong, and they eventually left him alone. . . .

From Michigan State, it was straight to P&G, where Ward confronted an old problem in a new guise. Instead of overt racism, Ward this time encountered the patronizing attitudes of P&G's efforts to hire minorities in those days, say people who were at the company at the time. Despite his B average in engineering and his having been the captain of a Big Ten basketball team, P&G was willing to hire him and a handful of other blacks only for its "qualifiable" program, an early version of affirmative action. "They brought us in under the stigma of being 'qualifiable,' " Ward says. "The idea was that there weren't qualified African Americans."

Ward nonetheless holds no grudge against P&G. In fact, he now praises the company as an early supporter of diversity. "If it were not for the so-called affirmative action of the '60s and '70s," he says, "people like me may not have ever gotten the opportunity to provide the leadership that we have now been able to give." . . .

Back at headquarters, Ward let people know he wanted much more than an engineering career. Floyd Dickens Jr, one of Ward's early supervisors, remembers a meeting in the '70s. Ward was wearing his usual gray suit, white shirt, and red tie. Dickens asked Ward about his goals, and Ward didn't mince words: By the age of 45, he wanted to be chief executive of a major US corporation.

It was an astonishingly bold ambition. When Ward came to P&G in 1970, he was one of just eight African American engineers in a department of around 1,200. In large companies, a black CEO seemed as likely as a black President of the [U.S.]. But that wasn't all. Dickens knew that engineers stood no chance of reaching the top of P&G. That was reserved for marketers and product developers, who knew how to bring money to the bottom line. "You're in the wrong organization if you want that," he told Ward.

So Ward pushed for a transfer that never came. Frustrated, he left P&G to take a job with Ford Motor Co. in 1977 and took his family back to Detroit. The move was a disaster. Ward became lost and struggled inside the massive auto company. A year later, he jumped at the chance to get back to P&G. All he wanted, he said, was, someday, an opportunity to transfer out of engineering.

He got it—and made the most of it. Over the next decade, Ward skipped from one field to the next, often stepping down a rung in the corporate hierarchy in order to earn his spurs. In 1984, for instance, he remade P&G's 100-year-old Ivorydale soap plant, which had been expanded in haphazard fashion over the years. Working with the unionized workforce, Ward redesigned the plant from top to bottom. "Lloyd is a high-energy, very focused, very competitive individual," says John E Pepper, chairman of P&G and Ward's former boss. By 1986, he had made the move to general management, heading up P&G's dishwashing unit.

But Ward was tiring of the P&G bureaucracy. In 1987, he was off again, this time for P&G's corporate opposite: the rough-and-ready culture of PepsiCo Inc., where Ward thrived. As head of Frito-Lay's western and central divisions, Ward led the charge against archrival Anheuser-Busch Cos.' Eagle Snacks. At the time, Eagle was trying to speed the launch of its new corn-chip brand by offering a free bag of potato chips with every purchase. When Ward heard about the strategy, he upped the ante. With a "supersize" bag of Frito-Lay chips, the company threw in a large bag of Doritos, a far more popular and established product than Eagle's entry. Unable to sell its brand, Eagle soon pulled back, and later Anheuser-Busch got out of the snack business altogether. "It was a major victory, and it was a lot of fun," says Ward.

Pep Talks. Pepsi was also the place where Ward began to polish his leadership skills. He was constantly out in the field trying to rev up the troops, even showing up at the loading docks to give an informal pep talk to workers there. Through it all, Ward's go-for-the-throat competitiveness and gung ho motivational tactics helped increase his division's overall market share in the region from 50% to 56%. "People in that division had decided that you couldn't grow market share because it was already so high," says Steven S Reinemund, chairman of Frito-Lay. "Lloyd didn't accept that. He went on a personal crusade."

Winning at business was hardly his only crusade. While at Pepsi, Ward got deeply involved in the Dallas community with his push to get more high school kids into college. Employees became mentors to students. They dropped in at school after work and on weekends to help with homework. Ward tutored kids in his office and brought members of the Dallas Mavericks basketball team to the school to give them a lift. And he whisked kids who passed a state test to a Six Flags amusement park on the Frito-Lay corporate jet. By 1996, 61% of the students passed the state's math test, up from 32% in 1994. "Dare to dream," Ward would tell them. "Learn to love adversity. Perform—good intentions are not enough." To this day, Ward urges self-reliance. "There are many who are systematically excluded. [But] the oppressed have to overcome the prejudices of society," Ward says. "Knock on the door, pull on the handle, and, if you have to, dismantle the hinge."

Meanwhile, Ward was intent on advancing his own career. So when a small Chicago search firm came calling in 1995, with an opportunity to interview for a job that could lead to the CEO's office, Ward convinced Lita [his wife] it was a good idea—even though it was in Newton, Iowa, 40 miles from Des Moines and a world away from big-city life in Dallas. It was a huge leap of faith: Ward was willing to leave a hot career at marketing heavyweight Pepsi to head the appliance division of a sleepy company personified by the hang-dog look of the Maytag repairman in TV ads. But the fast-track shot at the CEO's job made it worthwhile for Ward.

It was also a big risk for Maytag leaders, who typically promoted carefully groomed insiders. CEO Hadley, for example, has been at the company for 40 years. This time, however, he instructed the board that his successor should be an outsider. The company needed "an extroverted marketing man," he says. . . .

In Newton, though, Ward's focus is all on the present. Once Hadley dumped unprofitable units and revamped products, Ward set about reinvigorating the company's unsophisticated marketing culture. He sped up the pace of product introductions: Maytag will launch 20 new products this year, up from only a few in the mid '90s. He lured more than a dozen executives, mostly from Pepsi and P&G, to Newton. He developed new consumer-research methods, sending observers into people's houses to watch them cook and clean, rather than simply asking them to fill out surveys. One result: a new $400 washer to help Maytag compete for the lower end of the business it had long shunned. "Ward has been able to almost reinvent Maytag," says Mike London, a senior vice-president at Best Buy Co., a major client. . . .

Still, Ward's hard-charging ways have led to occasional mis-steps. "There were a few rough spots in front of a dealer group here and there," Beer says. And while Hadley and Ward speak highly of each other, their relationship has been tense at times, say other Maytag executives. Hadley is the veteran, bowing out on a high note and reluctant to relinquish control. Ward is the outsider, fond of shaking things up. "His style is very different from mine," says Hadley. "He holds meetings I wouldn't hold. He invites more people than I would invite. He says to me: 'You have to go out and sell your program.' " Says Ward: "Succession is hard at this level."

Differences aside, the results have made both men look smart. And Maytag's remarkable run has at last paid off for Ward. In May, Maytag's board gathered to announce that Lloyd Ward would become the company's ninth chief executive. Afterward, Lloyd and Lita celebrated at a posh Des Moines restaurant.

When Lloyd and Lita got home that night, exhausted, they climbed the stairs to their bedroom and collapsed in two facing chairs. Neither said anything. "We just looked at each other," Lloyd says. The silence lasted for more than five minutes. Their journey was complete. They had made it to the top, together. Rubert Ward would have been proud. It may not have been "Ward & Sons," but a member of the family finally had a business of his own.

Questions for Discussion

1. What role did Ward's upbringing play in his rise to CEO of Maytag? Discuss.

2. Citing examples, which different leadership traits and styles were exhibited by Lloyd Ward?

3. What did you learn about leadership from this case? Use examples to reinforce your conclusions.

4. Does Ward appear to display more transactional or charismatic leadership? Explain.

5. What career advice can you take from the manner in which Lloyd Ward rose to the top position at Maytag?

PERSONAL AWARENESS AND GROWTH EXERCISE

How Ready Are You to Assume the Leadership Role?

Objectives
1. To assess your readiness for the leadership role.

2. To consider the implications of the gap between your career goals and your readiness to lead.

Introduction
Leaders assume multiple roles. Roles represent the expectations that others have of occupants of a position. It is important for potential leaders to consider whether they are ready for the leadership role because mismatches in expectations or skills can derail a leader's effectiveness. This exercise assesses your readiness to assume the leadership role.[87]

Instructions
For each statement, indicate the extent to which you agree or disagree with it by selecting one number from the scale provided. Circle your response for each statement. Remember, there are no right or wrong answers. After completing the survey, add your total score for the 20 items, and record it in the space provided.

1 = Strongly disagree
2 = Disagree
3 = Neither agree nor disagree
4 = Agree
5 = Strongly agree

1. It is enjoyable having people count on me for ideas and suggestions.	1 — 2 — 3 — 4 — 5
2. It would be accurate to say that I have inspired other people.	1 — 2 — 3 — 4 — 5
3. It's a good practice to ask people provocative questions about their work.	1 — 2 — 3 — 4 — 5
4. It's easy for me to compliment others.	1 — 2 — 3 — 4 — 5
5. I like to cheer people up even when my own spirits are down.	1 — 2 — 3 — 4 — 5
6. What my team accomplishes is more important than my personal glory.	1 — 2 — 3 — 4 — 5
7. Many people imitate my ideas.	1 — 2 — 3 — 4 — 5
8. Building team spirit is important to me.	1 — 2 — 3 — 4 — 5
9. I would enjoy coaching other members of the team.	1 — 2 — 3 — 4 — 5
10. It is important to me to recognize others for their accomplishments.	1 — 2 — 3 — 4 — 5
11. I would enjoy entertaining visitors to my firm even if it interfered with my completing a report.	1 — 2 — 3 — 4 — 5
12. It would be fun for me to represent my team at gatherings outside our department.	1 — 2 — 3 — 4 — 5
13. The problems of my teammates are my problems too.	1 — 2 — 3 — 4 — 5
14. Resolving conflict is an activity I enjoy.	1 — 2 — 3 — 4 — 5

15. I would cooperate with another unit in the organization even if
     I disagreed with the position taken by its members.   1 — 2 — 3 — 4 — 5
16. I am an idea generator on the job.   1 — 2 — 3 — 4 — 5
17. It's fun for me to bargain whenever I have the opportunity.   1 — 2 — 3 — 4 — 5
18. Team members listen to me when I speak.   1 — 2 — 3 — 4 — 5
19. People have asked me to assume the leadership of an
     activity several times in my life.   1 — 2 — 3 — 4 — 5
20. I've always been a convincing person.   1 — 2 — 3 — 4 — 5

                                                                            Total score: _____

Norms for Interpreting the Total Score[88]
90–100   = High readiness for the leadership role
60–89   = Moderate readiness for the leadership role
40–59   = Some uneasiness with the leadership role
39 or less = Low readiness for the leadership role

Questions for Discussion
1. Do you agree with the interpretation of your readiness to assume the leadership role? Explain why or why
    not.

2. If you scored below 60 and desire to become a leader, what might you do to increase your readiness to lead?
    To answer this question, we suggest that you study the statements carefully—particularly those with low
    responses—to determine how you might change either an attitude or a behavior so that you can realistically
    answer more questions with a response of "agree" or "strongly agree."

3. How might this evaluation instrument help you to become a more effective leader?

GROUP EXERCISE

Exhibiting Leadership within the Context of Running a Meeting[89]

Objectives
1. To consider the types of problems that can occur when running a meeting.
2. To identify the leadership behaviors that can be used to handle problems that occur in meetings.

Introduction
Managers often find themselves playing the role of formal or informal leader when participating in a planned
meeting (e.g., committees, work groups, task forces, etc.). As a leader, individuals often must handle a
number of interpersonal situations that have the potential of reducing the group's productivity. For example, if
an individual has important information that is not shared with the group, the meeting will be less productive.
Similarly, two or more individuals who engage in conversational asides could disrupt the normal functioning
of the group. Finally, the group's productivity will also be threatened by two or more individuals who argue or
engage in personal attacks on one another during a meeting. This exercise is designed to help you practice
some of the behaviors necessary to overcome these problems and at the same time share in the responsibility
of leading a productive group.[90]

Instructions

Your instructor will divide the class into groups of four to six. Once the group is assembled, briefly summarize the types of problems that can occur when running a meeting—start with the material presented in the preceding introduction. Write your final list on a piece of paper. Next, for each problem on the group's list, the group should brainstorm a list of appropriate leader behaviors that can be used to handle the problem. Try to arrive at a consensus list of leadership behaviors that can be used to handle the various problems encountered in meetings.

Questions for Discussion

1. What type of problems that occur during meetings are most difficult to handle? Explain.

2. Are there any particular leader behaviors that can be used to solve multiple problems during meetings? Discuss your rationale.

3. Was there a lot of agreement about which leader behaviors were useful for dealing with specific problems encountered in meetings? Explain.

NOTES

1   Excerpted from J Martin, "Tomorrow's CEOs," *Fortune,* June 24, 1996, pp 78–79. © 1996 Time Inc. Reprinted by permission.

2   See S Lieberson and J F O'Connor, "Leadership and Organizational Performance: A Study of Large Corporations," *American Sociological Review,* April 1972, pp 117–30.

3   Results are presented in D Jacobs and L Singell, "Leadership and Organizational Performance: Isolating Links between Managers and Collective Success," *Social Science Research,* June 1993, pp 165–89.

4   C A Schriesheim, J M Tolliver, and O C Behling, "Leadership Theory: Some Implications for Managers," *MSU Business Topics,* Summer 1978, p 35.

5   T Peters and N Austin, *A Passion for Excellence* (New York: Random House, 1985), pp 5–6.

6   See H Mintzberg, "Covert Leadership: Notes on Managing Professionals," *Harvard Business Review,* November–December 1998, pp 140–47.

7   B M Bass, *Bass & Stogdill's Handbook of Leadership: Theory, Research, and Managerial Applications,* 3rd ed, (New York: Free Press, 1990), p 383.

8   For a thorough discussion about the differences between leading and managing, see G Weathersby, "Leading vs. Management," *Management Review,* March 1999, p 5; R J House, and R N Aditya, "The Social Scientific Study of Leadership: Quo Vadis?" *Journal of Management,* pp 409–73; and A Zalesnik, "Managers and Leaders: Are They Different?" *Harvard Business Review,* May–June 1977, pp 67–78.

9   See the related discussion in F E Fiedler, "Research on Leadership Selection and Training: One View of the Future," *Administrative Science Quarterly,* June 1996, pp 241–50.

10 The role of leadership within organizational change is discussed by O Harari, "Why Do Leaders Avoid Change," *Management Review,* March 1999, pp 35–38; and J P Lotter, *Leading Change* (Boston: Harvard Business School Press, 1996).

11 K Western, "No Matter What It Takes, I'll Do It," *The Arizona Republic,* August 1, 1993, p F1.

12 For complete details, see R M Stogdill, "Personal Factors Associated with Leadership: A Survey of the Literature," *Journal of Psychology,* 1948, pp 35–71; and R M Stogdill, *Handbook of Leadership* (New York: Free Press, 1974).

13 Excerpted from T A Stewart, "The Contest for Welch's Throne Begins: Who Will Run GE?" *Fortune,* January 11, 1999, p 27.

14 See R D Mann, "A Review of the Relationships between Personality and Performance in Small Groups," *Psychological Bulletin,* July 1959, pp 241–70.

15 See D A Kenny and S J Zaccaro, "An Estimate of Variance Due to Traits in Leadership," *Journal of Applied Psychology,* November 1983, pp 678–85 . Results from a more recent verification can be found in S J Zaccaro, R J Foti, and D A Kenny, "Self-Monitoring and Trait-Based Variance in Leadership: An Investigation of Leader Flexibility across Multiple Group Situations," *Journal of Applied Psychology,* April 1991, pp 308–15.

16 See A J Kinicki, P W Hom, M R Trost, and K J Wade, "Effects of Category Prototypes on Performance-Rating Accuracy," *Journal of Applied Psychology,* June 1995, pp 354–70; J S Phillips and R G Lord, "Schematic Information Processing and Perceptions of Leadership in Problem-Solving Groups," *Journal of Applied Psychology,* August 1982, pp 486–92; and R J Foti, S L Fraser, and R G Lord, "Effects of Leadership Labels and Prototypes on Perceptions of Political Leaders," *Journal of Applied Psychology,* June 1982, pp 326–33.

17   See R J Hall, J W Workman, and C A Marchioro, "Sex, Task, and Behavioral Flexibility Effects on Leadership Perceptions," *Organizational Behavior and Human Decision Processes,* April 1998, pp 1–32; and R G Lord, C L De Vader, and G M Alliger, "A Meta-Analysis of the Relation between Personality Traits and Leadership Perceptions: An Application of Validity Generalization Procedures," *Journal of Applied Psychology,* August 1986, p 407.

18   Results can be found in J M Kouzes and B Z Posner, *The Leadership Challenge* (San Francisco: Jossey-Bass, 1995).

19   Gender and the emergence of leaders was examined by A H Eagly and S J Karau, "Gender and the Emergence of Leaders: A Meta-Analysis," *Journal of Personality and Social Psychology,* May 1991, pp 685–710; and R K Shelly and P T Munroe, "Do Women Engage in Less Task Behavior Than Men?" *Sociological Perspectives,* Spring 1999, pp 49–67.

20   See A H Eagly, S J Karau, and B T Johnson, "Gender and Leadership Style among School Principals: A Meta-Analysis," *Educational Administration Quarterly,* February 1992, pp 76–102.

21   Results can be found in A H Eagly, S J Karau, and M G Makhijani, "Gender and the Effectiveness of Leaders: A Meta-Analysis," *Psychological Bulletin,* January 1995, pp 125–45.

22   Excerpted from H Lancaster, "Managing Your Career: To Get Shipped Abroad, Women Must Overcome Prejudice at Home," *The Wall Street Journal,* June 29, 1999, p B1.

23   "Colin Powell's Thoughts on Leadership," *Industry Week,* August 19, 1996, p 57.

24   This research is summarized and critiqued by E A Fleishman, "Consideration and Structure: Another Look at Their Role in Leadership Research," in *Leadership: The Multiple-Level Approaches,* eds F Dansereau and F J Yammarino (Stamford, CT: JAI Press, 1998), pp 51–60; and Bass, *Bass & Stogdill's Handbook of Leadership: Theory, Research, and Managerial Applications,* ch. 24.

25   See V H Vroom, "Leadership," in *Handbook of Industrial and Organizational Psychology,* ed M D Dunnette (Chicago: Rand McNally, 1976).

26   R R Blake and J S Mouton, "A Comparative Analysis of Situationalism and 9,9 Management by Principle," *Organizational Dynamics,* Spring 1982, p 23.

27   Ibid., pp 28–29. Also see R R Blake and J S Mouton, "Management by Grid Principles or Situationalism: Which?" *Group & Organization Studies,* December 1981, pp 439–55.

28   Ibid., p 21.

29   Excerpted from R J Grossman, "Heirs Unapparent," *HR Magazine,* February 1999, p 39.

30   See Bass, *Bass & Stogdill's Handbook of Leadership: Theory, Research, and Managerial Applications,* chaps. 20–25.

31   The relationships between the frequency and mastery of leader behavior and various outcomes were investigated by F Shipper and C S White, "Mastery, Frequency, and Interaction of Managerial Behaviors Relative to Subunit Effectiveness," *Human Relations,* January 1999, pp 49–66.

32   F E Fiedler, "Job Engineering for Effective Leadership: A New Approach," *Management Review,* September 1977, p 29.

33   Excerpted from C Hymowitz, "In the Lead: How Cynthia Danaher Learned to Stop Sharing and Start Leading," *The Wall Street Journal,* March 16, 1999, p B1.

34   For more on this theory, see F E Fiedler, "A Contingency Model of Leadership Effectiveness," in *Advances in Experimental Social Psychology,* vol. 1, ed L Berkowitz (New York: Academic Press, 1964); F E Fiedler, *A Theory of Leadership Effectiveness* (New York: McGraw-Hill, 1967).

35   Additional information on situational control is contained in F E Fiedler, "The Leadership Situation and the Black Box in Contingency Theories," in *Leadership Theory and Research: Perspectives and Directions,* eds M M Chemers and R Ayman (New York: Academic Press, 1993), pp 2–28.

36   See L H Peters, D D Hartke, and J T Pohlmann, "Fiedler's Contingency Theory of Leadership: An Application of the Meta-Analyses Procedures of Schmidt and Hunter," *Psychological Bulletin,* March 1985, pp 274–85. The meta-analysis was conducted by C A Schriesheim, B J Tepper, and L A Tetrault, "Least Preferred Co-Worker Score, Situational Control, and Leadership Effectiveness: A Meta-Analysis of Contingency Model Performance Predictions," *Journal of Applied Psychology,* August 1994, pp 561–73.

37   A recent review of the contingency theory and suggestions for future theoretical development is provided by R Ayman, M M Chemers, and F Fiedler, "The Contingency Model of Leadership Effectiveness: Its Levels of Analysis," in *Leadership: The Multiple-Level Approaches,* eds Dansereau and Yammarino, pp 73–94; and R P Vecchio, "Some Continuing Challenges for the Contingency Model of Leadership," in *Leadership: The Multiple-Level Approaches,* eds Dansereau and Yammarino, pp 115–24.

38   For more detail on this theory, see R J House, "A Path–Goal Theory of Leader Effectiveness," *Administrative Science Quarterly,* September 1971, pp 321–38.

39   Adapted from R J House and T R Mitchell, "Path–Goal Theory of Leadership," *Journal of Contemporary Business,* Autumn 1974, p 83.

40   See R Hooijberg, "A Multidirectional Approach toward Leadership: An Extension of the Concept of Behavioral Complexity," *Human Relations,* July 1996, pp 917–46.

41   P Sellers, "Pepsico's New Generation," *Fortune,* April 1, 1996, pp 112, 114.

42   Results can be found in P M Podsakoff, S B MacKenzie, M Ahearne, and W H Bommer, "Searching for a Needle in a Haystack: Trying to Identify the Illusive Moderators of Leadership Behaviors," *Journal of Management,* 1995, pp 422–70.

43   A thorough discussion of this theory is provided by P Hersey and K H Blanchard, *Management of Organizational Behavior: Utilizing Human Resources,* 5th ed (Englewood Cliffs, NJ: Prentice-Hall, 1988).

44   A comparison of the original theory and its latent version is provided by P Hersey and K Blanchard, "Great Ideas Revisited," *Training & Development,* January 1996, pp 42–47.

45 Results can be found in J R Goodson, G W McGee, and J F Cashman, "Situational Leadership Theory," *Group & Organization Studies,* December 1989, pp 446–61.

46 The first study was conducted by R P Vecchio, "Situational Leadership Theory: An Examination of a Prescriptive Theory," *Journal of Applied Psychology,* August 1987, pp 444–51. Results from the study of nurse executives can be found in C Adams, "Leadership Behavior of Chief Nurse Executives," *Nursing Management,* August 1990, pp 36–39.

47 See D C Lueder, "Don't Be Misled by LEAD," *Journal of Applied Behavioral Science,* May 1985, pp 143–54; and C L Graeff, "The Situational Leadership Theory: A Critical View," *Academy of Management Review,* April 1983, pp 285–91.

48 For details on these different theories, see J McGregor Burns, *Leadership* (New York: Harper & Row, 1978); N M Tichy and M A Devanna, *The Transformational Leader* (New York: John Wiley & Sons, 1986); J M Kouzes and B Z Posner, *The Leadership Challenge: How to Get Extraordinary Things Done in Organizations* (San Francisco: Jossey-Bass, 1990); B Bass and B J Avolio, "Transformational Leadership: A Response to Critiques," in *Leadership Theory and Research: Perspectives and Directions,* eds M M Chemers and R Ayman (New York: Academic Press, 1993), pp 49–80; B Nanus, *Visionary Leadership* (San Francisco: Jossey-Bass, 1992); and B Shamir, R J House, and M B Arthur, "The Motivational Effects of Charismatic Leadership: A Self-Concept Based Theory," *Organization Science,* November 1993, pp 577–94.

49 Shamir, House, and Arthur, "The Motivational Effects of Charismatic Leadership: A Self-Concept Based Theory," p 578.

50 Excerpted from A Bianco, "The Rise of a Star," *Business Week,* December 21, 1998, pp 61, 63.

51 This discussion is based on D A Waldman and F J Yammarino, "CEO Charismatic Leadership: Levels-of-Management and Levels-of-Analysis Effects," *Academy of Management Review,* April 1999, pp 266–85.

52 Nanus, *Visionary Leadership,* p 8.

53 See Ibid; and W L Gardner and B J Avolio, "The Charismatic Relationship: A Dramaturgical Perspective," *Academy of Management Review,* January 1998, pp 32–58.

54 N Deogun, "Bitter Medicine: Network of Doctors, Touted as a Panacea, Develops Big Problems," *The Wall Street Journal,* August 26, 1996, p A1.

55 See G Fuchsberg, " 'Visioning' Missions Becomes Its Own Mission," *The Wall Street Journal,* January 7, 1994, p B1.

56 Results can be found in B Shamir, E Zakay, E Breinin, and M Popper, "Correlates of Charismatic Leader Behavior in Military Units: Subordinates' Attitudes, Unit Characteristics, and Superiors' Appraisals of Leader Performance," *Academy of Management Journal,* August 1998, pp 387–409.

57 Results can be obtained from T G DeGroot, D S Kiker, and T C Cross, "A Meta-Analysis to Review the Consequences of Charismatic Leadership," paper presented at the annual meeting of the Academy of Management, Cincinnati, Ohio, 1996.

58 Supporting research can be found in R Pillai and J R Meindl, "Context and Charisma: A 'Meso' Level Examination of the Relationship of Organic Structure, Collectivism, and Crisis to Charismatic Leadership," *Journal of Management,* 1998, 643–71; and J C Wofford, V L Goodwin, and J L Whittington, "A Field Study of a Cognitive Approach to Understanding Transformational and Transactional Leadership," *Leadership Quarterly,* 1998, pp 55–84.

59 See K B Lowe, K G Kroeck, and N Sivasubramaniam, "Effectiveness Correlates of Transformational and Transactional Leadership: A Meta-Analytic Review of the MLQ Literature," *Leadership Quarterly,* 1996, pp 385–425.

60 See D I Jung and B J Avolio, "Effects of Leadership Style and Followers' Cultural Orientation on Performance in Group and Individual Task Conditions," *Academy of Management Journal,* April 1999, pp 208–18; and A J Dubinsky, F J Yammarino, M A Jolson, and W D Spangler, "Transformational Leadership: An Initial Investigation in Sales Management," *Journal of Personal Selling & Sales Management,* Spring 1995, pp 17–31.

61 Results can be found in R J House, W D Spangler, and J Woycke, "Personality and Charisma in the US Presidency: A Psychological Theory of Leader Effectiveness," *Administrative Science Quarterly,* September 1991, pp 364–96.

62 See B M Bass, "Does the Transactional-Transformational Leadership Paradigm Transcend Organizational and National Boundaries?" *American Psychologist,* February 1997, pp 130–39.

63 See B Shankar Pawar and K K Eastman, "The Nature and Implications of Contextual Influences on Transformational Leadership: A Conceptual Examination," *Academy of Management Review,* January 1997, pp 80–109; and P Sellers, "What Exactly Is Charisma?" *Fortune,* January 15, 1996, pp 68–75.

64 Supporting research is summarized by Bass and Avolio, "Transformation Leadership: A Response to Critiques," pp 49–80. The effectiveness of leadership training is discussed by J Huey, "The Leadership Industry," *Fortune,* February 21, 1994, pp 54–56.

65 The ethics of charismatic leadership is discussed by D Sankowsky, "The Charismatic Leader as Narcissist: Understanding the Abuse of Power," *Organizational Dynamics,* Spring 1995, pp 57–71.

66 These recommendations were derived from J M Howell and B J Avolio, "The Ethics of Charismatic Leadership: Submission or Liberation," *The Executive,* May 1992, pp 43–54.

67 See F Dansereau, Jr, G Graen, and W Haga, "A Vertical Dyad Linkage Approach to Leadership within Formal Organizations," *Organizational Behavior and Human Performance,* February 1975, pp 46–78; and R M Dienesch and R C Liden, "Leader–Member Exchange Model of Leadership: A Critique and Further Development," *Academy of Management Review,* July 1986, pp 618–34.

68 These descriptions were taken from D Duchon, S G Green, and T D Taber, "Vertical Dyad Linkage: A Longitudinal Assessment of Antecedents, Measures, and Consequences," *Journal of Applied Psychology,* February 1986, pp 56–60.

69 Supportive results can be found in C Hui, K S Law, and Z X Chen, "A Structural Equation Model of the Effects of Negative Affectivity, Leader–Member Exchange, and Perceived Job Mobility on In-Role and Extra-Role Performance: A Chinese Case," *Organizational Behavior and Human Decision Processes,* January 1999, pp 3–21; C A Schriesheim, L L Neider, and T A Scandura, "Delegation and Leader–Member Exchange: Main Effects, Moderators, and Measurement Issues," *Academy of Management Journal,* June 1998, pp 298–318; and H J Klein and J S Kim, "A Field

Study of the Influence of Situational Constraints, Leader–Member Exchange, and Goal Commitment on Performance," *Academy of Management Journal,* February 1998, pp 88–95.

70   See D A Hoffman and F P Morgeson, "Safety-Related Behavior as a Social Exchange: The Role of Perceived Organizational Support and Leader–Member Exchange," *Journal of Applied Psychology,* April 1999, pp 286–96.

71   Turnover studies were conducted by G B Graen, R C Liden, and W Hoel, "Role of Leadership in the Employee Withdrawal Process," *Journal of Applied Psychology,* December 1982, pp 868–72; G R Ferris, "Role of Leadership in the Employee Withdrawal Process: A Constructive Replication," *Journal of Applied Psychology,* November 1985, pp 777–81. The career progress study was conducted by M Wakabayashi and G B Graen, "The Japanese Career Progress Study: A 7-Year Follow-Up," *Journal of Applied Psychology,* November 1984, pp 603–14.

72   A review of this research can be found in R T Sparrowe and R C Liden, "Process and Structure in Leader–Member Exchange," *Academy of Management Review,* April 1997, pp 522–52.

73   Supporting evidence can be found in S J Wayne, L M Shore, and R C Liden, "Perceived Organizational Support and Leader–Member Exchange: A Social Exchange Perspective," *Academy of Management Journal,* February 1997, pp 82–111; and S J Wayne and G R Ferris, "Influence Tactics, Affect, and Exchange Quality in Supervisor-Subordinate Interactions: A Laboratory Experiment and Field Study," *Journal of Applied Psychology,* October 1990, pp. 487–99.

74   See S G Green, S E Anderson, and S L Shivers, "Demographic and Organizational Influences on Leader–Member Exchange and Related Work Attitudes," *Organizational Behavior and Human Decision Processes,* May 1996, pp 203–14.

75   The reliability and validity of this measure is provided by R C Liden and J M Maslyn, "Multidimensionality of Leader–Member Exchange: An Empirical Assessment through Scale Development," *Journal of Management,* 1998, pp 43–72.

76   These recommendations are from R P Vecchio, "Are You In or Out with Your Boss?" *Business Horizons,* November–December 1986, pp 76–78.

77   For an expanded discussion of this model, see S Kerr and J Jermier, "Substitutes for Leadership: Their Meaning and Measurement," *Organizational Behavior and Human Performance,* December 1978, pp 375–403.

78   See J P Howell, P W Dorfman, and S Kerr, "Moderator Variables in Leadership Research," *Academy of Management Review,* January 1986, pp 88–102.

79   Results can be found in Podsakoff, MacKenzie, Ahearne, and Bommer, "Searching for a Needle in a Haystack: Trying to Identify the Illusive Moderators of Leadership Behaviors."

80   For details of this study, see P M Podsakoff, S B MacKenzie, and W H Bommer, "Meta-Analysis of the Relationship between Kerr and Jermier's Substitutes for Leadership and Employee Job Attitudes, Role Perceptions, and Performance," *Journal of Applied Psychology,* August 1996, pp 380–99.

81   See the related discussion in J P Howell, D E Bowen, P W Dorfman, S Kerr, and P M Podsakoff, "Substitutes for Leadership: Effective Alternatives to Ineffective Leadership," in *Leadership: Understanding the Dynamics of Power and Influence in Organizations,* ed R P Vecchio (Notre Dame, IN: University of Notre Dame Press, 1997), pp 381–95.

82   An overall summary of servant leadership is provided by L C Spears, *Reflections on Leadership: How Robert K Greenleaf's Theory of Servant-Leadership Influenced Today's Top Management Thinkers* (New York: John Wiley & Sons, 1995).

83   J Stuart, *Fast Company,* September 1999, p 114.

84   See E McShulskis, "HRM Update: Coaching Helps, But Is Not Often Used," *HRMagazine,* March 1966, pp 15–16; and L McDermott, "Wanted: Chief Executive Coach," *Training & Development,* May 1996, pp 67–70.

85   For a discussion of superleadership, see C C Manz and H P Sims, Jr, "SuperLeadership: Beyond the Myth of Heroic Leadership," in *Leadership: Understanding the Dynamics of Power and Influence in Organizations,* ed Vecchio, pp 411–28; and C C Manz and H P Sims, Jr, *Superleadership: Leading Others to Lead Themselves* (New York: Berkley Books, 1989).

86   Excerpted from D Leonhardt, "His Remarkable Journey to Become Maytag's CEO: The Sage of Lloyd Ward," *Business Week,* August 9, 1999, pp 59–70.

87   The scale used to assess readiness to assume the leadership role was taken from A J DuBrin, *Leadership: Research Findings, Practice, and Skills* (Boston: Houghton Mifflin Company, 1995), pp 10–11.

88   The norms were taken from Ibid.

89   This exercise was based on one contained in L W Mealiea, *Skills for Managers in Organizations* (Burr Ridge, IL: Irwin, 1994), pp 96–97.

90   The introduction was quoted from Ibid., p 96.

Part 2

Introduction to Communication

An effective manager spends more time communicating - informing, persuading, inspiring, and listening - than doing anything else. Communication skills are the manager's most important asset or biggest liability. Recent studies show that managers spend from 66 to 80 percent of their time in communication with superiors, subordinates, peers, and outside constituents. If managers do not understand the processes involved in good communications, their best-laid plans can fail.

Communication is the process through which managers coordinate, lead, influence, and coach their subordinates. The ability to communicate effectively is the characteristic judged by managers to be most critical in determining managerial success. This ability involves a broad array of activities, from writing to face-to-face interaction to speech making to the use of symbolic gestures.

Communication skills can make or break a career - and an organization. Communication is essential to management because it encompasses all aspects of an organization and pervades all organizational activity; it is the process by which things get done. Yet, communication is a complicated and dynamic process with many factors influencing its effectiveness. First, communication is a process in which senders, messages, channels, and receivers do not remain constant or static. Second, communication is complex. A number of communication theorists suggest that even in a simple two-person interaction, there are many variables, such as the individuals, the setting, the experiences each person has had, and the nature of the task; that affect the efficiency and effectiveness of the process. Third, communication is symbolic. We use a wide variety of arbitrary words and signs to convey meaning to those with whom we are communicating. While there is some agreement about the meaning of most words and signs, there is also a wide variety of interpretation that may be made, and the words and signs may change over time.

Part 2 is devoted to providing an understanding of communication and to the task of developing excellence in managerial communication. This part begins with Chapter 5 which presents an understanding of basic communication foundations including a communication process, barriers to communication, and how to overcome them. Communication is a two way process. In addition to being able to express oneself well, one must also be an effective listener. Therefore, the listening process is examined in Chapter 6 with attention given to how one might become a more effective listener. Throughout a career in the business world, successful individuals will be required to make presentations – both oral and written. Making effective oral presentations is presented in Chapter 7. Part 2 concludes with three application chapters: Chapter 8 - writing quality letters, memos, and reports, Chapter 9 - interviewing, and Chapter 10 - meetings.

Chapter 5

The Communication Process

SOURCE: John M. Ivancevich and Michael T. Matteson, *Organizational Behavior and Management,* 5th ed., Chapter 13, McGraw-Hill 2002, 1999.

Learning Objectives

After completing this chapter, you should be able to:

- Explain the elements in the communication process.
- Compare the four major directions of communication.
- Describe the role played by interpersonal communication in organizations.
- Discuss multicultural communication.
- Identify significant barriers to effective communication.
- Describe ways in which communication in organizations can be improved.
- Define the following key terms:

communication	**feedback loop**	**nonverbal messages**
communicator	**filtering**	**receiver**
decoding	**medium**	**selective listening**
encoding	**message**	**source credibility**
exception principle	**noise**	**value judgements**

The focus of this chapter is the process of organizational communication. Communicating, like the process of decision making, pervades everything that all organizational members—particularly managers—do. The managerial functions of planning, organizing, leading, and controlling all involve communicative activity. In fact, communication is an absolutely essential element in all organizational processes.

THE IMPORTANCE OF COMMUNICATION

Communication is the glue that holds organizations together. Communication assists organizational members to accomplish both individual and organizational goals, implement and respond to organizational change, coordinate organizational activities, and engage in virtually all organizationally relevant behaviors. Yet, as important as this process is, breakdowns in communication are pervasive. The anonymous wit who said, "I know you believe you understand what you think I said, but I am not sure you realize that what you heard is not what I meant," was being more than humorous; she or he was describing what every one of us has experienced: a failure to communicate.

To the extent that organizational communications are less effective than they might be, organizations will be less effective than they might be. For example, in many companies, new-employee orientation programs represent the first important opportunity to begin the process of effective communication with employees. At Marriott International, the worldwide hotel and resort chain, 40 percent of new employees who leave the organization do so during the first three months on the job. At least that had been true historically. Recently, the rate of departures has been significantly reduced because Marriott has embarked on a concerted effort to improve the content and manner in which it communicates with new employees during orientation. In addition to formally providing more information, each new employee is assigned a "buddy" who serves as a vital communication link to which the newcomer has unrestricted access. Marriott helps ensure that its frontline service personnel communicate effectively with their guests by first ensuring that Marriott communicates effectively with its employees, starting from their very first day on the job.

It would be extremely difficult to find an aspect of a manager's job that does not involve communication. Serious problems arise when directives are misunderstood, when casual kidding in a work group leads to anger, or when informal remarks by a top-level manager are distorted. Each of these situations is a result of a breakdown somewhere in the process of communication.

Accordingly, the pertinent question is not whether managers engage in communication because communication is inherent to the functioning of an organization. Rather, the pertinent question is whether managers will communicate well or poorly. In other words, communication itself is unavoidable in an organization's functioning; only *effective* communication is avoidable. *Every manager must be a communicator.* In fact, everything a manager does communicates something in some way to somebody or some group. The only question is: "With what effect?" While this may appear an overstatement at this point, it will become apparent as you proceed through the chapter. Despite the tremendous advances in communication and information technology, communication among people in organizations leaves much to be desired.[1] It is a process that occurs within people.

FIGURE 5–1   **THE COMMUNICATION PROCESS**

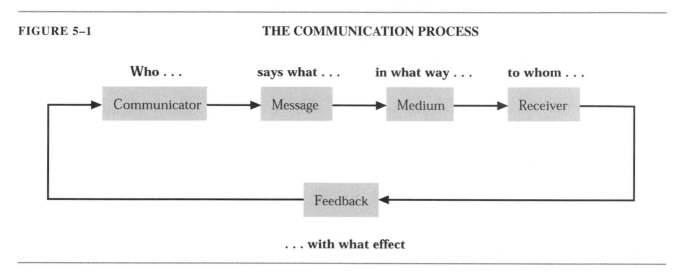

THE COMMUNICATION PROCESS

The general process of communication is presented in Figure 5-1. The process contains five elements—the communicator, the message, the medium, the receiver, and feedback. It can be simply summarized as: Who . . . says what . . . in what way . . . to whom . . . with what effect?[2] To appreciate each element in the process, we must examine how communication works.

How Communication Works

Communication experts tell us that effective communication is the result of a common understanding between the communicator and the receiver. In fact, the word **communication** is derived from the Latin *communis,* meaning "common." The communicator seeks to establish a "commonness" with a receiver. Hence, we can define communication as the *transition of information and understanding through the use of common symbols.* The common symbols may be verbal or nonverbal. You will see later that in the context of an organizational structure, information can flow up and down (vertical), across (horizontal), and down and across (diagonal).

The most widely used contemporary model of the process of communication has evolved mainly from the work of Shannon and Weaver and Schramm.[3] These researchers were concerned with describing the general process of communication that could be useful in all situations. The model that evolved from their work is helpful for understanding communication. The basic elements include a communicator, an encoder, a message, a medium, a decoder, a receiver, feedback, and noise. The model is presented in Figure 5-2. Each element in the model can be examined in the context of an organization.

The communication process works extremely well at the world's largest food producer, Nestlé. The company has entered the e-revolution by using the Web for continuous communication. Nestlé provides store owners the option of ordering its chocolates and other products via a Web site: Nestlé EZ Order. The system will eliminate most of the 100,000 phoned or faxed orders a year from mom-and-pop shops.[4] Nestlé buyers have purchased cocoa beans and other raw ingredients on a country-by-country basis with little information about how colleagues were buying the same products. Now they share price information via the Net and pick suppliers offering the best deals.

Nestlé has traditionally processed its own cocoa butter and powder and manufactured most of its own chocolate. The Web now lets Nestlé communicate regularly with suppliers, making outsourcing a viable option. In the past, Nestlé guessed at how many Kit Kat Crunch bars it might be able to sell in a promotion. Today, electronic links with supermarkets and other partners provides it with real-time feedback and information.

The Nestlé approach involves each of the elements in the communication process. The difference with Nestlé today and Nestlé yesterday is that some of the firm's exchanges of messages and feedback are performed electronically. Nestlé believes that face-to-face and electronic communicators are needed to operate a profitable business around the world.

The Elements of Communication

Communicator

In an organizational framework, the communicator *is an employee with ideas, intentions, information, and a purpose for communicating.*

Encoding

Given the communicator, an **encoding** process must take place that *translates the communicator's ideas into a systematic set of symbols*—into a language expressing the communicator's purpose. For example, a manager often takes accounting information, sales reports, and computer data and translates them into one message. The function of encoding, then, is to provide a form in which ideas and purposes can be expressed as a message.

Message

The result of the encoding process is the message. The purpose of the communicator is expressed in the form of the **message**—either *verbal* or *nonverbal*. Managers have numerous purposes for communicating, such as to have others understand their ideas, to understand the ideas of others, to gain acceptance of themselves or their ideas, or to produce action. The message, then, is what the individual hopes to communicate to the intended receiver, and the exact form it takes depends, to a great extent, on the medium used to carry the message. Decisions relating to the two are inseparable.

Not as obvious, however, are *unintended messages* that can be sent by silence or inaction on a particular issue as well as decisions of which goals and objectives not to pursue and which method not to utilize. For example, a decision to utilize one type of performance evaluation method rather than another may send a "message" to certain people. Messages may also be designed to appear on the surface to convey certain information, when other information is what is really being conveyed. Related to this are messages designed to protect the sender, rather than to facilitate understanding by the receiver. Organizational Encounter 5-1 provides some examples of these latter types of messages.

FIGURE 5–2   **A COMMUNICATION MODEL**

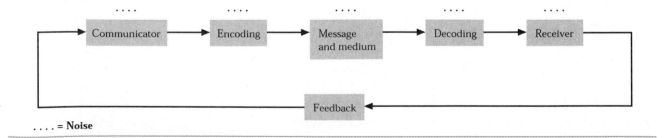

Medium

The **medium** *is the carrier of the message.* Organizations provide information to members in a variety of ways, including face-to-face communications, telephone, group meetings, memos, policy statements, reward systems, production schedules, and sales forecasts. The arrival of electronic media based upon the computer and telecommunication technologies has increased interest in the role of the medium in various aspects of organizational communications.[5]

Decoding-Receiver

For the process of communication to be completed, the message must be decoded in terms of relevance to the receiver. **Decoding** *is a technical term for the receiver's thought processes.* Decoding, then, involves interpretation. **Receivers** *interpret (decode) the message in light of their own previous experiences and frames of reference.* Thus, a salesperson is likely to decode a memo from the company president differently than a production manager will. A nursing supervisor is likely to decode a memo from the hospital administrator differently than the chief of surgery will. The closer the decoded message is to the intent desired by the communicator, the more effective is the communication. This underscores the importance of the communicator being "receiver-oriented."

Feedback

Provision for feedback in the communication process is desirable. One-way communication processes are those that do not allow receiver-to-communicator feedback. This may increase the potential for distortion between the intended message and the received message. A **feedback loop** *provides a channel for receiver response that enables the communicator to determine whether the message has been received and has produced the intended response.* Two-way communication processes provide for this important receiver-to-communicator feedback.[6]

For the manager, communication feedback may come in many ways. In face-to-face situations, direct feedback through verbal exchanges is possible, as are such subtle means of communication as facial expressions of discontent or misunderstanding. In addition, indirect means of feedback (such as declines in productivity, poor quality of production, increased absenteeism or turnover, and lack of coordination and/or conflict between units) may indicate communication breakdowns.

ORGANIZATIONAL ENCOUNTER 5–1

CONFUSING THE PEOPLE AND CLOUDING THE ISSUE

Unfortunately, not all organizational communications are meant to clarify; sometimes they are designed to confuse. At other times, protecting the communicator may be the primary objective. Some words and phrases are so frequently used to convey a meaning other than the apparent one that their use has become institutionalized. Below are some humorous examples of alternative interpretions to what otherwise appear as straightforward words or messages.

It is in process—It's so wrapped up in red tape that the situation is hopeless.

We will look into it—By the time the wheel makes a full turn we assume you will have forgotten about it.

Under consideration—Never heard of it.

Under active consideration—We're looking in our files for it.

We are making a survey—We need more time to think of an answer.

Let's get together on this—I'm assuming you're as confused as I.

For appropriate action—Maybe you'll know what to do with this.

Note and initial—Let's spread the responsibility for this.

It is estimated—This is my guess.

We are aware of it—We had hoped that the person who started it would have forgotten about it by now.

We will advise you in due course—If we figure it out, we'll let you know.

Give us the benefit of your thinking—We'll listen to you as long as it doesn't interfere with what we have already decided to do.

She is in conference—I don't have any idea where she is.

We are activating the file—We're faxing it to as many people as we can think of.

Let me bring you up to date—We didn't like what you were going to do, so we already did something else.

A reliable source—The person you just met.

An informed source—The person who told the person you just met.

An unimpeachable source—The person who started the rumor to begin with.

Noise

In the framework of human communication, **noise** *can be thought of as those factors that distort the intended message.* Noise may occur in each of the elements of communication. For example, a manager who is under a severe time constraint may be forced to act without communicating or may communicate hastily with incomplete information. Or a subordinate may attach a different meaning to a word or phrase than was intended by the manager.

The elements discussed in this section are essential for communication to occur. They should not, however, be viewed as separate. They are, rather, descriptive of the acts that have to be performed for any type of communication to occur. The communication may be vertical (superior–subordinate, subordinate–superior) or horizontal (peer–peer). Or it may involve one individual and a group. But the elements discussed here must be present.

Nonverbal Messages

The *information sent by a communicator that is unrelated to the verbal information*—that is, **nonverbal messages** or nonverbal communication—is a relatively recent area of research among behavioral scientists. The major interest has been in the *physical* cues that characterize the communicator's physical presentation. These cues include such modes of transmitting nonverbal messages as head, face, and eye movements, posture, distance, gestures, voice tone, and clothing and dress choices.[7] Nonverbal messages themselves are influenced by factors such as the gender of the communicator.[8]

Some nonverbal messages are spontaneous and unregulated expressions of emotion, while others are conscious and deliberately presented.[9] Through nonverbal behavior, particularly body movements, we say, "Help me, I'm lonely. Take me, I'm available. Leave me alone, I'm depressed." We act out our state of being with nonverbal body language. We lift one eyebrow for disbelief. We rub our noses for puzzlement. We clasp our arms to isolate ourselves or to protect ourselves. We shrug our shoulders for indifference, wink one eye for intimacy, tap our fingers for impatience, slap our forehead for forgetfulness.[10]

Nonverbal messages may differ from other forms of communication behavior in several ways. For example, nonverbal behavior can be difficult to suppress (e.g., an involuntary frown indicating displeasure). Such unconscious behavior can contradict the message the communicator is sending verbally. Another way in which nonverbal messages differ from other forms is that they are more apparent to the people who observe them than they are to the people who produce them. This can make it very difficult for the sender to know how successfully she or he produced the nonverbal message that was intended. Finally, many nonverbal messages are susceptible to multiple interpretations. Even something as common as a smile may have many different meanings. Smiles may indicate genuine happiness, contempt, deceit, fear, compliance, resignation—even, on occasion, anger.

Research indicates that facial expressions and eye contact and movements generally provide information about the *type* of emotion, while such physical cues as distance, posture, and gestures indicate the *intensity* of the emotion. These conclusions are important to managers. They indicate that communicators often send a great deal more information than is obtained in verbal messages. To increase the effectiveness of communication, a person must be aware of the nonverbal as well as the verbal content of the messages.

When verbal and nonverbal messages conflict, receivers tend to place more faith in nonverbal cues. When this type of conflict occurs, a judgment on what message to decipher is going to be made. Thus, examining nonverbal and verbal cues is constantly occurring. Some of the most common nonverbal cues people study include eye contact, facial expressions (the human face displays over 250,000), posture, and gestures. Being aware of these main cue initiators is important. For example, sustained eye contact in some cultures is considered impolite. While the thumbs up for a successful effort is a cue in the United States for a "job well done," it is an "obscene" gesture in Spain and parts of Latin America.

Being aware of nonverbal messages requires an awareness of their existence and importance. A good way to examine your own nonverbal impression and presence is to videotape yourself making a formal presentation. The review of the videotape will help determine the alignment of verbal and nonverbal messages.

COMMUNICATING WITHIN ORGANIZATIONS

The design of an organization should provide for communication in four distinct directions: downward, upward, horizontal, and diagonal. Since these directions of communication establish the framework within which communication in an organization takes place, let us briefly examine each one. This examination will enable you to better appreciate the barriers to effective organizational communication and the means to overcome them.

Downward Communication

This type of communication *flows downward from individuals in higher levels of the hierarchy to those in lower levels.* The most common forms of downward communication are job instructions, official memos, policy statements, procedures, manuals, and company publications. In many organizations, **downward communication** often is both inadequate and inaccurate, as evidenced in the often-heard statement among organization members that "we have absolutely no idea what's happening." Such complaints indicate inadequate downward communication and the need of individuals for information relevant to their jobs. The absence of job-related information can create unnecessary stress among organization members.[11] A similar situation is faced by a student who has not been told the requirements and expectations of an instructor.

Upward Communication

An effective organization needs **upward communication** as much as it needs downward communication. In such situations, *the communicator is at a lower level in the organization than the receiver.* Some of the most common upward communication flows are suggestion boxes, group meetings, and appeal or grievance procedures. In their absence, people somehow find ways to adopt nonexistent or inadequate upward communication channels. This has been evidenced by the emergence of "underground" employee publications in many large organizations.

Upward communication serves a number of important functions. Organizational communication researcher Gary Kreps identifies several:[12]

1. It provides managers with feedback about current organizational issues and problems and information about day-to-day operations that they need for making decisions about directing the organization.

2. It is management's primary source of feedback for determining the effectiveness of its downward communication.

3. It relieves employees' tensions by allowing lower-level organization members to share relevant information with their superiors.
4. It encourages employees' participation and involvement, thereby enhancing organizational cohesiveness.

Horizontal Communication

Often overlooked in the design of most organizations is provision for **horizontal communication**. When the chairperson of the accounting department communicates with the chairperson of the marketing department concerning the course offerings in a college of business administration, the flow of communication is horizontal. Although vertical (upward and downward) communication flows are the primary considerations in organizational design, effective organizations also need horizontal communication. Horizontal communication—for example, communication between production and sales in a business organization and among the different departments or colleges within a university—is necessary for the coordination and integration of diverse organizational functions.

Since mechanisms for assuring horizontal communication ordinarily do not exist in an organization's design, its facilitation is left to individual managers. *Peer-to-peer communication* often is necessary for coordination and also can provide social need satisfaction.

Diagonal Communication

While it is probably the least-used channel of communication in organizations, **diagonal communication** is *important in situations where members cannot communicate effectively through other channels.* For example, the comptroller of a large organization may wish to conduct a distribution cost analysis. One part of that task may involve having the sales force send a special report directly to the comptroller rather than going through the traditional channels in the marketing department. Thus, the flow of communication would be diagonal as opposed to vertical (upward) and horizontal. In this case, a diagonal channel would be the most efficient in terms of time and effort for the organization.

Communicating Externally

Organizations are involved in communicating externally to present products and services, to project a positive image, to attract employees, and to gain attention. The typical external communication program includes four distinct programs:

*   Public relations which involves the communication of a positive image, exemplary corporate/organization citizenship, and promotion of an identity as a contributor to society and the immediate community. If a full-time public relations staff is not used, some type of arrangement with a professional firm may be used.

*   Advertising involves illustrating products or services in a positive manner. This form of communication is designed to attract customers, clients, or patients.

*   Promoting the culture and opportunities available to prospective employees. This communication is designed to attract employee talent to sustain and grow the organization.

*   Customer/Client/Patient surveys to gather feedback about the experience of external constituents with the organization. This information is used to make modifications or changes in service, products, or relationships.

Each of these four communication programs is used to collect or disseminate information. The internal and external communication programs provide ideas, information, connections, and insight into what individuals and groups are saying, what is important, and what needs modification.

Information Richness and Information Technologies

There are many different ways to communicate within an organization and externally to various constituents. Communication media differ in their information richness. The richness of communication involves how much information can be effectively transmitted.[13] A media that enables high richness, such as face-to-face interaction, is more likely to result in common understanding between individuals or a group when compared to a low-in-richness media, such as a standard written memo.

Face-to-face communication is high in richness because verbal and nonverbal cues can be exchanged and observed. This form of communication is also in "real time" and consequently permits on-the-spot feedback. If a person fails to understand a communication, request for clarification can immediately be presented.

Information richness is low in the case of a memo to a general population (e.g., a department, the entire project team, a subsidiary company). The impersonal nature of this type of communication is obvious. A specific individual is not being addressed, so feedback is not likely to occur in this type of communication.

The Internet

The Internet has its origins in a late 1960s Department of Defense program to devise communications capable of surviving a military attack. In 1969, the first version of the Internet, then referred to as the Advanced Research Project Agency network (ARPA net), connected four host computers. The Internet body is run by the Internet Society Operating Committee. The average U.S. user has six sessions, surfs about 32 minutes each time, and looks at about 232 pages per week. There were in January 2001 over 144 million Internet users in the United States.[14]

The term Internet is used to cover many services and information technologies. The World Wide Web (www) is the service that currently has the most applicable communication protocols and technology for business on the Internet. Internet services include electronic mail (e-mail), newsgroups, and chat rooms. The Web brings graphics, interaction, and hyperlinking capabilities to the Internet and allows for multimedia content such as voice and video. A common mistake is to think that the Internet and the Web are the same.

An intranet is a private protected electronic communication system within an organization. If it is connected to the Internet, it has its privacy protected by what are called firewalls. A firewall is a network mode set up internally to prevent traffic to cross into the private domain. Intranets are used to communicate such things as proprietary organizational information, company plans, confidential medical records, training programs, compensation data, and company records.

Electronic Mail (e-mail)

Communication that is transmitted through personal computers is referred to as e-mail or messaging. Senders transmit messages by typing the message on their computer and sending it to a receiver's electronic address. It is estimated that 94 million users sent over 5.5 trillion e-mail messages in 1999.[15]

A few years ago e-mail users sent out unedited, poorly written messages on the fly. This type of sloppiness has been attacked and is discouraged in organizations. The privacy of e-mail is another serious issue. Supervisors, colleagues, and others can access e-mail messages. Consequently, care must be exercised in properly using e-mails as a communication approach. E-mail etiquette suggestions are spelled out in Organizational Encounter 5-2. These are only a few suggestions that should be considered before preparing and sending e-mails.

Astute users of e-mail communications have learned about the dangers. Messages can travel anywhere so they must be carefully written. Also, even erased messages can remain on disk drives. Colonel Oliver North during the Iran Contra hearings found that "deleted files" could be extracted from computers.

Websense Inc. is a maker of employee monitoring software. This software identifies improper use of the Internet and personal (not work-related) e-mails. Nearly one-third of those companies polled by Websense had fired workers for improper use of the Internet. Nearly three-quarters of major U.S. companies are now recording and reviewing employees' communications, including e-mail, telephone calls, and Internet connections. For example, Chevron and Microsoft both settled sexual harassment lawsuits for $2.2 million apiece as a result of internally circulated e-mails that could have created hostile work environments.[16]

E-mail is an effective way of communicating simple messages. Complex data and information should probably be sent in hard copy documents. Think simple. Secure your e-mails. Always use correct and professional language in preparing and sending e-mails.

Voice Mail

Voice mail links a telephone system to a computer that digitizes and stores incoming messages. Some systems use automated means, allowing callers to reach any associated extension by pushing specific touch-tone telephone buttons. Interactive systems allow callers to receive information from a database. For example, a golf resort in California uses voice mail to answer questions about its five courses. You touch numbers that answer questions, provide tee times, and provide golf tips.

Voice mail serves many functions, but one of the most important is message storage. Incoming messages are delivered without interrupting receivers and allow for communicators to focus on the reason for the call. Voice mail minimizes inaccurate message-taking and time-zone difference barriers.

Videoconferencing and Teleconferencing

Videoconferencing refers to technologies associated with viewing, and teleconferencing refers to technologies primarily associated with speaking. Often the terms are used interchangeably. Both technologies enable individuals to conduct meetings without getting together face to face.

Some technologies enable participants to interact at the same time even when they are in different places. HighTech Campus, a Dallas and Houston e-learning training company, conducts 80 percent of its executive operating meetings through videoconferencing. The remainder of times, executives meet in either Dallas or Houston. Travel expenses and travel time have been greatly reduced since HighTech Campus began using videoconferencing in June 2000.[17]

Electronic Meetings

Electronic meeting software (EMS) uses networked computers to automate meetings. A large screen at the front of the room is the focal point. The screen serves as an electronic flip chart displaying comments, ideas, and responses of participants. Meetingware allows facilitators to poll meeting participants, analyze voting results, and create detailed reports.

ORGANIZATIONAL ENCOUNTER 5–2

E-MAIL NETIQUETTE SUGGESTIONS

Practicing some simple procedures can improve the effectiveness and quality of e-mail communications in an organization. Consider these rules as just a start of sound e-mail practices.

- Reading other people's e-mail is unethical and should be avoided.
- If an e-mail has an attachment, do not open it if the sender is unknown. Viruses (software that can infect, freeze, or destroy programs) can be included in the attachment.
- Don't send an e-mail you wouldn't want to have published.
- Keep it short, to the point, and free of any vulgarity.
- Don't send a single personal message on a company computer.
- Use grammatically correct, properly formatted, and concise messages.
- Respond as soon as possible in a courteous way to e-mails.
- Never respond to an e-mail when you are angry.
- Avoid forwarding an e-mail sent to you without receiving permission from the original sender.

Meetingware is helpful when large groups must reach decisions quickly. Meeting participants can simultaneously instead of one-by-one provide a vote, an opinion, or an idea. At Hewlett-Packard, meetingware has accelerated new product development by 30 percent.[18] Structured electronic meetings are 20 to 30 percent shorter than face-to-face meetings.

Advancements in information technologies are continuing and are providing organizational members with additional ways to communicate. Technologies, however, will not solve all communication problems. Overloading employees with new "toys," additional information, and technologies to learn can result in less efficiency. There is also the social interaction and personal touch that can be lost by relying solely on electronic technologies for communication. Electronic communication omits many verbal and most nonverbal cues that people use to acquire feedback. Guarding against anonymity and depersonalization are concerns when using many of the information technologies such as e-mail, videoconferencing, and electronic meetings.

INTERPERSONAL COMMUNICATIONS

Within an organization, communication flows from individual to individual in face-to-face and group settings. Such flows are termed interpersonal communications and can vary from direct orders to casual expressions. Interpersonal behavior could not exist without interpersonal communication. In addition to providing needed information, interpersonal communication also influences how people feel about the organization. For example, research indicates that satisfaction with communication relationships affects organizational commitment.[19]

The problems that arise when managers attempt to communicate with other people can be traced to *perceptual differences* and *interpersonal style differences*. We know that each manager perceives the world in terms of his or her background, experiences, personality, frame of reference, and attitude. The primary way in which managers relate to and learn from the environment (including the people in that environment) is through information received and transmitted. And the way in which managers receive and transmit information depends, in part, on how they relate to two very important senders of information—*themselves* and *others*.

In research involving interpersonal communications, it has been found that only 7 percent of the "attitudinal" meaning of a message comes from words spoken. Over 90 percent of meaning results from nonverbal cues.[20] These silent signals exert a strong influence on the receiver. However, interpreting them is by no means scientifically based. For example, does a downward glance during a brief encounter in an office mean modesty, embarrassment, a lack of respect, or fatigue?

Multicultural Communication

An often-repeated and much-enjoyed joke in Latin America and Europe poses this question: "If someone who speaks three languages is called trilingual, and someone who speaks two languages is called bilingual, what do you call someone who speaks only one language?" The answer is "an American." Although certainly not universally true, nonetheless, this story makes a telling point. While the average European speaks several languages, the typical American is fluent only in English. In a recent year, 23,000 American college students were studying Japanese; in the same year, 20 million Japanese were studying English.[21]

In the international business environment of today—and even more so, of tomorrow—foreign language training and fluency is a business necessity. It is true that English is an important business language and that many foreign business people speak it fluently. The fact remains, however, that the vast majority of the world's population neither speak nor understand English. Nor is language per se the only barrier to effective cross-cultural communications; in fact, it may be one of the easiest difficulties to overcome. There are numerous cultural-related variables that can hinder the communication process, not the least of which is *ethnocentrism.*

Ethnocentrism is the tendency to consider the values, norms, and customs of one's own country to be superior to those of other countries. Ethnocentrism need not be explicit to create communication problems. Implicit assumptions based on an ethnocentric view make it less likely that we will have sufficient cultural sensitivity even to be aware of possible differences in points of view, underlying assumptions, interpretation, or other factors that may create communication difficulties. Consider the following true incident involving an Indian and an Austrian.

> When asked if his department could complete a project by a given date, a particular Indian employee said "Yes" even when he knew he could not complete the project, because he believed that his Austrian supervisor wanted "yes" for an answer. When the completion date arrived and he had not finished the project, his Austrian supervisor showed dismay. The Indian's desire to be polite—to say what he thought his supervisor wanted to hear—seemed more important than an accurate assessment of the completion date.[22]

Both of the individuals depicted in this incident were operating from their own cultural frame of reference. The Austrian valued accuracy; for the Indian, politeness was the central value. By not being sensitive to the possibility of cultural differences, both contributed to the unfortunate misunderstanding.

Numerous other examples are possible. Words and phrases do not mean the same to all people. If, during an attempt to work out a business deal, for example, an American were to tell another American "That will be difficult," the meaning is entirely different than if a Japanese were to use that phrase. To the American it means the door is still open, but perhaps some compromise needs to be made. To the Japanese it clearly means "no"; the deal is unacceptable.[23] As another example, consider eye contact. Americans are taught to maintain good eye contact, and we may unconsciously assume those who do not look us in the eye are dishonest, or at least rude. In Japan, however, when speaking with a superior it is customary to lower ones' eyes as a gesture of respect. Organizational Encounter 5-3 describes further examples of language and other problems in cross-cultural communication contexts.

In spite of innumerable differences, multicultural communication can be successful. Business people from different cultures effectively and efficiently communicate with each other hundreds, perhaps thousands, of times every business day. By and large, the senders and receivers of those successful communications figure some, or all, of the following attributes:

1. They have made it a point to familiarize themselves with significant cultural differences that might affect the communication process. They do this through study, observation, and consultation with those who have direct or greater experience with the culture than do they.

2. They make a conscious, concerted effort to lay aside ethnocentric tendencies. This does not mean they must agree with values, customs, interpretations, or perspectives different from their own; awareness, not acceptance, is what is required to facilitate communications.

3. Perhaps most importantly, despite their efforts at doing what is described in the above two points, they maintain a posture of "knowing they do not know." This simply means that in the absence of direct, usually extensive, ongoing exposure to another culture, there will be nuances in the communication process of which they may well be unaware. Rather than assuming understanding is complete unless demonstrated otherwise, they assume it is incomplete until shown otherwise.

In the two chapter sections that follow, you will be able to identify barriers to effective communications, which may be especially relevant in multicultural contexts, as well as find techniques for improving communications, which are particularly important in the same contexts.

Four Seasons, the luxury hotel chain, understands multicultural communication very well. In recruiting and selecting overseas managers, Four Seasons's profile includes strong listening skills, alertness to body language, and open minds.[24] Four Seasons believes that culture is learned and that open-mindedness allows managers to learn new attitudes to deal with diversity of customers.

BARRIERS TO EFFECTIVE COMMUNICATION

A good question at this point is: "Why does communication break down?" On the surface, the answer is relatively easy. We have identified the elements of communication as the communicator, encoding, the message, the medium, decoding, the receiver, and feedback. If noise exists in these elements in any way, complete clarity of meaning and understanding will not occur. A manager has no greater responsibility than to develop effective communications. In this section, we discuss several barriers to effective communication that can exist both in organizational and interpersonal communications.

ORGANIZATIONAL ENCOUNTER 5–3

CROSS-CULTURAL COMMUNICATION PROBLEMS

Communicating exactly what you want to communicate, rather than more, less, or something altogether different, can be a challenge when the communication takes place within a single culture. Achieving the desired results cross-culturally can present special problems.

Many of the difficulties encountered with cross-cultural communications stem from the fact that there are different languages involved and direct translation is not always feasible. American automobile manufacturers have learned this lesson. When Ford Motor Company introduced its Fiera truck line in some developing countries, it discovered that Fiera is a Spanish slang word meaning "ugly woman." Chevrolet discovered that in Italian Chevrolet Nova translates as "Chevrolet no go." Similarly, GMs "Body by Fisher" logo translates in at least one language into "Corpse by Fisher." Such problems are of course not restricted to car makers. Coca-Cola, for example, has had its share of translation problems. In Chinese, Coca-Cola becomes "Bite the head of a dead tadpole." In some parts of Asia the familiar Coke advertising slogan "Coke adds life" is translated as "Coke brings you back from the dead."

Language translation problems are not the only source of problems. Head, hand, and arm gestures may mean different things in different cultures. In some countries, for example, moving ones' head from side to side means "yes," while bobbing it up and down means "no." Just the reverse of U.S. meaning. Or take the familiar A-OK gesture. In the United States it means things are fine, or everything is working. In France it has no such meaning; it simply means "zero." In Japan, on the other hand, it is a symbol representing money. There it may be used to indicate that something is too expensive. And in Brazil, the gesture is interpreted as obscene.

Many other aspects of the communication process can cause difficulties. Different cultural interpretations of the significance of eye contact, the physical distance maintained between two people talking with one another, and differences in accepted forms of address are but a few examples. Effective cross-cultural communications require that we become less ethnocentric and more culturally sensitive.

Frame of Reference

Different individuals can interpret the same communication differently depending on their previous experiences. This results in variations in the encoding and decoding process. Communication specialists agree that this is the most important factor that breaks down the "commonness" in communications. When the encoding and decoding processes are not alike, communication tends to break down. Thus, while the communicator actually is speaking the "same language" as the receiver, the message conflicts with the way the receiver "catalogs" the world. If a large area is shared in common, effective communication is facilitated. If a large area is not shared in common—if there has been no common experience—then communication becomes impossible or, at best, highly distorted.

The important point is that communicators can encode and receivers can decode only in terms of their experiences. As a result, distortion often occurs because of differing frames of reference. People in various organizational functions interpret the same situation differently. A business problem will be viewed differently by the marketing manager than by the production manager. An efficiency problem in a hospital will be viewed by the nursing staff from its frame of reference and experiences, which may result in interpretations different from those of the physician staff. Different levels in the organization also will have different frames of reference. First-line supervisors have frames of reference that differ in many respects from those of vice presidents. They are in different positions in the organization structure, and this influences their frames of reference. As a result, their needs, values, attitudes, and expectations will differ, and this difference will often result in unintentional distortion of communication. This is not to say that either group is wrong or right. All it means is that, in any situation, individuals will choose the part of their own past experiences that relates to the current experience and is helpful in forming conclusions and judgments.

Selective Listening

A vital part of the communication process involves listening. In fact about 75 percent of communication is listening. Most people only spend between 30 and 40 percent of their time listening.[25] This means that there are a lot of listening errors and deficiencies. Most speakers talk at a rate of about 150 words per minute. A good listener can process and understand oral communication at a rate of about 400 words per minute.

Listening takes place in four phases—perception, interpretation, evaluation, and action. Barriers can obstruct and block the listening process. The meaning attached to a manager's request is colored by a person's cultural, educational, and social frames of reference. Thus, interpretation of the manager's meaning may be different because of frame-of-reference differences.

The method of evaluation used is influenced by attitudes, preferences, and experience. The type of action taken involves memory and recall. Sometimes memory failures do not permit the best actions.

Selective listening *is a form of selective perception in which we tend to block out new information, especially if it conflicts with what we believe.* When we receive a directive from management, we notice only those things that reaffirm our beliefs. Those things that conflict with our preconceived notions we either do not note at all or we distort to confirm our preconceptions.

For example, a notice may be sent to all operating departments that costs must be reduced if the organization is to earn a profit. The communication may not achieve its desired effect because it conflicts with the "reality" of the receivers. Thus, operating employees may ignore or be amused by such information in light of the large salaries, travel allowances, and expense accounts of some executives. Whether they are justified is irrelevant; what is important is that such preconceptions result in breakdowns in communication.

A few worthwhile listening pointers are apparent in observing Oprah Winfrey, the celebrated talk show host. Oprah blocks out distractions and focuses on the talker (guest, audience member); she is always actively involved with great eye contact, listens emphatically without interrupting, and paraphrases her guest's comments and ideas. She is a master at making sure the speaker is understood. Managers could learn a lot about listening in general, selective listening, and emphatic listening from Oprah. Her style and approach make guests feel important, welcomed, and understood.

Value Judgments

In every communication situation, **value judgments** are made by the receiver. This basically *involves assigning an overall worth to a message prior to receiving the entire communication.* Value judgments may be based on the reciver's evaluation of the communicator or previous experiences with the communicator, or on the message's anticipated meaning. For example, a hospital administrator may pay little attention to a memorandum from a nursing supervisor because "she's always complaining about something." A college professor may consider a merit evaluation meeting with the department chairperson as "going through the motions" because the faculty member perceives the chairperson as having little or no power in the administration of the college. A cohesive work group may form negative value judgments concerning all actions by management.

Source Credibility

Source credibility i*s the trust, confidence, and faith that the receiver has in the words and actions of the communicator.* The level of credibility the receiver assigns to the communicator in turn directly affects how the receiver views and reacts to words, ideas, and actions of the communicator.

Thus, how subordinates view a communication from their manager is affected by their evaluation of the manager. This, of course, is heavily influenced by previous experiences with the manager. Again we see that everything done by a manager communicates. A group of hospital medical staff who view the hospital administrator as less than honest, manipulative, and not to be trusted are apt to assign nonexistent motives to any communication from the administrator. Union leaders who view management as exploiters and managers who view union leaders as political animals are likely to engage in little real communication.

Filtering

Filtering, a common occurrence in upward communication in organizations, refers to *the manipulation of information so that the receiver perceives it as positive.* Subordinates cover up unfavorable information in messages to their superiors. The reason for filtering should be clear; this is the direction (upward) that carries control information to management. Management makes merit evaluations, grants salary increases, and promotes individuals based on what it receives by way of the upward channel. The temptation to filter is likely to be strong at every level in the organization.

At General Electric, under the strong leadership of Jack Welch, filtering has sometimes been a problem. CEO Welch has a reputation for being tough, aggressive, impatient, and intimidating, which has led to his being both highly admired and feared. He also has a reputation for sometimes terminating people for delivering bad news.[26] When GE senior executives (or anyone else) are apprehensive about communicating information to a superior, filtering can and does occur.

In-Group Language

Each of us undoubtedly has had associations with experts and been subjected to highly technical jargon, only to learn that the unfamiliar words or phrases described very simple procedures or familiar objects. Many students are asked by researchers to "complete an instrument as part of an experimental treatment." The student soon learns that this involves nothing more than filling out a paper-and-pencil questionnaire.

Often, occupation, professional, and social groups develop words or phrases that have meaning only to members. Such special language can serve many useful purposes. It can provide members with feelings of belongingness, cohesiveness, and, in many cases, self-esteem. It also can facilitate effective communication within the group. The use of in-group language can, however, result in severe communication breakdowns when outsiders or other groups are involved. This is especially the case when groups use such language in an organization, not for the purpose of transmitting information and understanding, but rather to communicate a mystique about the group or its function.

Status Differences

Organizations often express hierarchical rank through a variety of symbols—titles, offices, carpets, and so on. Such status differences can be perceived as threats by persons lower in the hierarchy, and this can prevent or distort communication. Rather than look incompetent, a nurse may prefer to remain quiet instead of expressing an opinion or asking a question of the nursing supervisor.

Many times superiors, in an effort to utilize their time efficiently, make this barrier more difficult to surmount. The governmental administrator or bank vice president may be accessible only by making an advance appointment or by passing the careful quizzing of a secretary. This widens the communication gap between superior and subordinates.

Time Pressures

The pressure of time is an important barrier to communication. An obvious problem is that managers do not have the time to communicate frequently with every subordinate. However, time pressures often can lead to far more serious problems than this. *Short-circuiting* is a failure of the formally prescribed communication system that often results from time pressures. What it means simply is that someone has been left out of the formal channel of communication who normally would be included.

For example, suppose a salesperson needs a rush order for a very important customer and goes directly to the production manager with the request since the production manager owes the salesperson a favor. Other members of the sales force get word of this and become upset over this preferential treatment and report it to the sales manager. Obviously, the sales manager would know nothing of the deal, since he or she has been short-circuited. In some cases, however, going through formal channels is extremely costly or is impossible from a practical standpoint. Consider the impact on a hospital patient if a nurse had to report a critical malfunction in life support equipment to the nursing team leader, who in turn had to report it to the hospital engineer, who would instruct a staff engineer to make the repair.

Communication Overload

One of the vital tasks performed by a manager in decision making, and one of the necessary conditions for effective decisions, is *information*.[27] Because of the advances in communication technology, the difficulty is not in generating information. In fact, the last decade often has been described as the "Information Era" or the "Age of Information." Managers often feel buried by the deluge of information and data to which they are exposed, and they cannot absorb or adequately respond to all of the messages directed to them. They "screen out" the majority of messages, which in effect means that these messages are never decoded. Thus, the area of organizational communication is one in which more is not always better. When Connecticut Bank and Trust Company surveyed its employees, it discovered that 40 percent of them were dissatisfied with the bank's internal communications. One major problem was communication overload in the form of too many memos. New guidelines were adopted which significantly improved employee satisfaction with communications while decreasing the number of memos sent by 57 percent.

The barriers to communication that have been discussed here, while common, are by no means the only ones. Examining each barrier indicates that they are either within individuals (e.g., frame of reference, value judgments) or within organizations (e.g., in-group language, filtering). This point is important because attempts to improve communication must, of necessity, focus on changing people and/or changing the organization structure.

IMPROVING COMMUNICATION IN ORGANIZATIONS

Managers striving to become better communicators have two separate tasks they must accomplish. First, they must improve their messages—the information they wish to transmit. Second, they must seek to improve their own understanding of what other people are trying to communicate to them. As organizations become increasingly diverse, the opportunities for communication breakdowns will most likely increase. Before examining the general means that managers can use to improve communication, consult the Management Pointer which presents some very specific ways to improve communication in diverse organizations. The bottom-line of this final section of the chapter is that managers must become better encoders and decoders. They must strive not only to be understood but also to understand. The techniques discussed here can contribute to accomplishing these two important tasks.

Organizational Encounter 5-4 on organizational communications illustrates that the company talk show can help employees identify more strongly with the firm.

MANAGEMENT POINTER 5–1

IMPROVING COMMUNICATION IN DIVERSE ORGANIZATIONS

Take a proactive approach to improve communications in a diverse organization. The following are successful ideas that have been implemented successfully in such organizations as Avon, Apple Computer, Digital Equipment, and Prudential Insurance.

1. Encourage employees to organize cultural communication networks. These networks help new employees adjust, arrange cultural events, and provide feedback to management.

2. Consider establishing a managerial position, the responsibility of which includes developing and overseeing multicultural and affirmative action programs.

3. Institute a mentor program whereby new minority employees are introduced to the company culture.

4. Celebrate cultural events such as Black History Month and Hispanic Heritage Week.

5. Conduct diversity-management workshops which allow managers to explore the meaning of being a minority in a majority society.

ORGANIZATIONAL ENCOUNTER 5–4

THE COMPANY TALK SHOW

It's 11am on a Wednesday, and Dan Hunt, president of Caribbean and Latin American operations for Nortel Networks, is live and on the air! Seated behind a stage-prop desk in the company's South Florida TV studio, the slender, articulate executive stares into a camera as he fields questions from Nortel employees - an audience every bit as tough as any that shows up for taping of The Tonight Show. A caller from Mexico wants to know the implications of a joint venture between Nortel rivals Motorola and Cisco. Hunt delivers a detailed answer. Someone asks about the new competitive threat posed by Lucent Technologies. After taking a breath, Hunt answers. Next comes a query about Nortel's new branding strategy. Hunt smiles and defers to the host of this corporate talk show, Emma Carrasco, vice president of marketing and communications, whom Hunt laughingly introduces as 'the mistress of all branding.'

Hunt isn't your standard talk-show guest. And this isn't your standard TV talk show. But it is an important corporate conversation. Once a month, Hunt and Carrasco broadcast the "Virtual Leadership Academy," an hour-long program that presents company spin and in-depth, highly usable information in an interactive, talk-show format. This morning's audience, consisting of 2,000 employees in 40 countries, has been treated to a conversational stew featuring industry news, a surprisingly interesting discussion of international tax strategy, and a chance to pepper Hunt and other Nortel executives with direct questions about the company and its competitors-all from the comfort of their regional offices. "We're always looking for ways to break down barriers in the company, and people are comfortable with the talk-show format," says Carrasco, who designed the program to tap into what she calls the "talk-show culture" of her audience. "People watch talk shows in every country in the region, and they've learned that it's okay to say what's on their minds. In fact, it's expected."

Nortel isn't the only company that is borrowing from talk-show culture to improve internal communication. Breaking the centuries-old convention of one-way, top-down, rigidly formulaic corporate monologues, smart organizations are experimenting with new, more interactive, less formal modes of talking to-and listening to-employees and customers. Not every company takes the talk-show model as literally as Nortel does - with its set, its TelePrompTers, and its commercial breaks. But at a time when all kinds of other boundaries in business are being bent, blended, and broken, the new metaphor for corporate communication is best described as "edutainment": the company as talk-show.

Think about it. In the Information Age, organizations that succeed are those that can quickly and effectively communicate critical knowledge to their constituents. And the best way to do that? Traditional top-down communication techniques-from shotgun memos to routinized meetings to heavily touted "knowledge management" systems - seem either heavily bureaucratic or unnecessarily technocentric. In the workplace, rigid hierarchies are giving way to informality and networks-which is another way of saying that relationships: between management and workers, between colleagues and, of course, between a company and its customers. And how do you build deep, valuable, personal relationships? Not through formal memos and structured meetings, but through repeated personal contact. Through informal contact. Through talk.

Following Up

Following up involves assuming that you are misunderstood and, whenever possible, attempting to determine whether your intended meaning actually was received. As we have seen, meaning often is in the mind of the receiver. An accounting unit leader in a government office passes on to staff members notices of openings in other agencies. While longtime employees may understand this as a friendly gesture, a new employee might interpret it as an evaluation of poor performance and a suggestion to leave.

Regulating Information Flow

The regulation of communication can ensure an optimum flow of information to managers, thereby eliminating the barrier of "communication overload." Communication is regulated in terms of both quality and quantity. The idea is based on the **exception principle** of management, *which states that only significant deviations from policies and procedures should be brought to the attention of superiors.* In terms of formal communication, then, superiors should be communicated with only on matters of exception and not for the sake of communication.

Utilizing Feedback

Earlier in the chapter, feedback was identified as an important element in effective two-way communication. It provides a channel for receiver response that enables the communicator to determine whether the message has been received and has produced the intended response.[28]

In face-to-face communication, direct feedback is possible. In downward communication, however, inaccuracies often occur because of insufficient opportunity for feedback from receivers. A memorandum addressing an important policy statement may be distributed to all employees, but this does not guarantee that communication has occurred. You might expect that feedback in the form of upward communication would be encouraged more in organic organizations, but the mechanisms discussed earlier that can be utilized to encourage upward communication are found in many different organization designs.

Empathy

Empathy involves being receiver-oriented rather than communicator-oriented. The form of the communication should depend largely on what is known about the receiver. Empathy requires communicators to place themselves in the shoes of the receiver in order to anticipate how the message is likely to be decoded. Empathy is the ability to put oneself in the other person's role and to assume that individual's viewpoints and emotions. Remember that the greater the gap between the experiences and background of the communicator and the receiver, the greater is the effort that must be made to find a common ground of understanding—where there are overlapping fields of experience.

Repetition

Repetition is an accepted principle of learning. Introducing repetition or redundancy into communication (especially that of a technical nature) ensures that if one part of the message is not understood, other parts will carry the same message. New employees often are provided with the same basic information in several different forms when first joining an organization. Likewise, students receive much redundant information when first entering a university. This is to ensure that registration procedures, course requirements, and new terms such as matriculation and quality points are communicated.

Encouraging Mutual Trust

We know that time pressures often negate the possibility that managers will be able to follow up communication and encourage feedback or upward communication every time they communicate. Under such circumstances, an atmosphere of mutual confidence and trust between managers and their subordinates can facilitate communication. Managers who develop a climate of trust will find that following up on each communication is less critical and that no loss in understanding will result among subordinates from a failure to follow up on each communication. This is because they have fostered high "source credibility" among subordinates.

Effective Timing

Individuals are exposed to thousands of messages daily. Many of these messages are never decoded and received because of the impossibility of taking them all in. It is important for managers to note that, while they are attempting to communicate with a receiver, other messages are being received simultaneously. Thus, the message that managers send may not be "heard." Messages are more likely to be understood when they are not competing with other messages.[29] On an everyday basis, effective communication can be facilitated by properly timing major announcements. The barriers discussed earlier often are the result of poor timing that results in distortions and value judgments.

Simplifying Language

Complex language has been identified as a major barrier to effective communication. Students often suffer when their teachers use technical jargon that transforms simple concepts into complex puzzles. Universities are not the only place where this occurs, however. Government agencies are also known for their often-incomprehensible communications. We already have noted instances where professional people use in-group language in attempting to communicate with individuals outside their group. Managers must remember that effective communication involves transmitting understanding as well as information. If the receiver does not understand, then there has been no communication. Managers must encode messages in words, appeals, and symbols that are meaningful to the receiver.

Using the Grapevine

The grapevine is an important information communication channel that exists in all organizations. It basically serves as a bypassing mechanism, and in many cases it is faster than the formal system it bypasses. The grapevine has been aptly described in the following manner: "With the rapidity of a burning train, it filters out of the woodwork, past the manager's office, through the locker room, and along the corridors." Because it is flexible and usually involves face-to-face communication, the grapevine transmits information rapidly. The resignation of an executive may be common knowledge long before it is officially announced.

On the other hand, the grapevine is not a formal channel of communications. Thus, there are those who believe that managers should avoid using the grapevine because to not do so borders on being unethical as well as potentially dangerous. The You Be the Judge examines the very real issue of what to do about the grapevine.

Promoting Ethical Communications

It is incumbent upon organizational members to deal ethically with one another in their communication transactions. Kreps postulates three broad principles which are applicable to internal organizational communications.[30] The first is that organizational members should not intentionally deceive one another. This may not be as simple a principle to conform to as it may seem. While lying clearly violates it, is communicating less than you know to be true a breach of ethics? There is no hard and fast answer. The second principle is that organization members' communication should not purposely harm any other organization member. This is known as nonmalfeasance, or refraining from doing harm. Finally, organization members should be treated justly. This too can be difficult, for justice is a relative principle that must be evaluated in a specific context.

Gathering information, data, and ideas from competitors has become a big business. Is it ethical? Spying on someone or another business is distasteful to some, but the price of surviving is necessary to others. Some managers propose that if the law is not broken, gathering intelligence through reviewing memos, posing as a customer, surfing a competitor's Web site, listening carefully to comments, attending trade shows, and talking to loose-lipped employees is all about business.

There is no one method of gathering intelligence, but a number of tools are available. Web monitoring services (www.knowx.com), books, Internet links, and books provide communication that might be useful.[31]

Competitive intelligence—a system for gathering information (all forms of communication) that affects a firm, analyzing the data, and taking action—is becoming an accepted practice. Used properly and with concern for ethical behavior, competitive intelligence can speed a firm's reaction to changes, help outmaneuver competitors, and protect a firm's own secrets.

An example of an unethical practice of competitive intelligence was discovered by the Granite Island Group in Gloucester, Massachusetts. The firm sweeps offices for technical surveillance devices. The firm found a videoconferencing camera that timed itself on and recorded a board meeting of a client. The investigators found that a rival competitor had set up a system to activate the camera remotely and look and listen in on the discussion.[32]

Competitive intelligence does not have to involve turning on cameras from a remote area. Listening to a rival's public statements, which is perfectly ethical, could reveal protected information. A West Coast provider of insurance in an interview gave information about a new wellness product. A Web-based monitoring service picked this information up. Competitors seized on the information and got to the market first with their own wellness protection policies.

In conclusion, it would be hard to find an aspect of a manager's job that does not involve communication. If everyone in the organization had common points of view, communicating would be easy. Unfortunately, this is not the case. Each member comes to the organization with a distinct personality, background, experience, and frame of reference. The structure of the organization itself influences status relationships and the distance levels between individuals, which in turn influence the ability of individuals to communicate.

WHAT TO DO ABOUT THE GRAPEVINE

There are those who believe that the grapevine—the gossip chain—is the speediest, most efficient channel of communication in an organization. Research also points out that it is accurate. At least 75 percent of the gossip that travels through the grapevine is said to be true. Thus, many believe that the grapevine is a very useful channel of communication and should, therefore, be utilized by managers. It can serve as an early warning system for employees, serving up bad news long before any formal announcements are made. It can promote closeness among employees allowing them to let off steam and alleviate stress. It provides managers the opportunity to float trial balloons (e.g., concerning a plan they're considering putting into action) and thus receive early indications of peoples' reactions. Finally, it can serve as a medium for building and maintaining a firm's culture. Via gossip, the company war stories and those stories that communicate the firm's values can be told.

On the other hand, there are those who believe that the grapevine carries a very costly downside—a negative impact on productivity. The argument is that gossip takes time and saps employee morale. While 75 percent of the grapevine gossip may be true, it is the remaining 25 percent that carries false and destructive rumors that employees spend costly time worrying about. As a result, managers spend a disproportionate amount of time dealing with situations caused by rumor and gossip, not reality. Managers may also be held personally liable for defamation as a result of workplace conversations that may disclose confidential information or start rumors. Finally, while managers have used the grapevine for years as an early warning system or break-it-to-them gently tool, it can no longer even serve in this capacity in many organizations because younger employees disbelieve all company communication, whether by official memo or gossip.

Because the grapevine is not likely to go away, it is important for management not to ignore it. What is your opinion of the grapevine as a communication tool for managers?

Source: "Who Pruned the Grapevine?" Across the Board, March 1997, pp. 55–56; M. K. Zackary, "The Office Grapevine: A Legal Noose?" Getting Results, August 1996, pp. 6–7; M. M. Kennedy, "The Unkindest Cut," Across the Board, June 1996, pp. 53–54; and G. J. Modic, "Grapevine Rated Most Believable," Industry Week, May 15, 1989, pp. 11–12.

In this chapter we have tried to convey the basic elements in the process of communication and what it takes to communicate effectively. These elements are necessary whether the communication is face-to-face or written and communicated vertically, horizontally, or diagonally within an organizational structure.

We discussed several common communication barriers and several means to improve communication. Figure 5-3 illustrates the means that can be used to facilitate more-effective communication. We realize that often there is not enough time to utilize many of the techniques for improving communication and that skills such as empathy and effective listening are not easy to develop. The figure does, however, illustrate the challenge of communicating effectively, and it suggests what is required. Figure 5-3 shows that communicating is a matter of transmitting and receiving. Managers must be effective at both. They must understand as well as be understood.

FIGURE 5–3

IMPROVING COMMUNICATIONS IN ORGANIZATIONS: (Narrowing the Communication Gap)

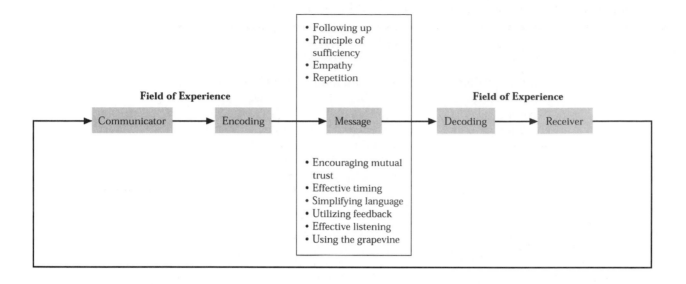

SUMMARY OF KEY CONCEPTS

1. Communication is one of the vital processes that breathe life into an organizational structure. The process contains five elements: the communicator who initiates the communication; the message, which is the result of encoding and which expresses the purpose of the communicator; the medium, which is the channel or carrier used for transmitting the message; the receiver for whom the message is intended; and feedback, a mechanism that allows the communicator to determine whether the message has been received and understood.

2. Communication flow moves in one of four directions. Downward communications are the most common, and include job instructions, procedures, and policies. An upward flow can be just as important, and may involve the use of suggestion boxes, group meetings, or grievance procedures. Horizontal and diagonal communications serve an important coordinative function.

3. Information technologies such as e-mails, voice mails, videoconferencing, and electronic meetings are becoming common in organizations of all sizes. Caution must be taken in how, when, and where these technologies are used.

4. Interpersonal communication is that which flows from individual to individual in face-to-face and group settings. In addition to providing needed information, interpersonal communication can also influence how people feel about the organization and its members. Interpersonal style is a term used to describe the way an individual prefers to relate to others in interpersonal communication situations.

5. In the international business environment of today, needing to communicate with members of other cultures is becoming commonplace. In addition to obvious language problems, different cultural customs, values, and perspectives can serve to complicate effective communications. A significant barrier is ethnocentrism, which is the tendency to consider the values of one's own country superior to those of other countries.

6. There are numerous barriers to effective communication. Among the more significant are frame of reference, selective listening, value judgments, source credibility, filtering, in-group language, status differences, time pressures, and communication overload.

7. Improving organizational communications is an ongoing process. Specific techniques for doing this include following up, regulating information flow, utilizing feedback, empathy, repetition, encouraging mutual trust, effective timing, simplifying language, effective listening, using the grapevine, and promoting ethical communications.

KEY TERMS

communication	feedback loop	nonverbal messages
communicator	filtering	receiver
decoding	medium	selective listening
encoding	message	source credibility
exception principle	noise	value judgements

DISCUSSION QUESTIONS

1. Can you think of a communication transaction you have been part of when an encoding or decoding error was made? Why did it happen, and what could have been done to avoid it?

2. Why do you think that downward communication is much more prevalent in organizations than upward communication? How easy would it be to change this?

3. Some claim that e-mail can take so much time reading and replying to that they are actually a drain on productivity. Do you agree? Why?

4. In your experience, which of the barriers to effective communication discussed in the chapter is responsible for the most communication problems? Which barrier is the hardest to correct?

5. Similarly, in your experience, which of the techniques for improving communication discussed in the chapter would solve the greatest number of problems? Which technique is the most difficult to put into practice?

6. Can you think of reasons why some individuals might prefer one-way communications when they are the sender, and two-way when they are the receiver? Explain.

7. A study once revealed that 55 percent of our communication time is spent transmitting and 45 percent is spent receiving. If true, what are the implications of this finding?

8. "Organizations should be less concerned with improving communication than with reducing the volume of information they disseminate to employees." Do you agree or disagree with this statement? Explain.

9. How does communication affect the interpersonal influence topics discussed?

10. Have you ever been in a cross-cultural communication situation? How effective was it? What was the most difficult aspect of the situation?

READING 5.1 Active Listening

Carl B. Rogers
Richard E. Farson
Source: Reprinted by permission of the Industrial Relations Center, The University of Chicago.

THE MEANING OF ACTIVE LISTENING

One basic responsibility of the supervisor or executive is the development, adjustment, and integration of individual employees. He tries to develop employee potential, delegate responsibility, and achieve cooperation. To do so, he must have, among other abilities, the ability to listen intelligently and carefully to those with whom he works. There are, however, many kinds of listening skills. The lawyer, for example, when questioning a witness, listens for contradictions, irrelevancies, errors, and weaknesses. But this is not the kind of listening skill we are concerned with. The lawyer usually is not listening in order to help the witness adjust or cooperate or produce. On the other hand, we will be concerned with listening skills which will help employees gain a clearer understanding of their situations, take responsibility, and cooperate with each other.

TWO EXAMPLES

The kind of listening we have in mind is called active listening. It is called active because the listener has a very definite responsibility. He does not passively absorb the words which are spoken to him. He actively tries to grasp the facts and the feelings in what he hears, and he tries, by his listening, to help the speaker work out his own problems.

To get a fuller picture of what is meant by active listening, let us consider two different approaches to the same work problem.

Example No. 1

FOREMAN: Hey, Al, I don't get this production order. We can't handle this run today. What do they think we are?

SUPERVISOR: But that's the order. So get it out as soon as you can. We're under terrific pressure this week.

FOREMAN: Don't they know we're behind schedule already because of that press breakdown?

SUPERVISOR: Look, Kelly, I don't decide what goes on upstairs. I just have to see that the work gets out, and that's what I'm gonna do.

FOREMAN: The guys aren't gonna like this.

SUPERVISOR: That's something you'll have to work out with them not me.

Example No. 2

FOREMAN: Hey, Ross, I don't get this production order. We can't handle this run today. What do they think we are?

SUPERVISOR: Sounds like you are pretty sore about it, Kelly.

FOREMAN: I sure am. We were just about getting back to schedule after that press breakdown. Now this comes along.

SUPERVISOR: As if you didn't have enough work to do, huh?

FOREMAN: Yeah, I don't know how I'm gonna tell the guys about this.

SUPERVISOR: Hate to face 'em with it now, is that it?

FOREMAN: I really do. They're under a real strain today. Seems like everything we do around here is rush, rush.

SUPERVISOR: I guess you feel like it's unfair to load anything more on them.

FOREMAN: Well, yeah, I know there must be plenty of pressure on everybody up the line, but—well, if
                that's the way it is—guess I'd better get the word to 'em.

There are obviously many differences between these two examples. The main one, however, is that Ross,
the supervisor in the second example, is using the active-listening approach. He is listening and responding in a
way that makes it clear that he appreciates both the meaning and the feeling behind what Kelly is saying.

Active listening does not necessarily mean long sessions spent listening to grievances, personal or otherwise.
It is simply a way of approaching those problems which arise out of the usual day-to-day events of any job.

To be effective, active listening must be firmly grounded in the basic attitudes of the user. We cannot employ
it as a technique if our fundamental attitudes are in conflict with its basic concepts. If we try, our behavior will
be empty and sterile, and our associates will be quick to recognize this. Until we can demonstrate a spirit which
genuinely respects the potential worth of the individual, which considers his rights and trusts his capacity for
self-direction, we cannot begin to be effective listeners.

WHAT WE ACHIEVE BY LISTENING

Active listening is an important way to bring about changes in people. Despite the popular notion that listening
is a passive approach, clinical and research evidence clearly shows that sensitive listening is a most effective
agent for individual personality change and group development. Listening brings about changes in people's
attitudes toward themselves and others; it also brings about changes in their basic values and personal philosophy.
People who have been listened to in this new and special way become more emotionally mature, more open to
their experiences, less defensive, more democratic, and less authoritarian.

When people are listened to sensitively, they tend to listen to themselves with more care and to make clear
exactly what they are feeling and thinking. Group members tend to listen more to each other, to become less
argumentative, more ready to incorporate other points of view. Because listening reduces the threat of having
one's ideas criticized, the person is better able to see them for what they are and is more able to feel that his
contributions are worthwhile.

Not the least important result of listening is the change that takes place with the listener himself. Besides
providing more information than any other activity, listening builds deep, positive relationships and tends to
alter constructively the attitudes of the listener. Listening is a growth experience.

These, then, are some of the worthwhile results we can expect from active listening. But how do we go about
this kind of listening? How do we become active listeners?

HOW TO LISTEN

Active listening aims to bring about changes in people. To achieve this end, it relies upon definite techniques—
things to do and things to avoid doing. Before discussing these techniques, however, we should first understand
why they are effective. To do so, we must understand how the individual personality develops.

The Growth of the Individual

Through all of our lives, from early childhood on, we have learned to think of ourselves in certain very definite
ways. We have built up pictures of ourselves. Sometimes these self-pictures are pretty realistic, but at other
times they are not. For example, an overage, overweight lady may fancy herself as a youthful, ravishing siren, or
an awkward teenager regard himself as a star athlete.

All of us have experiences which fit the way we need to think about ourselves. These we accept. But it is
much harder to accept experiences which don't fit. And sometimes, if it is very important for us to hang on to
this self-picture, we don't accept or admit these experiences at all.

These self-pictures are not necessarily attractive. A man, for example, may regard himself as incompetent
and worthless. He may feel that he is doing his job poorly in spite of favorable appraisals by the company. As
long as he has these feelings about himself, he must deny any experiences which would seem not to fit this self-
picture—in case any might indicate to him that he is competent. It is so necessary for him to maintain this self-

picture that he is threatened by anything which would tend to change it. Thus, when the company raises his salary, it may seem to him only additional proof that he is a fraud. He must hold on to this self-picture because, bad or good, it's the only thing he has by which he can identify himself.

This is why direct attempts to change this individual or change his self-picture are particularly threatening. He is forced to defend himself or to completely deny the experience. This denial of experience and defense of the self-picture tend to bring on rigidity of behavior and create difficulties in personal adjustment.

The active-listening approach, on the other hand, does not present a threat to the individual's self-picture. He does not have to defend it. He is able to explore it, see it for what it is, and make his own decision about how realistic it is. And he is then in a position to change.

If I want to help a man reduce his defensiveness and become more adaptive, I must try to remove the threat of myself as his potential changer. As long as the atmosphere is threatening, there can be no effective communication. So I must create a climate which is neither critical, evaluative, nor moralizing. It must be an atmosphere of equality and freedom, permissiveness and understanding, acceptance and warmth. It is in this climate and this climate only that the individual feels safe enough to incorporate new experiences and new values into his concept of himself. Let's see how active listening helps to create this climate.

What to Avoid

When we encounter a person with a problem, our usual response is to try to change his way of looking at things—to get him to see his situation the way we see it or would like to see it. We plead, reason, scold, encourage, insult, prod—anything to bring about a change in the desired direction, that is, in the direction we want him to travel. What we seldom realize, however, is that, under these circumstances, we are usually responding to our own needs to see the world in certain ways. It is always difficult for us to tolerate and understand actions which are different from the ways in which we believe we should act. If, however, we can free ourselves from the need to influence and direct others in our own paths, we enable ourselves to listen with understanding and thereby employ the most potent available agent of change.

One problem the listener faces is that of responding to demands for decisions, judgments, and evaluations. He is constantly called upon to agree or disagree with someone or something. Yet, as he well knows, the question or challenge frequently is a masked expression of feelings or needs which the speaker is far more anxious to communicate than he is to have the surface questions answered. Because he cannot speak these feelings openly, the speaker must disguise them to himself and to others in an acceptable form. To illustrate, let us examine some typical questions and the types of answers that might best elicit the feelings beneath them.

These responses recognize the questions but leave the way open for the employee to say what is really bothering him. They allow the listener to participate in the problem or situation without shouldering all responsibility for decision making or actions. This is a process of thinking with people instead of for or about them.

Passing judgment, whether critical or favorable, makes free expression difficult. Similarly, advice and information are almost always seen as efforts to change a person and thus serve as barriers to his self-expression and the development of a creative relationship. Moreover, advice is seldom taken and information hardly ever utilized. The eager young trainee probably will not become patient just because he is advised that "the road to success in business is a long, difficult one, and you must be patient." And it is no more helpful for him to learn that "only one out of a hundred trainees reaches a top management position."

Interestingly, it is a difficult lesson to learn that positive evaluations are sometimes as blocking as negative ones. It is almost as destructive to the freedom of a relationship to tell a person that he is good or capable or right, as to tell him otherwise. To evaluate him positively may make it more difficult for him to tell of the faults that distress him or the ways in which he believes he is not competent.

Encouragement also may be seen as an attempt to motivate the speaker in certain directions or hold him off, rather than as support. "I'm sure everything will work out O.K." is not a helpful response to the person who is deeply discouraged about a problem.

In other words, most of the techniques and devices common to human relationships are found to be of little use in establishing the type of relationship we are seeking here.

What to Do

Just what does active listening entail, then? Basically, it requires that we get inside the speaker, that we grasp, from his point of view, just what it is he is communicating to us. More than that, we must convey to the speaker that we are seeing things from his point of view. To listen actively, then means that there are several things we must do.

Listen for Total Meaning

Any message a person tries to get across usually has two components: the content of the message and the feeling or attitude underlying this content. Both are important; both give the message meaning. It is this total meaning of the message that we try to understand. For example, a machinist comes to his foreman and says, "I've finished that lathe setup." This message has obvious content and perhaps calls upon the foreman for another work assignment. Suppose, on the other hand, that he says, "Well, I'm finally finished with that damned lathe setup." The content is the same, but the total meaning of the message has changed—and changed in an important way for both the foreman and the worker. Here, sensitive listening can facilitate the relationship. Suppose the foreman were to respond by simply giving another work assignment. Would the employee feel that he had gotten his total message across? Would he feel free to talk to his foreman? Will he feel better about his job, more anxious to do good work on the next assignment?

Now, on the other hand, suppose the foreman were to respond with, "Glad to have it over with, huh?" or "Had a pretty rough time of it?" or "Guess you don't feel like doing anything like that again," or anything else that tells the worker that he heard and understands. It doesn't necessarily mean that the next work assignment need be changed or that he must spend an hour listening to the worker complain about the setup problems he encountered. He may do a number of things differently in the light of the new information he has from the worker—but not necessarily. It's just that extra sensitivity on the part of the foreman which can transform an average working climate into a good one.

Respond to Feelings

In some instances, the content is far less important than the feeling which underlies it. To catch the full flavor or meaning of the message, one must respond particularly to the feeling component. If, for instance, our machinist had said, "I'd like to melt this lathe down and make paper clips out of it," responding to content would be obviously absurd. But to respond to his disgust or anger in trying to work with his lathe recognizes the meaning of this message. There are various shadings of these components in the meaning of any message. Each time, the listener must try to remain sensitive to the total meaning the message has to the speaker. What is he trying to tell me? What does this mean to him? How does he see this situation?

Not All Cues

Not all communication is verbal. The speaker's words alone don't tell us everything he is communicating. And hence, truly sensitive listening requires that we become aware of several kinds of communication besides verbal. The way in which a speaker hesitates in his speech can tell us much about his feelings. So, too, can the inflection of his voice. He may stress certain points loudly and clearly and may mumble others. We should also note such things as the person's facial expressions, body posture, hand movements, eye movements, and breathing. All of these help to convey his total message.

WHAT WE COMMUNICATE BY LISTENING

The first reaction of most people when they consider listening as a possible method for dealing with human beings is that listening cannot be sufficient in itself. Because it is passive, they feel, listening does not communicate anything to the speaker. Actually, nothing could be farther from the truth.

By consistently listening to a speaker, you are conveying the idea that: "I'm interested in you as a person, and I think that what you feel is important. I respect your thoughts, and even if I don't agree with them, I know that they are valid for you. I feel sure that you have a contribution to make. I'm not trying to change or evaluate you. I just want to understand you. I think you're worth listening to, and I want you to know that I'm the kind of a person you can talk to."

The subtle but most important aspect of this is that it is the demonstration of the message that works. While it is most difficult to convince someone that you respect him by telling him so, you are much more likely to get this message across by really behaving that way—by actually having and demonstrating respect for this person. Listening does this most effectively.

Like other behavior, listening behavior is contagious. This has implications for all communication problems, whether between two people or within a large organization. To ensure good communication between associates up and down the line, one must first take the responsibility for setting a pattern of listening. Just as one learns that anger is usually met with anger, argument with argument, and deception with deception, one can learn that listening can be met with listening. Every person who feels responsibility in a situation can set the tone of the interaction, and the important lesson in this is that any behavior exhibited by one person will eventually be responded to with similar behavior in the other person.

It is far more difficult to stimulate constructive behavior in another person but far more profitable. Listening is one of these constructive behaviors, but if one's attitude is to "wait out" the speaker rather than really listen to him, it will fail. The one who consistently listens with understanding, however, is the one who eventually is most likely to be listened to. If you really want to be heard and understood by another, you can develop him as a potential listener, ready for new ideas, provided you can first develop yourself in these ways and sincerely listen with understanding and respect.

TESTING FOR UNDERSTANDING

Because understanding another person is actually far more difficult than it at first seems, it is important to test constantly your ability to see the world in the way the speaker sees it. You can do this by reflecting in your own words what the speaker seems to mean by his words and actions. His response to this will tell you whether or not he feels understood. A good rule of thumb is to assume that you never really understand until you can communicate this understanding to the other's satisfaction.

Here is an experiment to test your skill in listening. The next time you become involved in a lively or controversial discussion with another person, stop for a moment and suggest that you adopt this ground rule for continued discussion: Before either participant in the discussion can make a point or express an opinion of his own, he must first restate aloud the previous point or position of the other person. This restatement must be in his own words (merely parroting the words of another does not prove that one has understood but only that he has heard the words). The restatement must be accurate enough to satisfy the speaker before the listener can be allowed to speak for himself.

This is something you could try in your own discussion group. Have someone express himself on some topic of emotional concern to the group. Then, before another member expresses his own feelings and thought, he must rephrase the meaning expressed by the previous speaker to that individual's satisfaction. Note the changes in the emotional climate and in the quality of the discussion when you try this.

PROBLEMS IN ACTIVE LISTENING

Active listening is not an easy skill to acquire. It demands practice. Perhaps more important, it may require changes in our own basic attitudes. These changes come slowly and sometimes with considerable difficulty. Let us look at some of the major problems in active listening and what can be done to overcome them.

The Personal Risk

To be effective at all in active listening, one must have a sincere interest in the speaker. We all live in glass houses as far as our attitudes are concerned. They always show through. And if we are only making a pretense of interest in the speaker, he will quickly pick this up, either consciously or unconsciously. And once he does, he will no longer express himself freely.

Active listening carries a strong element of personal risk. If we manage to accomplish what we are describing here—to sense deeply the feeling of another person, to understand the meaning his experiences have for him, to see the world as he sees it—we risk being changed ourselves. For example, if we permit ourselves to listen our way into the psychological life of a labor leader or agitator—to get the meaning which has life for him—we risk coming to see the world as he sees it. It is threatening to give up, even momentarily, what we believe and start thinking in someone else's terms. It takes a great deal of inner security and courage to be able to risk one's self in understanding another.

For the supervisor, the courage to take another's point of view generally means that he must see himself through another's eyes—he must be able to see himself as others see him. To do this may sometimes be unpleasant, but it is far more difficult than unpleasant. We are so accustomed to viewing ourselves in certain ways—to seeing and hearing only what we want to see and hear—that it is extremely difficult for a person to free himself from his needs to see things these ways.

Developing an attitude of sincere interest in the speaker is thus no easy task. It can be developed only by being willing to risk seeing the world from the speaker's point of view. If we have a number of such experiences, however, they will shape an attitude which will allow us to be truly genuine in our interest in the speaker.

Hostile Expressions

The listener will often hear negative, hostile expressions directed at himself. Such expressions are always hard to listen to. No one likes to hear hostile words. And it is not easy to get to the point where one is strong enough to permit these attacks without finding it necessary to defend oneself or retaliate.

Because we all fear that people will crumble under the attack of genuine negative feelings, we tend to perpetuate an attitude of pseudo peace. It is as if we cannot tolerate conflict at all for fear of the damage it could do to us, to the situation, to the others involved. But of course the real damage is done to all these by the denial and suppression of negative feelings.

Out-of-Place Expressions

There is also the problem of out-of-place expressions—expressions dealing with behavior which is not usually acceptable in our society. In the extreme forms that present themselves before psychotherapists, expressions of sexual perversity or homicidal fantasies are often found blocking to the listener because of their obvious threatening quality. At less extreme levels, we all find unnatural or inappropriate behavior difficult to handle. That is, anything from an off-color story told in mixed company to a man weeping is likely to produce a problem situation.

In any face-to-face situation, we will find instances of this type which will momentarily, if not permanently, block any communication. In business and industry, any expressions of weakness or incompetency will generally be regarded as unacceptable and therefore will block good two-way communication. For example, it is difficult to listen to a supervisor tell of his feelings of failure in being able to "take charge" of a situation in his department, because all administrators are supposed to be able to "take charge."

Accepting Positive Feelings

It is both interesting and perplexing to note that negative or hostile feelings or expressions are much easier to deal with in any face-to-face relationship than are truly and deeply positive feelings. This is especially true for the businessman, because the culture expects him to be independent, bold, clever, and aggressive and manifest no feelings of warmth, gentleness, and intimacy. He therefore comes to regard these feelings as soft and inappropriate. But no matter how they are regarded, they remain a human need. The denial of these feelings in himself and his associates does not get the executive out of the problem of dealing with them. They simply become veiled and confused. If recognized, they would work for the total effort; unrecognized, they work against it.

EMOTIONAL DANGER SIGNALS

The listener's own emotions are sometimes a barrier to active listening. When emotions are at their height, which is when listening is most necessary, it is most difficult to set aside one's own concerns and be understanding. Our emotions are often our own worst enemies when we try to become listeners. The more involved and invested we are in a particular situation or problem, the less we are likely to be willing or able to listen to the feelings and attitudes of others. That is, the more we find it necessary to respond to our own needs, the less we are able to respond to the needs of another. Let us look at some of the main danger signals that warn us that our emotions may be interfering with our listening.

Defensiveness

The points about which one is most vocal and dogmatic, the points which one is most anxious to impose on others—these are always the points one is trying to talk oneself into believing. So one danger signal becomes apparent when you find yourself stressing a point or trying to convince another. It is at these times that you are likely to be less secure and consequently less able to listen.

Resentment of Opposition

It is always easier to listen to an idea which is similar to one of your own than to an opposing view. Sometimes, in order to clear the air, it is helpful to pause for a moment when you feel your ideas and position being challenged, reflect on the situation, and express your concern to the speaker.

Clash of Personalities

Here again, our experience has consistently shown us that the genuine expression of feelings on the part of the listener will be more helpful in developing a sound relationship than the suppression of them. This is so whether the feelings be resentment, hostility, threat, or admiration. A basically honest relationship, whatever the nature of it, is the most productive of all. The other party becomes secure when he learns that the listener can express his feelings honestly and openly to him. We should keep this in mind when we begin to fear a clash of personalities in the listening relationship. Otherwise, fear of our own emotions will choke off full expression of feelings.

LISTENING TO OURSELVES

To listen to oneself is a prerequisite for listening to others. And it is often an effective means of dealing with the problems we have outlined above. When we are most aroused, excited, and demanding, we are least able to understand our own feelings and attitudes. Yet, in dealing with the problems of others, it becomes most important to be sure of one's own position, values, and needs.

The ability to recognize and understand the meaning which a particular episode has for you, with all the feelings which it stimulates in you, and the ability to express the meaning when you find it getting in the way of active listening will clear the air and enable you once again to be free to listen. That is, if some person or situation touches off feelings within you which tend to block your attempts to listen with understanding, begin listening to yourself. It is much more helpful in developing effective relationships to avoid suppressing these feelings. Speak them out as clearly as you can and try to enlist the other person as a listener to your feelings. A person's listening ability is limited by his ability to listen to himself.

ACTIVE LISTENING AND COMPANY GOALS

How can listening improve production?

We're in business, and it's a rugged, fast, competitive affair. How are we going to find time to counsel our employees?

We have to concern ourselves with organizational problems first.

We can't afford to spend all day listening when there's a job to be done.

What's morale got to do with production?

Sometimes we have to sacrifice an individual for the good of the rest of the people in the company.

Those of us who are trying to advance the listening approach in industry hear these comments frequently. And because they are so honest and legitimate, they pose a real problem. Unfortunately, the answers are not so clear-cut as the questions.

INDIVIDUAL IMPORTANCE

One answer is based on an assumption that is central to the listening approach. That assumption is: The kind of behavior which helps the individual will eventually be the best thing that could be done for the group. Or saying it another way: The things that are best for the individual are best for the company. This is a conviction of ours, based on our experience in psychology and education. The research evidence from industry is only beginning to come in. We find that putting the group first, at the expense of the individual, besides being an uncomfortable individual experience, does not unify the group. In fact, it tends to make the group less a group. The members become anxious and suspicious.

We are not at all sure in just what ways the group does benefit from a concern demonstrated for an individual, but we have several strong leads. One is that the group feels more secure when an individual is being listened to and provided for with concern and sensitivity. And we assume that a secure group will ultimately be a better group. When each individual feels that he need not fear exposing himself to the group, he is likely to contribute more freely and spontaneously. When the leader of a group responds to the individual, puts the individual first, the other members of the group will follow suit and the group will come to act as a unit in recognizing and responding to the needs of a particular member. This positive, constructive action seems to be a much more satisfying experience for a group than the experience of dispensing with a member.

LISTENING AND PRODUCTION

Whether listening or any other activity designed to better human relations in an industry actually raises production—whether morale has a definite relationship to production—is not known for sure. There are some who frankly hold that there is no relationship to be expected between morale and production—that the production often depends upon the social misfit, the eccentric, or the isolate. And there are some who simply choose to work in a climate of cooperation and harmony, in a high-morale group, quite aside from the question of increased production.

A report from the Survey Research Center[33] at the University of Michigan on research conducted at the Prudential Life Insurance Company lists seven findings relating to production and morale. First-line supervisors in high-production work groups were found to differ from those in low-production work groups in that they:

1. Are under less close supervision from their own supervisors.

2. Place less direct emphasis upon production as the goal.

3. Encourage employee participation in the making of decisions.

4. Are more employee-centered.

5. Spend more of their time in supervision and less in straight production work.

6. Have a greater feeling of confidence in their supervisory roles.

7. Feel that they know where they stand with the company.

After mentioning that other dimensions of morale, such as identification with the company, intrinsic job satisfaction, and satisfaction with job status, were not found significantly related to productivity, the report goes on to suggest the following psychological interpretation:

People are more effectively motivated when they are given some degree of freedom in the way in which they do their work than when every action is prescribed in advance. They do better when some degree of decision making about their jobs is possible than when all decisions are made for them. They respond more adequately when they are treated as personalities than as cogs in a machine. In short, if the ego motivations of self-determination, or self-expression, of a sense of personal worth can be tapped, the individual can be more effectively energized. The use of external sanctions or pressuring for production may work to some degree, but not to the extent that the more internalized motives do. When the individual comes to identify himself with his job and with the work of his group, human resources are much more fully utilized in the production process.

The Survey Research Center has also conducted studies among workers in other industries. In discussing the results of these studies, Robert L. Kahn writes:

> In the studies of clerical workers, railroad workers, and workers in heavy industry, the supervisors with the better production records gave a larger proportion of their time to supervisory functions, especially the interpersonal aspects of their jobs. The supervisors of the lower-producing sections were more likely to spend their time in tasks which the men themselves were performing, or in the paperwork aspects of their jobs.[34]

MAXIMUM CREATIVENESS

There may never be enough research evidence to satisfy everyone on this question. But speaking from a business point of view, in terms of the problem of developing resources for production, the maximum creativeness and productive effort of the human beings in the organization are the richest untapped source of power still existing. The difference between the maximum productive capacity of people and that output which industry is now realizing is immense. We simply suggest that this maximum capacity might be closer to realization if we sought to release the motivation that already exists within people rather than try to stimulate them externally.

This releasing of the individual is made possible, first of all, by sensitive listening, with respect and understanding. Listening is a beginning toward making the individual feel himself worthy of making contributions, and this could result in a very dynamic and productive organization. Competitive business is never too rugged or too busy to take time to procure the most efficient technological advances or to develop rich raw-material resources. But these in comparison to the resources that are already within the people in the plant are paltry. This is industry's major procurement problem.

G. L. Clemens, president of Jewel Tea Co., Inc., in talking about the collaborative approach to management, says:

> We feel that this type of approach recognizes that there is a secret ballot going on at all times among the people in any business. They vote for or against the supervisors. A favorable vote for the supervisor shows up in the cooperation, teamwork, understanding, and production of the group. To win this secret ballot, each supervisor must share the problems of his group and work for them.[35]

The decision to spend time listening to his employees is a decision each supervisor or executive has to make for himself. Executives seldom have much to do with products or processes. They have to deal with people who must in turn deal with people who will deal with products or processes. The higher one goes up the line, the more one will be concerned with human relations problems, simply because people are all one has to work with. The minute we take a man from his bench and make him a foreman, he is removed from the basic production of goods and now must begin relating to individuals instead of nuts and bolts. People are different from things, and our foreman is called upon for a different line of skills completely. His new tasks call upon him to be a special kind of person. The development of himself as a listener is a first step in becoming this special person.

EXERCISE 5.1 YOUR COMMUNICATION STYLE

To determine your preferred communication style, select the one alternative that most closely describes what you would do in each of the 12 situations below. Do not be concerned with trying to pick the correct answer; select the alternative that best describes what you would actually do. Circle the letter a, b, c, or d.

1. Wendy, a knowledgeable person from another department, comes to you, the engineering supervisor, and requests that you design a special product to her specifications. You would:
    a. Control the conversation and tell Wendy what you will do for her.
    b. Ask Wendy to describe the product. Once you understand it, you would present your ideas. Let her realize that you are concerned and want to help with your ideas.
    c. Respond to Wendy's request by conveying understanding and support. Help clarify what is to be done by you. Offer ideas, but do it her way.
    d. Find out what you need to know. Let Wendy know you will do it her way.

2. Your department has designed a product that is to be fabricated by Saul's department. Saul has been with the company longer than you have; he knows his department. Saul comes to you to change the product design. You decide to:
    a. Listen to the change and why it would be beneficial. If you believe Saul's way is better, change it; if not, explain why the original idea is superior. If necessary, insist that it be done your way.
    b. Tell Saul to fabricate it any way he wants to.
    c. You are busy; tell Saul to do it your way. You don't have the time to listen and agree with him.
    d. Be supportive; make changes together as a team.

3. Upper management has a decision to make. They call you to a meeting and tell you they need some information to solve a problem they describe to you. You:
    a. Respond in a manner that conveys personal support and offer alternative ways to solve the problem.
    b. Respond to their questions.
    c. Explain how to solve the problem.

    d. Show your concern by explaining how to solve the problem and why it is an effective solution.

4. You have a routine work order. The work order is to be replaced verbally and completed in three days. Sue, the receiver, is very experienced and willing to be of service to you. You decide to:
    a. Explain your needs, but let Sue make the other decisions.
    b. Tell Sue what you want and why you need it.
    c. Decide together what to order.
    d. Simply give Sue the order.

5. Work orders from the staff department normally take three days; however, you have an emergency and need the job today. Your colleague Jim, the department supervisor, is knowledgeable and somewhat cooperative. You decide to:
    a. Tell Jim that you need it by three o'clock and return at that time to pick it up.
    b. Explain the situation and how the organization will benefit by expediting the order. Volunteer to help any way you can.
    c. Explain the situation and ask Jim when the order will be ready.
    d. Explain the situation and together come to a solution to your problem.

6. Danielle, a peer with a record of high performance, has recently had a drop in productivity. Her problem is affecting her performance. You know Danielle has a family problem. You:
    a. Discuss the problem; help Danielle realize the problem is affecting her work and yours. Supportively discuss ways to improve the situation.
    b. Tell the boss about it and let him decide what to do about it.
    c. Tell Danielle to get back on the job.
    d. Discuss the problem and tell Danielle how to solve the work situation; be supportive.

7. You are a knowledgeable supervisor. You buy supplies from Peter regularly. He is an excellent salesperson and very knowledgeable about your situation. You are placing your weekly order. You decide to:
    a. Explain what you want and why: Develop a supportive relationship.
    b. Explain what you want and ask Peter to recommend products.
    c. Give Peter the order.
    d. Explain your situation and allow Peter to make the order.

8. Jean, a knowledgeable person from another department, has asked you to perform a routine staff function to her specifications. You decide to:
    a. Perform the task to her specification without questioning her.
    b. Tell her that you will do it the usual way.
    c. Explain what you will do and why.
    d. Show your willingness to help; offer alternative ways to do it.

9. Tom, a salesperson, has requested an order for your department's services with a short delivery date. As usual, Tom claims it is a take-it-or-leave-it offer. He wants your decision now, or within a few minutes, because he is in the customer's office. Your action is to:
    a. Convince Tom to work together to come up with a later date.
    b. Give Tom a yes or no answer.
    c. Explain your situation and let Tom decide if you should take the order.

10. As a time-and-motion expert, you have been called in regard to a complaint about the standard time it takes to perform a job. As you analyze the entire job, you realize the one element of complaint should take longer, but other elements should take less time. The end result is a shorter total standard time for the job. You decide to:
    a. Tell the operator and foreman that the total time must be decreased and why.
    b. Agree with the operator and increase the standard time.
    c. Explain your findings. Deal with the operator and/or foreman's concerns, but ensure compliance with your new standard.
    d. Together with the operator, develop a standard time.

11. You approve budget allocations for projects. Marie, who is very competent in developing budgets, has come to you. You:
    a. Review the budget, make revisions, and explain them in a supportive way. Deal with concerns, but insist on your changes
    b. Review the proposal and suggest areas where changes may be needed. Make changes together, if needed.
    c. Review the proposed budget, make revisions, and explain them.
    d. Answer any questions or concerns Marie has and approve the budget as is.

12. You are a sales manager. A customer has offered you a contract for your product with a short delivery date. The offer is open for days. The contract would be profitable for you and the organization. The cooperation of the production department is essential to meet the deadline. Tim, the production manager, and you do not get along very well because of your repeated requests for quick delivery. Your action is to:
    a. Contact Tim and try to work together to complete the contract.
    b. Accept the contract and convince Tim in a supportive way to meet the obligation.
    c. Contact Tim and explain the situation. Ask him if you and he should accept the contract, but let him decide.
    d. Accept the contract. Contact Tim and tell him to meet the obligation. If he resists, tell him you will go to the boss.

To determine your preferred communication style, in the chart below, circle the letter you selected as the alternative you chose in situations 1–12. The column headings indicate the style you selected.

	Autocratic	Consultative	Participative	Laissez-Faire
1.	a	b	c	d
2.	c	a	d	b
3.	c	d	a	b
4.	d	b	c	a
5.	a	b	d	c
6.	c	b	a	b
7.	c	a	b	d
8.	b	c	d	a
9.	b	d	a	c
10.	a	c	d	b
11.	c	a	b	d
12.	d	b	a	c

Total

CASE 5.1   THE ROAD TO HELL

John Baker, chief engineer of the Caribbean Bauxite Company Limited of Barracania in the West Indies, was making his final preparations to leave the island. His promotion to production manager of Keso Mining Corporation near Winnipeg—one of Continental Ore's fast-expanding Canadian enterprises—had been announced a month before, and now everything had been tidied up except the last vital interview with his successor, the able young Barracanian Matthew Rennalls. It was vital that this interview be a success and that Rennalls leave Baker's office uplifted and encouraged to face the challenge of his new job. A touch on the bell would have brought Rennalls walking into the room, but Baker delayed the moment and gazed thoughtfully through the window, considering just exactly what he was going to say and, more particularly, how he was going to say it.

Baker, an English expatriate, was 45 years old and had served his 23 years with Continental Ore in many different places: the Far East; several countries of Africa; Europe; and, for the last two years, the West Indies. He had not cared much for his previous assignment in Hamburg and was delighted when the West Indian appointment came through. Climate was not the only attraction. Baker had always preferred working overseas in what were called the developing countries because he felt he had an innate knack—more than most other expatriates working for Continental Ore—of knowing just how to get on with regional staff. Twenty-four hours in Barracania, however, soon made him realize that he would need all of his innate knack if he were to deal effectively with the problems in this field that now awaited him.

At his first interview with Glenda Hutchins, the production manager, the whole problem of Rennalls and his future was discussed. There and then it was made quite clear to Baker that one of his most important tasks would be the grooming of Rennalls as his successor. Hutchins had pointed out that not only was Rennalls one of the brightest Barracanian prospects on the staff of Caribbean Bauxite—at London University he had taken first-class honors in the B.Sc. engineering degree—but, being the son of the minister of finance and economic planning, he also had no small political pull.

Caribbean Bauxite had been particularly pleased when Rennalls decided to work for it rather than for the government in which his father had such a prominent post. The company ascribed his action to the effects of its vigorous and liberal regionalization program that, since World War II, had produced 18 Barracanians at the middle-management level and given Caribbean Bauxite a good lead in this respect over all other international concerns operating in Barracania. The success of this timely regionalization policy had led to excellent relations with the government—a relationship that gained added importance when Barracania, three years later, became independent, an occasion that encouraged a critical and challenging attitude toward the role foreign interest would have to play in the new Barracania. Hutchins, therefore, had little difficulty convincing Baker that the successful career development of Renalls was of the first importance.

The interview with Hutchins was now two years in the past, and Baker, leaning back in his office chair, reviewed just how successful he had been in the grooming of Rennalls. What aspects of the latter's character had helped, and what had hindered? What about his own personality? How had that helped or hindered? The first item to go on the credit side, without question, would be the ability of Rennalls to master the technical aspects of his job. From the start he had shown keenness and enthusiasm, and he had often impressed Baker with his ability in tackling new assignments and the constructive comments he invariably made in departmental discussions. He was popular with all ranks of Barracanian staff and had an ease of manner that stood him in good stead when dealing with his expatriate seniors.

These were all assets, but what about the debit side? First and foremost was his racial consciousness. His four years at London University had accentuated this feeling and made him sensitive to any sign of condescension on the part of expatriates. Perhaps to give expression to this sentiment, as soon as he returned home from London, he threw himself into politics on behalf of the United Action Party, who were later to win the preindependence elections and provide the country with its first prime minister.

The ambitions of Rennalls—and he certainly was ambitious—did not, however, lie in politics. Staunch nationalist he was, but he saw that he could serve himself and his country best—for was not bauxite responsible for nearly half the value of Barracania's export trade?—by putting his engineering talent to the best use possible. On this account, Hutchins found that he had an unexpectedly easy task in persuading Rennalls to give up his political work before entering the production department as an assistant engineer.

It was, Baker knew, Rennall's well-repressed sense of racial consciousness that had prevented their relationship from being as close as it should have been. On the surface, nothing could have seemed more agreeable. Formality between the two was minimal. Baker was delighted to find that his assistant shared his own peculiar "shaggy dog" sense of humor, so jokes were continually being exchanged. They entertained one another at their houses and often played tennis together—and yet the barrier remained invisible, indefinable, but ever present. The existence of this screen between them was a constant source of frustration to Baker, since it indicated a weakness which he was loath to accept. If successful with people of all other nationalities, why not with Rennalls?

At least he had managed to break through to Rennalls more successfully than had any other expatriate. In fact, it was the young Barracanian's attitude—sometimes overbearing, sometimes cynical—toward other company expatriates that had been one of the subjects Baker raised last year when he discussed Rennall's staff report with him. Baker knew, too, that he would have to raise the same subject again in the forthcoming interview, because Martha Jackson, the senior drafter, had complained only yesterday about the rudeness of Rennalls. With this thought in mind, Baker leaned forward and spoke into the intercom: "Would you come in, Matt, please? I'd like a word with you." Rennalls came in, and Baker held out a box and said, "Do sit down. Have a cigarette."

He paused while he held out his lighter, and then went on. "As you know, Matt, I'll be off to Canada in a few days' time, and before I go, I thought it would be useful if we could have a final chat together. It is indeed with some deference that I suggest I can be of help. You will shortly be sitting in this chair and doing the job I am now doing, but I, on the other hand, am 10 years older, so perhaps you can accept the idea that I may be able to give you the benefit of my long experience."

Baker saw Rennalls stiffen slightly in his chair as he made this point, so he added in explanation, "You and I have attended enough company courses to remember those repeated requests by the personnel manager to tell people how they are getting on as often as the convenient moment arises, and not just the automatic once a year when, by regulation, staff reports have to be discussed."

Rennalls nodded his agreement, so Baker went on, "I shall always remember the last job performance discussion I had with my previous boss back in Germany. She used what she called the 'plus and minus technique.' She firmly believed that when seniors seek to improve the work performance of their staff by discussion, their prime objective should be to make sure the latter leave the interview encouraged and inspired to improve. Any criticism, therefore, must be constructive and helpful. She said that one very good way to encourage a person—and I fully agree with her—is to discuss good points, the plus factors, as well as weak ones, the minus factors. So I thought, Matt, it would be a good idea to run our discussion along these lines."

Rennalls offered no comment, so Baker continued. "Let me say, therefore, right away, that as far as your own work performance is concerned, the pluses far outweigh the minuses. I have, for instance, been most impressed with the way you have adapted your considerable theoretical knowledge to master the practical techniques of your job—that ingenious method you used to get air down to the fifth shaft level is a sufficient case in point. At departmental meetings I have invariably found your comments well taken and helpful. In fact, you will be interested to know that only last week I reported to Ms. Hutchins that, from the technical point of view, she could not wish for a more able person to succeed to the position of chief engineer."

"That's very good indeed of you, John," cut in Renalls with a smile of thanks. "My only worry now is how to live up to such a high recommendation."

"Of that I am quite sure," returned Baker, "especially if you can overcome the minus factor which I would like now to discuss with you. It is one that I have talked about before, so I'll come straight to the point. I have noticed that you are more friendly and get on better with your fellow Barracanians than you do with Europeans. In point of fact, I had a complaint only yesterday from Ms. Jackson, who said you had been rude to her—and not for the first time, either.

"There is, Matt, I am sure, no need for me to tell you how necessary it will be for you to get on well with expatriates, because until the company has trained up sufficient men of your caliber, Europeans are bound to occupy senior positions here in Barracania. All this is vital to your future interests, so can I help you in any way?"

While Baker was speaking on this theme, Rennalls sat tensed in his chair, and it was some seconds before he replied. "It is quite extraordinary, isn't it, how one can convey an impression to others so at variance with what one intends? I can only assure you once again that my disputes with Jackson—and you may remember also Godson—have had nothing at all to do with the color of their skins. I promise you that if a Barracanian had behaved in an equally peremptory manner, I would have reacted the same way. And again, if I may say it within these four walls, I am sure I am not the only one who has found Jackson and Godson difficult. I could mention the names of several expatriates who have felt the same. However, I am really sorry to have created this impression of not being able to get on with Europeans—it is an entirely false one—and I quite realize that I must do all I can to correct it as quickly as possible. On your last point, regarding Europeans holding senior positions in the company for some time to come, I quite accept the situation. I know that Caribbean Bauxite—as it has been for many years now—will promote Barracanians as soon as their experience warrants it. And, finally, I would like to assure you, John—and my father thinks the same, too—that I am very happy in my work here and hope to stay with the company for many years to come."

Rennalls had spoken earnestly, and Baker, although not convinced by what he had heard, did not think he could pursue the matter further except to say, "All right, Matt, my impression may be wrong, but I would like to remind you about the truth of that old saying 'What is important is not what is true, but what is believed.' Let it rest at that."

But suddenly Baker knew that he did not want to "let it rest at that." He was disappointed once again at not being able to break through to Rennalls and at having again had to listen to his bland denial that there was any racial prejudice in his makeup.

Baker, who had intended to end the interview at this point, decided to try another tack. "To return for a moment to the plus and minus technique I was telling you just now, there is another plus factor I forgot to mention. I would like to congratulate you not only on the caliber of your work, but also on the ability you have shown in overcoming a challenge that I, as a European, have never had to meet.

"Continental Ore is, as you know, a typical commercial enterprise—admittedly a big one—that is a product of the economic and social environment of the United States and western Europe. My ancestors have all been brought up in this environment of the past 200 or 300 years, and I have, therefore, been able to live in a world in which commerce (as we know it today) has been part and parcel of my being. It has not been something revolutionary and new that has suddenly entered my life. In your case," went on Baker, "the situation is different, because you and your forebears have only had some 50 and not 200 or 300 years. Again, Matt, let me congratulate you—and people like you—on having so successfully overcome this particular hurdle. It is for this very reason that I think the outlook for Barracania—and particularly Caribbean Bauxite—is so bright."

Rennalls had listened intently, and when Baker finished, he replied, "Well, once again, John, I have to thank you for what you have said, and, for my part, I can only say that it is gratifying to know that my own personal effort has been so much appreciated. I hope that more people will soon come to think as you do."

There was a pause, and, for a moment, Baker thought hopefully that he was about to achieve his long-awaited breakthrough. But Rennalls merely smiled back. The barrier remained unbreached. There were some five minutes' cheerful conversation about the contrast between the Caribbean and Canadian climates and whether the West Indies had any hope of beating England in the Fifth Test before Baker drew the interview to a close. Although he was as far from ever knowing the real Rennalls, he was nevertheless glad that the interview had run along in this friendly manner and, particularly, that it had ended on such a cheerful note.

This feeling, however, lasted only until the following morning. Baker had some farewells to make, so he arrived at the office considerably later than usual. He had no sooner sat down at his desk than his secretary walked into the room with a worried frown on her face. Her words came fast. "When I arrived this morning, I found Mr. Rennalls already waiting at my door. He seemed very angry and told me in quite a peremptory manner that he had a vital letter to dictate that must be sent off without any delay. He was so worked up that he couldn't keep still and kept pacing about the room, which is most unlike him. He wouldn't even wait to read what he had dictated. Just signed the page where he thought the letter would end. It has been distributed, and your copy is in your tray."

Puzzled and feeling vaguely uneasy, Baker opened the envelope marked "Confidential" and read the following letter:

FROM: Assistant Engineer

TO: The Chief Engineer
Caribbean Bauxite
Limited

SUBJECT: Assessment of Interview
Between Messrs. Baker and Rennals

DATE: 14th August 1982

It has always been my practice to respect the advice given me by seniors, so after our interview, I decided to give careful thought once again to its main points and so make sure that I had understood all that had been said. As I promised you at the time, I had every intention of putting your advice to the best effect.

It was not, therefore, until I had sat down quietly in my home yesterday evening to consider the interview objectively that its main purport became clear. Only then did the full enormity of what you said dawn on me. The more I thought about it, the more convinced I was that I had hit upon the real truth—and the more furious I became. With a facility in the English language which I—a poor Barracanian—cannot hope to match, you had the audacity to insult me (and through me every Barracanian worth his salt) by claiming that our knowledge of modern living is only a paltry 50 years old, while yours goes back 200 to 300 years. As if your materialistic commercial environment could possibly be compared with the spiritual values of our culture! I'll have you know that if much of what I saw in London is representative of your boasted culture, I hope fervently that it will never come to Barracania. By what right do you have the effrontery to condescend to us? At heart, all you Europeans think us barbarians, or, as you say amongst yourselves, we are "just down from the trees."

Far into the night I discussed this matter with my father, and he is as disgusted as I. He agrees with me that any company whose senior staff think as you do is no place for any Barracanian proud of his culture and race. So much for all the company claptrap and specious propaganda about regionalization and Barracania for the Barracanians.

I feel ashamed and betrayed. Please accept this letter as my resignation, which I wish to become effective immediately.

cc: Production Manager
Managing Director

Case Questions

1. What, in your opinion, did Baker hope to accomplish as a result of his conversation with Rennalls? Did he succeed? Why or why not?

2. Did nonverbal communications play a part in this case? Be specific and give examples.

3. What could Baker and Rennalls have done to improve the situation described in this case?

READING REFERENCES

1. "Productivity, Supervision, and Employee Morale." Human Relations, Series I, Report 1 (Ann Arbor: Survey Research Center, University of Michigan).

2. Robert L. Kahn, "The Human Factors Underlying Industrial Productivity." Michigan Business Review, November 1952.

3. G. L. Clemens, "Time for Democracy in Action at the Executive Level" (Address given before the AMAPersonnel Conference, February 28, 1951).

NOTES

1. James M. Kouzes, "Link Me to Your Leader," Business 2.0, October 2000, pp. 292-95.

2. These five questions were first suggested in H. D. Lasswell, Power and Personality (New York: W. W. Norton, 1948), pp. 37–51.

3. Claude Shannon and Warren Weaver, The Mathematical Theory of Communication (Urbana: University of Illinois Press, 1948); and Wilbur Schramm, "How Communication Works," in The Process and Effects of Mass Communication, Wilbur Schramm, ed. (Urbana: University of Illinois Press, 1953), pp. 3–26.

4. William Echikson, "Nestlé: An Elephant Dances," Business Week, December 11, 2000, pp. EB44-EB48.

5. Carol Saunders and Jack Jones, "Temporal Sequences in Information Acquisition for Decision Making: A Focus on Source and Medium," Academy of Management Review, January 1990, pp. 29–46.

6. Thad B. Green and Jay T. Knippen, Breaking the Barrier to Upward Communication (Westport, CT: Quorim, 1999).

7. E. Kiritani, Body Language, Journal of Japanese Trade & Industry, January-February 1999, pp. 50-52.

8. Dorothy Leeds, "Body Language: Actions Speak Louder Than Words," National Underwriter, May 1995, pp. 18-19.

9. G. Hofstede, "The Universal and the Specific in 21st Century Management," Organizational Dynamics, Summer 1999, pp. 34-44.

10. Leeds, "Body Language."

11. J.R. Carlson and R.W. Zmud, "Channel Expansion Theory and the Experimental Nature of Media Richness Perceptions," Academy of Management Journal, 1999, pp. 153-70.

12. Gary L. Kreps, Organizational Communication (New York: Longman, 1990), p. 203.

13. G.S. Russ, R.L. Deft, and R.H. Lengel, "Media Selection and Managerial Characteristics in Organizational Communications," Management Communication Quarterly, 1990, pp. 151-75.

14. "Internet at a Glance," Business 2.0, October 10, 2000, p. 282.

15. Richard Gibson, "Merchants Mull the Long and the Short of Lines," Wall Street Journal, September 1998, B11.

16. Michelle Conlin, "Workers, Surf at Your Own Risk," Business Week, June 12, 2000, pp. 105-06.

17. See www.hightechcampus.com for a look at this e-learning company and its products and services.

18. See www.hp.com and annual report 1997 of Hewlett-Packard.

19. J.M. Putti, S. Aryee, and J. Phua, "Communication Relationship Satisfaction and Organizational Commitment," Group and Organizational Studies, March 1990, pp. 44-52.

20. Mary Ellen Guffey, Business Communication (Cincinnati, OH: South-Western, 2000), p. 50.

21. Phillip Harris and Robert Moran, Managing Cultural Differences, 3rd ed. (Houston: Gulf Publishing, 1991).

22. Nancy Adler, International Dimensions of Organizational Behavior, 2nd ed. (Boston PWS-Kent, 1991), P. 131.

23. Jeswald Salacusse, Making Global Deals (Boston: Houghton Mifflin, 1991).

24. See www.fourseasons.com.

25. M.P. Nichols, The Lost Art of Listening (New York: Guilford, 1995).

26. Amy Barrett, "Jack's Risky Last Act," Business Week, November 6, 2000, pp. 40-45.

27. For a review of developments in decision making and communication, see Janet Fulk and Brian Boyd, "Emerging Theories of Communication in Organizations," Journal of Management, June 1991, pp. 407-46.

28. C.D. Mortenson, Miscommunication (Thousand Oaks, CA: Sage, 1997).

29. D.T. Hall, K. L. Otazo, and G.P. Hollenbeck, "Behind Closed Doors: What Really Happens in Executive Coaching," Organizational Dynamics, Winter 1999, pp. 39-53.

30. Kreps, *Organizational Communication*, pp. 250-51.

31. Carole Ashfinaze, "Spies Like Us," *Business Week*, June 12, 2000, pp. F24-F32.

32. Ibid.

33. "Productivity, Supervision, and Employee Morale." *Human Relations, Series I, Report I* (Ann Arbor: Survey Research Center, University of Michigan).

34. Robert L. Kahn, "The Human Factors Underlying Industrial Productivity." *Michigan Business Review*, November 1952.

35. G.L. Clemens, "Time for Democracy in Action at the Executive Level" (Address given before the AMA Personnel Conference, February 28, 1951).

Chapter 6

Effective Listening

SOURCE: Kitty O. Locker and Stephen K. Kaczmarek, *Business Communication: Building Critical Skills*, Module 17, © McGraw- Hill, 2001.

Learning Objectives

- Listen rather than simply hear.
- Listen actively.
- Continue to learn how to build goodwill

Start by Asking These Questions
- What do good listeners do?
- What is active listening?
- How do I show people that I'm listening to them?
- Can I use these techniques if I really disagree with someone?

Listening is the form of communication we practice most often. Yet because we rarely have formal training in it, it may be one that we do most poorly. Listening is even more crucial on the job than it is in classes, but it may also be more difficult.

- In class you're encouraged to take notes. But you can't whip out a notepad every time your boss speaks.
- Many classroom lectures are well organized, with signposts and repetition of key points to help hearers follow. But conversations usually wander. A key point about when a report is due may be sandwiched in among statements about other due dates for other projects.
- In a classroom lecture you're listening primarily for information. In interchanges with friends and co-workers, you need to listen for feelings, too. Feelings of being rejected or overworked need to be dealt with as they arise. But you can't deal with a feeling unless you are aware of it.

To receive a message, the receiver must first perceive the message, then decode it (that is, translate the symbols into meaning), and then interpret it. In interpersonal communication, **hearing** denotes perceiving sounds. **Listening** means decoding and interpreting them correctly.

WHAT DO GOOD LISTENERS DO?

They consciously follow four practices.

Good listeners pay attention, focus on the other speaker(s) in a generous way rather than on themselves, avoid making assumptions, and listen for feelings as well as for facts.

Pay Attention.

Good listening requires energy. You have to resist distractions and tune out noise, whether the rumble of a truck going by or your own worry about whether your parking meter is expiring.

Some listening errors happen because the hearer wasn't paying enough attention to a key point. After a meeting with a client, a consultant waited for the client to send her more information that she would use to draft a formal proposal to do a job for the client. It turned out that the client thought the next move was up to the consultant. The consultant and the client had met together, but they hadn't remembered the same facts.

To avoid listening errors caused by inattention,

- Before the meeting, anticipate the answers you need to get. Make a mental or paper list of your questions. When is the project due? What resources do you have? What is the most important aspect of this project, from the other person's point of view? During a conversation, listen for answers to your questions.

- At the end of the conversation, check your understanding with the other person. Especially check who does what next.

- After the conversation, write down key points that affect deadlines or how work will be evaluated.

Focus on the Other Speaker(s) in a Generous Way.

Some people listen looking for flaws. They may focus on factors other than the substance of the talk: "What an ugly tie." "She sounds like a little girl." "There's a typo in that slide." Or they may listen as if the discussion were a war, listening for points on which they can attack the other speaker. "Ah hah! You're wrong about *that*!" Good listeners, in contrast, are more generous. They realize that people who are not polished speakers may nevertheless have something to say. Rather than pouncing on the first error they hear and tuning out the speaker while they wait impatiently for their own turn to speak, good listeners weigh all the evidence before they come to judgment. They realize that they can learn something even from people they do not like.

To avoid listening errors caused by self-absorption,

- Focus on the substance of what the speaker says, not his or her appearance or delivery.

- Spend your time evaluating what the speaker says, not just planning your rebuttal.

- Consciously work to learn something from every speaker.

Avoid Making Assumptions.

Many listening errors come from making faulty assumptions. In 1977 when two Boeing 747 jumbo jets ran into each other on the ground in Tenerife, the pilots seem to have heard the control tower's instructions. The KLM pilot was told to taxi to the end of the runway, turn around, and wait for clearance. But the KLM pilot didn't interpret the order to wait as an order he needed to follow. The Pan Am pilot interpreted *his* order to turn off at the "third intersection" to mean the third *unblocked* intersection. He didn't count the first blocked ramp, so he was still on the main runway when the KLM pilot ran into his plane at 186 miles an hour. The planes exploded in flames; 576 people died.[1]

In contrast, asking questions can provide useful information. Magazine advertising account representative Beverly Jameson received a phone call from an ad agency saying that a client wanted to cancel the space it had bought. Jameson saw the problem as an opportunity: "Instead of hearing 'cancel,' I heard, 'There's a problem here—let's get to the root of it and figure out how to make the client happy.' " Jameson met with the client, asked the right questions, and discovered that the client wanted more flexibility. She changed some of the markets, kept the business, and turned the client into a repeat customer.[2]

To avoid listening errors caused by faulty assumptions,

- Don't ignore instructions you think are unnecessary. Before you do something else, check with the order giver to see if in fact there is a reason for the instruction.

- Consider the other person's background and experiences. Why is this point important to the speaker? What might he or she mean by it?

- Paraphrase what the speaker has said, giving him or her a chance to correct your understanding.

Listen for Feelings as Well as Facts.

Sometimes, someone just needs to blow off steam, to vent. Sometimes, people just want to have a chance to fully express themselves; "winning" or "losing" may not matter. Sometimes, people may have objections that they can't quite put into words.

To avoid listening errors caused by focusing solely on facts,

- Consciously listen for feelings.
- Pay attention to tone of voice, facial expression, and body language.
- Don't assume that silence means consent. Invite the other person to speak.

WHAT IS ACTIVE LISTENING?

Feeding back the literal meaning, or the emotional content, or both.

In **active listening,** receivers actively demonstrate that they've heard and understood a speaker by feeding back either the literal meaning or the emotional content or both. Other techniques in active listening are asking for more information and stating one's own feelings.

Five strategies create active responses:

- Paraphrase the content. Feed back the meaning in your own words.

- Mirror the speaker's feelings. Identify the feelings you think you hear.

- State your own feelings. This strategy works especially well when you are angry.

- Ask for information or clarification.

- Offer to help solve the problem.

Instead of simply mirroring what the other person says, many of us immediately respond in a way that analyzes or attempts to solve or dismiss the problem. People with problems need first of all to know that we hear that they're having a rough time. Figure 6-1 lists some of the responses that block communication. Ordering and interrogating all tell the other person that the speaker doesn't want to hear what he or she has to say. Preaching attacks the other person. Minimizing the problem suggests that the other person's concern is misplaced. Even advising shuts off discussion. Giving a quick answer minimizes the pain the person feels and puts him or her down for not seeing (what is to us) the obvious answer. Even if it is a good answer from an objective point of view, the other person may not be ready to hear it. And sometimes, the off-the-top-of-the-head solution doesn't address the real problem.

Active listening takes time and energy. Even people who are skilled active listeners can't do it all the time. Furthermore, as Thomas Gordon and Judith Gordon Sands point out, active listening works only if you genuinely accept the other person's ideas and feelings. Active listening can reduce the conflict that results from miscommunication, but it alone cannot reduce the conflict that comes when two people want apparently inconsistent things or when one person wants to change someone else.[3]

HOW DO I SHOW PEOPLE THAT I'M LISTENING TO THEM?

Acknowledge their comments in words, in nonverbal symbols, and in actions.

Active listening is a good way to show people that you are listening. Referring to another person's comment is another way: "I agree with Diana that . . . ."

Figure 6-1   BLOCKING RESPONSES VERSUS ACTIVE LISTENING

Blocking Response	Possible Active Response
Ordering, threatening "I don't care how you do it. Just get that report on my desk by Friday."	**Paraphrasing content** "You're saying that you don't have time to finish the report by Friday."
Preaching, criticizing "You should know better than to air the department's problems in a general meeting."	**Mirroring feelings** "It sounds like the department's problems really bother you."
Interrogating "Why didn't you *tell* me that you didn't understand the instructions?"	**Stating one's own feelings** "I'm frustrated that the job isn't completed yet, and I'm worried about getting it done on time."
Minimizing the problem "You think *that's* bad. You should see what *I* have to do this week."	**Asking for information or clarification** "What parts of the problem seem most difficult to solve?"
Advising "Well, why don't you try listing everything you have to do and seeing which items are most important?"	**Offering to help solve the problem together** "Is there anything I could do that would help

Source: The 5 responses that block communication are based on a list of 12 in Thomas Gordon and Judith Gordon Sands, *P.E.T. in Action* (New York: Wyden, 1976), 117–18

Acknowledgment responses—nods, *uh huh*'s, smiles, frowns—also help carry the message that you're listening. However, listening responses vary in different cultures. Research has found that European Americans almost always respond nonverbally when they listen closely, but that African Americans respond with words rather than nonverbal cues. This difference in response patterns may explain the fact that some European Americans think that African Americans do not understand what they are saying. Studies in the mid-1970s showed that white counselors repeated themselves more often to black clients than to white clients.[4] Similarly, black supervisors may want verbal feedback when they talk to white subordinates who only nod.

The mainstream U.S. culture shows attention and involvement by making eye contact, leaning forward, and making acknowledgment responses. However, some cultures show respect by looking down. In a multicultural workforce, you won't always know whether a colleague who listens silently as you talk agrees with what you say or disagrees violently but is too polite to say so. The best thing to do is to observe the behavior, without assigning a meaning to it: "You aren't saying much." Then let the other person speak.

Of course, if you go through the motions of active listening but then act with disrespect, people will not feel as though you have heard them. Acting on what people say is necessary for people to feel completely heard.

CAN I USE THESE TECHNIQUES IF I REALLY DISAGREE WITH SOMEONE?

Yes!

Most of us do our worst listening when we are in highly charged emotional situations, such as talking with someone with whom we really disagree, getting bad news, or being criticized. Certainly you don't need to listen to a radio talk show host whose views you deplore. But at work, you do need to listen even to people with whom you have major conflicts.

Building a Critical Skill

Leading by Listening

Until January 1999, D. Michael Abrashoff was captain of the USS *Benfold,* a $1 billion warship in the U.S. Navy. Abrashoff practiced what he called "grassroots leadership": seeing the ship through the eyes of the crew.

"Soon after arriving at this command . . . I realized that my job was to listen aggressively. . . . I decided to interview five people a day . . . ask[ing] three simple questions: What do you like most about the *Benfold?* What would you change if you could? . . .

"I tackled the most demoralizing things first—like chipping and painting. Because ships sit in salt water and rust, . . . my youngest sailors—the ones I wanted most to connect with—were spending entire days sanding down rust and repainting the ship. It was a huge waste of physical effort." Abrashoff had all the metal parts replaced with stainless steel and then painted with a rust inhibitor. "The entire process cost just $25,000, and that paint job is good for 30 years. The kids haven't picked up a paintbrush since. And they've had a lot more time to learn their jobs. . . .

"A lot of them wanted to go to college. But most of them had never had a chance to take the SAT. So I posted a sign-up sheet to see how many would take the test if I could arrange it. Forty-five sailors signed up. I then found an SAT administrator through our base in Bahrain and flew him out to the ship to give the test. That was a simple step for me to take, but it was a big deal for morale. . . .

"Most ships report several family problems during every deployment, and most of those problems result from lack of communication. I created an AOL account for the ship and set up a system for sending messages daily through a commercial satellite. That way, sailors can check in with their families, take part in important decisions, and get a little peace of mind."

In the Navy as a whole, only 54% of sailors sign up for a third tour of duty. Under Abrashoff's command, 100% of career sailors signed on for an additional tour. Because recruiting and training cost the Navy at least $100,000 a sailor, Abrashoff estimates that the *Benfold*'s retention rate saved the Navy $1.6 million in 1998. Meanwhile, *Benfold* sailors were promoted at twice the rate of the Navy's average. Sailors were so productive that in fiscal 1998 the *Benfold* returned $600,000 of its $2.4 million maintenance budget and $800,000 of its $3 million repair budget to the Navy.

Source: "The Most Important Thing a Captain Can Do Is to See the Ship from the Eyes of the Crew," *Fast Company,* April 1999, 114–26

At a minimum, good listening enables you to find out why your opponent objects to the programs or ideas you support. Understanding the objections to your ideas is essential if you are to create a persuasive campaign to overcome those objections.

Good listening is crucial when you are criticized, especially by your boss. You need to know which areas are most important and exactly what kind of improvement counts. Otherwise, you might spend your time and energy changing your behavior, but changing it in a way that wasn't valued by your organization.

Listening can do even more. Listening to people is an indication that you're taking them seriously. If you really listen to the people you disagree with, you show that you respect them. And taking that step may enable them to respect you and listen to you.

SUMMARY OF KEY POINTS

- In interpersonal communication, **hearing** denotes perceiving sounds. **Listening** means decoding and interpreting them correctly.

- Good listeners pay attention, focus on the other speaker(s) in a generous way rather than on themselves, avoid making assumptions, and listen for feelings as well as for facts.

- To avoid listening errors caused by inattention,

    - Be conscious of the points you need to know and listen for them.

    - At the end of the conversation, check your understanding with the other person.

    - After the conversation, write down key points that affect deadlines or how work will be evaluated.

- To avoid listening errors caused by self-absorption,

    - Focus on the substance of what the speaker says, not his or her appearance or delivery.

    - Spend your time evaluating what the speaker says, not just planning your rebuttal.

    - Consciously work to learn something from every speaker.

- To reduce listening errors caused by misinterpretation,

    - Don't ignore instructions you think are unnecessary.

    - Consider the other person's background and experiences. Why is this point important to the speaker?

    - Paraphrase what the speaker has said, giving him or her a chance to correct your understanding.

- To avoid listening errors caused by focusing solely on facts,

    - Consciously listen for feelings.

    - Pay attention to tone of voice, facial expression, and body language (p. 00).

    - Don't assume that silence means consent. Invite the other person to speak.

- In **active listening,** receivers actively demonstrate that they've heard and understood a speaker by feeding back either the literal meaning or the emotional content or both. To do this, hearers can

    - Paraphrase the content.

    - Mirror the speaker's feelings.

    - State your own feelings.

    - Ask for information or clarification.

    - Offer to help solve the problem.

QUESTIONS FOR COMPREHENSION

1. What is the difference between hearing and listening?

2. What do good listeners do?

3. What is active listening?

QUESTIONS FOR CRITICAL THINKING

1. Why is listening such hard work?

2. How do you show someone that you are listening?

3. What are the people and circumstances in your life where you find it most difficult to listen? Why do you find it difficult?

4. Think of a time when you really felt that the other person listened to you, and a time when you felt unheard. What are the differences in the two situations?

QUESTIONS FOR BUILDING SKILLS

1. What skills have you read about in this module?

2. What skills are you practicing in the assignments you're doing for this module?

3. How could you further develop the skills you're working on?

EXERCISES AND PROBLEMS

1. Identifying Responses That Show Active Listening

Which of the following responses show active listening? Which block communication?

1) Comment: Whenever I say something, the group ignores me.

   Responses: a. That's because your ideas aren't very good. Do more planning before group meetings.

   b. Nobody listens to me, either.

   c. You're saying that nobody builds on your ideas.

.2) Comment: I've done more than my share of work on this project. But the people who have been freeloading are going to get the same grade I worked so hard to earn.

   Responses: a. Yes, we're all going to get the same grade.

   b. Are you afraid we won't do well on the assignment?

   c. It sounds like you feel resentful.

3) Comment: My parents are going to kill me if I don't have a job lined up at the end of this term.

   Responses: a. You know they're exaggerating. They won't *really* kill you.

   b. Can you blame them? I mean, you've been in school for six years. Surely you've learned something to make you employable!

   c. If you act the way in interviews that you do in our class, I'm not surprised. Companies want people with good attitudes and good work ethics.

2. Practicing Active Listening

Go around the room for this exercise. In turn, let each student complain about something (large or small) that really bothers him or her. Then the next student(s) will

a. Offer a statement of limited agreement that would buy time.

b. Paraphrase the statement.

c. Check for feelings that might lie behind the statement.

d. Offer inferences that might motivate the statement.

3. Interviewing Workers about Listening

Interview someone who works in an organization about his or her on-the-job listening. Possible questions to ask include the following:

• Whom do you listen to as part of your job? Your superior? Subordinates? (How many levels down?) Customers or clients? Who else?

• How much time a day do you spend listening?

• What people do you talk to as part of your job? Do you feel they hear what you say? How do you tell whether or not they're listening?

• Do you know of any problems that came up because someone didn't listen? What happened?

• What do you think prevents people from listening effectively? What advice would you have for someone on how to listen more accurately?

As Your Instructor Directs,

a. Share your information with a small group of students in your class.

    b.   Present your findings orally to the class.

    c.   Present your findings in a memo to your instructor.

    d.   Join with other students to present your findings in a group report or presentation.

4. Reflecting on Your Own Listening

Keep a listening log for a week. Record how long you listened, what barriers you encountered, and what strategies you used to listen more actively and more effectively. What situations were easiest? Which were most difficult? Which parts of listening do you need to work hardest on?

As Your Instructor Directs,

    a.   Share your information with a small group of students in your class.

    b.   Present your findings orally to the class.

    c.   Present your findings in a memo to your instructor.

    d.   Join with other students to present your findings in a group report or presentation.

5. Reflecting on Acknowledgment Responses

Try to be part of at least three conversations involving people from more than one culture. What acknowledgment responses do you observe? Which seem to yield the most positive results? If possible, talk to the other participants about what verbal and nonverbal cues show attentive listening in their cultures.

As Your Instructor Directs,

    a.   Share your information with a small group of students in your class.

    b.   Present your findings orally to the class.

    c.   Present your findings in a memo to your instructor.

    d.   Join with other students to present your findings in a group report or presentation.

NOTES

1.   For a full account of the accident, see Andrew D. Wolvin and Caroline Gwynn Coakely, *Listening,* 2nd ed. (Dubuque, IA: William C. Brown, 1985), 6.

2.   "Listen Up and Sell," *Selling Power,* July/August 1999, 34.

3.   Thomas Gordon with Judith Gordon Sands, *P.E.T. in Action* (New York: Wyden, 1976), 83.

4.   Molefi Asante and Alice Davis, "Black and White Communication: Analyzing Work Place Encounters," *Journal of Black Studies* 16, no. 1 September 1985): 87–90. Decision-Making and Its Role in Leadership Perception," *Communication Quarterly* 30, no. 4 (Fall 1982): 374–75; Dennis S. Gouran and B. Aubrey Fisher, "The Functions of Human Communication in the Formation, Maintenance, and Performance of Small Groups," in *Handbook of Rhetorical and Communication Theory,* ed. Carroll C. Arnold and John Waite Bowers (Boston: Allyn and Bacon, 1984), 640; and Curt Bechler and Scott D. Johnson, "Leadership and Listening: A Study of Member Perceptions," *Small Group Research* 26, no. 1 (February 1995): 77–85.

Chapter 7

Making Effective Presentations

SOURCE: Kitty O. Locker and Stephen K. Kaczmarek, *Business Communication: Building Critical Skills*, Module 20, © McGraw- Hill, 2001.

Learning Objectives

After studying this chapter, you should be able to:
- Turn material from a paper document into a presentation.
- Plan and deliver oral presentations.
- Develop a good speaking voice.
- Give group presentations.

Start by Asking These Questions:

- What decisions do I need to make as I plan a presentation?

- How should I organize a presentation?

- How can I create a strong opening and close?

- What are the keys to delivering an effective presentation?

- How should I handle questions from the audience?

- What are the guidelines for group presentations?

Making a good oral presentation is more than just good delivery: It also involves developing a strategy that fits your audience and purpose, having good content, and organizing material effectively. The choices you make in each of these areas are affected by your purposes, the audience, and the situation.

Giving a presentation is in many ways very similar to writing a message. The other modules in this book—on analyzing your audience, using you-attitude and positive emphasis, developing reader benefits, designing slides, overcoming objections, doing research, and analyzing data—remain relevant as you plan an oral presentation.

Oral presentations have the same three basic purposes that written documents have: to inform, to persuade, and to build goodwill. Like written messages, most oral presentations have more than one purpose.

Informative presentations inform or teach the audience. Training sessions in an organization are primarily informative. Secondary purposes may be to persuade new employees to follow organizational procedures, rather than doing something their own way, and to help them appreciate the organizational culture.

Persuasive presentations motivate the audience to act or to believe. Giving information and evidence is an important means of persuasion. In addition, the speaker must build goodwill by appearing to be credible and sympathetic to the audience's needs. The goal in many presentations is a favorable vote or decision. For example, speakers making business presentations may try to persuade the audience to approve their proposals, to adopt their ideas, or to buy their products. Sometimes the goal is to change behavior or attitudes or to reinforce existing attitudes. For example, a speaker at a meeting of factory workers may stress the importance of following safety procedures. A speaker at a church meeting may talk about the problem of homelessness in the community and try to build support for community shelters for the homeless.

Goodwill presentations entertain and validate the audience. In an after-dinner speech, the audience wants to be entertained. Presentations at sales meetings may be designed to stroke the audience's egos and to validate their commitment to organizational goals.

Make your purpose as specific as possible.

Weak:	The purpose of my presentation is to discuss saving for retirement.
Better:	The purpose of my presentation is to persuade my audience to put their 401K funds in stocks and bonds, not in money market accounts and CDs.
or	The purpose of my presentation is to explain how to calculate how much money someone needs to save in order to maintain a specific lifestyle after retirement.

Note that the purpose *is not* the introduction of your talk; it is the principle that guides your decisions as you plan your presentation.

WHAT DECISIONS DO I NEED TO MAKE AS I PLAN A PRESENTATION?

Choose your main point, the kind of presentation, and ways to involve the audience.

An oral presentation needs to be simpler than a written message to the same audience. Identify the one idea you want the audience to take home. Simplify your supporting detail so it's easy to follow. Simplify visuals so they can be taken in at a glance. Simplify your words and sentences so they're easy to understand.

Presentation coach Jerry Weissman helped client David Angel simplify his description of his company:[1]

Too complicated:	Information Storage Devices provides voice solutions using the company's unique, patented multilevel storage technique.
Simple:	We make voice chips. They're extremely easy to use. They have unlimited applications. And they last forever.

Analyze your audience for an oral presentation just as you do for a written message. If you'll be speaking to co-workers, talk to them about your topic or proposal to find out what questions or objections they have. For audiences inside the organization, the biggest questions are often practical ones: Will it work? How much will it cost? How long will it take?[2]

Think about the physical conditions in which you'll be speaking. Will the audience be tired at the end of a long day of listening? Sleepy after a big meal? Will the group be large or small? The more you know about your audience, the better you can adapt your message to the audience.

Choosing the Kind of Presentation

Choose one of three basic kinds of presentations: monologue, guided discussion, or sales. In a **monologue presentation,** the speaker speaks without interruption; questions are held until the end of the presentation, where the speaker functions as an expert. The speaker plans the presentation in advance and delivers it without deviation. This kind of presentation is the most common in class situations, but it's often boring for the audience. Good delivery skills are crucial, since the audience is comparatively uninvolved.

Linda Driskill suggests that **guided discussions** offer a better way to present material and help an audience find a solution it can "buy into." In a guided discussion, the speaker presents the questions or issues that both speaker and audience have agreed on in advance. Rather than functioning as an expert with all the answers, the speaker serves as a facilitator to help the audience tap its own knowledge. This kind of presentation is excellent for presenting the results of consulting projects, when the speaker has specialized knowledge, but the audience must implement the solution if it is to succeed. Guided discussions need more time than monologue presentations, but produce more audience response, more responses involving analysis, and more commitment to the result.[3]

A **sales presentation** is a conversation, even if the salesperson stands up in front of a group and uses charts and overheads. The sales representative uses questions to determine the buyer's needs, probe objections, and gain temporary and then final commitment to the purchase. Even in a memorized sales presentation, the buyer will talk at least 30% of the time. In a problem-solving sales presentation, the buyer may talk 70% of the time.

Adapting Your Ideas to the Audience

Measure the message you'd like to send against where your audience is now. If your audience is indifferent, skeptical, or hostile, focus on the part of your message the audience will find most interesting and easiest to accept.

Don't seek a major opinion change in a single oral presentation. If the audience has already decided to hire some advertising agency, then a good pre-sentation can convince them that your agency is the one to hire. But if you're talking to a small business that has always done its own ads, limit your purpose. You may be able to prove that an agency can earn its fees by doing things the owner can't do and by freeing the owner's time for other activities. A second presentation may be needed to prove that an ad agency can do a *better* job than the small business could do on its own. Only after the audience is receptive should you try to persuade the audience to hire your agency rather than a competitor.

FIGURE 7-1   POWERPOINT SLIDES FOR AN INFORMATIVE PRESENTATION

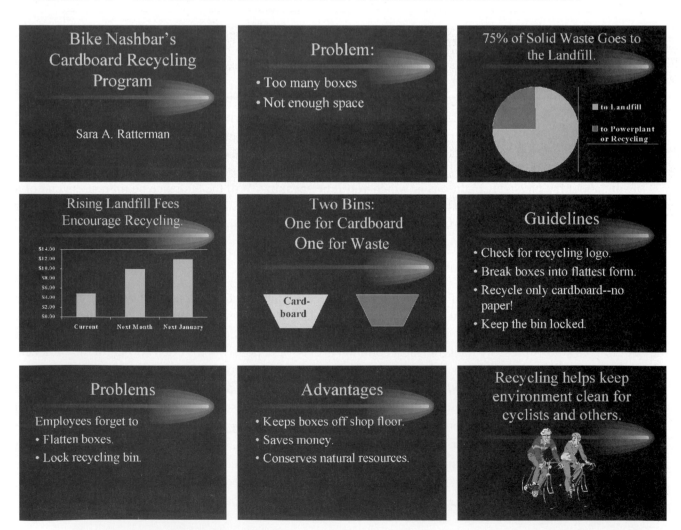

Make your ideas relevant to your audience by linking what you have to say to the audience's experiences and interests. Showing your audience members that the topic affects them directly is the most effective strategy. When you can't do that, at least link the topic to some everyday experience.

Planning Visuals and Other Devices to Involve the Audience

Visuals can give your presentation a professional image. A 1986 study found that presenters using overhead transparencies were perceived as "better prepared, more professional, more persuasive, more credible, and more interesting" than speakers who did not use visuals. They were also more likely to persuade a group to adopt their recommendations. Colored overhead transparencies were most effective in persuading people to act.[4]

A 2000 study found that in an informative presentation, multimedia (PowerPoint slides with graphics and animation) produced 5% more learning than overheads made from the slides and 16% more learning than text alone. In a sales presentation, multimedia (PowerPoint slides with graphics, animation, and video) motivated 58% more students to choose that bank compared to overheads and 60% more compared to text alone. Although the two banks offered identical fees and services, students said that the bank represented by the multimedia presentation "was more credible, was more professional and offered better ser-vices and fees."[5]

Use at least 18-point type for visuals you prepare with a word processor. When you prepare slides with PowerPoint, Corel, or another presentation program, use at least 24-point type for the smallest words.

Well-designed visuals can serve as an outline for your talk, see Figure 7-1, eliminating the need for additional notes. Plan at most one visual for every minute of your talk, plus two visuals to serve as title and conclusion. Don't try to put your whole talk on visuals. Visuals should highlight your main points, not give every detail.

Use these guidelines to create and show visuals for presentations:

- Make only one point with each visual. Break a complicated point down into several visuals.

- Give each visual a title that makes a point.

- Limit the amount of information on a visual. Use 35 words or less; use simple graphs, not complex ones.

- Don't put your visual up till you're ready to talk about it. Leave it up until your next point; don't turn the projector or overhead off.

Visuals work only if the technology they depend on works. When you give presentations in your own office, check the equipment in advance. When you make a presentation in another location or for another organization, arrive early so that you'll have time not only to check the equipment but also to track down a service worker if the equipment isn't working. Be prepared with a backup plan to use if you're unable to show your slides or videotape.

You can also involve the audience in other ways.

- A student giving a presentation on English-French business communication demonstrated the differences in U.S. and French handshakes by asking a fellow class member to come up to shake hands with her.

- Another student discussing the need for low-salt products brought in a container of Morton salt, a measuring cup, a measuring spoon, and two plates. As he discussed the body's need for salt, he measured out three teaspoons onto one plate: the amount the body needs in a month. As he discussed the amount of salt the average U.S. diet provides, he continued to measure out salt onto the other plate, stopping only when he had 11/4 pounds of salt—the amount in the average U.S. diet. The demonstration made the discrepancy clear in a way words or even a chart could not have done. [6]

- To make sure that his employees understood where money went, the CEO of a specialty printing shop in Algoma, Wisconsin, printed up $2 million in play money and handed out big cards to employees marked *Labor, Depreciation, Interest,* and so forth. Then he asked each "category" to come up and take its share of the revenues. The action was more dramatic than a color pie chart could ever have been.[7]

- Another speaker who was trying to raise funds used the simple act of asking people to stand to involve them, to create emotional appeal, and to make a statistic vivid:

> [A speaker] was talking to a luncheon club about contributing to the relief of an area that had been hit by a tornado. The news report said that 70% of the people had been killed or disabled. The room was set up ten people at each round table. He asked three persons at each table to stand. Then he said, ". . . You people sitting are dead or disabled. You three standing have to take care of the mess. You'd need help, wouldn't you?"[8]

HOW CAN I CREATE A STRONG OPENING AND CLOSE?

Brainstorm several possibilities. The following four modes can help.

The beginning and end of a presentation, like the beginning and end of a written document, are positions of emphasis. Use those key positions to interest the audience and emphasize your key point. You'll sound more natural and more effective if you talk from notes but write out your opener and close in advance and memorize them. (They'll be short: just a sentence or two.)

Brainstorm several possible openers for each of the four modes: startling statement, narration or anecdote, question, or quotation. The more you can do to personalize your opener for your audience, the better. Recent events are better than things that happened long ago; local events are better than events at a distance; people they know are better than people who are only names.

Startling Statement

> Twelve of our customers have canceled orders in the past month.

This presentation to a company's executive committee went on to show that the company's distribution system was inadequate and to recommend a third warehouse located in the southwest.

Narration or Anecdote

> A mother was having difficulty getting her son up for school. He pulled the covers over his head.
>
> "I'm not going to school," he said. "I'm not ever going again."
>
> "Are you sick?" his mother asked.
>
> "No," he answered. "I'm sick of school. They hate me. They call me names. They make fun of me. Why should I go?"
>
> "I can give you two good reasons," the mother replied. "The first is that you're 42 years old. And the second is *you're the school principal.*"[9]

This speech to a seminar for educators went on to discuss "the three knottiest problems in education today." Educators had to face those problems; they couldn't hide under the covers.

Question

> Are you going to have enough money to do the things you want to when you retire?

This presentation to a group of potential clients discusses the value of using the services of a professional financial planner to achieve one's goals for retirement.

Building a Critical Skill

Finding Your Best Voice

A good voice supports and enhances good content. Your best voice will manipulate pitch, intonation, tempo, and volume. Sound energetic and enthusiastic.

Pitch

Pitch measures whether a voice uses sounds that are low (like the bass notes on a piano) or high. Low-pitched voices are usually perceived as being more authoritative, sexier, and more pleasant to listen to than are high-pitched voices. Most voices go up in pitch when the speaker is angry or excited; some people raise pitch when they increase volume. Women whose normal speaking voices are high may need to practice projecting their voices to avoid becoming shrill when they speak to large groups.

To find your best pitch, try humming. The pitch where the hum sounds loudest and most resonant is your best voice.

Intonation

Intonation marks variation in pitch, stress, or tone. Speakers who use many changes in pitch, stress, and tone usually seem more enthusiastic; often they also seem more energetic and more intelligent. Someone who speaks in a monotone may seem apathetic or unintelligent. Non-native speakers whose first language does not use tone, pitch, and stress to convey meaning and attitude may need to practice varying these voice qualities.

Avoid raising your voice at the end of a sentence, however. In English, a rising intonation signals a question. Therefore, speakers who end sentences on higher tones sound as though they're unsure of what they're saying.

Tempo

Tempo is a measure of speed. In a conversation, match your tempo to the other speaker's to build rapport. In a formal presentation, vary your tempo. Speakers who speak quickly and who vary their volume during the talk are more likely to be perceived as competent.

Volume

Volume is a measure of loudness or softness. Very soft voices, especially if they are also breathy and high-pitched, give the impression of youth and inexperience. People who do a lot of speaking to large groups need to practice projecting their voices so they can increase their volume without shouting.

Source: George B. Ray, "Vocally Cued Personality Prototypes: An Implicit Personality Theory Approach," *Communication Monographs* 53, no. 3 (1986): 266–76, and Jacklyn Boice, "Verbal Impressions," *Selling Power,* March 2000, 69.

Quotation

> According to Towers Perrin, the profits of Fortune 100 companies would be 25% lower—they'd go down $17 billion—if their earnings statements listed the future costs companies are obligated to pay for retirees' health care.

This presentation on options for health care for retired employees urges executives to start now to investigate options to cut the future cost.

Your opener should interest the audience and establish a rapport. Some speakers use humor to achieve those goals. However, an inappropriate joke can turn the audience against the speaker. Never use humor that's directed against the audience. In contrast, speakers who can make fun of themselves almost always succeed:

> It's both a privilege and a pressure to be here.[10]

Humor isn't the only way to set an audience at ease. Smile at your audience before you begin; let them see that you're a real person and a nice one.

The end of your presentation should be as strong as the opener. For your close, you could do one or more of the following:

• Restate your main point.

• Refer to your opener to create a frame for your presentation.

• End with a vivid, positive picture.

• Tell the audience exactly what to do to solve the problem you've discussed.

The following close from a fund-raising speech combines a restatement of the main point with a call for action, telling the audience what to do.

> Plain and simple, we need money to run the foundation, just like you need money to develop new products. We need money to make this work. We need money from you. Pick up that pledge card. Fill it out. Turn it in at the door as you leave. Make it a statement about your commitment . . . make it a big statement.[11]

When you write out your opener and close, be sure to use oral rather than written style. As you can see in the example close above, oral style uses shorter sentences and shorter, simpler words than writing does. Oral style can even sound a bit choppy when it is read by eye. Oral style uses more personal pronouns, a less varied vocabulary, and more repetition.

HOW SHOULD I ORGANIZE A PRESENTATION?

Start with the main point. Often, one of five standard patterns will work.

Most presentations use a direct pattern of organization, even when the goal is to persuade a reluctant audience. In a business setting, the audience members are in a hurry and know that you want to persuade them. Be honest about your goals, and then prove that your goal meets the audience's needs too.

In a persuasive presentation, start with your strongest point, your best reason. If time permits, give other reasons as well and respond to possible objections. Put your weakest point in the middle so that you can end on a strong note.

Often one of five standard patterns of organization will work.

• **Chronological.** Start with the past, move to the present, and end by looking ahead.

• **Problem-Causes-Solution.** Explain the symptoms of the problem, identify its causes, and suggest a solution. This pattern works best when the audience will find your solution easy to accept.

• **Excluding alternatives.** Explain the symptoms of the problem. Explain the obvious solutions first and show why they won't solve the problem. End by discussing a solution that will work. This pattern may be necessary when the audience will find the solution hard to accept.

• **Pro-Con.** Give all the reasons in favor of something, then those against it. This pattern works well when you want the audience to see the weaknesses in its position.

• **1-2-3.** Discuss three aspects of a topic. This pattern works well to organize short informative briefings. "Today I'll review our sales, production, and profits for the last quarter."

Early in your talk—perhaps immediately after your opener—provide an **overview of the main points** you will make.

> First, I'd like to talk about who the homeless in Columbus are. Second, I'll talk about the services The Open Shelter provides. Finally, I'll talk about what you—either individually or as a group—can do to help.

An overview provides a mental peg that hearers can hang each point on. It also can prevent someone missing what you are saying because he or she wonders why you aren't covering a major point that you've saved for later.[12]

Offer a clear signpost as you come to each new point. A **signpost** is an explicit statement of the point you have reached. Choose wording that fits your style. The following statements are four different ways that a speaker could use to introduce the last of three points:

> So much for what we're doing. Now let's talk about what you can do to help.
>
> You may be wondering, what can I do to help?
>
> As you can see, the Shelter is trying to do many things. We could do more things with your help.

WHAT ARE THE KEYS TO DELIVERING AN EFFECTIVE PRESENTATION?

Turn your fear into energy, look at the audience, and use natural gestures.

Audience members want the sense that you're talking directly to them and that you care that they understand and are interested. They'll forgive you if you get tangled up in a sentence and end it ungrammatically. They won't forgive you if you seem to have a "canned" talk that you're going to deliver no matter who the listeners are or how they respond. You can convey a sense of caring to your audience by making direct eye contact and by using a conversational style.

Transforming Fear

Feeling nervous is normal. But you can harness that nervous energy to help you do your best work. As one student said, you don't need to get rid of your butterflies. All you need to do is make them fly in formation. To calm your nerves as you prepare to give an oral presentation,

- Be prepared. Analyze your audience, organize your thoughts, prepare visual aids, practice your opener and close, check out the arrangements.

- Use only the amount of caffeine you normally use. More or less may make you jumpy.

- Avoid alcoholic beverages.

- Relabel your nerves. Instead of saying, "I'm scared," try saying, "My adrenaline is up." Adrenaline sharpens our reflexes and helps us do our best.

Just before your presentation,

- Consciously contract and then relax your muscles, starting with your feet and calves and going up to your shoulders, arms, and hands.

- Take several deep breaths from your diaphragm.

During your presentation,

- Pause and look at the audience before you begin speaking.

- Concentrate on communicating well.

- Use body energy in strong gestures and movement.

Using Eye Contact

Look directly at the people you're talking to. In one study, speakers who looked more at the audience during a seven-minute informative speech were judged to be better informed, more experienced, more honest, and friendlier than speakers who delivered the same information with less eye contact.[13] An earlier study found that speakers judged sincere looked at the audience 63% of the time, while those judged insincere looked at the audience only 21% of the time.[14]

The point in making eye contact is to establish one-on-one contact with the individual members of your audience. People want to feel that you're talking to them. Looking directly at individuals also enables you to be more conscious of feedback from the audience, so that you can modify your approach if necessary.

Standing and Gesturing

Stand with your feet far enough apart for good balance, with your knees flexed. Unless the presentation is very formal or you're on camera, you can walk if you want to. Some speakers like to come in front of the lectern to remove that barrier between themselves and the audience.

Build on your natural style for gestures. Gestures usually work best when they're big and confident.

Using Notes and Visuals

Unless you're giving a very short presentation, you'll probably want to use notes. Even experts use notes. The more you know about the subject, the greater the temptation to add relevant points that occur to you as you talk. Adding an occasional point can help to clarify something for the audience, but adding too many points will destroy your outline and put you over the time limit.

Put your notes on cards or on sturdy pieces of paper. Most speakers like to use 4-by-6-inch or 5-by-7-inch cards because they hold more information. Your notes need to be complete enough to help you if you go blank, so use long phrases or complete sentences. Under each main point, jot down the evidence or illustration you'll use. Indicate where you'll refer to visuals.

Look at your notes infrequently. Most of your gaze time should be directed to members of the audience. Hold your notes high enough so that your head doesn't bob up and down like a yo-yo as you look from the audience to your notes and back again.

If you have lots of visuals and know your topic well, you won't need notes. If possible, put the screen to the side so that you won't block it. Face the audience, not the screen. With transparencies, you can use color marking pens to call attention to your points as you talk. Show the entire visual at once: don't cover up part of it. If you don't want the audience to read ahead, prepare several visuals that build up. In your overview, for example, the first visual could list your first point, the second the first and second, and the third all three points.

Keep the room lights on if possible; turning them off makes it easier for people to fall asleep and harder for them to concentrate on you.

HOW SHOULD I HANDLE QUESTIONS FROM THE AUDIENCE?

Anticipate questions that might be asked. Be honest. Rephrase biased or hostile questions.

Prepare for questions by listing every fact or opinion you can think of that challenges your position. Treat each objection seriously and try to think of a way to deal with it. If you're talking about a controversial issue, you may want to save one point for the question period, rather than making it during the presentation. Speakers who have visuals to answer questions seem especially well prepared.

During your presentation, tell the audience how you'll handle questions. If you have a choice, save questions for the end. In your talk, answer the questions or objections that you expect your audience to have. Don't exaggerate your claims so that you won't have to back down in response to questions later.

During the question period, don't nod your head to indicate that you understand a question as it is asked. Audiences will interpret nods as signs that you agree with the questioner. Instead, look directly at the questioner. As you answer the question, expand your focus to take in the entire group. Don't say, "That's a good question." That response implies that the other questions have been poor ones.

If the audience may not have heard the question or if you want more time to think, repeat the question before you answer it. Link your answers to the points you made in your presentation. Keep the purpose of your presentation in mind, and select information that advances your goals.

If a question is hostile or biased, rephrase it before you answer it. "You're asking whether . . . ." Or suggest an alternative question: "I think there are problems with both the positions you describe. It seems to me that a third solution which is better than either of them is . . . ."

Occasionally someone will ask a question that is really designed to state the speaker's own position. Respond to the question if you want to. Another option is to say, "I'm not sure what you're asking" or even "That's a clear statement of your position. Let's move to the next question now." If someone asks about something that you already explained in your presentation, simply answer the question without embarrassing the questioner. No audience will understand and remember 100% of what you say.

If you don't know the answer to a question, say so. If your purpose is to inform, write down the question so that you can look up the answer before the next session. If it's a question to which you think there is no answer, ask if anyone in the room knows. When no one does, your "ignorance" is vindicated. If an expert is in the room, you may want to refer questions of fact to him or her. Answer questions of interpretation yourself.

At the end of the question period, take two minutes to summarize your main point once more. (This can be a restatement of your close.) Questions may or may not focus on the key point of your talk. Take advantage of having the floor to repeat your message briefly and forcefully.

WHAT ARE THE GUIDELINES FOR GROUP PRESENTATIONS?

In the best presentations, voices take turns within each point.

Plan carefully to involve as many members of the group as possible in speaking roles.

The easiest way to make a group presentation is to outline the presentation and then divide the topics, giving one to each group member. Another member can be responsible for the opener and the close. During the question period, each member answers questions that relate to his or her topic.

In this kind of divided presentation, be sure to

- Plan transitions.

- Enforce time limits strictly.

- Coordinate your visuals so that the presentation seems a coherent whole.

- Practice the presentation as a group at least once; more is better.

The best group presentations are even more fully integrated: together, the members of the group

- Write a very detailed outline.

- Choose points and examples.

- Create visuals.

Then, *within* each point, speakers take turns. This presentation is most effective because each voice speaks only a minute or two before a new voice comes in. However, it works only when all group members know the subject well and when the group plans carefully and practices extensively.

Whatever form of group presentation you use, be sure to introduce each member of the team to the audience at the beginning of the presentation and to use the next person's name when you change speakers: "Now, Jason will explain how we evaluated the Web pages." Pay close attention to who is speaking. If other members of the team seem uninterested in the speaker, the audience gets the sense that that speaker isn't worth listening to.

SUMMARY

- **Informative presentations** inform or teach the audience. **Persuasive presentations** motivate the audience to act or to believe. **Goodwill presentations** entertain and validate the audience. Most oral presentations have more than one purpose.

- An oral presentation needs to be simpler than a written message to the same audience.

- In a **monologue presentation,** the speaker plans the presentation in advance and delivers it without deviation. In a **guided discussion,** the speaker presents the questions or issues that both speaker and audience have agreed on in advance. Rather than functioning as an expert with all the answers, the speaker serves as a facilitator to help the audience tap its own knowledge. A **sales presentation** is a conversation using questions to determine the buyer's needs, probe objections, and gain provisional and then final commitment to the purchase.

- Adapt your message to your audience's beliefs, experience, and interests.

- Use the beginning and end of the presentation to interest the audience and emphasize your key point.

- Using visuals makes a speaker seem more prepared, more interesting, and more persuasive.

- Use a direct pattern of organization. Put your strongest reason first.

- Limit your talk to three main points. Early in your talk—perhaps immediately after your opener—provide an **overview of the main points** you will make. Offer a clear signpost as you come to each new point. A **signpost** is an explicit statement of the point you have reached.

- To calm your nerves as you prepare to give an oral presentation,

  - Be prepared. Analyze your audience, organize your thoughts, prepare visual aids, practice your opener and close, check out the arrangements.

  - Use only the amount of caffeine you normally use.

  - Avoid alcoholic beverages.

  - Relabel your nerves. Instead of saying, "I'm scared," try saying, "My adrenaline is up." Adrenaline sharpens our reflexes and helps us do our best.

Just before your presentation,

- Consciously contract and then relax your muscles, starting with your feet and calves and going up to your shoulders, arms, and hands.

- Take several deep breaths from your diaphragm.

  During your presentation,

- Pause and look at the audience before you begin speaking.

- Concentrate on communicating well.

- Use body energy in strong gestures and movement.

- Convey a sense of caring to your audience by making direct eye contact with them and by using a conversational style.

- Treat questions as opportunities to give more detailed information than you had time to give in your presentation. Link your answers to the points you made in your presentation.

- Repeat the question before you answer it if the audience may not have heard it or if you want more time to think. Rephrase hostile or biased questions before you answer them.

- The best group presentations result when the group writes a very detailed outline, chooses points and examples, and creates visuals together. Then, within each point, voices trade off.

QUESTIONS FOR COMPREHENSION

1. How are monologue presentations, guided discussions, and sales presentations alike and different?

2. What are the four modes for openers?

3. What does maintaining eye contact and smiling do for a presentation?

QUESTIONS FOR CRITICAL THINKING

1. If you use presentation software, will you automatically have strong visuals?

2. Why should you plan a strong close, rather than just saying, "Well, that's it"?

3. Why does an oral presentation have to be simpler than a written message to the same audience?

4. What are the advantages and disadvantages of using humor?

QUESTIONS FOR BUILDING SKILLS

1. What skills have you read about in this module?

2. What skills are you practicing in the assignments you're doing for this module?

3. How could you further develop the skills you're working on?

EXERCISES AND PROBLEMS

1.   MAKING A SHORT ORAL PRESENTATION

As Your Instructor Directs,

Make a short (2- to 5-minute) presentation, with three to eight slides, on one of the following topics:

a.   Explain how what you've learned in classes, in campus activities, or at work will be useful to the employer who hires you after graduation.

b.   Profile someone who is successful in the field you hope to enter and explain what makes him or her successful.

c.   Describe a specific situation in an organization in which communication was handled well or badly.

d.   Make a short presentation based on one of the following:

•   Discuss three of your strengths.

•   Analyze your boss.

•   Explain a "best practice" in your organization.

•   Tell your boss about a problem in your unit and recommend a solution.

•   Explain one of the challenges (e.g., technology, ethics, international competition) that the field you hope to enter is facing.

•   Profile a company you would like to work for and explain why you think it would be a good employer.

•   Explain your interview strategy.

2.   MAKING A LONGER ORAL PRESENTATION

As Your Instructor Directs,

Make a 5- to 12-minute presentation on one of the following. Use visuals to make your talk effective.

a.   Show why your unit is important to the organization and either should be exempt from downsizing or should receive additional resources.

b.   Persuade your supervisor to make a change that will benefit the organization.

c.   Persuade your organization to make a change that will improve the organization's image in the community.

d.   Persuade classmates to donate time or money to a charitable organization. (Read Module 11.)

e.   Persuade an employer that you are the best person for the job.

f.   Use another problem based on one of the following:

•   Analyze a discourse community.

- Analyze an organization's corporate culture.

- Present a Web page you have designed.

- Summarize the results of a survey you have conducted.

- Summarize the results of your research.

3.   MAKING A GROUP ORAL PRESENTATION

As Your Instructor Directs,
Make a 5- to 12-minute presentation using visuals.

- Show how cultural differences can lead to miscommunication.

- Evaluate the design of three Web pages.

- Recommend an investment for your instructor.

- Recommend ways to retain workers.

- Present brochures you have designed to the class.

- Summarize the results of your research.

- Share the advice of students currently on the job market.

NOTES

1.   Dan Gillmor, "Putting on a Powerful Presentation," *Hemispheres,* March 1996, 31.

2.   Carol Hymowitz, "When You Tell the Boss, Plain Talk Counts," *The Wall Street Journal,* June 16, 1989, B1.

3.   Linda Driskill, "How the Language of Presentations Can Encourage or Discourage Audience Participation," paper presented at the Conference on College Composition and Communication, Cincinnati, OH, March 18–21, 1992.

4.   "A Study of the Effects of the Use of Overhead Transparencies on Business Meetings," Wharton Applied Research Center, reported in Martha Jewett and Rita Margolies, eds., *How to Run Better Business Meetings: A Reference Guide for Managers* (New York: McGraw-Hill, 1987), 109–110, 115.

5.   Tad Simons, "Multimedia or Bust?" *Presentations,* February 2000, 44, 49–50.

6.   Stephen E. Lucas, *The Art of Public Speaking,* 2nd ed. (New York: Random House, 1986), 248.

7.   John Case, "A Company of Businesspeople," *Inc.,* April 1993, 90.

8.   Edward J. Hegarty, *Humor and Eloquence in Public Speaking* (West Nyack, NY: Parker, 1976), 204.

9.   Ray Alexander, *Power Speech: Why It's Vital to You* (New York: AMACOM, 1986), 156.

10. Robert S. Mills, conversation with Kitty O. Locker, March 10, 1988.

11. Phil Theibert, "Speechwriters of the World, Get Lost!" *The Wall Street Journal,* August 2, 1993, A10.

12. Some studies have shown that previews and reviews increase comprehension; other studies have found no effect. For a summary of the research see Kenneth D. Frandsen and Donald R. Clement, "The Functions of Human Communication in Informing: Communicating and Processing Information," *Handbook of Rhetorical and Communication Theory,* ed. Carroll C. Arnold and John Waite Bowers (Boston: Allyn and Bacon, 1984), 340–41.

13.   S. A. Beebe, "Eye Contact: A Nonverbal Determinant of Speaker Credibility," *Speech Teacher* 23 (1974): 21–25; cited in Marjorie Fink Vargas, *Louder than Words* (Ames, IA: Iowa State University Press, 1986), 61–62.

14. J. Wills, "An Empirical Study of the Behavioral Characteristics of Sincere and Insincere Speakers" Ph.D. dissertation, University of Southern California, 1961; cited in Marjorie Fink Vargas, *Louder than Words* (Ames, IA: Iowa State University Press, 1986), 62.

Chapter 8

Communication Applications: Letters, Memos and Reports

SOURCE: Kitty O. Locker and Stephen K. Kaczmarek, *Business Communication: Building Critical Skills,* Modules 9, 10, 22, 23, 24 © McGraw- Hill, 2001.

Learning Objectives:

After studying this chapter, you should be able to:

- Choose and use standard formats.
- Use nonsexist courtesy titles.
- Create a professional image.
- Write effective subject lines.
- Organize informative and positive messages.
- Continue to develop strong reader benefits.
- Write goodwill endings.
- Write common kinds of informative and positive messages.
- Continue to analyze business communication situations.
- Find information online and in print.

- Write questions for surveys and interviews.
- Analyze information.
- Document sources.
- Use the Internet for research.
- Organize information in reports.
- Create a good writing style for reports.
- Ask good questions on the job.
- Use your time efficiently when you write reports.
- Set up the parts of a full formal report.
- Continue to create a professional image

Start by Asking These Questions:

- What are the standard formats for letters?
- What courtesy titles should I use?
- How should I set up memos?
- How should I set up e-mail messages?
- What's the best subject line for an informative or positive message?
- How should I organize informative and positive messages?
- When should I use reader benefits in informative and positive messages?
- What kinds of informative and positive messages am I likely to write?
- How can PAIBOC help me write informative and positive messages?
- How can I find information online and in print?
- How do I write questions for surveys and interviews?
- How do I decide whom to survey or interview?
- How should I analyze the information I've collected?
- How should I document sources?
- What are the basic strategies for organizing information?
- Do different kinds of reports use different patterns of organization?
- Should I use the same style for reports as for other business documents?
- I've never written anything so long. How should I organize my time?
- How do I create each of the parts of a formal report?

FORMATS FOR LETTTERS, MEMOS, AND E-MAIL MESSAGES

Letters normally go to people outside your organization; **memos** go to other people in your organization. In very large organizations, corporate culture determines whether people in different divisions or different locations feel close enough to each other to write memos. Letters and memos do not necessarily differ in length, formality, writing style, or pattern of organization. However, letters and memos do differ in format. **Format** means the parts of a document and the way they are arranged on the page.

WHAT ARE THE STANDARD FORMATS FOR LETTERS?

Block and modified block.

The two most common letter formats are **block,** sometimes called full block (see Figure 8-2), and **modified block** (see Figure 8-3). Your organization may make minor changes from the diagrams in margins or spacing.

Figure 8-1 shows how the formats differ.

Use the same level of formality in the **salutation,** or greeting, as you would in talking to someone on the phone: *Dear Glenn* if you're on a first-name basis, *Dear Mr. Helms* if you don't know the reader well enough to use the first name.

Sincerely and *Cordially* are standard **complimentary closes.** When you are writing to people in special groups or to someone who is a friend as well as a business acquaintance, you may want to use a less formal close. Depending on the circumstances, the following informal closes might be acceptable: *Yours for a better environment,* or even *Ciao.*

In **mixed punctuation,** a colon follows the salutation and a comma follows the close. In a sales or fund-raising letter, it is acceptable to use a comma after the salutation to make the letter look like a personal letter rather than like a business letter. In **open punctuation,** omit all punctuation after the salutation and the close. Mixed punctuation is traditional. Open punctuation is faster to type.

A **subject line** tells what the letter is about. Subject lines are required in memos; they are optional in letters. Good subject lines are specific, concise, and appropriate for your purposes and the response you expect from your reader.

- When you have good news, put it in the subject line.

- When your information is neutral, summarize it concisely in the subject line.

- When your information is negative, use a negative subject line if the reader may not read the message or needs the information to act, or if the negative is your error.

- When you have a request that will be easy for the reader to grant, put either the subject of the request or a direct question in the subject line.

- When you must persuade a reluctant reader, use a common ground, a reader benefit, or a directed subject line that makes your stance on the issue clear.

A **reference line** refers the reader to the number used on the previous correspondence this letter replies to, or the order or invoice number which this letter is about. Very large organizations, such as the IRS, use numbers on every piece of correspondence they send out so that it is possible quickly to find the earlier document to which an incoming letter refers.

Although not every example uses the same devices to provide visual impact, both formats can use headings, lists, and indented sections for emphasis.

Each format has advantages. Block format is the format most frequently used for business letters; readers expect it; it can be typed quickly since everything is lined up at the left margin. Modified block format creates a visually attractive page by moving the date and signature block over into what would otherwise be empty white space. Modified block is a traditional format; readers are comfortable with it.

Figure 8-1   Differences between Letter Formats

	Block	**Modified Block**
Date and signature block	Lined up at left margin	Lined up 1/2 or 2/3 over to the right
Paragraph indentation	None	Optional
Subject Line	Optional	Rare

The examples of the formats in Figures 8-2 and 8-3 show one-page letters on company letterhead. **Letterhead** is preprinted stationery with the organization's name, logo, address, and phone number. Figure 8-4 shows how to set up modified block format when you do not have letterhead. (It is also acceptable to use block format without letterhead.)

When your letter runs two or more pages, use a heading on the second page to identify it. Putting the reader's name helps the writer, who may be printing out many letters at a time, to make sure the right second page gets in the envelope. Note even when the signature block is on the second page, it is still lined up with the date.

Reader's Name
Date
Page Number

or

Reader's Name Page Number   Date

When a letter runs two or more pages, use letterhead only for page 1. (See Figures 8-5 and 8-6.) For the remaining pages, use plain paper that matches the letterhead in weight, texture, and color.

Set side margins of 1" to 1 1/2" on the left and 3/4" to 1" on the right. If your letterhead extends all the way across the top of the page, set your margins even with the ends of the letterhead for the most visually pleasing page. The top margin should be three to six lines under the letterhead, or 2" down from the top of the page if you aren't using letterhead. If your letter is very short, you may want to use bigger side and top margins so that the letter is centered on the page.

Many letters are accompanied by other documents. Whatever these documents may be—a multi-page report or a two-line note—they are called **enclosures,** since they are enclosed in the envelope. The writer should refer to the enclosures in the body of the letter: "As you can see from my résumé, ..." The enclosure line is usually abbreviated: *Encl.* (see Figure 8-3). The abbreviation reminds the person who seals the letter to include the enclosure(s).

Sometimes you write to one person but send copies of your letter to other people. If you want the reader to know that other people are getting copies, list their names on the last page. The abbreviation *cc* originally meant *carbon copy* but now means *computer copy*. Other acceptable abbreviations include *pc* for *photocopy* or simply *c* for *copy*. You can also send copies to other people without telling the reader. Such copies are called **blind copies.** Blind copies are not mentioned on the original; they are listed on the copy saved for the file with the abbreviation *bc* preceding the names of people getting these copies.

You do not need to indicate that you have shown a letter to your superior or that you are saving a copy of the letter for your own files. These are standard practices.

Figure 8-2
Block Format on Letterhead (mixed punctuation; collection letter)

100 Freeway Exchange
Provo, UT 84610

Line up everything at left margin

Northwest Hardware Warehouse

(801) 555-4683

↕ *2–6 spaces depending on length of letter*

June 20, 2001

1"–1 1/2"

Mr. James E. Murphy , Accounts Payable   *Title could be on a separate line*
Salt Lake Equipment Rentals
5600 Wasatch Boulevard
Salt Lake City , Utah 84121

Use first name in salutation if you'd use it on the phone

Dear Jim: *Colon in mixed punctuation*

The following items totaling $393.09 are still open on your account.   *¶ 1 never has a heading*

Invoice #01R-784391 *Bold heading*

After the bill for this invoice arrived on May 14, you wrote saying that the material had not been delivered to you. On May 29, our Claims Department sent you a copy of the delivery receipt signed by an employee of Salt Lake Equipment. You have had proof of delivery for over three weeks, but your payment has not yet arrived.   *5/8" – 1"*

Please send a check for $78.42.   *Single-space paragraphs*
Double-space between paragraphs

Triple-space before new heading

Voucher #59351

Do not indent paragraphs

The reference line on your voucher #59351, dated June 11, indicates that it is the gross payment for invoice #01G-002345. However , the voucher was only for $1171.25, while the invoice amount was $1246.37. Please send a check for $75.12 to clear this item.

Voucher #55032

Voucher #55032 dated June 15, subtracts a credit for $239.55 from the amount due. Our records do not show that any credit is due on this voucher. Please send either an explanation or a check to cover the $239.55 immediately.

Total Amount Due   *Headings are optional in letters*

Please send a check for $393.09 to cover these three items and to bring your account up to date.

↕ *2–3 spaces*
Sincerely,

3–4 spaces

[signature: Neil Hutchinson]

Neil Hutchinson
Credit Representative

cc: Joan Stottlemyer, Credit Manager

Leave bottom margin of 3–6 spaces— more if letter is short

Figure 8-3
Modified Block Format on Letterhead (mixed punctuation; letter of recommendation)

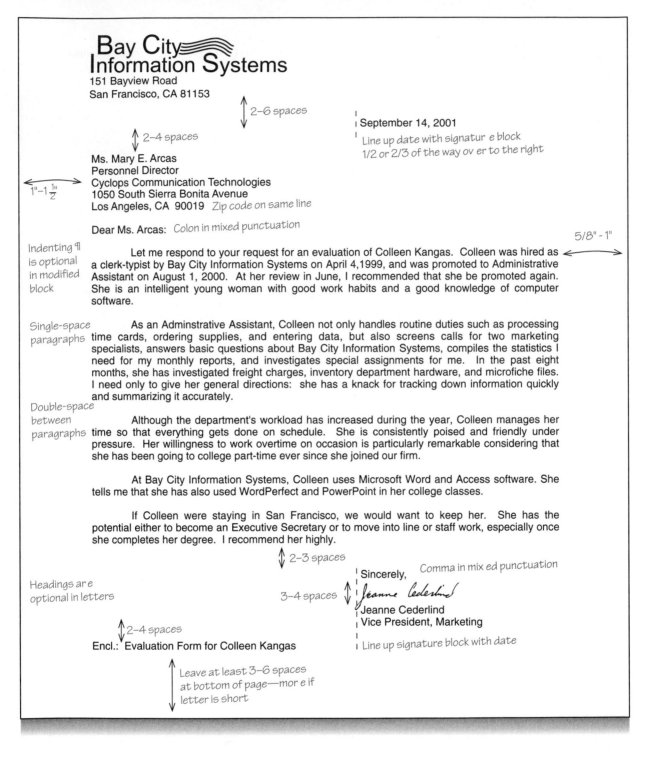

Figure 8-4
Modified Block Format without Letterhead (open punctuation; claim letter)

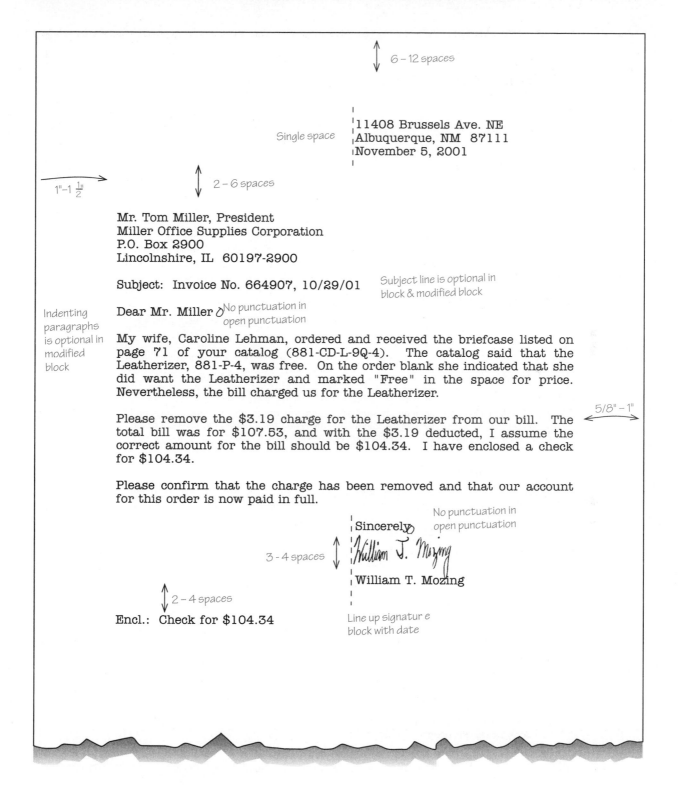

6 – 12 spaces

Single space

11408 Brussels Ave. NE
Albuquerque, NM 87111
November 5, 2001

1"–1 ½"

2 – 6 spaces

Mr. Tom Miller, President
Miller Office Supplies Corporation
P.O. Box 2900
Lincolnshire, IL 60197-2900

Subject: Invoice No. 664907, 10/29/01

Subject line is optional in block & modified block

Indenting paragraphs is optional in modified block

Dear Mr. Miller

No punctuation in open punctuation

My wife, Caroline Lehman, ordered and received the briefcase listed on page 71 of your catalog (881-CD-L-9Q-4). The catalog said that the Leatherizer, 881-P-4, was free. On the order blank she indicated that she did want the Leatherizer and marked "Free" in the space for price. Nevertheless, the bill charged us for the Leatherizer.

Please remove the $3.19 charge for the Leatherizer from our bill. The total bill was for $107.53, and with the $3.19 deducted, I assume the correct amount for the bill should be $104.34. I have enclosed a check for $104.34.

5/8" – 1"

Please confirm that the charge has been removed and that our account for this order is now paid in full.

Sincerely

No punctuation in open punctuation

3 - 4 spaces

William T. Mozing

2 – 4 spaces

Encl.: Check for $104.34

Line up signature block with date

Figure 8-5
Second Page of a Two-Page Letter, Block Format (mixed punctuation; informative letter)

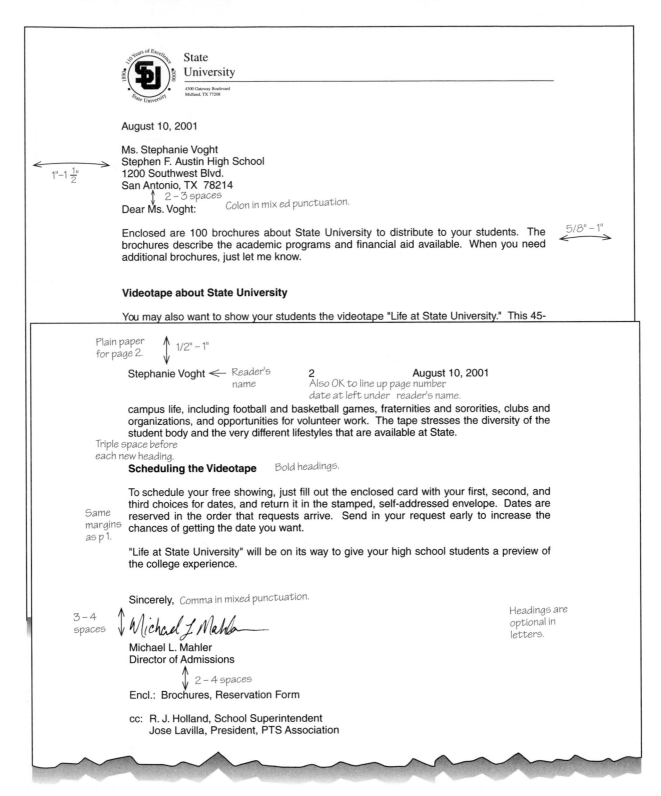

State
University

4300 Gateway Boulevard
Midland, TX 77208

August 10, 2001

Ms. Stephanie Voght
Stephen F. Austin High School
1200 Southwest Blvd.
San Antonio, TX 78214

Dear Ms. Voght: *Colon in mixed punctuation.*

2 – 3 spaces

1"–1 ½"

Enclosed are 100 brochures about State University to distribute to your students. The brochures describe the academic programs and financial aid available. When you need additional brochures, just let me know.   *5/8" – 1"*

Videotape about State University

You may also want to show your students the videotape "Life at State University." This 45-

Plain paper for page 2.   *1/2" – 1"*

Stephanie Voght ← *Reader's name*   2   August 10, 2001

Also OK to line up page number date at left under reader's name.

campus life, including football and basketball games, fraternities and sororities, clubs and organizations, and opportunities for volunteer work. The tape stresses the diversity of the student body and the very different lifestyles that are available at State.

Triple space before each new heading.

Scheduling the Videotape   *Bold headings.*

To schedule your free showing, just fill out the enclosed card with your first, second, and third choices for dates, and return it in the stamped, self-addressed envelope. Dates are reserved in the order that requests arrive. Send in your request early to increase the chances of getting the date you want.

Same margins as p 1.

"Life at State University" will be on its way to give your high school students a preview of the college experience.

Sincerely, *Comma in mixed punctuation.*

3 – 4 spaces

Michael L. Mahler
Director of Admissions

Headings are optional in letters.

2 – 4 spaces

Encl.: Brochures, Reservation Form

cc: R. J. Holland, School Superintendent
    Jose Lavilla, President, PTS Association

Figure 8-6
Second Page of a Two-Page Letter, Modified Block Format (mixed punctuation; goodwill letter)

Glenarvon Carpets

1500 Summit Avenue   *(612) 555-1002*
Minneapolis, MN 55401   *Fax (612) 555-4032*

November 8, 2001
Line up date with signature block.

↕ *2 – 4 spaces*

Mr. Roger B. Castino
Castino Floors and Carpets
418 E. North Street
Brockton, MA 02410

Dear Mr. Castino:

Indenting paragraphs is optional in modified block.

Welcome to the team of Glenarvon Carpet dealers!

Your first shipment of Glenarvon samples should reach you within ten days. The samples include new shades in a variety of weights. With Glenarvon Carpets, your customers can choose matching colors in heavy-duty weights for high-traffic areas and lighter, less expensive weights for less-used rooms.

Plain paper for page 2   ↕ *1/2" – 1"*

Mr. Roger B. Castino   Center 2   November 8, 2001
← *Reader's name*

territory. In addition, as a dealer you receive

*   Sales kit highlighting product features
*   Samples to distribute to customers
*   Advertising copy to run in local newspapers
*   Display units to place in your store.

Indent or center list to emphasize it.

Use same margins as p 1.

The Annual Sales Meeting each January keeps you up-to-date on new products while you get to know other dealers and Glenarvon executives and relax at a resort hotel.

Make your reservations now for Monterey January 10-13 for your first Glenarvon Sales Meeting!

Cordially, *Comma in mixed punctuation.*

3 – 4 spaces ↕

Barbara S. Charbonneau

Barbara S. Charbonneau
Vice President, Marketing

Line up signature block with date in heading and on . p 1.

↕ *1 – 4 spaces*

Encl.: Organization Chart
Product List
National Advertising Campaigns in 2001
1 – 4 spaces
cc: Nancy Magill, Northeast Sales Manager
Edward Spaulding, Sales Representative

↕ *3 – 6 spaces — more if second page isn't a full page.*

Building a Critical Skill

Creating a Professional Image, 1

The way you and your documents look affects the way people respond to you and to them. Every organization has a dress code. One young man was upset when an older man told him he should wear wing-tip shoes. He was wearing leather shoes but not the kind that said "I'm promotable" in that workplace. Dress codes are rarely spelled out; the older worker was doing the young man a favor by being direct. If you have a mentor in the organization, ask him or her if there are other ways you can make your appearance even more professional. If you don't have a mentor, look at the people who rank above you. Notice clothing, jewelry, and hairstyles. If you're on a budget, go to stores that sell expensive clothing to check the kind of buttons, the texture and colors of fabric, the width of lapels and belts. Then go to stores in your price range and choose garments that imitate the details of expensive clothing.

Documents need to look professional, too. Now that most documents are keyed in on computers and printed on laser printers, we don't need to worry about whited-out errors or uneven key strokes. We do need to make sure that the ink or toner is printing evenly and that the document uses a standard format. Some organizations prescribe a standard format for documents. If your organization does, follow it. If you have your choice, use one of the formats in this book. They're widely used in businesses, so they communicate a message of competence.

States with names of more than five letters are frequently abbreviated in letters and memos. The U.S. Postal Service abbreviations use two capital letters with no punctuation. See Figure 8-7.

WHAT COURTESY TITLES SHOULD I USE?

Use "Ms." unless a woman has a professional title or prefers a traditional title.
Use "Mr." unless a man has a professional title.

Letters require courtesy titles in the salutation *unless* you're on a first-name basis with your reader. Use the first name only if you'd use it in talking to the person on the phone.

When You Know the Reader's Name and Gender

When you know your reader's name and gender, use courtesy titles that do not indicate marital status: *Mr.* for men and *Ms.* for women. There are, however, two exceptions:

1. Use professional titles when they're relevant.

   Dr. Kristen Sorenson is our new company physician.

   The Rev. Robert Townsley gave the invocation.

2. If a woman prefers to be addressed as *Mrs.* or *Miss,* use the title she prefers rather than *Ms.* (You-attitude takes precedence over nonsexist language: address the reader as she—or he—prefers to be addressed.)

   To find out if a woman prefers a traditional title,

   a. Check the signature block in previous correspondence. If a woman types her name as *(Miss) Elaine Anderson* or *(Mrs.) Kay Royster,* use the title she designates.

   b. Notice the title a woman uses in introducing herself on the phone. If she says, "This is Robin Stine," use *Ms.* when you write to her. If she says, "I'm Mrs. Stine," use the title she specifies.

   c. Check your company directory. In some organizations, women who prefer traditional titles can list them with their names.

   d. When you're writing job letters or other crucial correspondence, call the company and ask the receptionist which title your reader prefers.

Figure 8-7   **Postal Service Abbreviations for States, Territories, and Provinces**

State Name	Postal Service Abbreviation	State Name	PostalService Abbreviation
Alabama	AL	Missouri	MO
Alaska	AK	Montana	MT
Arizona	AZ	Nebraska	NE
Arkansas	AR	Nevada	NV
California	CA	New Hampshire	NH
Colorado	CO	New Jersey	NJ
Connecticut	CT	New Mexico	NM
Delaware	DE	New York	NY
District of Columbia	DC	North Carolina	NC
Florida	FL	North Dakota	ND
Georgia	GA	Ohio	OH
Hawaii	HI	Oklahoma	OK
Idaho	ID	Oregon	OR
Illinois	IL	Pennsylvania	PA
Indiana	IN	Rhode Island	RI
Iowa	IA	South Carolina	SC
Kansas	KS	South Dakota	SD
Kentucky	KY	Tennessee	TN
Louisiana	LA	Texas	TX
Maine	ME	Utah	UT
Maryland	MD	Vermont	VT
Massachuettes	MA	Virginia	VA
Michigan	MI	Washington	WA
Minnesota	MN	West Virginia	WV
Mississippi	MS	Wisconsin	WI
		Wyoming	WY

Territory	Postal Service Abbreviation	Province Name	PostalService Abbreviation
Guam	GU	Alberta	AB
Puerto Rico	PR	British Columbia	BC
Virgin Islands	VI	Labrador	LB
		Manitoba	MB
		New Brunswick	NB
		Newfoundland	NF
		Northwest Territories	NT
		Nova Scotia	NS
		Ontario	ON
		Prince Edward Island	PE
		Quebec	PQ
		Saskatchewan	SK
		Yukon Territory	YT

Ms. is particularly useful when you do not know what a woman's marital status is. However, even when you happen to know that a woman is married or single, **you still use *Ms.* unless you know that she prefers another title.**

In addition to using parallel courtesy titles, use parallel forms for names.

Not Parallel	**Parallel**
Members of the committee will be Mr. Jones, Mr. Yacone, and Lisa.	Members of the committee will be Mr. Jones, Mr. Yacone, and Ms. Melton. *or* Members of the committee will be Irving, Ted, and Lisa.

When You Know the Reader's Name but Not the Gender

When you know your reader's name but not the gender, either
1. Call the company and ask the receptionist, or
2. Use the reader's full name in the salutation:

   Dear Chris Crowell:

   Dear J. C. Meath:

When You Know neither the Reader's Name nor Gender

When you know neither the reader's name nor gender, you have three options:
1. Use the reader's position or job title:

   Dear Loan Officer:

   Dear Registrar:

2. Use a general group to which your reader belongs:

   Dear Investor:

   Dear Admissions Committee:

3. Omit the salutation and use a subject line in its place:

   Subject: Recommendation for Ben Wandell

HOW SHOULD I SET UP MEMOS?

The standard memo format mimics block format but has no salutation, close, or signature.

Memos omit both the salutation and the close. Memos never indent paragraphs. Subject lines are required; headings are optional. Each heading must cover all the information until the next heading. Never use a separate heading for the first paragraph.

Figure 8-8 illustrates the standard memo format typed on a plain sheet of paper. Note that the first letters of the reader's name, the writer's name, and the subject phrase are lined up vertically. Note also that memos are usually initialed by the To/From block. Initialing tells the reader that your have proofread the memo and prevents someone's sending out your name on a memo you did not in fact write.

Some organizations have special letterhead for memos. When *Date/To/From/Subject* are already printed on the form, the date, writer's and reader's names, and subject may be set at the main margin to save typing time. (See Figure 8-9.)

Some organizations alter the order of items in the *Date/To/From/Subject* block. Some organizations ask employees to sign memos rather than simply initialing them. The signature goes below the last line of the memo, starting halfway over on the page, and prevents anyone adding unauthorized information.

If the memo runs two pages or more, use a heading at the top of the second and subsequent pages (see Figure 8-10). Since many of your memos go to the same people, putting a brief version of the subject line will be more helpful than just using "All Employees."

Brief Subject Line
Date
Page Number

or

Brief Subject Line   Page Number   Date

HOW SHOULD I SET UP E-MAIL MESSAGES?

Formats are still evolving.

Most e-mail programs prompt you to supply the various parts of the format. For example, a blank Eudora screen prompts you to supply the name of the person the message goes to and the subject line. *Cc* denotes computer copies; the recipient will see that these people are getting the message. *Bcc* denotes blind computer copies; the recipient does not see the names of these people. Most e-mail programs also allow you to attach documents from other programs. Thus you can send someone a document with formatting, drafts of PowerPoint slides, or the design for a brochure cover. The computer program supplies the date and time automatically. Some programs allow you to write a message now and program the future time at which you want it to be sent.

Some aspects of e-mail format are still evolving. In particular, some writers treat e-mail messages as if they were informal letters; some treat them as memos. Even though the e-mail screen has a "To" line (as do memos), some writers still use an informal salutation, as in Figure 8-11. The writer in Figure 8-11 ends the message with a signature block. You can store a signature block in the e-mail program and set the program to insert the signature block automatically. In contrast, the writer in Figure 8-12 omits both the salutation and his name. When you send a message to an individual or a group you have set up, the "From:" line will have your name and e-mail address. If you post a message to a group someone else has set up, such as a listserv, be sure to give at least your name and e-mail address at the end of your message, as some listservs strip out identifying information when they process messages.

When you hit "reply," the e-mail program automatically uses "Re:" (Latin for *about*) and the previous subject. The original message is set off with carats (see Figure 8-13). You may want to change the subject line to make it more appropriate for your message.

If you prepare your document in a word processor, use two-inch side margins to create short line lengths. If the line lengths are too long, they'll produce awkward line breaks as in Figure 8-13. Use two- or three-space tab settings to minimize the wasted space on the screen.

Figure 8-8
Memo Format (on plain paper; direct request)

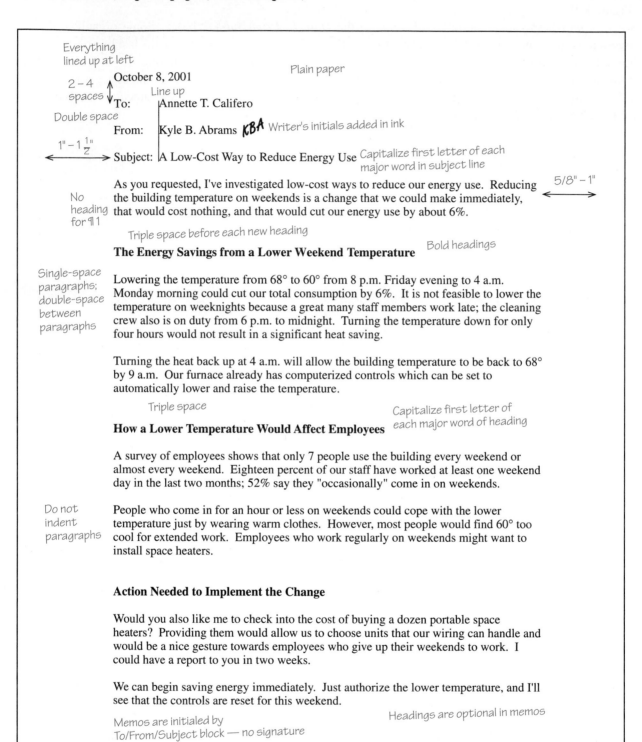

Everything lined up at left

Plain paper

2 – 4 spaces

October 8, 2001

Line up

To: Annette T. Califero

Double space

From: Kyle B. Abrams *KBA*   Writer's initials added in ink

1" – 1½"

Subject: A Low-Cost Way to Reduce Energy Use   Capitalize first letter of each major word in subject line

As you requested, I've investigated low-cost ways to reduce our energy use. Reducing the building temperature on weekends is a change that we could make immediately, that would cost nothing, and that would cut our energy use by about 6%.

5/8" – 1"

No heading for ¶ 1

Triple space before each new heading

The Energy Savings from a Lower Weekend Temperature   Bold headings

Single-space paragraphs; double-space between paragraphs

Lowering the temperature from 68° to 60° from 8 p.m. Friday evening to 4 a.m. Monday morning could cut our total consumption by 6%. It is not feasible to lower the temperature on weeknights because a great many staff members work late; the cleaning crew also is on duty from 6 p.m. to midnight. Turning the temperature down for only four hours would not result in a significant heat saving.

Turning the heat back up at 4 a.m. will allow the building temperature to be back to 68° by 9 a.m. Our furnace already has computerized controls which can be set to automatically lower and raise the temperature.

Triple space

Capitalize first letter of each major word of heading

How a Lower Temperature Would Affect Employees

A survey of employees shows that only 7 people use the building every weekend or almost every weekend. Eighteen percent of our staff have worked at least one weekend day in the last two months; 52% say they "occasionally" come in on weekends.

Do not indent paragraphs

People who come in for an hour or less on weekends could cope with the lower temperature just by wearing warm clothes. However, most people would find 60° too cool for extended work. Employees who work regularly on weekends might want to install space heaters.

Action Needed to Implement the Change

Would you also like me to check into the cost of buying a dozen portable space heaters? Providing them would allow us to choose units that our wiring can handle and would be a nice gesture towards employees who give up their weekends to work. I could have a report to you in two weeks.

We can begin saving energy immediately. Just authorize the lower temperature, and I'll see that the controls are reset for this weekend.

Memos are initialed by To/From/Subject block — no signature

Headings are optional in memos

Figure 8-9
Memo Format (on memo letterhead; good news)

Kimball,
Walls, and
Morganstern

Date: March 15, 2002   *Line up horizontally with printed Date/To/From/Subject*

To: Annette T. Califero

From: Kyle B. Abrams *KBA* *Writer's initials added in ink*

*Capitalize first
letter of each major
word in subject line*

Subject: The Effectiveness of Reducing Building Temperatures on Weekends

Triple space

*Margin lined up
with items in
To/From/Subject
block to save
typing time*

Reducing the building temperature to 60° on weekends has cut energy use by 4% compared to last year's use from December to February and has saved our firm $22,000.

This savings is particularly remarkable when you consider that this winter has been colder than last year's, so that more heat would be needed to maintain the same temperature.

5/8" – 1"

Fewer people have worked weekends during the past three months than during the preceding three months, but snow and bad driving conditions may have had more to do with keeping people home than the fear of being cold. Five of the 12 space heaters we bought have been checked out on an average weekend. On one weekend, all 12 were in use and some people shared their offices so that everyone could be in a room with a space heater.

Fully 92% of our employees support the lower temperature. I recommend that we continue turning down the heat on weekends through the remainder of the heating season and that we resume the practice when the heat is turned on next fall.

Headings are optional in memos

Figure 8-10
Option 2 for Page 2 of a Memo (direct request)

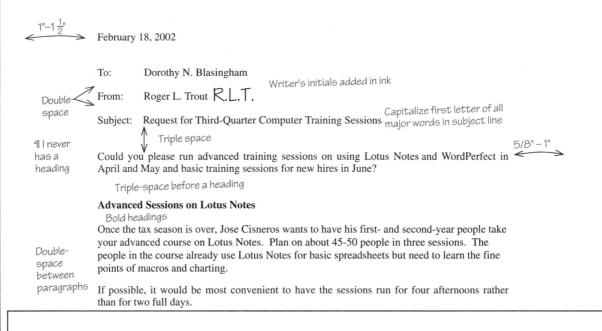

$1"–1\frac{1}{2}"$

February 18, 2002

To: Dorothy N. Blasingham

Writer's initials added in ink

Double-space

From: Roger L. Trout R.L.T.

Subject: Request for Third-Quarter Computer Training Sessions

Capitalize first letter of all major words in subject line

¶ I never has a heading

Triple space

Could you please run advanced training sessions on using Lotus Notes and WordPerfect in April and May and basic training sessions for new hires in June?

$5/8" – 1"$

Triple-space before a heading

Advanced Sessions on Lotus Notes
Bold headings

Once the tax season is over, Jose Cisneros wants to have his first- and second-year people take your advanced course on Lotus Notes. Plan on about 45-50 people in three sessions. The people in the course already use Lotus Notes for basic spreadsheets but need to learn the fine points of macros and charting.

Double-space between paragraphs

If possible, it would be most convenient to have the sessions run for four afternoons rather than for two full days.

Plain paper for page 2

$1/2" – 1"$

Dorothy N. Blasingham

Brief subject line or reader's name

2 *Page number*

February 18, 2002

Also OK to line up page number, date at left under reader's name

Same margins as p 1.

before the summer vacation season begins.

Orientation for New Hires

Capitalize first letter of all major words in heading

With a total of 16 full-time and 34 part-time people being hired either for summer or permanent work, we'll need at least two and perhaps three orientation sessions. We'd like to hold these the first, second, and third weeks in June. By May 1, we should know how many people will be in each training session.

Would you be free to conduct training sessions on how to use our computers on June 8, June 15, and June 22? If we need only two dates, we'll use June 8 and June 15, but please block off the 22nd too in case we need a third session.

Triple-space before a heading

Request for Confirmation

Let me know whether you're free on these dates in June, and which dates you'd prefer for the sessions on Lotus Notes and WordPerfect. If you'll let me know by February 25, we can get information out to participants in plenty of time for the sessions.

Thanks!

Memos are initialed by To/From/Subject block

Headings are optional in memos

Figure 8-11
A Basic E-Mail Message in Eudora (direct request)

To: larenzor@artemis.com   *The writer can type in the e-mail address directly.*
From: Sacha Zevchik <zevchik.2@acme.com>   *System puts in writer's name and e-mail address.*
Subject: Please Protect Computers
Cc:
Bcc:
Attached: *Write your message below the line.*

_____

Roger-- *Some writers use an informal salutation to make the message friendlier.*

No need to indent paragraphs. Just a reminder: when your workers install the ceiling insulation next week, be sure to have them put plastic sheeting over the desks and computers to protect them from sawdust, insulation, and debris.

Thanks!

Sacha Zevchik   *The writer creates the signature block*
Administrative Assistant   *once, then can use it automatically.*
Voice: 630-555-1000 ext. 117   *Some e-mail programs permit you to*
Fax: 630-555-2391   *store several signature blocks with*
E-Mail: zevchik.2@acme.com   *different levels of formality.*

Figure 8-12
An E-Mail Message with an Attachment (direct request)

To: TAC <tac@acme.com>   *E-mail programs allow you to create "nicknames" or "aliases" for individuals*
From: Keith Lee <lee.526@acme.com> *and names for groups. "TAC" sends messages to everyone on the "Technology Advisory Committee"*
Subject: Please Comment on Draft
Cc:
Bcc: *Above the line, use the "attach" icon—the path on your computer*
Attached: D:\comm\personalcomputer.draft   *is inserted*

_____

Attached is the current draft on personally-owned computers that people bring into the office.

Many e-mail programs support hyperlinks. Readers can click here
The file is in WordPerfect: *(the path where the message is stored on the recipient's*

c:\attachments\personalcomputer.draft   *computer) to go to the document.*

Please send me any changes by 10 a.m. Thursday—I'll collate them and bring them to our meeting Thursday afternoon.

This writer omits salutation and signature block.

Figure 8-13
An E-Mail Reply with Copies (response to a complaint)

Hitting "Reply" Produces "Re" and the original subject line.

When you "reply," the system inserts the recipient's e-mail address.

To: Ellen Oshio <ellen_oshio@gte.net>
From: Mary Monroe <mary_monroe.custserv@acme.com>
Subject: (Re:) Problems with Customer Service Reps
Cc: all.custserv@acme.com
Bcc: Wade <wade_palmer@acme.com>
Attached:

Recipient sees "cc"—will know it is going to the whole department.

Recipient doesn't see "Blind copies"

Using the reader's name in ¶1 makes the message more friendly.

Thank you, Ms. Oshio, for letting us know about the problem you've had. We're certainly not glad that there *is* a problem, but if there is one, we want to fix it—and we can do that only when we know what the problem is.

When you reply to a message, put your response first.

Of course we want our customer service representatives to be polite and professional. I apologize for the responses you've had. I'll work with all our reps to polish our phone skills. When you call our Customer Service line, we want you to get service that's just as good as the high-quality bath and kitchen fixtures you recommend to your clients!

Rather than using a signature block, this writer just types her name and job title.

Mary Monroe
Customer Service Manager

P.S. The Lifetime Brass Finish is currently scheduled for June 1 availability. I'll let you know a month from now if that date is going to hold.

Space between your message and the original message to make yours easier to read.

At 11:01 AM 4/27/1999 -0500, you wrote:

System inserts date, time of original message.

Carats denote a message written by the recipient (or forwarded from someone else).

>I don't want to switch suppliers, but recent experiences with your reps have
>just about made me change my mind. I just don't want to do business with them
anymore.

>As you know, the Lifetime Brass Finish has missed several roll-out dates. Those
>delays have been bad enough. But even worse have been my encounters with
>your customer reps. The reps I dealt with were curt and more concerned with
>justifying their mistakes than satisfying my needs.

>Today, I had another distasteful encounter with a customer service rep (Danielle was
>her name) who was rude and unprofessional—in fact, she hung up on me when I asked her
>last name. The woman had no business handling customer complaints because she seemed
>to take them personally. She accused me of "yelling" at her and then lectured me on
>her status as a human being. I am never rude or abusive to people; such behavior isn't
>nice and would ruin my own credibility.

These odd, distracting line breaks result when you receive a message whose line lengths are too long for your e-mail program. To avoid them, use short line lengths when you compose e-mail messages.

>I think you should know that, at least in their dealings with me, some of your reps
>are not serving your interests well (and I have told them that on several occasions).

INFORMATIVE AND POSITIVE MESSAGES

We categorize messages both by the author's purposes and by the initial response we expect from the reader. When we need to convey information to which the reader's basic reaction will be neutral, the message is informative. If we convey information to which the reader's reaction will be positive, the message is a positive or good news message. Neither message immediately asks the reader to do anything. However, you may well want the reader to save the information and to act on it later on. You usually do want to build positive attitudes toward the information you are presenting, so in that sense, even an informative message has a persuasive element.

Informative and positive messages include:

- Acceptances.

- Positive answers to reader requests.

- Information about procedures, products, services, or options.

- Announcements of policy changes that are neutral or positive.

- Changes that are to the reader's advantage.

Even a simple informative or good news message usually has several purposes:

Primary Purposes:

> To give information or good news to the reader or to reassure the reader.

> To have the reader read the message, understand it, and view the information positively.

> To deemphasize any negative elements.

Secondary Purposes:

> To build a good image of the writer.

> To build a good image of the writer's organization.

> To cement a good relationship between the writer and reader.

> To reduce or eliminate future correspondence on the same subject so the message doesn't create more work for the writer.

WHAT'S THE BEST SUBJECT LINE FOR AN INFORMATIVE OR POSITIVE MESSAGE?

One that contains the basic information or good news.

A **subject line** is the title of a document. It aids in filing and retrieving the document, tells readers why they need to read the document, and provides a framework in which to set what you're about to say.

Subject lines are standard in memos. Letters are not required to have subject lines. However, a survey of business people in the Southwest found that 68% of them considered a subject line in a letter to be important, very important, or essential; only 32% considered subject lines to be unimportant or only somewhat important.[1]

A good subject line meets three criteria: it is specific, concise, and appropriate to the kind of message (positive, negative, persuasive).

Making Subject Lines Specific

The subject line needs to be specific enough to differentiate that message from others on the same subject, but broad enough to cover everything in the message.

Too general:	Training Sessions
Better:	Dates for 200—Training Sessions
or:	Evaluation of Training Sessions on Conducting Interviews
or:	Should We Schedule a Short Course on Proposal Writing?

Making Subject Lines Concise

Most subject lines are relatively short—usually no more than 10 words, often only 3 to 7 words.[2]

Wordy:	Survey of Student Preferences in Regards to Various Pizza Factors
Better:	Students' Pizza Preferences
or:	The Feasibility of a Cassano's Branch on Campus
or:	What Students Like and Dislike about Giovanni Pizza

If you can't make the subject both specific and short, be specific.

Making Subject Lines Appropriate for the Pattern of Organization

In general, do the same thing in your subject line that you would do in the first paragraph.

When you have good news for the reader, build goodwill by highlighting it in the subject line. When your information is neutral, summarize it concisely for the subject line.

HOW SHOULD I ORGANIZE INFORMATIVE AND POSITIVE MESSAGES?

Put the good news and a summary of the information first.

The patterns of organization in this module and the modules that follow will work for 70 to 90% of the writing situations most people in business, government, and nonprofit organizations face. Using the appropriate pattern can help you compose more quickly and create a better final product.

- Be sure you understand the rationale behind each pattern so that you can modify the pattern if necessary. (For example, if you write instructions, any warnings should go up front, not in the middle of the message.)

- Not every message that uses the basic pattern will have all the elements listed. The elements you do have will go in the order presented in the pattern.

- Sometimes you can present several elements in one paragraph. Sometimes you'll need several paragraphs for just one element.

Present informative and positive messages in the following order:

Subject: Discount on Rental Cars Effective January 2

Starting January 2, as an employee of Amalgamated Industries you can get a 15% discount on cars you rent for business or personal use from Roadway Rent-a-Car.

Subject: Update on Arrangements for Videoconference with France

In the last month, we have chosen the participants and developed a tentative agenda for the videoconference with France scheduled for March 21.

1. **Give any good news and summarize the main points.** Share good news immediately. Include details such as the date policies begin and the percent of a discount. If the reader has already raised the issue, make it clear that you're responding.

2. **Give details, clarification, background.** Don't repeat information from the first paragraph. Do answer all the questions your reader is likely to have; provide all the information necessary to achieve your purposes. Present details in the order of importance to the reader.

3. **Present any negative elements—as positively as possible.** A policy may have limits; information may be incomplete; the reader may have to satisfy requirements to get a discount or benefit. Make these negatives clear, but present them as positively as possible.

4. Explain any reader benefits. Most informative memos need reader benefits. Show that the policy or procedure helps readers, not just the company. Give enough detail to make the benefits clear and convincing. In letters, you may want to give benefits of dealing with your company as well as benefits of the product or policy.

    In a good news message, it's often possible to combine a short reader benefit with a goodwill ending in the last paragraph.

5. **Use a goodwill ending: positive, personal, and forward-looking.** Shifting your emphasis away from the message to the specific reader suggests that serving the reader is your real concern.

Figure 8-14 summarizes the pattern. Figures 8-15 and 8-16 illustrate two ways that the basic pattern can be applied.

The letter in Figure 8-15 authorizes a one-year appointment that the reader and writer have already discussed and describes the organization's priorities. Since the writer knows that the reader wants to accept the job, the letter doesn't need to persuade. The opportunity for the professor to study records that aren't available to the public is an implicit reader benefit; the concern for the reader's needs builds goodwill.

The memo in Figure 8-16 announces a new employee benefit. The first paragraph summarizes the policy. Paragraphs 2 to 5 give details. Negative elements are in paragraphs 3 to 5, stated as positively as possible. The last section of the memo gives reader benefits and shows that everyone—even part-timers who are not eligible for reimbursement—will benefit from the new program.

WHEN SHOULD I USE READER BENEFITS IN INFORMATIVE AND POSITIVE MESSAGES?

When you want readers to view your policies and your organization positively.

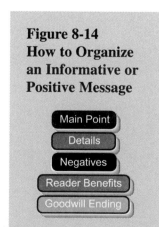

**Figure 8-14
How to Organize
an Informative or
Positive Message**

Main Point
Details
Negatives
Reader Benefits
Goodwill Ending

Not all informative and positive messages need reader benefits. You don't need reader benefits when

- You're presenting factual information only.
- The reader's attitude toward the information doesn't matter.
- Stressing benefits may make the reader sound selfish.
- The benefits are so obvious that to restate them insults the reader's intelligence.

You do need reader benefits when

- You are presenting policies.
- You want to shape readers' attitudes toward the information or toward your organization.
- Stressing benefits presents readers' motives positively.
- Some of the benefits may not be obvious to readers.

Messages to customers or potential customers sometimes include a sales paragraph promoting products or services you offer in addition to the product or service that the reader has asked about. Sales promotion in an informative or positive message should be low-key, not "hard sell."

Reader benefits are hardest to develop when you are announcing policies. The organization probably decided to adopt the policy because it appeared to help the organization; the people who made the decision may not have thought at all about whether it would help or hurt employees. Yet reader benefits are most essential in this kind of message so readers see the reason for the change and support it.

When you present reader benefits, be sure to present advantages to the reader. Most new policies help the organization in some way, but few workers will see their own interests as identical with the organization's. Even if the organization saves money or increases its profits, workers will benefit directly only if they own stock in the company, if they're high up enough to receive bonuses, if the savings enables a failing company to avoid layoffs, or if all of the savings goes directly to employee benefits. In many companies, any money saved will go to executive bonuses, shareholder profits, or research and development.

Develop reader benefits for informative and positive messages. Be sure to think about intrinsic benefits of your policy, that is, benefits that come from the activity or policy itself, apart from any financial benefits. Does a policy improve the eight hours people spend at work?

WHAT KINDS OF INFORMATIVE AND POSITIVE MESSAGES AM I LIKELY TO WRITE?

Transmittals, confirmations, summaries, adjustments, and thank-you notes

Many messages can be informative, negative, or persuasive depending on what you have to say. A transmittal, for example, can be positive when you're sending glowing sales figures or persuasive when you want the reader to act on the information. A performance appraisal is positive when you evaluate someone who's doing superbly, negative when you want to compile a record to justify firing someone, and persuasive when you want to motivate a satisfactory worker to continue to improve. A collection letter is persuasive; it becomes negative in the last stage when you threaten legal action. Each of these messages is discussed in the module for the pattern it uses most frequently. However, in some cases you will need to use a pattern from a different module.

Transmittals

When you send someone something in an organization, attach a memo or letter of transmittal explaining what you're sending. A transmittal can be as simple as a small yellow Post-it™ note with "FYI" written on it ("For Your Information") or it can be a separate typed document, especially when it transmits a formal document such as a report.

Organize a memo or letter of transmittal in this order:

1. Tell the reader what you're sending.

2. Summarize the main point(s) of the document.

3. Indicate any special circumstances or information that would help the reader understand the document. Is it a draft? Is it a partial document that will be completed later?

4. Tell the reader what will happen next. Will you do something? Do you want a response? If you do want the reader to act, specify exactly what you want the reader to do and give a deadline.

Frequently, transmittals have important secondary purposes, such as building goodwill and showing readers that you're working on projects they value.

Figure 8-15   A Positive Letter

Interstate
Fidelity
Insurance Company

100 Interstate Plaza
Atlanta, GA 30301
404-555-5000
Fax: 404-555-5270

March 8, 2001

Professor Adrienne Prinz
Department of History
Duke University
Durham, North Carolina 27000

Dear Professor Prinz:

Good news   Your appointment as archivist for Interstate Fidelity Insurance has been approved. When you were in Atlanta in December, you said that you could begin work June 1. We'd like you to start then if that date is still good for you.   *Tactful*

The Board has outlined the following priorities for your work: *Assumes reader's primary interest is the job*

Negative about lighting and security presented impersonally   1. **Organize and catalogue the archives.** You'll have the basement of the Palmer Building for the archives and can requisition the supplies you need. You'll be able to control heat and humidity; the budget doesn't allow special lighting or security measures.

Details   2. **Prepare materials for a 4-hour training session in October** for senior-level managers. We'd like you to cover how to decide what to send to the archives. If your first four months of research uncover any pragmatic uses for our archives (like Wells Fargo's use of archives to teach managers about past pitfalls), include those in the session.

3. **Write an article each month for the employee newsletter** describing the uses of the archives. When we're cutting costs in other departments, it's important to justify committing funds to start an archive program.

4. **Study the IFI archives to compile** information that (a) can help solve current management problems, (b) could be included in a history of the company, and (c) might be useful to scholars of business history.

These provisions will appeal to the reader   5. **Begin work on a corporate history of IFI.** IFI will help you find a publisher and support the book financially. You'll have full control over the content.

Salary is deemphasized to avoid implying that reader is "just taking the job for the money"

Negative that reader will have to reapply presented as normal procedure   Your salary will be $23,000 for six months; your contract can be renewed twice for a total of 18 months. You're authorized to hire a full-time research assistant for $8,000 for six months; you'll need to go through the normal personnel request process to request that that money be continued next year. A file clerk will be assigned full-time to your project. You'll report to me. At least for the rest of this calendar year, the budget for the Archives Project will come from my department.

Figure 8-15   A Positive Letter (Continued)

Professor Adrienne Prinz
March 8, 2001
Page 2

IFI offices are equipped with Pentium computers with FoxPro, WordPerfect, and Excel. Is there
any software that we should buy for cataloguing or research? Are there any office supplies that
we need to have on hand June 1 so that you can work efficiently?

In the meantime,

1. Please send your written acceptance right away.

2. Let me know if you need any software or supplies.

3. Send me the name, address, and Social Security number of your research assistant by May 1
    so that I can process his or her employment papers.

Goodwill ending

4. If you'd like help finding a house or apartment in Atlanta, let me know. I can give you the
    name of a real estate agent.

On June 1, you'll spend the morning in Personnel. Stop by my office at noon. We'll go out for lunch and then I'll
take you to the office you'll have while you're at IFI.

Welcome to IFI!

Cordially,

Cynthia Yen

Cynthia Yen
Director of Education and Training

Confirmations

Many informative messages record oral conversations. These messages are generally short and give only the
information shared orally; they go to the other party in the conversation. Start the message by indicating that it
is a confirmation, not a new message:

As we discussed on the phone today, . . .

As I told you yesterday, . . .

Attached is the meeting schedule we discussed earlier today.

Figure 8-16   A Positive Memo

Memo

January 26, 2001

To: All Crossroads Counselling Center Employees

From: Darlene Bonifas, Director of Human Resources   *DB*

Subject: New Tuition Reimbursement Program   *Good news in subject line and first paragraph*

Starting February 1st, full-time employees who have worked at Crossroads three months or more can be reimbursed for up to $3500 a year for tuition and fees when you take courses related to your current position (including courses needed to keep your licenses), courses that would prepare you for another position you might someday hold at Crossroads, or courses required for a job-related degree program.

You can take the courses at any level: high school, college, or graduate school. You can find a selection of catalogs from nearby schools and colleges in the Office of Human Resources.

How to Apply for the Program   *Headings chunk material and provide good visual impact*

To apply, pick up an application form in the Office of Human Resources, fill it out, and have it signed by your immediate supervisor. Return it to the Office of Human Resources at least two weeks before classes start: your application must be <u>approved before classes start</u>.

How to Get Reimbursed   *Negatives presented as positively as possible*

You'll be reimbursed when you <u>earn a "C" grade or better</u> in the course. Just bring the following documents to the Office of Human Resources:
1. A copy of the approved application.
2. An official grade report.
3. A statement of the tuition and fees paid.

If you are eligible for other financial aid (scholarships, grants, or veterans' benefits), you will be reimbursed for the tuition and fees not covered by that aid, up to $3500 during one calendar year. Reimbursements for undergraduate and basic education programs are currently tax-free.

Figure 8-16   A Positive Memo (Continued)

All Employees—New Tuition Reimbursement Program
January 26, 2001
Page 2

*page 2 of memo
doesn't use
letterhead*

Goals of the Program

This program will help us stay on top of developments in our field. For example, we're working with more and more people who have tested HIV-positive. Some counselors might want to take courses on medical treatments for AIDS. The more we understand about the physical pressures our clients are under, the better we can help them cope with their emotional challenges. Knowing that AIDS leaves patients exhausted may help us understand why someone needs a little extra time or tolerance during an appointment.

Courses about anxiety and stress could help us deal with the increasing number of clients who fear that their jobs will disappear. Perhaps someone would like to take a course in money management or career counseling so that we could offer practical as well as psychological advice. Counselors may want to become registered to administer the MBTI or learn how to use computers to score the MMPI.

Jargon appropriate for the audience

Reader Benefits

Counselors can use this program to earn their doctorates so that they can be the primary psychologist seeing a patient. Having more certified counselors would enable us to enlarge our practice.

Including Benefits for people who are not eligible to participate

But courses don't have to relate to psychology and counselling. Maybe someone would like to learn how to use advanced features in WordPerfect, Access, or Excel. (Could someone learn how to improve our database or chart our client profiles?) Management courses might help us run a tighter ship. And interpersonal courses might sharpen our skills so that we do an even better job of working together to solve problems.

In spite of cutbacks by some insurance providers last fall, Crossroads continues to be financially as well as professionally strong. This program gives us the opportunity to build on our strength as we prepare to help people in Columbus face the challenges of the new millennium.

Goodwill ending

Summaries

You may be asked to summarize a conversation, document, or an outside meeting for colleagues or superiors. (Minutes of an internal meeting are usually more detailed.)

In a summary of a conversation for internal use, identify

- The people who were present
- The topic of discussion
- Decisions made
- Who does what next.

To summarize a document

1. Start with the main point.
2. Give supporting evidence and details.
3. Evaluate the document, if your audience asks for evaluation.
4. Identify the actions that your organization should take based on the document. Should others in the company read this book? Should someone in the company write a letter to the editor responding to this newspaper article? Should your company try to meet with someone in the organization that the story is about?

Adjustments and Responses to Complaints

A study sponsored by Travelers Insurance showed that when people had gripes but didn't complain, only 9% would buy from the company again. But when people did complain—and their problems were resolved quickly— 82% would buy again.[3]

When you grant a customer's request for an adjusted price, discount, replacement, or other benefit to resolve a complaint, do so in the very first sentence.

Don't talk about your own process in making the decision. Don't say anything that sounds grudging. Give the reason for the original mistake only if it reflects credit on the company. (In most cases, it doesn't, so the reason should be omitted.)

Thank-You and Congratulatory Notes

Sending a thank-you note will make people more willing to help you again in the future. Thank-you letters can be short but must be prompt. They need to be specific to sound sincere.

Congratulating someone can cement good feelings between you and the reader and enhance your own visibility. Again, specifics help.

Avoid language that may seem condescending or patronizing. A journalism professor was offended when a former student wrote to congratulate her for a feature article that appeared in a major newspaper. As the professor pointed out, the letter's language implied that the writer has more status than the person being praised. The praiser was "quite impressed," congratulated the professor on reaching a conclusion that the praiser had already reached, and assumed that the professor would have wanted to discuss matters with the praiser. To the reader, "Keep up the good work!" implied that the one cheering her on had been waiting for ages at the finish line.[4]

> Your Visa bill for a night's lodging has been adjusted to $63. Next month a credit of $37 will appear on your bill to reimburse you for the extra amount you were originally asked to pay.

Building a Critical Skill

Writing a Goodwill Ending, 2

Goodwill endings focus on the business relationship you share with your reader. When you write to one person, a good last paragraph fits that person specifically. When you write to someone who represents an organization, the last paragraph can refer to your company's relationship to the reader's organization. When you write to a group (for example, to "All Employees") your ending should apply to the whole group.

Possibilities include complimenting the reader for a job well done, describing a reader benefit, or looking forward to something positive that relates to the subject of the message.

For example, consider possible endings for a letter answering the question, "When a patient leaves the hospital and returns, should we count it as a new stay?" For one company, the answer was that if a patient was gone from the hospital overnight or longer, the hospital should start a new claim when the patient was readmitted.

Weak closing paragraph:	Should you have any questions regarding this matter, please feel free to call me.
Goodwill ending:	Many employee-patients appreciate the freedom to leave the hospital for a few hours. It's nice working with a hospital which is flexible enough to offer that option.
Also acceptable:	Omit the paragraph; stop after the explanation.

Some writers end every message with a standard invitation:

If you have questions, please do not hesitate to ask.

That sentence lacks positive emphasis. But saying "feel free to call"—though more positive—is rarely a good idea. Most of the time, the writer should omit the sentence. Don't make more work for yourself by inviting calls to clarify simple messages.

One of the reasons you write is to save the time needed to tell everyone individually. People in business aren't shrinking violets; they will call if they need help. Do make sure your phone number is in the letterhead or is typed below your name. You can also add your e-mail address below your name.

HOW CAN PAIBOC HELP ME WRITE INFORMATIVE AND POSITIVE MESSAGES?

The PAIBOC questions help you examine the points your message should include.

Before you tackle the assignments for this module, examine the following problem. See how the PAIBOC questions probe the basic points required for a solution. Study the two sample solutions to see what makes one unacceptable and the other one good. Note the recommendations for revision that could make the good solution excellent.[5] The checklist in Figure 8-19 can help you evaluate a draft.

Problem

Interstate Fidelity Insurance (IFI) uses computers to handle its payments and billings. There is often a time lag between receiving a payment from a customer and recording it on the computer. Sometimes, while the payment is in line to be processed, the computer sends out additional notices: past-due notices, collection letters, even threats to sue. Customers are frightened or angry and write asking for an explanation. In most cases, if they just waited a little while, the situation would be straightened out. But policyholders are afraid that they'll be without insurance because the company thinks the bill has not been paid.

IFI doesn't have the time to check each individual situation to see if the check did arrive and has been processed. It wants you to write a letter that will persuade customers to wait. If something is wrong and the payment never reached IFI, IFI would send a legal notice to that effect saying that the policy would be canceled by a certain date (which the notice would specify) at least 30 days after the date on the original premium bill.

Continuing customers always get this legal notice as a third chance (after the original bill and the past-due notice).

Prepare a form letter that can go out to every policyholder who claims to have paid a premium for automobile insurance and resents getting a past-due notice. The letter should reassure readers and build goodwill for IFI.

Analysis of the Problem

P What are your **purposes** in writing or speaking?

To reassure readers: they're covered for 30 days. To inform them they can assume everything is OK unless they receive a second notice. To avoid further correspondence on this subject. To build goodwill for IFI: (a) we don't want to suggest IFI is error-prone or too cheap to hire enough people to do the necessary work; (b) we don't want readers to switch companies; (c) we do want readers to buy from IFI when they're ready for more insurance.

A Who is (are) your **audience(s)**? How do the members of your audience differ from each other? What characteristics are relevant to this particular message?

Automobile insurance customers who say they've paid but have still received a past-due notice. They're afraid they're no longer insured. Since it's a form letter, different readers will have different situations: in some cases payment did arrive late, in some cases the company made a mistake, in some the reader never paid (check lost in mail, unsigned, bounced, etc.)

I What **information** must your message include?

Readers are still insured. We cannot say whether their checks have now been processed (company doesn't want to check individual accounts). Their insurance will be canceled if they do not pay after receiving the second past-due notice (the legal notice).

B What reasons or reader **benefits** can you use to support your position?

Computers help us provide personal service to policyholders. We offer policies to meet all their needs. Both of these points would need specifics to be interesting and convincing.

O What **objections** can you expect your reader(s) to have? What negative elements of your message must you deemphasize or overcome?

Computers appear to cause errors. We don't know if the checks have been processed. We will cancel policies if their checks don't arrive.

C How will the **context** affect the reader's response? Think about your relationship to the reader, morale in the organization, the economy, the time of year, and any special circumstances

The insurance business is highly competitive—other companies offer similar rates and policies. The customer could get a similar policy for about the same money from someone else. Most people find that money is tight, so they'll want to keep insurance costs low. On the other hand, the fact that prices are steady or rising means that the value of what they own is higher—they need insurance more than ever.

Many insurance companies are refusing to renew policies (car, liability, malpractice insurance). These refusals to renew have gotten lots of publicity, and many people have heard horror stories about companies and individuals whose insurance has been canceled or not renewed after a small number of claims. Readers don't feel very kindly toward insurance companies.

People need car insurance. If they have an accident and aren't covered, they not only have to bear the costs of that accident alone but also (depending on state law) may need to place as much as $50,000 in a state escrow account to cover future accidents. They have a legitimate worry.

Discussion of the Sample Solutions

The solution in Figure 8-17 is unacceptable. The blue marginal comments show problem spots. Since this is a form letter, we cannot tell customers we have their checks; in some cases, we may not. The letter is far too negative. The explanation in paragraph 2 makes IFI look irresponsible and uncaring. Paragraph 3 is far too negative. Paragraph 4 is too vague; there are no reader benefits; the ending sounds selfish.

A major weakness with the solution is that it lifts phrases straight out of the problem; the writer does not seem to have thought about the problem or about the words he or she is using. Measuring the draft against the answers to the questions for analysis suggests that this writer should start over.

The solution in Figure 8-18 is much better. The gray marginal comments show the letter's strong points. The message opens with the good news that is true for all readers. (Whenever possible, one should use the good news pattern of organization.) Paragraph 2 explains IFI's policy. It avoids assigning blame and ends on a positive note. The negative information is buried in paragraph 3 and is presented positively: The notice is information, not a threat; the 30-day extension is a "grace period." Telling the reader now what to do if a second notice arrives eliminates the need for a second exchange of letters. Paragraph 4 offers benefits for using computers, since some readers may blame the notice on computers, and offers benefits for being insured by IFI. Paragraph 5 promotes other policies the company sells and prepares for the last paragraph.

As the blue comments indicate, this good solution could be improved by personalizing the salutation and by including the name and number of the local agent. Computers could make both of those insertions easily. This good letter could be made excellent by revising paragraph 4 so that it doesn't end on a negative note, and by using more reader benefits. For instance, do computers help agents advise clients of the best policies for them? Does IFI offer good service—quick, friendly, nonpresssured—that could be stressed? Are agents well trained? All of these might yield ideas for additional reader benefits.

Figure 8-17
An Unacceptable Solution to the Sample Problem

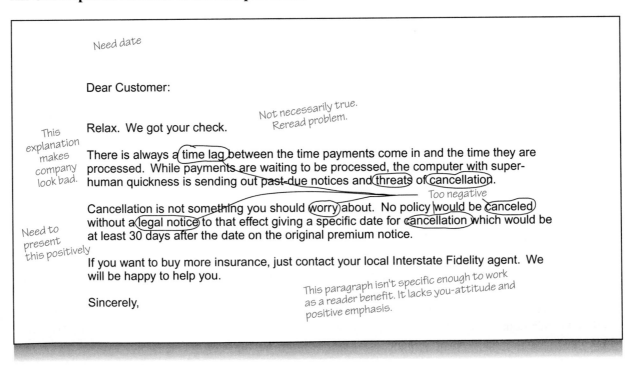

Figure 8-18
A Good Solution to the Sample Problem

Need date

Dear Customer: *Better: use computer to personalize. Put in name and address of a specific reader*

Your auto insurance is still in effect.   *Good ¶ 1. True for all readers*

Good to treat notice as information, tell reader what to do if it arrives

Past-due notices are mailed out if the payment has not been processed within three days after the due date. This may happen if a check is delayed in the mail or arrives without a signature or account number. When your check arrives with all the necessary information, it is promptly credited to your account.   *Good you-attitude*

Even if a check is lost in the mail and never reaches us, you still have a 30-day grace period. If you do get a second notice, you'll know that we still have not received your check. To keep your insurance in force, just stop payment on the first check and send a second one.

Benefits of using computers

Computer processing of your account guarantees that you get any discounts you're eligible for: multicar, accident-free record, good student. If you have a claim, your agent uses computer tracking to find matching parts quickly, whatever car you drive. You get a check quickly—usually within 3 working days—without having to visit dealer after dealer for time-consuming estimates.   *Better to put in agent's name, phone number*
Too negative

Need to add benefits of insuring with IFI

Today, your home and possessions are worth more than ever. You can protect them with Interstate Fidelity's homeowners' and renters' policies. Let your local agent show you how easy it is to give yourself full protection. If you need a special rider to insure a personal computer, a coin or gun collection, or a fine antique, you can get that from IFI, too.   *Good specifics*

Whatever your insurance needs—auto, home, life, or health—one call to IFI can do it all.   *Acceptable ending*

Sincerely,

Figure 8-19
Checklist for Informative and Positive Messages

☐ In positive messages, does the subject line give the good news? In either message, is the subject line specific enough to differentiate this message from others on the same subject?

☐ Does the first paragraph summarize the information or good news? If the information is too complex to fit into a single paragraph, does the paragraph list the basic parts of the policy or information in the order in which the memo discusses them?

☐ Is all the information given in the message? [What information is needed will vary depending on the message, but information about dates, places, times, and anything related to money usually needs to be included. When in doubt, ask!]

☐ In messages announcing policies, is there at least one reader benefit for each segment of the audience? Are all reader benefits ones that seem likely to occur in this organization?

☐ Is each reader benefit developed, showing that the benefit will come from the policy and why the benefit matters to this organization? Do the benefits build on the job duties of people as this organization and the specific circumstances of the organization?

☐ Does the message end with a positive paragraph—preferably one that is specific to the readers, not a general one that could fit any organization or policy?

And, for all messages, not just informative and positive ones,

☐ Does the message use you-attitude and positive emphasis?

☐ Is the style easy to read and friendly?

☐ Is the visual design of the message inviting?

☐ Is the format correct?

☐ Does the message use standard grammar? Is it free from types?

Originality in a positive or informative message may come from

☐ Creating good headings, lists, and visual impact.

☐ Developing reader benefits.

☐ Thinking about readers and giving details that answer their questions and make it easier for them to understand and follow the policy.

FINDING, ANALYZING, AND DOCUMENTING INFORMATION

Research for a report may be as simple as getting a computer printout of sales for the last month; it may involve finding online or published material or surveying or interviewing people. Secondary research retrieves information that someone else gathered. Library research and online searches are the best known kinds of secondary research. Primary research gathers new information. Surveys, interviews, and observations are common methods for gathering new information for business reports.

HOW CAN I FIND INFORMATION ONLINE AND IN PRINT?

Learn how to do keyword searches.

Figures 8-20, 8-21, and 8-22 list a few of the hundreds of online and print resources.

To use a computer database and Web search engines efficiently, identify the concepts you're interested in and choose keywords that will help you find relevant sources. **Keywords** are the terms that the computer searches for. If you're not sure what terms to use, check the *ABI/Inform Thesaurus* for synonyms and the hierarchies in which information is arranged in various database.

Figure 8-20   Sources for Electronic Research

These CD-ROM databases are available in many university libraries:

ABI/Inform (indexes and abstract 800 journals in management and business)

Biological and Agricultural Index

Black Studies on Disc

CINAHL (nursing and allied health)

ComIndex (indexes and abstracts journals in communication)

ERIC (research on education and teaching practices in the United States and other countries)

Foreign Trade and Economic Abstracts

GPO on SilverPlatter (government publications)

Handbook of Latin American Studies

LEXIS/NEXIS Services

Newspaper Abstracts

PAIS International-Public Affairs Information Service

Peterson's College Database

Social Sciences Index

Wilson Business Abstracts

Women's Resources International

Figure 8-21   Sources for Web Research

Subject Matter Directories
AccountingNet
  accounting.pro2net.com
FINWeb
  www.finweb.com
International Business Kiosk
  www.webcom.com/one/world
International business sources on the WWW
  ciber.bus.msu.edu/busres.htm
Marketing, Research, Advertising, Selling, Promotion & More
  www.knowthis.com
The WWW Virtual Library
  www.vlib.org

News Sites
AJR NewsLink (links to U.S., Canadian, and international newspapers, magazines, and resources online)
  ajr.newslink.org/menu.html
Business Week Online
  www.businessweek.com
CNN/CNNFN
  www.cnn.com (news)
  www.cnnfn.com (financial news)
National Public Radio
  www.npr.org
The New York Times on the Web
  www.nyt.com
The Wall Street Journal Interactive Edition
  www.interactive.wsj.com/home.html

U.S. Government Information
EDGAR Online (SEC's online database)
  www.edgar-online.com
  www.sec.gov/edgarhp.htm
FEDSTATS (links to 70 U.S. government agencies)
  www.fedstats.gov
STAT-USA (fast-breaking statistics on U.S. trade and economy)
  www.stat-usa.gov
U.S. Census (including Data FERRET)
  www.census.gov
U.S. government publications (search databases online)
  www.access.gpo.gov
U.S. Small Business Administration
  www.sbaonline.sba.gov
White House Briefing Room (economic issues)
  www.whitehouse.gov/fsbr/esbr.html

Reference Collections
Britannica Online
  www.eb.com:180
CEO Express
  www.ceoexpress.com
Hoover's Online (information on more than 13,000 public and private companies worldwide)
  www.hoovers.com
Liszt (mailing lists)
  www.liszt.com
Reference Desk
  www.refdesk.com

Figure 8-22   Print Sources for Research

Indexes:
  Accountants' Index
  Business Periodicals Index
  Canadian Business Index
  Hospital Literature Index
  Personnel Management Abstracts

Facts, figures, and forecasts (also check the Web):
  Almanac of Business and Industrial Financial Ratios
  Moody's Manuals
  The Statistical Abstract of the U.S.

U.S. Census reports (also available on the Web):
  Census of Manufacturers
  Census of Retail Trade

International business and government:
  Canada Year Book
  Dun and Bradstreet's Principal International Businesses
  European Marketing Data and Statistics
  Statistical Yearbook of the United Nations

HOW DO I WRITE QUESTIONS FOR SURVEYS AND INTERVIEWS?

Test your questions to make sure they're neutral and clear.

A **survey** questions a large group of people, called **respondents** or **subjects**. The easiest way to ask many questions is to create a **questionnaire**, a written list of questions that people fill out. An **interview** is a structured conversation with someone who will be able to give you useful information. Surveys and interviews can be useful only if the questions are well designed.

Phrase questions in a way that won't bias the response. Avoid questions that make assumptions about your subjects. The question "Does your spouse have a job outside the home?" assumes that your respondent is married.

Use words that mean the same thing to you and to the respondents. Words like *often* and *important* mean different things to different people. Whenever possible, use more objective measures:

Vague: Do you use the Web often?

Better: How many hours a week do you spend on the Web?

Closed questions have a limited number of possible responses. **Open questions** do not lock the subject into any sort of response. Figure 8-23 gives examples of closed and open questions. Closed questions are faster for subjects to answer and easier for researchers to score. However, since all answers must fit into chosen categories, they cannot probe the complexities of a subject. You can improve the quality of closed questions by conducting a pretest with open questions to find categories that matter to respondents.

When you use multiple-choice questions, make sure that only one answer fits in any one category. In the following example of overlapping categories, a person who worked for a company with exactly 25 employees could check either *a* or *b*. The resulting data would be unreliable.

Building a Critical Skill

Using the Internet for Research, 3

Most research projects today include the Internet. However, don't rely solely on the Internet for research. Powerful as it is, the Internet's just one tool. Your public or school library, experts in your company, journals and newspapers, and even information in your files are others.

Finding Web Pages

Use root words to find variations. A root word such as stock followed by the plus sign (stock1) will yield stock, stocks, stockmarket, and so forth.

Use quotation marks for exact terms. If you want only sites that use the term "business communication," put quotes around the term.

Uncapitalize words. Capitalizing words limits your search to sites where the word itself is capitalized; if the word doesn't have to be capitalized, don't. Some search engines group related sites based on keywords. Look for these links at the top of your search engine. If you get a broken or dead link, try shortening the URL. For example, if www.mirror. com/newinfo/index.html no longer exists, try www.mirror.com. Then check the site map to see whether it has the page you want.

Evaluating Web Pages

Anyone can post a Web site, and no one checks the information for accuracy or truthfulness. By contrast, many print sources, especially academic journals, have an editorial board that reviews manuscripts for accuracy and truthfulness. The review process helps ensure that information meets high standards. For a list of Web sites about evaluating information, see www.vuw.ac.nz/~agsmith/evaln/ evaln.htm.

Use reputable sources. Start with sites produced by universities and established companies or organizations. Be aware, however, that such organizations are not going to post information that makes them look bad. To get "the other side of the story," you may need to monitor listservs or to access pages critical of the organization. (Search for "consumer opinion" and the name of the organization.)

Look for an author. Do individuals take "ownership" of the information? What are their credentials? How can you contact them with questions? Remember that ".edu" sites could be from students not yet expert on a subject.

Check the date. How recent is the information?

Check the source. Is the information adapted from other sources? If so, try to get the original.

Compare the information with other sources. Internet sources should complement print sources. If facts are correct, you'll likely find them recorded elsewhere.

Overlapping categories:	Indicate the number of full-time employees in your company on May 16: __a. 0-25 __b. 25-100 __c. 100-500 __d. over 500
Discrete categories:	Indicate the number of full-time employees in your company on May 16: __a. 0-25 __b. 26-100 __c. 101-500 __d. over 500

Branching questions direct different respondents to different parts of the questionnaire based on their answers to earlier questions.

Figure 8-23   Closed and Open Questions

Closed Questions

Are you satisfied with the city bus service? (yes/no)

How good is the city bus service?

Excellent 5 4 3 2 1 Terrible

Indicate whether you agree or disagree with each of the following statements about city bus service:

A   D   The schedule is convenient for me.

A   D   The routes are convenient for me.

A   D   The drivers are courteous.

A   D   The buses are clean.

Rate each of the following improvements in the order of their importance to you (1 = most important, 6 = least important)

_____ Buy new buses.

_____ Increase non-rush-hour service on weekdays.

_____ Increase service on weekdays.

_____ Provide earlier and later service on weekdays.

_____ Buy more buses with wheelchair access.

_____ Provide unlimited free transfers.

Open Questions

How do you feel about the city bus service?

Tell me about the city bus service.

Why do you ride the bus? (or, Why don't you ride the bus?)

What do you like and dislike about the city bus service?

How could the city bus service be improved?

---

10. Have you talked to an academic advisor this year?
yes _____ no _____
(if "no," skip to question 14.)>>

Use closed multiple-choice questions for potentially embarrassing topics. Seeing their own situation listed as one response can help respondents feel that it is acceptable. However, very sensitive issues are perhaps better asked in an interview, where the interviewer can build trust and reveal information about himself or herself to encourage the interviewee to answer.

Generally, put early in the questionnaire questions that will be easy to answer. Put questions that are harder to answer or that people may be less willing to answer (e.g., age and income) near the end of the questionnaire. Even if people choose not to answer such questions, you'll still have the rest of the survey filled out.

If subjects will fill out the questionnaire themselves, pay careful attention to the physical design of the document. Use indentations and white space effectively; make it easy to mark and score the answers. Include a brief statement of purpose if you (or someone else) will not be available to explain the questionnaire or answer questions. Pretest the questionnaire to make sure the directions are clear. One researcher mailed out a two-page questionnaire without pretesting it. Twenty-five respondents didn't answer the questions on the back of the first page.[6]

HOW DO I DECIDE WHOM TO SURVEY OR INTERVIEW?

Use a random sample for surveys, if funds permit.
Use a judgment sample for interviews.

The **population** is the group you want to make statements about. Depending on the purpose of your research, your population might be all Fortune 1000 companies, all business students at your college, or all consumers.

Defining your population correctly is crucial to getting useful information. For example, Microscan wanted its sales force to interview "customer defectors." At first, salespeople assumed that a "defector" was a former customer who no longer bought anything at all. By that definition, very few defectors existed. But then the term was redefined as customers who had stopped buying *some* products and services. By this definition, quite a few defectors existed. And the fact that each of them had turned to a competitor for some of what they used to buy from Microscan showed that improvements-and improved profits-were possible.[7]

Because it is not feasible to survey everyone, you select a sample. If you take a true random sample, you can generalize your findings to the whole population from which your sample comes. In a **random sample**, each person in the population theoretically has an equal chance of being chosen. When people say they did something *randomly* they often mean *without conscious bias*. However, unconscious bias exists. Someone passing out surveys in front of the library will be more likely to approach people who seem friendly and less likely to ask people who seem intimidating, in a hurry, much older or younger, or of a different race, class, or sex. True random samples rely on random digit tables, generated by computers and published in statistics texts and books such as *A Million Random Digits*.

A **convenience sample** is a group of respondents who are easy to get: students who walk through the student center, people at a shopping mall, workers in your own unit. Convenience samples are useful for a rough pretest of a questionnaire. However, you cannot generalize from a convenience sample to a larger group.

A **judgment sample** is a group of people whose views seem useful. Someone interested in surveying the kinds of writing done on campus might ask each department for the name of a faculty member who cared about writing, and then send surveys to those people. Judgment samples are often good for interviews, where your purpose is to talk to someone whose views are worth hearing.

HOW SHOULD I ANALYZE THE INFORMATION I'VE COLLECTED?

Look for answers to your research questions, patterns, and interesting nuggets.

As you analyze your data, look for answers to your research questions and for interesting nuggets that may not have been part of your original questions but emerge from the data. Such stories can be more convincing in reports and oral presentations than pages of computer printouts.

Understanding the Source of the Data

If your report is based upon secondary data from library and online research, look at the sample, the sample size, and the exact wording of questions to see what the data actually measure. Some studies bias results by limiting the alternatives. Ninety percent of students surveyed by Levi Strauss & Co. said Levi's 501 jeans would be the most popular clothes this year. But the Levi's were the only brand of jeans on the list of choices.[8]

Identify the assumptions used in analyzing the data. When studies contradict each other, the explanation sometimes lies in the assumptions. For example, a study that found disposable diapers were better for the environment than cloth diapers assumed that a cloth diaper lasted for 92.5 uses. A study that found that cloth diapers were better assumed that each cloth diaper lasted for 167 uses.[9]

Evaluating online sources, especially Web pages, can be difficult, since anyone can post pages on the Web or contribute comments to chat groups. Check the identity of the writer: is he or she considered an expert? Can you find at least one source printed in a respectable newspaper or journal that agrees with the Web page? If a comment appeared in chat groups, did others in the group support the claim? Does the chat group include people who could be expected to be unbiased and knowledgeable? Especially when the issue is controversial, seek out opposing views.

Analyzing Numbers

Many reports analyze numbers-either numbers from databases and sources or numbers from a survey you have conducted.

If you've conducted a survey, your first step is to transfer the responses on the survey form into numbers. For some categories, you'll assign numbers arbitrarily. For example, you might record men as "1" and women as "2"-or vice versa. Such assignments don't matter, as long as you're consistent throughout your project. In these cases, you can report the number and percentage of men and women who responded to your survey, but you can't do anything else with the numbers.

When you have numbers for salaries or other figures, start by figuring the average, or mean, the median, and the range. The **average** or **mean** is calculated by adding up all the figures and dividing by the number of samples. The **median** is the number that is exactly in the middle. When you have an odd number of observations, the median will be the middle number. When you have an even number, the median will be the average of the two numbers in the center. The **range** is the high and low figures for that variable.

Finding the average takes a few more steps when you have different kinds of data. For example, it's common to ask respondents whether they find a feature "very important," "somewhat important," or "not important." You might code "very important" as "3," "somewhat important" as "2," and "not important" as "1." To find the average in this kind of data,

1. For each response, multiply the code by the number of people who gave that response.
2. Add up the figures.
3. Divide by the total number of people responding to the question.

For example, suppose you have surveyed 50 people about the features they want in a proposed apartment complex.

The average gives an easy way to compare various features. If the party house averages 2.3 while extra parking for guests is 2.5, you know that your respondents would find extra parking more important than a party house. You can now arrange the factors in order of importance:

Often it's useful to simplify numerical data: round it off and combine similar elements. Then you can see that one number is about 2-1/2 times another. Charting it can also help you see patterns in your data. Look at the raw data as well as at percentages. For example, a 50% increase in shoplifting incidents sounds alarming-but an increase from two to three shoplifting incidents sounds well within normal variation.

Table 4. "How Important Is Each Factor to You in Choosing an Apartment?"

n =50; 3 ="Very Important"	
Extra parking for guests	2.5
Party house	2.3
Pool	2.2
Convenient to bus line	2.0

Analyzing Words

If your data include words, try to find out what the words mean to the people who said them. Respondents to Whirlpool's survey of 180,000 households said that they wanted "clean refrigerators." After asking more questions, Whirlpool found that what people really wanted were refrigerators that looked clean, so the company developed models with textured fronts and sides to hide fingerprints.[10] Also try to measure words against numbers. When he researched possible investments, Peter Lynch found that people in mature industries were pessimistic, seeing clouds. People in immature industries saw pie in the sky, even when the numbers weren't great.[11]

Look for patterns. If you have library sources, on which points do experts agree? Which disagreements can be explained by early theories or numbers that have now changed? By different interpretations of the same data? Having different values and criteria? In your interviews and surveys, what patterns do you see?

- Have things changed over time?
- Does geography account for differences?
- What similarities do you see?
- What differences do you see?
- What confirms your hunches?
- What surprises you?

Checking Your Logic

Don't confuse causation with correlation. **Causation** means that one thing causes or produces another. **Correlation** means that two things happen at the same time. One might cause the other, but both might be caused by a third.

For example, suppose that you're considering whether to buy cell phones for everyone in your company, and suppose that your surveys show that the people who currently have cell phones are, in general, more productive than people who don't use cell phones. Does having a cell phone lead to higher productivity? Perhaps. But perhaps productive people are more likely to push to get cell phones from company funds, while less productive people are more passive. Perhaps productive people earn more and are more likely to be able to buy their own cell phones if the organization doesn't provide them.

Consciously search for at least three possible causes for each phenomenon you've observed and at least three possible solutions for each problem. The more possibilities you brainstorm, the more likely you are to find good options. In your report, mention all of the possibilities; discuss in detail only those that will occur to readers and that you think are the real reasons and the best solutions.

When you have identified patterns that seem to represent the causes of the problem or the best solutions, check these ideas against reality. Can you find support in the quotes or in the numbers? Can you answer counterclaims? If you can, you will be able to present evidence for your argument in a convincing way.

If you can't prove the claim you originally hoped to make, modify your conclusions to fit your data. Even when your market test is a failure, you can still write a useful report.

- Identify changes that might yield a different result (for example, selling the product at a lower price might enable the company to sell enough units).
- Discuss circumstances that may have affected the results.
- Summarize your negative findings in progress reports to let readers down gradually and to give them a chance to modify the research design.
- Remember that negative results aren't always disappointing to the audience. For example, the people who commissioned a feasibility report may be relieved to have an impartial outsider confirm their suspicions that a project isn't feasible.[12]

HOW SHOULD I DOCUMENT SOURCES?

Use APA or MLA format.

The two most widely used formats for endnotes and bibliographies in reports are those of the American Psychological Association (APA) and the Modern Language Association (MLA). Figure 8-24 shows the APA and MLA formats for books, government documents, journal and newspaper articles, online sources, and interviews.

In a good report, sources are cited and documented smoothly and unobtrusively. **Citation** means attributing an idea or fact to its source **in the body of the report**. "According to the 2000 Census . . ." "Jane Bryant Quinn argues that . . . " Citing sources demonstrates your honesty, enhances your credibility, and protects you from charges of plagiarism. **Documentation** means providing the bibliographic information readers would need to go back to the original source. Note that citation and documentation are used in addition to quotation marks. If you use the source's exact words, you'll use the name of the person you're citing and quotation marks in the body of the report; you'll indicate the source in parentheses and a list of References or Works Cited. If you put the source's idea into your own words, or if you condense or synthesize information, you don't need quotation marks, but you still need to tell whose idea it is and where you found it.

Indent long quotations on the left and right to set them off from your text. Indented quotations do not need quotation marks; the indentation shows the reader that the passage is a quote. Since many readers skip quotes, always summarize the main point of the quotation in a single sentence before the quotation. End the sentence with a colon, not a period, since it introduces the quote.

Interrupt a quotation to analyze, clarify, or question it.

Use square brackets around words you add or change to clarify the quote or make it fit the grammar of your sentence. Omit any words in the original source that are not essential for your purposes. Use ellipses (spaced dots) to indicate omissions.

Figure 8-24   APA and MLA Formats for Documenting Sources

APA Format

APA internal documentation gives the author's last name and the date of the work in parentheses in the text. A comma separates the author's name from the date (Pagel & Westerfelhaus, 1999). The page number is given only for direct quotations (Katz, 1998, p. 74). If the author's name is used in the sentence, only the date is given in parentheses. A list of References gives the full bibliographic citation, arranging the entries alphabetically by the author's last name and using hanging indents.

The References contain only items which are generally available. Therefore e-mail messages, interviews, and postings on listserves to which one must subscribe are not listed. Instead, these are cited as personal communications in the body: (Kitty Locker to Mike Garafano, personal communication, June 9, 2000).

In a double-spaced document, double space References as well. In a single-spaced document, double space between entries.

Web page
Creation/update date   *Period after year in parentheses*
American Express. (1998). Creating an effective business plan. Retrieved June 15, 2000 from the World Wide Web: http://home3.americanexpress.com/smallbusiness/resources/ starting/biz_plan   ← *No punctuation*
Break Web page address at a slash, period, or hyphen.

Article   *Last name first for all authors*   *Ampersand*
from Atre, T., Auns, K., Badenhausen, K., McAuliffe, K., Nikolov, C., & Ozanian, M. K. (1996, May 20).
an electronic Sports stocks and bonds. *Financial World,* p. 53 (11). General Reference Center Gold (GPIP).
database   *Starting page   Number of pages in article.   Name of database*

Article in an edited book
Burnett, R. E. (1993). Conflict in collaborative decision-making. In N. R. Blyler & C. Thralls (Eds.), *Professional communication: The social perspective* (pp. 144-162). Newbury Park, CA: Sage.
In book titles, capitalize only the first words of the title and subtitle.

Book or pamphlet
with Citibank. (1994). *Indonesia: An investment guide.* [Jakarta]: Author.
a corporate author   *Square brackets for information you add.*

House Select Committee on Children, Youth, and Families. (1991). *Babies and briefcases: Creating*
Government *a family-friendly workplace for fathers.* Hearing before the Select Committee on Children,
document Youth, and Families, House of Representatives, One Hundred Second Congress, first session, hearing held in Washington, DC, June 11, 1991. Washington: Government Printing Office.
No abbreviations

Book
Katz, S. M. (1998). *The dynamics of writing review: Opportunities for growth and change in the workplace.* Greenwich, CT: Ablex   *Give state when city is not well known.*

Capitalize first and main words of journal, newspaper titles
Article   *Comma even when only two authors*
in a Pagel S., & Westerfelhaus, R. (1999). Read the book or attend the seminar? Charting ironies in how
scholarly managers prefer to learn. *The Journal of Business Communication, 36*(2), 163-193.   *Repeat "1" in "193."*
journal   *Year first*   *comma   Volume number.   Issue number.*

Petzinger, T., Jr. (1999, April 2). New business leaders find greater profit mixing work, caring. *The*
Article *Wall Street Journal,* p. B1.   *No quotes for title of article.*
in a newspaper
or magazine   *"p." or "pp." for newspapers and magazines when you do not give a volume number.*

Figure 8-24   APA and MLA Formats for Documenting Sources (continued)

MLA Format

MLA internal documentation gives the author's last name and page number in parentheses in the text. Unlike APA, the year is not given, and no comma separates the name and page number (Katz 74). If the author's name is used in the sentence, only the page number is given in parentheses. A list of Works Cited gives the full bibliographic citation, arranging the entries alphabetically by the author's last name.

In a double-spaced document, double space Works Cited as well. In a single-spaced document, double space between entries.

Web page   *Put title in quote. Capitalize all main words.*   *Creation/ update date*   *Date you visited site*

American Express. "Creating an Effective Business Plan." 1998. 15 June 2000.   *URL in angle brackets*
<http://home3.americanexpress.com/smallbusiness/resources/starting/biz_plan>.

Article from   *Last name first only for first author*   *"and"*
an   Atre, Tushar, Kristine Auns, Kirt Badenhausen, Kevin McAuliffe, Christopher Nikolov, and Michael K.
electronic   Ozanian. "Sports Stocks and Bonds." *Financial World* 20 May 1996, 53 (11). General
database   Reference Center (GPIP). 30 Mar. 1997. *Date you visited site.*   *Number of pages in article*
Posting to a listserv   *Abbreviate month*   *Page article starts*

Bowman, Joel P. "Re: 'They' as Singular." 23 Mar. 1999. Online posting. BizCom.
Article in an edited book   *Date posted.*   *Name of listserv.*

Burnett, Rebecca E. "Conflict in Collaborative Decision-Making." *Professional Communication: The*
Date after   *Social Perspective.* Ed. Nancy Roundy Blyler and Charlotte Thralls. Newbury Park, CA:
publisher   Sage, 1993. 144-62. *Omit "1" in "162"*

Book or pamphlet with a corporate author
Citibank. *Indonesia: An Investment Guide.* [Jakarta:] Citibank, 1994.
Interview   *Use square brackets for information you add.*

Drysdale, Andrew. Telephone interview. 12 Apr. 1999.

Book   *Capitalize all main words in book title*
Katz, Susan M. *The Dynamics of Writing Review: Opportunities for Growth and Change in the*
Workplace. Greenwich, CT: Ablex, 1998.
Give state when city is not well known.
E-Mail

Locker, Kitty O. "How Do I Get Printer Fixed?" E-mail to Mike Garafano and Cheryl Frasch, 9 June,
2000.

Article   *Comma*   *Period*
in a   Pagel, Sonya, and Robert Westerfelhaus. "Read the Book or Attend the Seminar? Charting Ironies in
journal   How Managers Prefer to Learn." *The Journal of Business Communication* 36.2 (1999): 163-93.

Article in a newspaper or magazine   *No punctuation*   *Period*   *Colon*
Petzinger, Thomas, Jr. "New Business Leaders Find Greater Profit Mixing Work, Caring." *The Wall
Street Journal,* 2 April 1999: B1. *No "p."*   *Put quotes around title of article*

Government document
United States. Cong. Select Committee on Children, Youth, and Families. *Babies and Briefcases:
Creating a Family-Friendly Workplace for Fathers. Hearings.* 102nd Cong., 1st sess.
Washington: GPO, 1991.
Abbreviate

SHORT REPORTS

Whenever you have a choice, write a short report rather than a long one. Never put information in reports just because you have it or just because it took you a long time to find it. Instead, choose the information that your reader needs to make a decision.

One report writer was asked to examine a building that had problems with heating, cooling, and air circulation. The client who owned the building wanted quick answers to three questions: Can we do it? What will it cost? When will it pay for itself? The client wanted a three-page report with a seven-page appendix showing the payback figures.[13] When Susan Kleimann studied reply forms for a hotel, its managers said they didn't want to read a report. So Kleimann limited the "report" to an executive summary with conclusions and recommendations. Everything else went into appendixes.[14]

Short reports normally use letter or memo format.

WHAT ARE THE BASIC STRATEGIES FOR ORGANIZING INFORMATION?

Try one of these seven patterns.

Seven basic patterns for organizing information are useful in reports:

1. Comparison/contrast.
2. Problem-solution.
3. Elimination of alternatives.
4. General to particular or particular to general.
5. Geographic or spatial.
6. Functional.
7. Chronological.

Any of these patterns can be used for a whole report or for only part of it.

1. Comparison/Contrast

Comparison/contrast takes up each alternative in turn, discussing strengths and weaknesses. Feasibility studies usually use this pattern.

A variation of the divided pattern is the **pro and con pattern**. In this pattern, under each specific heading, give the arguments for and against that alternative.

Whatever information comes second will carry more psychological weight. This pattern is least effective when you want to deemphasize the disadvantages of a proposed solution, for it does not permit you to bury the disadvantages between neutral or positive material.

2. Problem-Solution

Identify the problem; explain its background or history; discuss its extent and seriousness; identify its causes. Discuss the factors (criteria) that affect the decision. Analyze the advantages and disadvantages of possible solutions. Conclusions and recommendations can go either first or last, depending on the preferences of your reader. This pattern works well when the reader is neutral.

3. Elimination of Alternatives

After discussing the problem and its causes, discuss the impractical solutions first, showing why they will not work. End with the most practical solution. This pattern works well when the solutions the reader is likely to favor will not work, while the solution you recommend is likely to be perceived as expensive, intrusive, or radical.

4. General to Particular or Particular to General

General to particular starts with the problem as it affects the organization or as it manifests itself in general and then moves to a discussion of the parts of the problem and solutions to each of these parts. Particular to general starts with the problem as the audience defines it and moves to larger issues of which the problem is a part. Both are good patterns when you need to redefine the reader's perception of the problem in order to solve it effectively.

5. Geographic or Spatial

In a geographic or spatial pattern, you discuss problems and solutions by units by their physical arrangement. Move from office to office, building to building, factory to factory, state to state, region to region, etc.

A sales report uses a geographic pattern of organization:

> Sales Have Risen in the European Economic Community
> Sales Have Fallen Slightly in Asia
> Sales Are Steady in North America

6. Functional

In functional patterns, discuss the problems and solutions of each functional unit. For example, a report on a new plant might divide data into sections on the costs of land and building, on the availability of personnel, on the conve-nience of raw materials, etc. A government report might divide data into the different functions an office performed, taking each in turn.

7. Chronological

A chronological report records events in the order in which they happened or are planned to happen.

DO DIFFERENT KINDS OF REPORTS USE DIFFERENT PATTERNS OF ORGANIZATION?

Yes. Work with the readers' expectations.

Informative, feasibility, and justification reports will be more successful when you work with the readers' expectations for that kind of report.

Informative and Closure Reports

An informative or closure report summarizes completed work or research that does not result in action or recommendation.

Figure 8-25
An Informative Memo Report Describing How a Company Solved a Problem

March 14, 2001

To: Kitty O. Locker

From: Sara A. Ratterman *SAR*   *Informal short reports use*
                                          letter or memo format.

First paragraph summarizes main points.

Subject: Recycling at Bike Nashbar

Two months ago, Bike Nashbar began recycling its corrugated cardboard boxes. The program was easy to implement and actually saves the company a little money compared to our previous garbage pickup.

Purpose and scope of report.

In this report, I will explain how, why, and by whom Bike Nashbar's program was initiated; how the program works and what it costs; and why other businesses should consider similar programs.

Bold headings.

The Problem of Too Many Boxes and Not Enough Space in Bike Nashbar

Cause of problem.

Every week, Bike Nashbar receives about 40 large cardboard boxes containing bicycles and other merchandise. As many boxes as possible would be stuffed into the trash bin behind the building, which also had to accommodate all the other solid waste the shop produces. Boxes that didn't fit in the trash bin ended up lying around the shop, blocking doorways, and taking up space needed for customers' bikes. The trash bin was only emptied once a week, and by that time, even more boxes would have arrived.

Triple space before heading.

The Importance of Recycling Cardboard Rather than Throwing It Away

Arranging for more trash bins or more frequent pickups would have solved the immediate problem at Bike Nashbar but would have done nothing to solve the problem created by throwing away so much trash in the first place.

Double space between paragraphs within heading.

Further seriousness of problem.

According to David Crogen, sales representative for Waste Management, Inc., 75% of all solid waste in Columbus goes to landfills. The amount of trash the city collects has increased 150% in the last five years. Columbus's landfill is almost full. In an effort to encourage people and businesses to recycle, the cost of dumping trash in the landfill is doubling from $4.90 a cubic yard to $9.90 a cubic yard next week. Next January, the price will increase again, to $12.95 a cubic yard. Crogen believes that the amount of trash can be reduced by cooperation between the landfill and the power plant and by recycling.

How Bike Nashbar Started Recycling Cardboard   *Capitalize first letter of major words in heading.*

Solution.

Waste Management, Inc., is the country's largest waste processor. After reading an article about how committed Waste Management, Inc., is to waste reduction and recycling, I decided to see whether Waste Management could recycle our boxes. Corrugated cardboard (which is what Bike Nashbar's boxes are made of) is almost 100% recyclable, so we seemed to be a good candidate for recycling.

Figure 8-25

An Informative Memo Report Describing How a Company Solved a Problem (continued)

Kitty O. Locker
March 14, 2001
Page 2

Reader's name, date, page number.

To get the service started,

1. I looked up Waste Management's phone number and called the company.

2. I met with a friendly sales rep, David Crogen, that same afternoon to discuss the service.

Waste Management, Inc., took care of all the details. Two days later, Bike Nashbar was recycling its cardboard.

How the Service Works and What It Costs   *Talking heads tell r eader what to expect in each section.*

Details of solution.   Waste Management took away our existing 8-cubic-yard garbage bin and replaced it with two 4-yard bins. One of these bins is white and has "cardboard only" printed on the outside; the other is brown and is for all other solid waste. The bins are emptied once a week, with the cardboard being taken to the recycling plant and the solid waste going to the landfill or power plant.

Since Bike Nashbar was already paying more than $60 a week for garbage pickup, our basic cost stayed the same. (Waste Management can absorb the extra overhead only if the current charge is at least $60 a week.) The cost is divided 80/20 between the two bins: 80% of the cost pays for the bin that goes to the landfill and power plant; 20% covers the cardboard pickup. Bike Nashbar actually receives $5.00 for each ton of cardboard it recycles.

Double space between paragraphs.

Each employee at Bike Nashbar is responsible for putting all the boxes he or she opens in the recycling bin. Employees must follow these rules:

- The cardboard must have the word "corrugated" printed on it, along with the universal recycling symbol.

Indented lists provide visual variety.

- The boxes must be broken down to their flattest form. If they aren't, they won't all fit in the bin and Waste Management would be picking up air when it could pick up solid cardboard. The more boxes that are picked up, the more money and space that will be made.

- No other waste except corrugated cardboard can be put in the recycling bin. Other materials could break the recycling machinery or contaminate the new cardboard.

- The recycling bin is to be kept locked with a padlock provided by Waste Management so that vagrants don't steal the cardboard and lose money for Waste Management and Bike Nashbar.

Figure 8-25
An Informative Memo Report Describing How a Company Solved a Problem (concluded)

Kitty O. Locker
March 14, 2001
Page 3

Dis-advantages of solution.

Minor Problems with Running the Recycling Program

The only problems we've encountered have been minor ones of violating the rules. Sometimes employees at the shop forget to flatten boxes, and air instead of cardboard gets picked up. Sometimes people forget to lock the recycling bin. When the bin is left unlocked, people do steal the cardboard, and plastic cups and other solid waste get dumped in the cardboard bin. I've posted signs where the key to the bin hangs, reminding employees to empty and fold boxes and relock the bin after putting cardboard in it. I hope this will turn things around and these problems will be solved.

Advantages of the Recycling Program

Advantages of solution.

The program is a great success. Now when boxes arrive, they are unloaded, broken down, and disposed of quickly. It is a great relief to get the boxes out of our way, and knowing that we are making a contribution to saving our environment builds pride in ourselves and Bike Nashbar.

Our company depends on a clean, safe environment for people to ride their bikes in. Now we have become part of the solution. By choosing to recycle and reduce the amount of solid waste our company generates, we can save money while gaining a reputation as a socially responsible business.

Why Other Companies Should Adopt Similar Programs

Argues that her company's experience is relevant to other companies.

Businesses and institutions in Franklin County currently recycle less than 4% of the solid waste they produce. David Crogen tells me he has over 8,000 clients in Columbus alone, and he acquires new ones every day. Many of these businesses can recycle a large portion of their solid waste at no additional cost. Depending on what they recycle, they may even get a little money back.

The environmental and economic benefits of recycling as part of a comprehensive waste reduction program are numerous. Recycling helps preserve our environment. We can use the same materials over and over again, saving natural resources such as trees, fuel, and metals and decreasing the amount of solid waste in landfills. By conserving natural resources, recycling helps the U.S. become less dependent on imported raw materials. Crogen predicts that Columbus will be on a 100% recycling system by the year 2020. I strongly hope that his prediction will come true and the future may start to look a little brighter.

Informative reports often include the following elements:
- Introductory paragraph summarizing the problems or successes of the project.
- Chronological account of how the problem was discovered, what was done, and what the results were.
- Concluding paragraph with suggestions for later action. In a recommendation report, the recommendations would be based on proof. In contrast, the suggestions in a closure or recommendation report are not proved in detail.

Figure 8-25 presents this kind of informative report.

Feasibility Reports

Feasibility reports evaluate several alternatives and recommend one of them. (Doing nothing or delaying action can be one of the alternatives.)

Feasibility reports normally open by explaining the decision to be made, listing the alternatives, and explaining the criteria. In the body of the report, each alternative will be evaluated according to the criteria. Discussing each alternative separately is better when one alternative is clearly superior, when the criteria interact, and when each alternative is indivisible. If the choice depends on the weight given to each criterion, you may want to discuss each alternative under each criterion.

Whether your recommendation should come at the beginning or the end of the report depends on your reader. Most readers want the "bottom line" up front. However, if the reader will find your recommendation hard to accept, you may want to delay your recommendation till the end of the report when you have given all your evidence.

Justification Reports

Justification reports recommend or justify a purchase, investment, hiring, or change in policy. If your organization has a standard format for justification reports, follow that format. If you can choose your headings and organization, use this pattern when your recommendation will be easy for your reader to accept:
1. **Indicate what you're asking for and why it's needed**. Since the reader has not asked for the report, you must link your request to the organization's goals.
2. **Briefly give the background of the problem or need**.
3. **Explain each of the possible solutions.** For each, give the cost and the advantages and disadvantages.
4. **Summarize the action needed to implement your recommendation.** If several people will be involved, indicate who will do what and how long each step will take.
5. **Ask for the action you want.**

If the reader will be reluctant to grant your request, use this variation of the problem-solving pattern:
1. **Describe the organizational problem (which your request will solve).** Use specific examples to prove the seriousness of the problem.
2. **Show why easier or less expensive solutions will not solve the problem.**
3. **Present your solution impersonally.**
4. **Show that the disadvantages of your solution are outweighed by the advantages.**
5. **Summarize the action needed to implement your recommendation.** If several people will be involved, indicate who will do what and how long each step will take.
6. **Ask for the action you want.**

How much detail you need to give in a justification report depends on your reader's knowledge of and attitude toward your recommendation and on the corporate culture. Many organizations expect justification reports to be short-only one or two pages. Other organizations may expect longer reports with much more detailed budgets and a full discussion of the problem and each possible solution.

SHOULD I USE THE SAME STYLE FOR REPORTS AS FOR OTHER BUSINESS DOCUMENTS?

Yes, with three exceptions.

Style also applies to reports, with three exceptions:
   1. **Use a fairly formal style, without contractions or slang.**
   2. **Avoid the word *you*.** In a document to multiple audiences, it will not be clear who you is. Instead, use the company name.
   3. **Include in the report all the definitions and documents needed to understand the recommendations.** The multiple audiences for reports include readers who may consult the document months or years from now. Explain acronyms and abbreviations the first time they appear. Explain the history or background of the problem. Add as appendices previous documents on which you build.

The following points apply to any kind of writing, but they are particularly important in reports.
   1. Say what you mean.
   2. Tighten your writing.
   3. Use transitions, topic sentences, and headings to make your organization clear to your reader.

Let's look at each of these principles as they apply to reports.

1. Say What You Mean.

Not-quite-right word choices are particularly damaging in reports, which may be skimmed by readers who know very little about the subject. Putting the meaning of your sentence in the verbs will help you say what you mean.

Vague: My report revolves around the checkout lines and the methods used to get price checks when they arise.

Better: My report shows how price checks slow checkout lines and recommends ways to reduce the number of price checks needed.

Sometimes you'll need to completely recast the sentence.

Incorrect: The first problem with the incentive program is that middle managers do not use good interpersonal skills in implementing it. For example, the hotel chef openly ridicules the program. As a result, the kitchen staff fear being mocked if they participate in the program.

Better: The first problem with the incentive program is that some middle managers undercut it. For example, the hotel chef openly ridicules the program. As a result, the kitchen staff fear being mocked if they participate in the program.

2. Tighten Your Writing.

Eliminate unnecessary words, use gerunds and infinitives, combine sentences, and reword sentences to cut the number of words.

Building a Critical Skill

Asking Specific and Polite Questions, 4

Learning to ask the right question the right way is a critical skill in business. Good business communicators use specificity and politeness.

Specificity

Vague questions often result in vague or rambling answers. Therefore, make sure you ask the right question for the kind of answer you want. To get a short answer,

- Give simple choices:

  When you work extra hours, would you prefer overtime pay or comp time (the same number of hours off)?

- Ask the real question.

  Not: When do you want to meet?

  But: Which day is best for you to meet?

- Ask for a quantifiable or measurable response, such as facts, dates, statistics, and so forth.

  What percentage of our customers are repeat business?

When you want longer, more qualitative answers, make your question specific enough for your audience to understand what you're asking:

- Start with one of the five Ws or H: Who, what, where, when, why, or how.

- Add concrete language that invites a qualified response:

  What reservations do you have about my proposal?

  Why do you want to work for this firm?

Politeness

Politeness is a matter of timing, tone, language, and culture (Module 3). Remember that when and how you ask the question are almost as important as the question itself. To increase your chances of not offending anyone,

- Use timing. Don't assault people with questions the moment they arrive or get up to leave. If someone is upset, give him or her time to calm down. Avoid questions when it's obvious someone doesn't want them.

- Keep questions to a minimum. Review all the resources at your disposal first to see if the answers are there.

- Avoid embarrassing or provocative questions. Even if you are comfortable discussing such issues, don't assume other people are.

- Avoid language that implies doubt, criticism, or suspicion.

  Rude: You don't really think you can handle this project, do you?

  Polite: How do you feel about managing this project?

- Use you-attitude and empathy. Try to look at situations from the other person's point of view, particularly if a conflict is involved.

  Because culture affects the rules of politeness-and culture changes-keep abreast of what is and isn't acceptable in society. Remember that different cultures have different concepts of politeness.

Wordy: Campus Jewelers' main objective is to increase sales. Specifically, the objective is to double sales in the next five years by becoming a more successful business.

Better: Campus Jewelers' objective is to double sales in the next five years.

3. Use Blueprints, Transitions, Topic Sentences, and Headings.

Blueprints are overviews or forecasts that tell the reader what you will discuss in a section or in the entire report. Make your blueprint easy to read by telling the reader how many points there are and numbering them. In the following example, the first sentence in the revised paragraph tells the reader to look for four points; the numbers separate the four points clearly. This overview paragraph also makes a contract with readers, who now expect to read about tax benefits first and employee benefits last.

Paragraph without numbers:	Employee Stock Ownership Programs (ESOPs) have several advantages. They provide tax benefits for the company. ESOPs also create tax benefits for employees and for lenders. They provide defense against takeovers. In some organizations, productivity increases because workers now have a financial stake in the company's profits. ESOPs are an attractive employee benefit and help the company hire and retain good employees.
Revised paragraph with numbers:	Employee Stock Ownership Programs (ESOPs) provide four benefits. First, ESOPs provide tax benefits for the company, its employees, and lenders to the plan. Second, ESOPs help create a defense against takeovers. Third, ESOPs may increase productivity by giving workers a financial stake in the company's profits. Fourth, as an attractive employee benefit, ESOPs help the company hire and retain good employees.

Transitions are words, phrases, or sentences that tell the reader whether the discussion is continuing on the same point or shifting points.

There are economic advantages, too.
(Tells the reader that we are still discussing advantages but that we have now moved to economic advantages.)

An alternative to this plan is . . . .
(Tells reader that a second option follows.)

These advantages, however, are found only in A, not in B or C.
(Prepares reader for a shift from A to B and C.)

A **topic sentence** introduces or summarizes the main idea of a sentence. Readers who skim reports can follow your ideas more easily if each paragraph begins with a topic sentence.

Hard to read (no topic sentence):	Another main use of ice is to keep the fish fresh. Each of the seven kinds of fish served at the restaurant requires one gallon twice a day, for a total of 14 gallons. An additional 6 gallons a day are required for the salad bar.
Better (begins with topic sentence):	Twenty gallons of ice a day are needed to keep food fresh. Of this, the biggest portion (14 gallons) is used to keep the fish fresh. Each of the seven kinds of fish served at the restaurant requires one gallon twice a day (7 X 2 = 14). An additional 6 gallons a day are required for the salad bar.

Headings are single words, short phrases, or complete sentences that indicate the topic in each section. A heading must cover all of the material under it until the next heading. For example, *Cost of Tuition* cannot include the cost of books or of room and board. You can have just one paragraph under a heading or several pages. If you do have several pages between headings you may want to consider using subheadings. Use subheadings only when you have two or more divisions within a main heading.

Topic headings focus on the structure of the report. As you can see from the following example, topic headings give very little information.

Recommendation
Problem
　Situation 1
　Situation 2
Causes of the Problem
　Background
　Cause 1
　Cause 2
Recommended Solution

Informative or **talking heads**, in contrast, tell the reader what to expect. Informative heads, like those in the examples in this chapter, provide an overview of each section and of the entire report:

Recommended Reformulation for Vibe Bleach
Problems in Maintaining Vibe's Granular Structure
　Solidifying during Storage and Transportation
　Customer Complaints about "Blocks" of Vibe in Boxes
Why Vibe Bleach "Cakes"
　Vibe's Formula
　The Manufacturing Process
　The Chemical Process of Solidification
Modifications Needed to Keep Vibe Flowing Freely

Headings must be parallel, that is, they must use the same grammatical structure. Subheads must be parallel to each other but do not necessarily have to be parallel to subheads under other headings.

LONG REPORTS

Formal reports are distinguished from informal letter and memo reports by their length and by their components. A full formal report may (but does not have to) contain all of the following components:

Cover

Title Page

Letter of Transmittal

Table of Contents

List of Illustrations

Executive Summary

Report Body

Introduction (Usually has subheadings for Purpose and Scope; may also have Limitations, Assumptions, and Methods.)

Background/History of the Problem (Serves as a record for later readers of the report.)

Body (Presents and interprets data in words and visuals. Analyzes causes of the problem and evaluates possible solutions. Specific headings will depend on the topic of the report.)

Conclusions (Summarizes main points of report.)

Recommendations (Recommends actions to solve the problem. May be combined with Conclusions; may be put before body rather than at the end.)

References or Works Cited (Documents sources cited in the report.)

Appendixes (Provide additional materials which the careful reader may want: transcript of an interview, copies of questionnaires, tallies of all the questions, computer printouts, previous reports.)

I'VE NEVER WRITTEN ANYTHING SO LONG. HOW SHOULD I ORGANIZE MY TIME?

Write parts as soon as you can.
Spend most of your time on sections that are important to your proof.

To use your time efficiently, think about the parts of the report before you begin writing. Much of the Introduction comes from your proposal with only minor revisions: Purpose, Scope, Assumptions, and Methods.

The bibliography from your proposal can form the first draft of your References or Works Cited.

Save a copy of your questionnaire or interview questions to use as an appendix. As you tally and analyze the data, prepare an appendix summarizing all the responses to your questionnaire, your figures and tables, and a complete list of References or Works Cited.

You can write the title page and the transmittal as soon as you know what your recommendation will be.

After you've analyzed your data, write the Executive Summary, the body, and the Conclusions and Recommendations. Prepare a draft of the table of contents and the list of illustrations.

When you write a long report, list all the sections (headings) that your report will have. Mark those that are most important to your reader and your proof, and spend most of your time on them. Write the important sections early. That way, you won't spend all your time on Background or History of the Problem. Instead, you'll get to the meat of your report.

HOW DO I CREATE EACH OF THE PARTS OF A FORMAL REPORT?

Follow the example here.

As you read each section below, you may want to turn to the corresponding pages of the long report in Figure 8-26 to see how the component is set up and how it relates to the total report.

Title Page

The Title Page of a report contains four items: the title of the report, whom the report is prepared for, whom it is prepared by, and the release date. Sometimes reports also contain a brief summary of the contents of the report; some title pages contain decorative artwork.

The title of the report should be as informative as possible.

Poor title: New Office Site

Better title: Why Dallas Is the Best Site for the New Info.com Office

In many cases, the title will state the recommendation in the report: "Why the United Nations Should Establish a Seed Bank." However, the title should omit recommendations when

- The reader will find the recommendations hard to accept.

- Putting all the recommendations in the title would make it too long.

- The report does not offer recommendations.

If the title does not contain the recommendation, it normally indicates what problem the report tries to solve.

Letter or Memo of Transmittal

Use a memo of transmittal if you are a regular employee of the organization for which you prepare the report; use a letter if you are not. The transmittal has several purposes: to transmit the report, to orient the reader to the report, and to build a good image of the report and of the writer.

Organize the transmittal in this way:

1. **Tell when and by whom the report was authorized and the purpose it was to fulfill.**

2. **Summarize your conclusions and recommendations.**

3. **Indicate minor problems you encountered in your investigation and show how you surmounted them.** Thank people who helped you.

4. **Point out additional research that is necessary, if any.**

5. **Thank the reader for the opportunity to do the work and offer to answer questions.** Even if the report has not been fun to do, expressing satisfaction in doing the project is expected.

Table of Contents

In the Table of Contents, list the headings exactly as they appear in the body of the report. If the report is shorter than 25 pages, list all the headings. In a very long report, list the two or three highest levels of headings.

List of Illustrations

Report visuals comprise both tables and figures. Tables are words or numbers arranged in rows and columns. Figures are everything else: bar graphs, pie charts, maps, drawings, photographs, computer printouts, and so forth. Tables and figures are numbered independently, so you may have both a "Table 1" and a "Figure 1." In a report with maps and graphs but no other visuals, the visuals are sometimes called "Map 1" and "Graph 1."

Building a Critical Skill

Creating a Professional Image, 5

Even on casual Fridays, most businesses still expect employees to be anything but casual with their work. Attention to detail, organization, accuracy, economy, and courtesy are the norm.

On casual days, don't dress as though you're planning to clean the garage. Instead, wear clothes in good repair that are one or two "notches" below what you'd wear on other days. If suits are the norm, choose blazers and slacks or skirts. If blazers and slacks or skirts are the norm, choose sweaters or knit sport shirts; khakis, simple skirts, or dressier jeans; or simple dresses. Wear good shoes and always be well groomed. Avoid anything that's ill-fitting or revealing.

Other symbols also convey professionalism. Your work area, for instance, says a lot about you. If your organization allows employees to personalize their desks or offices with photographs, knickknacks, and posters, don't display so much that you seem frivolous. And never display offensive photos or slogans, even in an attempt to be funny. One local government supervisor, known for being strict, put a poster of Adolph Hitler on his door to make light of his reputation. He so offended others that he lost his job. The same caution goes for screen savers and radio stations. It isn't professional to play a morning "shock jock" who uses coarse language and offensive stereotypes.

If your organization allows employees to listen to music, keep the volume at a reasonable level. If your organization allows, consider wearing headphones.

Avoid playing computer games, surfing the Web inappropriately, or ordering personal items on company time.

Keep your voicemail message succinct and professional-find out what co-workers say in theirs.

Keep your desk organized. File papers; keep stacks to a minimum. Throw away anything you don't need. Don't store food in your office. Clean periodically. Water your plants.

The volume of your voice can also disturb others. While most people wouldn't shout across an office, many of us don't realize how loud our voices can be when we're excited or happy. Keep personal conversations to a minimum, in person and on the phone.

Learn the culture of your organization and fit into it as much as you can. When in doubt, follow the lead of someone the organization respects.

Whatever you call the illustrations, list them in the order in which they appear in the report; give the name of each visual as well as its number.

Executive Summary

An Executive Summary tells the reader what the document is about. It summarizes the recommendation of the report and the reasons for the recommendation.

To market life insurance to mid-40s urban professionals, Interstate Fidelity Insurance should advertise in upscale publications and use direct mail.

Network TV and radio are not cost-efficient for reaching this market. This group comprises a small percentage of the prime-time network TV audience and a minority of most radio station listeners. They tend to discard newspapers and general-interest magazines quickly, but many of them keep upscale periodicals for months. Magazines with high percentages of readers in this group include *Architectural Digest, Bon Appétit, Golf Digest, Metropolitan Home, Southern Living, and Smithsonian*. Most urban professionals in their mid-40s already shop by mail and respond positively to well-conceived and well-executed direct mail appeals.

Any advertising campaign needs to overcome this group's feeling that they already have the insurance they need. One way to do this would be to encourage them to check the coverage their employers provide and to calculate the cost of their children's expenses through college graduation. Insurance plans that provide savings and tax benefits as well as death benefits might also be appealing.

Introduction

The **Introduction** of the report contains a statement of purpose and scope and may include all the parts in the following list.

- **Purpose.** Identify the organizational problem the report addresses, the technical investigations it summarizes, and the rhetorical purpose (to explain, to recommend).

- **Scope.** Identify the topics the report covers. For example, Company XYZ is losing money on its line of radios. Does the report investigate the quality of the radios? The advertising campaign? The cost of manufacturing? The demand for radios? If the report was authorized to examine only advertising, then one cannot fault the report for not considering other factors.

- **Limitations.** Limitations make the recommendations less valid or valid only under certain conditions. Limitations usually arise because time or money constraints haven't permitted full research. For example, a campus pizza restaurant considering expanding its menu may not have enough money to take a random sample of students and townspeople. Without a random sample, the writer cannot generalize from the sample to the larger population.

  Many recommendations are valid only for a limited time. For example, a store wants to know what kinds of clothing will appeal to college men. The recommendations will remain in force only for a short time: Three years from now, styles and tastes may have changed.

- **Assumptions**. Assumptions are statements whose truth you assume and which you use to support your conclusions and recommendations. If they are wrong, the conclusion will be wrong too. For example, recommendations about what cars appeal to drivers ages 18 to 34 would be based on assumptions both about gas prices and about the economy. If gas prices radically rose or fell, the kinds of cars young adults wanted would change. If there were a major recession, people wouldn't be able to buy new cars.

- **Methods.** Tell how you chose the people for a survey, focus groups, or interviews and how, when, and where they were interviewed.

  Omit Methods if your report is based solely on library and online research. Instead, simply cite your sources in the text and document them in References or Works Cited.

Background or History

Even though the current audience for the report probably knows the situation, reports are filed and consulted years later. These later audiences will probably not know the background, although it may be crucial for understanding the options that are possible.

In some cases, the History may cover many years. For example, a report recommending that a U.S. hotel chain open hotels in Vietnam will probably give the history of that country for at least the last hundred years. In other cases, the Background or History is much briefer, covering only a few years or even just the immediate situation.

Conclusions and Recommendations

Conclusions summarize points made in the body of the report; **Recommendations** are action items that would solve or partially solve the problem. Number the recommendations to make them easy to discuss. If the recommendations will seem difficult or controversial, give a brief paragraph of rationale after each recommendation. If they'll be easy for the audience to accept, you can simply list them without comments or reasons. The recommendations will also be in the Executive Summary and perhaps in the title and the transmittal.

Figure 8-26   A Long Report

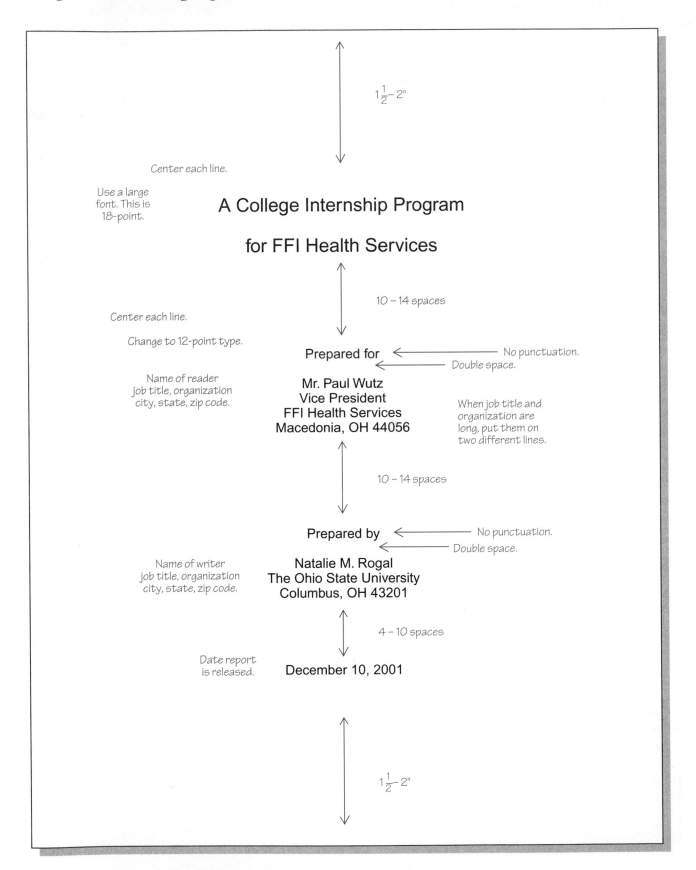

$1\frac{1}{2}- 2"$

Center each line.

Use a large
font. This is
18-point.

A College Internship Program

for FFI Health Services

10 – 14 spaces

Center each line.

Change to 12-point type.

Prepared for   ← No punctuation.
← Double space.

Name of reader
job title, organization
city, state, zip code.

Mr. Paul Wutz
Vice President
FFI Health Services
Macedonia, OH 44056

When job title and
organization are
long, put them on
two different lines.

10 – 14 spaces

Prepared by   ← No punctuation.
← Double space.

Name of writer
job title, organization
city, state, zip code.

Natalie M. Rogal
The Ohio State University
Columbus, OH 43201

4 – 10 spaces

Date report
is released.

December 10, 2001

$1\frac{1}{2}- 2"$

Figure 8-26   A Long Report *(continued)*

You may also design a letterhead for yourself, especially if you're assuming that you are doing the report as a consultant.

This letter uses modified block format (see Figure 9.4). Block format is also acceptable.

1470 Highland Street
Columbus, OH 43201
December 10, 2001

Mr. Paul Wutz
Vice President
FFI Health Services
8635 Crow Drive, Suite 105
Macedonia, OH 44056

Dear Mr. Wutz:

In paragraph 1, release the report. Note when and by whom the report was authorized. Note report's purpose.

Here is the report you authorized in October exploring the kind of internship program that might be best for FFI.

FFI Health Services can benefit from establishing an internship program while providing a valuable service to students. To establish an internship program, you should

Give recommendations or thesis.

- Use the guidelines suggested by Ohio State's Professional Experience Program.

- Pilot the program, focusing on finance and computer science majors the first summer.

- Set intern salaries at $9-$10 an hour for all majors except computer science. Start computer science majors at at least $15 an hour.

- Survey your staff to find out which employees would like to supervise and mentor interns.

- Publicize the program on the Web as well as in Ohio State's Career Services Center. Conduct further research on the best way to reach computer science majors.

- Conduct further research to identify schools other than Ohio State which would also be good sources of interns.

Thank people who helped you.

The information for this report came from online and print sources, a survey of 150 Ohio State students, and an interview with Mindy Kannard of Career Services at The Fisher College of Business. I especially appreciate the guidance of Ms. Kannard and others involved in the Professional Experience Program.

Thank the reader for the opportunity to do the research.

Thank you for the opportunity to conduct this research. I appreciate the chance to apply my experience helping to run an internship program last summer. If you have any questions about the material in this report, please call me.

Offer to answer questions about the report. Answers would be included in your fee—no extra charge!

Sincerely,

Natalie Rogal

Natalie Rogal

Center page number at the bottom of the page. Use a lower-case Roman numeral.

Figure 8-26   A Long Report *(continued)*

Intro begins on page "1".

Indent subheads.

Capitalize first letter of each major word in headings.

Some reports have separate sections for "Conclusions" and "Recommendations"

Headings or subheadings must be parallel within a section. Here, headings are nouns and noun (gerund) phrases. Questions and complete sentences can also be used.

Add a "List of Illustrations" at the bottom of the Table of Contents or on a separate page if the report has graphs and other visuals. Omit "List of Illustrations" if you have only tables.

Line up right margin (justify).

ii

Figure 8-26   A Long Report *(continued)*

**A College Internship Program
for FFI Health Services**

*Report
title.*

Executive Summary

Start with recommendations or thesis.

FFI Health Services should create a college internship program following the model outlined in Ohio State's Professional Experience Program. Following this program will cover the basics of a sound internship program and will enable FFI to hire interns at The Ohio State University.

*Provide
brief
support
for each
recom-
mendation*

FFI can eventually offer internships in eight areas: accounting, computer science, finance, fulfillment, human resources, marketing, transportation logistics, and Web maintenance. FFI does work in each of these areas and could benefit both from the projects that interns might complete and from the opportunity to make permanent hires in these areas. In its first year, however, the internship program should focus on two or three main areas of employment to pilot the program. Finance and computer science are FFI's areas of greatest need.

Since the best students have several options, FFI should offer interns a competitive wage. The average intern earned between \$8 and \$9 last summer, so FFI Health Services should set intern pay at \$9-\$10 an hour for all majors except computer science. To hire the best computer science majors will require starting salaries of at least \$15 an hour. Providing housing would make the internships more attractive and would enlarge the pool of applicants.

One person should not attempt to supervise all of the interns, even during the first summer when there may be only two or three interns. FFI will need to conduct internal research to determine how potential supervisors and mentors feel about working closely with interns. Acting as a mentor should be a voluntary position to ensure active and enthusiastic guidance for the intern.

Participating in the Professional Experience Program will mean that FFI's job descriptions will be available to students who come to the Fisher College of Business Career Services Center looking for internships. However, other kinds of publicity are also desirable so that FFI can have the widest pool of applicants from which to choose. Announcing the internships on FFI's Web site is an obvious step and would bring up FFI's internships when students do Web searches for "internships." Many other companies already give information about internships on Web sites. If computer majors remain in such high demand, FFI will need to do something special to attract them. Further research will be needed to determine what kind of niche FFI can develop.

FFI may want to recruit at other schools besides Ohio State. More research needs to be done to determine the optimal places for FFI Health Services to recruit student interns. Since students may not be able to relocate for the summer or may only move if given a substantial pay incentive, recruiting at colleges in Cleveland and in Tampa may make sense. In addition, it would be useful to identify any colleges that offer majors in managed care. Such colleges would be a good source of students who would be interested in the kind of work FFI does.

*Language in Executive Summary
can come from report. Make sure
any repeated language is well-
written!*

iii

*The Executive Summary
contains the logical skeleton of
the report: the recommendation(s)
and evidence supporting them.*

Figure 8-26   A Long Report *(continued)*

A College Internship Program for FFI Health Services   Page 1

Introduction

Many companies use internship programs to recruit and "try out" students who will eventually become permanent employees. Internships are so popular that they have increased 37% in the last five years (Ferguson, 1998). FFI Health Services is interested in creating a college internship program that will attract quality applicants.

Purpose

The purpose of this report is to recommend a college internship program that will meet FFI's needs.

Scope

In this report, I will focus on three topics: models of internships, what Ohio State students want from internships, and the kinds of internship experiences FFI Health Services can offer. My information about models for internships comes largely from The Fisher College of Business' Professional Experience Program (PEP). PEP suggests activities for interns and outlines the features for an internship program. I also use anecdotal evidence about common internship problems and how FFI can avoid them.

I discuss what Ohio State students want from the internship experience based on a survey of 150 Ohio State students. I discuss how students view internships, what students want from a summer experience, and their willingness to accept internships at FFI. Finally, based on interviews with staff members, especially Paul Wutz, I discuss the kinds of internship experiences FFI can offer.

I will also briefly discuss the general advantages of internships and how the internship program could be publicized.

I will not discuss the financial feasibility of the program or at what schools the company should focus its recruiting efforts.

Assumptions

My recommendations are based on three assumptions:

- The job market will remain tight, making it difficult to find qualified applicants. The tight job market makes an internship program especially desirable. If the job market changed so that there were many more applicants than jobs, FFI might be able to hire managers more easily without needed to "grow" its own managers.

- FFI's central office will remain in Macedonia, Ohio, making it desirable to recruit students from The Ohio State University. If the central office moved, students from other universities might be more desirable than Ohio State students as interns.

- Ohio State students' preferences regarding internships are typical of students at other universities.

Figure 8-26   A Long Report *(continued)*

If you use only library and online sources, you do not need a "Methodology" section. Instead, briefly describe your sources in a paragraph under "Purpose."

A College Internship Program for FFI Health Services   Page 2

Even if it focuses on Ohio State students, FFI will hire interns from other universities as well and should investigate preferences at other universities.

Methodology   *If you collected original data (surveys, interviews, or observations), tell how you chose whom to study, what kind of a sample you used, and on what date(s) you collected the information.*

Information for this report comes from print and online sources, interviews, and a survey of 150 Ohio State University students. I was unable to take a random sample of business students because the Fisher College of Business does not make available a directory of its students. Thus it was necessary for me to use a convenience sample. I chose to survey students on November 20, 2001, at the Ohio Union during a Career Fair. To get the desired number in the sample I asked every student who walked by if he or she had a few minutes to fill out a survey.   *Summarize the demographic information about your respondents.*

The students who responded represent a wide variety of majors and interests. Two-thirds of the students in my sample were juniors and seniors; 32% had an internship last summer. (See Appendix A for all of the raw data from the survey.)   *Refer to your Appendixes in the text of your report.*

Limitations   *If your report has limitations, state them.*
Giving the number makes it easier for the reader to read the paragraph.

My research has <u>four</u> limitations. First, I surveyed students only at The Ohio State University, and FFI will probably want to recruit from other universities as well. Second, at Ohio State, FFI is probably most interested in interns from the Colleges of Business and of Engineering, where Computer Science is housed. Yet my sample covers a wide variety of colleges and has no Engineering students at all. Third, the fact that my survey is based on a convenience sample means that we cannot generalize from my survey to all Ohio State students. Indeed, respondents' demographics show that the students I surveyed are not representative. The College of Social and Behavioral Sciences has the most undergraduate majors at Ohio State, yet it is not the College with the most students in my sample. Fourth, my survey may have interviewer error, which results from the interviewer answering questions differently for different people. Some respondents asked for clarification on some questions while others did not. I tried to answer consistently but my wording was open to interpretation and may have affected the responses. This source of error probably did not significantly affect the accuracy.

Criteria   *Triple-space (2 empty spaces) before new head. Double-space after head before paragraph.*

According to Paul Wutz, the two most important criteria for an internship program are that (1) supervising interns take as little time as possible and (2) the program yield permanent promotable workers. A less important criterion is that interns be able to complete some of the projects that full-time FFI personnel have not had time to do.

Background on FFI Health Services

FFI Health Services contracts with companies to manage prescription benefits. FFI enables employers to give employees prescription coverage at a very reasonable price. Employees can order deeply discounted prescription drugs on FFI's Web site.

Figure 8-26   A Long Report *(continued)*

A College Internship Program for FFI Health Services   Page 3

The company is five years old and started with two employees. FFI Health Services has experienced explosive growth. It now employs 50 people in two offices, one in Macedonia, Ohio, and the other in Tampa, Florida. Hiring qualified personnel is a challenge. Current hiring procedures include running classified advertisements or conducting nationwide searches depending on the type of position to be filled. Some specialized positions such as computer programmers are in such high demand that FFI Health Services does not always feel it is getting the best candidates.

Use talking heads. Note how much more informative this is than "Advantages".

General Benefits of College Internship Programs

Begin most paragraphs with topic sentences.

Businesses benefit enormously from hiring interns. Students are good, productive employees who are positively inclined toward work that is related to their career interests. They can serve as temporary staff or provide assistance for ongoing or special projects. Hiring interns also increases access for hiring women and minorities. Students cost less to hire than regular permanent employees and improve morale in the workplace. Furthermore, student employees bring new ideas and technology to the work site (Ohio State, 1998).

Other benefits include recruiting opportunities. When interns become full-time employees, they need less training and orientation into the company. "Research shows that the turnover rate of employees who have had co-op/internship experience with the organization is significantly less than that for those who did not have this type of job-related opportunity" (Ohio State, 1998, "Criteria and Guidelines").

APA format calls for page numbers when you quote a source. This Web source doesn't have page numbers, but the student gives the subpage from which the quote was taken.

A Model Internship Program

When starting a new internship program, a company can benefit by following a model. The Director of the Professional Experience Program (PEP) at Ohio State works with employers to design internships that benefit both the company and the student. The PEP Employer Handbook offers extensive, specific guidelines for employers. In addition, several articles suggest general guidelines for successful internships.

Spell out term the first time you use it, with the abbreviation in parentheses. Then you can use the abbreviation by itself.

Intern Duties

When author's name is in the sentence, use only year and page number in parentheses.

Appropriate job duties are at the heart of a successful internship program. Admitting that gofer and grunt work are "ubiquitous" in internships, Martha Stone argues that the best internships provide "planned, hands-on" tasks in the field of the student's major (1998, p. 8). Some companies ask interns to do small projects that no one in the organization has time for, but that the organization wants to have done.

Another option is to give interns the same kinds of jobs that entry-level employees would have. Allegiance Healthcare (Watson, 1998), Micron Technology (King, 1997), and Aetna are three of the many companies that take this approach. Aetna's actuarial interns analyze data, improve processes, and "mak[e] things happen" (1999, "Qualifications and Rewards"). One intern reports,   *Use square brackets for your changes in quoted text.*

Quote when the source is especially credible for the point you want to make.

As an Aetna actuarial intern, I worked closely with the other actuaries in my area. I helped to develop a reserving system and price a new contract. I began contributing to the area on my first day, which really surprised me. I worked side-by-side with the other actuaries in the area, as well as the other non-financial areas. What I did really made a difference. My technical, communication, and analytical skills were appreciated and demanded. (1999, "On the Job with Aetna Actuarial Interns")

This quote comes from the Web and has no page number. Title of subpage makes it easy for reader to find page on which quote appears.

Figure 8-26   A Long Report (*continued*)

The Professional Experience Program requires that the employer submit a one-page job description. Examples of job duties in past internships include the following:

Accounting
- Perform inventory costing and cost accounting
- Prepare monthly and year-end close-outs
- Prepare and produce financial statements for reports
- Implement and audit programs to verify accuracy
- Coordinate procurement and transmittal records for audit
- Use Excel, Lotus 1-2-3 and other business software

Periods could be used to end each line. But because this is part of a quote, give text exactly as it appears in the source.

Finance
- Prepare program management cost estimates for projects
- Perform Capital Investment Analysis—analyze the Net Present Value and Internal Rate of Return   *This line could be tightened—"Analyze Capital Investments."*
- Gather financial and accounting data for financial planning and analysis purposes
- Prepare Cost of Capital Estimates
- Prepare Monthly Cash Budgets

But because this is part of a quote, give it exactly as in the source. If you make changes, put them in square brackets [ ].

Human Resources
- Train employees on writing and supervisory skills
- Redesign clerical salary structures
- Evaluate and track recruiting efforts
- Develop a guide for cooperative education
- Assist with targeted selection recruiting plan
- Conduct grievance and disciplinary interviews (Ohio State, 1998, "Job Descriptions")

Other duties are also possible. For example, the Professional Experience Program guidelines suggest that employers may want to ask interns to present their projects to other managers or to employees within the department, both to inform other employees and to enhance students' communication skills.

As these job descriptions suggest, interns can be assigned the same work that might be given to entry-level employees. One question that a company might have is whether college interns who have not yet graduated can really do the work normally assigned to college graduates. Anecdotal evidence suggests that they can. According to Mindy Kannard, Director of Ohio State's Professional Experience Program, "We have very few problems" (personal communication, November 1, 2001). Testimonials from companies that have hired interns are even more positive. According to Heidi A. Willis, Internship Coordinator for American Backhaulers,

When the source is in the paragraph, the parentheses come before the period at the end of the sentence.

Long quotations are indented; no quotation marks necessary.

> Implementing a successful internship program was effortless with the help of the Career Services staff. Students from OSU's Fisher College of Business selected to join our internship team have an elevated level of maturity, a hearty appetite for success, and an active desire to convert learned theories into working ideas. (Ohio State, "Testimonials")

Note that the source parenthesis goes after the period at the end of the sentence in indented quotes.

Program Features

Employers who work with Ohio State's Professional Experience Program must supervise and evaluate interns. Setting appropriate salaries is also important.

Figure 8-26   A Long Report *(continued)*

Third-level headings have periods even when they are not complete sentences.

Quote when you can't think of any better words than those in the source.

Supervising Interns. Interns must receive supervision that is "on-going, consistent and positive" (Ohio State, 1998, "Criteria & Guidelines." At the beginning of the assignment, orientation should include identifying the "key players," the chain of command, office policy (for example, time sheets, overtime, and sick leave), and the corporate culture (including appropriate dress). Ideally, the supervisor or someone else should mentor the intern, not merely give an assignment and disappear. Students benefit from learning not only what is needed, but also why it's needed—how it fits into the larger picture of the company's goals. Identifying specific learning goals can help interns budget their time and also makes evaluation easier.

Mr. Wutz has assumed that since FFI does not have a Human Resources department, he would have to do all the work of supervising and evaluating interns. However, this work could be done by people in the areas in which the interns are working. Because the mentor provides guidance and acts as a "go-to" person for addressing concerns and questions, a mentor working in the same area as the student is ideal. It is important that each student be matched with an enthusiastic mentor who will take an active role in guiding the student's development and providing career advice.

Evaluating Interns. Interns should be evaluated midway through the work period and again at the end. The evaluation should be based on specific goals established earlier. Areas for evaluation might include quality of work, enthusiasm toward assignments, comprehension and knowledge, organizational skills, and judgment. Objectives set forth at the onset of the internship should be reiterated at the interim evaluation and discussed again before the student returns to school. The supervisor should discuss the evaluation with the student and provide constructive criticism and encouragement.

The Professional Experience Program provides a sample form which the employer can use (www.cob.ohio-state.edu/careers/pep/EmpEvual.htm). Employers can also use another evaluation instrument but must turn in some form of written evaluation to the Fisher College of Business Career Services Center.

Setting Salary. The Professional Experience Program at Ohio State gives useful suggestions for setting interns' salaries. While the initial salary should be high enough to attract quality applicants, it should be low enough so that wages can be raised commensurate with increased responsibilities developed should the student be hired again for another internship or hired as a permanent employee.

Second-level heads are flush with the left margin and bolded. Triple-space before new head; double-space after.

Common Problems

Some of the possible problems, such as not giving interns substantive work assignments, can be prevented by following the guidelines for the Professional Experience Program. Professor Dawn Kalmuth, who teaches a class for interns, reports that most interns experience situations in which they feel uncertain. Discussions among interns are helpful in understanding situations, brainstorming alternatives, and developing strategies for implementing the preferred alternative. Some interns find that their supervisors are not in fact very knowledgeable and that they need to seek information from more active (but busier) people. Some interns have been given huge assignments which require massive overtime. Other interns are asked to pick up a project started by a former intern without adequate documentation about what has been done and why. Still other interns experience problems that might be encountered by full-time employees, including sexual harassment (Dawn Kalmuth, personal communication, November 12, 2001). Telling the intern about company channels for dealing with problems and good communication between the intern and his or her mentor or supervisor is essential.

APA format for phone calls, conversations and other sources which the reader cannot check.

Figure 8-26   A Long Report *(continued)*

Heading must cover everything under that heading until the next head or subhead at that level.

Making Internships Attractive to Ohio State Students

Few of the people I surveyed—only 15%—had heard of FFI Rx Managed Care. Companies with strong internship programs are "overwhelmed with applications" ("Internships," 1997, p. 102), but it will be a while before FFI commands that kind of interest. To get off to a good start, FFI's internship program should be attractive to Ohio State students.

When an article has no author, use the first word of the title to identify it.

Providing Good Experience

In terms of accepting a specific internship, the students I surveyed ranked experience as most important, as Table 1 shows.

Refer to Tables in your text.

Table 1. How Important Are Various Criteria in Accepting a Specific Internship?

Rank	Criterion	Average; N = 150 (3 = Very impt., 2 = Somewhat impt., 1 = Not impt.)
1	Gaining experience	2.99
2	Quality of mentoring	2.92
3	Building connections	2.73
4	Chance of getting a job with that company	2.57
5	Prestige of company	2.43
6	Location where you live now	2.36
7	Money	2.22

Compare Table 1 with the raw data for Question 10 in Appendix A (p. 11 of report). Here, the items have been re-arranged to go from the highest to the lowest score.

This emphasis on gaining experience is consistent with the reports of people who had internships last summer. The top four benefits of their internships, according to the people who had them last summer, were "looks good on my résumé, work related to my major, chance to explore my interests," and "made connections." (See Table 2.) If FFI provides internships that give students experience related to their majors, it can attract interns even though it is not yet well known.

Table 2. What Were the Most Beneficial Aspects of Your Internship?

Rank	Aspect	N = 48 n	%
1	Looks good on my résumé	42	86%
2	Work related to my major	41	85%
3	Chance to explore my interests	35	73%
4	Made connections	34	71%
5	Worked with clients	22	46%
6	Likely to get a job offer/got a job offer	15	31%

"N" is the total number of people responding to the question; "n" is the number of people giving a particular response. Giving percentages makes it easier for readers to understand data.

Surprisingly, as Table 1 shows, "chance of getting a job with that company" ranked only fourth out of seven criteria. Fewer than a third of the students who had internships got or expected to get a job offer from that company (Table 2). This emphasis on experience rather than employment will work to FFI's benefit. Only 13% of the students I surveyed were "very interested" in a career in managed care, with a full 47% "not interested." But since students do not necessarily expect to work permanently at the site of their internships, they probably will be

Quote to give the exact wording of survey questions, so reader can interpret data accurately.

Figure 8-26   A Long Report *(continued)*

willing to accept any internship that gives them good experience. Then, a good internship experience can convince students that FFI is a good employer.

Part of providing good experience is assigning students to a good mentor. Some companies assign interns to otherwise unproductive people (Dawn Kalmuth, personal communication, November 12, 2001). However, this is a mistake. FFI should assign its most effective people as mentors, so that students have the best internship experience possible.

FFI's greatest needs are computer personnel, including a Web weaver, and finance personnel (Paul Wutz, personal communication, November 18, 2001). The company also could offer internships in accounting, fulfillment, human resources, marketing, and transportation logistics. Each of these areas could offer solid experience to college students while meeting FFI's needs.

Providing Competitive Pay

Begin most paragraphs with topic sentences. Numbering your points helps the reader.

My survey indicates three points in regards to pay. First, students who did not have internships last summer made an average of $7.67 per hour. The average wage for students with internships was $8.20. The highest-paid interns seem to be those majoring in Management Information Sciences (MIS): One respondent reported that computer science interns received $2,500 a month plus a bonus. Second, the survey demonstrates that only 20% of the respondents could afford to take an unpaid internship next summer. However, 49% could afford to take an internship paying only the minimum wage next summer. Third, while money is the least important of the seven criteria in choosing whether to accept a specific internship, it is at least "somewhat important" to most students. Therefore, FFI should offer competitive wages to attract the best students.

Here published, online, and survey data are combined.

Some internship programs provide more than just an hourly wage. Micron Technology provides corporate housing (King, 1997). Aetna provides not only housing but also round-trip travel to and from its corporate headquarters (Aetna, 1999). Only 15% of the students I surveyed said they could definitely take a job in Cleveland next summer. These may well be students who live in Cleveland. Providing housing and round-trip transportation could win over many of the students who say they "could not" take a job in Cleveland.

Vary paragraph lengths to provide good visual impact.

Finding a Niche for FFI Internships

Not every idea needs a source. Use your knowledge of people and of business.

Don't need author's name in parentheses if name is used in the sentence.

Simply announcing the internships may not be enough to get high-demand students such as MIS majors. If FFI develops an image or "niche" it will stand a better chance of attracting the strongest students. Natalie Engler (1998) shows the lengths to which some companies go. Sapient Corporation conducts "Super Saturdays" eight times a year. These team-based exercises are designed not only to test students' skills but, more importantly, to develop a good impression of Sapient. In one exercise, teams of six were asked to design and build a gift made out of Legos for a book-writing marine biologist. Sapient has used these Super Saturdays to attract employees. The company has added 300 people in the last year and has a very low rate of turnover.

Vary sentence length and sentence structure.

What sets Allegiance Healthcare's internships apart is its on-campus "virtual internship" program. Allegiance installed workstations on campus which students used to complete Allegiance projects throughout the school year (Watson, 1998). Thus Allegiance's location was immaterial; students did not need to relocate. An added benefit to Allegiance was that the interns' work could continue year-round.

Since most students don't know about FFI and don't come to the hiring process interested in managed care, it would be useful for FFI to develop some "gimmick" that could set it apart in students' minds.

Figure 8-26   A Long Report (*continued*)

Conclusions repeat points made in the report.
Recommendations are actions the readers should take.

12 pt. Conclusions and Recommendations

11 pt.   I recommend that FFI Health Services establish an internship program following the model outlined in the Professional Experience Program. Following this program will cover the basics of a sound internship program and will enable FFI to hire interns at The Ohio State University. Decisions to be made include choosing which positions to offer interns, deciding how much to pay them, identifying supervisors and mentors within each department, and determining how to publicize the program and at which colleges to recruit.

List in the order in which you'll discuss them.

1. Choosing Positions for Interns

Some companies ask for Conclusions and Recommendations at the beginning of reports.

FFI should eventually offer internships in eight areas: accounting, computer science, finance, fulfillment, human resources, marketing, transportation logistics, and Web maintenance. FFI does work in each of these areas and could benefit both from the projects that interns might complete and from the opportunity to make permanent hires in these areas.

In its first year I recommend that the internship program focus on two or three main areas of employment. For instance, hiring only finance and computer science majors will give FFI Health Services the opportunity to pilot the program. This strategy will help to ensure that each intern gets the necessary attention and career-related experience. Also, FFI Health Services can detect and correct any flaws in the initial program.

2. Setting Intern Salaries

My survey indicates that only 20% of students could afford to take an unpaid internship, and 51% would not be able to work for minimum wage. Since the best students have several options, FFI should offer interns a competitive wage. Because the average intern earned between $8 and $9 last summer, I recommend that FFI Health Services set intern pay at $9-$10 an hour for all majors except computer science. To hire the best computer science majors will require starting salaries of at least $15 an hour. Providing housing would make the internships more attractive and would enlarge the pool of applicants.

3. Choosing Supervisors and Mentors

Numbering the issues makes it easy for readers to discuss them.

One person should not attempt to supervise all of the interns, even during the first summer when there may be only two or three interns. I suggest conducting internal research to determine how potential supervisors and mentors feel about working closely with interns. Acting as a mentor should be a voluntary position to ensure active and enthusiastic guidance for the intern. Supervisors should be made familiar with assignment and evaluation procedures and should feel comfortable with their role in the internship program. Willing and dedicated supervisors and mentors will make for a more effective program.

4. Publicizing the Program

Participating in the Professional Experience Program will mean that FFI's job descriptions will be available to students who come to the Fisher College of Business Career Services Center looking for internships. However, other kinds of publicity are also desirable so that FFI can have the widest pool of applicants from

Figure 8-26   A Long Report *(continued)*

which to choose. Announcing the internships on FFI's Web site is an obvious step and would bring up FFI's internships when students do Web searches for "internships." Many other companies already give information about internships on Web sites. If computer majors remain in such high demand, FFI will need to do something special to attract them. Further research will be needed to determine what kind of niche FFI can develop.

5. Recruiting Interns

While my research focuses on Ohio State students, FFI may want to recruit at other schools. More research needs to be done to determine the optimal places for FFI Health Services to recruit student interns. Since students may not be able to relocate for the summer or may only move if given a substantial pay incentive, recruiting at colleges in Cleveland and in Tampa may make sense. In addition, it would be useful to identify any colleges that offer majors in managed care. Such colleges would be a good source of students who would be interested in the kind of work FFI does.

> Because many readers turn to the "Recommendations"
> first, provide a brief rationale for each. The ideas in
> this section must be logical extensions of the points
> made and supported in the body of the report.

Figure 8-26   A Long Report (*continued*)

Treat short Web pages like journal articles.   **References**   *APA Format*

Aetna. (1999). Actuarial internships. Retrieved November 4, 2000 from the World Wide Web: http:/www.aetna.com/working/interns.htm

When you use two sets of pages that are part of one Web site, combine them in a single entry.

Engler, N. (1998, March 23). We want you! (Please?!?) *Computerworld,* pp. 72-73.

Ferguson, L. H. (1998, April). Guidelines for a safety internship program in industry. *Professional Safety, 43*(no. 4), 22-25.

Give the page number(s) without "p." when you give the volume and issue number.

Internships identify promising future employees among college students. (1997, April). *HRMagazine, 42*(4), 102. *Start with the title of the article when no author is given.*

King, J. (1997, February 17). Companies use interns as hiring pool. *Computerworld,* pp. 63, 65.

Use "pp." when you don't have volume and issue number.

Ohio State University, Fisher College of Business. (1998). *The professional experience program: Employer handbook.* Retrieved November 4, 2000 from the World Wide Web: http:/www.cob.ohio-state.edu/ careers/pep/

Stone, M. L. (1998, June). How to offer successful internships. *Advertising Age's Business Marketing,* p. 8.

Watson, S. (1998, September 21). Changing perceptions. *Computerworld,* pp. C2-C4.

Month or date of issue goes after year.

Underline titles of magazines, journals, and books if you don't have italics.

List all the printed and online sources cited in your report. Do not list sources you used for background but did not cite. Do not list interviews, phone calls, or other information to which the reader has no access.

Figure 8-26   A Long Report *(continued)*

A College Internship Program for FFI Health Services   Page 11

*Tell how many
people responded.*   **Appendix A: Raw Survey Data**

N = 150. Percentages sometimes total more than 100% due to rounding.

1. Major (Grouped by College)
    Agriculture   *Also give*   7 (5%)
    Arts   *percentages.* 11 (7%)
    Business   35 (23%)
    Human Ecology   15 (10%)
    Humanities   41 (27%)
    Math & Physical Sciences 23 (15%)
    Social & Behav. Sciences 18 (12%)

2. Rank: First-Year   15 (10%)
             Sophomore   34 (23%)
             Junior   47 (31%)
             Senior   54 (36%)

3. How important is it to you to have one or
    more internships before you graduate?
    80 (53%) Very important
    57 (38%) Somewhat important
    14 (9%)   Not important

4. Did you have an internship last summer?
    48 (32%) Yes
    103 (68%) No (skip to Question 6)

5. What were the most beneficial aspects
    of your internship? (Check all that apply.)
    41 (85%) Work related to my major
    15 (31%) Likely to get a job offer/
        got a job offer
    35 (73%) Chance to explore my interests
    34 (71%) Made connections
    22 (46%) Worked with clients
    42 (86%) Looks good on my résumé

6. How much money did you make last
    summer? (Approximate hourly rate,
    before taxes)
    Intern: average $8.20/hr
    Non-intern: average $7.67/hr

    ■ Check here if you did not make any
    money last summer.
    3 interns; 9 non-interns

7. For next summer, could you afford to
    take an unpaid internship?
    30 (20%) Yes   120 (80%) No

8. For next summer, could you afford to
    take an internship paying only the
    minimum wage?
    73 (49%) Yes   76 (51%) No

10. How important is each of the following
    criteria in choosing whether to accept a
    specific internship?

	Very impt. (3)	Some impt. (2)	Not impt. (1)
			Average
a. Money			2.22
b. Prestige of company			2.43
c. Location near where you live now			2.36
d. Quality of mentoring			2.92
e. Building connections			2.73
f. Chance of getting a job with that company			2.57
g. Gaining experience			2.99

11. How interested are you in a career in
    managed care?
    19 (13%) Very interested
    63 (42%) Somewhat interested
    71 (47%) Not interested

12. Could you take a job in Cleveland next
    summer?
    22 (15%) Definitely
    70 (47%) Maybe
    58 (39%) No

13. Have you heard of FFI Rx Managed
    Care?
    23 (15%) Yes
    122 (81%) No

Include a copy of your survey with the raw data. Here, the format is changed a bit to make room for the data.

Figure 8-26   A Long Report *(continued)*

Appendix B: Responses to Open-Ended Question

"Whether or not I could take an unpaid internship or one paying minimum wage would depend on the type of internship and how relevant the experience would be."

"I wish internships would pay."

"I might sacrifice money for one summer if the internship was worth it in terms of gaining experience."

"Just as long as it dealt with my career field, I would be interested in taking an internship."

"It was told to me that internships are as important as some classes. Yet students who work themselves through college cannot afford some of these do to pay. Companies need to start making it worth the while for the working student."

Give responses verbatim—errors and all!

"Another important factor in deciding whether or not to accept a specific internship would be how enjoyable and comfortable the atmosphere is."

"I'll only work where it is warm!"

"Everyone should intern at least one quarter."

"I feel internships are *extremely* important!"

"MIS majors can make $33,000 or $2500 + bonus a month for internships."

"Philosophy students don't do internships, too much like work."

"I think internships are very important."

"Internships give you a taste for what your career will be like and what it's like to work in the 'real world.'"

Provide the text of survey comments so
readers get a sense of the flavor of responses.

SUMMARY

- Block and modified block are the two standard letter formats.

- Use *Ms.* as the courtesy title for a woman, unless she has a professional title, or unless she prefers a traditional title.

- Use *Mr.* as the courtesy title for a man, unless he has a professional title.

- In a list of several people, use parallel forms for names. Use either courtesy titles and last names for everyone, or use first names for everyone. For example, it's sexist to use "Mr." for each man in a document that calls all the women by their first names.

- Memos omit both the salutation and the close. Memos never indent paragraphs. Subject lines are required; headings are optional. Each heading must cover all the information until the next heading. Never use a separate heading for the first paragraph.

- A subject line is the title of a document. A good subject line meets three criteria: it's specific; it's reasonably short; and it's adapted to the kind of message (positive, negative, persuasive). If you can't make the subject both specific and short, be specific.

- The subject line for an informative or positive message should highlight any good news and summarize the information concisely.

- Informative and positive messages normally use the following pattern of organization:

  1. Give any good news and summarize the main points.

  2. Give details, clarification, background.

  3. Present any negative elements—as positively as possible.

  4. Explain any reader benefits.

  5. Use a goodwill ending: positive, personal, and forward-looking.

- Use reader benefits in informative and positive messages when

- You are presenting policies.

- You want to shape readers' attitudes toward the information or toward your organization.

- Stressing benefits presents readers' motives positively.

- Some of the benefits may not be obvious to readers.

- Use the PAIBOC questions to examine the basic points needed for successful informative and positive messages.

- To decide whether to use a Web site as a source in a research project, evaluate the site's authors, objectivity, information, and revision date.

- A survey questions a large group of people, called respondents or subjects. A questionnaire is a written list of questions that people fill out. An interview is a structured conversation with someone who will be able to give you useful information.

- Closed questions have a limited number of possible responses. Open questions do not lock the subject into any sort of response. Branching questions direct different respondents to different parts of the questionnaire based on their answers to earlier questions.

- In a random sample, each person in the population theoretically has an equal chance of being chosen. Only in a random sample is the researcher justified in inferring that the results from the sample are also true of the population from which the sample comes. A convenience sample is a group of subjects who are easy to get. A judgment sample is a group of people whose views seem useful.

- Causation means that one thing causes or produces another. Correlation means that two things happen at the same time. One might cause the other, but both might be caused by a third.

- Citation means attributing an idea or fact to its source in the body of the report. Documentation means providing the bibliographic information readers would need to go back to the original source.

- Comparison/contrast takes up each alternative in turn. The pro and con pattern divides the alternatives and discusses the arguments for and against that alternative. A problem-solving report identifies the problem, explains its causes, and analyzes the advantages and disadvantages of possible solutions. Elimination identifies the problem, explains its causes, and discusses the least practical solutions first, ending with the one the writer favors. General to particular begins with the problem as it affects the organization or as it manifests itself in general, then moves to a discussion of the parts of the problem and solutions to each of these parts. Particular to general starts with specific aspects of the problem, then moves to a discussion of the larger implications of the problem for the organization. Geographical or spatial patterns discuss the problems and solutions by units. Functional patterns discuss the problems and solutions of each functional unit.

- Reports use the same style as other business documents, with three exceptions:

  1. Reports use a more formal style than do many letters and memos.

  2. Reports rarely use the word you.

  3. Reports should be self-explanatory.

- To create good report style,

  1. Say what you mean.

  2. Tighten your writing.

  3. Use blueprints, transitions, topic sentences, and headings.

- Headings are single words, short phrases, or complete sentences that cover all of the material under it until the next heading. Informative or talking heads tell the reader what to expect in each section.

- The Title Page of a report contains the title of the report, whom the report is prepared for, whom it is prepared by, and the release date.

- The title of a report should contain the recommendation unless

  - The reader will find the recommendations hard to accept.

  - Putting all the recommendations in the title would make it too long.

  - The report does not offer recommendations.

- If the report is shorter than 25 pages, list all the headings in the Table of Contents. In a long report, pick a level and put all the headings at that level and above in the Contents.

- Organize the transmittal in this way:

  1. Release the report.

  2. Summarize your conclusions and recommendations.

  3. Mention any points of special interest. Indicate minor problems you encountered in your investigation and show how you surmounted them. Thank people who helped you.

  4. Point out additional research that is necessary, if any.

  5. Thank the reader for the opportunity to do the work and offer to answer questions.

- The **Introduction** of the report contains a statement of Purpose and Scope. The **Purpose** statement identifies the organizational problem the report addresses, the technical investigations it summarizes, and the rhetorical purpose (to explain, to recommend). The **Scope** statement identifies the topics the report covers. The

Introduction may also include **Limitations**, problems or factors that limit the validity of the recommendations; **Assumptions**, statements whose truth you assume, and which you use to prove your final point; and **Methods**, an explanation of how you gathered your data.

- A **Background** or **History** section is included because reports are filed and may be consulted years later.

- **Conclusions** summarize points made in the body of the report; **Recommendations** are action items that would solve or partially solve the problem.

QUESTIONS FOR COMPREHENSION

1. When do you send a letter? When do you send a memo?

2. What are the differences between block and modified block letter formats?

3. What are the differences between block format for letters and the formats for memos?

4. What is the Postal Service abbreviation for your state or province?

5. What are the three criteria for good subject lines?

6. How should you organize a positive or informative message?

7. How do specific varieties of informative and positive messages adapt the basic pattern?

8. What is the difference between open and closed questions?

9. What is the difference between the mean and the median?

10. What is the difference between correlation and causation?

11. What are the seven basic patterns for organizing information?

12. What is a blueprint?

13. What is a talking head?

14. What parts of the report come from the proposal, with some revision?

15. How do you decide whether to write a letter or memo of transmittal?

16. How should you organize a transmittal?

17. What goes in the Executive Summary?

QUESTIONS FOR CRITICAL THINKING

1. Which letter format do you prefer? Why?

2. What are the advantages in telling your reader who is getting copies of your message?

3. Does following a standard format show a lack of originality and creativity?

4. What's wrong with the subject line "New Policy"?

5. Is it unethical to "bury" any negative elements in an otherwise positive or informative message?

6. Why is it important to recognize the secondary as well as the primary purposes of your message?

7. Are you more likely to need reader benefits in informative letters or memos? Why?

8. Why do you need to know the exact way a question was phrased before using results from the study as evidence?

9. How do you decide whether a Web site is an acceptable source for a report?

10. Why should you test a questionnaire with a small group of people before you distribute it?

11. Why should you look for alternate explanations for your findings?

12. Why shouldn't you put all the information you have into a report?

13. Why do reports often use a more formal style than other business documents?

14. Why should you avoid you in reports?

15. Why are topic sentences especially useful in reports?

16. How do you decide what headings to use in the body of the report?

17. How do you decide how much background information to provide in a report?

18. How much evidence do you need to provide for each recommendation you make?

QUESTIONS FOR BUILDING SKILLS

1. What skills have you read about in this module?

2. What skills are you practicing in the assignments you're doing for this module?

3. How could you further develop the skills you're working on?

EXERCISES AND PROBLEMS

1. Revising a Letter
Your assistant gives you the following letter to sign:

Dear Ms. Hebbar:

I received your request to send a speaker to participate in "Career Day" at King Elementary School next month. I am pleased to be able to send Audrey Lindstrom to speak at your school about her job at the child care center.

Audrey has been working in the child care center for over five years. She trains contracted center personnel on policies and procedures of the department.

Another commitment later that day will make it impossible for her to spend the whole day at your school. She will be happy to spend two hours with your class participating in the event.

Call Audrey to coordinate the time of the program, the expected content, and the age group of the audience.

Your students will see the importance of trained day care providers in our neighborhoods.

Thank you for asking our agency to be part of your school's special event. Our future lies in the hands of today's students.

Sincerely,

This draft definitely needs some work. It lacks you-attitude and positive emphasis, it isn't well-organized, and it doesn't have enough details. "Ms. Lindstrom" would be more professional than "Audrey." And more information is needed. Exactly when should she show up? Will she be giving a speech (how long?), speaking as a member of a panel, or sitting at a table to answer questions? Will all grade levels be together, or will she be speaking to specific grades? Will all students hear each speaker, or will there be several concurrent speakers from which to choose?

As Your Instructor Directs
    a. Write a memo to your subordinate, explaining what revisions are necessary.
    b. Revise the letter.

2. Responding to a Supervisor's Request

You've received this e-mail message from your supervisor:

Subject: Need "Best Practices"

Please describe something our unit does well—ideally something which could be copied by or at least applied to other units. Our organization is putting together something on "Best Practices" so that good ideas can be shared as widely as possible.

Be specific. For example, don't just say "serve customers"—explain exactly what you do and how you do it to be effective. Anecdotes and examples would be helpful.

Also indicate whether a document, a videotape, or some other format would be the best way to share your practice. We may use more than one format, depending on the response.

I need your answer asap so that I can send it on to my boss.

Answer the message, describing something that you or others in your unit do well.

3. Accepting Suggestions

Your city government encourages money-saving suggestions to help balance the city budget. The suggestion committee, which you chair, has voted to adopt five suggestions.

1. Direct deposit paychecks to save distribution and printing costs. Suggested by Poh-Kim Lee, in Recreation and Parks.

2. Buy supplies in bulk. Suggested by Jolene Zigmund, in Maintenance.

3. Charge nearby towns and suburbs a fee for sending their firefighters through the city fire academy. Suggested by Charles Boxell, in Fire Safety.

4. Set up an honor system for employees to reimburse the city for personal photocopies or phone calls. Suggested by Maria Echeverria, in Police.

5. Install lock boxes so that meter readers don't have to turn off water valves when people move. This causes wear and tear, and broken valves must be dug up and replaced. Suggested by Travis Gratton, in Water Line Maintenance.

Each suggester gets $100. The Accounting Department will cut checks the first of next month; checks should reach people in interoffice mail a few days later.

As Your Instructor Directs,
    a. Write to one of the suggesters, giving the good news.

    b. Write to all employees, announcing the award winners.

4. Giving Good News

Write to a customer or client, to a vendor or supplier, or to your boss announcing good news. Possibilities include a product improvement, a price cut or special, an addition to your management team, a new contract, and so forth.

5. Easing New Hires' Transition into Your Unit

Prepare a document to help new hires adjust quickly to your unit. You may want to focus solely on work procedures; you may also want to discuss aspects of the corporate culture.

6. Announcing a Change in Group Life Insurance Rates

Your organization provides group life insurance to your salaried employees, worth 2.5 times the employee's annual salary. Hourly employees who worked 30 hours or more a week in the last year receive life insurance equal to what the person was paid in the last year. The premium that the organization pays has been considered taxable income. The exact value is listed on the pay stub in the box labeled "Employer-Paid Benefits." Now, the Internal Revenue Service has announced a reduction in the rates used to calculate the taxable value of this employer-provided life insurance. As a result, the value of the insurance will be slightly lower, and therefore all of the taxes based on pay will be slightly lower: federal, state, city, medicare hospitalization insurance, and school district taxes. These changes will be effective in the paycheck issued at the end of this month for employees paid monthly and in the paycheck issued 10 days from now for employees paid biweekly.

Write a memo to all employees, explaining the change.

7. Introducing a Wellness Program

The very best way for a company to save money on health insurance costs is to have healthy employees. Studies show that people who smoke, who are moderate or heavy drinkers, who are overweight, and who do not exercise regularly have significantly higher health care costs: They visit doctors more often, need more prescription drugs, and are hospitalized more often and for longer periods of time.

Your company has decided to launch a comprehensive wellness program in an effort to get employees to adopt healthier lifestyles. Employees in your organization pay about 40% of the cost of their health insurance; the organization pays the rest. On January 1 (or July 1) rates are going up, as they have every year for the last nine years. Singles will pay $75 a month; people who also insure a spouse or partner pay $160 a month; the cost for the employee and one child is $150 a month; the family rate is $250 a month.

People who follow good health practices don't have to pay that much. You'll give a $100 rebate (annually) to each employee who doesn't smoke or use chewing tobacco. Employees who don't drink to excess (more than an average of at least 6 ounces of beer or 3 ounces of wine or 1.5 ounces of hard liquor a day) and who don't use illegal drugs can also get $100, as can those whose cholesterol isn't over 150. Employees who exercise at least 30 minutes a day, three times a week will get rebates of $50. Exercise doesn't have to be difficult: Walking and gardening count. Another rebate of $50 is available for a waist-to-hip ratio not over 0.8 for women or 0.95 for men.

As part of the wellness program, the company cafeteria will focus on serving healthier foods and the company will offer twice-yearly heath fairs with free routine immunizations, flu shots, and mammograms for employees and dependents. These parts of the program will begin next month.

Write a memo to all employees informing them about the wellness program and the rates for insurance. Hints:

- Pick an organization you know something about to use for this message.

- Much of the program is described negatively. How can you present it positively?

- Specify when the next health fair is and when the new rates start. If the financial program's start is several months away, suggest that people begin to change habits now.

- If the organization saves money, will employees benefit?

- Why don't people already follow healthy practices? What can you do to overcome these objections?

- Saving money may not motivate everyone. Offer intrinsic benefits as well.

8. Explaining Packing Material

Your organization ships thousands of boxes to fill orders from catalogs and from your Web site. To cushion items, you fill the empty spaces around the items with plastic "popcorn." Some customers have written to complain about the plastic, which is not biodegradable. Some have asked you to use real popcorn, paper, or starch (which will degrade when wet). However, these materials cushion less well than plastic does (so that more items are damaged during shipment) and weigh more (so that shipping costs are higher). In addition, popcorn is subject to Food and Drug Administration regulations, which you do not want to monitor; paper fill creates dust and thus is a health hazard for packers; and starch doesn't work in very humid or very dry climates. You want to use one packing material for all boxes, wherever they are going.

Customers who mail some packages themselves could save and reuse the plastic packaging material. If they can't reuse it, they may be able to recycle it. They can call the local solid waste department or garbage company to find out. Or they could call the National Plastic Loose-Fill Collection Program, which accepts and reuses the material. People can call 1-800-828-2214 between 9 a.m. and 6 p.m., Eastern time, to find the closest of the 3,500 locations in the United States.

As Your Instructor Directs,

    a.   Write a letter to one customer who has complained, showing why you are continuing to use plastic fill.

    b.   Prepare a one-page document to be included in every package, explaining your decision about packaging.

9. Reminding Guests about the Time Change

Twice a year the switch to and from daylight-saving time affects people in the United States. The time change can be disruptive for hotel guests, who may lose track of the date, forget to change the clocks in their rooms, and miss appointments as a result.

Prepare a form letter to leave in each hotel room reminding guests of the impending time change. What should guests do?

    Write the letter.

Hints:

- Use an attention-getting page layout so readers don't ignore the message.

- Pick a specific hotel or motel chain you know something about.

- Use the letter to build goodwill for your hotel or motel chain. Use specific references to services or features the hotel offers, focusing not on what the hotel does for the reader, but on what the reader can do at the hotel.

10. Confirming a Reservation

Most travelers phone 13 months in advance to reserve rooms at Signal Mountain Lodge in Grand Teton National Park. Once you process the credit card (payment for the first night), you write to confirm the reservation.

The confirmation contains the amount charged to the credit card, the date on which the reservation was made, the confirmation number, the kind of room (Lakefront Retreat or Mountainview Retreat), and the dates the guest will be arriving and leaving.

In addition, the letter needs to give several pieces of general information. The amount of the deposit and the amount quoted per night is the rate for the current calendar year. However, the guest will be charged the rate for the calendar year of the stay, which is likely to increase about 4% to 5%. In addition to paying the new rate for each additional night, the guest will need to pay the difference between the amount of the deposit and the new rate for the first night.

Anyone who wants a refund must cancel the reservation in writing four days prior to the scheduled arrival date. Cancellations may be faxed: The fax number is on the letterhead the letter will be printed on.

Parking is limited. People who bring big motorhomes, boats, or camp trailers may have to park in the main parking area rather than right by their cabins.

All of the rooms are cabin style with three to four rooms in each building. There are no rooms in a main lodge. People will need to walk from their cabins to the restaurants, unless they do their own cooking.

Both Lakefront and Mountainview Retreats have kitchenettes with microwaves, but guests must bring their own cooking utensils, dishes, supplies, and food. The bedroom area (with a king-size bed in the Lakefront Retreats and a queen-size bed in the Mountainview Retreats) has a sliding divider that can separate it from the sitting area, which has a sofa bed.

Since the deposit pays for the first night (less any increase in room rate), the room will be held regardless of the time of arrival. Check-in time is 3 p.m.; earlier room availability cannot be guaranteed. Checkout time is 11 a.m.

All cabins are nonsmoking. Smoking is permitted on the decks of the Lakefront Retreats or the porches of the Mountainview Retreats.

The guest should present the confirmation letter when checking in.

As Your Instructor Directs,

a. Write a form letter that can be used for one type of room (either Lakefront or Mountainview Retreat). Indicate with square brackets material that would need to be filled in for each guest (e.g., "arriving [date of arrival] and departing [date of departure]").

b. Write a letter to Stephanie Simpson, who has reserved a Lakefront Retreat room arriving September 18 and departing September 20. Her credit card is being billed for $183.75 ($175 plus tax—the current rate). Her address is 3122 Ellis Street, Stevens Point, WI 54481.

11. Lining up a Consultant to Teach Short Courses in Presentations

As Director of Education and Training you oversee all in-house training programs. Five weeks ago, Runata Hartley, Vice President for Human Resources, asked you to set up a training course on oral presentations. After making some phone calls, you tracked down Brian Barreau, a professor of Communication at a nearby college.

"Yes, I do short courses on oral presentations," he told you on the phone. "I would want at least a day and a half with participants—two full days would be better. They need time to practice the skills they'll be learning. I'm free Thursdays and Fridays. I'm willing to work with up to 20 people at a time. Tell me what kind of presentations they make, whether they know how to use PowerPoint, and what kinds of things you want me to emphasize. I'll need a videocamera to record each participant's presentations and a tape for each person. My fee is $2,000 a day."

You told him you thought a two-day session would be feasible, but you'd have to get back to him after you got budget approval. You wrote a quick memo to Runata explaining the situation and asking about what the session should cover.

Two weeks ago, you received this memo.

I've asked the Veep for budget approval for $4000 for a two-day session plus no more than $500 for all expenses. I don't think there will be a problem.

We need some of the basics: how to plan a presentation, how to deal with nervousness. Adapting to the audience is a big issue: our people give presentations to varied audiences with very different levels of technical knowledge and interest. Most of our people have PowerPoint on their computers, but the slide shows I've seen have been pretty amateurish.

I don't want someone to lecture. I don't want some ivory tower theorist. We need practical exercises that can help us practice skills that we can put into effect immediately.

Attached is a list of 18 people who can attend a session Thursday and Friday of the second week of next month. Note that we've got a good mix of people. If the session goes well, I may want you to schedule additional sessions.

Today, you got approval from the Vice President to schedule the session and pay Professor Barreau's fee and reimburse him for expenses to a maximum of $500. He will have to keep all receipts and turn in an itemized list of expenses to be reimbursed; you cannot reimburse him if he does not have receipts.

You also need to explain the mechanics of the session. You'll meet in the Conference Room, which has a screen and flip charts. You have an overhead projector, a slide projector, a video camera, and a VCR, but you need to reserve these if he wants to use them. Will he bring his own laptop computer, or does he want you to provide the computer?

Write to Professor Barreau. You don't have to persuade him to come since he's already informally agreed, but you do want him to look forward to the job and to do his best work.

Hints:

- Choose an organization you know something about.

- What audiences do people speak to? How formal are these talks? What are their purpose(s)?

- Is this session designed to hone the skills of people who are competent, or is it designed to help people who are very weak, perhaps even paralyzed by fright?

- What role do presentations play in the success of the organization and of individuals in it?

- Check the calendar to get the dates. If there's any ambiguity about what "the second week of next month" is, "call" Runata to check.

12. Answering an International Inquiry

Your business, government, or nonprofit organization has received the following inquiries from international correspondents. (You choose the country the inquiry is from.)

1. Please tell us about a new product, service, or trend so that we can decide whether we want to buy, license, or imitate it in our country.

2. We have heard about a problem [technical, social, political, or ethical] which occurred in your organization. Could you please tell us what really happened and estimate how it is likely to affect the long-term success of the organization?

3. Please tell us about college programs in this field. We are interested in sending some of our managers to your country to complete a college degree.

4. We are considering setting up a plant in your city. We have already received adequate business information. However, we would also like to know how comfortable our nationals will feel. Do people in your city speak our language? How many? What opportunities exist for our nationals to improve their English? Does your town already have people from a wide mix of nations? Which are the largest groups?

5. Our organization would like to subscribe to an English-language trade journal. Which one would you recommend? Why? How much does it cost? How can we order it?

As Your Instructor Directs,

a. Answer one or more of the inquiries. Assume that your reader either reads English or can have your message translated.

b. Write a memo to your instructor explaining how you've adapted the message for your audience.

Hints:

- Even though you can write in English, English may not be your reader's native language. Write a letter that can be translated easily.

- In some cases, you may need to spell out background information that might not be clear to someone from another country.

13. Writing a Thank-You Letter

Write a thank-you letter to someone who has helped you achieve your goals.

As Your Instructor Directs,

    a. Turn in a copy of the letter.

    b. Mail the letter to the person who helped you.

    c. Write a memo to your instructor explaining the choices you made in writing the thank-you letter.

14. Evaluating Web Pages

Today you get this e-mail from your boss:

Subject: Evaluating Our Web Page

Our CEO wants to know how our Web page compares to those of our competitors. I'd like you to do this in two steps. First, send me a list of your criteria. Then give me an evaluation of two of our competitors and of our own pages. I'll combine your memo with others on other Web pages to put together a comprehensive evaluation for the next Executive Meeting.

As Your Instructor Directs,

    a. List the generic criteria for evaluating a Web page. Think about the various audiences for the page and the content that will keep them coming back, the way the page is organized, how easy it is to find something, the visual design, and the details, such as a creation/update date.

    b. List criteria for pages of specific kinds of organizations. For example, a nonprofit organization might want information for potential and current donors, volunteers, and clients. A financial institution might want to project an image both of trustworthiness and as a good place to work.

    c. Evaluate three Web pages of similar organizations. Which is best? Why?

15. Creating a Human Resources Web Page

As firms attempt to help employees balance work and family life (and as employers become aware that personal and family stresses affect performance at work), Human Resource Departments sponsor an array of programs and provide information on myriad subjects. However, some people might be uncomfortable asking for help, either because the problem is embarrassing (who wants to admit needing help to deal with drug or spouse abuse or addiction to gambling?) or because that focusing on nonwork issues (e.g., child care) might lead others to think they aren't serious about their jobs. The World Wide Web allows organizations to post information that employees can access privately—even from home.

Create a Web page that could be posted by Human Resources to help employees with one of the challenges they face. Possible topics include

- Appreciating an ethnic heritage.
- Buying a house.
- Caring for dependents: child care, helping a child learn to read, living with teenagers, elder care, and so forth.
- Dealing with a health issue: exercising, having a healthy diet, and so forth.
- Dealing with a health problem: alcoholism, cancer, diabetes, heart disease, obesity, and so forth.
- Dressing for success or dressing for casual days.
- Managing finances: basic budgeting, deciding how much to save, choosing investments, and so forth.
- Nourishing the spirit: meditation, religion.

- Planning for retirement.
- Planning vacations.
  - Reducing stress.
  - Resolving conflicts on the job or in families.

Assume that this page can be accessed from another of the organization's pages. Offer at least seven links. (More is better.) You may offer information as well as links to other pages with information. At the top of the page, offer an overview of what the page covers. At the bottom of the page, put the creation/update date and your name and e-mail address.

As Your Instructor Directs

a. Turn in two laser copies of your page(s). On another page, give the URLs for each link.

b. Turn in one laser copy of your page(s) and a disk with the HTML code and .gif files.

c. Write a memo to your instructor (1) identifying the audience for which the page is designed and explaining (2) the search strategies you used to find material on this topic, (3) why you chose the pages and information you've included, and (4) why you chose the layout and graphics you've used.

d. Present your page orally to the class.

Hints:

- Pick a topic you know something about.
- Realize that audience members will have different needs. You could explain the basics of choosing day care or stocks, but don't recommend a specific day care center or a specific stock.
- If you have more than nine links, chunk them in small groups under headings.
- Create a good image of the organization.

16. Evaluating Survey Questions

Evaluate each of the following questions. Are they acceptable as they stand? If not, how can they be improved?

a. Questionnaire on grocery purchases.

1. Do you usually shop at the same grocery store?

   a.   Yes

   b.   No

2. How much is your average grocery bill?

   a.   Under $25

   b. $25-50

   c. $50-100

   d. $100-150

   e.   Over $150

b. Survey on technology

1. Would you generally welcome any technological advancement that allowed information to be sent and received more quickly and in greater quantities than ever before?

2. Do you think that all people should have free access to all information, or do you think that information should somehow be regulated and monitored?

c. Survey on job skills

How important are the following skills for getting and keeping a professional-level job in U.S. business and industry today?

	Low				High
Ability to communicate	1	2	3	4	5
Leadership ability	1	2	3	4	5
Public presentation skills	1	2	3	4	5
Selling ability	1	2	3	4	5
Teamwork capability	1	2	3	4	5
Writing ability	1	2	3	4	5

17. Evaluating Web Sites

Evaluate seven Web sites related to the topic of your report. For each, consider
- Author(s)
- Objectivity
- Information
- Revision date.

Based on these criteria, which sites are best for your report? Which are unacceptable? Why?

As Your Instructor Directs,
   a. Share your results with a small group of students.
   b. Present your results in a memo to your instructor.
   c. Present your results to the class in an oral presentation.

18. Designing Questions for an Interview or Survey

Submit either a one- to three-page questionnaire or questions for a 20- to 30-minute interview AND the information listed below for the method you choose.

Questionnaire
   1. Purpose(s), goal(s)
   2. Subjects (who, why, how many)
   3. How and where to be distributed
   4. Rationale for order of questions, kinds of questions, wording of questions

Interview
   1. Purpose(s), goal(s)
   2. Subject (who and why)
   3. Proposed site, length of interview
   4. Rationale for order of questions, kinds of questions, wording of questions, choice of branching or follow up questions

As Your Instructor Directs,
a. Create questions for a survey on one of the following topics:
- Survey students on your campus about their knowledge of and interest in the programs and activities sponsored by a student organization.

- Survey workers at a company about what they like and dislike about their jobs.

- Survey people in your community about their willingness to pay more to buy products using recycled materials and to buy products that are packaged with a minimum of waste.

- Survey students and faculty on your campus about whether adequate parking exists.

- Survey two groups on a topic that interests you.

b. Create questions for an interview on one of the following topics:

- Interview an international student about the form of greetings and farewells, topics of small talk, forms of politeness, festivals and holidays, meals at home, size of families and roles of family members in his or her county.

- Interview the owner of a small business about the problems the business has, what strategies the owner has already used to increase sales and profits and how successful these strategies were, and the owner's attitudes toward possible changes in product line, decor, marketing, hiring, advertising, and money management.

- Interview someone who has information you need for a report you're writing.

19. Explaining "Best Practices"

Write a report explaining the "best practices" of the unit where you work that could also be adopted by other units in your organization.

20. Recommending Action

Write a report recommending an action that your unit or organization should take. Address your report to the person who would have the power to approve your recommendation. Possibilities include

- Hiring an additional worker for your department.
- Making your organization more family-friendly.
- Making a change that will make the organization more efficient.
- Making changes to improve accessibility for customers or employees with disabilities.

21. Writing up a Survey

Survey two groups of people on a topic that interests you. Possible groups are men and women, people in business and in English programs, younger and older students, students and townspeople. Non-random samples are acceptable.

As Your Instructor Directs,

a. Survey 40 to 50 people.

b. Team up with your classmates. Survey 50 to 80 people if your group has two members, 75 to 120 people if it has three members, 100 to 150 people if it has four members, and 125 to 200 people if it has five members.

c. Keep a journal during your group meetings and submit it to your instructor.

d. Write a memo to your instructor describing and evaluating your group's process for designing, conducting, and writing up the survey.

As you conduct your survey, make careful notes about what you do so that you can use this information when you write up your survey. If you work with a group, record who does what. Use complete memo format. Your subject line should be clear and reasonably complete. Omit unnecessary words such as "Survey of." Your first paragraph serves as an introduction, but it needs no heading. The rest of the body of your memo will be divided into four sections with the following headings: Purpose, Procedure, Results, and Discussion.

In your first paragraph, briefly summarize (not necessarily in this order) who conducted the experiment or survey, when it was conducted, where it was conducted, who the subjects were, what your purpose was, and what you found out.

In your **Purpose** section, explain why you conducted the survey. What were you trying to learn? Why did this subject seem interesting or important?

In your **Procedure** section, describe in detail exactly what you did.

In your **Results** section, first tell whether your results supported your hypothesis. Use both visuals and words to explain what your numbers show. Process your raw data in a way that will be useful to your reader.

In your **Discussion** section, evaluate your survey and discuss the implications of your results. Consider these questions:

1. Do you think a scientifically valid survey would have produced the same results? Why or why not?

2. Were there any sources of bias either in the way the questions were phrased or in the way the subjects were chosen? If you were running the survey again, what changes would you make to eliminate or reduce these sources of bias?

3. Do you think your subjects answered honestly and completely? What factors may have intruded? Is the fact that you did or didn't know them, were or weren't of the same sex relevant?

4. What causes the phenomenon your results reveal? If several causes together account for the phenomenon, or if it is impossible to be sure of the cause, admit this. Identify possible causes and assess the likelihood of each.

5. What action should be taken?

The discussion section gives you the opportunity to analyze the significance of your survey. Its insight and originality lift the otherwise well-written memo from the ranks of the merely satisfactory to the ranks of the above-average and the excellent.

22. Writing a Report Based on Your Knowledge and Experience
Write a report on one of the following topics.

1. What should a U.S. or Canadian manager know about dealing with workers from _____ [you fill in the country or culture]? What factors do and do not motivate people in this group? How do they show respect and deference? Are they used to a strong hierarchy or to an egalitarian setting? Do they normally do one thing at once or many things? How important is clock time and being on time? What factors lead them to respect someone? Age? Experience? Education? Technical knowledge? Wealth? Or what? What conflicts or miscommunications may arise between workers from this culture and other workers due to cultural differences? Are people from this culture pretty similar in these beliefs and behaviors, or is there lots of variation?

2. Describe an ethical dilemma encountered by workers in a specific organization. What is the background of the situation? What competing loyalties exist? In the past, how have workers responded? How has the organization responded? Have "whistle-blowers" been rewarded or punished? What could the organization do to foster ethical behavior?

3. Describe a problem or challenge encountered by an organization where you've worked. Show why it needed to be solved, tell who did what to try to solve it, and tell how successful the efforts were. Possibilities include

   • How the organization is implementing work teams, downsizing, or a change in organizational culture.

   • How the organization uses e-mail or voice mail, statistical process control, or telecommuting.

   • How managers deal with stress, make ethical choices, or evaluate subordinates.

   • How the organization is responding to changing U.S. demographics, the Americans with Disabilities Act, international competition and opportunities, or challenges from dot.com companies.

As Your Instructor Directs,

Turn in the following documents for Problems 23 through 25:

a. The approved proposal

b. Two copies of the report, including

> Cover
>
> Title Page
>
> Letter or Memo of Transmittal
>
> Table of Contents
>
> List of Illustrations
>
> Executive Summary
>
> Body (Introduction, all information, recommendations). Your instructor may specify a minimum length, a minimum number or kind of sources, and a minimum number of visuals.
>
> References or Works Cited
>
> Appendixes, if useful or relevant

c. Your notes and rough drafts.

23. Writing a Feasibility Study

Write an individual or group report evaluating the feasibility of two or more alternatives. Explain your criteria clearly, evaluate each alternative, and recommend the best course of action. Possible topics include the following:

1. Is it feasible for a local restaurant to open another branch? Where should it be?

2. Is it feasible to create a program to mentor women and traditionally underrepresented groups in your organization?

3. Is it feasible to create or enlarge a day care center for the children of students?

4. Is it feasible to start a monthly newsletter for students in your program?

5. With your instructor's permission, choose your own topic.

24. Writing a Library Research Report

Write an individual or group library research report. Possible topics include the following:

1. **Taxing Internet Sales.** You are an aide to one of your state's members of Congress. "Please write a report for me on whether we should tax sales on the Internet. I want to know about the effect of our current policy on state revenues and on the overall economy." Start with "The Great Internet Tax Debate," *Business Week,* March 27, 2000, 228-36.

2. **Culturally Sensitive Healthcare.** You work for a health maintenance organization (HMO). Your boss says, "Our biggest opportunity for growth is among people of color. But we know that to reach underrepresented groups and immigrants, we need to be more culturally sensitive. Tell us how we need to adapt our marketing and our health care to reach one specific group." Start with Roberto Suro, "Beyond Economics," *American Demographics*, February 2000, 47-55.

3. **Staffing the Military.** For the last several years, most branches of the U.S. military have not been able to recruit and retain as many men and women as they need. Your boss, one of your state's senators, says, "I'm not sure more pay is the answer. Look into the topic. I want to know how bad the problem is and what its causes are." Start with "Pushing the Pay Envelope," *Business Week,* March 8, 1999, 92-94.

4. **Hiring the Poor.** Your employer supports moving people off welfare and is interested in hiring poor people. "Some of the stuff I've read suggests that we need to be advocates for the people we hire. I'd like to know what's involved. Would you write a report on the challenges people coming off welfare in our area are likely to face and what our company would need to do to help them move successfully into work?" Start with Donna Fenn, "Give Me Your Poor," *Inc.*, June 2000, 97-105.

5. With your instructor's permission, choose your own topic.

25. Writing a Recommendation Report

Write an individual or group recommendation report. Possible topics include the following:

1. Recommending Courses. What skills are in demand in your community? What courses at what levels should the local college offer?

2. **Improving Sales and Profits.** Recommend ways a small business in your community can increase sales and profits. Focus on one or more of the following: the products or services it offers, its advertising, its decor, its location, its accounting methods, its cash management, or any other aspect that may be keeping the company from achieving its potential. Address your report to the owner of the business.

3. **Increasing Student Involvement.** How could an organization on campus persuade more of the students who are eligible to join or to become active in its programs? Do students know that it exists? Is it offering programs that interest students? Is it retaining current members? What changes should the organization make? Address your report to the officers of the organization.

4. **Evaluating a Potential Employer.** What training is available to new employees? How soon is the average entry-level person promoted? How much travel and weekend work are expected? Is there a "busy season," or is the workload consistent year-round? What fringe benefits are offered? What is the corporate culture? Is the climate nonracist and nonsexist? How strong is the company economically? How is it likely to be affected by current economic, demographic, and political trends? Address your report to a college placement office; recommend whether it should encourage students to work at this company.

5. With your instructor's permission, choose your own topic.

NOTES

1. Thomas L. Fernandez and Roger N. Conaway, "Writing Business Letters II: Essential Elements Revisited," *1999 Refereed Proceedings, Association for Business Communication Southwest Region*, ed. Marsha L. Bayless, 65–68.

2. In a study of 483 subject lines written by managers and MBA students, Priscilla S. Rogers found that the average subject line was five words; only 10% of the subject lines used 10 or more words ("A Taxonomy for Memorandum Subject Lines," *Journal of Business and Technical Communication* 4, no. 2 [September 1990]: 28–29).

3. Richard C. Whitely, *The Customer-Driven Company* (Reading, MA: Addison-Wesley, 1991), 39–40.

4. Deborah Tannen, *That's Not What I Meant: How Conversational Style Makes or Breaks Your Relations with Others* (New York: Morrow, 1986), 108.

5. An earlier version of this problem, the sample solutions, and the discussion appeared in Francis W. Weeks and Kitty O. Locker, *Business Writing Cases and Problems* (Champaign, IL: Stipes, 1980), 40–44.

6. Janice M. Lauer and J. William Asher, *Composition Research: Empirical Designs* (New York: Oxford University Press, 1986), 66.

7. Frederick F. Reichheld, "Learning from Customer Defects," *Harvard Business Review,* March–April 1996, 56–69.

8. Cynthia Crossen, "Margin of Error: Studies Galore Support Products and Positions, But Are They Reliable?" *The Wall Street Journal,* November 14, 1991, A1, A7.

9. Cynthia Crossen, "Diaper Debate: A Case Study of Tactical Research," *The Wall Street Journal,* May 17, 1994, B8.

10. "Whirlpool: How to Listen to Consumers," *Fortune,* January 11, 1993, 77.

11. Peter Lynch with John Rothchild, *One Up on Wall Street: How to Use What You Already Know to Make Money in the Market* (New York: Simon and Schuster, 1989), 187.

12. Patricia Sullivan, "Reporting Negative Research Results," and Kitty O. Locker to Pat Sullivan, June 8, 1990.

13. Michael L. Keene to Kitty Locker, May 17, 1988.

14. Susan D. Kleimann, "The Need to Test Forms in the Real World," Association for Business Communication Annual Convention, Orlando, FL, November 1–4, 1995.

Chapter 9

Communication Applications: Interviewing

SOURCE: Michael S. Hanna and Gerald L. Wilson, *Communicating in Business and Professional Settings*, 4th ed., Chapters 10-11, © McGraw-Hill, 1998, 1991, 1988, 1984.

Learning Objectives:

After completing this chapter, you should be able to:

- Cite the specific purposes interviews serve in organizations.
- Establish a purpose, select and schedule questions, and plan an interview in order to achieve a predetermined goal.
- Cite the specific purposes of a performance appraisal interview.
- Identify several strategies likely to produce a positive performance appraisal climate.
- Explain the techniques critical to employee-centered problem solving.
- Create and implement a plan to conduct an employee-centered appraisal interview.
- Develop and implement a plan for participating, as an employee, in an appraisal interview.
- Explain the importance of job descriptions, initial questions, EEOC guidelines, and setting to the interviewer in preparing for an interview.
- Distinguish among legal and illegal questions that might be asked in an employment interview and formulate appropriate answers to difficult and/or illegal employment interview questions.
- Do a preinterview informational interview.
- Do a self-analysis of job skills.
- Prepare a cover letter and résumé for a selection interview.
- Research an organization to gather preemployment information.
- Prepare for and practice typical questions asked by employment recruiters.
- Prepare a list of questions to ask an employment recruiter.
- Develop interviewer strategies for beginning an interview, motivating an interviewee to talk, avoiding various kinds of biases, and concluding the interview.
- Develop interviewer methods that allow careful interpretation of data collected from an interviewee.
- Identify the rules of behavior that should be observed during an interview.
- Prepare a strategy for handling a group interview.
- Define the following key terms:

closed question information	**problem-solving interview**
in-depth gathering interview	**schedule**
open question	**secondary question**
performance appraisal interview	**selection interview**
persuasive interview	**survey interview**
primary question	**topical pattern**

Mark and Sandra Sanford are entrepreneurs. In addition to holding full-time jobs, they maintain a business devoted to publishing a business directory. However, when you ask them, as we did, what they do for a living, you do not hear about their full-time jobs or their own small business. Instead they both respond, in unison and with confidence, that they are in the "informational interviewing business."

They explain that informational interviewing is one of the most important occupations in America's service-related economy. They point out that every business is only as profitable as the information gathered to provide a factual and interpretive basis for decision making, problem solving, and strategic planning. Persons who are skilled in locating and eliciting information are therefore highly valued.

Phil Williams, a senior at an eastern university, was heavily into the process of interviewing. Using the university's placement service, he had scheduled three interviews for the day. The last offered the most promising career opportunity. The interview had been with a well-established firm that was large enough to give him the opportunity to move up quickly in the organization. Phil was confident after the interview because he believed that he had made a good impression. He also had worked hard in school and knew that his credentials were very competitive. The interview reinforced his excitement about taking a job with the firm. The interviewer, the same man who would be his supervisor, seemed impressive and personable. Phil could actually imagine working for this man who behaved so competently during the interview. Phil was offered the job, and he accepted it. Interviews can be exciting for the interviewee if the interviewer understands his or her role and performs it well.

You may not have had much reason to think about the role of the interviewer or interviewee because most of us have not had extensive experience with these roles. Yet, these skills are most important for you to acquire.

TYPES OF INTERVIEWS

Interviews in organizations have six general purposes: (1) selecting members, (2) appraising performance, (3) in-depth information gathering, (4) collecting survey information, (5) problem solving, and (6) persuasion.

Selection Interview

Our students seem especially interested in the **selection interview** because they have apprehensions about the process. This type of interview is *conducted for the purpose of making a decision about the interviewee's qualifications for membership in some program, group, or organization*. Because of its "either/or" decision outcome, the selection interview tends to be a highly planned, narrowly purposeful activity that separates it from all other interviewing types and formats.

Performance Appraisal Interview

The **performance appraisal** *is the tool by which you and your work will be evaluated*. Thus, skill in this type of interview is one of the most essential skills an employee of any company can master, regardless of position, occupation, or profession.

Unlike selection interviews, there is seldom an either/or decision in appraisal interviews. Instead, the performance appraisal interview tends to focus on encouraging the employee and solving performance difficulties. As many authorities have pointed out, the performance appraisal is the chief communication mechanism by which organizations either improve or fail.[1]

You can transfer performance appraisal skills into any interpersonal setting where attitudes, values, beliefs, and behavior are issues. Performance appraisal skills are also useful when you help others solve problems.

In-depth Information Gathering Interview

The **in-depth information gathering interview** is used by newspaper and television reporters, radio personalities, academic researchers, popular authors, technical writers, advertising and marketing specialists, actors and directors, and organizational consultants and trainers. This kind of interview is designed *to acquire information about a* *subject, process, or person.* It is characterized by asking and answering both planned and spontaneous questions. When done well, it has the smooth flow of informal, intelligent conversation.

One of the attractive features of mastering the in-depth information gathering interview is that its skills transfer nicely to interpersonal conversations with new acquaintances, friends, and colleagues. Learning how to ask questions during this type of interview is a skill that you can practice every day in a variety of settings.

Survey Interview

Collecting survey data, such as buying habits, attitudes toward a new zoning policy, thoughts and feelings about a national problem, is a very specialized skill. The characteristics of a **survey interview** are essentially *similar to an in-depth information gathering interview, with two differences.* First, the survey interview generally lasts a shorter time. Second, it is *usually accompanied by some paper-and-pencil instrument for recording responses to brief preplanned, pretested questions.*

If you plan to pursue a career in marketing, advertising, or public relations, these interviewing skills will form a valuable part of your education. You will use them often on the job. If your career plans do not include these professions, the skills acquired will still be valuable because they will help you evaluate the quality of surveys conducted by others.

Counseling/Problem-Solving Interview

Interviews can be used to make a decision about a course of action. When the intent of the interviewer is to work through some difficulty with an interviewee, it is a **problem-solving interview** situation.

Counselors and supervisors use problem-solving *interviews to help employees overcome work and personal problems.* Nonprofit agencies use them to determine ways to acquire funding for programs. Health care professionals use them to deal productively with patients and clients. Managers use them to prevent problems from interrupting work and to reach deadlines.

Clearly, skills used in problem-solving interviews can be applied in many situations. They are useful as reasoning and motivating tools, as ways to overcome conflict, and as ways to negotiate outcomes. Problem solving is one of the contemporary hallmarks of a well-educated, communicatively competent individual.

Persuasive Interview

In a **persuasive interview** *the interviewer tries to exert influence over the interviewee.* The interviewer attempts to lead the interviewee to think, feel, and act in a preplanned way.

Selling is one of the most common persuasive interviews. Over 6 million people in the United States work in sales. Beyond selling products, many of us sell ideas. We persuade our bosses to do things that we think will make our work more productive. We persuade friends, parents, children, and colleagues to help us with our projects. Recruiters persuade candidates to take jobs. Health care professionals persuade their patients and clients to follow prescribed advice. Our world is filled with opportunities to use persuasive interviews.

GENERAL APPROACHES TO INTERVIEWS

Interviews may take either a directive or nondirective approach or some combination of these. Using a *directive approach,* the interviewer begins by establishing the purpose of the interview. A directive interviewer generally controls the interview by structuring the event and by asking nearly all the questions. In contrast, using a *nondirective approach,* the interviewer turns over control of the interview to the interviewee. For example, a supervisor, Linda, may perceive that the interviewee, George, needs to vent some dissatisfaction in an appraisal interview before productive discussion can take place. Linda might begin with, "I sense that you may have some things you want to say to me, George. Why don't you begin?"

In spite of the fact that the interviewee is allowed to control the interview, the interviewer has a reason for calling the interview and that usually means the interviewer influences to some degree the direction the interview will take.

The purpose of the interview will usually determine the approach. A directive approach may be used for in-depth probing, survey, employment/selection, and persuasive interviews. A nondirective approach is useful for some counseling, performance appraisal, and problem-solving interviews.

BEGINNING THE INTERVIEWS

Organizational research studies,[2] as well as practical experience, show that there are three interrelated goals for the opening of an interview:

1. To make the interviewee feel welcomed and relaxed.

2. To provide the interviewee with a sense of purpose.

3. To preview some of the major topics to be covered.

You will want to help the interviewee feel welcomed and relaxed. People generally perform better when they are not experiencing too much tension. The opening of an interview should provide a climate that allows participants to relax.

How is this goal accomplished? While the answer to this question depends largely on the personalities of the individuals involved, in general, it is easier for an interviewee to feel comfortable if the interviewer is relaxed. It is advisable, of course, for both parties to be well prepared for the interview.

Nonverbal cues such as a smile, a friendly facial expression, eye contact, a firm handshake, or open gestures set the tone. Introduce yourself. Greet the other person by name if possible. A polite inquiry such as, "How is it going today for you?" will help establish the relationship.

The second major goal of an effective opening should be to provide a sense of purpose and direction. This is primarily the responsibility of the interviewer, who must, early on, state the purpose of the interview and try to provide any additional information relevant to that purpose. For instance, during employment interviews the interviewer often will establish the purpose early on by describing the company and the job description and by explaining in general terms what type of employee is being sought. During an appraisal interview the supervisor might establish the purpose by explaining the policies concerning performance appraisals and by letting the interviewee know how she or he plans to proceed. During in-depth informational interviews the purpose should be stated clearly and directly soon after greetings have been made. Any questions about uses of the information should be answered. During survey and problem-solving interviews, the purpose should be followed by an explanation of how the interview will proceed.

The third major goal of an interview opening should be to preview the internal divisions of the interview. This allows the interviewer to understand the structure for his or her questions and will help the interviewee see the direction the interview will take. Previews serve as markers for people and therefore should make use of numerical references (e.g., first, second, third) and key words that will be easily recalled (e.g., education, work experience, future goals). Limit the number of markers in the preview to between two and four for easy recall.

DEVELOPING THE PATTERN OF QUESTIONING

The opening of the interview establishes rapport, suggests the purpose, and describes the topics to be pursued. In this section we will describe two interrelated concerns about interview questions: (1) organization and (2) structure.

Selecting a Pattern of Organization

These four basic patterns of organization are used to guide topic development.

Topical pattern

This pattern is based on the assumption that an interviewer wants to explore more than one area. We suggest you limit the number of topics to five or fewer and order them logically. The topic pattern is also widely used in performance appraisal interviews. The supervisor has a list of topics (performance categories) such as attitude toward work, relationship with others, willingness to work overtime, performance of established duties, and training needs. Because there are a variety of topics, the topical pattern is appropriate.

Time

Chronology is useful in a wide range of interviews, both as a general organizing device and as a way to pursue a subunit of questioning. An interviewer can organize topics by dates. So, for example, a person in a computer firm interviewing a development expert for a technical document might use the time sequence to develop questions concerning a product development and implementation cycle.

The time pattern is useful in an employment interview. The interviewer might begin with high school education, move to early work experience, then take up college education, and so forth. Thus, the topics of the interview are arranged chronologically. Each topic can also be patterned chronologically.

Cause to effect

The idea of this sequence is to discuss causes prior to effects and then to link causes to effects. When an effect is very dramatic, the cause-effect order may be reversed with good results.

For example, let's assume you are the supervisor of a manufacturing operation that has experienced a work slowdown. You are interviewing workers about the situation to find out what is causing the problem. You would briefly describe the slowdown and then pursue questions related to causes. After the causes have been identified, you pursue the effects these causes are creating and then link causes to effects.

Problem/solution

The problem-solving structure is appropriate, as its name implies, for problem-solving interviews. The goal is to help the interviewee overcome a problem by naming its causes and effects. Problem/solution is also useful as a subunit structure for information gathering, employment, performance appraisal, and persuasive interviews.

The problem-solving structure supposes that identification of a problem and how it is defined will lead to a solution. When using this structure, it is helpful to divide the body of your interview into a discussion of the problem and a discussion of the solution. Then, link the solution sequence to the problem sequence. Sometimes the problem, its significance, and solutions are developed in a series of interviews.

These four strategies suggest the available ways of planning for the developmental questioning sequence of the body of an interview.

Determining the Kind of Structure Needed

Structure can be characterized by the terms *nonscheduled, moderately scheduled, highly scheduled,* and *standardized.* The term **schedule** is used by interviewers to denote the list of questions to be used.

Nonscheduled

A nonscheduled interview has no preplanned questions. The interviewer may have a general goal for the interview but has not written out specific questions. Thus, the interview is guided by a series of topics that may or may not be written. As a result, the interviewer has nearly complete freedom in phrasing and posing questions. This style of interview is useful when not much is known about the interviewee or that person's grasp of a topic.

Moderately Scheduled

A moderately scheduled interview contains major topics along with possible probing or secondary questions for each. It is one of the most often used interviewing formats. It saves preparation time, and its flexibility encourages a positive relational climate. That is, it encourages interviewees to be open, to elaborate on answers given, and to provide important details and examples.

Employment interviewers use this format in all phases of the selection process. Appraisal, problem-solving, and persuasive interviews can benefit from this approach. In-depth interviewers find the method especially helpful too.

However attractive this approach may seem, there are times when a less flexible schedule is needed.

Highly Scheduled

A highly scheduled interview contains all the questions, including those to be used for probing, ordered and worded as they will be asked. This approach is recommended for screening interviews when, for example, the group or organization wants to compare qualifications of candidates. Tightly controlled or stringent conditions may mandate such interviews. For example, when an organization is involved with regulative agencies, questions must be tightly monitored. Follow-up or probing questions may also need to be specified. The screening interview is generally followed by a callback interview that can be more flexible.

Highly Scheduled, Standardized

The highly scheduled, standardized interview is used on occasions where there is a need to quantify answers. This format is used for surveys and in some health care interviews. It provides not only questions worded as they will be asked but also optional answers. The purpose of a survey interview is to determine how a sample population responds to the same series of carefully worded questions.

The choice of which interviewing schedule to use should be based on the particular demands of the situation. Figure 9-1 provides a summary.

FIGURE 9-1   SUMMARY OF STRUCTURAL CHOICES FOR INTERVIEWS

Context	Appropriate Type of Format
Screening/recruitment	Highly scheduled
Employment	Moderately scheduled
Appraisal	Moderately scheduled
Survey	Highly scheduled, standardized
Problem-solving	Moderately scheduled
In-depth information gathering	Moderately scheduled or highly scheduled
Persuasive	Moderately scheduled

CONCLUDING THE INTERVIEW

The conclusion of an interview also requires structure. The goals for an interview closing are similar to those of an opening.

There are three important aims that govern the closing phase in most interviews. First, the interviewer should review the major topics and the responses given to them. This procedure allows modification or changes in answers if necessary. Second, the interviewer should provide opportunity to add information that may have been left out. Valuable additional information can be obtained by asking a simple question: "Is there anything else we need to discuss regarding [name the topic or purpose] that you would like to bring up?"

Third, formally end the interview. An announcement that the interview is over takes the form of a simple "thank you," a handshake, and walking the interviewee out of the office.

THE QUESTIONING PROCESS

A skilled interviewer needs a thorough understanding of open and closed questions, of primary and secondary questions, and when to use each.

Open Questions

An **open question** *asks for broad, general information.* A reporter might say, "Tell me about your inventions." The purpose of an open question is to allow the respondent freedom to answer in his or her own way. Open questions generally produce a great deal of information, organized by the interviewee's own thought process. It is possible to control how much freedom you give a respondent by using one of two different types of open questions: highly open and moderately open.

Highly Open Questions

A *highly open question* suggests a general topic area but allows almost complete freedom of response. An example: "Tell me about yourself." A survey question might be, "What has been your experience with our call-waiting service?" The engineering department head might ask an employee to describe his performance. All of these are highly open because of the freedom of response they allow.

Moderately Open Questions

A *moderately open question* is used to produce a less lengthy and more focused answer. Instead of "Tell me about yourself," a recruiter might say, "Tell me why you chose to go to school at Northern Illinois University." Instead of "What has been your experience with our call-waiting service," the interviewer might ask, "How have you responded to the interruption by our call-waiting signal?"

Here are some guidelines that will help you decide how to ask open questions.

When to Use Open Questions

1. When you want to relax the interviewee, and when the question is easy to answer. (Often an interview will begin with such a question.)

2. When you want to discover what the interviewee thinks is important.

3. When you want to evaluate the communication skills of the interviewee.

4. When you want to evaluate what the interviewee knows.

5. When you are interested in the interviewee's values or feelings.

6. When you wish to open a new area of questioning and intend to follow up with questions prompted by the information the interviewee provides.

Remember, since the respondent has greater control when you use an open question, that person may not choose to talk about the information you want. You may have to take control by asking more specific questions. Also realize that it is difficult to code and tabulate, or record, the kind of information received from an open question. Juan Blackwell, an interviewer from a personnel department, was investigating employee complaints. He said, "Millie, you have been working for us for twenty years and we value your opinion. Tell me, do you know of any problems in the plant?" Then Millie began. Ten minutes later she stopped.

Open questions sometimes present problems in interviews where different interviewers will be collecting information for comparison. Different interviewers may not record enough information from different, or even the same, questions to make comparisons. Even if each interviewer does an adequate job of recording, they may not all select the same kind of information. It is best to use a standard interview schedule if you are using more than one interviewer.

Closed Questions

A *closed question* *narrows response options to a specific area*, so it gives the interviewer more focus on specific information wanted. A law-enforcement officer used a series of closed questions in an on-the-job interview with a driver he stopped.

> **OFFICER:** Good afternoon, sir. Do you know the speed limit on this street?
> **DRIVER:** I believe it is 40.
> **OFFICER:** The limit here is 35. Did you see the speed limit sign in the last block?
> **DRIVER:** No, I didn't.
> **OFFICER:** How fast do you think you were going?
> **DRIVER:** Between 40 and 45.
> **OFFICER:** I clocked you at 47.

Moderately Closed Questions

A *moderately closed question* asks the respondent to supply a particular piece of information. For example, a marketing representative asked a consumer, "What other brands of toothpaste have you tried?" A sales representative asked, "How many computers are in operation in your department?"

Highly Closed Questions

A *highly closed question* implies a very limited response or supplies a short list of responses from which the respondent selects. You will find this type of question in multiple-choice examinations. The highly closed question is most appropriate for surveys. Here is an example of two highly closed questions:

> What is your yearly salary?
> _____ Under $5,000   _____ $20,001 to $30,000
> _____ $5,000 to $10,000   _____ $30,001 to $40,000
> _____ $10,001 to $20,000   _____ Over $40,000
>
> Which of these is the most important as you look at a prospective employer?
> _____ Growth industry   _____ Responsibility/challenge
> _____ National reputation   _____ Location of facility

Another format for a highly closed question is a *rating scale.* Here is an example of this kind of scale using "satisfied" and "dissatisfied" as endpoints.
On a scale of 1 to 5, with 1 being very satisfied and 5 being very dissatisfied, how satisfied are you with your job?

> Satisfied   1   2   3   4   5   Dissatisfied

A third format for a highly closed question asks the interviewee to *rank order* a series of responses. For example,

> Rank order these in order of importance with respect to your work.
> _____ Challenge   _____ Opportunity for advancement
> _____ Job security   _____ Opportunity to be involved

A final type of highly closed question is the *bipolar* question. Such questions limit the respondent to one of two answers. For example, a nurse might ask, "Do you think you can continue working if I give you some Tylenol?"

This type of question assumes that there is no middle ground. The question, "Do you think that inflation will be higher or lower next year?" assumes the answer is not "about the same."

So closed questions provide distinct advantages when you use them effectively, but they can also create problems because of the information you collect. Most of the problems associated with closed questions are related to the control exerted by the question. First, the controlled nature of the responses makes it easy for an interviewee who does not know about a topic to fake understanding. It does not necessarily take any knowledge of the topic to say yes or no, to agree or disagree.

Second, the limited nature of these responses does not allow the respondent to reveal some information that might affect the results. That is, the interviewee may wish to volunteer information but has no convenient way to do so.

Third, there is not much opportunity to build rapport when closed questions comprise the major part of an interview. Lack of response freedom and response flexibility can be frustrating for the interviewee. The respondent may end up thinking the interviewer is the focus of the interview and the interviewer does not care about how the questions are answered.

Finally, closed questions do not allow the interviewer to assess how the interviewee is feeling. Both verbal and nonverbal cues are limited.

When to Use Closed Questions

There are five guidelines to keep in mind when you use closed questions:

1. When you want to have control over both the questions and the answers.

2. When you need specific information and the time for interviews is short.

3. When you are administering multiple interviews and ease of coding, tabulating, analyzing, and replicating are important.

4. When you are not particularly interested in "why" and when the feelings behind the interviewee's answer are not important.

5. When you think the interviewers you will use in multiple interviews are not particularly skilled.

Primary and Secondary Questions

The *primary* designation is given *to any question that initiates a new line of inquiry.* A **primary question** makes sense when taken by itself. For example, a physician said, "Tell me about the pain in your arm." This was a primary question. When she asked, "How often does it bother you?" she asked a secondary question.

Secondary questions derive their significance from the function they perform in the sequence of questions. **Secondary questions** follow primary questions; *they are questions that probe deeper.* There are four kinds of secondary (probing) questions, which are designated by the word *probe.*

The Elaboration Probe

An *elaboration probe* is used to encourage a respondent to provide additional information. Here are two examples:

> A selection interviewer, in response to the interviewee's statement, "I had trouble with my boss," said, "Tell me more about that."
>
> A supervisor who discovered during a performance appraisal interview that a coworker was distracting the interviewee asked, "What else is there to this?"

"What happened next?" "Go on." "Is there more to say about this?" are all examples of elaboration probes.

Clarification Probe

A *clarification probe* seeks further information when a respondent gives a vague answer. An exit interview provides an example.

> **INTERVIEWER:** Tell me why you want to leave your position.
> **INTERVIEWEE:** Well, it has to do with pace. The pace is too much for me.
> **INTERVIEWER:** I don't understand what you mean by pace. Would you say more?

Sometimes an answer is clear, but you want to know the feeling or attitude represented. You might attempt to get at the feeling as this interviewer did:

> **INTERVIEWER:** Tell me why you want to leave your position.
> **INTERVIEWEE:** It has to do with my relationship with my supervisor. I feel held back.
> **INTERVIEWER:** Why do you say "held back"?

Other examples abound:

> In a performance appraisal interview, the interviewer responded, "You say you think your work is average. What do you mean by 'average work'?"
> A candidate for a secretarial job was asked, "What do you mean by 'I get upset when my boss pressures me'?"
> A supervisor asked her employee about a recent argument with a coworker: "Why did you react that way?"

Reflective Probe

The *reflective probe* (also called a "mirror question") feeds back what the interviewee said, to gain clarification. It is also used to check the accuracy of a statement.

A salesperson used this internal summary with a customer who was buying prizes for use in a safety campaign.

> Okay, George, let's review the plan. You want 300 key rings with the company logo for employees who have not had an accident during the last quarter. Then you want 100 wooden plaques with the logo and the inscription, "Six-Month Safety Club." Finally, you want three dozen lightweight jackets in forest green with the logo on the front right for those who have had an accident-free year?

The reflective probe may also be used to check the interviewer's understanding of a response to a primary question.

> **EMPLOYEE:** I think I've been on time to work lately.
> **SUPERVISOR:** So, you haven't been late in the past three months?
> **EMPLOYEE:** That's right.

Clearinghouse Probe

The interviewer asks a *clearinghouse question* to allow a respondent to tell anything that might remain unsaid.

One journalist we know typically closes her interviews with a clearinghouse statement along these lines: "I appreciate all the information you have given me about the services you provide for the deaf. Is there anything else you would like me to know about deafness that would be of interest to the community?"

Now we turn to the performance appraisal context for an in-depth look at how to plan, carry out, and participate in this important interview.

THE PERFORMANCE APPRAISAL INTERVIEW

Suppose that midway through this course your instructor called your name and asked to speak to you, saying, "It's midterm and I've decided to give oral evaluations so students will have the opportunity to know how they are doing and how to improve where necessary. When can you come by my office so that we can talk?" If your experience is like ours, your initial response to this proposition is likely to be a mild anxiety reaction. The thought of being appraised often produces anxiety, stress, and sometimes defensiveness. Much of your self-concept is invested in being a student. Check out how this notion applies to you by filling in these blanks.

> When I seriously think about sitting across from my professor and talking about my effort in this course, I feel _____, _____, and _____.

While we cannot predict your answer, we are concerned that a performance appraisal has the potential for producing anxiety.

Research bares this notion that performance appraisals are anxiety-producing and are avoided when possible. Investigators C. O. Longenecker, H. P. Sims, and D. A. Gioia note that nearly every executive dreads performance appraisals at some time or other. They hate both giving them and getting them.[3] Further, there are some good grounds for these feelings. Evidence suggests that appraisals are often not the straightforward assessment they ought to be. T. A. Judge and G. R. Ferris found that performance appraisals are influenced by the supervisor's liking of the subordinate as well as similarity in demographic features.[4] The appraisal process can even be a "political" activity. One supervisor remarked, "I will use the review process to do what is best for my people and my division. . . ." Accurately describing an employee's performance is really not as important as generating ratings that keep things cooking.[5]

The irony in this situation is that the appraisal interview can and ought to produce a different effect. Accept, for a moment, that people do identify with their work. Part of that identification will necessarily reside in their ability to do the work with which they identify. Consequently, most people want to do well. The appraisal process ought to help them do well.

You can see, too, the logic in the notion that supervisors also want people to do well. Supervisors have a goal—to make the maximum contribution their section can make to the organization. If the performance appraisal system is working properly, it ought to accomplish this goal without distorting subordinate appraisals.

It follows that performance appraisals ought to help the individual employee do well, allow the supervisor to do well, and ultimately, cause the organization to do well. We think these objectives can be achieved and that subordinates can come away from the process feeling OK about themselves if performance appraisals are carried out effectively.

This section focuses on the elements of an effective appraisal interview and offers practical suggestions for preparing for and conducting these interviews. We describe some commonly accepted goals for appraisal interviews and then compare these with some of the approaches in use. Next, we present our approach—the employee-centered problem-solving interview—in three parts: discussion of the climate, presentation of effective techniques, and suggestions about the format of the interview.[6] Finally, we discuss how you can do better in a performance appraisal interview.

Goals for Performance Appraisal Interviews

Andrew Domico, who works for a large paper manufacturing company in Mobile, Alabama, was recently promoted. Apparently he had not realized that his promotion would also bring him the responsibility for talking with the seven people he supervised about their performance on the job. Like many supervisors, Andy felt uneasy about the task, and for a long time he had been avoiding the inevitable. When he could no longer put off the appraisal interviews, he came to us for advice. We suggested that he begin by listing as many goals as he could think of for these interviews.

Appraisal interviews are performed to achieve a number of purposes:[7]

1. To help the employee to do the job better.
2. To give the employee a clear picture of how well he or she is doing.
3. To build stronger, closer relationships with the employee.
4. To develop practical plans for improvement.
5. To recognize employee accomplishments.
6. To communicate the need for improvement.
7. To counsel and provide help.

8. To discover what employees are thinking.

9. To let the employee know what is expected.

10. To set objectives for future performance.

11. To warn or threaten.

12. To reveal the employee's ideas, feelings, and/or problems.

13. To discover the aspirations of the employee.

14. To determine training needs.

Although some of these objectives (for example, threatening) might not always be desirable, most of them are usually appropriate. Because this is so, the work of the supervisor is both difficult and complicated. The number of goals and the fact that some of them further the employee's development while others further only the aims of the organization complicate the performance appraisal task still further.

The Employee-Centered Problem-Solving Interview

Three things are important for a successful performance appraisal interview: a favorable climate, appropriate techniques, and the necessary structure.

Climate

Andy will have created a positive climate if his employee (1) achieves a high level of participation in the interview, (2) does not feel defensive, and (3) feels supported.

A significant body of research concludes that, in general, the more employees participate in the appraisal process, the more satisfied they are with the appraisal interview *and* the supervisor.[8] An interview in which the employee does most of the talking is probably employee-centered. Such an interview also appears to increase the employee's commitment to carrying out the goals discussed, but "airtime" measures might be misleading.[9] If during much of the time the employee is giving defensive reactions, these objectives might not be met.[10]

Andy can reduce defensive behavior by avoiding activities that promote defensiveness. Two researchers have reasoned that because employees are generally apprehensive about being appraised, reduction of the number of negative criticisms and removal of the discussion of salary from the appraisal can reduce defensiveness.[11] Beyond this, be sure to practice effective conflict management.

Andy can also use supportive behavior. W. F. Nemeroff and Kenneth Wexley found that supportive appraisal behavior (taking the attitude of helper, treating the appraisee as equal, showing respect for the appraisee) yielded more satisfaction with respect to the session and with the supervisor.[12] In addition, Gary Latham and Lise Saari found that supportive behavior resulted in higher goals being set.[13]

Techniques

Here are several important techniques that Bill needs to practice to be successful:

Give the employee a worksheet before the interview that allows the person to think about performance issues. Ronald Burke and his associates found that doing this was associated with a positive outcome.[14] A worksheet might include these questions:

1. What are your duties and responsibilities?

2. What are the problems you encounter on the job?

3. What is the quality of your performance with respect to your duties?

4. How do you see your work in comparison to others in similar positions?

The chief advantage of this procedure is that it gives the employee an opportunity to prepare and therefore to be more active in the interview.

Encourage rather than praise. Herbert Meyer, Emanual Kay, and John French discovered that praise had little effect on the outcome of a performance appraisal.[15] Richard Farson suggested that praise can have negative outcomes and often causes defensiveness.[16] Praise may be viewed by the appraisee as threatening—a statement of superiority. Further, Farson notes that praise may increase the distance between the supervisor and employee and also decrease contact between the two. Meyer and his associates concluded in their essay in the *Harvard Business Review* that praise was not useful "because it was regarded as the sandwich which surrounds the raw meat."[17]

Encouragement is a desirable alternative to praise. As a supervisor, you can be sensitive to employees' areas of accomplishment and affirm their sense of pride in what they have done well. When the employee is reviewing areas of strength, you can acknowledge these. For example, you might say, "You seem pleased by the way you handled that." Or when the employee mentions an accomplishment, you can say, "I appreciate what you did." Although the source of the compliment is the supervisor, the recognition has come from the employee. Thus the possibility of interpreting a remark as manipulative is lessened.

Listen actively and feed back the employee's important ideas. Active listening is an interpersonal skill in which the listener paraphrases what is heard and feeds it back to the speaker. Paraphrasing is casting what you have heard in your own words; it is not parroting. The employee is encouraged by paraphrase because it makes clear that the supervisor listened well enough to understand. The technique also provides the employee an opportunity to correct any faulty impressions.

Keep the interview employee-centered. The focus of the interview should be on the *employee's* reasoning, analysis, and solutions, when possible. Suppose you say to an employee, "I noticed that you've been late to work the past two days. I want you to get up earlier in the morning so that you can get here on time!" This is clearly not focused on his or her reasoning or analysis or solutions. Another way of saying this is, "I noticed that you've been late to work the past two days. I'm wondering what the problem is and if there is something either you or I can do to solve it." This presents the problem from the employee's view and is therefore likely to cause less resentment. This approach has been shown to yield better performance.[18]

Do not criticize too much. Giving few instead of many criticisms produces less defensiveness and a greater chance of your employee's achieving improvement.[19] Research found that those areas of the job that were most criticized were the ones in which least improvement was made. When similar areas received less criticism, more improvement was noted. Likewise, the overall number of criticisms was positively correlated with the number of defensive reactions by the employee.[20]

When you do discuss areas where improvement is needed, Jack Gibb's advice about maintaining a supportive climate, summarized in Figure 9-2, seems sensible.[21] You will be more successful if you are able to be supportive of the other person.

Discuss salary in an interview that is separate from the performance appraisal interview. If you talk about salary in an appraisal interview, you may destroy the frame of mind to discuss improvements.[22] The salary interview should come *after* the formal performance appraisal interview. If a salary discussion precedes the interview, the latter may turn into a session where your employee seeks to justify a greater increase or find out why you gave only a limited one. It may also increase the employee's tension. Your goal is to improve the employee's productivity, happiness, and self-worth; it is *not* to debate salary or justify yourself.

Establish specific goals and performance objectives. There is clear evidence that *setting specific goals is very important to improvement.*[23] Meyer, Kay, and French discovered that setting specific goals for improvement yielded twice as much improvement as did talking of general goals or criticizing without any goal discussion.[24] For example, it is more likely that workers will increase production if you jointly set goals. It is better to say, "We agree, then, that you will try to increase your production to 150 units a day by the end of the next month" than to say, "We agree, then, that you will increase your production." Both of these represent goals, but the first will motivate the employee more.

Establish regular checkpoints to review employee progress toward the goals. Appraisal systems that do not emphasize periodic checking on goal accomplishment *do not serve to motivate the employee.* Alva Kindall and James Gatza include this as one of the important steps, suggesting that there are often logical checking points in the completion of a project, or other company-imposed reporting dates.[25] Since each organization is different in this regard, we are unable to suggest a universally applicable periodic schedule. We think, however, that either the supervisor or the employee should initiate the suggestion that such a schedule be agreed upon. We cannot think of a situation in which the suggestion, if initiated by an employee, would be seen as negative.

Conduct interviews at least twice a year. Waiting a year to talk again about an employee's performance has drawbacks. People forget objectives and commitments over a long period. In addition, situations can change. Old goals may no longer be applicable.[26] So we think it is well to conduct at least two appraisal interviews each year, and perhaps more.

FIGURE 9-2	DOS AND DON'TS IN APPRAISAL INTERVIEWS

Dos	Don'ts
Describe the employee's behavior.	Evaluate.
Share the discussion of the problem, soliciting the employee's ideas and suggestions.	Give advice.
Be straightforward in reporting your feelings and in structuring the interview.	Be manipulative and appear to employ some secret strategy.
Put yourself in the place of the employee—empathize.	Appear neutral and unconcerned.
Project a sense of equality.	Pull rank or act superior.
Remain open to new ideas and be tentative in your suggestions.	Maintain rigid positions with respect to your ideas; exhibit defensiveness-arousing uncertainty.

Be consistent in your style. Try to achieve consistency between your usual interaction style and the employee-centered style you use in the appraisal interview. If you do not practice a problem-solving, coaching orientation in day-to-day activities, this style will seem insincere in the interview. Meyer and his associates suggest that you talk regularly with the employee about the job and play the role of helper rather than judge in the process of problem resolution.[27] This concept of helper is consistent with the role of the supervisor in the employee-centered appraisal interview.

Frank J. Landy and his associates suggest that several of these appraisal techniques work together to create a sense of fairness and accuracy.[28] In a questionnaire administered to 356 employees of a large manufacturing firm, the employees identified frequency of evaluation, identification of goals to eliminate weaknesses, and supervisor's knowledge of a subordinate's level of performance and duties as being related to their perceptions of the fairness and accuracy of the performance evaluation.

Structure of the Plan
The likelihood of the supervisor's being successful without some clear plan and approach in mind seems doubtful. We offer the following plan as one likely to achieve the goals of an appraisal interview.

Ask the employee to prepare for the interview. The employee could profit by spending some time considering these four questions prior to the actual interview:

1. What are my important job duties and responsibilities?

2. What are the major problems I encounter on the job?

3. How does my job performance meet the job goals and duties?

4. How does my performance compare to that of others doing similar work?

Establish or reestablish goals related to the specific job. Ask the employee:

1. What things does a person in this job need to do to be successful?

2. What do you think are the most difficult parts of your job?

3. What are the less difficult parts of your job?

Have the employee analyze performance. A study by Ronald J. Burke and his associates found that subordinates who were encouraged to talk about their ideas were more likely than those who weren't to see their supervisors as helpful, constructive, and willing to assist them in resolving job problems.[29]

Ask the employee:

1. Which of the activities you listed do you think you were most successful with? Least successful with?

2. Would you take each of the difficult and less difficult parts of your job that you listed and talk with me about how you see yourself handling each?

If the employee has missed a key issue, an appropriate response might be: "I have been thinking about what is important in a job like yours and have been wondering if [you name it] might also be important. What do you think?" (Employee talks.) Then, "How well do you see yourself doing this duty?"

Summarize any difficulties with performance that came out of the analysis. Examine your findings. Summarize the difficulties you've identified. Then explore alternative solutions with the employee through brainstorming. You might say, "You have listed these difficulties—_____, _____, and _____. I'm wondering what you think you might do to overcome [name the difficulty]."

Give some suggestions if the employee is unable to make any. You might say: "I have thought some about the difficulties you suggest. I can think of a solution or two that might be helpful. I wonder what you think of each of these." You can then reveal the tentative ideas.

Assist the employee in selecting a solution. In this step you review the ways the employee has suggested that the problem might be resolved. Then ask: "Which of these ideas do you think are best? Which are most reasonable?"

Attempt to get the employee to consider the outcome of the selected solution. The employee needs to know what it will take to do whatever he or she has agreed to. This important step is a transition to the next step, goal setting. It also may lead to the selection of a different solution. The employee may discover the favored solution is not practical or workable. Ask: "What are the likely results if you do [describe the solution]?"

Establish new goals and obtain the employee's commitment. Goal setting is a very important part of the plan. Remember these goals must be accepted by the employee if maximum motivation is to come from the goal setting. A goal is more likely to be accomplished when it is perceived to be under a person's control.[30] Notice that the goal-setting question is followed by the questions that seek to gain commitment to them. The three questions you will want to ask are (1) "What have you decided to do?" (2) "When will you do it?" and (3) (if the interviewee has not improved after previous appraisals) "What shall I do if you don't do what you say you will do?"

Plan for training if it appears to be the solution. You should keep training in mind as you conduct performance appraisal interviews. Sometimes employees do not know how to do certain aspects of the job as well as they should. This may become evident as they tell you about steps toward achieving a particular goal. Motivation alone will not solve a performance problem if there is also a training problem.

Plan with the employee for follow-up. Determine how you will know when the employee has met the goal and when it would be appropriate to check on goal accomplishment. The employee can help. Ask: "How will you know when you have achieved these goals? When shall we get back together to see how you are doing?"

Let the employee know you will help. The employee is likely to feel supported if you offer help. In a recent study, Gary Blau found that such an offer is especially important when the task is complex or ambiguous.[31] You have greater expertise, power, and control, and it may be comforting to the employee to know that you are available if needed. You might say, "Be sure to let me know if I can help you achieve these goals."

Keep in mind the main rationale for employee-centered problem solving is employee self-development. Each time employees move through this sequence, they learn to solve work problems.

A Successful Evaluation System

Your organization may not have set procedures that you are asked to follow. Here we present the evaluation procedure used by McCormack & Dodge, a fast-growing computer software company in Huntsville, Alabama, as an example of a system that follows an employee-centered philosophy. Figure 9-3 reproduces their rating instructions. A study of this figure can help you draw maximum benefit from an evaluation.

FIGURE 9-3 MCCORMACK & DODGE PERFORMANCE EVALUATION

The employee information and signature section across the top of the inside pages of the evaluation form will be completed as follows:

Please print: _____ Signatures: _____ Date:
Employee Name _____ Employee_____

Reviewing Manager_____ Manager _____

Department/Cost Center _____ Next Level Manager _____

Date of hire _____ Personnel _____

Managers evaluate each performance factor on two scales. The first scale is a determination of how heavily each item should be weighted, or how important it is in relation to all other factors. The second scale is a determination of how well the employee performs in relation to the manager's expectations:

These performance factors are *weighted* as:

Critical: the performance factor is absolutely vital to job performance. *Each* factor weighted as critical is unquestionably necessary to fulfilling the function of that job. The evaluation of the employee's performance would alter significantly if the employee did not meet the manager's expectations in those critical areas.

Important: the performance factor is very significant to job performance. Each is important, but *no one single* factor is critical to job performance. Rather, the successful performance of an individual is determined by the *overall* accomplishment of *all* important components.

Desirable: the performance factor is included in the evaluation, not as a necessary component to the job, but as a complementary component. It would be positive if the individual performed at or above the manager's expectations for these factors, but the overall impression of performance would not alter significantly if the individual did not perform well for these factors.

The performance factors are then *rated* as:

1. Exceeds expectations: the employee *consistently* and *significantly* exceeds the expectations of performance for this factor—*unusually high level of excellence.*

2. Meets expectations: the employee demonstrates good performance for this factor. The manager's standards are essentially met.

   A rating of "(2) Meets expectations" does not mean average or mediocre performance. Expectation standards for performance are high and should be communicated as such.

3. Does not meet expectations: the employee does not meet expectations of performance for this factor. Improvement is required.

   The Plus (+) or Minus (-) signs allow for further indication of how well each factor was performed.

(Figure 9-3 continued on the next page)

(Figure 9-3 continued from previous page)

The performance appraisal includes three categories of *performance factors:*

I.   *General performance factors:* job components that apply to all positions, such as quality of work, organizing skills, initiative.

    (1)   *Job knowledge:* depth of understanding of the content and procedures of the job and of the field of specialization.

    (2)   *Quality of work:* thoroughness, accuracy, and completeness exhibited in routine assignments and special projects.

    (3)   *Responsiveness to supervision:* timeliness of pursuing and completing tasks and objectives; acceptance of responsibility.

    (4)   *Organizing skills:* planning, scheduling, coordinating tasks and assignments effectively.

    (5)   *Judgment:* analyzing and evaluating situations; success in reaching correct and optimum decisions.

    (6)   *Attitude:* ability and desire to cooperate with others toward the best interest of all concerned.

    (7)   *Initiative:* ability to organize and develop constructive ideas; to perform new or assigned tasks in a self-directed manner.

    (8)   *Self-development:* desire to improve performance and to strengthen both personal and job skills.

    (9)   *Communication skills:* ability to communicate with superiors, peers, and subordinates.

    (10)   *Supervisory skills* (if applicable): *Human Factors:* ability to select, motivate, and develop subordinates.

    (11)   *Supervisory skills* (if applicable): *Managerial Factors:* skill in planning, organizing, controlling, and coordinating departmental activities; cost control effectiveness.

II. *Performance to job standards:* the standard functions of the employee's job. Any individual in a particular job should be rated on the standards of the job which are taken from the job description.

III. *Performance to goals and objectives:* the goals that the manager and the employee have *previously* determined. These should be relevant to the particular employee's performance, as opposed to being generic to the job description.

Comments

The manager's comments are *required* for all factors weighted as critical and any factors that exceed or did not meet expectations. Any additional comments related to performance of an individual in each performance category are welcomed.

The purpose of the comment sections is to document for the employee *why* the manager chose to put an *X* in the box for that factor. What was going through the manager's mind when he or she decided to put an *X* in:

Exceeds expectations—What did the employee do above and beyond the expectations for the factor?

Did not meet expectations—What was not accomplished? How could the employee improve performance?

An *X* in the box simply indicates the result of the manager's decision—not the reasons why that decision was made. Neither praise (exceeds expectations) nor criticism (did not meet expectations) really alters performance.

It simply makes the employee feel good or bad for a short period of time. By providing information as to *why* performance was rated as it was, an employee can understand what actions need to be continued or improved. These comments make the "performance to goals and objectives" section much easier to complete and to relate the goals and objectives to actual performance.

SOURCE: Used by permission of McCormack & Dodge Corporation, Natick, MA.

Participating Effectively As the Interviewee

Suppose that you are now employed part-time as a salesperson by Retailers Unlimited. You are particularly pleased by this job as you intend to make your career retail sales. You hope to be invited to participate in their management training program upon graduation. You are required to participate in the appraisal process at Retailers even though you are part-time. Retailers believes that these interviews are a good way to keep their employees informed and motivated. The situation can best be summed up as one in which you want to do a good job and also want to be perceived as a person who has management potential.

Suppose we substitute the word *internship* for *part-time worker.* You might prefer to imagine yourself in an internship, facing a midway evaluation. Try to think about what you would do to make your interview successful. Are you able to formulate ideas about how you would approach this communication problem? Can you translate these into a specific plan? The remainder of this chapter presents a plan that you can use as your guide.

Conducting a Self-Assessment

Answer the following questions in writing and think about the implications of your answers:

1. What are my principal duties?

2. How well have I carried out each of these duties?

3. How does my performance compare with that of my coworkers in similar jobs?

4. What problems have I encountered on the job?

5. What are several approaches I might employ to deal with these problems?

6. Would I promote myself if I were the boss? Why? Why not?

We believe these questions cover most of the central concerns of supervisors, and they will help you anticipate what you probably will be asked. You will also find them helpful if you must evaluate others.

Asking Informational Questions

It is generally important not to challenge or argue unless that is unavoidable. In asking questions, keep these guidelines in mind:

1. Try to get the interviewer to give you as much information as possible about your performance. If the employer is not following an employee-centered plan, you may hear evaluative comments about your performance.

2. Try to get the employer to give specific examples to illustrate what is meant, if possible.

3. Try to get specific suggestions about what you can do to improve.

4. Summarize what you think you have heard to discover if you really do understand.

5. Be prepared to discuss your performance difficulties. An interviewer following an employee-centered style will try to get you to think about any problems in your performance.

6. If you think that the interviewer and you have reached similar conclusions about what you can do, check it out by restating the conclusions.

7. Ask for information and suggestions from the interviewer if the interview seems to be stalled. Avoid questions or statements that challenge. Examples of informational, as opposed to challenging, statements are given in Figure 9-4

You might wish to avoid challenging your employer because it is difficult to challenge without creating defensiveness. We do not believe, however, that you should avoid challenging altogether. If you think it is necessary, keep in mind Jack Gibb's supportive and defensive behavior categories. Figure 9-5 gives some examples of how you might use supportive categories in a conversation about your performance.

Applying the Principles of Language Use

The basic principles of language are:

1. Personalize your communication.

2. Realize when you make an inference and choose words to reflect this.

3. Clarify the fact that you are hearing an inference when that is what it is.

4. When it seems appropriate to report your feelings, do so precisely, before explaining and interpreting them.

5. Say explicitly what you want rather than what you do not want.

6. State your wants in terms of actions you can control.

You may want to review the material on interviews in the beginning of this chapter before you participate in a performance appraisal interview.

FIGURE 9-4   EXAMPLES OF INFORMATIONAL AND CHALLENGING STATEMENTS

Informational	**Challenging**
I'm wondering what I have been doing that leads you to that conclusion?	I don't see how you can say that! How do you know?
Would you describe some specific difficulties you have observed so I can know how to improve?	What do *you* want me to do?
Looking at my performance, can you suggest particular things you'd like me to do that I'm not now doing?	I'll do anything you say. You're the boss!
Sometimes people do things that irritate or frustrate others. Am I doing anything you'd like me not to do?	And I'll refrain from doing what you tell me not to do. You're the boss.

FIGURE 9-5   EXAMPLES OF SUPPORTIVE STATEMENTS

Category	**Example**
Description	From my perspective, this is what I thought I was doing.
Provisionalism	There are several ways of attacking this problem. I thought that what I did had a good chance of working even though other methods might also work. What other methods would you suggest?
Equality and problem orientation	I recognize your point of view on this issue and wonder if there is some way we can work together on this problem.
Empathy	I believe we both want to get the best product from our effort, and I am beginning to understand how difficult it is to coordinate our effort. If we can find a specific solution to this problem, it will help us achieve this optimum effort.

PREPARING FOR THE INTERVIEW: THE INTERVIEWER

A novice may think that the interviewer's part is easy. It is not. Many candidates have bad experiences with interviews through no fault of their own. Applicants often turn down job offers because they cannot imagine working for an organization that would use incompetent recruiters. If you work long enough for a company, you will be involved in selecting new professionals. What we say here can serve as a reference when you are called upon to conduct an employment interview.

In preparing for an interview, recruiters need to follow a certain sequence of steps, including:
1. Consulting the job description.
2. Deciding on a structure for the interview and preparing initial questions.
3. Checking Equal Employment Opportunity Commission (EEOC) guidelines.
4. Arranging the setting.

Consulting the Job Description

Many job descriptions are out-of-date or do not correspond to the job's actual duties. Do some checking. In *How Effective Executives Interview,* Walter Mahler gives a list of steps to follow for updating the specifications for executive positions.[32] With a little imagination you will be able to adapt the list that follows, which is based on his list, to your situation.
1. Do not leave updating the job description to the staff. It is your responsibility.
2. Check your list with other people who are familiar with the job.
3. Look at business or operating objectives.
4. Check to see if the position description is up-to-date.
5. Consider what factors contributed to the success and failure of present and past incumbents.
6. Analyze relevant competitors of the company. What personnel factors, if any, might give them an advantage?
7. Give attention to future changes that might occur in the job.
8. Separate critical qualifications from those that would be nice to have.

With the job description and the answers to these questions in hand, you are ready to prepare a chart of the responsibilities and qualities needed. The two-column list in Figure 9-6, for a departmental secretary in a university setting, is a useful model. Upon completion of the analysis, you are ready for the next steps.

FIGURE 9-6   TWO-COLUMN JOB ANALYSIS

Job Responsibilities	Qualities Needed
Greet people and make them feel comfortable	Articulateness, good communication skills, personableness, self-assurance
Solve problems for students and faculty	Attentiveness to detail, good judgment, ability to be convincing but not pushy, analytical mindedness
Type and reproduce handouts and tests for classroom use	Ability to pass typing test, follow a list of priorities, and be punctual
Take dictation and produce departmental correspondence	Ability to pass shorthand test, transcribe accurately, and spell and punctuate
Keep departmental records, including financial records	Honesty, mathematical accuracy
Manage interpersonal relations among departmental personnel	Liking for people, integrity, ability to be supportive, social sensitivity
Supervise student workers	Ability to organize, plan; tactfulness, good judgment

Assessing Corporate Culture

The interviewer will find it easy to discover what the organization thinks about recruiting. There are likely to be some published procedures that reflect the organization's cultural expectations. Further, a person who is asked to take part in recruiting will undoubtedly have been in the organization long enough to understand what is expected. Beyond this, a recruiter will have access to those who routinely do this kind of work. If you are asked to help interview, find out what managers are looking for in a successful candidate. Ask also what causes disinterest in a candidate.

Reviewing the Résumé and Application Form

This process involves reading the applicant's letter, résumé, and application form (if your organization uses one). Look for continuity in the person's work and employment experience. Do you notice time gaps? You will want to probe these gaps to see if they are related to the way the candidate might perform. Consider the variety of reasons a person might not have been employed. A person may have been in school, been laid off, been fired, quit to take an extended vacation, been sitting around the house, been in jail, and so forth. Each of these possibilities has some potential consequence for hiring. A person may be laid off because of circumstances or perhaps because the work he was doing just wasn't that valuable. A person may have been between jobs and taken the opportunity to enrich herself, or she may have just sat around doing nothing. You will want to know what the person was doing during gaps in employment and the reasons for that choice.

Examine the candidate's references if they are included. Are these people in a position to observe the candidate's skills? Sometimes a candidate includes personal friends, clergy, and neighbors; these are not going to be helpful to you.

Next, check the candidate's reference letters. Most reference letters are positive—after all, who would ask a person who might reveal damaging information to write on his or her behalf? Sometimes these letters can be useful though. A middle-of-the-road letter, one that is not somewhat glowing, can be a bad sign. Notice if any of the letters speak specifically about outstanding contributions and/or past performance. Make a note of such comments, as these are areas that you may choose to pursue. For example, an interviewer for a small tool manufacturer noticed that a reference talked about a sales award. Questions were framed to probe this: "Tell me about how you came to win a sales contest." "Who was involved in the competition?" "What do you think it takes to win such an award?"

Look to see what kinds of educational experiences the person has had. Generally, this information is limited to the names of the schools and courses of study. Try to assess the quality of these programs from your organization's perspective.

Finally, check the application form, if there is one. Look here for completeness. Are all necessary blanks filled in? If not, there may be a reason for leaving a blank. Make a note of missing information in case you decide to interview the candidate later. Check also for the same kinds of information discussed above.

Structuring the Interview and Preparing Initial Questions

Generally you should work for a moderate degree of structure in your interviews, especially if you will be seeing a number of candidates. Research shows that structuring an interview will (1) force you to be more consistent, (2) cause you to talk less, and (3) allow you to achieve higher agreement with other interviewers, if you are part of a team of interviewers.[33] We think that planning topics and questions is a good idea. Cal Downs found that certain topics arise in most selection interviews.[34] Although not all were initiated by the interviewer, the topics most often covered, in order of the frequency discussed, are:

1. Job expectations

2. Academic background

3. Knowledge about job and company

4. Scholastic record

5. Work experience

6. Geographical preference

7. Interviewing for other jobs

8. Family background

9. Goals

10. Extracurricular activities

11. Strengths and/or weaknesses

12. Salary expectations

Framing questions for each topic is often difficult for an inexperienced interviewer. We recommend that you structure your interview by content area, taking advantage of the list of questions in Figure 9-7. Use it as a start, but tailor the questions to the job description. Also, keep in mind you may want to eliminate some of the less relevant content areas, especially if you are limited in time. And, of course, you will not necessarily want to ask all the questions in an area.

It is often useful to begin questioning in a content area by asking a broad question, such as "Tell me about your communication major." When you ask an unfocused question like this, applicants must focus and organize ideas and tell you what *they* think is important. This allows you to check their ability to analyze and organize—important communication skills you will want to evaluate. But limit the number of questions of this kind. They do not give you the specific information needed to compare candidates.

Ask some relatively easy questions early in the interview. Save the difficult questions for later, when candidates have begun to warm up to handling questions. Keep in mind that your structure has to be flexible. If a candidate is having difficulty with certain types of questions, be flexible enough to shift away from these questions. Come back to them later and try asking them in a different way.

Reviewing EEOC Guidelines

Discrimination in employment based on race, color, religion, sex, marital status, or national origin is forbidden by Title VII of the Civil Rights Act of 1964. In 1967, employment discrimination based on age was outlawed. Discrimination against handicapped people was attacked by the Rehabilitation Act of 1973, and again in 1990 by the Americans with Disabilities Act. In 1974, Congress provided for preference in employment and promotions for veterans of the Vietnam era by the Vietnam Era Veterans Readjustment Assistance Act.

Congress has produced this legislation and created governmental policing agencies to enforce the law in order to provide an opportunity for *all* qualified Americans to work. The principal governmental agency charged with policing the law is the EEOC. This agency has the power to bring those not in compliance to court. Thus, a series of court rulings has led to a set of guidelines and the following list of illegal areas of questioning:[35]

1. Change of name (may reveal national origin).

2. Maiden or former name of spouse (may reveal marital status).

3. Previous foreign address (may reveal national origin).

4. Birthplace of applicant, applicant's spouse, parents, or relatives (may reveal national origin).

5. Applicant's religion.

6. Applicant's complexion or color of skin

7. Applicant's citizenship or national origin.*

8. Applicant's foreign military service.

9. Name and address of relative to be notified (may reveal foreign-born parents). You can ask for *person* to be notified.

* Can ask if they have a legal right to work in the United States. This allows conformance with the Immigration Reform Act of 1987

FIGURE 9-7   QUESTIONS AND FOLLOW-UP QUESTIONS FOR SELECTION INTERVIEWS

I. Education

1. Why did you select your major area of study?
2. Why did you select your college/university?
3. If you were starting college again, what would you do differently? Why?
4. What subjects were most interesting? Useful? Why?
5. What subjects were least interesting? Useful? Why?
6. What classes/subjects did you do well in? Why?
7. What classes/subjects were difficult for you? Why?
8. Other than the courses you studied, what is the most important thing you learned from your college experience?
9. What did you learn from your extracurricular activities?
10. What would be your advice to an entering college student regarding participation in extracurricular activities?
11. What elective coursework did you take? Why did you select these courses?
12. What does it mean to you to have a college degree?
13. How did you finance your college education?

II. Experience

14. Describe each of your work experiences.
15. What do you see as your strengths as an employee?
16. You say that a strength you have is _____. Give me some indication, perhaps an example, that illustrates this strength.
17. Describe the employee you most enjoy working with.
18. Describe the employee you least like working with.
19. What is an ideal boss like?
20. What traits in a boss do you least like?
21. What were the best aspects of your last job?
22. What were the worst aspects of your last job?
23. What were some of your achievements in your last job?
24. What were some of the disappointments in your last job?
25. Do you see yourself as a leader/manager of people? Explain your answer.
26. What kind of work situations would you like to avoid? Why?
27. What skills are needed to be successful as a _____?
28. What are some of the pressures you've encountered in your work experience?
29. How have you worked to manage these work-related pressures?
30. In considering potential employers, what are the most important characteristics? What is *the most important*?
31. What frustrations have you encountered in your work experience? How have you handled these frustrations?
32. What aspects of your last job were difficult for you?
33. Sometimes a work assignment requires frequent travel. How do you react to the prospect of frequent travel?
34. How would you evaluate the progress you made in your last job?
35. Do you think the progress you made in your last job is representative of your ability? Why? Why not?
36. How can a boss help an employee develop his or her capabilities?
37. What areas has your boss suggested you improve? What did you do to improve?
38. Most employees and bosses have some disagreements. What are some things that you and your boss have disagreed about?
39. What does it take to be a good leader?

III. Position and Company

40. Why did you select this company?
41. Why did you decide to apply for this particular position?
42. How do you see yourself being qualified for this position?
43. What about this position is especially attractive to you?

(Figure 9-7 continued on next page)

(Figure 9-7 continued from previous page.)

44. What do you see in the position that is not attractive to you?
45. Why should I hire you?
46. Tell me what you know about our company.
47. Are you willing to relocate?

IV. Self-Evaluation

48. Tell me a little bit about yourself. Describe yourself.
49. If you could relive your life, what might you do differently?
50. What do you see as your strengths? Good qualities? Talents? How do you know that you possess these? Give examples of each.
51. What do you see as your weak points? Areas for improvement? Things you have difficulty doing? What have you done to deal with these?
52. In what areas of work do you lack confidence? Explain. What are you doing about these?
53. In what areas of work are you most confident?
54. Describe a specific work problem you had. Tell what you did to solve this problem.
55. What traits or skills are most important to being successful? Why? Evaluate yourself in relation to these traits or skills.
56. What do you consider to be your greatest work achievement? Why?
57. What does it mean to you to be a self-starter? Do you see yourself as a self-starter? Explain.
58. What factors in a work situation provide motivation for you?
59. Where do you see yourself being in your profession in five years? In ten years? How did you establish these goals? What will you need to do to achieve these goals?
60. What are your salary expectations for this position? Starting salary? Salary in five years?
61. Elaborate on the career objective you presented in your résumé.
62. What has influenced you most to select your particular career goal?

VI. Military Service

63. What kind of specific responsibilities did you have in the service?
64. What traits make a successful leader in the (name branch of service)?
65. What did you learn about work from your tour of duty?
66. What traits are needed to be a successful military person?
67. What traits detract from success as a military person?

10. Applicant's arrest or conviction record—unless you can prove that it is a business necessity (particularly true of arrest record).

11. Applicant's height—unless height can be demonstrated to be a bona fide occupational qualification.

In the search for a position in marketing, a young woman reported being asked: "Do you plan to have a family? And, if so, what are your plans for caring for the children while you work?"

These questions, of course, do not in any way relate to whether the individual is qualified for the position. Moreover, they are not only impertinent but illegal. The candidate handled the question well, we thought: "If you don't mind a preface remark about the illegality of that question, then I will tell you what our plans are in that regard."

The reason we think her answer was a particularly good one is that it took all possibilities into account. She served notice that she understood the law and that she was assertive enough to deal with infractions directly in a relatively high-risk situation. She also was able to show that she was tolerant of ignorance but prepared to treat the ignorance with information. Finally, she communicated that she would answer the question because she felt it was innocent enough.

The test you should keep in mind when asking interview questions is this: "Does this information pertain to a *bona fide occupational qualification?*" In other words, does the information really tell anything about the applicant's qualifications for this job? Sometimes employers are curious about arrangements for child care, plans women may have for childbearing, marriage plans, divorces, activities related to activist groups, and the like. None of these relate *directly* to legal employment considerations and therefore they are none of the employer's business. They are very good grounds for an EEOC complaint and therefore you should avoid them. A summary of the laws with respect to equal employment is provided in Figure 9-8.

Keep in mind that any particular list of laws provides general guidelines. Court interpretations of the laws allow the employer to know what specific lines of questioning are illegal. Some state laws may be more restrictive than those passed by Congress. You should check with the personnel office for the most recent interpretation of the law.

Arranging the Setting

How you arrange the setting in which an interview occurs will have an impact on it. Try to arrange for privacy. We know there will be situations in which privacy is impossible, but at least stay out of the flow of traffic. You may desire some degree of formality in the setting for a variety of reasons. If you are interviewing someone who will work for you, you may wish for the formality of your office. Keep in mind that the choice to stay behind your desk will communicate something about you.

Some college recruiters recommend that an interviewer aim at informality because it will relax the candidate. If this is what you want, you might arrange for seating that is more direct and an atmosphere that is less imposing than your office. Try moving away from your desk and setting chairs so that they are fairly equal—perhaps at 90-degree angles with a coffee table in between and indirect lighting. Your organization may have a suitable room that is used for this purpose. One interviewer we know often takes a candidate to the company cafeteria to have coffee.

We have looked at an employment interview from both the candidate's and the employer's point of view. The focus has been primarily on *preparation.* The second half of this chapter addresses what goes on during an employment interview.

PREPARING FOR THE INTERVIEW: THE INTERVIEWEE'S RESPONSIBILITIES

Consider how you planned for the last interview you had. How did you secure the interview? What did you do to get ready? Check to see how closely the following describes your preparation. If it was for a nonprofessional position, did you just put on appropriate clothing and go to the interview? If it was for a professional position, did you prepare a résumé, consider questions you might be asked, put on appropriate clothing, and go to the interview?

We recommend a six-step plan:

1. Doing preinterview informational interviewing

2. Doing a self-analysis

3. Preparing a résumé (data sheet) and cover letter

4. Researching the various organizations to which you might apply

5. Preparing and practicing for typical questions asked by employers

6. Preparing a list of questions you might ask an employer

Conducting Preinterview Informational Interviews

Interview one or two professionals who are actually working in the field of your choice. This interview ought to take place several months before you begin making appointments for interviews. Otherwise, it could be perceived as a ploy and may keep you from being considered seriously by firms where you have conducted informational interviews.

FIGURE 9-8   FEDERAL LAWS THAT APPLY TO SELECTION INTERVIEWS AND EMPLOYMENT

Civil Rights Act (1866)

This legislation gave all persons the same contractual rights as "white citizens." It was the first law that prohibited discrimination.

Equal Pay Act (1963, 1972)

This act made it unlawful to pay different hourly rates for the same work on the basis of sex. It amended the Fair Labor Standards Act. It exempts academic, administrative, and professional employees from the overtime provisions of that act. The Wage-Hour Division of the Labor Department administers this act.

Civil Rights Act (1964, 1972)

This comprehensive act forbade employment or membership discrimination by employers, employment agencies, and unions on the basis of race, color, religion, sex, or national origin. It established the Equal Employment Opportunity Commission. (An amendment in 1972 allowed the EEOC to initiate court action to force compliance.) Provisions of this act are administered by the Office of Civil Rights of the Department of Health and Human Services and the EEOC.

Age Discrimination in Employment Act (1967, 1978)

This act makes it unlawful to discriminate against applicants or employees who are between forty and sixty-five years of age. (In 1978, this act was amended to raise the age to seventy years, but exempted employees covered by collective bargaining contracts.) Some job categories are exempted if a bona fide occupational qualification is involved. The act applies to employers with twenty or more employees. The Wage-Hour Division of the Labor Department administers the act.

Equal Employment Opportunity Act (1972)

This act amended Title VII of the 1964 act to broaden coverage and to give the EEOC authority to bring lawsuits. It also included educational institutions under Title VII. EEOC has administrative authority.

Amendments to Higher Education Act of 1965 (1972)

These amendments prohibit sex discrimination in federally assisted educational programs and allow educational institutions to fall under the Equal Pay Act. Sex discrimination provisions are enforced by the Department of Education.

Rehabilitation Act (1973)

This act mandates affirmative action to employ and promote qualified handicapped persons. It applies to federal contract holders employing fifty or more persons. Departments of Labor and Health and Human Services administer this act.

Vietnam Era Veterans Readjustment Assistance Act (1974)

Employers with government contracts of $10,000 or more must take affirmative action to employ and promote Vietnam era veterans. Enforced by Labor Department when complaints are received.

Immigration Reform and Control Act (1987)

This act prohibits discrimination on the basis of citizenship, providing an alien has a work permit and appropriate visa. Enforced by the Labor Department and Health and Human Services Department.

Americans with Disabilities Act (1990)

This act requires equal access to employment and "reasonable accommodations" for persons with disabilities. A disability is any physical or mental impairment that substantially limits one or more major life activity. Job candidates can only be questioned about their ability to perform essential job functions. If a person indicates during the application process a need for reasonable accommodation—for example, an interpreter for a deaf person—the employer is obligated to provide it at its own expense.

One complaint of interviewers is that college students do not have practical experience. A fact-finding interview can give you a great deal of information about what a particular field of work is like. Here are some good questions to ask the professional:

1. What is a typical day like?

2. What kinds of skills are most valuable?

3. What kinds of coursework were most valuable?

4. What are the most difficult problems that you have to face?

5. How do you manage these problems successfully?

6. What are the most rewarding parts of your job? Why?

7. What are typical starting salaries? What are salaries after five years?

8. Which are the major firms or organizations in this city who employ people in your profession?

9. What are some other job titles for people with your training?

10. What would be a reasonable career goal for a person in this position—say, in five years? in ten years?

11. What professional organizations would a person in your position join?

12. What are the main benefits of working for a company like [name the company]?

You can see the value in knowing this kind of information. Some professionals will be flattered if you ask for a short interview; others will not be willing to take the time. As an alternative, you might persuade a student group to sponsor a program during which professionals would address these questions.

Conducting a Self-Analysis

There are two areas in which analysis would be helpful as you begin to plan for an employment interview; those personal characteristics of yours that might be valuable and the preferences you have for a job and organization. All of us have strengths that would make us good employees. The problem comes in identifying these strengths. Figure 9-9 presents a list of traits developed by Lois Einhorn for the Career Center at Indiana University. Rate yourself on each of these categories. Remember that careful evaluation produces the most useful results. Now take each trait you rated yourself highly on and write down a work or school example that illustrates the trait. Remember that most employers ask about your strengths. So pick two or three of your strengths and be prepared to give good examples.

Now rate your preferences in Figure 9-10, which lists characteristics of jobs and companies. Check the items according to their relative importance to you. Analysis of this information will help you decide which companies you'd like to interview.

Tom Reardon has discovered some interesting correlations between students' grade point average (GPA) and the organizational characteristics these students valued.[36] The lists in Figure 9-11 differ on the basis of whether the respondents are above-average or average students. We think it is interesting to see which items each category of student values.

One group of researchers speculates that the questions asked by the applicant help to reveal the person's motivation.[37] This idea supports Reardon—if high GPA people are highly motivated. Often you will be given an opportunity to ask questions, and what you ask will tell something about your personal orientation. We will return to this issue later.

Continue your analysis of your own strengths and weaknesses by asking yourself about your training and experience. This will lead to a résumé. Begin by listing the courses that relate to your designated professional goal. In which of these courses did you excel? How were your grades in these courses? Were there any special projects that allowed you to gain practical experience? Might any of your college professors be helpful to you in locating a job?

Figure 9-9

INVENTORY OF PERSONAL TRAITS

Trait	Poor		Average		Excellent
	1	2	3	4	5
1. Dependable	( )	( )	( )	( )	( )
2. Honest	( )	( )	( )	( )	( )
3. Motivated	( )	( )	( )	( )	( )
4. Assertive	( )	( )	( )	( )	( )
5. Outgoing	( )	( )	( )	( )	( )
6. Persistent	( )	( )	( )	( )	( )
7. Conscientious	( )	( )	( )	( )	( )
8. Ambitious	( )	( )	( )	( )	( )
9. Punctual	( )	( )	( )	( )	( )
10. Creative	( )	( )	( )	( )	( )
11. Intelligent	( )	( )	( )	( )	( )
12. Mature	( )	( )	( )	( )	( )
13. Emotionally stable	( )	( )	( )	( )	( )
14. Enthusiastic	( )	( )	( )	( )	( )
15. Flexible	( )	( )	( )	( )	( )
16. Realistic	( )	( )	( )	( )	( )
17. Responsible	( )	( )	( )	( )	( )
18. Serious	( )	( )	( )	( )	( )
19. Pleasant	( )	( )	( )	( )	( )
20. Sincere	( )	( )	( )	( )	( )
21. Analytical	( )	( )	( )	( )	( )
22. Organized	( )	( )	( )	( )	( )
23. Having a good appearance	( )	( )	( )	( )	( )
24. Able to get along with coworkers	( )	( )	( )	( )	( )
25. Able to get along with supervisors	( )	( )	( )	( )	( )
26. Having oral communication skills	( )	( )	( )	( )	( )
27. Having written communication skills	( )	( )	( )	( )	( )
28. Having good references	( )	( )	( )	( )	( )
29. Having good school attendance	( )	( )	( )	( )	( )
30. Having good job attendance	( )	( )	( )	( )	( )
31. Willing to work long hours	( )	( )	( )	( )	( )
32. Willing to work evenings and weekends	( )	( )	( )	( )	( )
33. Willing to relocate	( )	( )	( )	( )	( )
34. Willing to travel	( )	( )	( )	( )	( )
35. Willing to commute a long distance	( )	( )	( )	( )	( )
36. Willing to start at the bottom and advance according to own merit	( )	( )	( )	( )	( )
37. Able to accept criticism	( )	( )	( )	( )	( )
38. Able to motivate others	( )	( )	( )	( )	( )
39. Able to follow through on something until it is done	( )	( )	( )	( )	( )
40. Able to make good use of time	( )	( )	( )	( )	( )
41. Goal- (or achievement-) oriented	( )	( )	( )	( )	( )
42. Healthy	( )	( )	( )	( )	( )
43. Able to take initiative	( )	( )	( )	( )	( )
44. Able to follow directions	( )	( )	( )	( )	( )
45. Detail-oriented	( )	( )	( )	( )	( )
46. Able to learn quickly	( )	( )	( )	( )	( )
47. Willing to work hard	( )	( )	( )	( )	( )
48. Having moral standards	( )	( )	( )	( )	( )
49. Poised	( )	( )	( )	( )	( )
50. Having growth potential	( )	( )	( )	( )	( )
51. Others	( )	( )	( )	( )	( )

SOURCE: Adapted from Lois Einhorn, Interviewing . . . A Job in Itself, pp. 4–5. Used by permission of the Career Center of Indiana University.

Consider your work background. If you have held a job, you are in a better position to be hired than a person who has never held a job. List all jobs you have held and the names of your supervisors. Would your supervisors describe you as a good employee? Why? What work skills did you display that might be valued by other employers? How do these skills relate to the strengths you discovered in your personal trait analysis? Have the jobs you held helped you to finance part of your education? If so, this is important to emphasize.

Were you involved in any extracurricular activities? (If not, get involved now—if it is not too late). Have you invested any time in community service projects? (This is easy to do because service groups are usually looking for help.) Have you held any leadership positions in clubs or organizations? If so, list them, and anything else which might be an asset. Put everything you can think of on your worksheet. You can sort through the information on your worksheet later.

Assessing Corporate Culture

Communication events within an organization always take place within its cultural context. Selection interviews should be more productive for the applicant who is informed about the organization's culture. However, the interviewee will find the task of discovering cultural expectations somewhat difficult. Obviously, an outsider does not have access to the information that normally would be available to an insider.

One source of information consists of public documents. You should obtain a copy of the organization's annual report. What kind of business does the organization do? If the business is one that relies heavily on direct sales to its customers, then this might be a cultural fit. Do the primary values of the culture center on customers and their needs? Success in this type of company depends on persistence. One more contact with the customer, a few more telephone calls, make this hard work. When you interview for a company where this is the overriding cultural model, find ways to show that you believe in hard work and are persistent.

Check the organization's recruitment materials. What do the brochures tell you? Is the presentation crisp and formal? Is it friendly and chatty? Are there any stories about organizational heroes? If so, what characteristics seem to be emphasized? Look to see how the materials talk about the organization itself and its relation to its consumers. Are there themes that will tell you something about the people? If it is a manufacturing firm, for example, does it say anything about management's attitudes toward workers? Does it say anything about the company's concern for customers? Does it brag about products and how they are being received by customers? Does it suggest that it views its products as being on the cutting edge in its industry? You will undoubtedly find themes. If the organization is clearly concerned about its relationships with customers, this then provides an area for you to demonstrate your interest. If you are asked what makes for a successful company, for example, you might reply, "A company that takes time to discover its customers' needs and then acts on them." (Of course, you would expand on this response somewhat.) If the organization prides itself as one whose products are on the cutting edge, then you would be advised to study and be knowledgeable about the most recent advances in the industry.

If you know someone who is a part of the organization, you may be able to discover additional information. Pay attention to where this person's place is in the organization. Can you discover what subculture the person represents? A line worker's perception of an organization and its culture may not be as valuable to you as that of a person at some level of management—especially if you are interested in a management traineeship. Begin your questioning by asking what it is like to work in the organization. Ask also what it takes to be successful in the organization. See if the person can also tell you about some of the organization's prominent members. Ask too about the things in which the company takes pride. Finally, be sure to ask what the company looks for in a new employee. The answers to these questions will help you know what special research you need to do to be prepared and to gain a sense of how to present yourself in the interview.

Preparing a Cover Letter and Résumé

The primary purpose of a cover letter and résumé is to persuade the recruiter to grant you an interview. If you answer an advertisement in a placement bulletin or a newspaper, you will be using both the cover letter and the résumé. The cover letter is important because it gives you the opportunity to show the employer that you can

FIGURE 9-10 PREFERENCES IN JOB CHARACTERIZATION

	Importance		
Factors	Not Important	Average Importance	Very Important
1. Challenge	( )	( )	( )
2. Responsibility	( )	( )	( )
3. Stability of company	( )	( )	( )
4. Security of job within company	( )	( )	( )
5. Size of company	( )	( )	( )
6. Training program	( )	( )	( )
7. Initial job duties	( )	( )	( )
8. Advancement opportunities	( )	( )	( )
9. Amount of contact with coworkers	( )	( )	( )
10. Amount of contact with the public	( )	( )	( )
11. Starting salary	( )	( )	( )
12. Financial rewards "down the road"	( )	( )	( )
13. Degree of independence	( )	( )	( )
14. Opportunity to show initiative	( )	( )	( )
15. Degree of employee involvement in decision making	( )	( )	( )
16. Opportunity to be creative	( )	( )	( )
17. Type of industry	( )	( )	( )
18. Company's reputation in the industry	( )	( )	( )
19. Prestige of job within the company	( )	( )	( )
20. Degree of results seen from job	( )	( )	( )
21. Variety of duties	( )	( )	( )
22. What the boss is like	( )	( )	( )
23. What the coworkers are like	( )	( )	( )
24. Suburban or metropolitan community	( )	( )	( )
25. Hours	( )	( )	( )
26. Benefits	( )	( )	( )
27. Commuting distance involved	( )	( )	( )
28. Amount of overnight travel involved	( )	( )	( )
29. Number of moves from one city to another	( )	( )	( )
30. Facilities of office or plant	( )	( )	( )
31. Spouse's desires	( )	( )	( )
32. Others (list)	( )	( )	( )

SOURCE: From Lois Einhorn, Interviewing . . . A Job in Itself, p. 3. Used by permission of the Career Center of Indiana University.

FIGURE 9-11 THE TOP TEN EMPLOYER CHARACTERISTICS STUDENTS WANT

Above-Average Students (3.2 to 4.0 GPA) (N = 325)
*1. Employer is in a growth industry.
2. Potential for advancement.
*3. Past history of growth/success.
*4. Opportunity for continued education
5. Salary.
†6. National or local reputation.
†7. Location of employer.
8. Fringe benefits.
†9. Responsibility/challenge/freedom.
10. Prestige of working for employer.

Average Students (2.0 to 3.2 GPA) (N = 443)
1. National or local reputation.
2. Location of employer.
3. Potential for advancement.
4. Salary.
5. Responsibility/challenge/freedom.
6. Fringe benefits.
7. Prestige of working for employer.
8. Employer is in a growth industry.
9. Past history of growth/success.
10. Opportunity for continued education.

*Significant at .01 level †Significant at .05 level
SOURCE: Reprinted from the Winter 1980 Journal of Career Planning & Employment with the permission of the College Placement Council, Inc.,

write well and that you can adapt your pr1esentation of yourself to a specific job. The résumé serves to highlight your background, educ ation, and achievements. Its primary purpose is to cause the interviewer to want a personal interview with you.

Attention to detail in résumé preparation is important. Even such things as securing high-quality photocopies of your résumé can make a difference. One research team, Charles P. Bird and Dawn D. Puglisi, found that professionals who were asked to judge candidates were unable to ignore the fact that the résumé of a superior candidate was a poor-quality photocopy.[38]

The Cover Letter

There are some rather specific conventions surrounding cover letters. Here are some of the important dos and don'ts:

1. Always send an original copy of the letter. Do not send a Xerox or a carbon copy. If you cannot type, hire a typist.

2. Address the cover letter to a real person. Do not send it to "Dear Sir or Madam." It is worth the effort and expense to call the firm and ask the receptionist for the correct name. Say, "I would like to address a letter to the person who hires people for [name the area]. Could you tell me this person's name, spell it, please, and give the person's title?"

3. Do not allow any misspelled words or excessive erasures or white-outs.

4. Follow one of the typical business letter formats. (The one we use in Figure 9-12 is always appropriate.)

5. Use high-quality, cotton-content paper, white or off-white. Do not use flashy colors or erasable bond.

6. Space the letter attractively on the page. Leave a little more margin at the top than at the sides; allow approximately one-inch margins on the sides. Confine the letter to one page and do not run it too close to the bottom.

Structure the letter to include at least three paragraphs. The first paragraph generally should state the purpose of the letter, the particular position for which you are applying, and how you came to know about the position. You might also tell, here, why you are interested in the particular employer, or you could start the second paragraph with this information.

The reasons you are interested in the particular position, the organization, and its products or services could begin the second paragraph. You should highlight your qualifications and explain how your academic background qualifies you to be a candidate for the position. If you have had work experience or have special qualifications, tell about these briefly and explain how they give you unique qualifications for the position. Refer the reader to the enclosed résumé that summarizes your qualifications, training, and experiences.

The third paragraph should ask for an interview and may suggest times when you are available. Repeat your telephone number in the letter and offer to provide any additional information that might be helpful in evaluating your credentials. Finally, close your letter with thanks and some statement about anticipating their future contact. Say in some way, "I look forward to hearing from you."

Figure 9-12 presents a cover letter. Remember that each cover letter is adapted to the particular job and should be freshly typed.

The Résumé

Imagine your résumé sandwiched in a stack of 200 others. What can you do to make it stand out as deserving of special attention? You can print your résumé on off-white paper. You can also give it some graphic appeal by using quality paper, allowing adequate margins, underlining various important parts, and the like. But beyond these considerations there are no guarantees. The average résumé in a stack of 200 will receive much less than a minute of attention. If you violate certain expectations, however, it will be rejected immediately.[39]

We think that the best way to call attention to your résumé is to anticipate the needs of the reader. Consider that résumés serve at least three purposes: to open the door to an interview, to provide an outline for the interview, and to act as a reminder of the interview. Therefore, the following concerns are important:

FIGURE 9-12   SAMPLE COVER LETTER

2000 Hillcrest Road
Mobile, Alabama 36609
February 10,19–

Mr. G. L. Rhodarty
Personnel Manager
XYZ Corporation
3000 Executive Park
Mobile, Alabama 36604

Dear Mr. Rhodarty:

Please consider my application for a position with your
company. I am especially interested in XYZ Corporation because
of its successful history and record of continuous growth and stability.
I will be graduated in May from the University of South Alabama with
a Bachelor of Arts degree in communication with an emphasis in
organizational communication.

The enclosed resume will give you the pertinent facts about
my education and past record of employment, which I believe qualify
me for a position with your company. My particular interests lie in the
areas of personnel development and training, especially human relations.
The confidence I feel in handling personnel contacts has been gained
from both my work experience and classes I have taken in communication
and psychology. The variety of my work experience has given me the
ability to adapt and relate to people easily and quickly. I am free to
travel if the position warrants it, and I like to travel.

I would appreciate the opportunity to discuss employment
possibilities with you personally in an interview. I believe that would
enable us to discuss more fully my training and experience. I may be
reached at the above address or at 334-111-2222. Thank you for your
consideration of my application.

Sincerely,

John Q. Student

FIGURE 9-13   RÉSUMÉ FACTORS THAT CAUSE DISINTEREST IN CANDIDATE

Factor that Causes Disinterest	Strongly Agree	Agree	Neutral	Disagree	Strongly Disagree
Poor grammar	44%	53%	2%	1%	—
Spelling errors	27	60	11	2	—
Poor organization	18	58	21	3	—
Overpromise	15	44	35	5	1%

SOURCE: Reprinted from the Fall 1979 *Journal of Career Planning &Employment* with the permission of the College Placement Council, Inc., copyright holder.

1. Neatness and attention to expectations of employers

2. Information retrieval

3. Completeness of information, in a condensed form

Some important research is helpful in understanding what employers expect. A number of researchers have examined these expectations.[40] Figure 9-13 presents the most common causes of disinterest in the candidate; Figure 9-14 suggests what data employers preferred to see in the résumé; and Figure 9-15 addresses the issue of résumé form. You can see there is considerable agreement about the causes of disinterest in candidates and about items to be included in the résumé. There is also fairly uniform agreement about the form the résumé should take.

The résumé is an information sheet. It should be designed in such a way that it gives the expected information in easy-to-read form. It should contain:

1. *Name, addresses, and telephone numbers.*

2. *Career objectives or goals.* This is usually the kind of job you are seeking.

3. *Educational background.* Degree(s), major, minor, special training, and other significant educational experiences are listed with their dates. Grade point average can be given here also. If it is not particularly impressive, omit it.

4. *Experience.* List the jobs you have had, beginning with the most recent and working backward. Include job title, name of employer, specific duties, and responsibilities. List special accomplishments.

5. *Honors.* List any special awards, recognitions, and scholarships.

6. *Activities.* Here list service clubs, preprofessional societies, other clubs, and interests. List any offices held or other leadership provided.

7. *References.* These may be given, but we recommend just saying "References furnished upon request."

Sometimes we are asked, "Should I put personal information on my résumé?" There is no "right" answer, but generally we would say no. Research shows that about 26 percent of employers expect it, but this is not a good enough reason to include it. It does add a personal touch that allows the employer to get a better picture of you. At the same time, it often includes irrelevant material that can be used for illegal discrimination. By giving birth date, you are, of course, stating your age. Height and weight are also irrelevant considerations unless you are applying for certain jobs. You will need to decide whether you want to include this information or not.

Figure 9-16 shows a sample résumé that reflects our suggestions. We think it is a good one and can be helpful in planning your own résumé. Figures 9-17 and 9-18 show some alternative ways of arranging information. Figure 9-17 is the first page of a résumé of a person who has had considerable experience. Note how he arranges his strengths so that they stand out. Figure 9-18 shows an emphasis on the applicant's administrative and human relations skills. This applicant is looking for a management position. As you can see by these examples, there are a number of ways to structure a résumé.

FIGURE 9-14   **EMPLOYER REACTION TO RÉSUMÉ DATA**

Résumé Item	Yes, Should Appear	No	No Opinion
Career objective	66%	8%	27%
Extracurricular activities	76%	15%	9%
College(s) attended	76%	3%	20%
College grade-point average	57%	14%	29%
Specific courses taken	57%	23%	20%
Interests and hobbies	53%	11%	37%
Honors/awards	56%	9%	35%
List of references	8%	47%	45%

SOURCE: Beverly Culwell, "Employer Preferences Regarding Résumés and Application Letters," unpublished paper, School of Business, Missouri Southern State College.

FIGURE 9-15   **AGREEMENT ON MATTERS OF FORM AND STYLE**

Form and/or Style Issue	Strongly Agree	Agree	Neutral	Disagree	Strongly Disagree
Résumés should be 8½" x 11"	79%	15%	6%	—	—
A résumé should be a maximum of two pages long	51%	32%	8%	5%	4%
I am unlikely to pursue a candidate whose résumé is more than two pages long	10%	27%	47%	16%	—
A résumé should be only one page long	36%	30%	24%	8%	2%
I am more likely to pursue a candidate whose résumé has graphic appeal	3%	31%	42%	22%	2%

SOURCE: Reprinted from the Fall 1979 *Journal of Career Planning & Employment* with the permission of the College Placement Council, Inc., copyright holder.

FIGURE 9-16   **SAMPLE RÉSUMÉ**

Applicant's Name

ADDRESSES:
Home
2000 Hillcrest Road
Mobile, Alabama 36609
334-111-2222

College
Smith Residence Center
University of South Alabama
334-222-3333

OBJECTIVES:
My immediate objective is to obtain a position in business in the field of public relations. My long-range goal is public relations management.

EDUCATION:
B.A., University of South Alabama, expected May 1997. Major area: Organizational communication and public relations. Minor area: Marketing

GPA:
Overall: 3.2; Major area: 3.5; Minor area: 3.0 (4.0 scale)

EXPERIENCE:
1996-97
Information clerk, Smith Residence Center. Responsible for answering phone and giving information.

1995-97
Editorial Staff, Vanguard, student weekly newspaper. Researched and wrote news stories and editorials, assisted in layout and design.

Summer 1994
Part-time assistant, public relations, Illinois Bell Telephone Company, Dekalb. Helped to design brochures; wrote a speech for use in the high school; edited in-house newspaper.

1993-94
Part-time salesperson, Hall's Shoe Store, Mobile. Sold men's and women's shoes, took departmental inventory.

Summer 1993
Lifeguard, municipal swimming pool, Mobile. Taught swimming and enforced water safety programs.

HONORS:
Dean's list for junior and senior years. Outstanding Student in Communication Arts, 1996-1997.

ACTIVITIES:
Member, Public Relations Council of Alabama, Student Chapter, 1994-1997, and vice-president 1996-1997.

REFERENCES:
Furnished upon request.

FIGURE 9-17   SAMPLE RÉSUMÉ

John J. Doe   Telephone: (334)-222-3344
1200 Vienna Boulevard
Mobile, Alabama 36609

JOB OBJECTIVE: A marketing management position with a
major industrial firm.

1994-1997   EDUCATION:
University of South Alabama, Mobile, Alabama
Master of Business Administration, General Business

1981-1986   University of Alabama, Tuscaloosa, Alabama
B.S., Chemical Engineering
Treasurer of Student Chapter AlChE, 1985-1986
Worked part-time earning 50 percent of college expenses

MAJOR STRENGTHS
Technical: Capable of working with large amounts of technical data;
able to compile, interpret, and present reports using computer data as
a base. Research capabilities: have know-how in generating technical
information systematically.
Verbal and Written: Able to prepare written sales proposals in a clear,
concise manner. Able to prepare marketing brochures to convey
strong points of the product.
Managerial: Able to oversee, manage, and direct work of others. Can
develop program projects in a professional manner. Able to work with
details of a large project comfortably. Pragmatic in making judgements
or reaching conclusions about matters requiring action; able to accept
consequences of my judgement and decisions.
Marketing: Capable of assessing the needs of customers; able to
suggest ways of improving current assessments and very much
involved with problem solving.
Creative: Able to conceive new ideas, develop programs, and
institute new procedures.
Social: Have ability to relate on a continuous basis with clientele
in a social setting.

EXPERIENCE
A.B.C. Corporation
 Mobile, Alabama
1993-Present   Demonstration Plant Supervisor. Direct the work of four professional
engineers gathering data for operation of the latest in Chlor-alkali
manufacturing equipment. Prepare and deliver technology
presentations to prospective licensees who visit the plant. Prepare
program objectives and coordinate plant operation with research program
conducted in Ohio. Prepare and manage both capital and operating
budgets in excess of $4 million annually. Review performance of
professional engineers annually. Compile data and interpret monthly
results in written reports to upper management.

FIGURE 9-18   **SAMPLE RÉSUMÉ**

JOHN DOE
1111 ZALE AVENUE
MOBILE, ALABAMA 36691
(334) 395-6161

JOB OBJECTIVE: Entry-level management track position in
personnel staffing.

EDUCATION
1993-1997   University of South Alabama, Mobile, Alabama
B.S.: Psychology, minor in Economics. GPA: 3.4 (A = 4). June 1997

SKILLS
ADMINISTRATIVE AND MANAGEMENT SKILLS

- Supervised staff, budgets, and facilities in business and nonprofit
Organizations.
- Directed programs for University Placement Office, planned
workshops, coordinated public relations, and evaluated effectiveness.
- Attended to detail. Challenged by making systems work. Gathered
sophisticated information as research assistant. Processed orders for
meat company, and routed truck logistics (increasing efficiency by
20 percent).

HUMAN RELATIONS AND COMMUNICATION SKILLS

- Able to communicate in speaking and writing - clearly, concisely,
and effectively.
- Attentive listener, able to help people "think out loud," reflect on
experiences, identify problems, and develop solutions.
- Seasoned interviewer, skills developed as stringer for newspaper.
- Able to develop rapport quickly and easily.

EXPERIENCE
Ponder Meat Company
Mobile, Alabama
1994-1997   Assistant Manager for Inventories. Enjoyed industrial side of
management by assisting in maintenance of inventories, processing
orders, and directing transportation strategies.
Counselors, Inc.
Mobile, Alabama
1992-1994   Supervisor of Training. Recruited, trained, and supervised staff for
program to educate high-risk students about self-management skills.
University of South Alabama
Mobile, Alabama
1991-1992   Placement Assistant. Worked part-time for several years to present
"Career Orientation" workshops to students.
Mobile Press-Register
Mobile, Alabama
1990-1991   Journalist. Worked as part-time "stringer," conducting interviews,
gathering facts, writing news and features. Published 50 articles.
Other Part-Time and Summer Experiences. Student intern in
psychology department; tutor in English, math, and other subjects;
waiter; and busboy.

INTERESTS AND ACTIVITIES
Vice-president, Senior Class in college.
Salutatorian in high school.
Active in Student Council, debate and swim teams at the University
of South Alabama.

CREDENTIALS AVAILABLE UPON REQUEST

Conducting the Job Search

At some time in the search for employment you will face the question, "Where should I begin looking for prospective employers?" This might be one of your first considerations or it might come after you have prepared credentials. There are many places for you to consider. You may be overwhelmed by the time it takes to conduct a vigorous search. But you can save time by understanding where to look for the most promising job opportunities.

The most promising source of jobs lies in the field that has the kind of job you want. When you are determined to stay in your local area, local sources are best. Figure 9-19 suggests local sources that may be most promising. You will want to pursue a different set of contact points if you are willing to move.

Researching the Organization

You will make a better impression than other candidates for the job if you carefully research the organization. Just as you are impressed when an interviewer takes the time to study your résumé thoroughly, employers are gratified when you have taken time to study their organization.

Organizations have been known to ask specific questions about an applicant's knowledge of their firm. One interviewer we know routinely says, "Tell me what our company's stock was selling for this morning." One of our students reported being asked by a paper company representative: "How much paper is produced in our mill across the street?" The student knew the answer because he had taken the time to read the trade journal. (He got the job too.)

There are two types of information you want to know: that which is public and that which only the employees of the organization know. Sources of public information are numerous. Consult your school's placement center; the Chamber of Commerce; the organization's annual report; *Thomas' Register of American Manufacturers; Moody's Industrial Manual; Standard and Poor's Industrial Index and Register;* Dun and Bradstreet's *Middle Market Directory, Million Dollar Directory, Reference Book; Fortune's Plant and Product Directory; US Industrial Outlook;* and *Business Index.* Also, check to see if the organization's business is the focus of a trade journal.

Here are some questions you will be able to answer from these sources:

1. Location of the organization's plants, offices, and branches

2. Age of the company and its history

3. Services the company offers or products it produces, and yearly sales

4. Growth and potential, and rank within its industry

5. Competitors in the industry

6. Information that is specific to a particular field, such as objectives, program, and funding sources for a social service agency; or circulation, affiliations with other media, competition, and growth history for a newspaper

Not surprisingly, sources of private information are not as accessible. You might get answers to some of these questions if you do informational interviewing. Check with alumni, friends, stockbrokers, and anyone else who might have experience with the firm. Sometimes a direct phone call to the personnel department of the company can be rewarding.

These are some questions to ask:

1. In your opinion, what kind of public image does the organization have?

2. Is there high turnover? If so, why?

3. What educational and training programs does the company have?

4. Will the organization help employees return to college for advanced study?

5. What is a realistic entry-level salary for a job in your profession?

6. What kind of benefits does the company offer?

7. What is the company's policy on transferring people to other locations?

8. What is the general work climate like?

9. Do subordinates participate in decisions?

10. What are the most serious problems faced by people in your part of the organization?

11. What is the company's stock selling for (on the day of the interview)?

You can see that some of these questions would *not* be appropriate to ask a recruiter. Yet often they are important for your future. We think doing your homework is just a common-sense thing to do, but it is also impressive to recruiters.

FIGURE 9-19   **WHERE TO SEARCH FOR JOB OPPORTUNITIES**

Where to Search and Success Rates

1. Professional placement agencies (1%)
2. State placement offices (2%)
3. University placement offices (10%)
4. Professional association placement services (AMA, SCA, ASTD) (40%)
5. Relatives (25%)
6. Professional associates, former colleagues, friends (75%)
7. Former teachers (30%)
8. Newspaper and magazine advertisements (25%)
9. Mass mailing to job lists (5%)
10. Mass mailing to the *Fortune 500* lists (5%)
11. People holding a similar job (50%)
12. Personnel directors (?)
13. Leads from former employers (5%)
14. Social acquaintances (clubs, PTA, Scouts, etc.) (10%)
15. Workshops or seminars (60% long term; 15% short term)
16. Take your classes on field trips (50% long term; 1% short term)
17. Create your own (1%)
18. Write corporate officers (5%)
19. Fellow students, fraternity brothers, or sorority sisters (60%)
20. Voluntary organizations (United Fund, Community Center, etc.) (15%)
21. Gimmicks (mailing your face in chairman or president's picture, etc.) (5%)
22. Work for the local Chamber of Commerce (15%)
23. Start your own business (10%)
24. Advertise your qualifications in journals, magazines, and other publications (2%)

SOURCE: Charles J. Stewart and William B. Cash, Jr., *Interviewing: Principles and Practices,* 4th ed., p. 213. Copyright © 1985 Wm. C. Brown Publishers, Dubuque, Iowa. All rights reserved. Reprinted by permission.

Preparing for and Practicing Typical Recruiter Questions

Ask people who have participated in a number of interviews if they were asked any surprise questions and they will tell you several that neither they nor you would have anticipated. For example, during a selection interview one of us reported to a dean that a graduate school friend was studying communication and the elderly. The next question from the dean was, "Why would anyone want to talk to old people anyway? They just want to be left alone." Then the dean paused for a response.

Obviously, we cannot prepare you for every question. There are, however, some very good lists of typical questions, such as the ones in Figure 9-20. Use these lists to prepare for unexpected questions. We suggest that you develop an answer to each question.

We recommend that you practice answering questions from the list we have provided. Videotape your answers if you can. If you cannot, at least audiotape the answers so that you can analyze both the verbal and the nonverbal content. (Ask a friend to play interviewer.) You may be surprised by what you hear. For example, taping may reveal that you are a person who chops your sentences with pauses. The interviewer may decide the excessive pauses mean you are unsure of yourself and your answers. This may merely be a habit you have acquired, but the interviewer does not know that. With a little effort you may eliminate this vocal pattern.

Then analyze your answers, keeping in mind that an organization wants to know that:

1. You have selected your profession for good reasons.

2. You have selected the organization for good reasons.

3. You are reasonably ambitious.

4. You are a hard worker.

5. You know your weaknesses and strengths.

6. You are working to correct any weaknesses.

7. You can be relied upon to do the job and to follow through.

8. You have some goals and they are reasonable.

9. You are trustworthy.

10. You like people and are likable.

11. You get along with people and will "fit" with other employees.

12. You will have the interests of the company in mind when you act.

See if your answers give evidence of some of these items. For example, telling the interviewer that you have been active in clubs and organizations will say that you probably like people. A steady work record will show that you believe in working. The fact that you have been successful in difficult courses and that you have carried out special projects in school will show that you are ambitious and probably a hard worker. The judgments recruiters make are based on their speculation about you. The decisions recruiters make are based upon what they *think* is true—although what they think may not actually be the case.

Questioning the Interviewer

What you ask the recruiter will tell much about you, although you will not always get the opportunity to ask questions. If you ask about salary, retirement, and other benefits, the recruiter may decide you are one of those people who is too concerned about what the company can do for the employee. Many recruiters view this as an inappropriate priority for a candidate. If you ask questions about things that a little research would have told you, you may be viewed negatively also.

Do ask questions that will point to your strengths, show that you have done research, and help you know when you can expect the recruiter to make a decision. You might want to ask, "Will I be involved in decisions in my department?" Or you might ask, "What kind of training and professional development opportunities are available as I progress in the organization?" Keep in mind that the recruiter may not be able to answer specific questions about your area. Here are some additional questions you might ask *if it seems appropriate*. (A note of caution: Do not ask so many questions that you appear to be quizzing the recruiter.)

1. What are some of the things that you have enjoyed most about working for XYZ Company?

2. Will there be a training program or period? If so, what can I expect?

3. If I do well in this initial position, what would be my next step?

4. Is there anything else you would find useful to have in evaluating my qualifications?

5. When might I expect to hear from you about your decision?

FIGURE 9-20   **TYPICAL INTERVIEW QUESTIONS**

1. What are your long-range and short-range goals and activities? When and why did you establish these goals? How are you preparing yourself to achieve them?

2. What specific goals, other than those related to your occupation, have you established for yourself for the next ten years?

3. What do you see yourself doing five years from now?

4. What do you really want to do in life?

5. What are your long-range career objectives?

6. How do you plan to achieve your career goals?

7. What are the most important rewards you expect in your business career?

8. What do you expect to be earning in five years?

9. Why did you choose the career for which you are preparing?

10. Which is more important to you, the money or the type of job?

11. What do you consider to be your greatest strengths and weaknesses?

12. How would you describe yourself?

13. How do you think a friend or professor who knows you well would describe you?

14. What motivates you to put forth your greatest effort?

15. How has your college experience prepared you for a business career?

16. Why should I hire you?

17. What qualifications do you have that make you think that you will be successful in business?

18. How do you determine or evaluate success?

19. What do you think it takes to be successful in a company like ours?

20. In what ways do you think you can make a contribution to our company?

21. What qualities should a successful manager possess?

22. Describe the relationship that should exist between a supervisor and those reporting to him or her.

23. What two or three accomplishments have given you the most satisfaction? Why?

24. Describe your most rewarding college experience.

25. If you were hiring a graduate for this position, what qualities would you look for?

26. Why did you select your college or university?

27. What led you to choose your field or major study?

28. What college subjects did you like best? Why?

29. What college subjects did you like least? Why?

30. If you could do so, how would you plan your academic study differently? Why?

31. What changes would you make in your college or university? Why?

32. Do you have plans for continued study? An advanced degree?

(Figure 9-20 continued on next page)

(Figure 9-20 continued from previous page)

33. Do you think that your grades are a good indication of your academic achievement?

34. What have you learned from participation in extracurricular activities?

35. In what kind of a work environment are you most comfortable?

36. How do you work under pressure?

37. In what part-time or summer jobs have you been most interested?

38. How would you describe the ideal job for you following graduation?

39. Why did you decide to seek a position with this company?

40. What do you know about our company?

41. What two or three things are most important to you in your job?

42. Are you seeking employment in a company of a certain size? Why?

43. What criteria are you using to evaluate the company for which you hope to work?

44. Do you have a geographical preference? Why?

45. Will you relocate? Does relocation bother you?

46. Are you willing to travel?

47. Are you willing to spend at least six months as a trainee?

48. Why do you think you might like to live in the community in which our company is located?

49. What major problem have you encountered and how did you deal with it?

50. What have you learned from your mistakes?

We think it would be helpful to you to add these additional, somewhat difficult questions to the list.

51. Did you do the best job you could in school? If not, why?

52. What kind of boss do you prefer? Why?

53. Describe a typical day of work at the XYZ Company for which you worked.

54. What are some of the important lessons you have learned from jobs you have held?

55. What types of books do you read? What was the last one you read?

56. What kinds of things cause you to lose your temper?

57. Are you a leader? Give an example.

58. Are you a creative person? Give an example of your creativity.

59. Are you analytical? Give an example.

60. What are the most important books in your field?

SOURCE: From *Northwestern Lindquist-Endicott Report* by Victor R. Lindquist, Northwestern University Placement Service, Evanston, Illinois. Used by permission.

The question about time frame is a good one. It implies a continuing relationship with the recruiter. It also allows you to know how to follow up on the interview, and when. A call to the recruiter toward the end of the time frame may allow you to find out if the job has already gone to another candidate. Employers operate in different ways. Some may not be planning to fill a position for a month or more; others will make a decision within a couple of weeks. You want to know when you can quit worrying about a particular position. The time-frame question provides another advantage, although you don't really need to use it in this way. You may prefer a position in one company but be offered a job with another. The time-frame question provides you an opportunity to contact the first company without seeming too anxious. If you are offered your second-choice job, we think you ought to call your first-choice employer and tell the interviewer the situation. Sometimes direct assertiveness will move an organization off dead center and into your camp. Besides, what have you got to lose?

MANAGING THE INTERVIEW: THE INTERVIEWER

Beginning the Interview

Some interviewers are tempted to try to relax the applicant by several minutes of small talk. We think this is not wise. Applicants realize that recruiters make decisions early in the interview, so they may think that this behavior is some sort of ploy. Small talk also makes some interviewees nervous as they wonder when the "real" interview will begin.

We think it is better to start by orienting the applicant and then asking an easy but substantive question. There are two perspectives on orienting the interviewee. Some recruiters prefer to discuss specific job qualifications late in the interview. They believe that early information about the job allows the candidate to pitch qualifications to the job—to "manufacture" qualifications to meet the situation. Other recruiters prefer to give job specifications and details first.

We believe that potential employees are entitled to some information about the job. You may not wish to be specific early on, but at least tell the person in general terms what is involved. Presumably you want to know why candidates think that they are qualified. How can this be accomplished if you do not give at least a general job description?

Use the orientation to set the tone of the interview. Tell the interviewee how you would like to be addressed. Give some indication of how you will proceed; you might say, "I'll begin by asking some questions about your education, move to your previous employment, then to your present work situation. After that, you can ask me questions." Gary Richetto and Joseph Zima suggest that this type of orientation is particularly important in cases where the interviewee is highly anxious.[41] A good opening question is, "Tell me a little about yourself." Most people can handle this question, and it gives a perspective on what the applicant sees as important.

Motivating the Interviewee to Talk

Avoid difficult questions in the first part of the interview; they increase the tension level and may cause the candidate to say less. Also, avoid sensitive areas of questioning until later. Bypass probing of unfavorable information that may come out early in the interview. For example, if the interviewee suggests that he or she has been fired from a job, you might say, "Many people experience difficulties with employers early in their careers. Let's talk about what you did in your next job." Later in the interview you may want to come back to probe this area.

Ask questions that are both open and clear. This means trying to avoid questions that can be answered by a yes or no. Encourage the applicant to tell you more by asking, "And what happened next?"[42] Be sure that you use questions rather than statements as you attempt to motivate the interviewee, and do not constantly interrupt. Interruptive statements are a significant predictor that the interviewee will judge the interviewer as not an empathic listener. Be careful not to be concerned about short pauses. Sometimes a pause merely means that the candidate is thinking about what else ought to be said. Wait.

Probing

Sometimes the interviewee cannot be motivated to tell you all you need to know about some area of concern. In this case you will need to know how to probe for more. Probing is accomplished by asking a chain of related questions. Probing requires careful and analytical listening. What you ask comes from what the candidate has just told you; you usually cannot plan these questions. Suppose you asked, "What were some of your favorite courses in your major?" You might follow by asking, "Why was your study of small group communication your favorite?" You might ask further, "How do you see these experiences you cite as being related to your professional goals?" Probing will allow you to analyze both communication skill and depth of thought.

Watch for answers to questions that do not answer what you asked. Do not assume that the person is avoiding a straight answer and do not blame the applicant for misinterpreting the question. You might say, "I guess I was not clear with that question. Let me try to rephrase it." If the person does not answer you directly the second time, make a mental note to come back to the topic later.

Avoiding Biases

Bias may inadvertently slip into an interview. One source of bias may be your own questioning. You may be telegraphing the preferred answer by the way you ask the question. For example, you might say, "That is interesting, tell me more about it." Or you might say, "I think that _____ is extremely important to job success. Tell me about your experience and training in this area." You can see how revealing your biases may lead interviewees to respond as they think you would like.

Another source of bias lies in the order in which you interview candidates. Researchers have found that the quality of preceding candidates can influence a recruiter's opinion of a current candidate. For example, Kenneth Wexley and his associates found that when an average candidate was preceded by two very good candidates, the average candidate seemed to be much better than he or she actually was.[43] This effect was observed mainly for average candidates and not for very good or very poor candidates. Being aware of such a bias is your best defense against it, but we also suggest that you review your work after each series of interviews.

Time of day can be a source of bias in conducting an interview. Harvey Tschirgi and Jon Huegli discovered that a high percentage of negative decisions were made just before the lunch hour and just before the end of the day.[44] Their hour-by-hour analysis, based on interviews conducted by seventeen private organizations at Ohio University, is displayed in Figure 9-21. Certainly it is not the case that the worst candidates always end up with interviews scheduled at these times!

Bias also creeps in when proper weight is not given to positive information. Thomas Hollmann investigated the claim that interviewers give too much weight to negative information, particularly if it comes early in the interview. He discovered that interviewers process negative information accurately, but they do not place enough weight on positive information.[45] In other words, the presence of negative information causes the recruiter to pay less attention to equally important positive information. The consequence is that interviewers let some very good candidates go. While employers cannot afford to ignore negative information, they can be aware of this processing bias.

Concluding the Interview

Keep in mind that whether you select or reject the candidate, you want the person to view your organization as attractive. The image of your company is important and you are its public relations officer in the interview. Try to end on a positive note. Do not stop the questioning with a series of difficult questions or probing of negative information. Move to an area where the candidate can experience pleasant, free-flowing conversation. Talk about the organization and why you enjoy working for it. You need to do some selling of the company in this interview, and this is a good place to say a little more about it. Mention the company's growth and image in the community. Talk about some of the company's key benefits. Do not overdo this, of course, but make your company sound like a good place to work.

FIGURE 9-21   HOUR-BY-HOUR ANALYSIS OF INTERVIEWS WITH RECORDED DECISIONS

Time of Day Interview Held	Number of Interviews	Number of Positive Decisions	Percentage of Positive Decisions	Number of Negative Decisions	Percentage of Negative Decisions
A.M.:					
9–10	22	12	55	10	45
10–11	22	14	64	8	36
11–12	12	4	33	8	67
P.M.					
12–1	4	3	75	1	25
1–2	17	9	53	8	47
2–3	23	15	65	8	35
3–4	21	13	62	8	38
4–5	15	5	33	10	67
5–6	4	1	33	2	67
Totals	140	76		63	

SOURCE: Reprinted from the Winter 1979 *Journal of Career Planning & Employment* with the permission of the College Placement Council, Inc., copyright holder.

Ask if there are any final questions. Then tell the candidate when you plan to make a decision. Give a time frame that encompasses a couple of weeks, but do not indicate that the person either will or will not be hired. You may think that this is the best candidate and say that, only to discover that the next candidate is even better! Or you might tell an average candidate that she or he does not have one of the important qualifications, later to discover that person is the preferred candidate.

Interpreting Interview Data

As soon as practical after the interview is complete, record your impressions. Your organization may have a form for this purpose. If not, you can make your own. Figure 9-22 shows a typical two-part evaluation form—the first part is a rating scale, the second a series of open questions. Use this check sheet in conjunction with the two-column job analysis you did before the interview for analysis of your data. Interpreting the data is not an easy task and is tied to the interviewer's value system. We cannot tell you what makes a good employee for a particular job; this depends on job and and situational constraints.[46] We do, however, have a few suggestions that will make the task easier.

Keep in mind the information we have presented about biases. Research about bias indicates that (1) a preceding candidate who is very good may make an average candidate look better, (2) the time of day in which you interview may bias choices, (3) the order in which you interview may cause a contrast effect, and (4) positive information may be given much less attention in the face of negative information.

Keep in mind that you may have biased the answers by the way you presented the question. Your perception of a candidate may be wrong because of bias you introduced. Be sure not to signal the appropriate response by the way you ask the question. Some candidates may be quicker than others to pick up on your cue and thus may appear to be the better candidate when they aren't.

Use several interviews for promising candidates. Often lower-level candidates get only a single interview. We think this can be a mistake. You will avoid some costly errors if you conduct several interviews. Many organizations have someone other than the initial contact conduct the second interview. The two then compare and contrast their impressions in the hope of arriving at the best applicant.

Prior to any interviewing, make a check sheet of qualifications with space to write about each. After each interview, fill the sheet out for the candidate. This will force you to consider the same qualities for each candidate. Thus you will have a basis for comparison after you have concluded a series of interviews.

Forcing yourself to write something about each interview will also cause you to think more carefully about the candidates, but be careful not to make any marks on the person's résumé or employment application form. The EEOC has discovered that certain employers marked applications in ways that signaled discrimination for blacks, women, Hispanics, and others. Any marks on résumés or applications may be suspect if EEOC decides to examine your firm's employment files. We advise that you keep the notes you make after the interview together in a file separate from the applicant's file. Also, do not write evaluative comments *during the interview*. Write factual information and not inferences. Notes taken *during the interview* become a part of the applicant's file, and an applicant who thinks you have illegally discriminated can legally demand to see them later.

Prepare a list of specific questions for use in the second interview. Attempts to match qualifications with a job description will usually produce some areas of uncertainty. The second interview allows you to gather additional data to strengthen your inferences that the preferred candidate is the right person for the job.

FIGURE 9-22 **APPLICANT EVALUATION FORM**

	Poor	Fair	Good	Very Good	Excellent
Preparation for the interview	____	____	____	____	____
Attitude	____	____	____	____	____
Level of maturity	____	____	____	____	____
Level of motivation	____	____	____	____	____
Selfconfidence	____	____	____	____	____
Ability to get along	____	____	____	____	____
Communication ability	____	____	____	____	____
Appearance	____	____	____	____	____
Knowledge of organization	____	____	____	____	____
Academic preparation	____	____	____	____	____
Work experiences	____	____	____	____	____

Answer these openended questions:

1. How well prepared was the applicant?
2. Describe the applicant's strengths.
3. Describe the applicant's weaknesses.
4. How does the applicant compare to the other applicants?
5. How well does the applicant's qualifications fit the organization's present and future needs?
6. What is the applicant's potential for development?
7. How well does the applicant understand what is required in this position?
8. How well does the applicant understand our organization?
9. Should we hire this person? Why? Or, why not?

MANAGING THE INTERVIEW: THE APPLICANT

You may be discouraged at this point because there is much to do merely to be prepared for the interview. Employment interviewing is complex, but there exists a good deal of help. For example, Northwestern University's Placement Service lists the most frequent complaints employers make about interviewees (see Figure 9-23).

These complaints can be avoided. The preparation we recommended will allow you to show that you are prepared and have appropriate interests and expectations. If you practice interviewing, you will sharpen your communication skills. Avoid giving reason for these complaints as you interview.

Asking Questions of the Interviewer

You will also want to ask some questions. We've already made a few suggestions in this regard. Ask about any special job responsibilities you might have. Ask about the organization's professional development and/or training programs. Ask about opportunities to advance with the company, assuming you do well on the job. *Do not* ask about company benefits or salary or what the company can do for you; if you are invited for a second interview, the matter of salary will be discussed. The employer will want you to know about remuneration so that you can evaluate its adequacy. Take a list of questions you have prepared, along with extra copies of your résumé, to the interview.

FIGURE 9-23   MOST FREQUENT INTERVIEWER COMPLAINTS ABOUT INTERVIEWEES

Rank	Complaint
1	Poor personality, manners; lack of poise, confidence; arrogant, egotistical, conceited
2	Poor appearance, lack of neatness, careless dress
3	Lack of enthusiasm, shows little interest, no evidence of initiative, lack of drive
4	Lack of goals and objectives, lack of ambition, poorly motivated, does not know interests, uncertain, indecisive, poor planning
5	Inability to express self well, poor oral expression, poor habits of speech
6	Unrealistic salary demands, overemphasis on money, more interested in salary than opportunity, unrealistic concerning promotion to top jobs
7	Lack of maturity, no leadership potential
8	Lack of extracurricular activities, inadequate reasons for not participating in activities
9	Failure to get information about our company, lack of preparation for the interview, inability to ask intelligent questions
10	Lack of interest in security and benefits, "what can you do for me" attitude
11	Objects to travel, unwilling to relocate

SOURCE: From *Northwestern Lindquist-Endicott Report* by Victor R. Lindquist, Northwestern University Placement Service, Evanston, Illinois. Used by permission.

Combating Gender, Ethnic, and Religious Bias

In an interview, you are likely to be asked illegal questions.[47] There aren't any perfect ways to handle these questions. There is always a risk. You may choose to answer the question and forget about the fact that it may create bias. If you answer the question directly, the employer may use your answer to actually discriminate against you. Or you may politely refuse to answer. If you avoid answering the question, the employer may not hire you because you were evasive. You will want to do a quick analysis of the interviewer's motives, as best as you can determine them, to make a decision about how you want to answer.

Research shows that when most interviewees are presented with an illegal question, they answer it straightforwardly.[48] We also know that typical interviewees experience illegal questions as inappropriate even if they do not understand that the questions are illegal.[49] These two statements taken together are a bit disturbing and lead to a question. Why do people who are uncomfortable with an illegal question answer it? It seems reasonable to suppose that they believe they have no other option if they are interested in securing employment. While we do not deny that the interviewee is at a disadvantage when asked an illegal question, we do think that there are options other than answering the question directly. There are a range of options to be used as the interviewee sees fit. We present options and examples for your consideration and practice.

These strategies convey messages that range from answering the question directly to addressing the perceived concern of the interviewer to terminating the interview. These strategies are based on the work of Joann Keyton and Jeff Springston.[50] The assumption for each strategy, except the terminating strategy, is that it is used with the goal of doing the least damage to the interviewee's candidacy.

Three criteria are offered for making a decision about which strategy will work best. These are: (1) the perceived use of the information, (2) the importance of the information asked for, and (3) the desire to secure the position.

Let's examine how these strategies might be used. First, what seems to be the interviewer's intent? The primary interest here is in whether the interviewer seems to want the information to discriminate illegally. Sometimes the tone of the interview will allow you to make this judgment. Second, how important is revealing the information? Perhaps the interviewee may judge that giving the information is not particularly important or objectionable. Third, how important is securing the position? The position may be so important to the interviewee that he or she is willing to risk providing the information to be viewed as cooperative.

Figure 9-24 presents eight response strategies with exemplary responses. These are meant to serve as a model for you to use in practicing response strategies.

We have provided some answers that students have reported using to illustrate these strategies. The first two questions were asked of a woman who was interviewing for a school system job. The last illegal question was asked by the owner of a grocery store in Illinois. The first question:

> Q: Are you married or single?
> A: That's a personal question. I'd be happy to answer any questions about my qualifications.

An alternative answer:

> A: If you're concerned about how my marital status might affect my staying with the school system, you should know that I am a professional and intend to continue working regardless of events in my personal life. I am single (or married).

The second question:

> Q: How old are your children? Who will be babysitting with them?
> A: I don't see how that information would be helpful in evaluating me as an employee, but I have children and have made arrangements for their care.

Alternative answers:

> A: I'm not sure what information you want by asking these questions. Could you tell me what it is you want to know?
> A: I'm not sure how these questions pertain to my qualifications. I'm, of course, willing to answer any question you'd like to ask about my training or experience.

The third question:

> Q: Do you participate actively in a church?
> A: My religious activities are personal. I do not mix my professional life with my personal life. I'd prefer to talk about my job qualifications.

Alternative answers:

> A: I'm not sure how this question relates to my qualifications. [Then you might say,] I prefer to pass on that one. [or] I'd prefer to tell you more directly what you want to know. [You could stop here.] I'd be happy to answer questions about my training and experience.
> A: [If you are sure you do not want the job and would like to put a stop to this kind of questioning, you might say,] This is a highly illegal question. It is interesting that your company uses such questions as a basis for hiring. I expect to file a complaint with the Equal Employment Opportunity Commission because you discriminate on an illegal basis. What is your name?

Sometimes an interviewer may ask an illegal question with the intent of getting at job-related information. An interviewer for an insurance company once asked about family ties. She was trying to determine social bases for finding clients and for selling insurance. If the interviewee understands the basis for what is being asked, an answer that will provide the information without giving out illegal information can be given.

There are many other illegal questions that might be asked. Remember that the answers to illegal questions asked by inexperienced interviewers may not be information used in making hiring decisions.[51] Sometimes the interviewer is just trying to be friendly and does not understand the law. You have to decide what the situation is and then formulate an answer.

Abiding by the Rules of the Game

Interviewees are often turned down for not observing the rules of behavior rather than because they do not have the qualifications. Some of the special rules you must observe and prepare for if you are to be successful are discussed below.

Be present at the appropriate time

Plan to arrive at least fifteen minutes ahead of the time of the interview. You may want to take care of personal needs, have trouble finding the office, or get stuck in traffic. Fifteen minutes is not much time, but it's enough to handle last-minute details. Most interviewers consider promptness very important.

Dress appropriately

Remember that proper hair length, appropriate use of colognes and perfumes, and other grooming are important concerns. Incidentally, we think it's good advice to remove any outside clothes—heavy coats, hats, and the like—before you enter the office for the interview.

Be friendly and responsive

Smile. Try to show that you are enjoying the conversation. Use gestures in your conversation that are appropriately smooth and emphatic. Make sure you get the interviewer's name right and use it once or twice—Mr. Smith and not John.

Do not take over the interview

Most interviewers expect to control the interview; let them. Also, don't interrupt the interviewer. Do not be surprised, however, if an interviewer expects you to carry the interview. Broad, general questions are often a signal of this situation.

Give more than one- or two-word answers to questions

Most interviewers will want you to talk. Very short answers show a lack of thoroughness and may mean that you cannot carry a conversation. Give the interviewer something with which to work. On the other hand, do not drone on forever with meaningless talk.

Avoid the negative

Do not criticize your present or past employers. Think of positive reasons for leaving. For example, tell the recruiter that you left to take a job that would allow you to grow professionally. If the situation was bad, you can mention it, but don't dwell on it or explain it in detail. Sometimes our students worry about having been fired from a position—that if the recruiter knew of the firing, it might damage their chances. Often they want to hide the fact. Our advice is that such an effort would be fruitless at best—and probably counterproductive. Lots of people get fired, and that fact suggests, or should suggest, that there is no disgrace involved. Moreover, every personnel director, and almost every interviewer, knows how to find out about a candidate's successes or failures on the job.

We would advise you not to hide a firing or dismissal. You can and should accentuate the positive side, but do not try to hide anything. The risk is too great. Suppose you hide a firing and someone in the organization discovers it later. The discovery is liable to cost your job.

Be prepared to sell yourself

The recruiter will ask what training you have had to prepare you to do the job. Do not brag. Say that you have had some very good educational and work experiences and that you have been successful. Mention that you believe you can do the job because of a successful experience that relates to the job and then describe it.

Show an interest in the company

Tell the employer that you want to work for the company (if you do) and why. Do not beg for a job, however. You may be asked why you selected to interview with this company. This is an opportunity to express interest. Take advantage of it.

Conform to the culture's norms if you can do so without violating your own ethic

Common sense and simple courtesy suggest these rules:

> Do not use profanity or slang, even if the interviewer does.
> Do not continue talking while the interviewer is studying your résumé.
> Do not try to interpret items on the résumé unless asked to do so.
> Do not lie.
> Do not look at your watch to keep track of the time.
> Do not talk about salary in the first interview until and unless the interviewer raises the issue.
> Do not appear to be too interested in telephone conversations that might take place during the interview.
> Do not fiddle with hair or clothing.
> Do not read papers on the interviewer's desk or pick up things on the desk.
> Do not smoke.
> Do not drink alcoholic beverages if, for instance, the interview takes place in a restaurant.

Take a few notes if you want. There may be some information you will want later. Be sure it is accurate; write it down. But do so courteously. Ask, "Do you mind if I jot a note or two?" You can also write some of the questions you will ask on the same pad. When you ask when the interviewer will get in touch with you, you may want to write the information down so you will remember it.

FIGURE 9-24   **EXEMPLARY RESPONSES TO ILLEGAL INTERVIEW QUESTIONS**

1. *Termination of the interview.*
   Example: "It's interesting that your company uses such questions as a basis for hiring. I expect to file a complaint with the Equal Employment Opportunity Commission because you discriminate on an illegal basis."

2. *Direct refusal.*
   Example: "I'm sorry, this is not a question that I am willing to answer."

3. *Direct refusal with reason.*
   Example: "I'm sorry, this is not a question that I am willing to answer because this information is personal."

4. *Asking how information relates to job qualification.*
   Example: "I am not sure how this question pertains to my qualifications for this job. I'd be happy to answer it if I can understand how it pertains to my qualifications."

5. *Telling that information is personal.*
   Example: "This information is personal. I don't mix my personal life with my professional life. I'd be happy to talk about my job qualifications."

6. *Acknowledging concern/asking for information.*
   Example: "I'm not sure what you want to know by asking this question. Could you tell me what it is you want to know?"

7. *Answering perceived concern.*
   Example: "I take it that your question about my plans for child care is a concern about the likelihood that I may be absent from work when they are ill. I want to assure you that I see myself as a professional person and will behave in a professionally responsible manner when they are ill."

8. *Answering the question and the perceived concern.*
   Example: "I am married. If you are concerned about how my marital status might affect my staying with the school system, I can assure you that I am a professional and intend to continue working regardless of the events in my personal life."

Handling the Group Interview

A popular kind of interviewing is the *group interview.* The personnel section arranges for several candidates to be interviewed as a group. This has several advantages for the organization, though it can be unnerving for the interviewees. The purpose of such an interview seems to be very much like the technique commonly referred to as the "stress interview." The organization wants to discover how the interviewees will handle themselves in a very stressful situation, what personality characteristics will emerge (who is willing to take charge, or who is willing to be thoughtful and cautious but assertive under pressure) or how the several interviewees vie for control of the situation. While this type of interview allows for comparisons and contrasts, it is not useful, in our opinion, because it produces a kind of tension in candidates not likely to be encountered in normal working situations. If you can avoid a group interview, we recommend that you do so. If you cannot—and there are some situations in which you will not be able to—then there are some techniques you can use to manage the situation:

1. Apply the suggestions we have made in the chapters on interpersonal communication and group participation and leadership. These may help you convey the impression you are a thoughtful, take-charge person.

2. Ask the interviewer—or some representative—before the interview why the company uses this technique. Most of the time the company knows why it is using some technique; and if you can discover it, you will be that much ahead. We think the direct approach is the best to discover why a company would use the group interview technique. You might say something like, "Mr. Jones, would you mind telling me what you are attempting to discover by using this method of interviewing? It would help me greatly to know how to

respond to the situation." Such a statement *is* a take-charge statement. It shows you are reflective, that you like to plan ahead, and that you are concerned about your image and like to live up to expectations. Even if the company representative declines to answer the question, you are still likely to earn some "points."

3. Prepare as you would normally prepare to answer the typical questions we suggest in the first part of the chapter.

4. Do organizational research. Many of the other candidates will not research the organization, and this will set you apart from them.

5. Listen carefully to the questions. Under these circumstances you will not want to ask that a question be repeated because you have not understood.

6. Pay close attention to what other candidates say. You may be asked to react to what they have said. If you have not been listening, then you will not be able to respond. Be sure you have paper so that you can take notes.

7. Be especially careful about the questions you ask. If you can think of an especially good question or two, be sure to word them carefully prior to the session. Write them down so that you have them ready and look for opportune moments to bring them up during the interview.

You may be able to turn a difficult situation into an advantageous one for you by following these suggestions.

SUMMARY

1. We have presented basic issues of the interviewing process. The interview's opening, schedule of questions, and closing must be planned. An opening should (1) make the interviewee feel welcomed and relaxed, (2) provide the interviewee a sense of purpose, and (3) preview the major topics to be covered. Closings should (1) review the major topics and responses, (2) provide opportunity to add information that may have been omitted, and (3) formally end the interview.

2. The schedule of questions might be ordered by topic, time, cause to effect, or problem/solution. Questions that are planned will be more open or less open depending on the interviewer's purpose. The specificity of the questions will range from questions drawn spontaneously during the interview to specifically worded questions and response categories written prior to the interview and used as written. Follow-up questions, both planned and unplanned, will be used to add depth and clarity to the interviewee's responses. Finally, a decision must be made as to how directive the interviewer will be in carrying out the interview.

3. We have presented each side of the performance appraisal interview because we believe you will experience both sides in your career. The first part of our presentation centered on the role of the supervisor in conducting performance appraisal interviews. We discussed the goals and perspectives managers might have for conducting these interviews.

4. Next, we looked at the employee-centered problem-solving approach as a method of meeting most of the goals of the interview. In this approach it is necessary to create a climate for the interview so that the employee participates actively, does not feel defensive, and does feel supported by the supervisor.

5. In carrying out the employee-centered problem-solving appraisal interview, you should employ these techniques:

   • Help the employee focus on duties and performance with respect to these.

   • Encourage rather than praise.

   • Listen actively and feed back the employee's important ideas.

   • Keep the perspective employee-centered.

- Do not criticize too much.

- Discuss salary in an interview separate from the appraisal interview.

- Establish specific goals and performance objectives.

- Establish checkpoints to review the employee's progress toward goals.

- Conduct interviews at least semiannually.

- Be consistent in your style.

6. In addition, we discussed a sequence to follow in planning the performance appraisal interview that includes these steps:

- Ask the employee to prepare for the interview by doing a self-analysis.

- Establish or reestablish goals related to the specific job.

- Have the employee analyze performance.

- Summarize any performance difficulties that came out of the analysis.

- Assist the employee in selecting a solution by reviewing the ideas.

- Attempt to get the employee to consider outcomes of solutions.

- Establish new goals and obtain the employee's commitment to the plan.

- Plan for training if it appears to be the solution to the problem.

- Plan with the employee for evaluation and follow-up.

- Let the employee know that you will help.

7. Finally, we offered a plan to use when you are the interviewee:
- Conduct a self-assessment.

- Ask informational questions.

- Apply the principles of language to be clear about your wants, needs, and feelings.

8. Selection interviews produce particular constraints on the communication process. We provided advice, based on our experience and what researchers have found, to help you know how to manage these communications.

9. The interviewer prepares carefully by (1) gathering information about and updating the job description, (2) deciding on the appropriate structure for the interview and initial questions, (3) reviewing EEOC guidelines to make sure no illegal questions are asked, and (4) considering and arranging the setting.

10. Key considerations for the interviewee are understanding the process, preparation, and practice. For the interviewee this means these six steps: (1) gathering information about the job and problems related to it through informational interviewing and library research, (2) doing a self-analysis to gain understanding of strengths and weaknesses, (3) preparing a résumé and cover letter that conform to the expectation of recruiters, (4) researching the organization by conducting interviews and library research, (5) preparing to answer employer questions by rehearsing answers to typical questions and self-criticism of taped responses, and (6) preparing a list of questions to ask an employer.

11. Interviewers must be concerned with techniques for conducting an employment interview. We presented strategies for motivating the interviewee, along with information about avoiding bias. We pointed out that both the beginning and ending of the interview are very important since they set the tone. They serve to relax the candidate, get the necessary information, and build a favorable image of the company. In interpreting the data the interviewer should keep in mind sources of bias. The interviewer can eliminate bias by following carefully worked-out check sheets listing the qualifications for the specific job and by conducting multiple interviews.

12. Interviewees ought to ask appropriate questions of the recruiter and present themselves well. They should handle illegal questions tactfully but firmly, based on the particular goal they have. They should follow the guidelines for appropriate interview behavior. Finally, they should use techniques for managing group interviews to turn them to their advantage.

RECOMMENDED READINGS

M. Beer. "Performance Appraisal." In J. W. Lorsch (ed.), *Handbook of Organizational Behavior.* Englewood Cliffs, N.J., Prentice Hall, 1987, pp. 286–300. This chapter is an excellent reference regarding issues of appraising performance.

Cal W. Downs, G. Paul Smeyak, and Ernest Martin. "Appraisal Interviews," "Counseling Interviews," and "Discipline Interviews." In *Professional Interviewing,* pp. 160–187, 188–207, 215–229. New York, Harper & Row, 1980. Downs and his associates offer additional material in these chapters on interviews.

William F. Eadie. "Defensive Communication Revisited: A Critical Examination of Gibb's Theory." *Southern Speech Communication Journal,* 47 (Winter 1982):163–177.

David W. Ewing, "How to Negotiate with Employees." *Harvard Business Review,* January–February 1983, pp. 103–110. This interesting essay presents a practicing manager's experience with handling complaints.

H. Lloyd Goodall, Jr., Gerald L. Wilson, and Christopher L. Waagen. "The Performance Appraisals Interview: An Interpretive Reassessment." *Quarterly Journal of Speech,* 72 (February 1986):74–87. These authors provide an interesting and useful perspective on the performance appraisal interview.

Gerald L. Wilson and H. Lloyd Goodall, Jr. *Interviewing In Context.* New York, McGraw-Hill, 1991. This book is an especially useful reference for answering specific questions about any of the topics discussed in this chapter.

W. E. Barlow and E. Z. Hane. "A Practical Guide to the Americans with Disabilities Act," *Personnel Journal,* 71 (1992):53–60.

Richard N. Bolles, *What Color Is Your Parachute? A Practical Manual for Job Hunters and Career-Changers.* Berkeley, Calif., Ten Speed Press, 1997. This guide to job hunting is updated every year.

Cal W. Downs, G. Paul Smeyak, and Ernest Martin. "The Selection Interview" and "Selection Interviews: The Interviewee's Perspective." In *Professional Interviewing.* New York, Harper & Row, 1980, pp. 107–139, 146–159. These chapters provide detailed descriptions of the employment selection process.

John D. Drake. *Interviewing for Managers.* New York, American Management Association, 1972. This is a good book for more help in conducting interviews.

Lois J. Einhorn, Patricia Hays Bradley, and John E. Baird, Jr. *Effective Employment Interviewing.* Glenview, Ill., Scott, Foresman, 1982. Here is a book written by communication studies scholars. Its principal author worked as a professional recruiter.

Gerald L. Wilson and H. Lloyd Goodall, Jr. *Interviewing in Context.* New York, McGraw-Hill, 1991. Chapters 6 and 7 focus on the selection interview, first from the interviewer and then from the interviewee perspective.

DISCUSSION QUESTIONS

With a small group of your classmates, plan an interview appraising the performance in your class to date of (a) your professor; (b) a classmate; and (c) yourself. Then answer the following questions and share your answers with your classmates.

• For each of the appraisals, what would be necessary to create a positive performance appraisal climate?

• Develop suggestions for encouraging each of the individuals.

• Does relative power and status influence the task of appraisal? How? What may be done to address power and status differences?

• Are there any significant differences to be found in the way the professor and the classmate might prepare for an appraisal interview?

1. If you had the opportunity to talk with a professional in your field, what questions would you want to ask that person, and why?

2. Develop a résumé that you might use to apply for a position. If you have not had extensive working experience, don't worry about it. Just include what you can to represent yourself. Bring copies of the résumé to class to share with other members. Share résumés, then discuss these questions:

   a. What features of the résumés seem attractive to you?

   b. What features seem to control eye movement and attention?

   c. Were some résumés easier to use than others? What are the differences?

3. Suppose you were going to interview the person whose résumé you found most attractive. What questions would you ask that individual? How did the résumé contribute to your selection of the questions you would ask?

4. Two or three pairs of students should role-play an interview while the class observes. Then the entire class should discuss the following questions:

   a. How effective were the questions asked by the interviewer and interviewee? Why do you think that?

   b. How successfully did the interviewer guide the exchange? Did the interviewee have any influence on guiding the exchange? If so, how?

   c. What suggestions would you make to the interviewee to improve the performance?

5. Review the questions provided in Figures 9-7 and 9-20. Pick out the five most difficult questions and answer them. Share your answers with the class.

6. Identify the two illegal questions you believe would be most difficult to handle. Share with the class how you might answer these.

INTERNET ACTIVITIES

1. Do you think the many commercial employment services available on the World Wide Web are helpful? How do you determine the qualifications and quality of the advice they provide? Check out (http://www.proactive-inst.com/) for an example.

2. Suppose your annual performance appraisal review resulted in the suggestion that you take a course about interpersonal communication in interview settings. Check out your local college or university's offerings on the Internet, and make notes to share with classmates. What did you discover about the institution? Who teaches the courses? Can you take such a course online? Where? How? How much will it cost?

3. You are going to interview for a position with an on-campus recruiter. In order to prepare you want to research the company, which you can do using the Internet. What can you find out from Moody's (http://www.moodys.com/) about your chosen company? How would that be useful?

4. Can you find any help on the World Wide Web for designing your résumé? Keep notes and report back to the class.

NOTES

1. H. Lloyd Goodall, Jr., Gerald L. Wilson, and Christopher L. Waagen, "The Performance Appraisal Interview: An Interpretive Assessment, *The Quarterly Journal of Speech,* 72 (1986): 74–87.

2. Meryl R. Lewis, "Surprise and Sense-Making: What Newcomers Experience On Entering Unfamiliar Organizational Settings," *Administrative Science Quarterly,* 23 (1980):225–251.

3. C. O. Longenecker, H. P. Sims, and D. A. Gioia, "Behind the Mask: The Politics of Employee Appraisal," *Academy of Management Executive,* 1 (1987):183–193.

4. T. A. Judge and G. R. Ferris, "Social Contexts of Performance Evaluation Decisions," *Academy of Management Journal,* 36 (1993):80–105.

5. Longenecker, Sims, and Gioia, op. cit.

6. Gerald L. Wilson and H. Lloyd Goodall, Jr., "The Performance Appraisal Interview: A Review of the Literature with Implications for Communication Research," Southern Speech Association Meeting, Winston-Salem, N.C., April 1985. Also, see Hermine Zagat Levine, "Consensus on Performance Appraisals at Work," *Personnel* (1986):63–71.

7. Compiled from suggestions by Cal W. Downs, Wil Linkugel, and David M. Berg, *The Organizational Communicator* (New York, Harper & Row, 1977), p. 104; Felix M. Lopez, Jr., *Personnel Interviewing* (New York, McGraw-Hill, 1965), p. 148; "Performance Appraisal and Review," (Ann Arbor, Mich., The Foundation for Research on Human Behavior, 1958).

8. See Norman R. F. Maier, *The Appraisal Interview* (New York, Wiley, 1958); A. R. Solem, "Some Supervisory Problems in Appraisal Interviewing," *Personnel Administration,* 23 (1960):27–40; M. M. Greller, "Subordinate Participation and Reactions to the Appraisal Interview," *Journal of Applied Psychology,* 60 (1975): 544–549; W. F. Nemeroff and K. N. Wexley, "Relationships between Performance Appraisal Interview Characteristics and Interview Outcomes as Perceived by Supervisors and Subordinates," paper presented at the 1977 Academy of Management Meeting, cited in R. J. Burke et al., "Characteristics of Effective Employee Performance Review and Development Interviews: Replication and Extension," *Personnel Psychology,* 31 (1978):903–905; and K. N. Wexley, J. P. Singh, and G. A. Yukl, "Subordinate Personality as a Moderator of the Effects of Participation in Three Types of Appraisal Interviews," *Journal of Applied Psychology,* 58 (1973):54–59.

9. Maier, op. cit., pp. 1–20; Solem, op. cit., pp. 27–40; Greller, op. cit., pp. 544–549.

10. Greller, op. cit., pp. 544–549.

11. E. F. Huse and Emanuel Kay, "Increasing Management Effectiveness through Work Planning," in *The Personnel Job: A Changing World* (New York, American Management Association, 1964).

12. Nemeroff and Wexley, op. cit.

13. Gary P. Latham and Lise M. Saari, "Importance of Supportive Relationships in Goal Setting," *Journal of Applied Psychology,* 64 (1979):151–156.

14. Burke et al., op. cit., pp. 903–919.

15. Herbert H. Meyer, Emanual Kay, and John R. P. French, Jr., "Split Roles in Performance Appraisal," *Harvard Business Review,* January–February 1965, pp. 123–129.

16. Richard E. Farson, "Praise Reappraised," *Harvard Business Review,* September–October 1963, pp. 61–66.

17. Meyer, Kay, and French, op. cit., p. 127.

18. Latham and Saari, op. cit.

19. Emanuel Kay, Herbert H. Meyer, and John R. P. French, Jr., "Effects of Threat in a Performance Appraisal Interview," *Journal of Applied Psychology,* 49 (October 1965):311–317.

20. Huse and Kay, op. cit.

21. J. R. Gibb, "Defensive Communication," *Journal of Communication,* 11, no. 3 (September 1961):141–148.

22. Meyer, Kay, and French, op. cit., pp. 124–127.

23. Feedback and goal setting have been found to be significantly related to subordinates' perception of equity and to the accuracy and clarity of information exchanged. See John M. Ivancevich, "Subordinates' Reaction to Performance Appraisal Interviews: A Test of Feedback and Goal Setting Techniques," *Journal of Applied Psychology,* 67 (1982):581–587.

24. Meyer, Kay, and French, op. cit.

25. Alva F. Kindall and James Gatza, "Positive Program for Performance Appraisal," *Harvard Business Review,* November–December 1963, p. 158.

26. Ibid.

27. Meyer, Kay, and French, op. cit.

28. Frank J. Landy, Janet Barnes-Farrell, and Jeanette N. Cleveland, "Perceived Fairness and Accuracy of Performance Evaluation: A Follow-Up," *Journal of Applied Psychology,* 65 (1980): 355–356.

29. Ronald J. Burke, William F. Weitzel, and Tamara Weir, "Characteristics of Effective Employee Performance Review and Development Interviews: One More Time," *Psychological Reports,* 47 (1980):683–695.

30. Mirian Erez and Frederick H. Kanfer, "Role of Goal Acceptance in Goal Setting and Task Performance," *Academy of Management Review,* 8 (1983):455.

31. Gary Blau, "The Effect of Source Competence on Worker Attitudes," *Journal of Applied Communication Research,* 14 (1986):33.

32. Walter R. Mahler, *How Effective Executives Interview* (Homewood, Ill., Dow Jones/Irwin, 1976), pp. 77–83.

33. D. P. Schwab and H. G. Heneman III, "Relationship between Interview Structure and Interviewer Reliability in an Employment Situation," *Journal of Applied Psychology,* 53 (1969):214–217.

34. Cal W. Downs, "A Content Analysis of Twenty Selection Interviews," *Personnel Administration and Public Personnel Review,* September 1972, p. 25.

35. For further analysis of illegal questions asked in employment interviews, see Fredric M. Jablin, "Use of Discriminatory Questions in Screening Interviews," *Personnel Administrator,* 27 (1982):41–44.

36. Thomas Reardon, "Preselection: How Students Prescreen Employers," *Journal of College Placement,* 40, no. 2 (Winter 1979):53–55.

37. Robert Gifford, Cheuk Fan Ng, and Margaret Wilkinson, "Nonverbal Cues in the Employment Interview: Links between Applicant Qualities and Interviewer Judgment," *Journal of Applied Psychology,* 70 (1985):735.

38. Charles P. Bird and Dawn D. Puglisi, "Method of Résumé Reproduction and Evaluations of Employment Suitability," *Journal of Business Communication,* 13 (1986):31–40.

39. Ibid.

40. Edward Rogers, "Elements of Efficient Job Hunting," *Journal of College Placement,* 40, no. 1 (Fall 1979):55–58; Victor R. Lindquist, *The North-Western Lindquist-Endicott Report.* The Placement Center, Northwestern University, 1988; Beverly Culwell, "Employer Preferences Regarding Résumés and Application Letters," unpublished paper, School of Business, Missouri Southern State College.

41. Gary M. Richetto and Joseph P. Zima, *Fundamentals of Interviewing* (Chicago, Science Research Associates, 1976).

42. Karen B. McComb and Fredric M. Jablin, "Verbal Correlates of Interviewer Empathic Listening and Employment Interview Outcomes," *Communication Monographs,* 51 (1984):367.

43. Kenneth N. Wexley et al., "Importance of Contrast Effects in Employment Interviews," *Journal of Applied Psychology,* 56 (1972): 45–48.

44. Harvey D. Tschirgi and Jon M. Huegli, "Monitoring the Employment Interview," *Journal of College Placement,* Winter 1979, p. 39.

45. Thomas D. Hollmann, "Employment Interviewers' Errors in Processing Positive and Negative Information," *Journal of Applied Psychology,* 56 (1972):130–134. See also Arthur A. Witkin, "Commonly Overlooked Dimensions of Employee Selection," *Personnel Journal,* 59 (1980): 573–588.

46. Donna Bogar Goodall and H. Lloyd Goodall, Jr., "The Employment Interview: A Selective Review of the Literature with Implications for Communication Research," *Communication Quarterly,* 30 (1982):116–124.

47. Jeff K. Springston and Joann Keyton, "The prevalence of potentially illegal questioning in pre-employment screening," in *Global Implications for Business Communications: Theory, Technology and Practice*, S. J. Bruno (ed.), Proceedings of the Association for Business Communication meeting (1988):247–263.

48. W. D. Siegfried and K. Wood, "Reducing College Student's Compliance with Inappropriate Interview Requests: An Educational Approach," *Journal of College Student Personnel*, 14 (1983):66–71.

49. Ibid.

50. Joann Keyton and Jeff K. Springston, "I Don't Want to Answer That! A Response Strategy Model for Potentially Discriminatory Questions," paper presented at the annual meeting of the Speech Association, San Francisco, November 1989.

51. For further counsel on answering illegal questions, see: Fredric M. Jablin and Craig D. Tengler, "Facing Discrimination in On-Campus Interviews," *Journal of College Placement*, 42 (1982):57–61.

Chapter 10

Communications Applications: Meetings

SOURCE: Kitty O. Locker and Stephen K. Kaczmarek, *Business Communication: Building Critical Skills*, Module 18, © McGraw- Hill, 2001.

Learning Objective

After studying this chapter, you should be able to:

- Plan a meeting.

- Lead a meeting.

- Be an effective participant in meetings.

- Take good meeting minutes.

- Network effectively

Start by Asking These Questions

- What planning should precede a meeting?

- When I'm in charge, how do I keep the meeting on track?

- What decision-making strategies work well in meetings?

- How can I be an effective meeting participant?

- What should go in meeting minutes?

- How can I use informal meetings with my boss to advance my career?

- Do virtual meetings require special consideration

Meetings have always taken a large part of the average manager's week. The increased number of teams means that meetings are even more frequent. A 1998 survey found that the average business person attended three meetings a week. As people are promoted, they generally attend more meetings. A fifth of the executives surveyed said they attend 11 or more meetings a week. When David House became CEO of Bay Networks in 1996, he figured that the company was spending, directly and indirectly, $87 million a year on staff meetings.[1] A variety of meetings are held in business, nonprofit, and government organizations.

- **Parliamentary meetings** are run under strict rules, like the rules of parliamentary procedure summarized in *Robert's Rules of Order.* Formal rules help the meeting run smoothly if the group is very large or if the agenda is very long. Motions must be made formally before an topic can be debated. Each point is settled by a vote. **Minutes** record each motion and the vote on it. Parliamentary meetings are often used by Boards of Directors and by legislative bodies such as the U.S. Congress and Senate, but they are rarely part of the day-to-day meetings common in most businesses and nonprofit organizations.

- **Regular staff meetings** are held to announce new policies and products, answer questions, share ideas, and motivate workers. For example, Microsoft Exchange Group's development team meets every morning to review daily software builds and to identify any issues that have come up in the last 24 hours. At Industrial Light & Magic's "Computer Graphics Weeklies," project teams present special-effects problems that they have solved or that they need help with. Other teams learn from them or help them solve it. On the first Friday of every month, all the employees of Employease, a four-year-old firm that helps companies automate Human Resource functions, gather to review financial updates, welcome new employees, build the corporate culture, and connect raw data to the company's long-term vision. The meetings mix "straight talk, town-hall discussion, and vaudeville."[2] A financial services company holds quarterly town-hall meetings for all employees, complete with staging, professional-quality videos, and question-and-answer sessions with the executive team.[3]

- **Team meetings** bring together team members to brainstorm, solve problems, and create documents. Meetings may be called on short notice when a problem arises that needs input from several people.

- **One-on-one meetings** are not always thought of as meetings, but they are perhaps the most common meetings of all. Employees talk by the water cooler or the refrigerator or ride up an elevator together. One person walks into another's office or cubicle to ask a question. A supervisor stops by a line worker to see how things are going and to "manage by walking around." These highly informal meetings can be crucial to your being seen as promotable.

Other kinds of meetings also are held. Many companies hold sales meetings for their sales staff. Conventions bring together workers in the same field from many different employers. Retreats allow a small group to get away for team-building, brainstorming, or long-range planning.

Any of these meetings may be supported with computers. Allstate and McKinsey & Co. are among the organizations that key in comments on a computer hooked up to a large overhead projector for all the participants to see. "People literally see themselves being heard. Related comments are identified, linked, and edited on screen. The digressions and tangents quickly become apparent." The resulting document can be posted on the company intranet for further discussion and comments.[4]

Other organizations use group support software. Each person sits at a workstation. Participants key in their own brainstorming ideas and comments. People can vote by ranking items on a 1- to-10 scale; the software calculates the averages.[5]

Speakerphones and conference calls allow people in different locations to participate in the same conversation. On-line meetings, such as those hosted by WebEx (www.webex.com), allow you to bring together five other participants for a simultaneous e-mail conversation in your own private chat room. Some computer systems support video as well as data or audio transmissions. Videoconferences provide high-quality video and audio transmissions.

The length and purposes of the meeting, the number of people who attend, the budget, and the available technology all affect outcomes. However, a number of principles apply to almost all meetings.

WHAT PLANNING SHOULD PRECEDE A MEETING?

Identify the purpose(s) and create an agenda.

Meetings can have at least six purposes:

- To share information.

- To brainstorm ideas.

- To evaluate ideas.

- To make decisions.

- To create a document.

- To motivate members.

When meetings combine two or more purposes, it's useful to make the purposes explicit. For example, in the meeting of a university Senate or a company's Board of Directors, some items are presented for information. Discussion is possible, but the group will not be asked to make a decision. Other items are presented for action; the group will be asked to vote. A business meeting might specify that the first half hour will be time for brainstorming, with the second half hour devoted to evaluation.

Intel's agendas also specify *how* decisions will be made. The company recognizes four different decision-making processes:

- Authoritative (the leader makes the decision alone).

- Consultative (the leader hears group comments, but then makes the decision alone).

- Voting (the majority wins).

- Consensus (discussion continues until everyone can "buy into" the decision).[6]

Specifying how input will be used makes expectations clear and focuses the conversation.

Once you've identified your purposes, think about how you can make them happen. Perhaps participants will need to receive and read materials before the meeting. Perhaps people should bring drafts to the meeting so that creating a document can go more quickly.

For team meetings called on short notice, the first item of business is to create an agenda. This kind of agenda can be informal, simply listing the topics or goals.

For meetings with more lead time, distribute an agenda several days before the meeting. (*Agenda* is Latin for "to be done.") If possible, give participants a chance to comment and revise the agenda in response to those comments. A good agenda indicates

- The time and place of the meeting.

- Whether each item is presented for information, for discussion, or for a decision.

- Who is sponsoring or introducing each item.

- How much time is allotted for each item.

Many groups put first routine items on which agreement will be easy. If there's a long list of routine items, save them till the end or, in a parliamentary meeting, dispense with them in an omnibus motion. An **omnibus motion** allows a group to approve many items together rather than voting on each separately. A single omnibus motion might cover multiple changes to operational guidelines, or a whole slate of candidates for various offices, or various budget recommendations.

Schedule controversial items early in the meeting, when people's energy level is high, and to allow enough time for full discussion. Giving a controversial item only half an hour at the end of the day or evening makes people suspect that the leaders are trying to manipulate them.

If you're planning a long meeting, for example, a training session or a conference, recognize that networking is part of the value of the meeting. Allow short breaks at least every two hours and generous breaks twice a day so participants can talk informally to each other. If participants will be strangers, include some social functions so they can get to know each other. If they will have different interests or different levels of knowledge, plan concurrent sessions on different topics or for people with different levels of expertise.

Allow for creativity and fun. Each Best Buy store chooses its own way to start monthly staff meetings. The Best Buy in Boca Raton, Florida, opens each 7:30 A.M. meeting with a talent show.[7]

You may want to leave five minutes at the end of the meeting to evaluate it. What went well? What could be better? What do you want to change next time?

WHEN I'M IN CHARGE, HOW DO I KEEP THE MEETING ON TRACK?

Pay attention both to task and to process.

Your goal as chair is to help participants deal with the issues in a way that is both timely and adequately thorough. When the issues are simple and clear-cut, running the meeting may require only that you introduce the person who introduces each issue, recognize people who want to speak, and remind the group of its progress. "We're a bit behind schedule. Let's see if we can get through the committee reports quickly." When the issues

Building a Critical Skill

Networking

Getting to know people within and beyond your own organization helps you build a network of contacts, colleagues, and friends.

In your own organization,

- Most days, have lunch with other people in your organization. At least once a month (more often is better), invite someone whom you don't know well. You can go someplace inexpensive or even bring brown-bag lunches. But don't work through lunch more than twice a week. Use the time to widen your circle of acquaintances at the place where you work.

- At a meeting, sit by someone you don't know well. Introduce yourself, and find out something about the other person.

To get to know other business people in your community,

- At events, sit with people you don't yet know. For example, if your company buys a table of 10 seats at a charity luncheon, ask the organizers to put two of you at each of five tables, so that you can use the lunch to network.

- Attend meetings of the trade association for your industry and meetings of business people specifically designed to network or to share ideas.

Join a listserv to get to know other people in your field. To find the appropriate listserv, visit www.liszt.com. As this book goes to press, it links to 178 business listservs.

When you meet new people, suggests Marc Kramer, don't waste your time talking about news, weather, and sports. Instead, talk about business. Ask strangers what they and their companies do. When you know someone's specialty, ask his or her opinion about challenges or events in that industry. After you find out about the other person, give a short, 60-second description of your work and your company. Then probe more deeply into the other person's experience and ideas. Find out what his or her position is. Exchange business cards. And ask for the names of other people in that organization whom you should talk to, depending on your own interests and your job.

Once you've established a contact, you need to nurture it. Some business people like to send a short follow-up message right after the first meeting. In some cases, you may want to set up occasional lunches with people—in your own or in other organizations—who are particularly useful and interesting. The very best follow-up is to send something the other person can truly use—information about a book or article, a URL, the address for a listserv you find useful. Think of networking not just as a way to meet people who can be useful to you but also a way that you can be more useful and visible in your own organization and in the community in which you live and work.

Source: Marc Kramer, *Power Networking: Using the Contacts You Didn't Even Know You Have to Succeed in the Job You Want* (Lincolnwood, IL: VGM Career Horizons, 1998

are complex, or when members have major disagreements, you may need to summarize issues or shape the discussion: "We're really talking about two things: whether the change would save money and whether our customers would like it. Does it make sense to keep those two together, or could we talk about customer reaction first, and then deal with the financial issues?"

As chair, you may want to make ground rules explicit. Ground rules vary considerably from company to company and sometimes even within organizations based on the corporate culture. In some meetings, participants are expected to stay for the entire session, even if not all agenda items are relevant to them personally. In others, people are free to attend just part of the meeting. In some cultures, participants are expected to give their full attention to the discussion. In others, it may be acceptable to check one's e-mail or even work on other projects during the meeting. Some organizations ask senior people to wait to speak until after junior people have spoken; others may expect senior people to speak first. If the issue is contentious, the chair may ask that speakers for and against a motion alternate. If no one remains on one side, then the discussion can stop.

Pay attention to people and process as well as to the task at hand. At informal meetings, a good leader observes nonverbal feedback and invites everyone to participate. If conflict seems to be getting out of hand, a leader may want to focus attention on the group process and ways that it could deal with conflict, before getting back to the substantive issues.

If the group doesn't formally vote, summarize the group's consensus after each point so that it is clear to everyone what decision has been made and who is responsible for implementing or following up on each item.

WHAT DECISION-MAKING STRATEGIES WORK WELL IN MEETINGS?

Try the standard agenda or dot planning.

Probably the least effective decision-making strategy is to let the person who talks first, last, loudest, or most determine the decision. Voting is quick but may leave people in the minority unhappy with and uncommitted to the majority's plan. Coming to consensus takes time but results in speedier implementation of ideas. Two strategies that are often useful in organizational groups are the standard agenda and dot planning.

The **standard agenda** is a seven-step process for solving problems.

1. Understand what the group has to deliver, in what form, by what due date. Identify available resources.

2. Identify the problem. What exactly is wrong? What question(s) is the group trying to answer?

3. Gather information, share it with all group members, and examine it critically.

4. Establish criteria. What would the ideal solution include? Which elements of that solution would be part of a less-than-ideal but still acceptable solution? What legal, financial, moral, or other limitations might keep a solution from being implemented?

5. Generate alternate solutions. Brainstorm and record ideas for the next step.

6. Measure the alternatives against the criteria.

7. Choose the best solution.[8]

Dot planning offers a way for large groups to choose priorities quickly. First, the group brainstorms ideas, recording each on pages that are put on the wall. Then each individual gets two strips of three to five adhesive dots in different colors. One color represents high priority, the other lower priority. People then walk up to the pages and affix dots by the points they care most about. Some groups allow only one dot from one person on any one item; others allow someone who is really passionate about an idea to put all of his or her dots on it. As Figure 10-1 shows, the dots make it easy to see which items the group believes are most important.

Figure 10-1   Dot Planning Allows Groups to Set Priorities Quickly

Here, gray dots mean "high priority;" black dots mean "low priority." One can see at a glance which items have widespread support, which are controversial, and which are low priority.

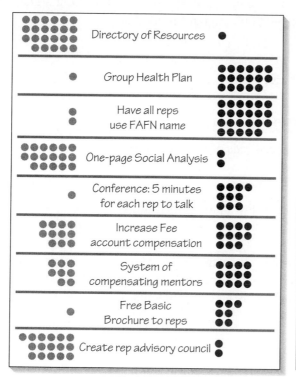

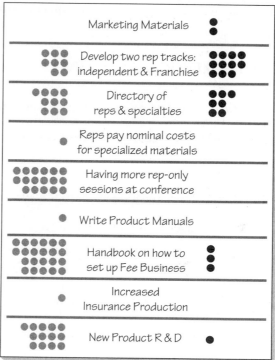

Source: "The Color-Coded Priority Setter," *Inc.,* June 1995, 70–71.

HOW CAN I BE AN EFFECTIVE MEETING PARTICIPANT?

Be prepared.

Take the time to prepare for meetings. Read the materials distributed before the meeting and think about the issues to be discussed. Bring those materials to the meeting, along with something to write on, and with, even if you're not the secretary.

In a small meeting, you'll probably get several chances to speak. Roger Mostvick and Robert Nelson found that the most influential people in a meeting are those who say something in the first five minutes of the meeting (even just to ask a question), who talk most often, and who talk at greatest length.[9]

In a large meeting, you may get just one chance to speak. Make notes of what you want to say so that you can be succinct, fluent, and complete.

It's frustrating to speak in a meeting and have people ignore what you say. Here are some tips for being taken seriously.[10]

- Show that you've done your homework. Laura Sloate, who is blind, establishes authority by making sure her first question is highly technical: "In footnote three of the 10K, you indicate. . . ."

- Link your comment to the comment of a powerful person. Even if logic suffers a bit, present your comment as an addition, not a challenge. For example, say, "John is saying that we should focus on excellence, AND I think we can become stronger by encouraging diversity."

- Find an ally in the organization and agree ahead of time to acknowledge each other's contributions to the meeting, whether you agree or disagree with the point being made. Explicit disagreement signals that the comment is worth taking seriously: "Duane has pointed out. . . , but I think that. . . ."

WHAT SHOULD GO IN MEETING MINUTES?

Topics discussed, decisions reached, and who does what next.

Meeting expert Michael Begeman suggests recording three kinds of information:

- Decisions reached.

- Action items, where someone needs to implement or follow up on something.

- Open issues—issues raised but not resolved.[11]

Minutes of formal meetings indicate who was present and absent and the wording of motions and amendments as well as the vote. Committee reports are often attached for later reference. For less formal meetings, brief minutes are fine. The most important notes are the decisions and assignments. Long minutes will be most helpful if assignments are set off visually from the narrative.

> We discussed whether we should switch from road to rail shipment.
> Action: Sue will get figures on cost for the next meeting.
> Action: Tyrone will conduct survey of current customers on-line to ask their opinions.

HOW CAN I USE INFORMAL MEETINGS WITH MY BOSS TO ADVANCE MY CAREER?

Plan scripts to present yourself positively.

You'll see your supervisor several times a week. Some of these meetings will be accidental: You'll meet by the coffeepot or ride up the elevator together. Some of them will be deliberately initiated: Your boss will stop by your workstation, or you'll go to your boss's office to ask for something.

You can take advantage of these meetings by planning for them. These informal meetings are often short. An elevator ride, for example, may last about three minutes. So plan 90-second scripts that you can use to give your boss a brief report on what you're doing, ask for something you need, or lay the groundwork for an important issue.

Planning scripts is especially important if your boss doesn't give you much feedback or mentoring. In this case, your boss probably doesn't see you as promotable. You need to take the initiative. Make statements that show the boss you're thinking about ways to work smarter. Show that you're interested in learning more so that you can be more valuable to the organization.

DO VIRTUAL MEETINGS REQUIRE SPECIAL CONSIDERATION?

Yes. Watch interpersonal communication. For important projects, build in some real meetings as well.

When you meet technologically rather than in person, you lose the informal interactions of going to lunch or chatting during a break. Those interactions not only create bonds, so that people are more willing to work together, but also give people a chance to work out dozens of small issues. Listening, teamwork, and the ability to resolve conflicts constructively become even more crucial.

Be aware of the limitations of your channel. When you are limited to e-mail, you lose both tone of voice and body language. In addition, e-mail messages are often more brusque than comments in person. Audio messages provide tone of voice but not the nonverbal signals that tell you whether someone wants to make a comment or understands what you're saying. Even videoconferencing gives you only the picture in the camera's lens. With any of these technologies, you'll need to attend specifically to interpersonal skills.

For an important project, in-person meetings are essential. In 1999, Lucent Technologies introduced a $1 million product called Bandwidth Manager. Its million lines of code were written in 18 months by 500 engineers in five U.S. states, the Netherlands, Germany, and India. Cultural differences existed even among the U.S. workers: Massachusetts workers got to work early and left on time; New Jersey workers stayed late. Time differences among India, Europe, and the United States meant that as one country's workers went home, in another time zone other workers took over the job. But the two team leaders learned that technology alone wasn't enough. Groups of managers met every other week in rotating cities, socializing as much as their busy schedules permitted. Those meetings helped the group find its "pace," using technology even more effectively to cut down on voice-mail tag and other problems. The project shipped on time, within budget, and with even more technical versatility than Lucent had hoped for.[12]

SUMMARY

- A good agenda indicates

    - The time and place of the meeting.

    - Whether each item is presented for information, for discussion, or for a decision.

    - Who is sponsoring or introducing each item.

    - How much time is allotted for each item.

- To make meetings more effective,

    - State the purpose of the meeting at the beginning.

    - Distribute an agenda that indicates whether each item is for information, for discussion, for action and how long each is expected to take.

    - Allow enough time to discuss controversial issues.

    - Pay attention to people and process as well as to the task at hand.

    - If you don't take formal votes, summarize the group's consensus after each point. At the end of the meeting, summarize all decisions and remind the group who is responsible for implementing or following up on each item.

- The **standard agenda** is a seven-step process for solving problems. In **dot planning** the group brainstorms ideas. Then each individual affixes adhesive dots by the points or proposals he or she cares most about.

- Minutes should record

  - Decisions reached.

  - Action items, where someone needs to implement or follow up on something.

  - Open issues—issues raised but not resolved.

QUESTIONS FOR COMPREHENSION

1. What should go in an agenda?

2. What are the seven steps in the standard meeting agenda?

3. When would dot planning be most effective?

4. What should go in minutes of a meeting?

QUESTIONS FOR CRITICAL THINKING

1. What opportunities do you have to network?

2. In the groups of which you're a member (at school, at work, and in volunteer organizations), what kinds of comments are most valued in meetings?

3. What is the best meeting you ever attended? What made it so effective?

QUESTIONS FOR BUILDING SKILLS

1. What skills have you read about in this module?
2. What skills are you practicing in the assignments you're doing for this module?
3. How could you further develop the skills you're working on?

EXERCISES AND PROBLEMS

1. Writing an Agenda
Write an agenda for your next collaborative group meeting.
As Your Instructor Directs,

   a. Write a memo to your instructor, explaining the choices you made.

   b. Share your agenda with the ones developed by others in your group. Use the agendas as drafts to help you create the best possible agenda.

   c. Present your best agenda to the rest of the class in a group oral presentation.

2. Taking Minutes

As Your Instructor Directs,

Have two or more people take minutes of each class or collaborative group meeting for a week. Compare the accounts of the same meeting.

- To what extent do they agree on what happened?
- Does one contain information missing in other accounts?
- Do any accounts disagree on a specific fact?
- How do you account for the differences you find?

3. Writing a Meeting Manual*

Create a manual for students next term telling them how to have effective meetings as they work on collaborative projects.

*Adapted from Miles McCall, Beth Stewart, and Timothy Clipson, "Teaching Communication Skills for Meeting Management," *1998 Refereed Proceedings, Association for Business Communication Southwestern United States*, ed. Marsha L. Bayless (Nacogdoches, TX), p. 68.

4. Planning Scripts for 3-Minute Meetings

Create a script for a 90-second statement to your boss

1. Describing the progress on a project you're working on.
2. Providing an update on a problem the boss already knows about.
3. Telling about a success or achievement.
4. Telling about a problem and asking approval for the action you recommend.
5. Asking for resources you need for a project.
6. Asking for training you'd like to get.
7. Laying the groundwork for a major request you need to make.

As Your Instructor Directs,

a. Discuss your scripts with a small group of other students.

b. Present your script to the class.

c. Write a memo to your instructor explaining the choices you have made in terms of content, arrangement, and word choice.

NOTES

1. "Why Making Meetings Better Matters," *Selling Power,*June 1999, 78; Roger K. Mosvick and Robert B. Nelson,We've Got to Start Meeting Like this: A Guide to Successful *Meeting Management,* rev. ed. (Indianapolis: Park Avenue, 1996), 26; Carl Quintanilla, "Work Week," *The Wall Street Journal,* July 14, 1998, A1; and Michael Warshaw, "HaveYou Been House-Trained?" *Fast Company,* October 1998, 46.

2. Cathy Olofson, "So Many Meetings, So Little Time," *Fast Company,* January/February 2000, 48; Cheryl Dahle, "Sneak Previews Make Good Project Reviews," *Fast Company,* July/August 1999, 66; and Cathy Olofson, "Thank God It's First Friday," *Fast Company,* April 2000, 74.

3. Andrea Williams, "The Rhetoric of Corporate Communications: A Case Study of a Canadian Employee Communications Program in a Global Financial Services Organization," Ph.D. dissertation, The Ohio State University, 2000, Chapter 5.

4. Michael Schrage, "Meetings Don't Have to be Dull," *The Wall Street Journal,* April 29, 1996, A12.

5. Eric Matson, "The Seven Deadly Sins of Meetings," *Fast Company Handbook of the Business Revolution,* 1997, 29.

6. Matson, 30.

7. "There's Something about Mary," *Fortune,* October 25, 1999, 368.

8. H. Lloyd Goodall, Jr., *Small Group Communications in Organizations* (Dubuque, IA: William C. Brown, 1985), 39–40.

9. Mosvick and Nelson, 177.

10. Cynthia Crossen, "Spotting Value Takes Smarts, Not Sight, Laura Sloate Shows," *The Wall Street Journal,* December 10, 1987, A1, A14; and Joan E. Rigdon, "Managing Your Career," *The Wall Street Journal*, December 1, 1993, B1.

11. Gina Imperator, "'You Have to Start Meeting Like This,'" *Fast Company*, April 1999, 204-10.

12. Thomas Petzinger, Jr., "With the Stakes High, a Lucent Duo Conquers Distance and Culture," *The Wall Street Journal,* April 23, 1999, B1.

Part 3

Introduction to Creative Thinking

Consider all of the decisions necessary to carry out the goals of any major effort - from launching a space satellite to marketing and producing a new line of automobiles to creating a new product. Managers responsible for these decisions rely on good decision-making skills.

A manager's responsibility as a decision maker is very important. While all managers are called upon to make decisions, the kinds of decisions that are required will vary with their level of authority and type of assignment. Poor decisions can be disastrous to a unit and to the organization as a whole. Good decisions help work flow and enable the organization to achieve its goals.

Decision making is the process through which managers identify and resolve problems and capitalize on opportunities. Managers may not always make the right decision, but they can use their knowledge of appropriate decision-making processes to increase the odds of success. Skill as a decision maker is a distinguishing characteristic of most successful managers. Decision making often begins with creative thinking.

Creative thinking has become more and more important in today's environment. As individuals seek an "edge" and organizations seek a competitive advantage, they can no longer be just like everyone else. Creative thinking is a way of gaining that edge and competitive advantage.

Part 3 begins with an examination of the Creative Thinking Process in Chapter 11. A common, everyday application of creative thinking may be found in how individuals and organizations solve problems and make decisions. Chapter 12 explores creative problem solving/ decision making including a focus on ethics. Part 3 concludes with a presentation, in Chapter 13, of another application of creative thinking – Total Quality Management (TQM). Both problem solving/ decision making and TQM may be significantly enhanced if fresh, new looks are taken, rather than doing things the way we have always done them.

Chapter 11

The Creative Thinking Process

SOURCE: Shani and Lau, *Organizational Behavior and Management*, 5th ed., Module 16, McGraw-Hill, 1999.

Learning Objectives:

After completing this chapter, you should be able to
- Describe the creative process.
- Identify the traits or characteristics that are related to individual creativity.
- Explain the difference between creativity and innovation.
- Describe the stages and the different types of innovation.
- Gain insight into the key elements that influence both the creativity and the innovation processes.
- Understand the interplay among human behavior, group behavior, creativity, and innovation.
- Define the following key terms:

Adaption–innovation model	Innovation
Administrative innovation	Innovation process
Creative process	Person–oriented creativity
Creativity	Process–oriented creativity
Creativity–relevant skills	Product innovation
Domain–relevant skills	Product–oriented creativity
Dual ladders	Radical innovation
Emotional intelligence	System–maintaining innovation (SMI)
Incremental innovation	System–transforming innovation (STI)
	Task motivation

Prechapter Preparation

ACTIVITY 11–1: Exploring Creativity in an Organizational Setting: 3M's Post–It Note Pads Case

---

OBJECTIVES:
a. To explore the organizational context for creativity and innovation.
b. To identify the variety of skills and competencies involved in creativity.

Task 1 (Homework):
Students are to read the case "3M Post–It Notes" and respond to the question at the end of the case.

Task 2:
Individuals are to share the answers in small groups. Each group is to develop a shared response, which will be presented and discussed with the class.

CASE: 3M's Post–It Note Pads

In 1922 Minnesota Mining and Manufacturing inventor Francis G. Okie was dreaming of ways to increase sandpaper sales, the company's major product at the time, when a novel thought struck him. Why not sell sandpaper as a replacement for razor blades? The idea was that people could rub their cheeks smooth. The idea never caught on, but Okie went on at 3M and eventually developed a waterproof sandpaper that became a major staple in the auto industry. Okie's failure is as much legend at 3M as is his successful idea.

The 3M Company was founded at the turn of the century by a doctor, a lawyer, two railroad executives, and a meat market manager on the shores of Lake Superior. Their purpose was to mine corundum, an abrasive used in sandpaper. Unfortunately, the corundum mine yielded a mineral of no value to the sandpaper industry. Most of the original investors left, and those who remained turned to inventing. Their first success was an abrasive cloth used in metal polishing. Then Okie's wet or dry sandpaper came along. Since then, 3M has never stopped.

William L. McKnight is the legendary spiritual father of the company. McKnight worked himself up from bookkeeper through sales to chairman and chief executive. As a salesman he pitched his products directly to furniture makers on the factory shop floors rather than to the purchasing agents.

This became the 3M approach — get close to the customer. Both scotch tape and masking tape were developed to meet individual customer's needs. Part of McKnight's manifesto was "If management is intolerant and destructively critical when mistakes are made, I think it kills initiative." In addition to tolerating mistakes, the company rarely hires from outside (never at the senior level). The turnover rate among managers and other professionals is less than 4 percent. Divisions are kept small so that division managers are on a first–name basis with their staffs.

Source: Background on 3M was drawn from "Masters of Innovation," *Business Week*, April 10, 1989, pp. 58–63. This case is a shorter and modified version of "3M's Little Yellow Note Pads: Never Mind I'll Do It Myself," in *Breakthroughs!*, eds. P. R. Nayak and J. M. Kerrengham (New York: Rawson Associates, 1988), pp. 50–73. Used by permission.

NEW PRODUCT DEVELOPMENT

A 3Mer comes up with an idea for a new product. He or she forms an action team by recruiting full–time members from technical areas, manufacturing, marketing, sales, and finance. The team designs the product and figures out how to produce and market it. Then the team develops new uses and line extensions. All members of the team are promoted and receive raises as the project develops. As sales grow, the product's originator can go on to become project manager, department manager, or division manager. There's a separate track for scientists who don't want to manage. The result is that there are 42 divisions. Each division must follow the 25 percent rule: A quarter of a division's sales must come from products introduced within the past five years. In addition, there is a 15 percent rule. Virtually anyone at the company can spend up to 15 percent of the workweek on anything he or she wants to as long as it's product related. Managers do not monitor very carefully their scientists' use of this 15 percent rule. If this policy were enforced rigidly, such action would undermine its intent and inhibit the creative energy of researchers. This practice (called "bootlegging" by members of the company) and the 25 percent rule are at the heart of one of 3M's most famous innovations, the yellow Post–It Note.

The Post–It Note

Unlike many of the incremental improvements and innovations made in product lines, the Post–It Note pad was unique, a product entirely unrelated to anything that had ever been developed or sold by 3M. Post–It Notes are ubiquitous in modern business because they do something no product ever did before. They convey messages in the exact spot where people want the messages, and they leave no telltale sign that the message was ever there at all.

This small but powerful idea was begun by a 3M chemist, Spencer Silver; refined by two scientists named Henry Courtney and Roger Merrill; and nurtured from embryo to offspring by Arthur L. Fry. Post–It revenues are estimated at as much as $300 million per year.

Post–It Notes started out as another oddball idea — an adhesive that didn't form a permanent bond — with no perceptible application. In 1964 Silver was working in 3M's central research labs on a program called Polymers for Adhesives. 3M regularly sought ways to improve its major products. Tapes and adhesives were 3M's primary product lines, and adhesives that created stronger bonds were actively sought. Silver found out about a family of monomers that he though might have potential as ingredients for polymer–based adhesives, and he began exploring them.

In the course of this exploration, Silver tried an experiment, just to see what would happen, with one of the monomers and then to see what would happen if a lot more of the monomer was added to the reaction mixture, rather than the amount dictated by conventional wisdom. This in itself was irrational, as in polymerization catalysis, the amounts of interacting ingredients were controlled in tightly defined proportions according to theory and experience. Silver says, "The key to the Post–It adhesive was doing the experiment. If I had sat down and factored it out beforehand, and thought about it, I wouldn't have done the experiment. If I had really seriously cracked the books and gone through the literature, I would have stopped. The literature was full of examples that said you can't do this." To Silver, science is one part meticulous calculation and one part fooling around.

Silver describes what happened with the unusual concoction as a "Eureka moment" — the emergence of a unique, unexpected, previously unobserved and reliable scientific phenomenon. "It's one of those things you look at and you say, This has got to be useful! You're not forcing materials into a situation to make them work. It wanted to do this. It wanted to make Post–It adhesive."

The adhesive became Silver's baby. Silver started presenting this discovery to people who shared none of his perceptions about the beauty of his glue. Interested in practical applications, they had only a passing appreciation for the science embodied in Silver's adhesive. More significantly, they were "trapped by the metaphor" that insists that the ultimate adhesive is one that forms an unbreakable bond. In addition, Silver was immersed in an organization whose lifeblood was tape of all kinds. In this atmosphere imagining a piece of paper that eliminated the need for tape is an almost unthinkable leap into the void.

Silver couldn't say exactly what it was good for. "But it has to be good for something," he would tell them. "Aren't there times," Silver would ask people, "when you want a glue to hold something for awhile but not forever? Let's think about those situations. Let's see if we can turn this adhesive into a product that will hold tight as long as people need it to hold but then let go when people want it to let go."

From 1968 to 1973, support for Silver's idea slipped away. The Polymers for Adhesives program ran out of funding and support, and the researchers were reassigned. Silver had to fight to get the money to get the polymer patented because there was no commercial application immediately present.

Silver was a quiet, well–behaved scientist with an amazing tolerance for rejection. Spencer Silver took his polymer from division to division at 3M, felling that there was something to be said for such a product. He was zealous in his pursuit because he was "absolutely convinced that this had some potential." The organization never protested his search. At every in–house seminar no one ever said to Silver, "Don't try. Stop wasting our time." In fact, it would have violated some very deeply felt principles of the company to have killed Silver's pet project. As long as Silver never failed in his other duties, he could spend as much time as he wanted fooling around with his strange adhesive.

The best idea Silver could come up with on his own was a sticky bulletin board, not a very stimulating idea even to Silver. But 3M did manufacture them, and a few were sold, though it was a slow–moving item in a sleepy market niche. Silver knew there had to be a better idea. "At times I was angry because this stuff is so obviously unique," said Silver. "I said to myself, Why can't you think of a product? It's your job!"

Silver had become trapped by a metaphor. The bulletin board, the only product he could think of, was coated with adhesive — it was sticky everywhere. The metaphor said that something is either sticky or not sticky. Something "partly sticky" didn't occur to him.

Silver and Robert Oliveira, a biochemist whom Silver met in his new research assignment, continued to try selling the idea. Geoff Nicholson, who was leading a new venture team in the commercial tapes division, agreed to see them. Nicholson knew nothing about adhesives and had just taken the position in commercial tapes. Silver and Oliveira were literally the first people to walk through his door. Nicholson says that he was "ripe for something new, different, and exciting. Most anybody who had walked in the door, I would have put my arms around them." Nicholson recruited a team to work on an application for the five–year old discovery. One of these people, Arthur Fry (a chemist, choir director, and amateur mechanic), would make the difference. Fry had "one of those creative moments" while singing in the choir of his church. "To make it easier to find the songs we were going to sing at each Sunday's service, I used to mark the places with little slips of paper. "Inevitably the little slips would flutter to the floor. The idea of using Silver's adhesive on these bookmarks took hold of him at one of these moments. Fry went to 3M, mixed up some adhesive and paper, and invented the "better bookmark." Fry realized that the primary application for the adhesive was not to put it on a fixed surface, such as the bulletin board, but on the paper itself. It was a moment of insight that contemplation did not seem to generate. Fry now has his own lab at 3M and often speaks to large groups of businesspeople about the climate for creativity at 3M. Silver is still in 3M's basement, working out of a cramped, windowless office in a large lab — a place where experimental ferment and scientific playfulness still reign.

The product was not perfected at the moment of Fry's discovery. It still took two more scientists on the Nicholson team — Henry Courtney and Roger Merrill — to invent a paper coating that would make the Post–It adhesive work. Silver said, "Those guys actually made one of the most important contributions to the whole project, and they haven't got a lot of credit for it. The Post–It adhesive was always interesting to people, but if you put it down on something and pulled it apart, it could stay with either side. It had no memory of where it should be. It was difficult to figure out a way to prime the substrate, to get it to stick to the surface you originally put it on. Roger and Hank invented a way to stick the Post–It adhesive down. And they're the ones who really made the breakthrough discovery because once you've learned that, you can apply it to all sorts of different surfaces."

To get the product to manufacturing, Fry brought together the production people, designers, mechanical engineers, product supervisors, and machine operators and let them describe the many reasons why something like that could not be done. He encouraged them to speculate on ways that they might accomplish the impossible. A lifelong gadgeteer, Fry found himself offering his own suggestions. "Problems are wonderful things to have, especially early in the game, when you really should be looking for problems," said Fry.

In trying to solve the problem of one difficult phase of production, Fry assembled a small–scale basic machine in his own basement, which was successful in applying adhesive to paper in a continuous roll. The only problem was that it wouldn't fit through his basement door. Fry accepted the consequences and bashed a hole through the basement wall. Within two years Fry and 3M's engineers had developed a set of unique, proprietary machines that are the key to Post–It Notes' consistency and dependability.

Discussion Questions

1. Describe the creative process that resulted in the Post–It Note pads as we know them today.

2. Identify the factors that fostered and hindered the creative process.

3. Described the characteristics of Spencer Silver.

INTRODUCTION

Organizational creativity and innovation are organizational processes that provoke continuing interest among managers and researchers alike.[1] At the surface level, organizational creativity and innovation are viewed as processes by which individuals working together in a complex social system create a valuable, useful new product, service, idea, procedure, or work process.[2] As such, they play a central role in the long–term survival of organizations and are key processes that must be managed.

Alvin Toffler described this growing turbulence in *Future Shock* in 1970, which was followed by *Third Wave* in 1980. He has now completed his trilogy with *Powershift*, which claims that the accelerated dissemination of information has resulted in a shift of power and wealth.[3] From the old smokestack era with mass production of individual models requiring timely planning and changeovers, we have moved into the new computer–driven economies that make possible designer production and services tailored to specific client needs. The power vested in the stable financial institutions, which existed with the old industrial giants, has been diluted by the shift to designer financial systems and currencies, making a multitude of new enterprises powerful in a global production market. Adding to this mix are the economic and political turbulence (resulting, for example, from the manipulation of budget deficits as special interest groups assert power with the aid of modern media methods) and the social turbulence, arising from changing population demographics and a highly pluralistic society.

There seems to be little question that you and your peers will experience environmental change at an augmented rate never before experienced by humankind. Similarly, organizations in all phases of their life cycles will experience this whirlpool–type environment. In the past organizational behavior practitioners have spoken of "coping with change" as a primary viewpoint for meeting this challenge, but more recently they have broadened this view to include a more proactive strategy of **innovation**, which emphasizes finding new products and new methods to enable organizations to maintain the lead in competitive endeavors. At present the buzzwords *creativity* and *innovation* fill the work world vocabulary. Organizations like Asian Brown Bovery (ABB), General Electric, Ford, IBM, Intel, and Coca–Cola send their employees to training programs where they learn techniques for becoming more creative in their thinking. Numerous games and software are now available to teach people how to become more creative. But let us turn first to defining and exploring the relevant concepts. Next we will present a summary of some of the literature that describes strategies being used in organizations to attain a competitive edge regarding creativity and innovation. We begin by discussing creativity as an aspect of individual effectiveness and then move on to describing innovation in organizational effectiveness.

WHAT IS CREATIVITY?

Recently, an interactionist model of creative behavior was proposed.[4] The interactionist view suggests that **creativity** *is the complex product of a person's behavior in a given situation.* The situation is characterized in terms of the contextual and social influences that either facilitate or hinder creative accomplishments. The person brings to the situation his or her cognitive abilities, personality traits, and noncognitive abilities. The interactionist view provides an integrative framework that combines important elements of personality, cognitive style and abilities and social psychology elements such as leadership dynamics, group dynamics, motivation, organizational elements such as work and organization design, and technology and information technology. Figure 11–1 captures the interactionist model of organizational creativity.

It is probably most useful to start with the view of cognitive psychology that the brain is a creative entity, continuously processing data for problem solving, understanding, and responding, mostly at the unconscious level. We are all creative because the brain is creative. Creative in this sense means processing data to come up with an answer, whether it be "get out of the way of that oncoming truck" (an unconscious response) or arithmetic reasoning (a primarily but not entirely conscious process). There is some evidence that individuals may be either right–brain or left–brain dominant. Right–brain dominant people tend to be more intuitive in their response to problem–solving and learning, and left–brain dominants more logical and rational. Right–brain dominants were thought to be more creative, but more evidence suggests that both sides must work together. Test your own brain dominance at http://www.mindmedia.com/brain.html.

FIGURE 11–1   CONCEPTUAL LINKS AMONG CREATIVE PERSONS, PROCESSSES, SITUATIONS AND PRODUCTS

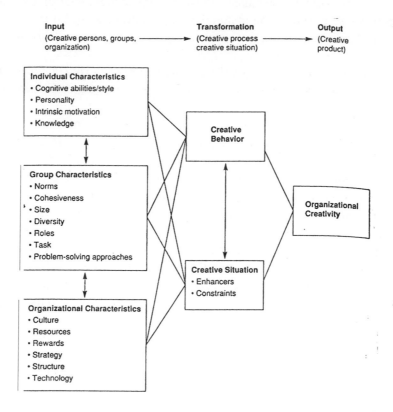

Source: R. W. Woodman, J. E. Sawyer, and R. W. Griffin, "Toward a Theory of Organizational Creativity," *Academy of Management Review* 18, no. 2 (1993), p. 309.

Webster's dictionary defines *creativity* as "the ability to bring something new into existence." Early experiments by Wolfgang Koehler add the element of "insight" to creativity.[5] Koehler placed a piece of fruit outside a chimpanzee's cage and beyond the reach of a stick in the chimp's hand. He placed a longer stick in the vicinity of the fruit. The chimp tried without success to reach the fruit with the short stick. After an extended pause, the chimp suddenly used the short stick to drag the longer one to him and then used the longer stick to haul in the fruit. This sudden flash of insight into the right answer has been referred to as the *aha process* or the *eureka process*.

Scientists long ago[6] developed a process to exploit the "insight" mechanism, and they show up on TV talk shows from time to time to tell about it. When confronted with a difficult problem, they systematically go through several stages:

1. Studying the problem area to realize its different aspects.

2. Saturating the brain with all available data.

3. Allowing incubation time during which the cognitive process at the unconscious level reform and reshape the data.

4. Awaiting enlightenment (insight).

5. Testing hypotheses.

This process is used in many professions. Engineers are intensely aware of this inventive approach. Judges most often do not give decisions until time for incubation is allowed. Architects work and rework designs. All of us do this naturally, but awareness and practice can augment our effectiveness in both our personal and our work lives. (The next time you write a term paper, follow this procedure. After time for incubation, you will be surprised how much better than expected the material will fall into meaningful form so that you can write an excellent paper.) For more information on how you use the creative process, go to http://snow.utoronto.ca/Learn2/creative.htm.

Defining **creativity** as we have used it *refers to brain functions of acquiring and processing data for purposes of problem solving, whether it be responses, answers, actions, or new ideas.* This involves both unconscious and conscious processes.

As we have seen, the interactionist view would advocate the need to stress that in working organizations, everyone has the potential for creativity — to solve problems and to give new ideas. Executives and managers with whom we have worked almost always are looking for "creative people," assuming that "you've either got it (creativity) or you haven't." The implication is that very few have it. Yet most consultant firms readily admit that their recommendations in managerial and organizational effectiveness surveys come primarily from internal sources: the employees they have interviewed. (Of course, these firms have performed the important function of judging the merits of each recommendation.)

There is further support for this idea. In Sternberg's studies, unskilled workers in a milk–processing plant always developed operating procedures that required the least physical efforts. The author reviewed other studies consistent with these findings and concluded, "Beneath the surface of adaptation, however, lie continuing acts of creativity — the invention of new ways of handling old and new problems. Since creativity is a term ordinarily reserved for exceptional individuals and extraordinary accomplishments, recognizing it in the practical problem–solving activities of ordinary people introduced a new perspective from which to grasp the challenge of the ordinary."[7]

Carrying this idea one step further, there is additional evidence for widespread creativity in the multitude of unique ways in which disgruntled workers can come up with methods to resist or even sabotage management.

We know that some people have more new ideas than others have, but we also want to point out that the widespread (and self–fulfilling) expectation system of management overlooks the major contributions that the whole body of the employee system has to offer.[8]

Distinguishing between Creativity and Innovation

Sociologists have long used concepts related to these subjects. Invention represents a completely new idea, often related to technology, that has an impact on societal institutions. **Innovation** *is the reforming or reworking of old ideas to come up with something new.* Both of these ideas would be included in our recent definition of creativity. We mention this here because the term *innovation* is currently being used in organizational settings in a trendy way to mean many things. In much of the literature discussing applications of creativity and innovation, the words are used loosely and often interchangeably. Current usage in organizational behavior defies definition of innovation as a concept. However, J. J. Kao's distinction between creativity and innovation is adequate for our purposes.[9] If creativity implies the vision of what is possible, then the term *innovation* suggests the implementation process by which inspiration leads to the practical results. Creativity involves problem solving that may lead to a useful idea. The term *innovation* is more suitably applied to decision–making processes: the decision to search for a new, useful idea; the decision to select the most useful idea; and the decision of how to implement the chosen idea.

Although creativity depends on many uncontrollable factors (such as the degree of knowledge available; the characteristics, skills, and motivation of the person or persons involved; and a good dose of chance or luck), innovation requires organizational choice and change that can be planned. Finally, an innovation when defined as implementation is not necessarily unique. Successful innovation may result from imitation or adoption of an innovation from another source.

Many people use the term *invention* when they are distinguishing creativity from innovation. However this distinction can be misleading about the nature of creativity. Most of us think of an invention as a tangible, usually technical, product or an idea that can be readily translated into a useful product. This is too limiting a view of creativity. Creativity involves characteristics of the individual exhibiting creative behavior and a process as well as a product.

Creativity can be defined from the person–oriented, process–oriented, and product–oriented perspectives. The **person–oriented approach** to creativity *studies patterns of personality traits and characteristics observed in individuals who exhibit creative behavior.* Such creative behavior might include the activities of inventing, designing, contriving, composing, and planning.[10] The **process–oriented approach to creativity** *examines the development of a new and valuable idea or product through the unique interaction of the individual with the available resources, settings, people, and situations.* The **product–oriented approach to creativity** *focuses on the production of novel and useful ideas by an individual or a small group of individuals working together.* A full understanding of creativity requires an integration of these orientations. An agreement seems to exist that the creative behavior, the creative interaction, and the creative idea need not be successful, commercial, or applied.

Innovation, in contrast, generally refers to the successful application of a new idea to the firm. Success in this case refers to the actual translation of the idea into a useful product or process. An innovation may or may not be profitable or beneficial to the firm. Innovation is a process of developing and implementing a new idea, whether it is a new technology, product, or organizational process. Obviously, creativity can be a part of this implementation process.[11] It may involve recombining old ideas in a new way, a scheme that challenges the present order, or an approach perceived as new by those involved.[12] Note that the idea need not be a breakthrough idea such as superconductivity or a completely new organizational model; it need only be new, or perceived as new, to the organization. Given these distinctions between creativity and innovation, we next examine people's orientation toward creativity.

The Creative Person

The stereotyped image we have of the creative person originates from the mad scientist, the crazy artist, the computer nerd, or the absent–minded professor. We typically think of a collection of personality traits that immediately sets the individual off from others. Do such stereotypes hold? Outstanding creative people have been studied across fields to try to determine the common traits. Unfortunately, the common traits do not come in a precise package that would help you to immediately identify a creative person.

The intelligence level has been of major interest. Exceptionally creative architects, mathematicians, scientists, and engineers usually score no higher on intelligence tests than their less creative peers do. Testing suggests that a certain level of intelligence is related to creativity, but the correlation between the two factors disappears when the person's IQ is above 120. This lack of correlation is particularly important to know in a work setting because managers tend to believe that only the brightest people are apt to be creative.

In general, the literature tends to show that expertise and intrinsic motivation are essential components of creativity — which is another way of saying that the individual has to know the field and want to do something about the problem. The following characteristics also have been related to creativity: high energy level, dedicated and effective work habits, a persistent and high level of curiosity, interest in reflective thinking, relatively little tie to reality, low level of sociability, unusual appreciation of humor, facility for producing humor, need for adventure, need for variety, self–confidence, tolerance of ambiguity, introversion, high need for autonomy, self–direction, and an impulsive personality. Emotional intelligence has recently been linked to effective creativity. Link: http://www.queendom.com/emotionaliq.html.

Emotional Intelligence and Creativity

Leadership and personality play critical roles in shaping human behavior at the workplace. As of late, one of the growing areas that seems to attract attention centers around the role that emotional intelligence plays in leadership and organizations.[13] *Emotional intelligence* is defined *as the ability to sense, understand, and effectively apply the power and acumen of emotions as a source of human energy, information, trust, creativity, and influence.*[14] In a recent book titled *Executive EQ: Emotional Intelligence in Leadership and Organizations*, the authors attempt to demonstrate "… how the science of emotional intelligence has enabled manager after manager, company after company, to begin capturing the single most powerful source of human energy, authenticity, and drive."[15] While the topic of emotional intelligence is beyond the scope of this book, and more empirical research is needed, we want to make the following points:

1. Creativity is one of the 21 scales that map out emotional intelligence.

2. Creativity seems to be influenced by the person's emotional intelligence level.

3. Creativity seems to be influenced by the supervisor/leader/coach's level of emotional intelligence.

4. The emotional intelligence level of the leaders influence the workplace context and dynamics.

Additional links for further investigation of emotional intelligence include the following: http://www.qmetricseq.com and http://www.207.200.142.6/egi–win/mhs.exe/ABIO17.

THE ORGANIZATIONAL CONTEXT OF CREATIVITY

Creativity involves a special kind of problem solving. In organizational settings, attempts have been made to identify potentially creative people by observing the problem–solving behavior. Yet as we have seen, individual creativity is a function of antecedent conditions (i.e., part reinforcement history), cognitive style and ability (i.e., divergent thinking), personality, relevant knowledge, motivation, social influences, and group, unit, and organizational actors.[16]

The Adaption–Innovation Model

The **adaption–innovation model** — and others — *identify two types of people within organizations: adaptors and innovators.*[17] *Adaptors* prefer structured situations, seek answers to the problem at hand, and are perceived by innovators as being rigid, conforming, "safe" people. *Innovators*, on the other hand, appreciate an unstructured work environment, seek to answer questions that have not yet been asked, and are perceived by adaptors as being impractical, abrasive risk takers. Although both types can be found in and are needed in all organizations, research has found that both are capable of generating original creative solutions but from different problem–solving orientations. (See Figure 11–2.)[18]

Motivation and Creativity

We have argued that the personality traits associated with creativity are not enough to guarantee creative behavior. What motivates a person to be creative? The process is complex and involves both intrinsic and extrinsic motivation as well as skills and abilities. The components of individual creativity are shown in Figure 11–3.[19] The framework clusters three components of individual creativity: domain–relevant skills, creativity–related skills and task motivation.

Domain–relevant skills are the general skills in the area (or domain) an individual must bring to the situation. If a person is working on the problem in microelectronics, then he or she must be knowledgeable, talented, and trained, for example, in electrical engineering.

Creativity–relevant skills are the "something extra" that makes the difference in creative performance. The individual's cognitive style is characterized by the ability to break out of old ways of thinking. The individual also depends on a *heuristic* (a general strategy that helps in approaching problems or tasks). A creative heuristic might be "when all else fails, try something counterintuitive" or "make the familiar strange." Finally, the individual's working style must be conducive to creativity. For example, persistence, a long attention span, and the ability to venture off in a new direction when the well–worn direction is not leading to a new idea are all characteristics of a creative work style. Creativity–relevant skills depend on training, experience, and the personality characteristics mentioned earlier.

FIGURE 11-2   CHARACTERISTICS OF ADAPTORS AND INNOVATORS

Implications	Adaptors	Innovators
For problem solving	Tend to take the problem as defined and generate novel, creative ideas aimed at "doing things better." Immediate high efficiency is the keynote of high adaptors.	Tend to redefine generally agreed on problems, breaking previously perceived restraints, generating solutions aimed at "doing things differently."
For solutions	Generally generate a few well–chosen and relevant solutions that they generally find sufficient but that sometimes fail to contain ideas needed to break the existing pattern completely.	Produce numerous ideas, many of which may not be either obvious or acceptable to others. Such a pool often contains ideas, if they can be identified, that may crack hitherto intractable problems.
For policies	Prefer well–established structured situations. Best at incorporating new data or events into existing structures of policies.	Prefer unstructured situations. Use new data as opportunities to set new structures or policies accepting the greater attendant risk.
For organizational "fit"	Essential to the ongoing functions, but in times of unexpected changes may have some difficulty moving out of their established role.	Essential in times of change or crisis, but may have some trouble applying themselves to ongoing organizational demands.
For potential creativity	Capable of generating original, creative solutions, but which reflect their overall approach to problem solving.	Capable of generating original, creative solutions that reflect their overall approach to problem solving.
For collaboration	High adaptors do not get along easily with innovators. Middle adaptors may act as bridges.	High innovators do not get along easily with adaptors. Middle innovators may act as bridges.
For perceived behavior	Seen by innovators as sound, conforming, safe, predictable, relevant, inflexible, wedded to the system, and intolerant of ambiguity.	Seen by adaptors as unsound, impractical, risky, abrasive, often shocking their opposites and creating dissonance.

Source: Adapted with permission from M. J. Kirton, "Adaptors and Innovators: Problem Solvers in Organizations," in *Innovation: A Cross–Disciplinary Perspective*, K. Gronhaug and G. Kaufmann, eds. (Oslo: Norwegian University Press, 1988), p. 72.

FIGURE 11-3   COMPONENTS OF INDIVIDUAL CREATIVITY

Domain-Relevant Skills	Creativity-Relevant Skills	Task Motivation
Includes	*Includes*	*Includes*
Knowledge about the domain	Appropriate cognitive style	Attitudes toward the task
Technical skills required	Implicit or explicit heuristics for generating novel ideas	Perceptions of own motivation for undertaking the task
Special domain–relevant "talent"	Conducive work style	
Depends on	*Depends on*	*Depends on*
Innate cognitive abilities	Training	Initial level of intrinsic motivation to the task
Innate perceptual and motor skills	Experience in idea generation	Presence or absence of salient extrinsic constraints in the social environment
Formal and informal education	Personality characteristics	Individual ability to cognitively minimize extrinsic constraints

Source: Adapted with permission from T. M. Amabile, "From Individual Creativity to Organizational Innovation," in *Innovation: A Cross–Disciplinary Perspective*, K. Gronhaug and G. Kaufmann, eds. (Oslo: Norwegian University Press, 1988), p. 149.

Regardless of the individual's skill level, it is **task motivation** *that determines if these skills will be fully utilized.* If a person is not motivated to do something, no amount of skills can compensate for the lack of motivation. The individual's attitude toward the task is simply the person's natural inclination either toward or away from the task — do I want to do this or not? The individual's perception of his or her motivation, however, depends on factors in the social and work environments. If an individual feels that there are extrinsic motivational factors in the environment intended to control his or her performance of the task (e.g., surveillance, evaluation, deadlines, competition, rewards, and restricted choices), his or her motivation to generate new ideas is likely to suffer. In contrast, if the person does not feel pressures to perform in a certain way or if the person is able to minimize or ignore such pressures, he or she is likely to have a higher level of motivation, even a "passion" for the project.

Creativity and Commitment

One additional element that may be related to the degree of intrinsic motivation is the individual's *commitment* to the organization (the degree to which an employee's personal goals are aligned with the organization's goals). Some authors have suggested that (1) there is a direct connection between level of commitment and motivation to engage in creative behaviors and (2) highly ideological organizations will produce more highly committed individuals.[20]

Creativity and Social Influence

What are the external influences that can operate on the individual, encouraging the display and development of creative potential in the organization? What can be done to increase creative behavior within the organization, that is, to turn a potentially creative person into an actively creative person? We have described some of the factors that can inhibit creativity, but several factors have been identified that have a positive effect on creative behavior. These factors can be organized into the general areas of freedom, support, and participation.[21]

Freedom
Freedom from external constraints can lead to creative behavior. The notion of freedom includes the following managerial actions:
1. Provide freedom to try new ways of performing tasks.
2. Permit activities or tasks to be different for different individuals.
3. Allow an appropriate amount of time for the accomplishment of tasks.
4. Allow time for non–task–related thinking and development of creative ideas.
5. Encourage self–initiated projects.
6. Respect an individual's need to work alone.
7. Encourage divergent activities by providing resources and room.

Support
Non–controlling support can be given in the following ways:
1. Support and reinforce unusual ideas and responses of individuals.
2. Communicate confidence in the individuals.
3. Tolerate complexity and disorder.
4. Provide constructive feedback.
5. Reduce concern over failure.

6. Create a climate of mutual respect and acceptance among individuals.

7. Encourage interpersonal trust.

8. Listen to individuals.

Participation

Involving the individual in the decision–making process as well as the problem–solving process (participation) provides motivation that encourages creative behavior. Participation can be enhanced in the following ways:

1. Encourage individuals to have choices and to be part of the goal–setting process.

2. Encourage involvement of those interested in the problem — don't limit involvement across jobs, departments, and divisions.

3. Challenge individuals to find new tasks and problems.

4. Encourage questioning.

5. Encourage a high quality of interpersonal relationships including a spirit of cooperation, open confrontation of conflicts, and the expression of ideas.

Freedom, support, and participation can be implemented in a variety of ways, depending on the situation. The application of these factors can reduce the extrinsic motivational factors that have a negative effect on creative performance.

DEVELOPING THE CREATIVE PROCESS WITHIN THE ORGANIZATION

The ways of increasing creativity listed previously make up the organizational environment in which the creative process is to take place. The organization must introduce into this context a learning model for operational use. Individuals and teams must be made aware of the **creative process**, which we described in our discussion at the beginning of the chapter, and they must make a systematic effort to allow it to work. Thus in stage 1 the problem is defined in all its dimensions, and decisions are made regarding who will be involved, who has the expertise, and what support is needed. Management needs to select people for participation who have the required domain–relevant skills and task motivation ensuring high–level involvement. In stage 2, data are collected and all available sources are explored. Again, domain–relevant skills and creativity–relevant skills are essential. Stage 3 allows a time lapse for the incubation of ideas and the injection of new data, with the recognition that there will be periods of no progress, that consultation and dialogues may be needed, and that dropping the effort temporarily may be useful. In stage 4, insight (hopefully) comes to the individual or the team in terms of useful ideas or solutions. Finally, in stage 5 some testing and verification is conducted to find out whether the idea will be useful and whether its implementation is possible.

Throughout the creative process, two types of thinking have been identified: divergent thinking and convergent thinking. Divergent thinking is creative thinking. By using divergent thinking, the individual creates new connections between ideas (as in making metaphors) and thinks of many possibilities and alternatives (as in brainstorming). In this type of thinking, a person's built–in censor is temporarily turned off. Convergent or critical thinking involves comparing and contrasting, improving and refining, screening, judging, selecting, and decision making. In the creative process, the individual moves back and forth between these types of thinking. In group settings, different individuals may be valued for their divergent or convergent skills.

Team Creativity

We have focused primarily on the role of the individual in creativity. We noted that under certain conditions teams can achieve *synergy* — a group solution superior to that of the most accurate member's solution. One reason for this superior group solution was that the pool of knowledge in the group was usually greater than that of any individual. Another reason was creativity: Individuals built on others' ideas and produced new ideas. Many factors were at work. There seems to be little doubt that the interactive group process can be productive. However, managers must examine the conditions under which teams can be expected to be more creative or solve problems better than individuals. Certainly the conditions must be right. Expertise is often a major factor for including team members.

From Creativity to Innovation

Once a creative idea has been developed and verified, how does it become meaningful to the organization? The creative process described previously is commonly perceived as the first step in the process of innovation. It is a necessary first step to innovation, whether the innovation is a groundbreaking internal discovery or an idea brought to the organization from the outside. How the process unfolds is a function of the type of innovation, the innovation process itself, and key elements that influence innovation. Innovation is rarely the work of one individual. As we saw in the 3M case, many people, from scientists to managers, were involved in bringing that creative idea to commercial fruition.

ORGANIZATIONAL INNOVATION

Types of Innovation

At the beginning of this module, we defined *innovation* as the successful application of a new idea to the firm. The idea may be a new technology, a new product, or a new organizational or administrative process. The innovation may be an imitation of a product, a person, or an idea used elsewhere, which becomes unique because it is placed within a new context.

We tend to think most often of innovations as **radical innovations** (discontinuous breakthroughs in technology).[22] Often, however, there is an **incremental innovation** (an improvement of a technology, product, or process). A series of incremental innovations can lead to radical innovation, as in the 3M case where Silver discovered the Post–It Note adhesive while experimenting on improving traditional adhesives. Another distinction is between process and product innovations. A zero–defect quality control system is an example of a **process innovation**. **Product innovation** are usually the more visible of the two types, but not necessarily the more important. A product innovation can require process innovation.

Administrative innovations often affect the organization as much or more than technological innovations. New incentive systems and new communication network systems are just two examples of administrative innovations, as are new marketing and sales techniques.

Finally, it is important to make a distinction between **system–maintaining innovation (SMI)** and **system–transforming innovation (STI)**. *SMI refers to new ideas that enhance or improve some aspect of the business without changing the overall nature of how the organization operates. STI refers to a new idea that affects the fundamental aspects of organizing, requiring change in several of the subsystems or segments of the organization in order to fully implement the innovation.*

Stages of the Innovation Process

Although there are many types of innovation, it is generally agreed that the **innovation process** for each is similar. Descriptions of the innovation process have been borrowed from many fields. Group development and problem–solving models,[23] decision process models,[24] and organizational change models[25] have all been applied to the innovation process. These models as well as innovation process models have traditionally viewed the innovation process as occurring in a linear fashion in a series of discrete stages, generally from idea generation to adoption to implementation.[26] Although these activities occur in innovation, there is little empirical evidence for their occurrence in discrete stages. More–recent research has found that the process is more "fluid" than stage theories would suggest.

The Minnesota Innovation Studies Program has been one of the most comprehensive research projects seeking to understand the process of innovation. Based on an in–depth review of longitudinal development of seven major innovations, the researchers of this study made six important observations about the process:

1. An initial shock to the organization precedes innovation. This shock may be new leadership, a product failure, a budget crisis, lack of market share, opportunity, or dissatisfaction of some kind.

2. Ideas proliferate.

3. While ideas are proliferating, setbacks and surprises are likely to occur.

4. These setbacks and surprises provide opportunities for trial–and–error learning and the blending of old and new ideas.

5. Restructuring of the organization at some or all levels occurs.

6. A hands–on approach of top management is evident all the way through the process.[27]

It is evident that this view of the innovation process is not a neat, step–by–step, easily planned activity. How the process unfolds is determined by the elements described next.

KEY ELEMENTS THAT INFLUENCE THE INNOVATION PROCESS

Key Players and Roles

The previous description of the innovation process emphasizes the important role of top management in influencing innovation. Top management not only provides resources for innovation but also provides a vision of the organization and its members as innovative. In addition, several roles required in the innovation process have been described. As early as 1931, the phenomenon of innovation was being studied by J. Schumpeter, an economist.[28] His basis "one–man theory" described characteristics of the "dynamic entrepreneur." This figure is still evident in small and new organizations. However, in larger organizations it makes sense to view a variety of individuals who participate by playing different roles.

The *product champion* is the one who promotes the innovation and overcomes resistance to change. The product champion may or may not have formal power and influence within the organization, but this person has top–management support, which is necessary for success.[29]

The *technical innovator* is the inventor or the person who makes the most significant technical contribution to the innovation. In the 3M case this role may have been shared by Silver and Fry.[30]

The *technological gatekeeper* has been identified as the person who has both technical know–how and formal influence channels to other parts of the organization.[31]

Atmosphere or Climate

The organizational factors that were discussed as positively influencing creativity — freedom, support, and participation — also influence innovation, which is reasonable because creativity and innovation are viewed as parts of the same process. The climate or culture of the organization (the visions and goals, strategies, style of leadership, work setting, characteristics of the individuals, type of work, way people organize to get the work done, qualitative features of the context, and the values and norms of the people) may promote or inhibit innovation. How to measure the creative climate of the organization has been problematic. Using questionnaires and interviews, researchers have had some success discriminating between working climates that are more or less favorable to innovative outcomes.[32]

Organization Design

The relationship between organization design and innovation isn't definite. An early study of organizational innovation identified organic versus mechanistic organizations as likely to encourage innovation.[33] Bureaucracy, with its formal hierarchical levels, has often been identified as the mechanistic organization, whereas the organic organization has been described as flat. However, other researchers have argued that no one form of organization is superior to another in terms of being conducive to innovation; rather, it is the links for collaboration and problem solving throughout the organization that are important.[34] Reorganization during the process of innovation is likely to result in different designs as well as structures.

Incentives, Rewards, and Evaluation

We have seen that expected evaluation has been found to have a detrimental effect on creativity and that external incentives must stimulate intrinsic motivation. It is not so clear how reward systems contribute to creative and innovative effort. One view is that rewards based on seniority rather than performance tend to inhibit innovation and creativity, whereas merit–based systems, in which individual performance is rewarded, stipulate creativity.

However, in Japan, where lifetime employment systems and seniority–based reward systems in large organizations are the norm, long–range thinking appears to be promoted, and there seems to be less necessity to resist new ideas (and freedom to fail) because a person's promotion and rewards are not based on short–term performance.[35] Innovative firms generally have innovative incentive and reward systems, which acknowledge both individual and group efforts in non–threatening ways.

Job Design, Job Rotation, and Careers

Jobs that offer intrinsic motivation to perform well, that involve the employee, and that provide variety and autonomy tend to increase innovative levels of activity. Recently, career planning involving **dual ladders** has gained a lot of attention. In a **dual–ladder system**, *a high–performing individual may choose to climb the managerial or technical ladder, depending on his or her own personal preferences and goals.* Companies such as 3M, Monsanto, Eastman Kodak, and General Mills have successfully implemented dual–ladder systems, which they've found lead to more open communications, are an aid in recruiting, and provide better advancement opportunities for people at all levels.[36] To be successful, the dual–ladder system requires the full commitment of management.

MANAGEMENT'S CHALLENGE

If creativity and innovation are both parts of a process that is becoming a greater and greater necessity in today's organizations, then managers must become aware of how this process can be managed. Innovation is not a simple, straightforward process. Innovation implies change, although not all change is innovation. Just as there is no one way to organize, there is no one way to encourage innovation. Innovation is risky, and the manager's role in this process can be likened to a balancing act. On the one hand, he or she must provide the stability, support, and security that free employees from the fear of failure. On the other hand, the manager must encourage risk taking, which is likely to result in new ideas that are beneficial to the organization as a whole.

Part of this challenge is to hire, train, and develop a set of individuals with not only a variety of specialized and technical skills and abilities but also skills in problem solving, communication, conflict resolution, and team building. Another part of the challenge is to retain these employees not only through innovative reward and incentive systems but also by providing the vision, resources, autonomy, and support they need.

This is far from an easy task. Innovative environments are turbulent, and the innovation process requires the management of change as an integral part of organizational and managerial routines. In addition to providing a free, supportive, and participative environment to encourage creative thinking, management must also deal with resistance to change, which is likely to occur in some parts of the organization when an innovation is developed.

All of these elements demand that the manager be involved in an ongoing, creative problem–solving process. Creativity and innovation rely on creative and innovative management processes.

Cautions on Creativity

When expectations for creativity and innovation in the work world are high, there are bound to be counterproductive excesses. Young people may feel they will not be regarded as having high potential if they are not offering new ideas; and managers can feel they are not providing a supportive climate if they do not try new ideas. A "change for the sake of change" approach can be disruptive and must be guarded against. "If it's not broken, don't fix it" is often good advice.

SUMMARY

In this module we have examined the organizational process that begins with creativity at the individual or team level and culminates in an innovation that contributes to the success of the organization as a whole. We have defined *creativity* as the brain functions of acquiring and processing data for the purposes of problem solving, whether it be responses, answers, actions, or new ideas. Creativity involves both unconscious and conscious processes. A five–stage process for the individual to utilize in producing creative reactions was given. Innovation, in contrast, was defined as the implementation process through which creative ideas are transformed into practical applications in the organization.

KEY TERMS AND CONCEPTS

Adaption–innovation model	Innovation
Creativity	Person–oriented creativity
Creativity–relevant skills	Process–oriented creativity
Domain–relevant skills	Product–oriented creativity
Dual ladders	System–maintaining innovation (SMI)
Emotional intelligence	System–transforming innovation (STI)
	Task motivation

DISCUSSION QUESTIONS

1. Creativity and innovation are different parts of the same process. Can an innovation occur without creativity? Discuss why or why not.

2. "The creative person is born, not made." Do you agree or disagree? Why?

3. Charlie likes to wrestle with a problem for several days or weeks, looking at it from all sides. Janet focuses on solving the problem efficiently and doesn't worry if she has considered all possible solutions. Which of the two is likely to be more creative? Why?

4. Sam loves his job because it is open–ended and he decides what to do each day. He works hard, often forgetting to quit at 5 P.M. Discuss Sam's motivation.

5. List the five steps in the creative process. Identify the skills required at each step.

6. Think of an innovation that you would consider radical. How does it differ from an incremental innovation?

7. Mr. Jones has just returned from a short course on innovative management and has decided to reorganize his firm to increase innovation. He has isolated the scientists and design engineers in one building so they won't be disturbed by the production people and the marketing and sales forces. Is Mr. Jone's plan likely to increase innovative activity? Why?

8. Two employees of a high–tech firm began their careers with the firm as design engineers. Both are highly skilled, creative workers. Employee A now manages the production research department. Employee B has a private lab in the basement. Both are very satisfied. Discuss career choices and personal and organizational factors that led to this situation.

9. You are designing a new incentive and reward system for a research and development lab. All the employees have advanced engineering degrees, and the market for their skills is very competitive. How would you structure such a system?

10. Mrs. White has just been hired to run a large, nationwide temporary employee company. The former CEO suggests to her that she might be interested in attending a seminar on managing innovation. Mrs. White laughs and says, "Why would I want to do that? We're not concerned with innovation around here. That's something for managers of high–tech companies." Do you agree or disagree with Mrs. White? Explain your answer.

ACTIVITY 11–2: DOWNSIZING AND CREATIVITY

OBJECTIVE:

To examine the relationship between company restructuring and creativity.

Task 1 (Individual):

Read the following section, connect to the 3M Web site, and answer the questions at the end of the section.1

Task 2:

Class discussion.

Current Events at 3M Company

In spite of 3M's legendary history of fostering entrepreneurial innovation within the company, 1988 revenues were flat. Projections of dependable earnings were down 3 percent. The slowdown of the Asian economies cost the company hundreds of millions in lost profits. Even though 30 percent of sales have come from products released in just the past four years, entrepreneurial freedom has caused some experiments to lie dormant in the lab for years. According to *U.S. News and World Report* (December 21, 1998, p. 50), the company's new product portfolio for the 1990s was "horrendous."

3M has introduced a new program call Pacing Plus, designed to identify high–potential products earlier and release them faster and to drop underperforming products. It hopes to reduce the workforce by 6 percent in response to slower growth, but through attrition rather than layoffs. In addition, 3M has increased the number of partnerships by 36 percent, abandoning its "go–it–alone" mindset. However, 3M continues to resist radical restructuring.

Continue to search for current information about 3M. You can connect to 3M at www.3M.com.

QUESTIONS:

1. What do you think is the effect of radical restructuring on creativity and the innovation process?

2. The pressure to innovate has increased at 3M. How will this environment affect the creativity and innovation process?

ACTIVITY 11–3: ORGANIZATIONAL INNOVATION:
Learning from the WWW

OBJECTIVE:

Reflecting on organizational innovation by learning from information on the WWW.

Task 1 (Individual):

Go to the Innovation Network Web site on articles and reports on organizational innovation: www.thinksmart.com.

What are some of the skills most critical to the organizations that were 1998 Land Award winners for innovation?

Task 2 (Team):

Each team is to share its learning and prepare a three–minute presentation based on its collective learning.

ACTIVITY 11–4: Making a Metaphor

OBJECTIVE:

To explore individual paradigms that affect individual creativity. A metaphor is a figure of speech in which we liken two objects or concepts that do not appear to be alike. Through metaphor we can make connections and discoveries that did not previously exist. We can make the familiar strange and thus challenge our way of thinking. In the 3M case, metaphors had to be changed so people could break through old mental sets.

Task 1:

Complete the following metaphors, choosing from one of the options given or making up your own.

Eating a fine dinner is like
a.   Throwing a javelin a long distance.
b.   Watching an hourglass drip sand.
c.   Reading a popular novel at the beach.
d.   Putting nail polish on your toes.

Raising a child is like
a.   Driving from Seattle to New York.
b.   Weeding your garden.
c.   Building a fire and watching it burn.
d.   Fishing for rainbow trout.

Playing a piano recital is like
a.   Investing in the stock market.
b.   Growing orchids.
c.   Driving through rush hour traffic with your gas gauge on empty.
d.   Fasting for three days.

Finding truth is like
a.   Making banana nut bread.
b.   Walking into a room and forgetting the reason why.
c.   Navigating a sailboat through a violent thunderstorm.
d.   Taking a test that has no wrong answers.

Task 2:

Share your metaphors with your group. Explain why you chose the metaphor you did. The instructor will facilitate a class discussion on the use of metaphors and creativity.

Source: This activity is adopted with permission from R. von Oeck, *A Kick in the Seat of the Pants* (New York: Warner Books, 1986), p. 72.

ACTIVITY 11–5: Fostering Creativity and Innovation in the Intercon Semiconductor Company

OBJECTIVE:

To identify the organizational elements that affect innovation and creativity.

Task 1:

a. Students are to read the Intercon Semiconductor Company case.
b. Students are to analyze the case and provide answers to President Bergman's dilemma.

Task 2:

Class discussion will be facilitated by the instructor.

CASE STUDY: THE INTERCON SEMICONDUCTOR COMPANY

BACKGROUND AND COMPANY EVOLUTION

Intercon was founded in 1961 as the first company worldwide to exclusively manufacture integrated circuits. The company's evolution resulted in six product line divisions and two specific market divisions. Each division designed, manufactured, and marketed its own products. The divisions were organized into the following groups: Metal–Oxide Semiconductor (MOS), Linear Large–Scale Integration (LSI) products group, Linear LSI, MOS Microprocessor, MOS Memory Bipolar Digital products groups, Logic, Bipolar LSI, Bipolar Memory, Military, and Automotive/Telecommunications. The Military and Automotive/Telecommunications divisions used products from each of the other six and packaged and tested them for their markets.

The company was headquartered on the East Coast with additional production facilities throughout the western United States and overseas.

In 1975, Intercon became a wholly owned subsidiary of U.S. Kunikon Corporation, a subsidiary of the European electrical and electronic multinational firm. Intercon operated independently of Kunikon, but relied on interchange of products and technology with Kunikon International.

The European firm bought and sold Intercon products under the Intercon name and supplied Intercon with innovative products. A Kunikon research laboratory located near Intercon headquarters housed scientists and technicians from both companies.

Intercon made most of its sales growth and reputation in bipolar technology, including programmable read–only memories (PROMs), integrated fuse logic (IFL), arrays, an 8–bit microcontroller family, emitter–coupled logic (ECL) and integrated shotkey logic (ISL) gate arrays, small–scale integration (SSI)/medium–scale integration (MSI) logic, and analog MSI/LSI circuits.

Though it was primarily seen as a generic transistor–transistor–logic (TTL) manufacturer, Intercon was developing as well into a producer of innovative very large scale integrated (VLSI) products and a supplier of metal–oxide semiconductor (MOS) products. Other developments included complementary MOS (CMOS) and n–channel MOS (NMOS) expertise and capacity. By 1983, production began of 256K NMOS read–only memories (ROMs), and the company achieved full production of MOS VLSI 8/16–bit microcomputers and peripherals. Intercon viewed its main strengths in production of MOS products including the 68000 16/32–bit microprocessor family, the NMOS and CMOS 8048/8051 8–bit midrange microcontroller family and static memory products such as ROMs, CMOS, EPROMs, CMOS static RAMs, and LSI CMOS and NMOS analog/digital signal processing circuits.

By 1983, Intercon had 18,000 employees and had grown since 1972 at a compounded annual growth rate of 26 percent (excluding the 1981–82 recession), outpacing industry growth by 7 percent. Revenues in 1983 were $600 million and were projected to triple by 1988.

Current Status of the Company

Once the boom years were over, the company faced not only shrinking markets but competition from abroad in production effectiveness and pricing as well. Intercon underwent a major reorganization and a new reporting structure. In August 1985, Intercon announced a zero–defects warranty on all of its semiconductor products. It was the first IC company to offer the warranty. According to Quality and Reliability Director W. A. Stephens, zero defects is "really a selfish thing. It is the best way and the most cost–effective way to run a company." The zero–defects warranty was the result of several years of attempts to improve quality control. In late 1979, a 14–step quality improvement process had been initiated, based on Philip Crosby's "zero defects" system. By 1985 the process of quality control had taken hold so that defects were eliminated at their source, through prevention, whereas previously a defect level of 1,000 parts per million had been acceptable.

Currently Intercon has over 15,000 employees, making it one of the largest companies in the semiconductor industry. Its relationship with the European–based Kunikon makes it the beneficiary of Kunikon's current overseas endeavors, including a joint venture with another multinational in the attempt to produce an unusually large memory chip. Kunikon is also researching gallium arsenide, which can process information 10 times faster than silicon; this is part of the corporate–directed effort to be first to the market with ultrahigh–speed superconductors, which will revolutionize the industry.

Intercon faces the same concerns that are faced by most large American–based semiconductor firms. In his April 1987 message, President Martin Bergman expressed the belief that Intercon had the fundamental strengths — the ability to respond quickly to the 1985 recession, the opportunities afforded by pooling strengths with Kunikon's worldwide organization, a zero–defects philosophy, and a nucleus of talented personnel — to respond to future shifts in the market.

Source: This case was developed by A. B. (Rami) Shani and C. Sexton.

Company Strategy

President Bergman believed that the restructuring of Intercon was designed to make it "more strategic, more competitive, and, ultimately, more profitable." According to VP of Sales and Marketing Mike Walker, there was one goal: "meeting the customer's every need. We have restructured this company with that single goal in mind."

A primary goal was to become a significant competitor in the worldwide market in MOS technology, while maintaining a leading edge in standard products in the linear division. LSI VP Martin Stanley remarked, "The challenge for us is to develop individual strategies within our product areas while maintaining a coordinated strategy between them — synergy in the marketplace that makes us as close to one–stop shopping as we can be."

Strategic Marketing Manager Linda Grant explained that "Learning the technology, our human resources, our processes, our customers, and our strengths and weaknesses in our markets is the beginning of developing strategic direction. Currently we are still a product–line–driven company. We have yet to develop the true market–driven–based strategy that is anchored in our strengths. Ideally we would try to match and deal with both a product and a market–based strategic plan. We don't have a clear direction where we are going to be or a clear sense of priority for the entire corporation. We don't have a cohesive overall priority–based strategy that is communicated by top management to the lower levels. Divisions do have their own strategies but we are not globally optimized without having the overall strategy and a clear set of priorities. We need to find the mechanism that will help us develop the shared vision for the entire corporation."

Business unit managers and functional managers within the units expressed concern over the market–driven orientation. "We need to be structured according to where the product is going. We lack product marketing engineers — people with engineering and technical backgrounds," stated Marketing Manager Martin. "We've still not made the full transition from our old philosophy. Products or devices fall between the cracks. Top management needs to decide whether we are market–driven or whether we can continue to drive the market. Doing both is confusing, both internally and in terms of our image."

The commitments to becoming a marketing–driven company and to having a zero–defects philosophy were considered key elements of strategy that would maintain and develop Intercon as the world leader in an industry where the large firms traditionally had difficulty in applying specifics because of the high degree of customer involvement. Application Specific Products (ASP) Marketing Manager Kelly Martin stated that the company "has the ability to bring something to the customer that he doesn't have — a highly reliable source of application–specific ICs."

Since the IC industry had become worldwide, a "global perspective and global presence" (in President Bergman's words) was required for success, and the relationship with Kunikon International afforded that presence and perspective. The relationship with North American Kunikon as well as the more recent relationship with Kunikon International were issues in the company strategy. According to R&D VP Paul Bracken, "I believe that once you are in the multinational company you can, if you learn the system and learn the roles, do almost everything that you want. The economic struggle between us and Kunikon can either hinder us or explode into hyperactivity and very innovative work and products. The current struggle for autonomy between us and U.S. Kunikon does not permit us to take part in the innovation process as it is currently being conducted in other parts of the world. By limiting contact, you actually hinder the innovation process."

Harvey Sparling, vice president of Consumer/Standard Linear Products, noted an additional adjustment was necessary as part of Kunikon International. "We have a four–year strategic plan which we review quarterly. Kunikon requires us to have a five– to eight–year strategic plan."

Company Design

Figure 11–4 shows the company prior to the recent major restructuring. The company was designed along functional lines with the two major product groups — MOS and Bipolar — determined by technology.

The new structure appearing in Figure 11–5 was designed to strip major product groups of their technological differences based on the major MOS and Bipolar technologies and restructure the company into groups differentiated by greater orientation to commodity versus leading–edge innovations products. The absolute number of divisions was reduced from eight to five to accommodate the pressure to find economies of scale. The technology development groups (which were previously separated within the two product groups) were combined into R&D. The new structure depended far more on integrated interfaces across functional groups within and across divisions and a more companywide team–oriented approach to making decisions about which new products to invest in.

The current design was both strongly supported and questioned. Sales and Marketing VP Walker expressed the belief that how well the firm assesses the environment is the key to its success. The current business unit design supports the attempt to get closer and sense the environment by developing a network of relationships with the entire industry and utilize the process to collect all the variable information.

However, Linear Division VP Jonathan Lee remarked, "When I compare the business unit organization with the functional–based organization, I strongly believe that the functional organization has more advantages. The business unit structure fosters independence that results in limited sharing across the business unit boundaries."

FIGURE 11-4   **INTERCON ORGANIZATIONAL CHART**

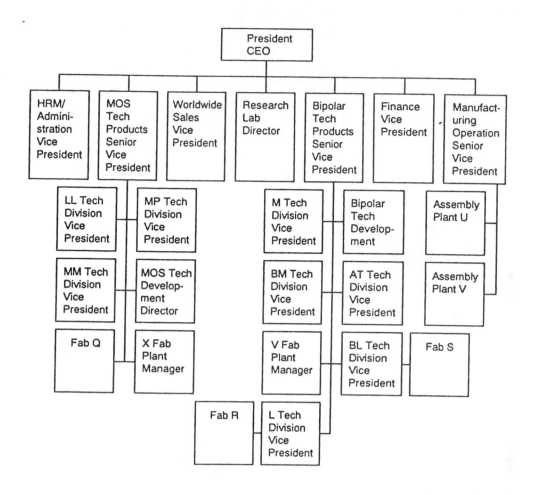

COMPANY INNOVATION

Although logic and bipolar memory were the mainstays of the company during its growth, Intercon sought to maintain its competitive edge by developing new products and areas of expertise. According to President Bergman, "The key to any company's success is product development, but we [need to] develop products that have clear and specific market segments to serve and that we are capable of manufacturing. The situation of the industry requires innovation, new product development, and a second–source house orientation. We need to make sure, however, that we keep developing new products in a timely fashion in order for us to continue our success and maintain our image. Designing the company so that it will accomplish innovation and will be a good second–source house is a challenge that we are still struggling with."

The company had committed major resources to innovation in the areas of application–specific and microprocessors. Moving from a technology–driven philosophy to a marketing–driven one had required, beyond product innovation, innovation in terms of methodology, processes, tools, strategy, and organizational structure.

According to R&D VP Bracken, "Innovation is more than the development of a concept into the product objectives specification that meets the business criteria and into product execution. It is actually the formulation of the concept itself. Management recognition and support of the new concept idea is innovation. It takes innovation on the part of management to recognize it."

FIGURE 11-5   **REVISED INTERCON ORGANIZATIONAL CHART**

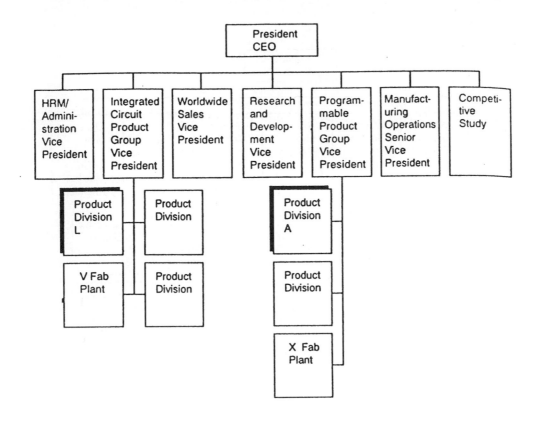

VP of Programmable Products Kurt Nilssen stated that the company had identified four basic needs, including innovation. "We have technological needs — technology that we want to demonstrate — and customer needs — we develop good relationships with the customers and they identify for us their needs or problems requiring solutions. We have pure research needs, and finally we have innovative needs, namely, artificial expert systems. We are convinced that this is the direction to go."

Consumer Standard Business Unit Manager Jay Samuelson asserted that innovation is "what causes things to happen — 25 percent of what we do should be geared toward this important asset."

COMPANY DIVISIONS

Figure 11–5 shows that currently there are two main product groups within the company and a total of five product divisions. The remainder of this case study will describe the dynamics of two major product divisions called Division L and Division A (one from each product group.) Because the company is so complex, it was felt that an in–depth description of two divisions, identified by corporate as representative samples of company divisions, be made rather than provide a broad, but necessarily shallow overview of every division within the company. Division L and Division A exhibit two parallel company orientations with different strategic orientations for interfacing with the company and its competitive environment.

Division L

Design: Division L is made up of independent business units based on product orientation and an integrative marketing department for the entire division. Each business unit includes its own marketing department, design department, product engineering department, and test engineering department. The current divisional struggle is shown in Figure 11–6.

FIGURE 11-6   **INTERCON DIVISION L**

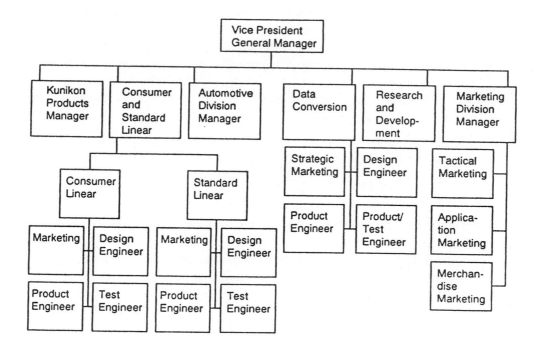

A key feature of the structure is the team concept. For example, the standard linear business unit is described as a *quality improvement team (QIT)*, and the functional areas within the unit are designated as *make certain teams (MCTs)*. Specific problem–solving activity is handled by *corrective action teams (CATs)*. Though the team concept is stressed, the issues of individual differences and competition across functional boundaries have arisen. According to Standard Linear Product Engineer Manager Duane Fulton, "It is a constant war around here. We don't share the same goals. People do not confront each other. Many of the battles are fought under the table. There is conflict suppression on every issue."

Standard Linear Marketing Manager Miles Wilson added, "We are very fragmented within the division. The structure creates too strong boundaries, yet the definition of territory is not as clear."

Strategy: Although Standard Linear Business Unit Manager Rex Fogelberg noted, "We need to find the balance between technological and market innovation so that we can meet the needs of both our customers and our people," the tension involved in creating this strategic balance between technology push and market pull is pronounced.

Design Engineer Manager Eli Chou commented, "The technological component should be represented higher up in the hierarchy. You cannot leave out the technology people. Marketing people tend to see what is out there now, what the customer wants. Technology tends to see what is in the future from a technology standpoint. Don't shut us middle management off by saying that we are marketing driven."

Division Manager Simon Adams summarized the division's concern over the market versus technology issue and the viability of the division and company's goals and strategies. "The movement toward vertical marketing and product–specific markets is a series of concentrated efforts being made by the company. Yet it is often asked around here whether this is the right way to go and, if so, how should we proceed?"

Innovation: Innovation in this division is identified primarily as an engineering/design process, yet Consumer/Linear Test Engineer George Gasparian remarked, "Product and test engineers should be involved in an earlier phase in a collaborative mode that might aid in stimulating design engineers to develop more innovative products."

Product Engineer Manager Fulton agreed. "The product engineer can be innovative by looking at the critical parameters within the time frame so that directions for their resolutions can emerge. The product engineer can be the igniter for innovation by the designers or test engineers."

Design Engineer Manager Sharad Johal expressed the sentiment that management "does not understand the problems that the design engineer faces. It is very hard to convince management to provide the funds to support the process. Management structure is not as responsive as it should be. Business managers dominate here. In other companies there is a technology director. Here we don't have that. The design manager feels alone. There is no forum for us, the middle management, to present our ideas or issues of technological challenges to the top. It is very difficult to get through to the hierarchy. It is like speaking two different languages."

Throughout the division, engineers and managers expressed their views of what management might do to foster innovation:

"Managers should allow innovation to happen by keeping control over the work and by making sure that the designers or engineers have adequate tools."

"Management needs to provide the freedom for development and at the same time create clearly defined boundaries so that things are not allowed to drift."

"Management needs fewer time constraints. We need to rethink the time structured into one's week if we're really committed to new ideas."

The Product Development Process (PDP): The PDP refers to the number and types of interactions and evaluations that occur between the initial formulation of an idea and its ultimate introduction into the market. It is an evolutionary process characterized by three major factors: research, development, and implementation. The PDP is variously described in the division. Some perceive it as beginning with the identification of new markets or a literature search for new ideas, while others see it as beginning with the new product release (NPR). Consumer/Standard Business Unit Manager Dave King identified 12 elements of the PDP (see Figure 11–7): the customer, marketing, design, characterization, data sheet specification, fabrication, die sort, assembly, final testing where cooperation takes place, quality assurance, production control, and sales — which lead directly back to the customer.

FIGURE 11-7   **PRODUCT DEVELOPMENT PROCESS, DIVISION L**

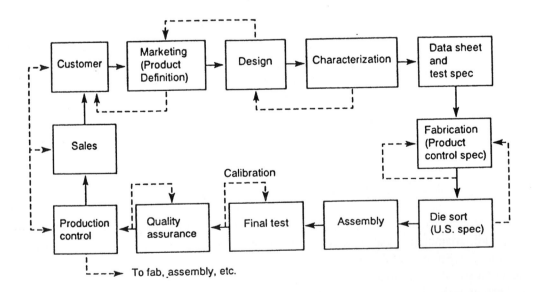

Although various stages of the PDP could be identified, a definite pattern was not always established. According to Marketing Division Manager Blake Lawler, "The PDP cannot always be sequential, especially in our case where the market moves too fast. As a result, there are times when the NPR is signed off after the product is already completely designed."

The importance of each phase and the order of the phases will vary throughout the division, depending on the function of the engineers. Test Engineer Gasparian felt that the "most critical and biggest problem is the phase where we determine how to test the product." Yet product engineer managers believed that product planning was the most critical.

The marketing–versus–technology question arises with regard to the PDP, ranging from marketing's "We are not fully incorporating the customer throughout the entire PDP," to Design Engineer Manager Johal's not seeing the need for "making the customer part of the PDP. The company probably has more to lose than to gain from it."

Business Unit Manager King remarked, "The design engineers are not close to the customers as they should be. We have a lot of holes in the specifications given by the marketing guys based on their understanding of the customers. It is at this stage that the discrepancy occurs around the interpretation of what the customer really needs."

Division Manager Adams main concern was "the relationship between the new product idea brought forward by the customer, the strategic marketing people, who believe they know the market (but who don't always know it), and design engineers, who are supposed to work together with the strategic marketing people and the customer. Being in the middle is problematic. Who has control over the product? Is it the customer, is it the engineer, or is it marketing?"

Division A

Design: The Structure in Division A is a combination of functional–based and product–based design. The Programmable Linear Devices (PLD) group, which is the strongest and most stable group, is organized along functional lines. The semicustom group is formulated along product lines. The reorganized structure of Division A is shown in Figure 11-8.

FIGURE 11-8   **INTERCON DIVISION A**

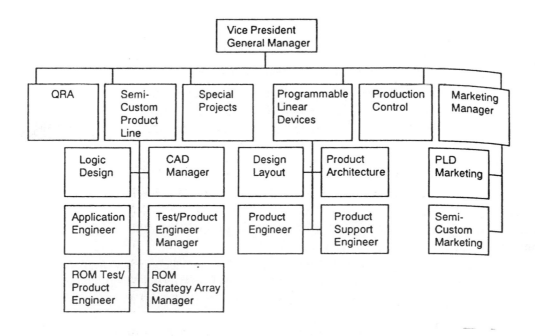

Division members expressed various concerns about the effect of company structure and design on their division. PLD Design Engineer Paul Sakamoto commented, "The structure of the company gets in the way. The decision–making process is hindering, delaying the decision is causing us a lot of damage. Top–level management should delegate decision–making authority to lower levels and not centralize more and more decision making at headquarters."

Marketing Manager Andrea White was optimistic about further changes in the structure of Division A's marketing group. "Currently I am working on redesigning the structure to include three subgroups: the strategic application group, the tactical marketing group, and the strategic business group. I believe this kind of design would help us accomplish our mission and position ourselves best in the marketplace and really enhance creativity and innovation. I believe that we can actually develop a long and lasting solid relationship with our customers."

Semicustom Business Unit Manager Al Younger commented on the effect of organizational structure on the ability to innovate. "We deliver sole–source products; therefore, we are limited in freedom to take risks. The bureaucratic procedures also hinder new product development. We need to try to minimize the bureaucratic process and to be sensitive to individual needs."

Strategy: The market–driven aspect of company strategy is emphasized here. PLD Engineer Sakamoto remarked that "We are a broad–line company, and as a result we are more market driven. For the PLD group, we are driving the market. Lack of focus or clear direction is one of our struggles. The currently shortsighted view of top management is hindering the entire process."

Various marketing personnel within the division made the following comments:

"There are things that we need to do to be viable in the market. The first priority is to satisfy customers, and the second priority is to develop new products and come up with new innovations."

"The real challenge is to go out and segment the market."

"We need to understand the marketplace first. Educating the customer is critical."

PLD Marketing Manager Rod Ellsworth commented, "Strategically, the technical reactive mode used to be our company's approach. Currently we are trying to break away from that mode. We have quarterly meetings with the field people and engineers to share ideas, and we make each party familiar with other current practices, thoughts, and ideas. In terms of decision making, a strategic roadmap is used as a criterion for making decisions."

The role management played within the company appeared to many to be the key to the success of its strategy. Design Engineer Manager Elliot Shields remarked, "Management today is entirely business bottom–line oriented. Managers truly don't understand the complexity of what we do. Top management must understand that we need to differentiate ourselves from other companies, not just through bottom–line production of the same product. Management wants quick returns and therefore it's very tough, if not impossible, to be very innovative."

Division Manager Mark Tenor noted, "Senior management should provide vision. We have had serious problems with it. It is our fault that we did not provide it for our employees. I know where we are going as a division. I still have a lot to do in developing shared vision throughout the division. We are only one year old as a division."

Innovation: In this division, the concept of innovation is frequently expressed in terms of product and technology development.

R&D VP Bracken described innovation as an "interactive process. It is the ability to manage the three groups: design, layout, and computer–aided design (CAD)."

PLD Design Engineer Sakamoto said, "Innovation is defining a new technology or process. Innovation is development of the right tool to integrate the products. Putting the tools in the design layout phase is where I will put my resources in order to foster innovation. We need to provide the design engineers with the state–of–the–art technological processes so that they can be innovative."

Time, freedom, recognition, and stimulation are seen as requirements for innovation. Sakamoto believed it was important to give people the freedom to do the job, assign people the responsibility to a part, and let them know that its success is dependent on them without a continuous need for monitoring its progress. Upper–level management should know and be familiar with what their people do. They need to express appreciation and recognition and to provide equitable rewards. Top–level management should be concerned about the company.

Design engineers were generally in agreement about criteria for innovation:

> "Stimulating the thinking process within the individual is critical for the manager in facilitating or fostering innovation. The challenge is to give people the time and the space that they need. Driving people to innovation is hindering innovation."

> "We need to find a way to recognize and acknowledge the innovative people and to provide people the time to think without special pressure. Short–term innovation is hindering the innovation process. Management needs to let people go and develop the product without too many other assignments. The tight schedule and the number of projects at any given time is hindering the ability to be really innovative."

Division Manager Tenor commented, "If innovation is a goal, we need to free the people that are innovative to do innovation. We need to free them from everyday operation functioning, and we truly need to stand behind them with the most updated state–of–the–art technology and processes."

Product Development Process (PDP): Some descriptions of the PDP in this division are of highly technical, specialized stages; others describe more of a flow from the customer through the process and back to the customer. R&D Specialist Kenny Walsh defined the PDP as "composed broadly of the following phases: idea, generation, new product review (NPR) document, NPR board review, design and layout, masks, fabrication, characterization phase, and code 1 (release for production)."

In contrast, Application Specific Marketing Manager White defined several phases in the PDP (see Figure 11–9): "In the stimulation source phase there are three elements: technology, study, competitive study, and a study they call seeing a 'better mouse trap.' Next we have the company phase, which leads to the idea generation element, which in turn leads to a feasibility assessment phase, followed by the initial market analysis phase. Market analysis is also exposure to the next phase, which is the customer."

The PDP is perceived to have a variety of strengths and weaknesses in this division. Design Engineer Manager Shields noted, "The time that it takes to pass the qualification process can take as much time as the entire design process. The more guidelines we have, the less flexible we are, and the less innovative we are going to be."

Semicustom Business Manager Younger felt that "Training the customer is the most critical thing. The customer will be as good as you train him. The company is not hiring the right people, the professional trainers."

Division Manager Tenor commented on two weak points that he felt were hindering the innovation in the PDP. "First and most critical is our technology: manufacturing technology, process development technology, and design development technology. We are not using the most up–to–date technology on all three fronts. Second, we are weak at the concept definition. The Japanese have put a lot of resources to develop the next–generation technology. We have done very little with it. Furthermore, their designers are coming up with very good and creative design which is relatively new. Historically, they are very good at duplicating our designs, but now their designs are coming from unique, innovative ideas."

Sakamoto also remarked about the lack of resources. "We don't have enough resources to evaluate the up–to–date tools that we might need or can use. Integration of tools across groups is problematic in the integration and interface between the design and marketing. It should be worked on continuously."

Besides resources, time was also perceived as a critical factor. According to Marketing Manager White, "The amount of time that it takes to make a decision, the time to market, is critical. Once you start the PDP, you can do all you can to reduce the time, but if it takes a year from the first idea to the start of the design, you lose your market. We have a lot of ideas that were proposed that took too long, about a year on average."

Design Manager Shields added that "The rest of the PDP is pushed hard to cut time. This is wrong. You force the designers into using tricks to enhance the process to look better than it really is."

FIGURE 11-9   **PRODUCT DEVELOPMENT PROCESS, DIVISION A**

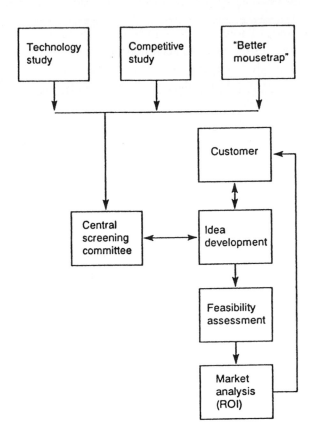

PRESIDENT BERGMAN'S DILEMMA

As President Bergman prepared to meet with his top executives, he wondered what steps should be taken next by the company. Three things particularly troubled him. First, how could he develop a better shared vision of the company's competitive strategy? Second, what could the company do to both foster and shorten the new product development process? Third, how could the company achieve optimal alignment of its competitive strategy, organization design, and new product development process while maintaining zero–defect production and increasing bottom–line profit?

* This module was revised by Dr. Carol Sexton. We are grateful to Carol.

NOTES

1. See, for example, S. G. Scott and R. A. Bruce, "Determinants of Innovative Behavior: A Path Model of Individual Innovation in the Workplace," *Academy of Management Journal* 37, no. 3 (1994), pp. 580–607; R. J. Sternberg, L. A. O'Hara, and T. I. Lubart, "Creativity as Investment," *California Management Review* 40, no. 1 (1997), 8–21; C. J. Nemeth, "Managing Innovation: When Less Is More," *California Management Review* 40, no. 1 (1997), pp. 59–74.

2. See, for example, R. W. Woodman, J. E. Sawyer, and R. W. Griffin, "Towards a Theory of Organizational Creativity," *Academy of Management Review* 18, no. 1 (1993), pp. 293–321; J. D. Couger, *Creativity and Innovation*, (Danvers, MA: Boyd & Fraser, 1996).

3. Alvin Toffler and Heide Toffler, *Powershift* (New York: Bantam Books, 1990); T. M. Amabile, "The Motivation to Be Creative," in *Frontiers of Creativity Research: Beyond the Basics*, ed. S. Isaksen (New York: Bearly Limited, 1987), pp. 223–54.

4. See R. W. Woodman and J. F. Schoenfeldt, "An Interactionist Model of Creative Behavior," *Journal of Creative Behavior* 24 (1990), pp. 279–90; and R. W. Woodman and J. E. Sawyer, *An Interactionist Model of Organizational Creativity,"* paper presented at the annual Academy of Management Meeting, Miami, 1991.

5. W. Koehler, *The Mentality of Apes* (London: Pelican, 1925/1957).

6. G. Wallas, "Stages of Control," *The Art of Thought* (New York: Harcourt Brace Jovanovich, 1926).

7. R. J. Sternberg, *The Nature of Creativity: Contemporary Psychological Perspectives* (New York: Cambridge University Press, 1988); R. J. Sternberg, and R. K. Wagner, *Practical Intelligence* (New York: Cambridge University Press, 1986).

8. D. Leonard and S. Straus, "Putting Your Company's Whole Brain to Work," *Harvard Business Review* (July–August 1997), pp. 111–21.

9. J. J. Kao, *Managing Creativity* (Englewood Cliffs, NJ: Prentice–Hall, 1991); D. Bohm, and F. D. Peat, *Science, Order, and Creativity* (New York: Bantam Books, 1987); J. R. Evans, *Creative Thinking* (Cincinnati: South Western, 1991).

10. J. P. Guilford, "Creativity," *American Psychologist* 14 (1950), pp. 469–79; J. P. Guilford, "Creativity Research: A Quarter Century of Progress," in *Perspectives in Creativity*, eds. I. A. Taylor and J. W. Getzels (New York: Aldine, 1975).

11. E. Rogers, *The Diffusion of Innovations*, 3rd ed. (New York: Free Press, 1983); A. H. Van de Ven, "Central Problems in the Management of Innovation," *Management Science* (May, 1986), pp. 590–607.

12. G. Zaltman, R. Duncan, and J. Holbek, *Innovations and Organizations* (New York: Wiley–Interscience, 1973).

13. P. Salovey and J. Myer, *Emotional Development and Emotional Intelligence*, (New York: Basic Books, 1997); H. Weisinger, *Emotional Intelligence at Work*, (San Francisco: Jossey–Bass, 1997).

14. R. Cooper, "Applying Emotional Intelligence in the Workplace," *Training & Development* (December 1997), pp. 31–38.

15. R. Cooper and A. Sawaf, *Executive EQ: Emotional Intelligence in Leadership and Organizations*, (New York: Grosset/Putman, 1998); R. Bar–On, "Bar–On Emotional Quotient Inventory" (1996).

16. Woodman, Sawyer, and Griffin, "Towards a Theory of Organizational Creativity," p. 296.

17. M. J. Kirton, "Adaptors and Innovators: Cognitive Style and Personality," in *Frontiers of Creative Research*, ed. S. Isaksen (New York: Bearly Limited, 1987), pp. 282–304.

18. M. J. Kirton, "Adaptors and Innovators: Problem Solvers in Organizations," in *Innovation: A Cross–Disciplinary Perspective*, eds. K. Gronhaug and G. Kaufmann (Norway: Norwegian University Press, 1988), p. 72.

19. T. M. Amabile, "The Motivation to be Creative," in *Frontiers of Creativity Research*, ed. S. Isaksen (New York: Bearly Limited, 1987), p. 223–54.

20. R. L. Kuhn and G. T. Geis, "A Cross–Organization Methodology for Assessing Creativity and Commitment," in *New Directions in Creative and Innovative Management*, eds. Yuji Ijiri and Robert Kuhn (Cambridge, MA: Ballinger Publishing Co., 1988), pp. 303–22.

21. S. G. Isaksen, "Educational Implications of Creativity Research: An Updated Rationale for Creative Learning," in *Frontiers of Creativity Research*, ed. S. Isaksen (New York: Bearly Limited, 1987), p. 149.

22. M. Tushman and D. Nadler, "Organizing for Innovation," *California Management Review* (Spring 1986), pp. 74–92; J. Galbraith, "Designing the Innovating Organization," *Organizational Dynamics* (Winter 1982), pp. 5–25.

23. K. Lewis, "Frontiers in Group Dynamics," *Human Relations* 1 (1947), pp. 5–41; R. F. Bales and F. L. Strodtbeck, "Phases in Group Problem–Solving," *Journal of Abnormal and Social Psychology* 46 (1951), pp. 485–95.

24. J. G. March and H. Simon, *Organizations* (New York: John Wiley & Sons, 1958); M. D. Cohen, J. G. March, and J. P. Olsen, "A Garbage Can Model of Organizational Choice," *Administrative Science Quarterly* 17 (1972), pp. 1–25.

25. G. W. Dalton, P. R. Lawrence, and L. E. Greiner, *Organizational Change and Development* (Homewood, IL: Dorsey Press, 1970).

26. W. J. Abernathy and J. M. Utterback, "Patterns of Industrial Innovation," in *Readings in the Management of Innovation*, eds. M. Tushman and W. Moore (Boston: Pitman 1975), pp. 97–150; M. Jelinek, and C. Bird–Schoonhoven, *Innovation Marathon: Lessons from High Technology Firms* (Oxford, England: Basil Blackwell, 1990); R. M. Kanter, "Innovation — The Only Hope for Times Ahead?" *Sloan Management Review* (Summer 1984), pp. 51–55.

27. R. Schroeder, A. H. Van de Ven, G. D. Scudder, and D. Polley, "The Development of Innovative Ideas," in *Research on the Management of Innovation: The Minnesota Studes*, eds. A. H. Van de Ven, H. Angle, and M. Poole (New York: Harper & Row, 1990), pp. 107–34.

28. J. Schumpeter, *Theorie der wirtschaftlichen Entwicklung. Eine Untersuchung uber Unternehmergewinn, Kapital, Kredit, Zins und den Konjunkturzyklus*, 3rd ed. (Munich: Duncker & Humblot, 1931).

29. A. K. Chakrabarti, "The Role of Champions in Product Innovation," *California Management Review* 17 (Winter 1974), pp. 58–62; Kjell Gronhaug, and Geir Kaufmann, *Innovation: A Cross–Disciplinary Perspective* (Oslo: Norwegian University Press, 1988).

30. T. J. Allen and S. I. Cohen, "Information Flow in Research and Development Laboratories," *Administrative Science Quarterly* 14 (1969), pp. 12–19.

31. G. Ekvall and Y. T. Andersson, "Working Climate and Creativity: A Study of an Innovative Newspaper Office," *Journal of Creative Behavior* 20 (1986), pp. 215–25; R. M. Burnside, T. M. Amabile, and S. S. Gryskiewicz, "Ássessing Organizational Climates for Creativity and Innovation: Methodological Review of Large Company Audits," in *New Directions in Creative and Innovative Management*, eds. Yuji Ijiri and Robert Kuhn (Cambridge, MA: Ballinger Publishing Co., 1988), pp. 169–86.

32. T. Burns and G. M. Stalker, *The Management of Innovation* (London: Tavistock Publications, 1961).

33. J. L. Pierce and A. L. Delbecq, "Organization Structure, Individual Attitudes, and Innovation," *Academy of Management Review* 2, (January 1977), pp. 27–37.

34. M. Jelinek and C. B. Schoonhoven, *Innovation Marathon* (Cambridge, MA: Basil Blackwell, 1990).

35. T. Kono, *Structure of Japanese Enterprises* (London: Macmillan, 1984).

36. M. F. Wolff, "Revamping the Dual Ladder at General Mills," *Research Management* (November 1979), pp. 8–11.)

Chapter 12

Problem Solving and Decision Making

SOURCE: Curtis W. Cook, Phillip L. Hunsaker and Robert E. Coffey, *Management and Organizational Behavior*, 3rd ed., Chapter 12, McGraw-Hill, 2001, 1997, 1994.

Learning Objectives

After studying this chapter, you should be able to:

- Explain the nature of managerial problem solving.

- Identify the five steps of the rational problem-solving process.

- Appreciate the value of ethics and morality in decision making.

- Describe the strengths and weaknesses of different decision styles.

- Utilize quality management tools for problem solving.

- Apply techniques to stimulate creativity and innovation.

- Define the following key terms:

brainstorming	**ethical dilemma**	**nominal group technique**
compensatory justice	**ethical reasoning**	**objective**
criteria	**ethics**	**Pareto chart**
decision making	**flowchart**	**problem solving**
decision styles	**Gantt chart**	**retributive justice**
Delphi technique	**group decision support systems**	**right**
distributive justice	**justice**	**satisficing**
ethical behavior	**morality**	**utilitarianism**
		utility

Groomed So Not to Marry: Porshe Claims Exemption from Merger Mania

Not too long ago, the production floor of Porsche's factory was not a pretty sight. Workers would storm off in a huff. Managers would fume. Voices would rise above the hum and bang of the line. Porsche's assembly line looked like a dark warehouse. On either side were shelves eight-feet high with huge parts bins filled with 28 days of inventory. To get a part, workers often had to climb ladders, wasting enormous amounts of time. Half-built engines sat on the side of the assembly line while workers left their work spaces to dig for parts, and others stood around waiting until they returned.

Porsche could afford this type of inefficiency in the early 1980s when the economic boom fueled sales to more than 50,000 vehicles a year. But then the recession of the early 1990s hit, and Porsche sales plummeted to 14,000 units in 1993, including a paltry 3,000 in the United States, its largest market. From the dizzying heights of the mid-1980s when American yuppies, not to mention staid German executives, had to have one, Porsche went to the brink of bankruptcy in 1992. Recession had crippled sales, and costs were out of control. That was when the company's family owners called in 43-year-old Mr. Wendelin Wiedeking to be Porsches's chief executive and solve its problems.

From the beginning, Wiedeking's idea was to bring in the Japanese. First, he eliminated one-third of his managers and gave those remaining new assignments, so that they would be struggling to learn new jobs "rather than waiting for me to make a mistake." Next, he took his management team on extensive tours of Japanese auto plants. They benchmarked by timing precisely how long it took Porsche to assemble body parts and engines and install carpeting and dashboards, then studied comparable times in Japan. On most tasks, Porsche was taking almost twice as long. These comparisons gave Porsche management a dramatic understanding of what had to be done.

In late 1992, Wiedeking brought the Shin-Gijutsu group, a cadre of former Toyota engineers, to the Porsche plant and gave them carte blanche to revitalize the system. It was a painful process. The Japanese engineers unleashed demanding explanations—scolding, lecturing, and browbeating some of Germany's finest automobile craftsman—about how poorly they were doing their jobs. But the result was the salvation of Porsche A.G., Germany's ultimate symbol of racing car performance and autobahn freedom.

With help from the Japanese engineers, assembly time for a car was reduced from 120 hours to 72. The number of errors per car fell 50 percent, to an average of three. The work force has shrunk 19 percent, to about 6,800 employees from more than 8,400 in 1992. Parts bins have been entirely eliminated and assemblers now only take the parts needed for each stage of assembly. The line itself has been shortened, and inventories have been cut back so much that factory space has been reduced by 30 percent. All of this means Porsche is making more cars at lower cost. And, the company recently reported its first profit in four years, after $300 million in losses.

Source: N.-C. Nash, "Putting Porsche in the Pink: German Craftsmanship Gets Japanese Fine-Tuning," The New York Times (January 20, 1996), pp.-17–18.

Individual, managerial, and organizational success all depend on making the right decisions at the right times.[1] But decision making is just one component of the problem-solving process. Unless a problem has been defined and its root causes identified, managers are unlikely to be able to make an appropriate decision about how to solve it. Effective managers, like Porsche's Wiedeking, know how to gather and evaluate information that clarifies a problem. They know the value of generating more than one action alternative and weighing all the implications of a plan before deciding to implement it. And they acknowledge the importance of following through. This chapter explains decision making and problem solving and offers some guidelines for eliminating barriers to effective problem solving.

WHAT ARE THE STEPS FOR RATIONAL PROBLEM SOLVING?

Problem solving *is the process of eliminating the discrepancy between actual and desired outcomes.* Although sometimes subconsciously, most people confront problems by first acknowledging that they exist. Next, the problem needs to be defined and analyzed. Then alternative solutions need to be generated. **Decision making—** *selecting the best solution from among feasible alternatives*—comes next. Finally, the solution needs to be implemented, which Europeans call "taking" a decision. For optimal problem solving, social scientists advocate the use of the rational problem-solving approach outlined in Figure 12–1.[2]

A problem exists whenever the actual situation is not what is needed or desired. For example, when a work project needs to be done by a certain deadline and information needed to complete the assignment has not been supplied, a problem exists.

FIGURE 12-1   THE RATIONAL PROBLEM SOLVING PROCESS

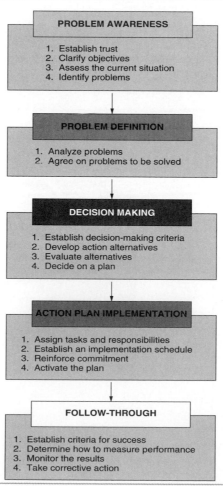

PROBLEM AWARENESS

1. Establish trust
2. Clarify objectives
3. Assess the current situation
4. Identify problems

PROBLEM DEFINITION

1. Analyze problems
2. Agree on problems to be solved

DECISION MAKING

1. Establish decision-making criteria
2. Develop action alternatives
3. Evaluate alternatives
4. Decide on a plan

ACTION PLAN IMPLEMENTATION

1. Assign tasks and responsibilities
2. Establish an implementation schedule
3. Reinforce commitment
4. Activate the plan

FOLLOW-THROUGH

1. Establish criteria for success
2. Determine how to measure performance
3. Monitor the results
4. Take corrective action

DYNAMICS OF DIVERSITY
Changing Corporate Culture at P&G

Changing the corporate culture can be a time consuming and exhaustive project according to both the former and present CEOs of Procter & Gamble (P&G). However, these two "costs" are minor when compared to the losses when, in a global economy, the corporation does not recognize the value generated by diversity. Therefore, a commitment, vision, and strategy to change a company culture will pay off in the end.

John Pepper, the former CEO of P&G from 1988 to 1989, set in motion the change in corporate culture by establishing a diversity task force, charged with creating a diversity plan for the corporation. By the time Durk Jager (the current CEO assumed control, the task force was making progress. Jager also added another component—diversity for the global organization. Jager felt that "Unless you have diversity in thinking, you will never get real diversity—racial or gender or national diversity."

P&G's strategy for diversity included several essential components.. First, rather than attempting to change the culture overnight, P&G set forth to incorporate diversity into the hiring process. P&G sought bright college recruits from diverse backgrounds who had the potential to rise to managerial-level positions throughout the organization. Secondly, accountability and performance were integrated into P&G's value system. P&G's chief executive consistently monitored the diversity effort, and diversity management was incorporated into the performance appraisals of managers. Futhermore, the ability to work within a diverse environment is part of everyone's appraisal. Thirdly, communication and leadership were seen as important success factors of the diversity strategy. A consistent and continual message from all management levels reinforced the task force's initiatives in the company.

This strategy would not immediately change P&G's culture, rather it was an investment toward the future. However, by the late 1990s, the diversity initiative yielded some positive results. Although still a relatively small percentage, the actual number of women in high-level management positions more than tripled. More importantly, however, was that the retention ratio of women increased significantly, matching the level of men. This implies that the women viewed P&G as a company that values diversity and would provide opportunities for women.

The initiative is still ongoing. P&G recently set forth their new Diversity in Organization 2005 under the leadership of LaVelle Bond, vice president of global diversity. The initiative stresses worldwide P&G diversity and includes objectives such as global diversity training and translating the company's values into measurable diversity objectives. The second objective is targeted especially for foreign countries, where a lack of education and opportunity has historically put women at a disadvantage compared to men. The goal is to make P&G "the company of choice."

Source: Margaret Blackburn White, "Organization 2005: New Strategies at P&G," *Diversity Factor* (Fall 1999), pp.16-20.

GTE Telephone Operations had nearly $16 billion in revenues in 1992. But, faced with increasing competition and the need to reduce costs, GTE has begun the process of re-engineering the entire company to better serve the customer with improved technology and more efficient business processes. One example of a re-engineered process is the new GTE Customer Care Center, where "front-end technicians" now have the ability to access customer records, remotely test lines, and fulfill most customers' repair requests while they are still on the telephone. (Photo: Eyewire.)

Problem Awareness

A major responsibility for all managers is to maintain a constant lookout for actual or potential problems. Managers do this by keeping channels of communication open, monitoring employees' current performance, and examining deviations from present plans as well as from past experience.[3] Four situations usually alert managers to possible problems: when there is a deviation from past experience, when there is a deviation from a set plan, when other people communicate problems to the manager, and when competitors outperform the overall organization.[4]

Being aware that problems exist is not always easy, however. People may be genuinely unaware of a problem's source or reluctant to acknowledge that a negative situation actually exists. The problem may appear threatening to them, they may fear reprisal from a supervisor for their share of the responsibility, or they may not want to be considered inept. The Dynamics of Diversity box shows how Proctor & Gamble identified and is solving the problem (rather, opportunity) of global diversity.

Establish Trust

When a problem involves others, they need to feel understood and accepted; they must have confidence that the problem can be resolved; they must trust management to see the problem as a learning experience and not as an excuse to punish someone.[5] People need to feel secure enough to acknowledge that a problem exists and to acknowledge their own contributions to it.

Clarify Objectives

> "Cheshie Puss," Alice began, "would you tell me, please, which way I ought to walk from here?"
> "That depends a good deal on where you want to get to," said the Cat.
> "I don't care where," said Alice.
> "Then it doesn't matter which way you walk," said the Cat.[6]

Unlike Alice, most of us have an **objective** or *desired outcome that we want to achieve*. If you don't know what your objectives are, it is difficult to know what your problems are, let alone what to do about them. Therefore, objectives must be set and clarified before a current situation can be assessed.

Setting objectives serves four main purposes.[7] First, it provides a clear, documented statement of what you intend to accomplish. Written objectives are a form of acknowledgment and reminder of commitment. Second, setting objectives establishes a basis for measuring performance. Third, knowing what is expected and desired provides positive motivation to achieve goals. And fourth, knowing exactly where you're going is much more likely to get you there than trying many different solutions in a haphazard way.

It is the manager's responsibility is to make sure that set objectives support overall organizational goals. To obtain commitment from employees, managers must define organizational objectives and point out how they support each employee's personal goals. Finally, the objectives for any particular person or group should mesh with the objectives of others who might be affected by them. One way to address these constraints is to conduct team goal-setting meetings so that all concerned parties can participate openly.

There is little motivational value in setting objectives that require nothing more than maintenance of present performance levels. On the other hand, very difficult objectives may appear unattainable and therefore be demoralizing. While objectives should foster an improvement over present performance, they should also be clearly achievable.

Assess the Current Situation

When evaluating the current situation, participants must focus on both the "what" and the "how" of performance from two viewpoints: that of the organization and that of the people involved. The immediate need is to determine if goals are met by the current situation. Do actual conditions match desired ones? If not, what are the differences? Mismatches usually show up clearly, but sometimes an inadequate current situation is taken for granted because it is how things have been for so long. If the matching process reveals discrepancies, the next step is to determine why.

Identify Problems

Serious mistakes can be made if managers act before they accurately identify all of the sources of a problem. To identify a problem accurately, it must be understood from all points of view.

The full determination of how a particular problem prevents people from accomplishing desired goals can be made only when all parties are free to participate in its identification without fear of being blamed or criticized. If problem solving is perceived as a joint learning experience, people will be much more likely to contribute needed information than if they fear punishment for disclosing information that may indicate they have made mistakes.

Problem identification and solution are much easier in routine than nonroutine situations. Routine problems are those that arise on a regular basis and can be solved through programmed decisions—standard responses based on procedures that have been effective in the past. One example of a programmed decision is a student's automatic probationary status when his or her grade point average sinks below a predetermined level. Another is the reordering of supplies as soon as inventory on hand falls below a certain quantity. Most routine problems are anticipated, which allows managers to plan in advance how to deal with them and sometimes to delegate problem solving to their subordinates.

Nonroutine problems are ones not anticipated by managers. They are unique. No standard responses to them exist. These types of problems require nonprogrammed decisions—innovative solutions tailored to fit specific dilemmas. The petroleum shortage of the late 1970s was a nonroutine problem that required new ways of distributing gasoline and transporting goods and people. Catastrophes always pose nonroutine problems. When an American Airlines DC-10 crashed in 1979, all the nation's DC-10s were grounded. Stranded ticket holders, shortages of long-range aircraft, and idle pilots and flight crews were just some of the nonroutine problems faced by decision makers at many levels.

One way to be prepared for potential problems and to be able to quickly identify their causes is to thoroughly understand the process involved. A **flow chart** *is a pictorial representation of all the steps of a process.* Flow charts document a process and help demonstrate how the various steps relate to each other. See Figure 12-2 for a sample flow chart involving quality inspection of incoming parts.

The flow chart is widely used in problem identification. The people with the greatest amount of knowledge about the process meet to first draw a flow chart of what steps the process actually follows. Then they draw a flow chart of what steps the process should ideally follow. By comparing the two charts they find differences, because that is where the problems arise.[8]

Problem Definition

If the problem is not defined clearly, any attempt at solving it will be doomed to fail because the parties involved won't really know what they are working on. All the remaining steps will be distorted because they will be based on insufficient or erroneous information. Lack of information often inhibits the generation of adequate alternatives and exploration of potentially negative consequences.

All necessary information should be gathered so that all relevant factors can be analyzed to determine the exact problem that must be solved. The goal is to determine the root causes of the problem. If instruction forms are constantly misinterpreted, for example, are the forms incomplete, or is the required information poorly supplied? Causes should not be assumed; instead, all plausible alternatives should be investigated before settling on the most probable cause(s).

Hasty assumptions can also result in symptoms being mistaken for sources of problems. When symptoms are eliminated, it is often mistakenly assumed that the problem has also been eliminated. This is like receiving medication from your doctor to control a skin rash, which is only a symptom that something is wrong. The medication clears the rash, but the actual cause of the problem isn't identified until you and/or the physician look for clues. When you discover that the onset of the rash coincided with the arrival of a new plant in your living room, you have identified the problem: an allergy to that plant.

FIGURE 12-2   **PROCESS FLOW DIAGRAM: Receiving Inspection**

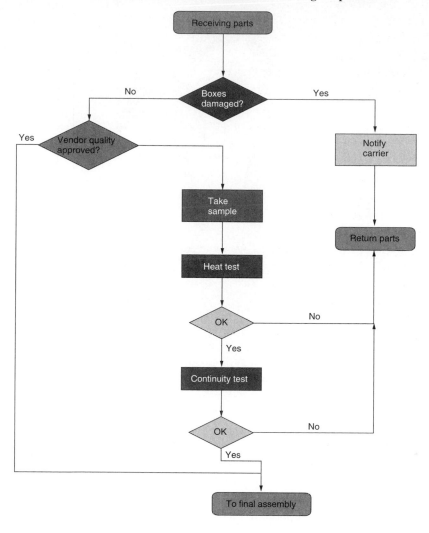

Source: Michael Brassard. The Memory Jogger: A Pocket Guide of Tools for Continuous Improvement (Methuen, MA: GOAL/QPC, 1988), p.-10.

Analyze Problems

Checking to make sure that the problem is defined accurately and analyzed completely provides a safeguard against incorrect assumptions, treatment of symptoms only, and incomplete understanding. The way a problem is actually defined has a major impact on what alternatives are considered, what decision is reached, and how the action plan is implemented. Failure to define an identified problem accurately can impede consideration and eventual application of the best solution.

Failure to thoroughly diagnose a problem can result from inadequate time and energy available to review all the possible causes and implications. Other times, underlying psychological reasons come into play, such as not wanting to know what the real problems are, fearing that we ourselves are to blame, being concerned that a close associate will be hurt, or anticipating that the problem will prove too enormous for us.

One technique for facilitating a thorough problem analysis is the *cause-and-effect diagram.*[9] A cause-and-effect diagram, or fishbone chart, is constructed to represent the relationship between some "effect" and all possible "causes" influencing it. As illustrated in Figure 12–3, the effect or problem is stated on the right side of the chart, and the major influences or causes are listed to the left. Although a problem may have various sources, the major causes can usually be summarized under the four "M" categories of *manpower, methods, machines, and material.* Data can then be gathered and shared to determine the relative frequencies and magnitudes of contribution of the different potential causes.

A TQM team at George Washington University Medical Center identified and analyzed a problem in the hospital's oncology unit: patients could sometimes wait up to 12 hours for elective chemotherapy. When the team dissected the process of admitting a patient to the hospital, they found it to be much more complicated than they had imagined. Team-suggested changes in the admissions process were implemented, and the average time between admission and start of chemo-theraphy decreased from 11 hours to less than 2 hours. (Photo: © Terry Ashe.)

Agree on Problems to Be Solved

If more than one problem has been identified and defined, the next step is to set priorities regarding which problem will be worked on first and which ones will be put aside temporarily or indefinitely. One criterion for rank ordering multiple problems is how much their solutions will contribute to desired objectives. The most important problems should be dealt with first, even if their solutions seem more difficult. One quality management tool that can help management do this is called Pareto analysis.

Pareto chart

A **Pareto chart** *is a vertical bar graph that indicates which problems, or causes of problems, should be solved first*. To construct a Pareto chart, the problems to be compared and rank ordered are determined by brainstorming and analyzing existing data. Then a standard for comparison, such as annual cost or frequency of occurrence, and the time period to be studied are selected. After necessary data for each category have been gathered, the frequency or cost of each category is compared to that for other categories. The categories are listed from left to right on the horizontal axis in order of decreasing frequency or cost.[10] A Pareto chart of field service customer complaints is illustrated in Figure 12–4.

Decision Making

After information has been gathered and goals have been clarified, situations assessed, and problems identified, the next step is to develop a particular course of action that will either restore formerly acceptable conditions or improve the situation in a significant way. Since there is usually more than one way to solve a problem, it is critical to keep open to all possible solutions and arrive at several alternatives from which to choose.

Establish Decision-Making Criteria

Decision-making criteria are statements of objectives that need to be met for a problem to be solved. Effective criteria should possess the following characteristics:

* *Specific, Measurable, and Attainable.* "I need to reduce scrap material waste by 10 percent, avoid a reduction in product quality, and increase production by 5 percent," is an example of a concise decision-making criteria statement. Decision-making criteria should be *specific:* "I will increase productivity by 5 percent," not just "I want to increase productivity." Second, they should be measurable: Saying you want to increase employee morale is not as good a criterion statement as saying that you will increase employee morale as indicated by a 4 percent reduction in absenteeism over the next three months. Third, to gain commitment to meeting criteria, there should be sufficient time, resources, and expertise available to make them attainable.

FIGURE 12-3   **CAUSE-EFFECT DIAGRAM (Fishbone Analysis)**

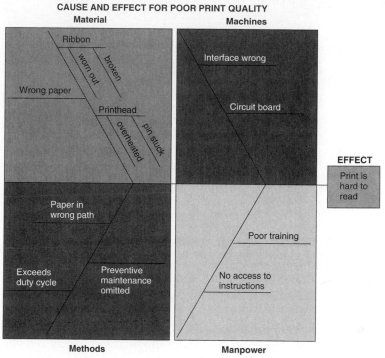

CAUSE AND EFFECT FOR POOR PRINT QUALITY

Source: Michael Brassard. *The Memory Jogger: A Pocket Guide of Tools for Continuous Improvement* (Methuen, MA: GOAL/QPC, 1988), p.26. Reprinted with permission from *The Memory Jogger*™. Copyright 1986 by GOAL/QPC.

- *Complementary.* The criteria must also complement one another. The achievement of one should not reduce the likelihood of achieving another. For example, you would not improve the quality and detail of your written reports at the expense of spending the necessary time with those who must interact with you.

- *Ethical.* Decision criteria should conform to what is considered morally right by society. Criteria should be legal, fair, and observant of human rights. Organizations need to establish a commonly agreed on set of ethical standards to guide decisions when individuals are confronted with conflicting obligations, cost-benefit trade-offs, and competing value choices. The following section on ethical decision making expands on the many dilemmas of applying moral criteria.

- *Acceptable.* Even the best technical decision will not be workable if it is unacceptable to the parties involved. You may be convinced, for example, that the best solution for meeting a production deadline without increasing costs is to have the department work weekends for the next month without additional compensation. But this is not a viable action plan because it will not be acceptable to those on whom its implementation depends. Negative reactions to changes can create more problems than are solved. Sensitivity to emotional factors, personal values, and individual objectives is vital in choosing a successful action plan.

Develop Action Alternatives

The value, acceptance, and implementation of an action plan are enhanced by involving all affected parties in the generation and analysis of alternatives. Acceptance can be tested by soliciting feedback to determine if those involved understand the potential benefits and to assess their readiness to make the necessary commitment. As many solutions as possible should be generated to avoid picking a premature solution that doesn't meet all long-run criteria. Techniques to facilitate this step are provided in the following section on how problems can be solved more effectively.

FIGURE 12-4   **PARETO CHART: Field Service Customer Complaints**
                                   (Rank Order by Frequency of Occurency)

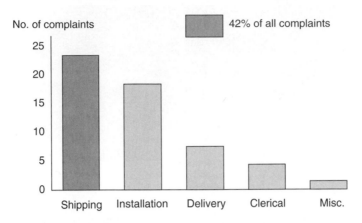

Source: Michael Brassard. *The Memory Jogger: A Pocket Guide of Tools for Continuous Improvement* (Methuen, MA: GOAL/QPC, 1988), p.26. Reprinted with permission from *The Memory Jogger™*. Copyright 1986 by GOAL/QPC.

Evaluate Benefits and Risks of Alternatives

It is important to look at all the long-run consequences of the alternatives being considered. This is sometimes overlooked because of our tendency to avoid spending extra time and energy and our fear of discovering negative consequences in preferred solutions.

Important criteria to consider in evaluating action alternatives are each alternative's *probability of success* and the associated *degree of risk* that negative consequences will occur. If the chance of failure is high and the related costs for an alternative are great, the benefits of an alternative may not justify its use. Risk can be personal as well as economic—just ask the person whose reputation is on the line or who is soon to undergo a performance review. The degree of risk can be separated into four categories: certainty, known risk, uncertainty, and turbulence.[11]

Certainty exists if the exact results of implementing a problem solution are known in advance. Certainty (of return) exists if you put your money in a savings account for one year, whereas it does not exist if you invest it in real estate or the stock market. Certainty is the exception rather than the rule in most managerial decision-making situations. Complete information and guaranteed outcomes are rare.

Known risk is present when the probability that a given alternative will produce specific outcomes can be predicted. For example, an executive may know that by taking a commercial airline flight tonight, he or she has a 99.5 percent probability of arriving on time for a business meeting in New York tomorrow morning. If the executive lives in San Diego, he or she will also know for certain that if the last flight is missed, the meeting tomorrow will also be missed. Probabilities based on historical records or statistical analyses are sometimes assigned to risky alternatives. At other times, probabilities are simply estimated through managerial intuition.

Uncertainty exists when decision makers are unable to assign any probabilities to the consequences associated with an alternative. Choices among uncertain alternatives are often based on intuition and hunches.

Turbulence occurs when the environment is rapidly changing and decision makers are not even clear about relevant variables, available solution options, or potential consequences of decisions. In times of recession, economic reforms, or military conflict, turbulence usually prevails.

Decide on a Plan

As alternatives are evaluated according to these criteria, many will be clearly unsatisfactory and can be eliminated. Sometimes the evaluation will reveal that one alternative is decidedly superior to all others. At other times none of the proposed action plans will be acceptable, signaling a need to develop additional alternatives. Most often, however, several alternatives will appear feasible, and the best one must be selected. Figure 12–5 illustrates a

FIGURE 12-5   DECISION-MAKING GRID

Alternatives	Criteria					
	Benefits	Probability of Success	Costs	Risks	Associated Consequences	Timing
Alternative A						
Alternative B						
Alternative C						

decision-making grid that summarizes the above criteria for evaluating alternatives. Such a grid can help to visualize which alternative offers the maximum benefits with minimal risks and costs. The decision-making goal is to select the best solution alternative for solving the entire problem without creating any additional negative consequences for anyone else in the organization.

Perfect Rationality. In a world of perfect rationality, all problems can be clearly defined, all information and alternatives are known, the consequences of implementing each alternative are certain, and the decision maker is a completely rational being who is concerned only about economic gain. These conditions of classical decision theory allow for an optimal solution to every problem and provide the basics for ideal management decision making. The real world, however, is made up of real people with real problems, and it rarely conforms to these ideal conditions.

Bounded Rationality. Behavioral decision theory has questioned the classical assumptions and recognized the real-world limitations to obtaining and processing all relevant information that might optimize decision making. Administrators exhibit bounded rationality when they reach satisfactory rather than "perfect" decisions. Bounded rationality is necessary in the face of constraints on time, money, and intellectual resources.[12] While the goal of the decision model presented here is to optimize decision outcomes, **satisficing**—*choosing the first satisfactory alternative that meets minimal requirements*—probably describes the majority of daily managerial decision making. See the Eye on Ethics box for a discussion about how the medical decisions can be bounded by financial conditions.

Action Plan Implementation

A decision and action plan are of little value unless they are effectively implemented. How the action plan is to be accomplished connects the decision with reality. Implementation includes assigning tasks and responsibilities and establishing an implementation schedule.

Assign Tasks and Responsibilities
It is important to clarify both verbally and in writing what each person involved will do to make the new action plan work. To avoid misunderstandings, it is essential to specify who is to do what, by when, and how.

Establish an Implementation Schedule
To be effectively implemented, all necessary tasks need a specified time schedule for completion. One way to do this is to start at an end point (the date by which the objective should be completed) and work backward. Action implementation steps can be listed in priority order and assigned reasonable time periods for completion, starting with the last step before the objective is accomplished.

FIGURE 12-6   SAMPLE GANTT CHART

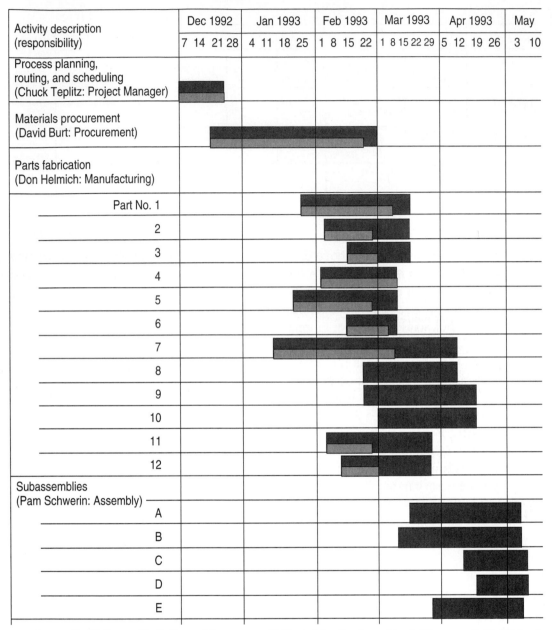

Activity description (responsibility)	Dec 1992	Jan 1993	Feb 1993	Mar 1993	Apr 1993	May
	7 14 21 28	4 11 18 25	1 8 15 22	1 8 15 22 29	5 12 19 26	3 10
Process planning, routing, and scheduling (Chuck Teplitz: Project Manager)						
Materials procurement (David Burt: Procurement)						
Parts fabrication (Don Helmich: Manufacturing)						
Part No. 1						
2						
3						
4						
5						
6						
7						
8						
9						
10						
11						
12						
Subassemblies (Pam Schwerin: Assembly) A						
B						
C						
D						
E						

Source: L.-W. Rue and L.-L. Byars, Management Skills and Applications, 6th ed. (Homewood, IL: Richard D. Irwin, 1992), p.-210. Adapted from Elwood S. Buffa, Modern Production Management, 4th ed. (New York: John Wiley & Sons, Inc., 1973), p.-576.

One of the earliest scheduling techniques was developed by Harry Gantt in the early 1900s. A **Gantt chart** *is a graphic planning and control method that breaks down a project into separate tasks and estimates the time needed for their completion.* The chart has a space for planned starting and completion dates and for actual dates filled in as implementation occurs. A sample Gantt chart appears in Figure 12–6.

Gantt charts help to make certain that all implementation tasks are considered in relationship to each other and that appropriate people are assigned to each task. They provide checkpoints for all tasks to ensure that they are finished on time. Gantt charts are developed by defining goals and setting completion dates and then bracketing time blocks based on the time required and completion date of each task.

Once an action plan is implemented, managers often move on to another task. It is of key importance, however, to follow through to be sure that the solution is working effectively and that no additional problems have been created. Follow-through is the final stage of the problem-solving process.

Follow-Through

Following-through entails the development and maintenance of positive attitudes in everyone involved in the implementation process. There are several guidelines to help establish the positive climate necessary for the implementation steps that follow:

- Visualize yourself in the position of those doing the implementing so that you understand their feelings and perspectives.

- Establish sincere respect and concern.

- Make sure necessary resources are available.

With this kind of positive climate set up, there are several sequential steps in the follow-through process. They include establishing the criteria for measuring success, monitoring the results obtained, and taking corrective action when necessary.

Establish Criteria for Measuring Success

Unless the circumstances have changed, the criteria for measuring problem-solving success are the time, quality, and quantity goals already developed in the action-planning stage. These criteria serve as *benchmarks* for measuring and comparing the actual results.

Monitor the Results

The data on the results can be compared with the established criteria. If the new performance meets the criteria, no further action is necessary other than continued monitoring. If the new results do not measure up, the next step is to determine why. Each implementation step may alter the problem situation in unanticipated ways.

WORLD WATCH

Corruption in Foreign Aid

The United States hoped that with the passage of the Foreign Corrupt Practices Act in 1977, other countries would follow suit. None have, however, which places American companies at a major disadvantage when operating in foreign countries with different views toward ethics. It takes only a casual vacation trip to Southeast Asia to see hundreds of copies of American products, some even with authentic-looking U.S. company logos on them. In this part of the world it is commonplace for foreign companies to have to pay bribes to be able to conduct business, but even some Westernized countries such as Germany permit legal tax deductions for bribes to win foreign business deals. How can American companies compete in such an environment?

However, the bribes and corrupt practices are not limited to private business alone. Rather, official U.S. government aid to foreign countries for infrastructure development projects (road and water plant construction, communication projects, etc.) has been diverted for nontargeted uses. In a recent study, the World Bank received some shocking news—40 percent of overseas firms (including some U.S. firms abroad) admitted to using bribery to win World Bank sponsored projects.

A new act is before Congress to combat the misuse of official funds from the United States—the Fair Competition in Foreign Commerce Act. The aim of this act is twofold. First, it will block U.S. Treasury funds from going to a country that does not have a third-party monitor in place. This action will require independent monitors to oversee the bidding on projects an disbursement of monies. Secondly, it will require recipient countries to establish their own anticorruption programs, including the use of third-party monitors.

While the aim of the Fair Competition in Foreign Commerce Act is twofold, so are the intended outcomes. This act will require countries to operate on a higher ethical level, eliminating bribery and the diverting of funds for nonspecified uses (especially since these are U.S. government funds). Secondly, it should place U.S. companies in a better position to compete with foreign firms when bidding on development contracts.

Source: Adapted from James Srodes, "Curbs on Foreign Bribery—and Foreign Aid," *World Trade* (Irvine: February 2000), p. 12.

Julia Butterfly Hill, environmental activist, sccaled an ancient redwood tree in Northern California's Humboldt County to protest the cutting down of redwoods by the Pacific Lumber Company. Faced with her own ethical dilemma, she chose to deal with this situation by doing something somewhat unorthodox (in the end she was in the tree for over two years) to draw attention to her cause in the hope that our remaining unprotected redwoods and forests would be protected in the future. (Photo: © Corbis.)

Take Corrective Action. The problem-solving process is a closed-loop system. If performance fails to match the success criteria, the problem needs to be identified by again applying the problem-solving process. For any new corrective action plan, new measures and schedules need to be determined and new data need to be gathered and tested against the criteria.

WHAT IS ETHICAL DECISION MAKING?

A large majority of American managers agree that unethical practices occur in business, and a substantial portion (about 65 percent) report that they have been pressured to compromise their own ethical standards when making organizational decisions.[13] Some of the underlying causes for individuals and organizations making poor choices when considering ethical issues are:[14]

- Individuals and/or organizations are sometimes immature.

- Economic self-interest is overwhelming.

- Special circumstances outweigh ethical concerns.

- Lack of education in the areas of morality and ethics.

- Potential rewards outweigh possible punishments for unethical behavior.

- The culture or mindset is that "All's fair in love, war, and business."

- Organizational pressure on individuals to commit unethical acts.

Ethics *is the discipline dealing with what is good and bad and with moral duty and obligations.* **Ethical behavior** *is that which conforms to accepted standards of conduct.* **Ethical reasoning** *involves sorting out the principles that help determine what is ethical when faced with an ethical dilemma.* An **ethical dilemma** *is a situation or problem facing an individual that involves complex and often conflicting principles of ethical behavior.* A classic example of an ethical dilemma would be the submarine commander who has to decide whether to stay afloat to save a downed pilot or to submerge immediately to avoid enemy aircraft. In business, ethical dilemmas often arise when managers face conflicting values. For example, a salesperson might face the dilemma of telling the truth about a product and thus losing a sale and his or her commission.

To prevent these ethical dilemmas, organizational decision makers need to prioritize all competing values and standards of behavior. A commonly agreed on set of ethical standards can then be developed to guide decisions when conflicting obligations, cost-benefit trade-offs, and competing value choices are present.[15] When thinking through particular dilemmas, the following questions can sharpen ethical sensitivity and moral awareness:[16]

- Does this decision or action meet the highest societal standards about how people should interact with each other?

- Does this decision or action agree with my religious teachings and beliefs (or with my personal principles and sense of responsibility?

- How will I feel about myself if I do this?

- Do we (or I) have a rule or policy for cases like this?

- Would I want everyone to make the same decision and take the same action if faced with these same circumstances?

- What are my true motives for considering this action?

Public Justification Criteria

One dilemma in determining ethical criteria concerns differences of opinion regarding what behaviors are appropriate. The rule of thumb in North American business culture is whether you would feel proud about your behavior if every detail was published in the newspaper the next day. Specific questions to ask yourself when contemplating an action using public justification criteria are:[17]

- How would I feel (or how will I feel) if (or when) this action becomes public knowledge?

- Will I be able to explain adequately to others why I have taken this action?

- Would others feel that my action or decision is ethical or moral?

This test does not eliminate ethical dilemmas between subcultures or different countries, however, because there are "readers" with very different values. An international example concerning different expectations about bribery is given in the World Watch box.

Values As Benchmarks

Since neither the home or host country values are absolute or hold for both countries, some type of transitional, or compromise criteria, need to be established in these situations that satisfy all parties concerned with the interactions. Nevertheless, there are some moral values that might be so important to a party that they should never be compromised. These are core values, or *absolute values*, like those established by the United Nations regarding basic human rights. *Compatible values* are statements of desirable ways of behaving that support absolute values. One example is a credo statement of a company that states how members should behave to live up to the company's absolute values. *Transitional values* are those that bend somewhat from absolute and compatible values to be more compatible with the different values of another culture. For example, the limits established for gift giving in the United States might be less than those allowed for Japan, where the custom is to be more extravagant. These are values in tension, which may or may not endure depending on the consequences. Finally, there are intolerable values that are so opposed to our core values that no interaction with the people holding them is possible. Countries allowing slave labor or dangerous procedures with high death rates would not be viable business partners for a company in a Judeo-Christian country.[18]

Applying Moral Frameworks to Ethical Decisions

Competing ethical criteria can also create ethical dilemmas within the same culture. Take the dilemma faced by John Higgins in the following situation.

John Higgins is director of research for a large electronics industry company. He recently promoted Mary Fernandez to head the design team charged with developing a critical component for a new radar system. He evaluated Mary as having superior knowledge of the technical elements in the project. However, he had begun to hear that the members of the all-male team were complaining about a woman leading them. There was

EYE ON ETHICS
Who (or What) Are Making Health Decisions?

In 1992, Cynthia Herdrich of Bloomington, Illinois, almost died because of a ruptured appendix. The real question is, Why did Cynthia not receive the necessary appendectomy before this life-threatening condition presented itself? Was it sudden, unforeseen condition, or had doctors already identified a potentially harmful situation and not acted upon it because of the cost?

Herdrich blamed her HMO for her ruptured appendix and sued. She felt her HMO was providing inadequate medical care because her doctor at the Carle Clinic waited to perform an ultrasound test "so the test could be performed at a facility owned by the HMO" (hence, reducing the cost of the test). However, the eight-day delay for the test was too long and her appendix ruptured. Later, she sued the HMO and claimed $35,000 in damages. Nevertheless, in February of 2000, her case is in front of the U.S. Supreme Court. The question in front of the judges is, Can patients sue HMOs that offer doctors financial incentives to reduce medical costs?

Currently, doctors receive financial incentives to reduce health care costs. However, what are the "costs" of these financial incentives provided by HMOs? According to Greg Bloche (Georgetown University law professor), "What matters is whether financial incentives put so much pressure on physicians that physicians can no longer act primarily overshadowing ethical or sound medical decisions?

It is foreseen that this question will continue to resurface as the United States reforms health care. The trade-off between costs and levels of care is continually debated. HMOs want lower costs, patients want the best health care at the lowest cost, and doctors are caught in the middle between HMOs and patients. Therefore, doctors are forced to make decisions that balance the needs of their patients with the financial needs (and incentives) of their patients' HMOs.

Sources: Article by Charles Bierbauer on CNN website (February, 23, 2000) — http://www.cnn.com/2000/HEALTH/02/23/scotus.hmos/index.html.

evidence that some team members were subtly sabotaging the project. John knew it was fair to give Mary this job based on her merits, but he also knew that the successful and quick completion of the project was essential both for the company's success and his own reputation. He wondered if he should remove Mary as team leader.[19]

John Higgins's problem is typical of the complex decisions managers face much of the time. These problems can be viewed from different points of view, including the economic, legal, and moral frameworks.[20] A strictly *economic* framing of this problem would consider what is most efficient and effective in terms of minimizing costs and maximizing efficiency and profits. From this point of view, Higgins would likely opt to remove Mary Fernandez as team leader. The *legal* view is concerned with whether or not a given act violates the law. Using a legal framework, Higgins would ask such questions as Would removing Fernandez be illegal because of gender discrimination? Does management have the legal right to assign duties? From this viewpoint, Higgins may need legal advice in making his decision. Viewing this problem from a *moral* framework raises a different set of questions. Two basic ones are: Would such a move be right? Would it be fair and just? A decision might be both economically wise and legal and still be immoral.

Some people believe that moral considerations apply to their personal lives but not to their business decisions. Those with this viewpoint believe that economic and legal considerations are the only relevant basis for making sound business decisions. What is most profitable overrides moral considerations, assuming legality. This does not mean such people believe business is an immoral activity. Rather, they would see it as amoral, which means business runs according to its own rules. They assume that laws provide the necessary rules for conducting business, so the relevant questions are: Is the behavior profitable? Is it legal? If John Higgins held this amoral view, he would likely replace Mary. However, he might believe that moral issues are relevant for work as well as for personal behavior. Managers face difficult decisions when they must balance moral considerations and organizational goals.

Morality

What, then, is a moral viewpoint? **Morality** *is a set of principles defining right and wrong behaviors.* A behavior is considered moral if it conforms to a standard of right behavior.[21] The concept of ethics is closely related to morality, and the terms moral and ethical are frequently used synonymously.

Some educators say ethics cannot be taught.[22] Their point, partially, is that people may be taught ethical behavior, but that there is no guarantee they will behave ethically. While this is true, the starting point is to teach people to recognize the ethical dimensions of a problem and to reason with ethical principles to decide on an ethical solution in a particular situation. A framework for applying moral principles to ethical dilemmas is presented below.

Moral Principles

When individuals are confronted with ethical dilemmas—situations that involve conflicting or competing moral interests—it is helpful to have guiding principles for reasoning through the dilemma. Three major sets of moral principles are utilitarianism, rights, and justice.

Utilitarianism

Utilitarianism means *to act in such a way that the greatest good is achieved for the greatest number.*[23] To use utilitarianism for reasoning through an ethical dilemma, begin by identifying alternative courses of action.[24] Then determine the benefits and harm resulting from each alternative for all relevant stakeholders. A stakeholder is any person or group that would be affected by the behavior resulting from a decision being made. Next select the alternative that encompasses the most benefits and least harm for the most stakeholders. This principle is similar to cost-benefit analysis, which is commonly used in business decision making. Utilitarianism guides the decision maker to choose the alternative that produces the greatest net social good when all the stakeholders are considered.

In the context of a moral decision, **social good** i*s defined in general terms such as happiness, benefit, or least harm.*[25] The broad nature of this definition sometimes makes application of the concept difficult, and people may differ in their assessments. It is easier to use the economics term, **utility**, but it has a narrower meaning, *referring to only the economic benefits realized in transactions*. It is much more difficult to measure happiness, benefit, or good. The greater the number of stakeholders affected by a decision, the more difficult is such measurement.

Another weakness of utilitarianism is its focus on outcomes and not on the means for achieving the ends. If utilitarianism is the only principle applied, some courses of action may be suggested that conflict with other ethical principles such as rights and justice. The Higgins-Fernandez case exemplifies this point. Higgins might reason that he, the other employees, and the company would best be served if the conflict surrounding Mary Fernandez were eliminated by removing her. However, such a decision would appear to violate Fernandez's rights, and many would question the fairness or justice of such a decision.

In spite of these limitations, the utilitarian principle can be useful. Its main value is that it helps guide decision makers to act in ways that lead to the greatest social good. Appropriate application of utilitarianism requires considering the impact of decisions on all stakeholders and reaching decisions that benefit the largest number. Questions to ask when applying utilitarianism might include:[26]

- What will be the short- and long-term consequences of this action?

- Who will benefit from this course of action?

- Who will be hurt?

- How will this action create good and prevent harm?

Rights

A second philosophical approach to reasoning about ethical dilemmas focuses on the rights of individuals. This approach is grounded in the work of Immanual Kant, the eighteenth century German philosopher who believed that each individual has a right to be treated with dignity and respect and as a free and equal person. A **right** *is a justified claim or entitlement that an individual can make to behave or to have others behave toward him or her in a certain way.*[27] The justification for such a claim is based on a standard accepted by a society. Sometimes these rights are explicitly stated. The Declaration of Independence identifies life, liberty, and the pursuit of happiness as "unalienable rights," and the United States Constitution sets forth the "Bill of Rights," which includes such things as the right of free speech and the "right to a speedy and public trial by an impartial jury" if accused of a crime. Interpretations of these specific rights have led to many additional legal and socially accepted moral rights.

Legal rights are codified in law, whereas *moral rights* are justified by society's generally accepted moral standards. An important basis for moral rights is Kant's principle that humanity must always be treated as an end, not merely as a means.[28] This implies that treating another as a means is to use that person for one's own gain. Treating the individual as an end implied respect by allowing the person to choose for herself or himself in order to satisfy personal needs and goals.

Rights impose corresponding duties. These duties may either be to refrain from certain behavior or to act out certain behavior. For example, an individual's right to privacy imposes on others the duty to refrain from violating that privacy. Kant's notion that each individual should be treated with respect suggests that each individual has a corresponding duty to treat others with respect. If society accepts that each individual has a right to education or medical care, there are corresponding duties to provide them for those who cannot provide for themselves.

The rights approach suggests that actions are wrong that violate the rights of individuals. However, individual rights sometimes conflict. For example, the right to associate freely with whomever one wants may conflict with the right not to be discriminated against. For example, should a private club be able to determine that only men can be members? In such cases the decision maker needs to determine which right is more important for sustaining human dignity. Is it free association or equality?[29]

The rights approach to ethical dilemmas indicates that it is morally wrong to interfere with the moral rights of an individual. However, consideration of individual rights alone is insufficient for ethical decision making because social costs must also be considered. Individual rights should not be achieved at an unreasonable cost to others in the society. The difficulty of defining, measuring, and balancing these rights sometimes make specific ethical decisions difficult. Both individual rights and the common good must be considered. Questions to ask when using the rights approach to solve ethical dilemmas include:[30]

- Would this action infringe or impinge on the moral rights or dignity of others?

- Would this action allow others freedom of choice in this matter?

- Would this action involve deceiving others in any way?

Justice

Justice has been connected with ethics and morality more than any idea in western civilization.[31] **Justice *is fairness*.** It means giving each person what he or she deserves.[32] Conflicts often develop when people disagree over how benefits and burdens should justly be distributed. The challenge is to determine morally what each person or group justly deserves.

One widely accepted principle that helps reason about such issues was stated by Aristotle over two thousand years ago. He postulated that equals should be treated equally and unequals unequally. Today, that principle is interpreted as meaning that "individuals should be treated the same, unless they differ in ways that are relevant to the situation in which they are involved."[33] For example, two people of different gender or race who perform equally should be compensated equally. However, two people who perform and contribute differently should be paid differently, even if they are of the same gender or race. Differences based on such criteria as contribution, need, and what one deserves are sometimes used to justify unequal treatment. For example, it is widely accepted that it is just for the government to treat poor people differently than those who are wealthy. However, many would agree that it is not just, or fair, to treat Mary Fernandez differently than her male colleagues only because of gender.

There are different types of justice.[34] The kind we have been talking about so far is **distributive justice**, *which refers to the fair distribution of benefits and burdens across a group or society.* A second kind of justice is **retributive justice**, *which is the fairness of blame or punishment for wrongdoers.* For example, most would say that firing an employee for making a relatively small mistake the first time would not be fair. On the other hand, if that employee had been adequately trained and had made a similar mistake before, and if the mistake was relatively expensive, termination might be just.

Compensatory justice *is concerned with the fairness of compensation awarded to those who have been injured.* For example, an employee who is terminated illegally is entitled to compensation for having been wronged. The extent of a compensation that is just depends on such factors as how long the employee goes without getting work, how long the employee had been with the employer, and how much hardship the illegal termination caused the employee.

Key questions to ask when making moral decisions are: Am I treating all people equally? If not, is such action justified? In business and other organizations people are often treated differently in terms of their pay, job responsibilities, and authority. If these differences are based on morally acceptable criteria, such as performance or experience, such unequal treatment is considered just. Differences of treatment based on such things as race, gender, religion, or age are not considered just in the United States. Morally acceptable criteria, however, are different in different countries. Questions to apply when deciding how to be just include:[35]

- Would I feel that this action was just (ethical or fair) if I were on the other side of the decision?

- How would I feel if this action were done to me or to someone close to me?

- Would this action or decision distribute benefits justly?

- Would it distribute hardships or burdens justly?

Cultural differences will make a difference in what is considered just, which can cause ethical dilemmas in international business transactions like those previously described in the Eye on Ethics box. The issue of bribery, for example, is one of the toughest to resolve in the international context. It regularly occurs in government as well as business even though it violates all of the economic, legal, and moral frameworks just discussed. The free market system is the best in the world for promoting efficient productivity, but it only works if transactions are based solely on price and quality considerations. No country in the world has laws that sanction bribery, so it is universally illegal. Furthermore, it violates the moral principles of justice (it is not fair), rights (those who produce the best quality with the lowest price are not necessarily rewarded), and utilitarianism (the greatest net social good for all stakeholders is not obtained).[36]

Arthur Andersen & Company, one of the major U.S. accounting firms, is trying to help solve this type of business ethics dilemma. Brainstorming with ethics experts from academia and business, it has developed a program promoting ethics education in business schools and in employee training programs. The sessions cover ethical issues in finance, marketing, management, and accounting, such as accepting gifts and tips, truthfulness in advertising, and sexual harassment.[37]

As we have seen, however, not all issues can be unequivocally solved by applying previously agreed on standards of conduct because such agreement is impossible. In such situations, the best that one can do is to refer to personal intuition and insight. Some questions to ask yourself when dealing with these ambiguous ethical dilemmas are:[38]

- Have I searched for all alternatives? Are there other ways to look at this situation? Have I considered all points of view?

- Even if I can rationalize this decision or action, and even if I could defend it publicly, does my inner sense tell me this is right?

- What does my intuition tell me is the ethical thing to do in this situation? Have I listened to my inner voice?

WHAT ARE INDIVIDUAL DIFFERENCES IN DECISION STYLES?[39]

Individuals do not always follow ethical guidelines or the rational problem-solving process just described. Even when they do, there are variances due to individual information-processing habits. Some differences involve satisficing versus optimizing preferences. Others are determined by the amount of information people prefer and the criteria they focus on when making decisions.

Decision styles refer to our *learned habits for processing decision-making information.* Whether one style is "better" than another depends on the particular situation in which it is used. There are two primary ways that people differ in their decision-making habits: (1)-in the amount of information they use and (2)-in the number of alternatives they develop to potentially solve a problem.

Employees can help to redesign operations and show how new designs should work. If management allows employees to create new ideas and focus on new ways of processing information, it may result in increased savings or increased revenues for the company just by shifting the focus of decision making.

Amount and Focus of Information Processing

Some people use a great deal of information in generating and evaluating alternatives, while others use very little. When faced with a problem, *a satisficer* uses just enough information to arrive at a feasible solution. The satisficer knows that more information about the problem might be available but decides that it is not worth the additional effort to obtain it.

A *maximizer*, on the other hand, continues to gather information until nothing new can be learned about the problem. A maximizer knows that a workable solution might be reached with less information but decides that important aspects of the problem might not be recognized unless all available information is considered.

Both methods are valuable in the appropriate situations. For example, the satisficer has an advantage when time is important, whereas the maximizer has an advantage when problems are complicated and there is little time pressure.

Solution focus refers to the number of alternatives that a person develops for dealing with a problem. *Unifocus* people are committed to one dominant criterion and consequently favor a single solution to a problem. *Multifocus* people, on the other hand, apply several criteria and generate several solutions to a problem. The unifocus approach has an advantage when efficiency is important, when it is possible to adopt only one solution, or when rules and regulations narrowly limit the range of choices. The multifocus approach has an advantage when there is a need to find new ways of doing things or it is important to "cover all the bases."

The Five Dominant Decision Styles

From these differences in amount of information used and solution focus, five fundamentally different decision styles emerge. Figure 12–7 illustrates the relationships among the five decision styles.

Decisive Style

Decisive persons use just enough information to reach one workable solution. Decisives are fast-thinking, action-oriented people who place high importance on efficiency, promptness, and reliability. They usually stick to one course of action for dealing with a particular problem.

Flexible Style

People with this style also use a minimal amount of information, but they are multifocused and so produce several solutions for a problem. Like Decisives, Flexibles are action oriented, but they place greater importance on adaptability than on efficiency. They like to keep their options open.

Hierarchic Style

People with the hierarchic style analyze a large amount of information thoroughly to develop a single best solution to a problem. They place great emphasis on logic and quality. Hierarchics tend to be slow to make decisions the first time they encounter a particular problem, but they speed up substantially after they develop a method for handling that type of problem.

Integrative Style

People with this style utilize a very large amount of information to produce multiple solutions to problems. Integratives value exploration, experimentation, and creativity. They look at problems from many points of view and see numerous options for dealing with a single problem. Consequently, they sometimes have difficulty deciding on only one solution, which makes them appear indecisive. To counter this tendency, Integratives sometimes try to implement several courses of action simultaneously.

Systemic Style

This two-stage decision style combines both integrative and hierarchic patterns. A person using the systemic style initially approaches a problem in the integrative way, viewing it from many points of view and exploring multiple solutions. After examining many options, however, the person becomes more hierarchic, subjecting various alternatives to a rigorous analysis that ends with a clearly prioritized set of solutions. The Systemic usually develops a very broad understanding of a problem. In many cases, Systemics examine multiple problems simultaneously to understand the broader implications of situations. Because of the thoroughness of their analyses, Systemics tend to be slow decision makers.

FIGURE 12-7   **INDIVIDUAL DECISION STYLES**

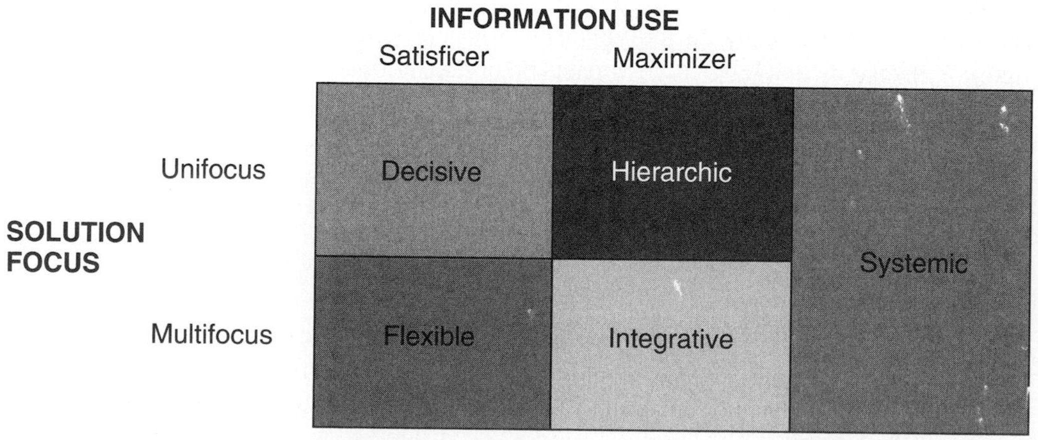

Backup Styles

Although most people have a clear predisposition toward one dominant decision style, many shift to a different "backup" style occasionally. The shift between dominant and backup styles is related to how much pressure a person experiences when making decisions.

Under the pressure of tight deadlines, high risk, and significant consequences, people tend to shift to the less complex decisive or flexible styles, which are easier and faster to use. These styles are also frequently used under low pressure if there is not enough information to employ a more complex style. Under moderate pressure, people tend to use the more complex systemic, integrative, or hierarchic styles because there is a lot of information available and sufficient time to analyze it in depth.

WHEN IS PARTICIPATION IMPORTANT FOR DECISION MAKING?

Who should be involved in the problem-solving process? Just the manager? A committee? A coalition of key individuals? The entire department? In 1992, General Motors was losing $2.5 million a day. To turn this negative trend around, employees were encouraged to participate wholeheartedly with GM management in a $3 billion gamble to build a tight, light, high-quality, peppy subcompact in competition with Tercel, Civic, and the rest of Japan's best. GM's approach was to merge management and labor into a team where they would make decisions and share the pains, gains, and profits. The result was a lean production facility, a familial management–labor structure, and an obsession with quality control. The product was the Saturn, which during its first nine months sold at twice the rate of Toyotas or Hondas.[40]

Degrees of Decision Participation

There is evidence that participation can enhance morale, satisfaction, and productivity, but in emergencies or when others do not have sufficient information, an autocratic decision may be more appropriate.[41] Victor Vroom and Phillip Yetton have developed a diagnostic framework for matching the amount of participation in decision making with situational requirements.[42] Their five possible decision-making processes described in Figure 12-8, vary in the degrees of participation they allow.

Criteria for Participation in Decision Making
When deciding how much participation to use when making a decision, several factors need to be considered. Three of the most important are the quality requirements, the degree that it is necessary for subordinates to accept the decision, and the time required to make the decision.

Quality Requirements
Whether a decision is best made by an individual or a group depends on the nature and importance of the problem. Important decisions that have large impacts on organizational goal achievement need to be the highest quality possible. In a complex situation, it is unlikely that any one individual will have all the necessary information to make a top-quality decision. Therefore, the decision maker should at least consult with others who are either closer to the problem or more "expert" in dealing with it. One person with appropriate knowledge and experience, on the other hand, can decide what to do to solve simple routine problems.

Acceptance Requirements
The effectiveness of the action plan decided on is a combination of its quality and the effort put into implementing it. A top-quality decision, if not implemented appropriately, will not be effective. A lower-quality decision that receives enthusiastic support from all involved may be more effective than a higher-quality alternative that implementers do not "buy into."

Those affected by a decision are usually more highly motivated to implement the action plan if they have had an opportunity to influence it. Being involved usually increases participants' understanding and generates a feeling of commitment to make "our" decision work, whereas an arbitrary, autocratic decision that is handed down often results in passive acceptance or even active resistance to implementation.

Time Requirements

Allocating problem solving and decision making to a group requires a greater investment of time in meetings that is unavailable for usual tasks. But the level of acceptance and probability of efficient execution is greater for participative decisions than autocratic methods. Also, a higher-quality decision may result from the inclusion of a variety of perspectives and approaches. It is important to determine if this additional time investment produces significantly higher degrees of quality, acceptance, and commitment.

Determining the Appropriate Amount of Participation in Decision Making

The specific needs for quality, acceptance, and time provide the impetus for choosing among the five degrees of participation in any given decision situation. Vroom and his colleagues have found that the answers to seven questions about decision quality and acceptance can indicate the most appropriate degree of participation in any given decision situation.[43] Figure 12-9 illustrates the appropriate sequence of these three questions regarding quality and four questions regarding acceptance in a decision-tree format.

It's possible that more than one style may be appropriate for a problem situation. In that case, the optimal style indicated by this model is the more autocratic one because it will require the least amount of time to implement. Therefore, the decision tree is most useful in situations where time is a critical factor. It does not take into consideration such long-term factors as morale or employee development. In a situation where increased group cohesiveness and worker morale are important, it may be more appropriate to choose a more time-consuming decision style that emphasizes team development. While the autocratic style takes far less time, it does not address the long-term developmental needs of the individuals involved.

FIGURE 12-8	**TYPES OF PARTICIPATION IN DECISIONS**

Key:	A = Automatic, C = Consultant, G = Group, I and II denote variations of a process
AI	You solve the problem or make the decision yourself, using information available at the time.
AII	You obtain the necessary information from your subordinate(s), then decide on the solution to the problem yourself. You may or may not tell your subordinates what the problem is in getting the information from them. The role played by your subordinates in making the decision is clearly one of providing the necessary information to you, rather than generating or evaluating alternative solutions.
CI	You share the problem with relevant subordinates individually, getting their ideas and suggestions without bringing them together as a group. Then you make the decision that may or may not reflect your subordinates' influence.
CII	You share the problem with your subordinates as a group, collectively obtaining their ideas and suggestions. Then you make the decision that may or may not reflect your subordinates' influence.
GII	You share the problem with your subordinates as a group. Together you generate and evaluate alternatives and attempt to reach agreement (consensus) on a solution. Your role is much like that of chairman. You do not try to influence the group to adopt "your" solution, and you are willing to accept and implement any solution that has the support of the entire group.

SOURCE: Reprinted from *Organizational Dynamics,* Spring 1973. © 1973 with permission from Elsevier Science.

FIGURE 12–9   DECISION TREE FOR DECISION-MAKING PARTICIPATION

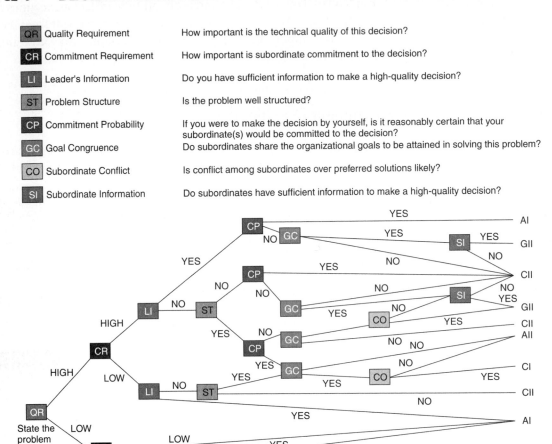

QR	Quality Requirement	How important is the technical quality of this decision?
CR	Commitment Requirement	How important is subordinate commitment to the decision?
LI	Leader's Information	Do you have sufficient information to make a high-quality decision?
ST	Problem Structure	Is the problem well structured?
CP	Commitment Probability	If you were to make the decision by yourself, is it reasonably certain that your subordinate(s) would be committed to the decision?
GC	Goal Congruence	Do subordinates share the organizational goals to be attained in solving this problem?
CO	Subordinate Conflict	Is conflict among subordinates over preferred solutions likely?
SI	Subordinate Information	Do subordinates have sufficient information to make a high-quality decision?

HOW CAN PROBLEMS BE SOLVED MORE EFFECTIVELY?

Techniques for avoiding groupthink and the liabilities of group decision making can enhance group problem-solving effectiveness. Other methods for solving problems better include encouraging creativity, structured processes for guiding interaction, and electronic information processing.

Encouraging Creativity

For organizations to creatively solve problems, managers must demonstrate that they value it and know how to deal with innovations when they are suggested. The Center for Creative Leadership has determined some characteristics of managers who generate creativity in their organizations.

Characteristics of Managers Who Generate Creativity.[44]

Managers who encourage creativity are willing to absorb risks taken by subordinates. They allow their people freedom, expect some errors, and are willing to learn from inevitable failures. Managers who are afraid of mistakes, on the other hand, restrict the freedom of their subordinates to experiment and be creative.

Productive managers of creativity can live with *half-developed ideas*. They do not insist that an idea be 100 percent proven before supporting its development. They are willing to listen to and encourage subordinates to press on with "half-baked" proposals that hold promise. They know that criticism can kill an innovation.

Creative managers have a feel for the times when the company rule book needs to be ignored and will *stretch normal policies* for the greater long-term good. Managers that permit no deviation from standard operating procedures will make predictable progress and avoid mistakes, but they will not obtain giant breakthroughs that calculated risk taking can promote.

Productive managers are *good listeners*. They listen to their staff, try to pull out good ideas, and build on suggestions. They do not try to impose new policies or procedures on people without listening to the other side first.

Creative managers *don't dwell on mistakes*. They are more future oriented than past oriented. They don't hold the mistakes of others against them indefinitely. They are willing to begin with the world as it is today and work for a better future. They learn from experience, but they do not wallow in the past.

When good ideas are presented, productive managers are willing to decide on the spot to try them without waiting for further studies. They are courageous enough to *trust their intuition* and commit resources to implementing promising innovations.

Finally, productive managers are *enthusiastic and invigorating*. They encourage and energize others. They enjoy using the resources and power of their position to push projects forward and make improvements.

YOUR TURN

How Creative Are You?

Place a check mark by the 10 words in the following list that best characterize you.

energetic	persuasive	observant	fashionable	self-confident
persevering	original	cautious	habit-bound	resourceful
egotistical	independent	stern	predictable	formal
informal	dedicated	factual	open-minded	forward-looking
tactful	inhibited	enthusiastic	innovative	poised
acquisitive	practical	alert	curious	organized
unemotional	dynamic	polished	courageous	clear-thinking
helpful	efficient	perceptive	quick	self-demanding
good-natured	thorough	impulsive	determined	understanding
realistic	modest	involved	flexible	absent-minded
sociable	well-liked	restless	retiring	

Scoring Key. For each of the following adjectives that you checked, give yourself 2 points:

energetic	resourceful	original	enthusiastic	dynamic
flexible	observant	independent	perceptive	innovative
persevering	dedicated	courageous	curious	self-demanding
involved				

For each of the following adjectives that you checked, give yourself 1 point:

thorough	determined	restless	informal	self-confident
alert	open-minded	forward-looking		

The rest of the adjectives receive no points.

Add up your total number of points: _____

Interpretation

16–20	Very creative
11–15	Above average
6–10	Average
1–5	Below average
0	Noncreative

Source: Adapted from Eugene Raudsepp, *How Creative Are You?* (New York: Putnam, 1981), pp.-22–24.

CHALLENGE OF CHANGE
Electronic Brainstorming

Electronic brainstorming is similar to the nominal group technique except that group members exchange ideas on interactive computer terminals instead of writing their ideas on paper. It is especially effective in groups larger than five members, where experiments have demonstrated that more unique and high-quality ideas are generated and members are more satisfied than when they use verbal brainstorming. Electronic brainstorming is not a face-to-face medium, which reduces the negative effects of ideas being blocked due to apprehension about their rejection.

Electronic brainstorming also enables widely dispersed group members to generate ideas interactively. In this application, electronic brainstorming is a sophisticated form of computer conferencing, wherein group members' ideas are automatically sent to each other's screens during the idea generation session. This process may be particularly helpful when people's schedules differ markedly because of time zones and workloads. It may offer an attractive alternative to conference calls that require everyone to be available to interact at the same time.

Finally, the simultaneity of input in electronic brainstorming also prevents one individual from dominating the idea generation process. Inputs tend to be evenly distributed over group members, which helps increase not only the number of ideas generated but also people's satisfaction with the process.

A new technology is also assisting in electronic brainstorming. A Group Support System (GSS), also called "groupware", is a suite of software tools running over a network to support a team working toward a goal or set of goals. Depending on the specific goal desired, the software will enable team members to work together on objects, list creation, graphics, presentations, idea sharing via conferencing or e-mail, etc. Furthermore, teamwork is generated using groupware since a large breadth of ideas are shared, team members can participate anonymously without fear of retaliation, and the convergence and divergence of ideas are not inhibited by personality conflicts.

In a recent experiment to test the effectiveness of a GSS, U.S. Military personnel used electronic brainstorming to generate ideas about an upcoming change of command. Additionally, electronic brainstorming was used to discuss methods of moving the U.S.S. Coronado. In both cases, ideas were generated and prioritzed according to urgency in a short period of time. Once the ideas were generated, electonic voting indicated which ideas the group favored. The personnel involved felt better that better ideas were generated in a more efficient manner via electronic brainstorming than via normal group methods.

Source: R.O. Brigss, M. Adkins, D. Mittleman, J. Kruse, et. al., "A Technology Transition Model Derived from Field Investigation of GSS Use Abroad the U.S.S. CORONADO," *Journal of Management Information Systems*, 15 (Winter 1998/1999), pp. 151-95; W.L. Tuller, P.A. Kaiser, and P.A. Balthazard, "Group Work and Electronic Meeting Systems: From Boardroom to Classroom," *Business Communication Quarterly* (New York: December 1998), pp. 53-65. R. Brent Gallupe et al., "Electronic Brainstorming and Group Size," *Academy of Management Journal* 35, no. 2 (1992), pp.-350–369.

To determine how creative you are, complete the Your Turn exercise. If your score is not as high as you would like, a number of ways to enhance creativity are described in the next section.

Promoting Creative Thinking in Organizations

To encourage creativity, a manager needs to provide a bureaucracy-free environment that tolerates diverse behavior. When a wealthy patron once asked Pablo Picasso what he could do to help him, Picasso looked at him and said succinctly, "Stand out of my light."[45] Several examples of how universities and businesses have promoted creativity by eliminating organizational barriers follow.[46]

In a course at the University of Houston, nicknamed Failure 101, students are requested to build the tallest structure possible out of ice-cream-bar sticks and then look for "the insight in every failure. Those who end up with the highest projects went through the most failures. Whoever followed a fixed idea from the outset never finished first."

Training students to learn from mistakes and try, try again may be good training for future careers in business. But "you can't just order up a good idea or spend money to find one," points out Jon Henderson, director of Hallmark's Creative Resources Center. "You have to build a supportive climate and give people the freedom to create things."

One famous example of how a creative climate can pay off is 3M in Minneapolis, where employees are encouraged to devote about 15 percent of their work time to non-job-related creative thinking. Doing "skunkworks duty," as it is known at 3M, has resulted in such creative products as Post-It notes, three-dimensional magnetic recording tape, and disposable medical masks. About 30 percent of total revenues is from new products developed in the past five years, and 3M figures that nearly 70 percent of its annual $12 billion in sales comes from creative ideas that originated with the work force.

At W.L. Gore & Associates, the company that brought us Teflon products, employees are urged to take risks. The feeling is that if they are not making mistakes, they are doing something wrong. This philosophy has propelled W.L.Gore from a glorified mom-and-pop operation to a company with 37 plants worldwide that turns out everything from electronics to dental products.

Despite the obvious benefits creative risk taking has brought to companies like 3M and W.L. Gore, not all managers are comfortable with the adjustments necessary for creating a climate that nurtures creativity. The Conference Board, a business research group, found that managers with negative feelings about creativity feel that it is uncontrollable, which is anathema for a manager whose job is to control. Consequently, many managers are fearful and unwilling to give up their power and control. But, according to founder Vieve Gore, it was the absence of direct control and deliberate structure that contributed to W.L. Gore's phenomenal creative success.

For managers who see the necessity for creativity but are still apprehensive, several structured alternatives to promoting problem-solving creativity exist that do not entail giving up control in the work environment.[47] Among them are brainstorming, the nominal group technique, and the Delphi technique.

Brainstorming

Brainstorming *is a demonstrated approach for achieving high participation and increasing the number of action alternatives.*[48] To engage in brainstorming sessions, people meet in small groups and feed off one another's ideas, which provide stimuli for more creative solutions. Rules for effective brainstorming promote the goal of quantity of ideas no matter how far fetched, allow no criticism or evaluation of ideas as they are generated, allow only one idea at a time from each person, and encourage people to build on each other's ideas.

Brainstorming groups are encouraged to be freewheeling and radical. Through use of a nonevaluative environment that is intentionally fun, brainstorming ensures involvement, enthusiasm, and a large number of solution alternatives.

Brainstorming generally works well in a participative, team-oriented climate where people are comfortable with each other and are committed to pulling together toward a common goal. In some situations it may not be effective, however. One example occurred in Paris, France, where the expatriate general manager from the United States attempted a brainstorming session with department managers and, instead of a number of excited ideas, was met with a room full of frowns and complete silence. When he inquired why there were no responses, he was told very seriously that he was the director general, and it was his job to tell them what to do. The staff's job was to follow orders and accept his suggestions, not to do his job for him.

At other times, a hostile or political climate might inhibit the free flow of ideas. In restrictive interpersonal climates, more structured techniques like the nominal group or Delphi group technique may be more effective. The recent development of electronic brainstorming, described in the Challenge of Change box, can also circumvent the need for face-to-face brainstorming meetings.

Nominal Group Technique

In the **nominal group technique**, *participants meet together in a highly structured format that governs the decision-making process.*[49] First, participants independently write down their ideas about the problem. Second, each presents one idea to the group in a round-robin fashion without discussion. These ideas are summarized and written on a flip chart or blackboard so all can see them. After a group discussion to clarify and evaluate the ideas, an independent ranking of the proposals takes place. These rankings are pooled to determine the proposal with the highest aggregate ranking, which is the group's decision.

The nominal group technique offers the advantages of multiple idea generation, balanced participation, and participant satisfaction. It is time consuming and does require participants to meet together at a common location. In any group decision-making situation, the advantages and disadvantages of a proposed technique should be weighed with respect to the nature of the participants and the specific decision being made.

Delphi Technique

In the **Delphi technique**, participants do not meet together but interact through a series of written judgments and suggestions.[50] After each participant has been presented with the problem, he or she writes down comments and possible solutions and sends them to a central location for recording and reproduction. Each participant then receives a copy of all other comments and solutions to use as a springboard for additional ideas or comments. These also are returned to the central location for compilation and reproduction, and an independent vote on solution priority is taken.

The Delphi technique allows for the pooling of a variety of ideas, viewpoints, independent feedback, and criticism at minimal expense, since participants do not have to congregate at a common meeting place. It does, however, take an extended period of time, and there is really no control over the decision-making process. Depending on the nature of the decision group, participants' lack of face-to-face interaction can be either an asset or a liability.

Group Decision Support Systems

Group decision support systems *are electronic and computer-supported data processing tools that can facilitate group decision making in certain situations.* "Same time–same place" interactions among team members can be facilitated by software tools such as mathematical models, spreadsheets, graphics packages, and electronic brainstorming activities. "Same place–different time" interactions are supported by such tools as retrieval systems for information sharing and display software. "Same time–different place" group interactions can be accomplished through videoconferencing, which combines audio and video communications. "Different time–different place" decision making can be helped by such mechanisms as electronic mail and groupware. Group decision support system tools have been shown to increase the efficiency of group problem solving, better document it, and produce higher-quality decisions.[51]

Porsche Claims Exemption from Merger Mania — A Second Look

Since 1996 peace prevails on the Porsche line. The production changes imposed by the Shin-Gijutsu group three years ago produce more cars faster with fewer people without losing technical sophistication and road performance. Putting the losses behind it, the company can now concentrate on developing new models and new markets. In 1997 Porsche sold over 10,000 of its new Boxter roadsters, its least expensive model that has been produced to go along with its reengineered, top-of-the-line 911s. Porsche sales rose 28 percent in the United States in 1999, the sixth consecutive year of record sales and the best year for the 911 coupe in 35 years. The company is also planning to introduce a sport-utility vehicle in early 2002 with typical Porsche high-performance characteristics.

The team of Japanese consultants now returns only about four times a year because the innovations they initiated are being continued by the German engineers. Workers on the line submit 2,500 suggestions a month. Porsche still hopes to strip another 10 hours off car-assemble time, making the company comparable to the best Japanese auto makers. Porsche is also working with its suppliers to cut costs and improve quality and deliveries. While it works away at this goal, Porsche has formed Porsche Consulting to spread to other German manufacturers the Japanese manufacturing concepts it has learned.

As other automakers have scurried to merge and acquire, foreseeing a future controlled by fewer than 10 mega-motor conglomerates, tiny Porsche has rescued itself, by itself, from near bankruptcy. Dismissing what seem impossible odds, Porsche declares it never will marry. Finances are in order, sales are strong and very profitable, and new products are coming. Porsche has restored its reputation as a clear-headed, focused, unique auto company.

Source: J. Mateja, "Image-conscious Porsche to Offer an All-Wheel SUV," The San Diego Union Tribune (May 13, 2000), p. WHEELS-8; J.R. Healey, "Groomed So Not to Marry: Porsche Claims Exemption from Merger Mania," USA Today (August 6, 1999); J. Kandell, "Ferdinand Porsche, Creator of the Sports Car That Bore His Name, Is Dead at 88," The New York Times (March 28, 1998). p.A12; and N.-C. Nash, "Putting Porsche in the Pink: German Graftsmanship Gets Japanese Fine-Tuning," The New York Times (January 20, 1996), pp.-17–18.

SUMMARY

1. The rational problem-solving process includes identifying the problem, clarifying objectives, analyzing alternatives, deciding on a solution, implementing the solution, and following through to ensure its effectiveness. To begin solving a problem, the current situation needs to be diagnosed to understand and define the problem as accurately as possible. Hasty assumptions often contribute to a failure to distinguish a problem's symptoms from its sources.

2. The immediate and long-term effects of all alternative solutions on other people and situations should be considered. Effective action plans contain measurable criteria and time lines. Involving the people affected by the plan in the analysis of alternatives and in decision making will build their commitment to its implementation.

3. When evaluating action plan alternatives, benefits are weighed against possible negative consequences. Other considerations include probability of success; associated risk factors; potential money, time, and energy costs; and the possible reactions of those affected.

4. Effective implementation of an action plan depends on the parties' commitment to make it work. Commitment to the agreed-on solution usually is gained when problems, needs, and objectives are identified mutually, and solutions are reached through participation and consensus of all involved. Specific tasks and responsibilities are assigned, schedules are established, and personal commitment is reinforced as the plan is activated.

5. The follow-through process involves the development of procedures to monitor and assist the implementation of the new action plan. A control process is applied to measure performance, monitor results, and take corrective actions when needed.

KEY TERMS

brainstorming	ethical reasoning	Pareto chart
certainty	ethics	problem solving
compensatory justice	flowchart	retributive justice
criteria	Gantt chart	right
decision making	group decision support systems	satisficing
decision styles	justice	social good
Delphi technique	known risk	turbulence
distributive justice	morality	uncertainty
ethical behavior	nominal group technique	utilitarianism
ethical dilemma	objective	utility

QUESTIONS FOR STUDY AND DISCUSSION

1. Explain why it is so important to establish an atmosphere of trust in situations of group problem solving. Can you cite situations where you have not trusted others with whom you were involved in solving a problem? Compare them with situations in which you have felt trust. Have you ever felt that others in a group distrusted you? Why?

2. What four purposes are served by clarifying objectives early in the problem-solving process? Whose objectives should be considered?

3. Explain this statement: "No problem solution can be better than the quality of diagnosis on which it is built."

4. With regard to selecting an action plan, indicate whether you agree or disagree with each of the following statements and why: (1)-Experience is the best teacher. (2)-Intuition is a helpful force. (3)-Advice from others is always beneficial. (4) Experiment with several alternatives.

5. What difficulties might you anticipate when using the rational problem-solving process? Why? What additional difficulties might arise because of personal attributes? Which of these have you experienced? Explain. What were the consequences? How can these difficulties be avoided?

6. Which decision style would be most effective at each stage of the rational problem-solving process? Why? Explain which decision style would be best for making decisions under emergency circumstances. Which is best for solving a complex problem requiring considerable creativity?

7. Explain under what circumstances you would want to use participation to solve a problem. When would you rather solve the problem individually?

8. How can a manager encourage creative problem solving by department members?

9. How would you, as a manager, motivate your employees to engage in ethical behavior?

PERSONAL SKILLS INVENTORY

1. **Apply all five steps in the problem-solving process.**
   a. *Problem awareness.* Focus on correctly identifying problems versus symptoms of problems. Assess the importance of the problem relative to overall goals of the team. Is it a "mission critical" problem or a relatively minor situation?

   b. *Problem definition.* As the saying goes, "garbage in equals garbage out." Make sure you correctly define the problem so you don't create new problems.

   c. *Decision making.* Establish good criteria for a decision. Then come up with alternative solutions and assess the impacts (both positive and negative) of each alternative. Choose the best alternative.

   d. *Action plan implementation.* Assign specific work assignments to the most appropriate people and determine how long the individual tasks will take. Once actions are under way, reinforce team commitment to the actions.

   e. *Follow-through.* Identify success criteria and measure the results against it. If the results do not match the success criteria, determine why and how far the results were off. Identify new actions that need to be taken.

2. **Use problem-solving tools.** Use flow charts to analyze processes, and cause-and-effect diagrams to uncover sources of problems. Use Pareto charts to identify graphically the major causes or priorities of problems. Use decision-making grids to establish criteria and alternatives for decisions. Use a Gantt chart to identify tasks and time lines for decision implementation.

3. **Identify the ethical concerns in each specific decision situation.** Ask yourself, If I made this decision and it was published in *The Wall Street Journal* tomorrow, how would I feel? How would others feel?

4. **Use the most appropriate personal decision-making style.** Examine the strengths and weaknesses of your dominant decision style. In situations where other decision styles are more appropriate, use them yourself or enlist others more comfortable with other styles to aid you in the decision process.

5. **Determine when and how much group participation is optimal in each decision situation.** Some decisions and problems require an autocratic approach, while others need a consultative or group approach. Recognize the difference in problems and the level of participation needed to be successful.

6. **Encourage creativity.** Show others that you value creativity by absorbing risks, living with half-developed ideas, stretching normal policies, being a good listener, not dwelling on mistakes, and committing resources to implementation of promising innovations.

7. **Use group decision making to enhance problem-solving effectiveness.** Use group techniques like brainstorming, the nominal group technique, and the Delphi technique to enhance creative group problem solving. If available, take advantage of computer-supported group decision support systems.

WWW EXERCISE

Manager's Internet Tools

Web Tips: Problem-Solving Skills on the Web This chapter provides a variety of tools for helping you solve problems and make decisions. They range from knowledge of the rational problem-solving process to group decision support systems consisting of electronic and computer-supported data processing tools. Today there are many more databases and information processing tools available on the Internet that can expand your problem-solving capabilities. Complete the exercises that follow to become more familiar with these alternatives.

World Wide Web Search There are many sites on the Internet, including many specific companies, devoted to improving problem-solving skills. Using a search engine, find some sites that are targeted to helping people develop their problem-solving skills. What do these sites and/or companies have to offer, and what are the similarities to the concepts presented in this chapter?

Specific Website—Creative Problem Solving Group—Buffalo The Creative Problem Solving Group—Buffalo is a consulting group that, among other things, helps organizations solve problems creatively. On their website, the company has a pictorial representation of its problem-solving methodology. Go to the company's website, examine its mission, and then look at its problem-solving methodology (in their Services section).
Company: http://www.cpsb.com/
Problem Solving: http://www.cpsb.com/cps.html

Discussion Questions

1. What are the key components to Buffalo's creative problem-solving approach? To what types of problems does the company think the model can be applied?

2. Is the model static, with defined beginning and end points, or is it a dynamic model? What difference does it make?

Specific Website—The Future Problem Solving Program The Future Problem Solving Program (FPSP) is an organization established to expand students' thinking on problems. The organization hopes to inspire students to look at problems in different lights, and generate new and creative solutions to problems. The organization developed a six-step process as a guideline for problem solving. Go to the FPSP website and examine its six-step process on the Overview page. Then, look at the graphical representation on its FPSP History page.
Company: http://www.fpsp.org/
Problem Solving: http://www.fpsp.org/overview/history.html

Discussion Questions

1. What are the key components of FPSP's approach to creative problem solving? Are they different from Buffalo's components identified in the previous website?

2. What are the differences in the two models, and what might account for the differences? What difference do they make?

PERSONAL SKILLS EXERCISE

Choosing a Decision Style[52]

Objective To learn how to apply the Vroom and Yetton decision participation model.

Preparation Review the section entitled "When Is Participation Important in Decision Making?" earlier in this chapter. Make sure you understand the five decision participation styles (Figure 12-8) and the decision participation tree (Figure 12-9).

Stage 1: Individual Case Analyses Individually read each of the hypothetical cases that follow. Decide which of the five decision participation styles from Figure 12-8 you would use in each situation. Record your decisions.

Case A You are a manufacturing manager in the northeastern division of a large electronics plant. Upper management is always searching for ways to increase efficiency.

Recently management installed new machines and introduced a simplified work system, but to everyone's surprise (including your own) the expected increase in productivity has not been realized. In fact, production has begun to drop, quality has fallen, and the number of employee resignations has risen.

You do not believe there is anything wrong with the machines. You have requested reports from other companies that are using them, and their responses confirm this opinion. You have also called in representatives from the firm that built the machines. These technicians have examined the machines thoroughly and report that they are operating at peak efficiency.

You suspect that some elements of the new work system may be responsible for the decreased output and quality, but this view is not shared by your five immediate subordinates—the four first-line supervisors who head your four production sections and your supply manager. They have attributed the drop in production to various factors: poor operators, insufficient training, lack of adequate financial incentives, and poor worker morale. Clearly, this is an issue about which there is considerable depth of individual feeling. There exists a high potential for discord among your five key subordinates, and this may be just the tip of the iceberg.

This morning you received a phone call from your division manager, who had just reviewed your production figures for the last six months and was clearly concerned. The division manager has indicated that the problem is yours to solve in any way that you think best but has requested that you report within a week what steps you plan to take.

Certainly you share your manager's concern and you know that, despite their differing views, your subordinates share it as well. Your problem is to decide what steps must be taken by whom in the effort to reverse the decline.

Case B You are the general foreman in charge of a large work gang that is laying an oil pipeline. It is now necessary to estimate your expected rate of progress in order to schedule material deliveries to the next field site. You know the nature of the terrain you will be traveling and have the historical data you need to compute the mean and variance in the rate of speed over that type of terrain. Given these two variables, it is a simple matter to calculate the earliest and the latest times at which materials and support facilities will be needed at the next site. It is important that your estimate be reasonably accurate. Underestimates result in idle workers, and overestimates result in securing materials for a period of time before they are to be used.

Up to this point, progress has been good. Your five group foremen and other members of the gang stand to receive substantial bonuses if the project is completed ahead of schedule.

Case C You are supervising the work of twelve engineers. All twelve have similar levels of formal training and work experience, a condition that enables you to use them interchangeably on most projects. Yesterday your manager informed you that a request had come in from an overseas affiliate for four engineers to go abroad on extended loan for a period of six to eight months. For a number of reasons, he argued (and you agreed) that this request should be met from your group.

All your engineers are capable of handling this assignment, and from the standpoint of present and future projects, there is no particular reason why any one should be retained over any other. The major problem is that the location of the overseas assignment is considered undesirable by most members of the organization.

Stage 2: Group Discussion After individuals have recorded their opinions of the most appropriate decision participation style to be used in each of these cases, proceed with the following steps:

1. Divide the class into groups of three to five people. Designate one person from each group to keep a record of each group's discussion.

2. Each person shares with others in the group why he or she chose a particular decision style for each of the three cases.

3. Focus on determining all the reasons people chose different decision styles. One person should write down the styles chosen for each case and note briefly the associated reasons. Important: The group should not try to reach a consensus; you merely want to discover how many different approaches were taken and why.

4. Using the decision-making tree in Figure 12-9, individually answer the questions at the top and work through the decision tree until you reach the recommended decision style for each of the three cases.

5. Repeat step 4 as a group. Now establish consensus as to the appropriate decision style prescribed by this model.

6. Check your answers with Vroom and Yetton's, which your instructor will provide. Discuss any variations and reread the chapter explanation if misunderstandings persist.

7. Discuss within the group how original decisions agreed with or varied from the Vroom and Yetton model. Speculate as to why. The recorder should note the outcome of this group discussion.

Stage 3: Class Discussion Reconvene as a class. Have the group recorders report group outcomes, including discrepancies between the original (individual) analyses and Vroom and Yetton's solutions. Note any sharp disparities among the groups' responses, and try to determine why they occurred. Participate in a class discussion based on the following questions:

1. To what extent do you agree with the model? What are its strengths and weaknesses in application?

2. Do you have a preferred decision style (AI, AII, CI, CII, GII)? Why or why not? Will knowledge of this model help you be more flexible in choosing a decision style?

3. How closely does your decision behavior match that prescribed by the model? What evidence do you have that you are concerned more with time (efficiency) or with participation in choosing a decision style?

TEAM EXERCISE

Ethical Decision Making [53]

Purpose. To practice stretching and expanding your moral reasoning and ethical judgment and to sharpen your ethical sensitivity and moral awareness. (Total time required is 55 to 110 minutes, depending on the number of cases assigned and the degree of class discussion.

Procedure. Participants assume that they are managers at Martin Marietta Corporation who are undertaking an ethics training session. The exercise consists of deciding on ethical courses of action for 10 minicases. (Time: 50 minutes: 5 minutes per case. If time is limited fewer cases can be used.)

Instructions. Form groups of 4 to 6 people and select a group leader who will lead the discussion of the first case. Your group will have 5 minutes to reach a decision for each case before moving on to the next one. Rotate leaders for the case discussions.

Note. These cases reflect real-life situations. Consequently, you may sometimes feel that a case lacks clarity or that the precise choice you would have made is not available. Some cases have more than one satisfactory solution and others have no good solutions. In all cases, however, you must **decide on the one best solution** from those presented.

Debriefing: After the decisions have been made for all of the cases, the class should discuss each case in order. For each case, groups share their decisions and explain why they think their choice is the best. Then the instructor provides the point values and rational assigned for each option by the Martin Marietta Corporation trainers. Each group keeps track of its score for each case. At the end of the discussion, groups add their points for all 10 cases and the group with the highest score wins. (Time: 60 minutes. Less time is required if fewer cases are assigned or the total class discussion of group answers is omitted).

Minicase 1. A defense program has not yet been formally approved nor have the funds been allocated. Nevertheless, because it all looks good and you need to get started in order to meet schedule, you start negotiating with a supplier. What do you tell the supplier?

Potential Answers.

A. "This is a 'hot' program for both of us. Approval is imminent. Let's get all the preliminary work under way."

B. "The program is a 'go.' I want you under contract as soon as possible."

C. "Start work and we will cover your costs when we get the contract."

D. "If you want to be part of the team on this important, great program, you, like us, will have to shoulder some of the start-up costs.

Minicase 2. Two of your subordinates routinely provide their children with school supplies from the office. How do you handle this situation?

Potential Answers.

A. Lock up the supplies and issue them only as needed and signed for.

B. Tell these two subordinates that supplies are for office use only.

C. Report the theft of supplies to the head of security.

D. Send a notice to all employees that office supplies are for office use only and that disregard will result in disciplinary action.

Minicase 3. Your operation is being relocated. The personnel regulations are complex and might influence your employees' decisions about staying on the "team." Relocating with no experienced staff would be very difficult for you. What do you tell your employees about their options?

Potential Answers.

A. State that the relocation regulations are complex: you won't go into them right now. However, you tell them that everything probably will come out OK in the end.

B. Suggest that they relocate with you, stating that a job in hand is worth an unknown in the bush.

C. Present them with your simplified version of the regulations and encourage them to come along.

D. Tell them only that you'd like them to relocate with you and conserve the team, which has worked so well together.

Minicase 4. Your price is good on a program contract you are bidding, but you think it will take you several months longer than your competitor to develop the system. Your client, the U.S. Army, wants to know the schedule. What do you say?

Potential Answers.

    A. Tell the Army your schedule is essentially the same as what you believe your competitor's will be.

    B. Show the Army a schedule the same as what you believe your competitor's is (but believing you can do better than what your engineers have told you).

    C. Explain to the Army the distinct advantage of your system irrelevant of schedule.

    D. Lay out your schedule even though you suspect it may cause you to lose points on the evaluation.

Minicase 5. A friend of yours wants to transfer to your division, but he may not be the best qualified for the job. You do have an opening, and one other person, whom you do not know, has applied. What do you do?

Potential Answers.

    A. Select the friend you know and in whom you have confidence.

    B. Select the other person, who you are told is qualified.

    C. Request a qualifications comparison of the two from the human resources department.

    D. Request the human resources department to extend the search for additional candidates before making the selection.

Minicase 6. Your new employee is the niece of the vice president of finance. Her performance is poor, and she has caused trouble with her co-workers. What do you do?

Potential Answers.

    A. Call her in and talk to her about her inadequacies.

    B. Ask the human resources department to counsel her and put her on a performance improvement plan.

    C. Go see her uncle.

    D. Maybe her problems are caused by the newness of the job; give her some time to come around.

Minicase 7. You work in finance. Another employee is blamed for your error involving significant dollars. The employee will be able to clear himself, but it will be impossible to trace the error back to you. What do you do?

Potential Answers.

    A. Do nothing. The blamed employee will be able to clear himself eventually.

    B. Assist the blamed employee in resolving the issue but don't mention your involvement.

    C. Own up the error immediately, thus saving many hours of work.

    D. Wait and see if the matter is investigated and at that time disclose your knowledge of the case.

Minicase 8. After three months you discover that a recently hired employee who appears to be very competent falsified her employment application in that she claimed she had a college degree when she did not. As her supervisor, what do you do?

Potential Answers.

    A. You are happy with the new employee, so you do nothing.

    B. Discuss the matter with the human resources department to determine company policy.

    C. Recommend that she be fired for lying.

    D. Consider her performance, length of service, and potential benefit to the organization before making any recommendation to anyone.

Minicase 9. A close relative of yours plans to apply for a vacancy in the department that you head. Hearing of this, what would you say to that person?

Potential Answers.

    A. "Glad to have you. Our organization always needs good people."

    B. "I would be concerned about the appearance of favoritism."

    C. "It would be best if you did not work for me."

    D. "If you get the job, expect no special consideration from me."

Minicase 10. A current supplier contacts you with an opportunity to use your expertise as a paid consultant to the supplier in matters not pertaining to your company's business. You would work only on weekends. You could:

Potential Answers.

    A. Accept the job if the legal department poses no objection.

    B. Accept the job.

    C. Report pertinent details to your supervisor.

    D. Decline the position.

CASE

DEALING WITH ACADEMIC DISHONESTY[54]

Someday it will happen to every professor. A student will turn in such an excellent, well-written paper that its authenticity is in serious doubt. Or, during a test, the professor looks up and sees one student copying from another, or from crib notes lying on the floor. A 1991 study of 31 U.S. colleges and universities found 67 percent of students said they have cheated at least once. About 40 percent of students cheat in a given term, and it isn't only the lazy student looking for a shortcut. In fact, over achievers are more likely to cheat than underachievers when a professor springs a test on them and they feel they're losing control of their ability to prepare for class. For example, a student who is taking 16 course-hours, working 30 hours a week, and still trying to have a social life may not feel adequately prepared for a test and feel pressured to cheat. The question is, What should professors do about it?

It seems unthinkable that a professor would ignore students whispering answers to one another during a test, or obviously copying from crib notes, yet some admit that they frequently overlook such dishonesty. Although cheating rates are rising nationwide, many professors turn a blind eye to it because it puts them in the uncomfortable role of police officer instead of educator. Most universities' academic dishonesty policies scare professors with onerous, ambiguous regulations. Professors typically don't know what to expect of the policies and often avoid dealing with them. Many fear that complex legal proceedings will hurt their reputations and feel that it's their word against the student's. Others have trouble with the penalties. Some believe that lowering students' grades is unlikely to stop them from cheating again, but having them expelled from the university is too severe.

University administrators are worried about these faculty attitudes towards cheating, and some feel that "academic dishonesty is one of the most serious problems facing higher education today." They know that many professors are anxiety-ridden about it and believe that it is reducing the validity of the education students are receiving.

Students at universities with honor codes are much less likely to cheat than those at schools without such codes. But this is no guarantee. According to Stanford University figures, honor code violations have shot up, from 20 in 1991 to 47 in 1995.

Many students report that there is a confusing lack of set rules about what professors define as cheating which makes cheating seem unimportant. Others, however, report that they rely on faculty to stop their classmates from cheating and express disappointment in the professors who let them get away with it. Professors, on the other hand, feel that it is a gray area which would be difficult to solve unless they prohibited all collaboration, which would be damaging academically because people learn a lot talking together.

Questions for Discussion

1. What types of student cheating behavior have you observed?

2. Whose responsibility is it to control cheating?

3. How can cheating be prevented?

4. How should cheating be dealt with when it is detected?

5. Apply the creative problem-solving process to develop an action plan to prevent the problem of academic cheating. Be prepared to present your plan to the class.

VIDEO CASE

Second City Theater and Heavenly Ski Resort

In a global economy, sound business decisions require consideration of a number of important factors that may potentially affect a company's ability to meet its goals. It is important to understand that the problem-solving process in business and the quality of managerial decisions can determine a company's success or failure. A recent study concluded that managers spend approximately 50 percent of their time dealing with the consequences of bad decision making.

In this video, case study examples of two successful businesses—the Second City Theater in Chicago, Illinois, and Heavenly Ski Resort in Lake Tahoe, Nevada—are presented to allow you to explore how effective decisions are made by managers operating in very different businesses and under very different conditions. It is evident that being aware of the many factors that impact the quality of decisions, and understanding the rational problem-solving process, can lead to more effective decisions, although different aspects of the process need to be emphasized in various circumstances.

Broadly defined, decision making is a process of choosing among alternative courses of action. In the business world, this process takes place under varying conditions of certainty and risk. Decision making is more likely to be effective when approached in a series of steps that explore and evaluate alternatives.

1. Identify the problem.

2. Generate alternative solutions.

3. Evaluate the alternatives.

4. Select the best alternative.

5. Implement the decision.

6. Evaluate the decision.

In order to evaluate a decision, managers must gather information that can shed light on its effectiveness. Although most managers would prefer to follow all these decision-making steps, time and circumstances don't always allow for it. This decision-making process can also be influenced by other important factors such as intuition, emotion and stress, confidence, and risk propensity.

Although Second City and Heavenly Lake Tahoe are very different businesses, they are both examples of companies that have made successful decisions under conditions of risk and uncertainty. Second City has grown from its roots as a small "mom and pop" theater, to a large, internationally known corporate enterprise. Rather than investing all its resources into its immensely popular Old Chicago Improv Theater, Second City has decided to translate its expertise into other ventures, such as television, corporate training, and other theaters in Toronto, suburban Chicago, and Detroit.

Joe Keefe, producer of Second City communications, said,

> So much of what we do is in having people approach the decision-making process from a group point of view, and allowing for input. It's difficult many times to find the time to listen to everyone but, I literally try to book out time weekly to meet with people. I meet with the directors after every project. I know what the heck happened: What do they think? How do they feel? What does the client feel? By the time you have all that information the decision is usually self evident. It's a matter of making certain that you get accurate information immediately, that your client response issues are done immediately and then your intuition will tell you what's the right thing to do. About 99.9 percent of my decisions are self evident once you have the right information.

Heavenly Lake Tahoe accommodates nearly 750,000 skiers per year and competes as one of eight large Tahoe-area resorts. Like the Second City Theater, managers at Heavenly must make decisions affecting the growth of the company under less than ideal conditions. Malcolm Tibbets, vice president of mountain operations, said,

> Quick decisions happen every hour of the day. Looking at the level of business coming into the base areas and making a quick decision to open an additional lift that was not otherwise scheduled or vice versa shutting down a lift in order to save some cost because the level of business is not going to warrant the operation of that lift. Whether to start the snow plows at midnight or wait until 3:00 in the morning. These kinds of decisions are continuous. You have to have people in positions that are unafraid to make those decisions without calling six people and wasting time collecting all the data. That's just part of the way this business works.

Although following the six decision-making steps may lead to a sounder decision-making process, theory doesn't always play out in practice. Management may follow some steps, but perhaps not all of them, depending on the factors affecting the decision-making process. In the words of Steve Jacobson, director of food and beverage at Heavenly,

> Most of the managers are encouraged to make a decision right away and don't hold on to the problem. It's such a fast pace that I want them to just go on to the next thing and not hold the problem back. I've empowered them to pretty much make their own decisions. They were hired to do a job so I let them do the job. If there's something wrong we can discuss that later, but business must go on.

In their day-to-day operations, both Second City Theater and Heavenly Lake Tahoe experience the need to make decisions in varying conditions of certainty, uncertainty, and risk. Both companies follow the steps of the decision-making model when feasible. Awareness of the nature of decision making, its important steps, and influential factors may help managers minimize the time they spend responding to the consequences of poor decision making. This can enable managers to spend more time maximizing opportunities for growth.

Discussion Questions

1. How does the six-step decision-making process compare to the rational problem-solving process described in this chapter? What additional considerations do you think would be helpful in making effective decisions?

2. Which decision-making environment, Second City Theater or Heavenly Lake Tahoe, do you think requires the most creativity? Why? In which situation is "intuition" most relevant? Why?

3. Which degrees of participation, autocratic, consultive, or group, do you think are most appropriate at Second City Theater versus Heavenly Lake Tahoe? Why do you say this?

NOTES

1. B. M. Bass, *Organizational Decision Making* (Homewood, IL: Richard D. Irwin, 1983).

2. E. R. Archer, "How to Make a Business Decision: An Analysis of Theory and Practice," *Management Review* (February 1980), pp.289-299.

3. W. F. Pounds, "The Process of Problem Finding," *Industrial Management Review* II (Fall 1969), pp.1-19.

4. Ibid.

5. P. L. Hunsaker and A. J. Alessandra, *The Art of Managing People* (New York: Simon & Schuster, 1986), pp.224-226.

6. Lewis Carroll, *Alice's Adventures in Wonderland* (New York: Viking Press, 1975), pp.22.

7. G. L. Morrisey, *Management by Objectives and Results for Business and Industry,* 2nd ed. (Reading, MA: Addison-Wesley, 1977).

8. Michael Brassard, *The Memory Jogger: A Pocket Guide of Tools for Continuous Improvement* (Methuen, MA: GOAL/QPC, 1988), pp.9-13.

9. Ibid., pp.24-29.

10. Ibid., pp.17-23.

11. S. M. Natale, C. F. OÆDonnell, and W. R. C. Osborne, Jr., "Decision Making: Managerial Perspectives," *Thought* 63, no. 248 (1990), pp.32-51.

12. H. A. Simon, *Administrative Behavior,* 2nd ed. (New York: Free Press, 1957).

13. J. Tsalikis and D. J. Fritzsche, "Business Ethics; A Literature Review with a Focus on Marketing Ethics," *Journal of Business Ethics* 8 (1989), pp.695-743.

14. O. C. Ferrell and G. Gardiner, *In Pursuit of Ethics: Tough Choices in the World of Work* (Springfield, IL: Smith Collins Company, 1991), pp.9-13.

15. Linda S. Klein, "Ethical Decision Making in a Business Environment," *Review of Business* 13, no. 3 (Winter 1991/1992), pp.27-29.

16. Sherry Baker, "Ethical Judgment," *Executive Excellence* (March 1992), pp.7-8.

17. Ibid., pp.7-8.

18. T. Donaldson, "Values in Tension: Ethics Away from Home," Kenneth Robinson Fellowship Lecture, University of Hong Kong (January 9, 1996).

19. Adapted from example in John R. Boatright, *Ethics and the Conduct of Business* (Englewood Cliffs, NJ: Prentice-Hall, Inc. 1993), p.1.

20. Ibid., pp.4-19.

21. Ibid., p.8.

22. James R. Rest, "Can Ethics Be Taught in Professional Schools? The Psychology Research," *Easier Said Than Done* (Winter 1988), pp.22-26.

23. John E. Fleming, "Business Ethics: An Overview," (University of Southern California, Unpublished paper, 1994) p.2.

24. "Thinking Ethically," *Issues in Ethics* 1, no. 2 (Santa Clara University, Center for Applied Ethics; Winter 1988), p.2.

25. Ibid.

26. Baker, "Ethical Judgment," pp.7-8.

27. "Rights Stuff," *Issues in Ethics* 3, no. 1 (Santa Clara University, Center for Applied Ethics; Spring 1990), pp.1, 6; and Fleming, op. cit., p.3.

28. Ibid., p.6.

29. Ibid.

30. Baker, "Ethical Judgment," pp.7-8.

31. "Justice and Fairness," *Issues in Ethics* 3, no. 1 (Santa Clara University, Center for Applied Ethics; Fall 1990), pp.1, 7.

32. Ibid.

33. Ibid.

34. Ibid.

35. Baker, "Ethical Judgment," pp.7-8.

36. T. Donaldson, "Values in Tension: Ethics Away from Home," Kenneth Robinson Fellowship Lecture, University of Hong Kong (January 9, 1996).

37. M. A. C. Fusco, "Ethics Game Plan: Taking the Offensive," *Business Week Careers* (Spring/Summer 1989), p.51.

38. Baker, "Ethical Judgment," pp.7-8.

39. The material in this section is summarized from M. J. Driver, K. R. Brousseau, and P. L. Hunsaker, *The Dynamic Decisionmaker* (New York: Jossey-Bass, 1993), pp.1-36.

40. Paul Dean, "Open-and-Shut for Value," *Los Angeles Times* (October 30, 1992), pp.E1, E6.

41. John L. Cotton, David A. Vollrath, and Kirk L. Froggatt, "Employee Participation: Diverse Forms and Different Outcomes," *Academy of Management Review* (January 1988), pp.8-22.

42. V. H. Vroom and A. J. Jago, *The New Leadership: Managing Participation in Organizations* (Englewood Cliffs, NJ: Prentice Hall, 1988).

43. Ibid.

44. David Campbell, "Some Characteristics of Creative Managers," *Center for Creative Leadership Newsletter* no. 1 (February 1978), pp.6-7.

45. Ibid., p.7.

46. The company examples in this section are from Jay Cocks, "Let's Get Crazy," *Time* (June 11, 1990), pp.40-41.

47. Maryam Alari, "Group Decision Support Systems: A Key to Business Team Productivity," *Journal of Information Systems Management* 8, no. 3 (Summer 1991), pp.36-41.

48. A. F. Osborn, *Applied Imagination* (New York: Scribners, 1957).

49. A. H. Van de Ven and Andre Delbecq, "The Effectiveness of Nominal, Delphi, and Interacting Group Decision-Making Processes," *Academy of Management Journal* 17 (1974), pp.605-621.

50. N. C. Dalkey and Olaf Helmer, "An Experimental Application of the Delphi Method to the Use of Experts," *Management Science* 9 (1963), pp.458-467.

51. Alari, "Group Decision Support Systems," pp.36-41.

52. The three cases in this exercise are from Victor H. Vroom and Arthur G. Jago, "Decision Making as a Social Process," *Decision Sciences* 5, no. 4 (October 1974), pp.734-769.

53. George Sammet, *Gray Matters: The Ethics Game* (Orlando, FL: Martin Marietta Corporation, 1992).

54. The case was prepared based on materials appearing in Bridget Murray, "Are Professors Turning a Blind Eye to Cheating?" *The APA Monitor* (January 1996), pp.1, 42; Don McBurney, "Cheating: Preventing and Dealing with Academic Dishonesty," *APS Observer* (January 1996), pp.32-35; and Jim Puzzanghera, "Misconduct Violations on the Rise at Stanford," *San Diego Union-Tribune* (February 9, 1996), pp.C-1, C-3.

Chapter 13

Total Quality Management (TQM)

SOURCE: William J. Stevenson, *Production Operations Management*, 6th ed., Chapter 11, McGraw-Hill, 2002, 1999.

LEARNING OBJECTIVES

After completing this chapter, you should be able to:

- Describe TQM.
- Give an overview of problem solving.
- Give an overview of process improvement.
- Describe and use various quality tools.
- Define the following key terms:

benchmarking	fishbone diagram	process improvement
brainstorming	flowchart	quality at the source
cause-and-effect diagram	histogram	quality circles
check sheet	interviewing	run chart
continuous improvement	kaizen	scatter diagram
control chart	Pareto anaylsis	total quality management
5W2H approach	plan-do-study-act cycle	

A primary role of management is to lead an organization in its daily operation and to maintain it as a viable entity into the future. Quality has become an important factor in both of these objectives.

Although ostensibly always an objective of business, customer satisfaction, *in customer terms,* became a specific goal in the late 1980s. Providing high quality was recognized as a key element for success. Most large corporations taking that path have documented their success. First, they survived the strong overseas competition that had set the high quality levels and now have regained some of their former markets. Smaller companies are also adopting similar goals.

Management, with a new approach, has played the critical role. The new approach is reflected in expressed changes in policy. The Ford Motor Company *operating philosophy* is a good example:

> The operating philosophy of Ford Motor Company is to meet customer needs and expectations by establishing and maintaining an environment which encourages all employees to pursue never-ending improvement in the quality and productivity of products and services throughout the corporation, its supply base, and its dealer organization.[1]

INTRODUCTION

The term **total quality management (TQM)** refers to a quest for quality in an organization. There are three key philosophies in this approach. One is a never-ending push to improve, which is referred to as *continuous improvement;* the second is the *involvement of everyone* in the organization; and the third is a goal of *customer satisfaction,* which means meeting or exceeding customer expectations. TQM expands the traditional view of quality—looking only at the quality of the final product or services—to *looking at the quality of every aspect of the process* that produces the product or service. TQM systems are intended to prevent poor quality from occurring.

We can describe the TQM approach as follows:

1. Find out what customers want. This might involve the use of surveys, focus groups, interviews, or some other technique that integrates the customer's voice in the decision-making process. Be sure to include the *internal customer* (the next person in the process) as well as the *external customer* (the final customer).

2. Design a product or service that will meet (or exceed) what customers want. Make it easy to use and easy to produce.

3. Design processes that facilitate doing the job right the first time. Determine where mistakes are likely to occur and try to prevent them. When mistakes do occur, find out why so that they are less likely to occur again. Strive to make the process "mistake-proof." This is sometimes referred to as a **fail–safing**: Elements are incorporated in product or service design which make it virtually impossible for an employee (or sometimes a customer) to do something incorrectly. The Japanese term for this is *pokayoke.* Examples include parts that fit together one way only and appliance plugs that can be inserted into a wall outlet the correct way only. Another term that is sometimes used is *foolproofing,* but use of this term may be taken to imply that employees (or customers) are fools—not a wise choice!

4. Keep track of results, and use them to guide improvement in the system. Never stop trying to improve.

5. Extend these concepts to suppliers and to distribution.

Many companies have successfully implemented TQM programs. Among them are General Electric and Motorola, both of which are known for their "six-sigma" programs, a term generally associated with extremely high process capability, but more appropriately referring to a quality program in general. In fact, competitive pressures and shorter product life cycles are leading a wide variety of companies to undertake TQM-type initiatives. General Electric puts selected employees through a high-level statistical training program. Upon completion, they are certified as "black belt" qualified. These employees then train others and also serve as consultants.

Successful TQM programs are built through the dedication and combined efforts of everyone in the organization. Top management must be committed and involved. If it isn't, TQM will become just another fad that quickly dies and fades away.

The preceding description provides a good idea of what TQM is all about, but it doesn't tell the whole story. A number of other elements of TQM are important, including:

1. *Continuous improvement.* The *philosophy* that seeks to improve all factors related to the process of converting inputs into outputs on an ongoing basis is called **continuous improvement**. It covers equipment, methods, materials, and people. Under continuous improvement, the old adage "If it ain't broke, don't fix it" gets transformed into "Just because it isn't broke doesn't mean it can't be improved."

   The concept of continuous improvement was not new, but it did not receive much interest in the United States for a while, even though it originated here. However, many Japanese companies used it for years, and it became a cornerstone of the Japanese approach to production. The Japanese use the term **kaizen** to refer to continuous improvement. The successes of Japanese companies caused other companies to reexamine many of their approaches. This resulted in a strong interest in the continuous improvement approach.

2. *Competitive benchmarking.* This involves identifying other organizations that are the best at something and studying how they do it to learn how to improve your operation. The company need not be in the same line of business. For example, Xerox used the mail-order company L.L. Bean to benchmark order filling.

3. *Employee empowerment.* Giving workers the responsibility for improvements and the authority to make changes to accomplish them provides strong motivation for employees. This puts decision making into the hands of those who are closest to the job and have considerable insight into problems and solutions.

4. *Team approach.* The use of teams for problem solving and to achieve consensus takes advantage of group synergy, gets people involved, and promotes a spirit of cooperation and shared values among employees.

5. *Decisions based on facts rather than opinions.* Management gathers and analyzes data as a basis for decision making.

6. *Knowledge of tools.* Employees and managers are trained in the use of quality tools.

7. *Supplier quality.* Suppliers must be included in quality assurance and quality improvement efforts so that their processes are capable of delivering quality parts and materials in a timely manner.

8. *Champion.* A TQM champion's job is to promote the value and importance of TQM principles throughout the company.

9. *Quality at the source.* **Quality at the source** refers to the philosophy of making each worker responsible for the quality of his or her work. This incorporates the notions of "do it right" and "if it isn't right, fix it." Workers are expected to provide goods or services that meet specifications and to find and correct mistakes that occur. In effect, each worker becomes a quality inspector for his or her work. When the work is passed on to the next operation in the process (the internal customer) or, if that step is the last in the process, to the ultimate customer, the worker is "certifying" that it meets quality standards.

This accomplishes a number of things: (1) it places direct responsibility for quality on the person(s) who directly affect it; (2) it removes the adversarial relationship that often exists between quality control inspectors and production workers; and (3) it motivates workers by giving them control over their work as well as pride in it.

> Sign on the wall of a company cafeteria
>
> Sometimes they can be cranky, and it may sometimes seem like they expect too much, but they do provide our paychecks and our benefits, such as sick leave, maternity leave, health insurance, and three weeks of paid vacation time each year. And what about all the new equipment we've been getting lately? They pay for that, too. And a lot more. So the next time you see them, give them a great big smile to show how much you appreciate them—our *customers!*

10. *Suppliers* are partners in the process, and long-term relationships are encouraged. This gives suppliers a vital stake in providing quality goods and services. Suppliers, too, are expected to provide quality at the source, thereby reducing or eliminating the need to inspect deliveries from suppliers.

Table 13-1   **Comparing the cultures of TQM and traditional organizations**

Aspect	Traditional	TQM
Overall mission	Maximize return on investment	Meet or exceed customer satisfaction
Objectives	Emphasis on short term	Balance of long term and short term
Management	Not always open; sometimes inconsistent objectives	Open; encourages employee input; consistent objectives
Role of manager	Issue orders; enforce	Coach, remove barriers, build trust
Customer requirements	Not highest priority; may be unclear	Highest priority; important to identify and understand
Problems	Assign blame; punish	Identify and resolve
Problem solving	Not systematic; individuals	Systematic; teams
Improvement	Erratic	Continuous
Suppliers	Adversarial	Partners
Jobs	Narrow, specialized; much individual effort	Broad, more general; much team effort
Focus	Product oriented	Process oriented

It would be incorrect to think of TQM as merely a collection of techniques. Rather, TQM reflects a whole new attitude toward quality. It is about the *culture* of an organization. To truly reap the benefits of TQM, the culture of an organization must change.

Table 13–1 illustrates the differences between cultures of a TQM organization and a more traditional organization.

OBSTACLES TO IMPLEMENTING TQM

Companies have had varying success in implementing TQM. Some have been quite successful, but others have struggled. Part of the difficulty may be with the process by which it is implemented rather than with the principles of TQM. Among the factors cited in the literature are:

1. Lack of a companywide definition of quality: Efforts aren't coordinated; people are working at cross-purposes, addressing different issues, using different measures of success.

2. Lack of a strategic plan for change: Lessens the chance of success; ignores need to address strategic implications of change.

3. Lack of a customer focus: Without this, there is a risk of customer dissatisfaction.

4. Poor interorganizational communication: The left hand doesn't know what the right hand is doing; frustration, waste, and confusion ensue.

5. Lack of employee empowerment: Gives the impression of not trusting employees to fix problems; adds "red tape" and delays solutions.

6. View of quality as a "quick fix": Needs to be a long-term, continuing effort.

7. Emphasis on short-term financial results: "Duct-tape" solutions often treat symptoms; spend a little now—a lot more later.

8. Inordinate presence of internal politics and "turf" issues: These can sap the energy of an organization and derail the best of ideas.

9. Lack of strong motivation: Managers need to make sure employees are motivated.

10. Lack of time to devote to quality initiatives: Don't add more work without adding additional resources.

11. Lack of leadership:[2] Managers need to be leaders.

This list of potential problems can serve as a guideline for organizations contemplating implementing TQM or as a checklist for those having trouble implementing it.

CRITICISMS OF TQM

TQM programs are touted as a way for companies to improve their competitiveness, which is a very worthwhile objective. Nonetheless, TQM programs are not without criticism. Some of the major ones are:

1. Blind pursuit of TQM programs: Overzealous advocates may focus attention on quality even though other priorities may be more important (e.g., responding quickly to a competitor's advances).

2. Programs may not be linked to the strategies of the organization in a meaningful way.

3. Quality-related decisions may not be tied to market performance. For instance, customer satisfaction may be carried to the extent that its cost far exceeds any direct or indirect benefit of doing so.

4. Failure to carefully plan a program before embarking on it can lead to false starts, employee confusion, and meaningless results.

Table 13-2		Basic steps in problem solving
	Step 1	**Define the problem and establish an improvement goal.** Give problem definition careful consideration; don't rush through this step because this will serve as the focal point of problem-solving efforts.
	Step 2	**Collect data.** The solution must be based on *facts*. Possible tools include check sheet, scatter diagram, histogram, run chart, and control chart.
	Step 3	**Analyze the problem.** Possible tools include Pareto chart, cause-and-effect diagram.
	Step 4	**Generate potential solutions.** Methods include brainstorming, interviewing, and surveying.
	Step 5	**Choose a solution.** Identify the criteria for choosing a solution. (Refer to the goal established in Step 1.) Apply criteria to potential solutions and select the best one.
	Step 6	**Implement the solution.** Keep everyone informed.
	Step 7	**Monitor the solution to see if it accomplishes the goal.** If not, modify the solution, or return to Step 1. Possible tools include control chart and run chart.

Note that there is nothing inherently wrong with TQM; the problem is how some individuals or organizations misuse it. Let's turn our attention to problem solving and process improvement.

PROBLEM SOLVING

Problem solving is one of the basic procedures of TQM. In order to be successful, problem-solving efforts should follow a standard approach. Table 13–2 describes the basic steps in the TQM problem-solving process.

An important aspect of problem solving in the TQM approach is *eliminating* the cause so that the problem does not recur. This is why users of the TQM approach often like to think of problems as "opportunities for improvement."

The Plan-Do-Study-Act Cycle

The **plan-do-study-act (PDSA)** cycle, also referred to as either the Shewhart cycle or the Deming wheel, is the conceptual basis for problem-solving activities. The cycle is illustrated in Figure 13–1. Representing the process with a circle underscores its continuing nature.

There are four basic steps in the cycle:

Plan. Begin by studying the current process. Document that process. Then collect data on the process or problem. Next, analyze the data and develop a plan for improvement. Specify measures for evaluating the plan.

Do. Implement the plan, on a small scale if possible. Document any changes made during this phase. Collect data systematically for evaluation.

Figure 13-1

A. The PDSA Cycle

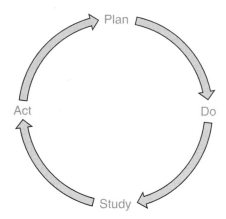

B. The PDSA cycle applied to problem solving.

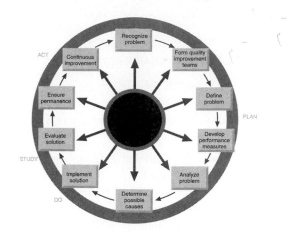

Source: Reprinted by permission of Prentice-Hall, Upper Saddle River, NJ. From Donna Summers, *Quality,* 2nd ed. (Upper Saddle River, NJ: Prentice Hall, 2000), p. 67.

Study.   Evaluate the data collection during the *do* phase. Check how closely the results match the original goals of the *plan* phase.

Act.   If the results are successful, *standardize* the new method and communicate the new method to all people associated with the process. Implement training for the new method. If the results are unsuccessful, revise the plan and repeat the process or cease this project.

FIGURE 13-2   The process improvement cycle is another version of the plan-do-study-act cycle

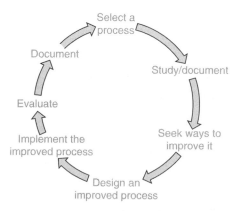

Table 13-3   **Overview of process improvement**

A. Process mapping

1. Collect information about the process; identify each step in the process. For each step, determine:

     The inputs and outputs.

     The people involved.

     All decisions that are made.

     Document such measures as time, cost, space used, waste, employee morale and any employee turnover, accidents and/or safety hazards, working conditions, revenues and/or profits, quality, and customer satisfaction, as appropriate.

2. Prepare a flowchart that *accurately* depicts the process; note that too little detail will not allow for meaningful analysis, and too much detail will overwhelm analysts and be counterproductive. Make sure that key activities and decisions are represented.

B. Analyze the process

1. Ask these questions about the process:
     Is the flow logical?
     Are any steps or activities missing?
     Are there any duplications?

2. Ask these questions about each step:
     Is the step necessary? Could it be eliminated?
     Does the step add value?
     Does any waste occur at this step?
     Could the time be shortened?
     Could the cost to perform the step be reduced?
     Could two (or more) steps be combined?

C. Redesign the process

Using the results of the analysis, redesign the process. Document the improvements; potential measures include reductions in time, cost, space, waste, employee turnover, accidents, safety hazards, and increases/improvements in employee morale, working conditions, revenues/profits, quality, and customer satisfaction.

In replicating successful results elsewhere in the organization, the cycle is repeated. Similarly, if the plan was unsuccessful and you wish to make further modifications, repeat this cycle.

Employing this sequence of steps provides a systematic approach to continuous improvement.

PROCESS IMPROVEMENT

Process improvement is a *systematic* approach to improving a process. It involves documentation, measurement, and analysis for the purpose of improving the functioning of a process. Typical goals of process improvement include increasing customer satisfaction, achieving higher quality, reducing waste, reducing cost, increasing productivity, and speeding up the process.

Table 13–3 provides an overview of process improvement, and Figure 11–2 shows its cyclical nature.

TOOLS

There are a number of tools that an organization can use for problem solving and process improvement. This section describes eight of these tools. The tools aid in data collection and interpretation, and provide the basis for decision making.

Figure 13–3   **The seven basic quality tools**

Flowchart

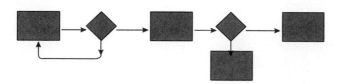

A diagram of the steps in a process

Check sheet

	Day			
Defect	1	2	3	4
A	///		////	/
B	//	/	//	///
C	/	////	//	////

A tool for organizing and collecting data; a tally of problems or other events by category

Histogram

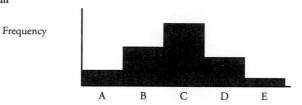

A chart that shows an empirical frequency distribution

Pareto chart

A diagram that arranges categories from highest to lowest frequency of occurrence

Scatter diagram

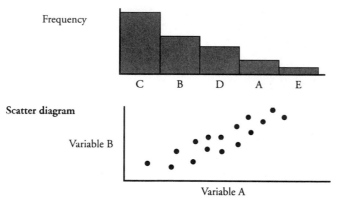

A graph that shows the degree and direction of relationship between two variables

Control chart

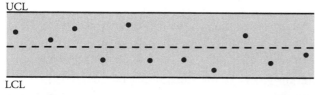

A statistical chart of time-ordered values of a sample statistic (e.g., sample means)

Cause–and–effect diagram

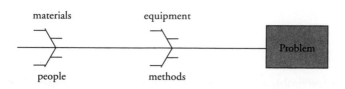

A diagram used to organize a search for the cause(s) of a problem; also known as a *fishbone* diagram

Figure 13-4   **A FLOWCHART**

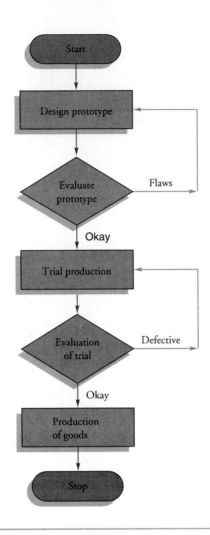

The first seven tools are often referred to as the *seven basic quality tools*. Figure 13–3 provides a quick overview of the seven tools.

Flowcharts

A **flowchart** is a visual representation of a process. As a problem-solving tool, a flowchart can help investigators in identifying possible points in a process where problems occur. Figure 13–4 illustrates a flowchart.

The diamond shapes in the flowchart represent decision points in the process, and the rectangular shapes represent procedures. The arrows show the direction of "flow" of the steps in the process.

To construct a simple flowchart, begin by listing the steps in a process. Then classify each step as either a procedure or a decision (or check) point. Try to not make the flowchart too detailed, or it may be overwhelming, but be careful not to omit any key steps.

Check Sheets

A **check sheet** is a simple tool frequently used for problem identification. Check sheets provide a format that enables users to record and organize data in a way that facilitates collection and analysis. This format might be one of simple checkmarks. Check sheets are designed on the basis of what the users are attempting to learn by collecting data.

Figure 13-5   **AN EXAMPLE OF A CHECK SHEET**

Day	Time	Missing label	Off-center	Smeared print	Loose or folded	Other	Total
M	8-9	IIII	II				6
	9-10		III				3
	10-11	I	III	I			5
	11-12		I		I	I (Torn)	3
	1-2		I				1
	2-3		II	III	I		6
	3-4		II	IIIII			8
Total		5	14	10	2	1	32

(Type of Defect spans the Missing label, Off-center, Smeared print, Loose or folded, and Other columns)

Figure 13-6   **A SPECIAL PURPOSE CHECK SHEET**

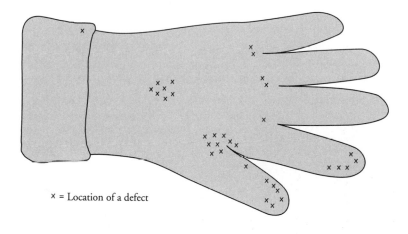

× = Location of a defect

Many different formats can be used for a check sheet and there are many different types of sheets. One frequently used form of check sheet deals with type of defect, another with location of defects. These are illustrated in Figures 13–5 and 13–6.

Figure 13–5 shows tallies that denote the type of defect and the time of day each occurred. Problems with missing labels tend to occur early in the day and smeared print tends to occur late in the day, whereas offcenter labels are found throughout the day. Identifying types of defects and when they occur can help in pinpointing causes of the defects.

Figure 13–6 makes it easy to see where defects on the product are occurring. In this case, defects seem to be occurring on the tips of the thumb and first finger, in the finger valleys (especially between the thumb and first finger), and in the center of the gloves. Again, this may help determine why the defects occur and lead to a solution.

Figure 13-7
A histogram

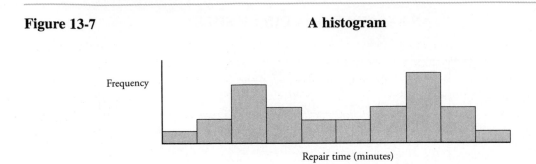

Figure 13-8
A Pareto diagram based on data in Figure 13–5

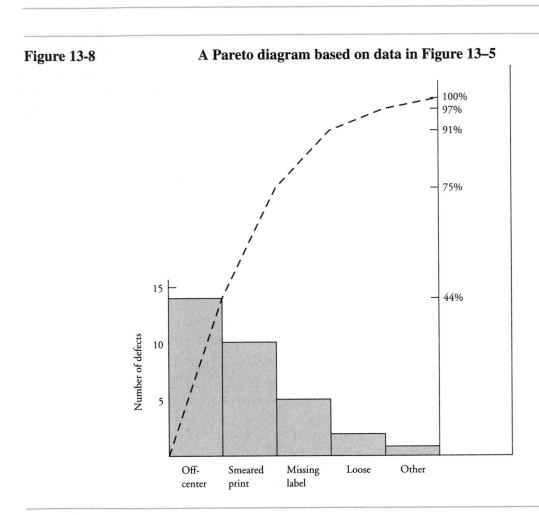

Histograms

A **histogram** can be useful in getting a sense of the distribution of observed values. Among other things, one can see if the distribution is symmetrical, what the range of values is, and if there are any unusual values. Figure 13–7 illustrates a histogram. Note the two peaks. This suggests the possibility of *two* distributions with different centers. Possible causes might be two workers or two suppliers with different quality.

Pareto Analysis

Pareto analysis is a technique for focusing attention on the most important problem areas. The Pareto concept, named after the nineteenth-century Italian economist Vilfredo Pareto, is that a relatively few factors generally account for a large percentage of the total cases (e.g., complaints, defects, problems). The idea is to classify the cases according to degree of importance, and focus on resolving the most important, leaving the less important. Often referred to as the 80–20 rule, the Pareto concept states that approximately 80 percent of the problems come from 20 percent of the items. For instance, 80 percent of machine breakdowns come from 20 percent of the machines, and 80 percent of the product defects come from 20 percent of the causes of defects.

Often, it is useful to prepare a chart that shows the number of occurrences by category, arranged in order of frequency. Figure 13–8 illustrates such a chart corresponding to the check sheet shown in Figure 13–5. The dominance of the problem with offcenter labels becomes apparent. Presumably, the manager and employees would focus on trying to resolve this problem. Once they accomplished that, they could address the remaining defects in similar fashion; "smeared print" would be the next major category to be resolved, and so on. Additional check sheets would be used to collect data to verify that the defects in these categories have been eliminated or greatly reduced. Hence, in later Pareto diagrams, categories such as "offcenter" may still appear but would be much less prominent.

Figure 13-9   **A scatter diagram**

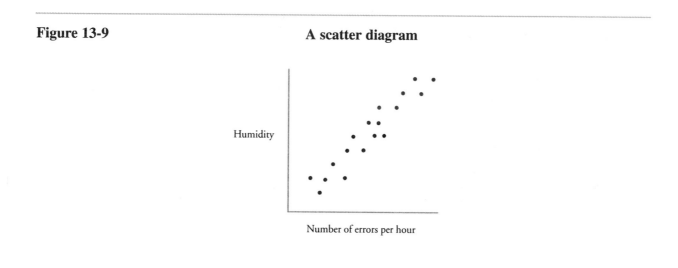

Figure 13-10   **A control chart**

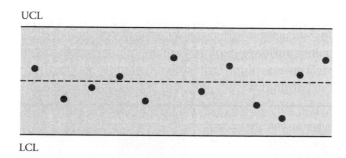

Scatter Diagrams

A **scatter diagram** can be useful in deciding if there is a correlation between the values of two variables. A correlation may point to a cause of a problem. Figure 13–9 shows an example of a scatter diagram. In this particular diagram, there is a *positive* (upward sloping) relationship between the humidity and the number of errors per hour. High values of humidity correspond to high numbers of errors, and vice versa. On the other hand, a *negative* (downward sloping) relationship would mean that when values of one variable are low, values of the other variable are high, and vice versa.

Figure 13-11   **One format of a cause-and-effect diagram**

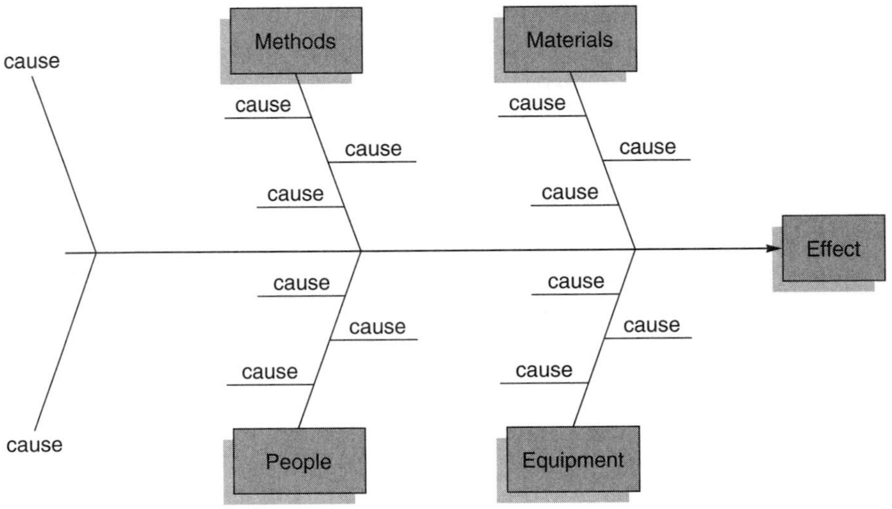

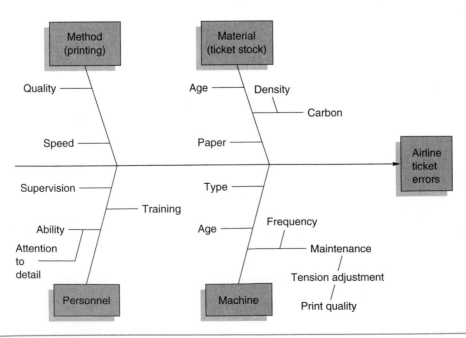

Figure 13-12   **Cause-and-effect diagram for airline ticket errors**

The higher the correlation between the two variables, the less scatter in the points; the points will tend to line up. Conversely, if there were little or no relationship between two variables, the points would be completely scattered. In Figure 13–9, the correlation between humidity and errors seems strong, because the points appear to scatter along an imaginary line.

Control Charts

A **control chart** can be used to monitor a process to see if the process output is random. It can help detect the presence of *correctable* causes of variation. Figure 13–10 illustrates a control chart. Control charts can also indicate when a problem occurred and give insight into what caused the problem.

Figure 13-13   **A run chart shows performance over time**

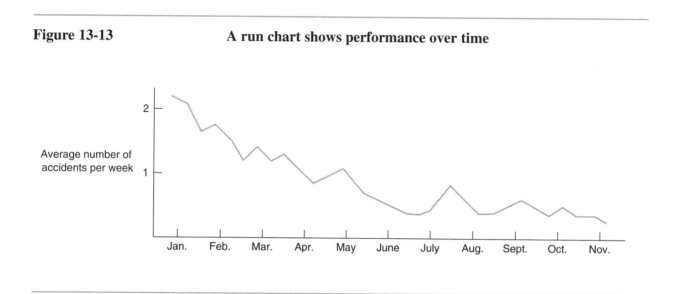

Cause-and-Effect Diagrams

A **cause-and-effect diagram** offers a structured approach to the search for the possible cause(s) of a problem. It is also known as a **fishbone diagram** because of its shape, or an *Ishikawa diagram,* after the Japanese professor who developed the approach to aid workers overwhelmed by the number of possible sources of problems when problem solving. This tool helps to organize problem-solving efforts by identifying *categories* of factors that might be causing problems. Often this tool is used after brainstorming sessions, to organize the ideas generated. Figure 13–11 illustrates one form of a cause-and-effect diagram.

An example of an application of such a cause-and-effect diagram is shown in Figure 13–12. Each of the factors listed in the diagram is a potential source of ticket errors. Some are more likely causes than others, depending on the nature of the errors. If the cause is still not obvious at this point, additional investigation into the *root cause* may be necessary, involving a more in-depth analysis. Often, more detailed information can be obtained by asking *who, what, where, when, why,* and *how* questions about factors that appear to be the most likely sources of problems.

Figure 13-14   Employing graphical tools in problem solving

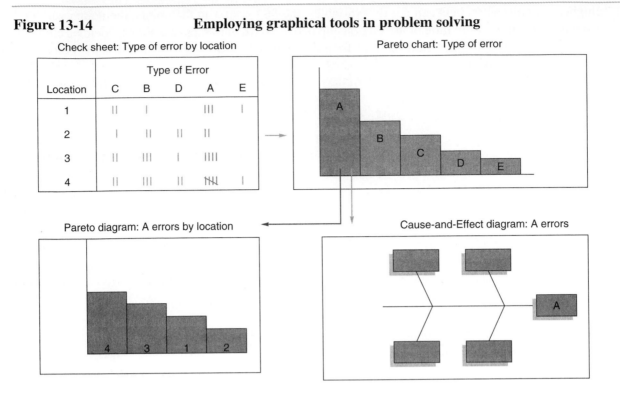

Check sheet: Type of error by location

Pareto chart: Type of error

Pareto diagram: A errors by location

Cause-and-Effect diagram: A errors

Figure 13-15   Comparison of before and after using Pareto charts

Before

100%

After

Improvement

100%

Figure 13-16   Using a control chart to track improvements

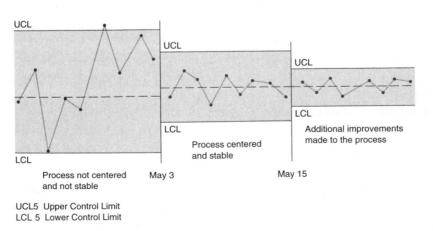

UCL

UCL

UCL

UCL

LCL

LCL

LCL

Process not centered
and not stable

May 3

Process centered
and stable

May 15

Additional improvements
made to the process

UCL5 Upper Control Limit
LCL 5 Lower Control Limit

Run Charts

A **run chart** can be used to track the values of a variable over time. This can aid in identifying trends or other patterns that may be occurring. Figure 13–13 provides an example of a run chart showing a decreasing trend in accident frequency over time. Important advantages of run charts are ease of construction and ease of interpretation.

Illustrations of the Use of Graphical Tools

This section presents some illustrations of the use of graphical tools in process or product improvement. Figure 13–14 begins with a check sheet that can be used to develop a Pareto chart of the types of errors found. That leads to a more focused Pareto diagram of the most frequently occurring type of error, followed (moving right) by a cause-and-effect diagram of the second most frequently occurring error. Additional cause-and-effect diagrams, such as errors by location, might also be used.

Figure 13–15 shows how Pareto charts measure the amount of improvement achieved in a before-and-after scenario of errors.

Figure 13–16 illustrates how control charts track two phases of improvement in a process that was initially out of control.

Methods for Generating Ideas

Some additional tools that are useful for problem solving and/or for process improvement are brainstorming, quality circles, interviewing, and benchmarking.

Brainstorming

Brainstorming *is a technique in which a group of people share thoughts and ideas on problems in a relaxed atmosphere that encourages unrestrained collective thinking.* The goal is to generate a free flow of ideas on identifying problems, and finding causes, solutions, and ways to implement solutions. In successful brainstorming, criticism is absent, no single member is allowed to dominate sessions, and all ideas are welcomed.

Quality Circles

One way companies have tapped employees for ideas concerning quality improvement is through **quality circles.** The circles comprise a number of workers who get together periodically to discuss ways of improving products and processes. Not only are quality circles a valuable source of worker input, they also can motivate workers, if handled properly, by demonstrating management interest in worker ideas. Quality circles are usually less structured and more informal than teams involved in continuous improvement, but in some organizations quality circles have evolved into continuous improvement teams. Perhaps a major distinction between quality circles and teams is the amount of authority given to the teams. Typically, quality circles have had very little authority to implement any but minor changes; continuous improvement teams are sometimes given a great deal of authority. Consequently, continuous improvement teams have the added motivation generated by *empowerment.*

The team approach works best when it reaches decisions based on consensus. This may involve one or more of the following methods:

1. *List reduction* is applied to a list of possible problems or solutions. Its purpose is to clarify items, and in the *process,* reduce the list of items by posing questions about affordability, feasibility, and likelihood of solving the problem for each item.

2. A *balance sheet* approach lists the pros and cons of each item and focuses discussion on important issues.

3. *Paired comparisons* is a process by which each item on a list is compared with every other item, two at a time. For each pair, team members select the preferred item. This approach forces a choice between items. It works best when the list of items is small: say, five or fewer.

Interviewing

Another technique a firm can use to identify problems or collect information about a problem is **interviewing.** Internal problems may require interviewing employees; external problems may require interviewing external customers.

Ideas for improvement can come from a number of sources: research and development, customers, competitors, and employees. Customer satisfaction is the ultimate goal of improvement activities, and customers can offer many valuable suggestions about products and the service process. However, they are unlikely to have suggestions for manufacturing processes.

Benchmarking

Benchmarking is an approach that can inject new energy into improvement efforts. Summarized in Table 13–4, benchmarking is the process of measuring an organization's performance on a key customer requirement against the best in the industry, or against the best in any industry. Its purpose is to establish a standard against which performance is judged, and to identify a model for learning how to improve. A benchmark demonstrates the degree to which customers of other organizations are satisfied. Once a benchmark has been identified, the goal is to meet or exceed that standard through improvements in appropriate processes.

The benchmarking process usually involves these steps:
1. Identify a critical process that needs improvement (e.g., order entry, distribution, service after sale).
2. Identify an organization that excels in the process, preferably the best.
3. Contact the benchmark organization, visit it, and study the benchmark activity.
4. Analyze the data.
5. Improve the critical process at your own organization.

Selecting an industry leader provides insight into what competitors are doing; but competitors may be reluctant to share this information. Several organizations are responding to this difficulty by conducting benchmarking studies and providing that information to other organizations without revealing the sources of the data.

Selecting organizations that are world leaders in different industries is another alternative. For example, the Xerox Corporation uses many benchmarks: For employee involvement, Procter & Gamble; for quality process, Florida Power and Light and Toyota; for high-volume production, Kodak and Canon; for billing collection, American Express; for research and development, AT&T and Hewlett-Packard; for distribution, L.L. Bean and Hershey Foods; and for daily scheduling, Cummins Engine.

The 5W2H Approach

Asking questions about the current process can lead to important insights about why the current process isn't working as well as it could, as well as potential ways to improve it. One method is called the **5W2H** (5 "w" words and 2 "h" words) approach (see Table 13–5).

OPERATIONS STRATEGY

In order for total quality management to be successful, it is essential that a majority of those in an organization "buy in" to the idea. Otherwise, there is a risk that a significant portion of the benefits of the approach will not be realized. Therefore, it is important to give this sufficient attention, and to confirm that concordance exists before plunging ahead. A key aspect of this is a "top-down" approach: Top management needs to be visibly involved and needs to be supportive, both financially and emotionally. Also important is education of managers and workers in the concepts, tools, and procedures of quality. Again, if education is incomplete, there is the risk that TQM will not produce the desired benefits.

Table 13-4   **The benchmarking approach**

1. What organization does it the best?
2. How do they do it?
3. How do we do it now?
4. How can we change to match or exceed the best?

Table 13-5   **The 5W2H approach**

Category	5W2H	Typical Questions	Goal
Subject	What?	What is being done?	Identify the focus of analysis.
Purpose	Why?	Why is this necessary?	Eliminate unnecessary tasks.
Location	Where?	Where is it being done? Why is it done there? Would it be better to do it someplace else?	Improve the location.
Sequence	When?	When is it done? Would it be better to do it at another time?	Improve the sequence.
People	Who?	Who is doing it? Could someone else do it better?	Improve the sequence or output.
Method	How?	How is it being done? Is there a better way?	Simplify tasks, improve output.
Cost	How much?	How much does it cost now? What would the new cost be?	Select an improved method.

Source: Adapted from Alan Robinson, *Continuous Improvement in Operations: A Systematic Approach to Waste Reduction* (Cambridge, MA: *Productivity Press, 1991), p. 246.*

SUMMARY

Total quality management is a never-ending pursuit of quality that involves everyone in an organization. The driving force is customer satisfaction; a key philosophy is continuous improvement. Training of managers and workers in quality concepts, tools, and procedures is an important aspect of the approach. Teams are an integral part of TQM.

Two major aspects of the TQM approach are problem solving and process improvement.

DISCUSSION AND REVIEW QUESTIONS

1. What are the key elements of the TQM approach? What is the driving force behind TQM?

2. Briefly describe each of the seven quality tools.

3. Briefly define or explain each of these tools:

   a. Brainstorming

   b. Benchmarking

   c. Run charts

4. Explain each of these methods:

   a. The plan-do-study-act cycle

   b. The 5W2H approach

5. List the steps of problem solving.

6. Select four tools and describe how they could be used in problem solving.

7. List the steps of process improvement.

8. Select four tools and describe how they could be used for process improvement.

MEMO WRITING EXERCISES

1. The vice president of manufacturing of your company, June Seymour, has asked you to write her a memo that lists the key elements of a total quality management approach and outlines the benefits and risks of adopting a TQM approach for the company.

    Write a one- to two-page memo to her.

2. You are an assistant to the production manager of a large company. The company wants to give worker teams in several departments additional authority and responsibility to see whether quality and productivity in those areas are increased. However, the proposal has met with resistance from both managers and worker teams.

    Write a one-page memo to Jeff Rogers, the production manager, discussing the probable causes of the resistance and potential solutions for overcoming it.

3. Select a task that you do on a regular basis, such as taking notes in class, doing a homework assignment, grocery shopping, or another task. Write a one-page, quality-at-the-source memo on the difficulties you might encounter by not doing it correctly the first time.

PROBLEMS

1. Make a check sheet and then a Pareto diagram for this car repair shop data.

Ticket No.	Work	Ticket No.	Work
1	Tires	16	Tires
2	Lube & oil	17	Lube & oil
3	Tires	18	Brakes
4	Battery	19	Tires
5	Lube & oil	20	Brakes
6	Lube & oil	21	Lube & oil
7	Lube & oil	22	Brakes
8	Brakes	23	Transmission
9	Lube & oil	24	Brakes
10	Tires	25	Lube & oil
11	Brakes	26	Battery
12	Lube & oil	27	Lube & oil
13	Battery	28	Battery
14	Lube & oil	29	Brakes
15	Lube & oil	30	Tires

2. An air-conditioning repair department manager has compiled data on the primary reason for 41 service calls for the previous week, as shown in the table. Using the data, make a check sheet for the problem types for each customer type, and then construct a Pareto diagram for each type of customer.

Job Number	Problem/ Customer Type	Job Number	Problem/ Customer Type	Job Number	Problem/ Customer Type
301	F/R	315	F/C	329	O/C
302	O/R	316	O/C	330	N/R
303	N/C	317	W/C	331	N/R
304	N/R	318	N/R	332	W/R
305	W/C	319	O/C	333	O/R
306	N/R	320	F/R	334	O/C
307	F/R	321	F/R	335	N/R
308	N/C	322	O/R	336	W/R
309	W/R	323	F/R	337	O/C
310	N/R	324	N/C	338	O/R
311	N/R	325	F/R	339	F/R
312	F/C	326	O/R	340	N/R
313	N/R	327	W/C	341	O/C
314	W/C	328	O/C		

Key: Problem type:
N = Noisy
F = Equipment failure
W = Runs warm
O = Odor

Customer type:
C = Commercial customer
R = Residential customer

3. Prepare a run chart for the occurrences of defective computer monitors based on the following data, which an analyst obtained from the process for making the monitors. Workers are given a 15-minute break at 10:15 A.M. and 3:15 P.M., and a lunch break at noon. What can you conclude?

Interval Start Time	Number of Defectives	Interval Start Time	Number of Defectives
8:00	1	1:00	1
8:15	0	1:15	0
8:30	0	1:30	0
8:45	1	1:45	1
9:00	0	2:00	1
9:15	1	2:15	0
9:30	1	2:30	2
9:45	2	2:45	2
10:00	3	3:00	3
10:30	1	3:30	0
10:45	0	3:45	1
11:00	0	4:00	0
11:15	0	4:15	0
11:30	1	4:30	1
11:45	3	4:45	3

4. Prepare a run diagram for this 911 call data. Use five-minute intervals (i.e., count the calls received in each five-minute interval. Use intervals of 0-4, 5-9, etc.). Note: Two or more calls may occur in the same minute; there were three operators on duty this night. What can you conclude from the run chart?

Call	Time	Call	Time
1	1:03	22	1:56
2	1:06	23	1:56
3	1:09	24	2:00
4	1:11	25	2:00
5	1:12	26	2:01
6	1:17	27	2:02
7	1:21	28	2:03
8	1:27	29	2:03
9	1:28	30	2:04
10	1:29	31	2:06
11	1:31	32	2:07
12	1:36	33	2:08

13	1:39	34	2:08
14	1:42	35	2:11
15	1:43	36	2:12
16	1:44	37	2:12
17	1:47	38	2:13
18	1:48	39	2:14
19	1:50	40	2:14
20	1:52	41	2:16
21	1:53	42	2:19

5. Suppose that a table lamp fails to light when turned on. Prepare a simple cause-and-effect diagram to analyze possible causes.

6. Prepare a cause-and-effect diagram to analyze the possible causes of late delivery of parts ordered from a supplier.

7. Prepare a cause-and-effect diagram to analyze why a machine has produced a large run of defective parts.

8. Prepare a scatter diagram for each of these data sets and then express in words the apparent relationship between the two variables. Put the first variable on the horizontal axis and the second variable on the vertical axis.

a. Age	24	30	22	25	33	27	36	58	37	47	54	28	42	55
Absenteeism rate	6	5	7	6	4	5	4	1	3	2	2	5	3	1

b. Temper. (F)	65	63	72	66	82	58	75	86	77	65	79
Error rate	1	2	0	0	3	3	1	5	2	1	3

9. Prepare a flowchart that describes going to the library to study for an exam. Your flowchart should include these items: finding a place at the library to study, checking to see if you have your book, paper, highlighter, etc., traveling to the library, and the possibility of moving to another location if the place you chose to study starts to get crowded.

10. College students trying to register for a course sometimes find that the course has been closed, or the section they want has been closed. Prepare a cause-and-effect diagram for this problem.

11. The county sheriff's department responded to an unusually large number of vehicular accidents along a quarter-mile stretch of highway in recent months. Prepare a cause-and-effect diagram for this problem.

CASE

Chick-n-Gravy Dinner Line

The operations manager of a firm that produces frozen dinners had received numerous complaints from supermarkets about the firms Chick-n-Gravy dinners. The manager then asked her assistant, Ann, to investigate the matter and to report her recommendations.

Ann's first task was to determine what problems were generating the complaints. The majority centered on five defects: underfilled packages, a missing item, spills/mixed items, unacceptable taste and improperly sealed packages.

Next, she took samples of dinners from the two production lines and examined each sample, making note of any defects that she found. A summary of those results is shown in the table.

The data resulted from inspecting approximately 800 frozen dinners. What should Ann recommend to the manager?

DEFECT OBSERVED

Date	Time	Line	Underfilled	Missing Item	Spill/ Mixed	Unacceptable Taste	Improperly Sealed
5/12	0900	1		✓✓	✓	✓✓✓	
5/12	1330	2			✓✓		✓✓✓
5/13	1000	2				✓	✓✓✓✓
5.13	1345	1	✓✓		✓✓		
5/13	1530	2		✓✓	✓✓✓		✓
5/14	0830	1		✓✓✓		✓✓✓	
5/14	1100	2	✓		✓	✓✓	
5/14	1400	1			✓		✓
5/15	1030	1		✓✓✓		✓✓✓✓✓	
5/15	1145	2			✓	✓✓	
5/15	1500	1	✓		✓		
5/16	0845	2				✓✓	✓✓
5/16	1030	1		✓✓✓	✓	✓✓✓	
5/16	1400	1					
5/16	1545	2	✓	✓✓✓✓✓	✓	✓	✓✓

CASE

Tip Top Markets

Tip Top Markets is a regional chain of supermarkets located in the Southeastern United States. Karen Martin, manager of one of the stores was disturbed by the large number of complaints from customers at her store, particularly on Tuesdays, so she obtained complaint records from the store's customer service desk for the last eight Tuesdays. These are shown below.

Assume you have been asked to help analyze the data and to make recommendations for improvement. Analyze the data using a check sheet, a Pareto diagram, and run charts. Then construct a cause-and-effect diagram for the leading category on your Pareto diagram.

On July 15, changes were implemented to reduce out-of-stock complaints, improve store maintenance, and reduce checkout lines/pricing problems. Do the results of the last two weeks reflect improvement?

Based on your analysis, prepare a list of recommendations that will address customer complaints.

June 1
out of orange yogurt
bread stale
checkout lines too long
overcharged
double charged
meat smelled strange
charged for item not purchased
could't find the sponges
meat tasted strange
store too cold
light out in parking lot
produce not fresh
lemon yogurt past sell date
couldn't find rice
milk past sale date
stock clerk rude
cashier not friendly
out of maple walnut ice cream

something green in meat
didn't like the music
checkout lines too slow

June 8
fish smelled funny
out of date bread
dented can
out of hamburger rolls
fish not fresh
cashier helpful
meat tasted bad
ATM ate card
slippery floor
music too loud
undercharged
out of roses
meat spoiled
overcharged on two items

store too warm
out of ice
telephone out of order
overcharged
rolls stale
bread past sale date

June 15
wanted smaller size
too cold in store
out of Wheaties
out of Minute Rice
cashier rude
fish tasted fishy
ice cream thawed
double charged on hard rolls
long wait at checkout
wrong price on item
overcharged

fish didn't smell right
overcharged on special
couldn't find aspirin
undercharged
checkout lines too long
out of diet cola
meat smelled bad
overcharged on eggs
bread not fresh
didn't like music
lost wallet
overcharged on bread

June 22
milk past sales date
store too warm
foreign object in meat
store too cold
eggs cracked
couldn't find lard
out of 42 oz. Tide
fish really bad
windows dirty
couldn't find oatmeal
out of Bounty paper towels
overcharged on orange juice
lines too long at checkout
couldn't find shoelaces
out of Smucker's strawberry jam
out of Frosty Flakes cereal
out of Thomas' English Muffins

June 29
checkout line too long
out of Dove soap
out of Bisquick
eggs cracked
store not clean
store too cold
cashier too slow
out of skim milk
charged wrong price
restroom not clean
could't find sponges
checkout lines too slow
out of 18 oz. Tide
out of Campbell's turkey soup
out of pepperoni sticks

checkout lines too long
meat not fresh
overcharged on melon

July 6
out of straws
out of bird food
overcharged on butter
out of masking tape
stockboy was helpful
lost child
meat looked bad
overcharged on butter
out of Swiss chard
too many people in store
out of bubble bath
out of Dial soap
store too warm
price not as advertised
need to open more checkouts
shopping carts hard to steer
debris in aisles
out of Drano
out of Chinese cabbage
store too warm
floors dirty and sticky
out of Diamond chopped walnuts

July 13
wrong price on spaghetti
water on floor
store looked messy
store too warm
checkout lines too long
cashier not friendly
out of Cheese Doodles
triple charged
out of Saran Wrap
out of Dove bars
undercharged
out of brown rice
out of mushrooms
overcharged
checkout wait too long
shopping cart broken
couldn't find aspirin
out of brown lunch bags
out of straws

July 20
out of low-salt pickles
checkout lines too slow
found keys in parking lot
lost keys
wrong price on sale item
overcharged on corn
wrong price on baby food
out of 18oz. Tide
out of green tea
checkout lines too long
out of romaine lettuce
out of large eggs
out of cranapple juice
out of pretzels
out of apricot jam
telephone out of order
out of cocktail sauce
water on floor
out of frozen onion rings
out of frozen squash
out of powdered sugar
out of nonfat peanut butter

July 27
out of dill pickles
reported accident in parking lot
wrong price on cranapple juice
out of carrot juice
out of licorice sticks
out of chocolate milk
out of Dove bars
windows dirty
out of iceberg lettuce
like store decorations
out of St. John's Wort
out of vanilla soy milk
wanted to know who won the lottery
store too warm
oatmeal spilled in bulk section
telephone out of order
out of Lava soap
water on floor
out of glazed donuts
out of baby carrots
spaghetti sauce on floor
out of Peter Pan crunchy peanut butter

READING 13.1

CALCOMP: DISASTER BECOMES SUCCESS

Michelle Vranizan

Flash back to the early 1980s. The only thing world-class about CalComp was the mess it was in. The company that practically invented the computer plotter—a device engineers and architects use to print intricate, oversized schematics—had become arrogant, inattentive and lazy.

Every last plotter that rolled off the assembly line didn't work well enough to ship without some rejiggering. A legion of field technicians was needed to make house calls on installed machines that malfunctioned every few weeks. Competitors such as Hewlett-Packard jumped into the breach, stealing dissatisfied customers. Flash forward to the CalComp of the 1990s, recognized as a leader in world-class manufacturing. No more mass assembly lines. No more bugs. No more field technicians.

Hewlett-Packard still sells more pen plotters. But CalComp is a strong No. 2 and has a tight grip on other segments of the plotter and digitizer business. Now bursting with confidence, the $525 million subsidiary of Lockheed Corp. is plowing into other areas of the multibillion dollar computer graphics industry.

The difference between the early 1980s and the 1990s?

Quality.

Specifically, a quality program spearheaded by then CalComp President William Conlin that permeates every square inch of the company's grassy Anaheim headquarters and the attitudes of its 2,800 employees.

At CalComp, quality boils down to pleasing customers with gracefully built, innovative products that work from the start, rarely break down, are competitively priced and are upgraded faster than the other guy's.

"We built a manufacturing system that improves every day," said Bernard Masson, senior vice president of the plotter division, which accounts for about 60 percent of CalComp's revenue. "The product we build tomorrow will be better than the ones we build today."

In the early 1970s and 1980s, CalComp's manufacturing process was fractured. Product design and manufacturing weren't coordinated. The company stockpiled parts and the plotter division alone had more than 650 suppliers. A plotter was only tested for imperfections after it was made.

The system worked as long as CalComp only sold 1,000 or so plotters a year to customers who used mainframes or minicomputers, also very temperamental machines prone to breakdowns.

Then along came personal computers, which worked straight out of the box. When personal computers became the preferred tools for engineering and graphics, CalComp managers realized the old way of doing things had to go.

Conlin signed on in late 1983 and CalComp took its first steps toward world-class manufacturing soon after. CalComp embraced the teachings of quality gurus such as W. Edwards Deming and Richard J. Schonberger, focusing first on the factory.

In the beginning, changes were simple, such as writing down the steps it took to assemble a plotter—something CalComp had never done before, Masson said.

Next, assembly workers were taught quality principles, given a say in how things were done and encouraged to catch mistakes on the line.

Other steps CalComp took:

1. When a new product is conceived, a team of more than a dozen people representing virtually every department shepherds it from development to delivery. With this kind of teamwork engineers don't end up designing parts that factory workers can't put together, said Linda Gronski, an operating unit manager in the plotter division.

2. Instead of stockpiling parts, CalComp cut inventories to the bare minimum and now takes delivery of just enough parts for the next week's work. Some suppliers even deliver parts on a daily basis.

3. CalComp put strict quality controls on suppliers and reduced its vendors in the plotter division to about 180. CalComp started a three-tier preferred-supplier program, dubbed "a mini-Malcolm Baldrige award" contest by one supplier. Parts from suppliers on the higher tier are expected to be so perfect CalComp doesn't even inspect them before building them into products.

By keeping inventories down, CalComp cut its overhead costs. It also can avoid writing off obsolete parts should demand shift suddenly and can direct energies to new products more quickly, company executives said.

Readjusting attitudes toward work was the most important part of the jump to quality, CalComp managers said.

Today, front-line workers are treated with as much respect as executives. Assembly workers are never reprimanded for stopping the line if they can't solve a problem. Gronski and other production managers wear beepers and are expected to attend to problems immediately.

Suppliers said they benefited from classes at CalComp on quality processes: They use the information to transform their businesses and attract other customers.

"When Xerox found out where we were with CalComp, they decided to send a team of people out to visit us," said Harry Esayian, owner of Zac Precision in Anaheim, which makes machine parts for dozens of CalComp products.

Draftsmen and engineers who use CalComp plotters and digitizers might be unfamiliar with the company's quality programs. But they appreciate the results.

"I'm always talking up the plotter because it's a good deal," said customer David Terry, who has a Santa Ana engineering firm that designs waste water-treatment plants. "They're low-cost and no-maintenance. We're real happy."

QUESTIONS

1. In general terms, what was wrong in the early 1980s at CalComp?

2. Specifically, what was wrong with:

    a. design and manufacturing?

    b. inventory?

    c. suppliers?

3. In general terms, what change helped to turn things around at CalComp?

4. What steps were taken to improve the situation?

5. What benefits have resulted from the changes?

Source: *The Orange County Register,* March 1, 1992.

READING 13.2

CONTINUOUS IMPROVEMENT ON THE FREE-THROW LINE

Timothy Clark and Andrew Clark

In 1924, Walter Shewhart developed a problem-solving method to continually improve quality by reducing variation (the difference between the ideal outcome and the actual situation). To help guide improvement efforts, Shewhart outlined a process referred to as the plan-do-study-act (PDSA) cycle. The PDSA cycle combined with the traditional concepts of decision making and problem solving are what my son and I used to continuously improve his basketball free-throw shooting.

Recognizing the Problem

Identify the facts. I had observed over a three-year period from 1991 to 1993 that in basketball games, my son Andrew's free-throw shooting percentage averaged between 45 percent and 50 percent.

Identify and define the process. Andrew's process for shooting free throws was simple: Go to the free-throw line, bounce the ball four times, aim, and shoot.

The desired outcome was a higher free-throw shooting percentage. An ideal outcome, or perfection, would be one in which 100 percent of the shots fall through the middle of the rim, land at the same spot on the floor every time, and roll straight back in the shooter's direction after landing.

Plot the points. To confirm my observations on the results of the current process, we went to the YMCA and Andrew shot five sets of 10 free throws

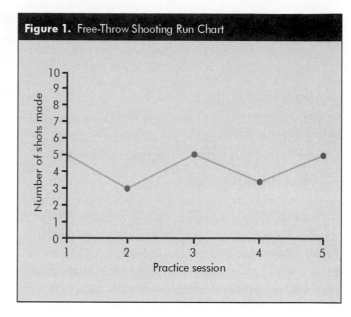

Figure 1. Free-Throw Shooting Run Chart

for a total of 50 shots. His average was 42 percent. Results were recorded on a run chart (see Figure 1). Based on this information as well as on past observations, I estimated the process was stable.

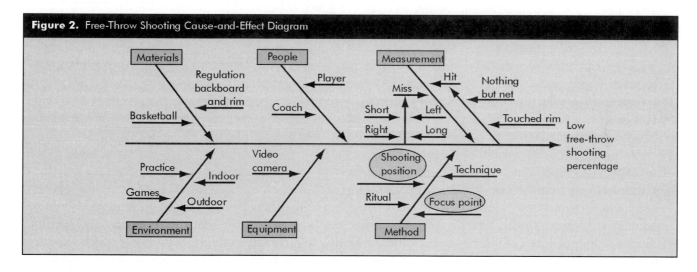

Figure 2. Free-Throw Shooting Cause-and-Effect Diagram

Decision Making

Identify the causes. Causes of variation in any process can be identified through the general categories of people, equipment, materials, methods, environment, and measurement. A cause-and-effect diagram is used to graphically illustrate the relationship between the effect—a low free-throw shooting percentage—and the principal causes (see Figure 2).

In analyzing my son's process, I noticed that he did not stand at the same place on the free-throw line every time. I believed his inconsistent shooting position affected the direction of the shot. If the shot goes left or right, there is a smaller probability that the ball will have a lucky bounce and go in. I also noticed that he didn't seem to have a consistent focal point.

Develop, analyze, and select alternatives. The alternatives selected for Andrew, a right-handed shooter, were for him to line up his right foot on the middle of the free-throw line, focus on the middle of the front part of the rim, and visualize the perfect shot before he released the ball. The modified process is:

1. Stand at the center of the free-throw line.

2. Bounce the ball four times.

3. Focus on the middle of the front part of the rim, and visualize a perfect shot.

4. Shoot.

Develop an action plan. The course of action at this point was for Andrew to shoot five more sets of 10 free throws to test the effectiveness of the changes.

Problem Solving

Implement the selected alternative and compare actual with expected results. The new process resulted in a 36 percent improvement in Andrew's average free-throw percentage at basketball practice, which raised his average to 57 percent (see Figure 3). The new process was first implemented in games toward the end of the 1994 season, and in the last three games, Andrew hit nine of his 13 free throws for a free-throw shooting average of 69 percent.

During the 1995 season, Andrew made 37 of his 52 free throws in games for an average of 71 percent. In one extremely close game where the other team was forced to foul Andrew's team in an effort to get the ball back, Andrew hit seven of his seven shots, which helped his team win the game. In team practices, the coaches had the players shoot two free throws and then rotate. For the entire season, Andrew hit 101 of 169 of his team practice free throws for an average of 60 percent.

As we monitored Andrew's process from March 17, 1994, to Jan. 18, 1996, we plotted the total number of practice shots made out of 50, using Shewhart's number-of-affected-units control chart (see Figure 4).

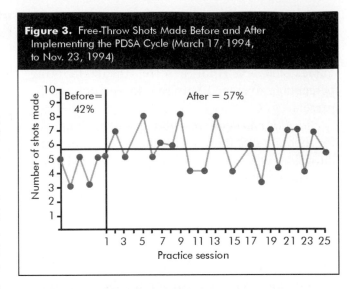

Figure 3. Free-Throw Shots Made Before and After Implementing the PDSA Cycle (March 17, 1994, to Nov. 23, 1994)

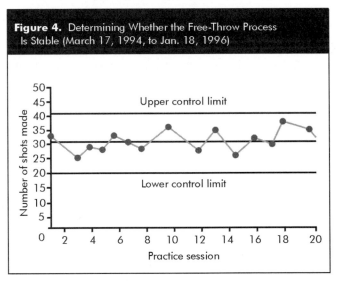

Figure 4. Determining Whether the Free-Throw Process Is Stable (March 17, 1994, to Jan. 18, 1996)

In the late summer of 1995, Andrew went to a basketball camp where he was advised to change his shooting technique. This change to his process reduced his shooting percentage during the 1996 season to 50 percent. This caused him to lose confidence in his shooting ability, and consequently, he took fewer shots. We then reinstalled his old process, and his shooting percentage returned to its former level. In one series of 50 practice free throws, he hit 35 of 50 shots for an average of 70 percent and in another set, he hit 32 of 50 for an average of 64 percent. During the remaining team practices, Andrew hit 14 of 20 of his practice free throws for an average of 70 percent. During the final three games, he hit two of three free throws for an average of 67 percent. During the 1996 and 1997 sea`sons, Andrew was a point guard and was responsible for controlling and distributing the ball. In this position, he had fewer opportunities to shoot free throws. Therefore, during the 1997 season, he had the opportunity to shoot only 12 free throws, but he made nine of them for an average of 75 percent.

Overall benefits. In addition to the tangible results, such as improved free-throw shooting, the intangible benefits were significant. For example, Andrew's confidence improved, and he learned how to determine when changes to his shooting technique resulted in improvement. W. Edwards Deming referred to this type of knowledge as profound.

CONTINUOUS IMPROVEMENT

Take appropriate action based on study results. In preparation for the 1998 season, Andrew's priorities for improvement are to continue to monitor his free-throw shooting to ensure it remains stable and to work on improving the shooting percentage of his two- and three-point shots.

Source: © 1997 American Society for Quality. Reprinted with permission.

READING 13.3

BENCHMARKING CORPORATE WEBSITES OF FORTUNE 500 COMPANIES

www.dow.com

More and more people are using the Internet. And when these people want information about a company's products or services, they often go to the company's website. In a study of the home pages of Fortune 500 companies, 13 factors were deemed critical to quality. Those factors, and the survey results, are shown below:

1. Use of meta tags (e.g., keywords used by search engines) Yes, 70%; no, 30%

2. Meaningful home page title Yes, 97%; no, 3%

3. Unique domain name Yes, 91%; no, 9%

4. Search engine site registration 97% (average)

5. Server reliability 99% (average)

6. Average speed of loading (seconds) 28k, 19.3; 56k, 10.9; T1, 2.6 sec.

7. Average number of bad links .40

8. Average number of spelling errors .16

9. Visibility of contact information Yes, 74%; no, 26%

10. Indication of last update date Yes, 17%; no, 63%

11. A privacy policy Yes, 53%; no, 47%

12. Presence of a search engine Yes, 59%; no, 41%

13. Translation to multiple languages Yes, 11%; no, 89%

The corporations are doing well on most factors, but they need improvement on the last five.

The list is a handy reference other organizations can use to benchmark their existing home pages to see where improvements are needed or to develop effective home pages.

QUESTION

Give one reason for the importance of each factor.

Source: Based on Nabil Tamimi, Murli Rajan, and Rose Sebastianelli, "Benchmarking the Home Pages of 'Fortune 500' Companies," *Quality Progress,* July 2000, pp. 47–51.

READING 13.3

MAKING QUALITY PAY: RETURN ON QUALITY

Start with an effective quality program. Companies that don't have the basics, such as process and inventory controls and other building blocks, will find a healthy return on quality elusive.

Calculate the cost of current quality initiatives. Cost of warranties, problem prevention, and monitoring activities all count. Measure these against the returns for delivering a product or service to the customer.

Determine what key factors retain customers—and what drives them away. Conduct detailed surveys. Forecast market changes, especially qual-ity and new-product initiatives of competitors.

Focus on quality efforts most likely to improve customer satisfaction at a reasonable cost. Figure the link between each dollar spent on quality and its effect on customer retention and market share.

Roll out successful programs after pilot-testing the most promising efforts and cutting the ones that don't have a big impact. Closely monitor results. Build word of mouth by publicizing success stories.

Improve programs continually. Measure results against anticipated gains. Beware of the competition's initiative and don't hesitate to revamp programs accordingly. Quality never rests.

When the "total quality" mantra swept U.S. boardrooms in the 1980s, few companies responded with the fervor and dedication of Varian Associates Inc. The scientific-equipment maker put 1,000 of its managers through a four-day course on quality. The company's Silicon Valley headquarters buzzed with quality-speak. Talk of work teams and cycle times replaced discussion of electrons and X-rays. There was even a mascot, Koala T—a manager who wore a koala costume and roamed Varian's cafeteria handing out homilies about quality.

And it wasn't just buzzwords and bear suits. Varian went about virtually reinventing the way it did business—with what seemed to be stunning results. A unit that makes vacuum systems for computer clean rooms boosted on-time delivery from 42 percent to 92 percent. The radiation-equipment-service department ranked No. 1 in its industry for prompt customer visits. The semiconductor unit cut the time it took to put out new designs by 14 days. W. Edwards Deming and J. M. Juran, the famous management consultants and leading prophets of quality, would have been proud.

But while Varian thought it was playing quality by the book, the final chapter didn't feature the happy ending the company expected. Obsessed with meeting production schedules, the staff in that vacuum-equipment unit didn't return customers' phone calls and the operation ended up losing market share. Radiation-repair people were so rushed to meet deadlines that they left before explaining their work to customers. Sure, Varian could boast about quality. But in 1990, its sales grew by a paltry 3 percent, to $1.3 billion. And Varian posted a $4.1 million loss after a $32 million profit in 1989. "All of the quality-based charts went up and to the right, but everything else went down," says Richard M. Levy, executive vice-president for quality.

Levy isn't the only one who's dismayed. Countless other managers have heeded the siren song of total quality management, or TQM, only to discover that quality doesn't necessarily pay. At Johnson & Johnson, quality teams for several product lines crisscrossed the country, benchmarking against other companies, but costs skyrocketed. In 1990, Wallace Co. won the Malcolm Baldrige National Quality Award. Two years later, the oil equipment company filed for Chapter 11 as the cost of its quality programs soared and oil prices collapsed.

Rallying Cry. Of course, the quest for quality doesn't always have unhappy results. Detroit, for instance, finally caught the quality wave in the 1980s, and it's hard not to shudder at the thought of how the Big Three would be faring today if they were still turning out Chevy Citations instead of Saturns. And much of the rest of U.S. industry would be locked out of the game in today's global economy without the quality strides of the past few years.

But at too many companies, it turns out, the push for quality can be as badly misguided as it is well-intended. It can be popular with managers and their consultants, but as at Varian, it can devolve into a mechanistic exercise that proves meaningless to customers. And quality that means little to customers doesn't produce a payoff in improved sales, profits, or market share. It's wasted effort and expense.

That's why a growing number of companies and management thinkers are starting to refine the notion. Today's rallying cry: return on quality. Concepts such as better product designs and swifter manufacturing aren't being rejected, but advocates of the new theory are abandoning the narrow statistical benchmarks worshipped by some TQM acolytes. Instead, managers are trying to make sure that the quality they offer is the quality their customers want. And they're starting to use sophisticated financial tools to ensure that quality programs have a payoff. Roland Rust, a Vanderbilt University professor of management and one of ROQ's chief apostles, says executives have to worry about only one thing: "If we're not going to make money off of it, we're not going to do it."

The ROQ revisionism is attracting a growing number of corporate devotees across a wide spectrum of industries. Banking giant NationsBank Corp., for example, now measures every improvement in service, from adding tellers to offering new mortgage products, in terms of added revenue. Telecommunications powerhouse GTE Corp. is looking for quality at reasonable costs. Even companies that were in the vanguard of the 1980s quality push are considering the benefits of ROQ. "We're trying to isolate quality improvements that just don't add any value to the service that is delivered to the customer," says Michael E. Reed, managing director of operations at Federal Express Corp.

For FedEx, a 1990 Baldrige recipient, that has meant rethinking its original quality goals. In its sorting operation, for example, FedEx stressed speed over accuracy. Workers met schedules, but the number of misdirected packages soared as they scrambled to meet deadlines. FedEx eventually fixed most errors, but redirecting each wayward package cost it some $50. Now, the Memphis-based shipper has eased the sorting crunch by investing $100 million in new equipment that routes packages to various destinations.

ROQ is more than just a new twist on an old theme. Many companies believe that applying a bottom-line discipline to quality is crucial at a time when the economy is rebounding and competition is growing. AT&T CEO Robert E. Allen, for example, receives a quarterly report from each of the company's 53 business units that spells out quality improvements and their subsequent financial impact.

Return Threshold. Everything from the installation of new technology to methods of improving billing accuracy is held up against an array of financial yardsticks, such as potential sales gains and return on capital. Based on its experience, AT&T has found that when customers perceive improved quality, it shows up in better financial results three months later. "This is the most important thing that AT&T has ever done," Allen told a meeting of top managers the day before his June board presentation.

To win approval from AT&T's top management these days, proponents of any new quality initiative must first demonstrate that the effort will yield at least a 30 percent drop in defects and a 10 percent return on investment. Ma Bell used those criteria last year to maintain its supremacy in the toll-free 800-number market. To reduce service outages—its customers' biggest complaint—AT&T mulled a vast modernization program. But it seemed unlikely that the staggering $1 billion-plus project would net enough new customers to clear the 10 percent investment-return threshold. Instead, Ma Bell invested $300 million in backup power equipment to guard against failures in its 800-number system. "It isn't the old 'Give me money and I'll fix it' stuff," says Phillip M. Scanlan, a corporate quality officer. "We're taking the cost out of making our system better."

Chasing Prizes. Of course, quality was always supposed to make bottom-line sense. In the Deming and Juran doctrines, empowered employees would make quicker and more market-based decisions. Faster and better manufacturing processes would lead to improved products and broader market share. That message was popularized by Deming in the 1950s, and it soon became the cornerstone of Japanese management theory. The quality theory emigrated to the U.S. in the 1980s as American companies tried to duplicate the Japanese miracle. For some of them, including Motorola, Intel, Hewlett-Packard, and General Electric, excellence became the norm. But others among the legions who followed Deming came to confuse process with purpose. Quality devotees grew obsessed with methodology—cost-cutting, defect reduction, quicker cycle times, continual improvement. Before too long, customer concerns seemed to fall by the wayside.

Quality became its own reward. Standards were more important than sales. And companies appeared more interested in chasing prizes than profits. Pleasing the International Standards Organization, which sets European quality standards, became a paramount concern for some companies. Meanwhile, Baldrige wannabes often tripped and fell as they tried to complete an obstacle course of requirements that emphasizes process over proceeds. "There's been an insufficient focus on the aspect of quality improvements that will make the largest contribution to overall financial performance," admits Curt W. Reimann, director of the Baldrige Quality Award.

The new focus on the relationship between quality and financial returns does have its detractors. Critics say it's just a smokescreen behind which companies are cutting back on their quality efforts. A healthier economy and ris-ing sales may be prompting them to slack off on the costly discipline of TQM. And some companies—Hewlett-Packard among them—argue it's a mistake to take a bean-counter's view of something as fundamental as quality. Yes, HP makes its decisions about quality based on sound business considerations. But that doesn't mean it takes out a calculator every time it launches a quality program. "Saying that this is a quality move and this is what it's worth is like saying, 'What's my left lung worth?'" says Richard LeVitt, director of corporate quality. "Quality is intrinsic to our whole business."

Ironing It Out. To its advocates, ROQ is about getting companies back to something that's equally intrinsic to everyone's business: customer focus. Instead of talking about attracting new customers with dazzling statistical displays of quality, ROQ emphasizes customer retention. After all, selling more to existing customers is a cheaper way to build market share than luring business away from competitors. "Customers are an economic asset. They're not on the balance sheet, but they should be," says Claess Fornell, a University of Michigan professor who is a leading ROQ advocate. Extensive surveying, perhaps even inviting customers into design and production processes, helps companies identify the key factors that affect customers' buying decisions.

QUESTIONS

1. According to the ROQ approach, how should a company decide which quality activities to fund?

2. What criticisms does the author level at those who don't use ROQ to guide quality efforts?

3. What risks are there in rigidly applying the ROQ approach?

READING 13.4

QUALITY PROGRAMS DON'T GUARANTEE RESULTS

U.S. companies have poured millions of dollars into quality programs in the last few years. Unfortunately, the programs do not always achieve the results companies expect. The McKinsey Consulting Group has developed several useful guidelines for executives concerning quality programs:

Don't promote continuous improvement if dramatic results are needed. Sagging sales and profits often imply the need for something more than incremental improvement. Continuous improvement programs should be reserved for those instances where an organization has already achieved substantial quality results but still wants to improve its operations.

Link quality programs to strategic planning. Then, set goals for the program, and evaluate senior management, based on how well those goals are met. However, let lower-level employees set their own goals in order to get them involved, and to motivate their best performance.

Focus programs on market "break points." Customers may not be able to perceive a difference between an on-time delivery performance of 90 percent and one of say, 95 percent, although they would perceive a difference in 90 percent versus 99 percent on-time delivery. So determine what the break points are, and don't waste resources on improving performance that does not achieve a higher break point.

Choose a single theme. It is important for everybody to be rowing in the same direction. Note, however, that a single focus does carry a risk: It may become an end in itself.

Emphasize results as well as the process. Focusing exclusively on the process carries the risk of diverting attention from results, and may also lead to excessive buildup in staff associated with the program. Instead, set specific goals in terms of *measurable* results.

Questions

1. List some of the ways a company can judge whether its quality program is working.

2. Explain the importance of measurements for quality programs.

3. For each guideline, explain the rationale.

READING 13.5

SWIMMING UPSTREAM

Theodore B. Kinni

An early convert to the philosophy of *kaizen,* Richard Chang has been preaching the gospel of continuous improvement for two decades. Founder of Irvine, Calif.-based Richard Chang Associates, Inc., a diversified organizational-consulting firm and publishing house, Mr. Chang currently serves as a senior examiner for the Malcolm Baldrige National Quality Award and judge for California's Governor's Golden State Quality Award. He is also a prolific writer, having penned 14 books himself. He is the publisher of The Practical Guide Book Series, a collection of four series including the eight-volume Quality Improvement Series—which covers process-improvement methodology, techniques, and tools. In the following interview he explains for IW readers how the spirit of kaizen is successfully infused throughout a small company.

IW: *What are the environmental prerequisites of kaizen?*

CHANG: Typically, you need to run a lean or even understaffed operation. . . . You have to make an investment in training and must also hire people who are open to continuous improvement—they are hard to find. . . . Finally, especially in a small company, the philosophy must come from the top. The CEO can't be a reactive firefighter, but must behave in a manner consistent with continuous improvement. Also, instead of taking a punishment approach, you have to look at problems and mistakes as learning opportunities.

IW: *If we can create such an environment, what's next?*

CHANG: Oftentimes, you would then create a sense of vision and core values that includes the principles of kaizen. You must also build reinforcement into your reward systems and align corporate goals with continuous improvement. Remember, kaizen has to be the way you run your business; it can't just be an extra program you tack on to the operation.

If you think of that as Phase One, Phase Two is then about building capacity. This is when you concentrate on the skills that make you capable of continuously improving the business. People tend to skip this—they want to get right to the results.

IW: *What would a typical continuous-improvement-initiative rollout look like?*

CHANG: We use a technique called discovery meetings. We simply gather groups of employees and ask them to think about areas that need improvement. It's just some downtime to sit and think. From that we can begin to look at opportunities for improvement.

IW: *Do discovery meetings turn into giant gripe sessions?*

CHANG: In the beginning, yes, you tend to get a lot of ideas connected to dissatisfaction. The first meeting or two may be mostly discovery baggage, but you have to let the emoting happen. We suggest making some quick fixes to help build confidence that we really plan to act on the results of these meetings. Soon, with some coaching and leading, the groups get to work processes and develop worthy opportunities.

IW: *How much of the workforce is involved in these meetings?*

CHANG: At the early stages, no more than 15 percent to 25 percent. I'm not an advocate of the blanket approach.

IW: *When improvement opportunities are established, what happens?*

CHANG: Put the teams to work on the problems they identified. Now is the perfect time to start training. This gives people the opportunity to learn and apply the learning at the same time.

When the projects are complete, and before the groups disband, have the teams collect feedback and data, and then transfer ownership of the process to them. Now they take responsibility for continuously improving the process and other members of the workforce can start their training.

IW: *Don't opportunities for improvement eventually dry up?*
CHANG: There is a certain point when the process capability might max out and the benefit you get from incremental improvements is not worth the cost. When your processes top out, that's when reengineering comes in. A complete overhaul, in turn, leads to more rounds of continuous improvement. That's how continuous improvement and reengineering complement each other.

IW: *Can you tip us off to the pitfalls?*
CHANG: There are five that I like to describe in medical terms. "Widespread implementation rash" is when companies try to do too much, too fast. This is a philosophy; you don't get in and get out. Then there is "key process selection deficiency"—don't improve the petty cash process, make the work important. "Elevated doses of training" is when people train the whole workforce before they have established the environmental conditions for success. "High count of quality teams" is when we get team mania. The goal is not to implement teams; it's to improve processes. Last is "persistent process measurement cost," which occurs when organizations start improving processes before they are measured. The result is that they have no way of knowing whether they got anything worthwhile accomplished.

IW: *If you only had a moment to sum up continuous improvement, what would you tell us?*
CHANG: I usually end my speeches with some version of this thought: Implementing continuous-improvement initiatives is like swimming upstream against the downward flow of habit.

Source: Reprinted with permission from *Industry Week,* January 23, 1995. Copyright Penton Publishing, Inc., Cleveland, Ohio.

SELECTED BIBLIOGRAPHY

Besterfield, Dale H., Carol Besterfield-Micha, Glen Besterfield, and Mary Besterfield-Sacre. *Total Quality Management.* 2nd ed. Englewood Cliffs, NJ: Prentice Hall, 1999.

Brassard, Michael, and Diane Ritter. *The Memory Jogger II: A Pocket Guide of Tools for Continuous Improvement and Effective Planning.* Methuen, MA: Goal/QPC, 1994.

Cappels, Thomas. *Financially Focused Quality: TQM in the 21st Century.* Boca Raton, FL: St. Lucie Press, 1999.

Gitlow, Howard, Alan Oppenheim, and Rosa Oppenheim. *Quality Management: Tools and Methods for Improvement.* 2nd ed. Burr Ridge, IL: Irwin, 1995.

Giffith, Gary K. *The Quality Technician's Handbook.* 4th ed. Upper Saddle River, NJ: Prentice Hall, 2000.

Harry, Mikel, and Richard Schroeder. *Six Sigma: The Breakthrough Management Strategy Revolutionizing the World's Top Corporations.* New York: Currency, 2000.

Hendricks, Kevin B., and Vinod R. Singhal. "Don't Count TQM Out." *Quality Progress,* April 1999, pp. 35–41.

Juran, Joseph M. *Juran's Quality Handbook.* New York: McGraw-Hill, 1999.

Lientz, B. P., and P. Rea. *How to Plan and Implement Business Process Improvement.* San Diego, CA: Harcourt Brace Professional Publications, 1998.

Lynch, R. L., and K. F. Cross. *Measure Up! Yardsticks for Continuous Improvement.* 2nd ed. Cambridge, MA: Blackwell, 1995.

Mears, P. *Quality Improvement Tools and Techniques.* New York: McGraw-Hill, 1995.

Mitra, Amitava. *Fundamentals of Quality Control and Improvement.* 2nd ed. Englewood Cliffs, NJ: Prentice Hall, 1998.

Oppenheim, Bohdan W., and Zbigniew H. Przasnyski. "Total Quality Requires Serious Training." *Quality Progress,* October 1999, pp. 63–73.

Salegna, Gary, and Farzaneh Fazel. "Obstacles to Implementing Quality." *Quality Progress,* July 2000, pp. 53–57.

Smith, Gerald. *Statistical Process Control and Process Improvement.* 3rd ed. Englewood Cliffs, NJ: Prentice Hall, 1997.

Stevenson, William J. "Supercharging Your Pareto Analysis." *Quality Progress,* October 2000, pp. 51–55.

Straker, D. *A Toolbook for Quality Improvement and Problem Solving.* New York: Prentice Hall, 1995.

Summers, Donna. *Quality.* 2nd ed. Upper Saddle River, NJ: Prentice Hall, 2000.

Part 4

Introduction to Adapting to Change

There are few guarantees in business, as in life. Change is inevitable. As we work within the twenty-first century, the ability of businesses to adapt to change is often integral to their survival. To be successful, management must also assist their employees in adapting to changes in the workplace.

Examples of major changes influencing businesses are the rapid development of technology, corporate mergers, consolidations, and the redesigning of organizations. The impact of technological advances on jobs, how information is disseminated, and how customers are served, has changed the nature of many businesses and facilitated globalization in the marketplace. Corporate mergers and acquisitions have created industry giants controlling diverse businesses and influencing the global economy. Many organizations are forced to adapt new systems, procedures, and policies as they redesign themselves. Transformations such as these require organizations and industries to examine how they meet the needs and expectations of their internal and external customers, and how they are positioned in a dynamic marketplace.

Part 4 focuses on the issues that influence change and how organizations and individuals can effectively develop to accommodate change. The part begins in Chapter 14 with an examination of change and organizational development including a look at the forces of change, how to manage change, and the impact of change on organizational development. Chapter 15 is an exploration of a major element of change in today's world – Managing Across Cultures. We live in a truly multicultural world and operate in a global economy. To understand that multicultural global economy is one of the keys to successfully adapting to change.

Change is often extremely stressful; therefore, the text concludes with Chapter 16 - Managing Stress. Stress is a significant factor in contemporary business causing many of the changes with which we are faced. Part 4 concludes with an examination of stress at work, looking at the major cause and effects of stress, and how to effectively manage stress.

Chapter 14

Change and Organizational Development

SOURCE: Steven L. McShane and Mary Ann VonGlinow, *Organizational Behavior*, Chapter 15, © McGraw-Hill, 2000.

Learning Objectives

After reading this chapter, you should be able to:

- Identify four forces for change in the business environment.

- Describe the elements of Lewin's force field analysis model.

- Outline six reasons why people resist organizational change.

- Discuss six strategies to minimize resistance to change.

- Outline the role of change agents.

- Define organization development.

- Discuss three things consultants need to determine in a client relationship.

- Explain how appreciative inquiry differs from the more traditional approach to OD.

- Discuss four ethical issues in organization development.

In the mid-1990s, senior executives at Royal Dutch/Shell realized that the giant Anglo-Dutch oil company had to change. Although still profitable, Shell was not responsive enough to global customers, and new competitors were grabbing market share. Shell's executives in London and The Hague spent two years reorganizing, downsizing, and educating several layers of management, but this top-down approach had minimal effect. Managers in charge of Shell's operations for a particular country resisted changes that threatened their autonomy, and headquarters managers couldn't break out of the routines that worked well in the past.

So Steve Miller, head of Shell's worldwide oil products business, decided to change the company from the bottom up. He and his executive team held several five-day workshops, each attended by six country teams of frontline people (e.g., gas station managers, truck drivers, marketing professionals). Participants at these "retailing boot camps" learned about worrisome competitive trends in their regions and were taught powerful marketing tools to identify new opportunities. The teams then returned home to study their market and develop proposals for improvement. For example, a team in South Africa proposed ways to increase liquid gas market share. Another team developed plans to increase gasoline sales in Malaysia.

Four months later, the teams returned for a second workshop where each proposal was critiqued by Miller's executive team in "fishbowl" sessions with the other teams watching. Videotapes from these sessions became powerful socialization tools for other employees back in the home country. Each team had 60 days to put its ideas into action, then return for a third workshop to analyze what worked and what didn't.

These workshops, along with field tours and several other grassroots activities, had a tremendous effect. Frontline employees developed an infectious enthusiasm and a stronger business approach to challenging the competition. "I can't overstate how infectious the optimism and energy of these committed employees was on the many managers above them," says Miller. The change process also resulted in solid improvements in profitability and market share in most regions where employees had attended the sessions.[1]

Change is difficult enough in small firms. At Shell and other large organizations, it requires monumental effort and persistence. Organizational change is also very messy. Although Steve Miller's change process sounds like a well-executed strategy, he later said that it was a "scary" experience with uncertain consequences. Even in successful firms, leaders need to overcome (or bypass) resistance to change. They need to give up control and move people out of their comfortable routines.

This chapter examines ways to bring about meaningful change in organizations. After considering some of the more significant forces for organizational change, we introduce Lewin's model of change and its component parts. This includes sources of resistance to change, ways to minimize this resistance, and stabilizing desired behaviors. The latter part of this chapter introduces the field of organization development (OD). In particular, we review the OD process, emerging OD strategies, and issues relating to OD effectiveness.

EXTERNAL FORCES FOR CHANGE

Today's business environment is changing so rapidly that it leaves everyone breathless. "The velocity of change is so rapid, so quick, that if you don't accept the change and move with the change, you're going to be left behind," says Ford CEO Jacques Nasser. W. Allen Schaffer, head of managed care at CIGNA Healthcare, Inc., agrees. "The pace of change is stunning," he says. "We have to reevaluate our strategic assumptions every six months."[2]

To illustrate the amount of churn and upheaval in the business environment, consider *Business Week*'s latest list of top-performing companies: Microsoft, Dell Computer, GAP, Oracle, and EMC.[3] Twenty years ago, these companies were either junior start-ups or nonexistent. Today, they are leaders in growth and profitability. And unless these firms anticipate and adapt to continual change, few of them will be on the list 20 years from now. As open systems, successful organizations monitor their environments and take appropriate steps to maintain a compatible fit with the new external conditions. This adaptability requires continual change. It is an ongoing process because environmental change does not end.

There are many forces for change in the external environment, but the prominent forces are computer technology, global and local competition, and demographics. Not surprisingly, most of these are emerging organizational behavior issues that we discussed in the opening chapter of this book.

Computer Technology

Computer technology seems to be the main reason why organizations are experiencing such dramatic and rapid environmental change. More specifically, the systems of networks that connect computers throughout the planet have dramatically reduced time and dissolved distances; this relates to the **law of telecosm,** which says that as the web of computer networks expands, distances will shrink and eventually become irrelevant.[4]

A few years ago "e-commerce" was a spelling mistake. Now, Amazon.com, Charles Schwab, and other companies are leveraging the power of the Internet to offer a variety of electronic commerce experiences. Intranets have also made it easy and inexpensive to transfer information throughout the organization.[5] Employees use intranet systems to directly access job-related information, bypassing supervisors who previously served as conduits. Suppliers are hooked up to computer-based networks—called *extranets*—to accelerate just-in-time delivery of goods. Major clients are also hooked up to the organization's product database for direct ordering and delivery.[6]

Computer technology does more than open up business opportunities. It forces corporate leaders to rethink how their organizations are configured, as well as what competencies and expectations employees must have in these emerging organizational forms.[7] It facilitates telecommuting and opens up new employment relationships with employees. It places more emphasis on knowledge management rather than physical presence and manufacturing capacity as a driver of competitive advantage. E-commerce, extranets, and other forms of networked computer technology are also creating new organizational structures in which small businesses are able to compete on a global level through network alliances.

Global and Local Competition

Increasing global and local competition are also powerful forces for organizational change.[8] Competitors are just as likely to be located in a distant part of the world than within your country. Emerging trading blocs in North America, Europe, the Asia-Pacific region, and other areas add another dimension to these competitive forces. As we learned in the opening story to this chapter, Shell's need for change arose mainly because new competitors were threatening the oil company's survival in France and other key markets.

Technology has played a role in increasing global and local competition. A few years ago, no one would have guessed that Internet upstart Amazon.com would be a threat to bookstore giants Barnes & Noble and Borders. AT&T executives would not have predicted that WorldCom would become a major competitor. And few could imagine that cable companies would somehow be competing with telephone companies.

Government deregulation and privatization have also fueled competition. Energy companies in several U.S. states now compete where they previously held monopolies. Post offices in Australia and the United Kingdom have also been forced to reinvent themselves as their governments open up some mail services to the private sector. Government-owned telephone companies in Singapore, Canada, and other countries have been transformed into private or semiprivate enterprises.[9]

Global and domestic competition often leads to corporate restructuring. To increase their competitiveness, companies reduce layers of management, sell entire divisions of employees, and reduce payroll through downsizing. Raytheon, Gillette, Levi Strauss, and many other firms have closed plants and laid off thousands of employees due to increased competition and other pressures to increase efficiency.[10]

Global competition has also fueled an unprecedented number of mergers and acquisitions in recent years. Daimler-Benz merged with Chrysler; British Petroleum merged with Amoco and Arco; General Electric acquires dozens of companies each year. Mergers potentially improve a company's competitive advantage through greater efficiency and global reach, but they also require dramatic changes in the way people work. When America Online acquired Netscape, for instance, Netscape's employees worried about losing their jobs and their Californian way of life.[11]

Demography

While firms adjust to global competition, they are also adapting to changes in the workforce. Employees are more educated and consequently expect more involvement and interesting work. Generation-X employees are less intimidated by management directives and they work to live more than live to work. In Japan, corporate leaders must adjust to a younger workforce that is more individualistic. In Singapore, once considered a country with a high respect for authority, younger employees are starting to openly question and debate with senior executives. Meanwhile, in many parts of the world, companies employ a far more diverse workforce than they did a few decades ago. These changes have put pressure on organizational leaders to alter work practices, develop more compatible structures and rewards, and discover new ways to lead.

LEWIN'S FORCE FIELD ANALYSIS MODEL

It is easy to see that these environmental forces push companies to change the way they operate. What is more difficult to see is the complex interplay of these forces against other organizational dynamics. Psychologist Kurt Lewin developed the force field analysis model to help us understand how the change process works (see Figure 14-1).[12] Although developed over 50 years ago, Lewin's **force field analysis** model remains the prominent way of viewing this process.

One side of the force field model represents the *driving forces* that push organizations toward a new state of affairs. We began this chapter by describing several driving forces in the external environment: computer technology, global and local competition, and demographics. Along with these external forces are driving forces that seem to originate from within the organization, such as competition across divisions of the company and the leader's need to impose his or her image on the organization.

The other side of Lewin's model represents the *restraining forces* that maintain the status quo. These restraining forces are commonly called "resistance to change" because they appear as employee behaviors that block the change process. Stability occurs when the driving and restraining forces are roughly in equilibrium; that is, they are of approximately equal strength in opposite directions.

Lewin's force field model emphasizes that effective change occurs by **unfreezing** the current situation, moving to a desired condition, and then **refreezing** the system so that it remains in this desired state. Unfreezing involves producing a disequilibrium between the driving and restraining forces. As we will describe later, this may occur by increasing the driving forces, reducing the restraining forces, or having a combination of both. Refreezing occurs when the organization's systems and structures are aligned with the desired behaviors. They must support and reinforce the new role patterns and prevent the organization from slipping back into the old way of doing things. This stabilization does not occur automatically; rather, organizational leaders must

Figure 14-1   **Lewin's force field analysis model**

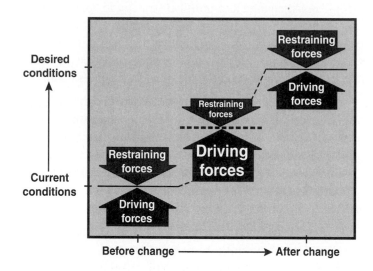

continuously restabilize the desired behaviors. Over the next few pages, we use Lewin's model to understand why change is blocked and how the process can evolve more smoothly.

Restraining Forces

When BP Norge introduced self-directed work teams (SDWTs) on its North Sea drilling rigs, the Norwegian subsidiary of British Petroleum faced more resistance from employees than from the infamous North Sea weather. Many skeptical employees claimed that previous attempts to create SDWTs didn't work. Others were convinced that they already had SDWTs, so why change anything? Several people complained that SDWTs required more responsibility, so they wanted more status and pay. Still others were worried that they lacked the skills to operate in SDWTs. Some BP Norge supervisors were slow to embrace SDWTs because they didn't want to give away their cherished power.[13]

BP Norge isn't the only organization in which employees seem to block the change process.[14] According to one recent survey, 43 percent of U.S. executives identify employee resistance as the main reason why their organization is not more productive.[15] This resistance takes many forms, including passive noncompliance, complaints, absenteeism, turnover, and collective action (e.g., strikes, walkouts). Some organizational behavior scholars point out that these actions do not necessarily represent employee resistance to change. Employees usually appreciate the need for change and actively embrace it when it does not threaten their own situation.[16] Rather, these behaviors indicate that restraining forces still exist in the organizational system. For example, resistance occurs because rewards discourage rather than encourage desired behaviors. Similarly, employee norms and roles may be incompatible with the desired state of affairs. These incompatible systems and structures produce obstacles to change, which manifest themselves in employee behavior.[17]

From this perspective, employee "resistance" represents symptoms of underlying restraining forces that need to be removed. Some employees are worried about the *consequences* of change, such as how the new conditions will take away their power and status. Others are concerned about the *process* of change itself, such as the effort required to break old habits and learn new skills. The main reasons why people create obstacles to change include direct costs, saving face, fear of the unknown, breaking routines, incongruent organizational systems, and incongruent team dynamics (see Figure 14-2).[18] We describe each briefly in the following paragraphs.

- *Direct costs*—People tend to block actions that result in higher direct costs or lower benefits than the existing situation. For instance, supervisors at BP Norge resisted self-directed work teams because they believed they would lose power as the change process empowered employees.

- *Saving face*—Some people resist change as a political strategy to "prove" that the decision is wrong or that the person encouraging change is incompetent. For example, senior executives in a manufacturing firm bought a computer system other than the one recommended by the information systems department. Soon after the system was in place, several information systems employees let minor implementation problems escalate to demonstrate that senior management had made a poor decision.

- *Fear of the unknown*—People resist change because they are worried that they cannot adopt the new behaviors. This fear of the unknown increases the *risk* of personal loss. This happened at a company where the owner wanted sales staff to telephone rather than personally visit prospective customers. These employees had little experience in telephone sales, so they argued against the need for using telephone calls. Some didn't even show up for the training program that taught them how to make telephone sales. "The salespeople were afraid of failing," explained the owner. "Each of them was very successful in the field, but they had never been exposed to a formalized telephone lead development program."[19]

- *Breaking routines*—We've described how organizations need to unlearn, not just learn.[20] This means that employees need to abandon the behavioral routines that are no longer appropriate. Unfortunately, people are creatures of habit. They like to stay within the comfort zones by continuing routine role patterns that make life predictable.[21] Consequently, many people resist organizational changes that force employees out of their comfort zones and require investing time and energy learning new role patterns.

- *Incongruent organizational systems*—Rewards, selection, training, and other control systems ensure that employees maintain desired role patterns. Yet the organizational systems that maintain stability also discourage employees from adopting new ways.[22] The implication, of course, is that organizational systems must be altered to fit the desired change. Unfortunately, control systems can be difficult to change, particularly when they have supported role patterns that worked well in the past.[23]

- *Incongruent team dynamics*—Teams develop and enforce conformity to a set of norms that guide behavior. However, conformity to existing team norms may discourage employees from accepting organizational change. Team norms that conflict with the desired changes need to be altered.

Figure 14-2   **Forces resisting organizational change**

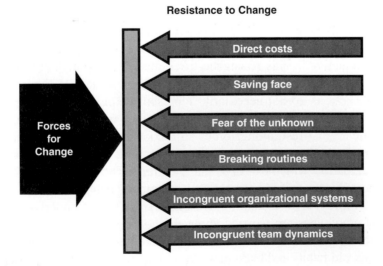

UNFREEZING, CHANGING, AND REFREEZING

According to Lewin's force field analysis model, effective change occurs by unfreezing the current situation, moving to a desired condition, and then refreezing the system so that it remains in this desired state. Unfreezing occurs when the driving forces are stronger than the restraining forces. This occurs by making the driving forces stronger, weakening or removing the restraining forces, or a combination of both. With respect to the first option, driving forces must certainly increase enough to motivate change. However, change rarely occurs by increasing driving forces alone because the restraining forces often adjust to counterbalance the driving forces. It is rather like the coils of a mattress. The harder corporate leaders push for change, the stronger the restraining forces push back. This antagonism threatens the change effort by producing tension and conflict within the organization.

The preferred option is to both increase the driving forces and reduce or remove the restraining forces. Increasing the driving forces creates an urgency for change, whereas reducing the restraining forces minimizes resistance to change.

Creating an Urgency for Change

Driving forces represent the booster rockets that push employees out of their comfort zones. They energize people to face the risks that change presents to them. Driving forces must be real, not contrived; otherwise, employees will doubt the change agent's integrity. Some threats are well known to employees. PepsiCo employees never forget about their archrivals at Coca-Cola. Bay Networks staff members are frequently reminded of competitive threats from Cisco Systems. However, many driving forces are unknown to employees beyond the top ranks of the organization. Thus, the change process must begin by informing employees about competitors, changing consumer trends, impending government regulations, and other driving forces.[24]

James Donald had to communicate the urgency for change when he took over Pathmark Stores. The New Jersey–based supermarket chain was in financial trouble, but few of the company's 28,000 employees knew about these problems. To get employees ready for change and to avoid bankruptcy, Donald prepared a video that told everyone about Pathmark's tremendous financial debt. Some employees quit, fearing that the company wasn't going to make it. But the remaining 99 percent quickly developed a commitment to get the company back to health.[25]

Customer driven change

Another powerful driver of change is customer expectations.[26] Dissatisfied customers represent a compelling force for change because of the adverse consequences for the organization's survival and success. Customers also provide a human element that further energizes employees to change current behavior patterns. Greg Brenneman and Gordon Bethune relied on customer complaints to motivate change at Continental Airlines. The executives took on the painful task of listening to customer complaints, and they communicated these problems to employees.[27]

Joel Kocher, CEO of Micron Electronics, also engaged in customer-driven change in his previous job as an executive with Power Computing. At a large employee meeting, Kocher read an angry customer letter. Then, to everyone's surprise, he brought the customer who wrote the letter into the meeting. "We actually brought the customer to the meeting, to personalize it for every single person in the room," says Kocher. "And it was very, very interesting to see the metamorphosis that occurred within the context of these several hundred people when you actually had a customer talking about how their foul-up had hurt this person and hurt their business."[28]

Reducing the Restraining Forces

Effective change involves more than making employees aware of the driving forces. It also involves reducing or removing the restraining forces. Figure 14-3 identifies six ways to overcome employee resistance. The first four—communication, training, employee involvement, and stress management—try to reduce the restraining

Figure 14-3   Methods for dealing with resistance to change

Strategy	Example	When used	Problems
Communication	Customer complaint letters shown to employees.	When employees don't feel an urgency for change, or don't know how the change will affect them.	Time consuming and potentially costly.
Training	Employees learn how to work in teams as company adopts a team-based structure.	When employees need to break old routines and adopt new role patterns	Time consuming and potentially costly.
Employee involvement	Company forms task force to recommend new customer service practices.	When the change effort needs more employee commitment, some employees need to save face, and/or employee ideas would improve decisions about the change strategy.	Very time consuming. Might also lead to conflict and poor decisions if employees' interests are incompatible with organizational needs.
Stress management	Employees attend sessions to discuss their worries about the change.	When communication, training, and involvement do not sufficiently ease employee worries.	Time consuming and potentially expensive. Some methods may not reduce stress for all employees.
Negotiation	Employees agree to replace strict job categories with multi-skilling in return for increased job security.	When employees will clearly lose something of value from the change and would not otherwise support the new conditions. Also necessary when the company must change quickly.	May be expensive, particularly if other employees want to negotiate their support. Also tends to produce compliance but not commitment to the change.
Coercion	Company president tells managers to "get on board" the change or leave.	When other strategies are ineffective and the company needs to change quickly.	Can lead to more subtle forms of resistance, as well as long-term antagonism with the change agent.

Sources: Adapted from J. P. Kotter and L. A. Schlesinger, "Choosing Strategies for Change," *Harvard Business Review* 57 (March–April 1979), pp. 106–14; P. R. Lawrence, "How to Deal with Resistance to Change," *Harvard Business Review* (May–June 1954), pp. 49–57.

forces and, if feasible, should be attempted first.[29] However, negotiation and coercion are necessary for people who will clearly lose something from the change and when the speed of change is critical.

Communication

Communication is the highest priority and first strategy required for any organizational change. It reduces the restraining forces by keeping employees informed about what to expect from the change effort. Although time consuming and costly, communication can potentially reduce fear of the unknown and develop team norms that are more consistent with the change effort.[30]

Du Pont recognized the importance of communication when it decided to outsource most of its 3,100 information systems (IS) employees to Computer Systems Corp. and other IS service firms. The chemical giant informed everyone of this decision six months before the change, and it continuously communicated with them throughout the process using e-mail, videos, and face-to-face meetings. By the time the transition took place, employees had a deeply embedded knowledge about what was happening and how it would affect them personally. The result was that 97 percent of Du Pont's IS staff went along with the change. "The communication was so thorough that, by the time we got the offer letter, it was an absolute nonevent," says an outsourced Du Pont employee.[31]

Training

The opening story to this chapter described how Steve Miller and other Royal Dutch/Shell executives brought about meaningful change by putting a cross-section of frontline employees through "retailing boot camps." These week-long sessions not only generated an urgency to change, but also taught employees valuable skills for the desired future. Retail boot camps and other forms of training are necessary so that employees learn the required skills and knowledge under the new conditions. When a company introduces a new sales database, for instance, representatives need to learn how to adapt their previous behavior patterns to benefit from the new system. Training is time consuming, but as employees learn new role patterns, they experience less stress and feel more comfortable with breaking previous routines.

Employee involvement

Employee involvement can be an effective way to reduce the restraining forces because it creates a psychological ownership of the decision. Rather than viewing themselves as agents of someone else's decision, staff members feel personally responsible for its success. Employee involvement also minimizes resistance to change by reducing problems of saving face and fear of the unknown.[32]

It's fairly easy for small organizations to involve everyone in the change process. But how do you apply employee involvement when there are thousands of employees? The answer is to involve as many people as possible through **search conferences.** Search conferences are large group sessions, usually lasting a few days, in which participants identify environmental trends and determine ways to adapt to those trends.[33] Search conferences are often known as "putting the entire system in the room" because they attempt to congregate representatives throughout the organization's entire system. This means involving as many employees as possible, along with others associated with the organization. For instance, Eicher Motors, a large manufacturer of light commercial vehicles in central India, holds an annual three-day search conference that includes a representation of suppliers, buyers, and shareholders as well as all employees.[34]

Various types of organizations, including Ford Motor Company, the U.S. Forest Service, a high school, and a religious order, have used search conferences to assist the change process.[35] Connections 14-1 describes how Keene State College and PECO Energy successfully involved most employees in the change process through these large group activities. Of course, search conferences and other forms of employee involvement require follow-up action by organizational leaders. If employees do not see meaningful decisions and actions resulting from these meetings, they begin to question the credibility of the process and are more cynical of similar change strategies in the future.

Stress management

For most of us, organizational change is a stressful experience.[36] It threatens our self-esteem and creates uncertainty about our future. Communication, training, and employee involvement can reduce some of these stressors, but companies sometimes need to introduce formal stress management programs to help employees cope with the changes. The Kerr Drug chain recognized this problem when it acquired 164 stores from J. C. Penney Co. Store managers and pharmacists had to install and operate new systems almost overnight without creating a disturbance to customers. They also had to adjust to Kerr's more customer-oriented culture. To help everyone cope, Kerr installed a toll-free telephone line, appropriately called "1-(800)-I've-Had-It." Employees who called this number

Connections 14-1   Keene State College and PECO Energy Get Everyone Involved in Change

Keene State College in New Hampshire brought together 350 faculty, staff, and administrators to identify shared and achievable goals for the learning institution's future. Administrators at the college concluded that the three day search conference—called "Speak Out"—would yield more meaningful ideas and generate more commitment to strategic decisions than if these decisions were made only by senior decision makers.

"Instead of appointing a committee to write an institutional plan," said Keene State College's president when opening the conference, "I am asking each of you to 'speak out' about the things you want changed and the things you value."

Keene State's participants discussed more than 100 issues during the sessions, some in small groups of three people, others in packed rooms with people spilling out the door. As Day Three came to a close, everyone voted on the top 10 to 15 issues. Over 100 people then grouped the dozens of discussion topics and mapped their relationships to one another.

PECO Energy, the Philadelphia-based electrical utility, required more than one search conference to restructure its human resource (HR) management group. With the help of consultants, four conferences were held over a five-month period to create a vision statement as well as design and implementation plan for the HR function. Each conference was attended by a broad cross-section of 200 employees, so that nearly 800 people participated altogether. Between these conferences, the company's other 7,000 employees contributed their ideas through videotapes, memos, and faxes.

The PECO Energy activity was structured with a specific agenda. Other search conferences merely gather the organization's representatives in a common location and let them determine the agenda. Most gatherings, however, create "max-mix" teams, whereby each table consists of a representation of people from different departments and levels of the organization.

Sources: P. D. Tolchinsky, "Still on a Winning Streak," *Workforce* 76 (September 1997), pp. 97–102; W. Kaschub, "PECO Energy Redesigns HR," *HR Focus* 74 (March 1997), p. 3; S. E. Brigham, "Large-Scale Events: New Ways of Working across the Organization," *Change* 28 (November 1996), pp. 28–34.

received informational or emotional support from human resource professionals at Kerr Drugs. "Sometimes they needed only a pat on the back or a hug because we were putting too many demands on them," explains Diane Eliezer, Kerr's director of marketing.[37]

Negotiation

Organizational change is, in large measure, a political activity.[38] People have vested interests and apply their power to ensure that the emerging conditions are consistent with their personal values and needs. Consequently, negotiation may be necessary for employees who will clearly lose out from the change activity. This negotiation offers certain benefits to offset some of the cost of the change.

Consider the experience of GE Capital Fleet Services. When the company removed two levels of management, it faced serious resistance from supervisors who worried that they would lose their status. After several months, senior executives negotiated with the supervisors and eventually created an intermediate manager position to overcome this resistance. "In our case, the decision to delayer was nonnegotiable," recalls a GE Capital manager. "As time was subsequently to show, however, we should have been prepared to negotiate on the number of layers to be eliminated."[39]

Coercion

Gordon Bethune and Greg Brenneman orchestrated a dramatic turnaround of Continental Airlines, but not everyone was ready for the change process. Fifty of the 61 executive officers were replaced with about 20 new people soon after Bethune and Brenneman became CEO and president, respectively.[40] This is not an isolated example.

One survey reported that two-thirds of senior management in large U.S. firms were replaced by the time the businesses were revived.[41]

We don't want to give you the impression that firing people is a valuable way to change organizations. On the contrary, this is a risky strategy because survivors (employees who are not fired) may have less trust in corporate leaders and engage in more political tactics to protect their own job security. More generally, various forms of coercion may change behavior through compliance, but it won't develop commitment to the change effort.

At the same time, coercion may be necessary when speed is essential and other tactics are ineffective. For example, it may be necessary to remove several members of an executive team who are unwilling or unable to change their existing mental models of the ideal organization. This is also a radical form of organizational "unlearning" because when executives leave, they take knowledge of the organization's past routines with them. This potentially opens up opportunities for new practices to take hold.[42]

Changing to the Desired Future State

Organizational change takes many forms. In our example of the Du Pont information systems employees who were outsourced, the actual changes were probably quite subtle at first. The outsourced employees still worked at Du Pont and probably kept their same desks, but their paychecks came from another company. Eventually, the change required new behaviors, such as calling their new employer rather than Du Pont about employment issues. Change was more dramatic at Royal Dutch/Shell. The company laid off many people and changed the organizational structure. When those actions didn't work, a representation of frontline employees diagnosed marketing opportunities and later implemented these ideas. Overall, change results in new behaviors that employees must learn and internalize.

Refreezing the Desired Conditions

After unfreezing and changing behavior patterns, we need to refreeze desired behaviors so that people do not slip back into their old work practices.[43] Refreezing occurs when organizational systems and team dynamics are realigned with the desired changes. Numerous systems and structures can "nail down" desired patterns of behavior. Organizational structure anchors new roles and behavior patterns. For example, companies that want to encourage decisions and actions that support customer service would redesign the organization around customers rather than specialized knowledge groups (e.g., marketing, engineering).

Organizational rewards are powerful systems that refreeze behaviors. If the change process is supposed to encourage efficiency, then rewards should be realigned to motivate and reinforce efficient behavior. Information systems play a complementary role in the change process, particularly as conduits for feedback.[44] Feedback mechanisms help employees learn how well they are moving toward the desired objectives, and they provide a permanent architecture to support the new behavior patterns in the long term. The adage "What gets measured, gets done" applies here. Employees concentrate on the new priorities when they receive a continuous flow of feedback about how well they are achieving those goals.

The dramatic turnaround of Continental Airlines illustrates how rewards and feedback refreeze desired behavior patterns. Continental had one of the worst performance records in the U.S. airline industry. It was particularly notorious for late arrivals and departures. To change Continental "from worst to first," incoming president Greg Brenneman offered every employee $65 for each month that the U.S. Department of Transportation (DOT) placed Continental in the top five airlines for on-time performance. Within months, the airline was regularly finishing first. The reward system—which cost $3 million in each successful month—aligned employees to the desired goals and the DOT's on-time performance feedback became symbolically meaningful. Both became important ingredients to refreeze Continental employees around efficiency and customer service.[45]

STRATEGIC VISIONS, CHANGE AGENTS, AND DIFFUSING CHANGE

Kurt Lewin's force field analysis model provides a rich understanding of the dynamics of organizational change. But the model overlooks three important ingredients in effective change processes: strategic visions, change agents, and diffusing change. Every successful change requires a clear, well-articulated vision of the desired future state. Indeed, a recent survey of executives in large U.S. firms found that the most important feature of successful change efforts was a clear vision of the proposed change.[46] This minimizes employee fear of the unknown and provides a better understanding about what behaviors employees must learn for the future state.[47] Strategic visions represent the goals that clarify role perceptions and thereby guide future behavior.

In the opening story, Steve Miller relied on retail boot camps to communicate and build commitment to his vision of Royal Dutch/Shell's future. When the city of Hampton, Virginia, began its change process, it formed a clear vision to become "the most livable city in Virginia." This image was understood and internalized by involving employees in the change process and continually communicating the vision statement. Departmental managers also worked out specific action plans to implement that vision. Moreover, employees were put into cross-department task forces responsible for moving the city toward this vision.

Change Agents

Organizational change also requires change agents to help form, communicate, and build commitment toward the desired future state. A **change agent** is anyone who possesses enough knowledge and power to guide and facilitate the change effort. Some organizations rely on external consultants to serve as change agents. However, change agents are typically people within the organization who possess the leadership competencies necessary to bring about meaningful change. Corporate executives certainly need to be change agents. However, as companies rely increasingly on self-directed work teams, every employee may become a change agent at one time or another.

Effective change agents are **transformational leaders**.[48] They form a vision of the desired future state, communicate that vision in ways that are meaningful to others, behave in ways that are consistent with the vision, and build commitment to the vision. Jacques Nasser, CEO of Ford Motor Company, has a reputation as a transformational leader. As we noted earlier, he effectively changed Ford Australia a few years ago and is now engaging Ford employees worldwide to become more proactive and entrepreneurial.[49]

Diffusion of Change

It is often better to test the transformation process with a pilot project, then diffuse what has been learned from this experience to other parts of the organization. The reason is that pilot projects are more flexible and less risky than centralized, organizationwide programs.[50] How are the results of pilot projects successfully diffused to other parts of the organization? Organizational behavior scholars offer several recommendations.[51] Generally, diffusion is more likely to occur when the pilot project is successful within one or two years and receives visibility (e.g., favorable news media coverage). These conditions tend to increase top management support for the change program and persuade other employees to support the change effort in their operations. Successful diffusion also depends on labor union support and active involvement in the diffusion process.

Another important condition is that the diffusion strategy isn't described too abstractly, because this makes the instructions too vague to introduce the change elsewhere. Neither should the strategy be stated too precisely, because it might not seem relevant to other areas of the organization. Finally, without producing excessive turnover in the pilot group, people who have worked under the new system should be moved to other areas of the organization. These employees transfer their knowledge and commitment of the change effort to work units that have not yet experienced it.

Figure 14-4   **The action research approach to organization development**

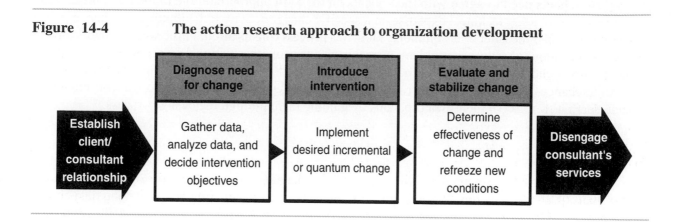

ORGANIZATION DEVELOPMENT

So far, we have discussed the dynamics of change that occur every day in organizations. However, an entire field of study, called **organization development (OD),** tries to understand how to manage planned change in organizations. OD is a planned systemwide effort, managed from the top with the assistance of a change agent, that uses behavioral science knowledge to improve organizational effectiveness.[52]

Organization development relies on many of the organizational behavior concepts described in this book, such as team dynamics, perceptions, job design, and conflict management. OD also takes an open systems perspective because it recognizes that organizations have many interdependent parts and must adapt to their environments. Thus, OD experts try to ensure that all parts of the organization are compatible with the change effort, and that the change activities help the company fit its environment.[53]

Most OD activities rely on **action research** as the primary blueprint for planned change. As depicted in Figure 14-4, action research is a data-based, problem-oriented process that diagnoses the need for change, introduces the OD activity, and then evaluates and stabilizes the desired changes.[54]

Action research is a highly participative process, involving the client throughout the various stages.[55] It typically includes an action research team consisting of people both affected by the organizational change and having the power to facilitate it. This participation is a fundamental philosophy of OD, but it also increases commitment to the change process and provides valuable information to conduct organizational diagnosis and evaluation. Let's look at the main elements of the action research process.

The Client-Consultant Relationship

The organization development process begins by forming a relationship between the client and consultant. External consultants might become change agents, but they are usually retained as facilitators to assist an internal change agent (usually a senior executive or team leader). Consultants need to determine three things when forming a client relationship in organization development: the client's readiness for change, the consultant's power base, and the consultant's role in the relationship.

First, consultants need to determine the client's readiness for change, including whether people are motivated to participate in the process, are open to meaningful change, and possess the abilities to complete the process. They watch out for people who enter the process with preconceived answers before the situation is fully diagnosed, or who intend to use the change effort to their personal advantage (e.g., closing down a department or firing a particular employee).

Second, consultants need to establish their power base in the client relationship.[56] Effective consultants rely on expertise and perhaps referent power to have any influence on the participants. However, they *should not* use reward, legitimate, or coercive power, because these bases may weaken trust and neutrality in the client-consultant relationship.

Lastly, consultants need to agree with their clients on the most appropriate role in the relationship.[57] This might range from providing technical expertise on a specific change activity to facilitating the change process. Many OD experts prefer the latter role, commonly known as **process consultation**.[58] Process consultation involves helping the organization solve its own problems by making it aware of organizational processes, the consequences of those processes, and the means by which they can be changed. Rather than providing expertise about the content of the change—such as how to introduce a quality management program—process consultants help participants learn how to solve their own problems by guiding them through the change process.[59]

Diagnose the Need for Change

Action research is a problem-oriented activity that carefully diagnoses the problem (or opportunity) through systematic analysis of the situation. *Organizational diagnosis* involves gathering and analyzing data about an ongoing system. Organizational diagnosis is important because it establishes the appropriate direction for the change effort.[60]

Data collection may occur through interviews, survey questionnaires, direct observation, analysis of documents, or any combination of these. The consultant typically organizes and interprets the data, then presents it to the client to identify symptoms, problems, and possible solutions. These results also become drivers for change. They motivate participants to support the change process because it allows them to see the need for change. The data analysis should be neutral and descriptive to avoid perceptual defensiveness. The information should also relate to factors over which participants have control.

Along with gathering and analyzing data, the diagnostic process involves agreement upon specific prescriptions for action, including the appropriate change method and the schedule for these actions. This process, known as *joint action planning,* ensures that everyone knows what is expected of them and that standards are established to properly evaluate the process after the transition.[61]

Introduce Change

Organization development is a process of altering specific system variables identified in the organizational diagnosis and planning stages. These changes might alter tasks, strategic organizational goals, system controls (e.g., rewards), attitudes, or interpersonal relationships.

An important issue is the appropriate amount of change. **Incremental change** is an evolutionary strategy whereby the change agent fine-tunes the existing organization and takes small steps toward the change effort's objectives.[62] Continuous improvement usually applies incremental change, because it attempts to make small improvements to existing work processes. Incremental change is generally less threatening and stressful to employees because they have time to adapt to the new conditions. Moreover, any problems in the process can be corrected while the change process is occurring, rather than afterwards.[63]

However, incremental change may be inadequate where companies face extreme environmental turbulence. Instead, companies may require **quantum change** in which they create a totally different configuration of systems and structures.[64] "We are at the beginning of a revolutionary time in business," warns Mort Meyerson, CEO of Perot Systems. "Many companies that have enjoyed decades of fabulous success will find themselves out of business in the next five years if they don't make revolutionary changes."[65]

Although restructuring, reengineering, and other forms of quantum change are sometimes necessary, they also present risks. One problem is that quantum change usually includes the costly task of altering organizational systems and structures. Many costs, such as getting employees to learn completely different roles, are not apparent until the change process has started. Another problem is that quantum change is usually traumatic and rapid, so change agents rely more on coercion and negotiation than employee involvement to build support for the change effort.[66] As we learn in the *Fast Company Online* feature in this chapter, Hewlett-Packard's Barbara Waugh believes that change is usually most effective when change agents create the right conditions for change, then start slow and work small.

Evaluate and Stabilize Change

Organization development activities can be very expensive, so measuring their effectiveness makes a great deal of sense. To evaluate an OD process, we need to recall its objectives that were developed during the organizational diagnosis and action planning stages. But even when these goals are clearly stated, the effectiveness of an OD activity might not be apparent for several years. It is also difficult to separate the effects of the activity from external factors (e.g., improving economy, introduction of new technology).

If the activity has the desired effect, then the change agent and participants need to stabilize the new conditions. This refers to the refreezing process that we described earlier. Rewards, information systems, team norms, and other conditions are redesigned so that they support the new values and behaviors. Even with stabilizing systems and structures in place, the desired conditions may erode without the ongoing support of a change champion. For example, ALCOA's magnesium plant in Addy, Washington, became a model of efficiency under the guidance of its plant manager and human resource manager. Then, ALCOA transferred both of them to other turnaround projects and reduced the number of department heads at the plant. This unintentionally had the effect of removing the change champions and undermining the previous four years of change effort. ALCOA "stripped away the leadership that could have supported the change efforts afterwards," says one of the original change agents.[67]

EMERGING TRENDS IN ORGANIZATION DEVELOPMENT

Organization development includes any planned change intended to make a firm more effective. In theory, this means that OD covers almost every area of organizational behavior, as well as many aspects of strategic and human resource management. In practice, OD consultants have favored one perspective and level of process more than others at various periods in OD's history.

Fast Company Online: Start Slow and Work Small

Barbara Waugh's official title is Worldwide Personnel Manager at HP Labs, a division of Hewlett-Packard. But her real job is to help the 1,200 scientists, engineers, and support staff engage in continual change. Most of us would call her a change agent, but Waugh disagrees. "The notion of a 'change agent' is problematic," she says. "You don't manage change. You help to create the conditions for it. You help people to do what they already want to do."

This point of clarification is a reflection of Waugh's two guiding principles for change. First, it would be up to the people of HP Labs to move the organization forward; she couldn't do the job for them. Second, deep-seated change could occur only as a result of incremental improvement: If you want to make a big difference, then you need to help people achieve little victories.

In other words, quantum change isn't part of Waugh's toolkit. "The way we've done it here is to start slow and work small. At some point, it begins to multiply, and you get transformation—almost before you realize it." That's why Waugh and HP Labs have spent the past five years cultivating more than 100 small, achievable, grassroots initiatives, all designed to make measurable improvements inside HP Labs. "It's better to do something small and conventional that can actually make a difference than to do something big and far-out that isn't going to go anywhere," explains Waugh.

Online Check-Up
1. This *Fast Company Online* feature describes Barbara Waugh's preference for incremental rather than quantum change. Explain her reasoning for this approach. Are there situations in which incremental change is inappropriate?
2. The full text of this *Fast Company* article describes several other activities that are part of Barbara Waugh's change initiatives. Identify these strategies and discuss their importance for minimizing resistance to change.

Source: Adapted from K. Mieszkowski, "Change: Barbara Waugh," *Fast Company,* issue 20 (December 1998).

Get the full text of this *Fast Company* article at www.mhhe.com/mcshane1e

When the field of organization development emerged in the 1940s and 1950s, OD practitioners focused almost exclusively on interpersonal and small group dynamics. Few OD activities were involved with macrolevel organizationwide changes. The field was equated with various forms of sensitivity training. **Sensitivity training** is an unstructured and agendaless session in which a small group of people meet face-to-face, often for a few days, to learn more about themselves and their relations with others.[68] Learning occurs as participants disclose information about themselves and receive feedback from others during the session.

Today, the reverse is true.[69] OD processes now are mostly aimed at improving service quality, corporate restructuring, and knowledge management. They are typically organizationwide, affecting organizational systems and structures with less emphasis on individual emotions and values.[70] And although surveys suggest that OD consultants still value their humanistic roots, there is also increasing awareness that the field's values have shifted more to a bottom-line focus.

There are numerous OD activities. In this section, we briefly discuss two emerging OD activities: parallel learning structures and appreciative inquiry.

Parallel Learning Structures

Executives at Europcar wanted to make the company's vehicle rental process more customer friendly and efficient. But the European vehicle rental company operated as a set of independent fiefdoms in each country. The only way to change this dispersed organization was to create a parallel learning structure in the form of a task force that represented these far-reaching and independent units. The Greenway Project, as it was called, brought together 100 representatives from Europcar's operations across the continent to design and implement a better car rental process. In spite of opposition from country managers protecting their turf, the Greenway project made significant progress over the 18-month mandate. Its members became committed to the new structure. Moreover, Greenway's members made the subsequent structural change easier because they became change champions throughout the system.[71]

The Greenway Project relied on an organization development process known as a parallel learning structure. **Parallel learning structures** are highly participative arrangements, composed of people from most levels of the organization who follow the action research model to produce meaningful organizational change. They are social structures developed alongside the formal hierarchy with the purpose of increasing the organization's learning.[72] Ideally, parallel learning structure participants are sufficiently free of the constraints of the larger organization that they may solve organizational issues more effectively.

The Greenway Project served as a parallel learning structure because it operated alongside the existing organization. Royal Dutch/Shell's retail boot camp teams, described at the beginning of this chapter, also represented a form of parallel structure because they worked outside the normal structure. These teams represented various countries and established a more entrepreneurial approach to getting things done at Shell. Shell separated these people from the traditional hierarchy so that it was easier to instill new attitudes, role patterns, and work behaviors. These teams became committed to the desired values and behaviors and later transmitted them to co-workers in the larger organization.

Appreciative Inquiry

The action research process described earlier in this chapter is based on the traditional problem-solving model. OD participants focus on problems with the existing organizational system and identify ways to correct those problems. Unfortunately, this deficiency model of the world—in which something is wrong that must be fixed—focuses on the negative dynamics of the group or system rather than its positive opportunities.

Appreciative inquiry tries to break out of the problem-solving mentality by reframing relationships around the positive and the possible.[73] It takes the view that organizations are creative entities in which people are capable of building synergy beyond their individual capabilities. To avoid dwelling on the group's own shortcomings, the process usually directs its inquiry toward successful events and successful organizations. This external focus becomes a form of behavioral modeling, but it also increases open dialogue by redirecting the group's attention away from its own problems. Appreciative inquiry is especially useful when participants

Figure 14-5   **The appreciative inquiry process**

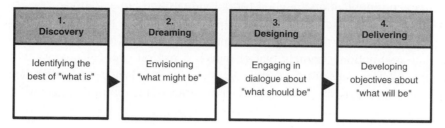

Source: Based on D. Whitney and C. Schau, "Appreciative Inquiry: An Innovative Process for Organization Change," *Employment Relations Today* 25 (Spring 1998), pp. 11–21; F. J. Barrett and D. L. Cooperrider, "Generative Metaphor Intervention: A New Approach for Working with Systems Divided by Conflict and Caught in Defensive Perception," *Journal of Applied Behavioral Science* 26 (1990), p. 229.

are aware of their "problems" or already suffer from enough negativity in their relationships. The positive orientation of appreciative inquiry enables groups to overcome these negative tensions and build a more hopeful perspective of their future by focusing on what is possible.

Figure 14-5 outlines the four main stages of appreciative inquiry.[74] The process begins with *discovery*—identifying the positive elements of the observed events or organization. This might involve documenting positive customer experiences elsewhere in the organization. Or it might include interviewing members of another organization to discover its fundamental strengths. As participants discuss their findings, they shift into the *dreaming* stage by envisioning what might be possible in an ideal organization. By directing their attention to a theoretically ideal organization or situation, participants feel safer revealing their hopes and aspirations than if they were discussing their own organization or predicament.

As participants make their private thoughts public to the group, the process shifts into the third stage, *designing*. Designing involves the process of **dialogue** in which participants listen with selfless receptivity to each others' models and assumptions and eventually form a collective model for thinking within the team.[75] In effect, they create a common image of what should be. As this model takes shape, group members shift the focus back to their own situation. In the final stage of appreciative inquiry, *delivering*, participants establish specific objectives and direction for their own organization based on their model of what will be.

Appreciative inquiry is a relatively new approach to organization development, but several organizations have already applied its basic principles. One of these is DPR, the fast-growing construction company in Redwood City, California. DPR begins the first five minutes of its problem-solving meetings by highlighting the project's successes. "There's nothing like a whiteboard covered with wins," explains DPR executive Lou Bainbridge. "It raises the energy level of your meetings and reminds people that they can succeed together."[76]

EFFECTIVENESS OF ORGANIZATION DEVELOPMENT

Is organization development effective? Considering the incredible range of organization development activities, answering this question is not easy. Nevertheless, a few studies have generally reported that some OD processes have a moderately positive effect on employee productivity and attitudes. According to some reviews, team building and intergroup mirroring produce the most favorable results when a single activity is applied.[77] Others report that self-directed work teams are very effective.[78] One of the most consistent findings is that OD has its greatest effectiveness when it includes two or more change processes.

Cross-Cultural Concerns with Organization Development

One significant concern with OD techniques originating from the United States is that they conflict with cultural values in other countries.[79] Some scholars argue that OD in North America assumes a particular model of change that is different from organizational change philosophies held by people in other cultures.[80] The North

American model of change is linear, as shown earlier in the force field analysis, and is punctuated by tension and conflict. Until recently, OD practitioners also embraced a humanistic approach with intergroup mirroring, sensitivity training, and other interpersonal processes. These practices are based on assumptions that open dialogue and conflict based on direct communication are good for individuals and organizations.

However, the linear and open conflict assumptions about change are not held in cultures with high power distance, saving face, and collectivism (a high need to maintain harmony). Instead, people in some countries work well with Confucian assumptions, namely that change is a natural cyclical process with harmony and equilibrium as the objectives.[81] This does not mean that OD is ineffective elsewhere. Rather, it suggests that the field needs to develop a more contingency-oriented perspective toward the cultural values of its participants.

Ethical Concerns with Organization Development

The field of organization development also faces ethical concerns with respect to some processes.[82] One ethical concern is that OD activities potentially increase management's power by inducing compliance and conformity in organizational members. This power shift occurs because OD initiatives create uncertainty and reestablish management's position in directing the organization. Moreover, because OD is a systemwide activity, it requires employee participation rather than allowing individuals to get involved voluntarily. Indeed, one of the challenges of OD consultants is to gain the support of those who are reluctant to engage in the process.

A second ethical concern is that OD activities may threaten the individual's privacy rights. The action research model is built on the idea of collecting information from organizational members, yet this requires employees to provide personal information that they may not want to divulge.[83] Some OD processes, such as sensitivity training, further threaten individual privacy rights by requiring participants to reveal their private lives. Consider the session attended by Jim Morgan, a copywriter for an advertising agency in London, England. "I saw adults 'confessing' (via a large PA system) to complete strangers about childhood sexual abuse, incidents where they were nearly murdered and all manner of dark secrets and fears, crying uncontrollably as they did so."[84]

A third concern with some OD activities is that they undermine the individual's self-esteem. The unfreezing process requires participants to disavow their existing beliefs, sometimes including their own competence at certain tasks or interpersonal relations. Sensitivity training and intergroup mirroring may involve direct exposure to personal critique by co-workers as well as public disclosure of one's personal limitations and faults. A more extreme example apparently occurred at SaskTel. As we read in Connections 14-2, consultants working at the government-owned telephone company in Saskatchewan, Canada, used OD tactics that allegedly included public ridicule and control over employees who participated in the project.

A fourth ethical dilemma facing OD consultants is their role in the client relationship. Generally, they should occupy "marginal" positions with the clients they are serving. This means that they must be sufficiently detached from the organization to maintain objectivity and avoid having the client become too dependent on them.[85] However, this can be a difficult objective to satisfy because of the politics of organizational change. OD consultants and clients have their own agendas, and these are not easily resolved without moving beyond the marginal positions that change agents should ideally attain.

The organization development practices described in this section facilitate the change process, and Lewin's force field analysis model provides a valuable template for understanding how the change process works. Still, you can see from reading this chapter that organizational change is easier said than done. Many corporate leaders have promised more change than they were able to deliver because they underestimated the time and challenges involved with this process. Probably the most difficult area of change is corporate culture.

Connections 14-2   Organization Development Behind Closed Doors at SaskTel

It all seemed quite normal on the surface. A group of employees and managers at SaskTel, the telephone provider in Saskatchewan, Canada, would form a cross-functional team under the guidance of Symmetrix, a U.S. consulting firm. Instead, according to participants, the organization development process may have wandered over the line of ethical conduct.

Symmetrix used a "greenhouse approach" by isolating the SaskTel employees in an office suite with paper taped over its glass walls so that no one could see inside. Participants say they were quarantined in small cubicles and were prevented from talking to each other. Moreover, Symmetrix refused to give reasons for assignments or why employees had to work long hours with tight deadlines at various times.

The project was supposed to last six weeks. Instead, it ended one year later, after participants united and forced SaskTel to get rid of Symmetrix. Of the 20 SaskTel employees who were involved in the project, nearly half took stress leave. The employees' union hired a university professor to evaluate the Symmetrix project. That report, along with internal documents, shocked SaskTel's board and ended the consultant's contract.

Symmetrix claims that the process was working and that the insults were the result of "political hoopla" and union-management problems. But employees say the problems were real. "There was always a manipulative pressure on the group to submit," says Gord Young, a SaskTel installer who participated in most of the Symmetrix project. "Team members regularly received insults in front of the group," recalls Kathryn Markus, a seven-year SaskTel manager. "The isolation, long hours, and purposeless activity left me feeling abandoned, betrayed, and frightened." Markus hasn't worked since she left the project.

Source: "Perils of Public Sector Work: A Case Study," *Consultants News*, April 1996, p. 5; S. Parker, Jr., "SaskTel Dials the Wrong Number," *Western Report*, February 26, 1996, pp. 14–17.

SUMMARY

Organizations face numerous forces for change because they are open systems that need to adapt to changing environments. Some current environmental dynamics include computer technology, globalization, competition, and demographics.

Lewin's force field analysis model states that all systems have driving and restraining forces. Change occurs through the process of unfreezing, changing, and refreezing. Unfreezing involves producing a disequilibrium between the driving and restraining forces. Refreezing occurs when the organization's systems and structures are aligned with the desired behaviors.

Almost all organizational change efforts face one or more forms of employee resistance. The main reasons why people resist change are direct costs, saving face, fear of the unknown, breaking routines, incongruent organizational systems, and incongruent team dynamics

Resistance to change may be minimized by keeping employees informed about what to expect from the change effort (communicating), teaching employees valuable skills for the desired future (training), involving them in the change process, helping employees cope with the stress of change, negotiating trade-offs with those who will clearly lose from the change effort, and using coercion sparingly and as a last resort.

A change agent is anyone who possesses enough knowledge and power to guide and facilitate the change effort. Change agents rely on transformational leadership to develop a vision, communicate that vision, and build commitment to the vision of a desirable future state.

Organization development (OD) is a planned systemwide effort, managed from the top with the assistance of a change agent, that uses behavioral science knowledge to improve organizational effectiveness.

When forming a client relationship, OD consultants need to determine the readiness for change, establish their power base in the client relationship, and understand their appropriate role in the change process. An important issue is whether change should be evolutionary (incremental change) or revolutionary (quantum change).

Appreciative inquiry focuses participants on the positive and possible. It tries to break out of the problem-solving mentality that dominates OD through the action research model. The four stages of appreciative inquiry include discovery, dreaming, designing, and delivering.

Organization development activities, particularly those with multiple parts, have a moderately positive effect on employee productivity and attitudes. However, there are some cross-cultural concerns with OD processes. Moreover, there are ethical concerns with some OD activities, including increasing management's power over employees, threatening individual privacy rights, undermining individual self-esteem, and making clients dependent on the OD consultant.

KEY TERMS

action research
appreciative inquiry
change agent
dialogue
force field analysis
incremental change
law of telcosm
organization development (OD)

parallel learning structures
process consultation
quantum change
refreezing
search conferences
sensitivity training
transformational leadership
unfreezing

DISCUSSION QUESTIONS

1. Chances are that the school you are attending is currently undergoing some sort of change to adapt more closely to its environment. Discuss the external forces that are driving these changes. What internal drivers for change also exist?

2. Use Lewin's force field analysis to describe the dynamics of organizational change at Royal Dutch/Shell described in the opening vignette to this chapter.

3. Senior management of a large multinational corporation is planning to restructure the organization. Currently, the firm is decentralized around geographical areas so that the executive responsible for each area has considerable autonomy over manufacturing and sales. The new structure will transfer power to the executives responsible for different product groups; the executives responsible for each geographic area will no longer be responsible for manufacturing in their area but will retain control over sales activities. Describe two types of resistance senior management might encounter from this organizational change.

4. Read again the organizational change process at Keene State College (Connections 14-1). Then explain how this process reduced resistance to change.

5. Web Circuits, Inc., is a manufacturer of computer circuit boards for high-technology companies. Senior management wants to introduce value-added management practices to reduce production costs and remain competitive. A consultant has recommended that the company start with a pilot project in one department. When the pilot project succeeds, the company can diffuse these practices to other areas of the organization. Discuss the merits of this recommendation and identify three conditions (other than the pilot project's success) that would make diffusion of the change effort more successful.

6. You are an organization development consultant who has been asked by the president of Southern Textiles, Inc., to explore "issues" that may account for poor sales in the company's Pacific-Northwest division. Before accepting this role, what three things should you consider when forming the client relationship? How would you determine whether the client-consultant is well suited to organization development?

7. Suppose that you are vice president of branch services at Humongus BankCorp. You notice that several branches have consistently low customer service ratings even though there are no apparent differences in resources or staff characteristics. Describe an appreciative inquiry process in one of these branches that might help to overcome these problems.

8. This chapter suggests that some organization development activities face ethical concerns. Yet, several OD consultants actively use these processes because they believe they benefit the organization and do less damage to employees than it seems on the surface. For example, some OD activities try to open up the employee's hidden area so that there is better mutual understanding with co-workers. Discuss the merits of this argument and identify where you think OD should limit this process.

CASE STUDY

TransAct Insurance Corporation

TransAct Insurance Corporation (TIC) provides automobile insurance throughout the southeastern United States. Last year a new president was brought in by TIC's Board of Directors to improve the company's competitiveness and customer service. After spending several months assessing the situation, the new president introduced a strategic plan to improve TIC's competitive position. He also replaced three vice presidents. Jim Leon was hired as vice president of claims, TIC's largest division with 1,500 employees, 50 claims center managers, and 5 regional directors.

Jim immediately met with all claims managers and directors, and visited employees at TIC's 50 claims centers. As an outsider, this was a formidable task, but his strong interpersonal skills and uncanny ability to remember names and ideas helped him through the process. Through these visits and discussions, Jim discovered that the claims division had been managed in a relatively authoritarian, top-down manner. He could also see that morale was extremely low and employee-management relations were guarded. High workloads and isolation (claims adjusters work in tiny cubicles) were two other common complaints. Several managers acknowledged that the high turnover among claims adjusters was partly due to these conditions.

Following discussions with TIC's president, Jim decided to make morale and supervisory leadership his top priority. He initiated a divisional newsletter with a tear-off feedback form for employees to register their comments. He announced an open-door policy in which any claims division employee could speak to him directly and confidentially without going first to the immediate supervisor. Jim also fought organizational barriers to initiate a flextime program so that employees could design work schedules around their needs. This program later became a model for other areas of TIC.

One of Jim's most pronounced symbols of change was the "Claims Management Credo" outlining the philosophy that every claims manager would follow. At his first meeting with the complete claims management team, Jim presented a list of what he thought were important philosophies and actions of effective managers. The management group was asked to select and prioritize items from this list. They were told that the resulting list would be the division's management philosophy and all managers would be held accountable for abiding by its principles. Most claims managers were uneasy about this process, but they also understood that the organization was under competitive pressure and that Jim was using this exercise to demonstrate his leadership.

The claims managers developed a list of 10 items, such as encouraging teamwork, fostering a trusting work environment, setting clear and reasonable goals, and so on. The list was circulated to senior management in the organization for their comment and approval and sent back to all claims managers for their endorsement. Once this was done, a copy of the final document was sent to every claims division employee. Jim also announced plans to follow up with an annual survey to evaluate each claims manager's performance. This worried the managers, but most of them believed that the credo exercise was a result of Jim's initial enthusiasm and that he would be too busy to introduce a survey after settling into the job.

One year after the credo had been distributed, Jim announced that the first annual survey would be conducted. All claims employees were to complete the survey and return it confidentially to the human resources department where the survey results would be compiled for each claims center manager. The survey asked the extent to which the manager had lived up to each of the 10 items in the credo. Each form also provided space for comments.

Claims center managers were surprised that the survey Jim had promised a year ago would be conducted, but they were even more worried about Jim's statement that the results would be shared with employees. What "results" would employees see? Who would distribute these results? What happens if a manager gets poor ratings from his or her subordinates? "We'll work out the details later," said Jim in response to these questions. "Even if the survey results aren't great, the information will give us a good baseline for next year's survey."

The claims division survey had a high response rate. In some centers, every employee completed and returned a form. Each report showed the claims center manager's average score for each of the 10 items and how many employees rated the manager at each level of the five-point scale. The reports also included every comment made by employees at that center.

No one was prepared for the results of the first survey. Most managers received moderate or poor ratings on the 10 items. Very few managers averaged above 3.0 (out of a five-point scale) on more than a couple of items. This suggested that, at best, employees were ambivalent about whether their claims center manager had abided by the 10 management philosophy items. The comments were even more devastating than the ratings. Comments ranged from mildly disappointed to extremely critical of their claims manager. Employees also described their long-standing frustration with TIC, high workloads, and isolated working conditions. Several people bluntly stated that they were skeptical about the changes that Jim had promised. "We've heard the promises before, but now we've lost faith," wrote one claims adjuster.

The survey results were sent to each claims manager, the regional director, and employees at the claims center. Jim instructed managers to discuss the survey data and comments with their regional manager and directly with employees. The claims center managers, who thought employees only received average scores, were shocked to learn that the reports included individual comments. Some managers went to their regional director, complaining that revealing the personal comments would ruin their careers. Many directors sympathized, but the results were already available to employees.

When Jim heard about these concerns, he agreed that the results were lower than expected and that the comments should not have been shown to employees. After discussing the situation with the regional directors, he decided that the discussion meetings between claims managers and their employees should proceed as planned. To delay or withdraw the reports would undermine the credibility and trust that Jim was trying to develop with employees. However, the regional director in that area attended the meeting in each claims center to minimize direct conflict between the claims center manager and employees.

Although many of these meetings went smoothly, a few created harsh feelings between managers and their employees. The source of some comments was easily identified by their content, and this created a few delicate moments in several sessions. A few months after these meetings, two claims center managers quit and three others asked for transfers back to nonmanagement positions in TIC. Meanwhile, Jim wondered how to manage this process more effectively, particularly since employees expected another survey the following year

.

Discussion Questions

1. Identify the forces pushing for change and the forces restraining the change effort in this case.

2. Was Jim Leon successful at bringing about change? Why or why not?

3. What should Jim Leon do now?

CASE STUDY

The taming of France Telecom

When Michel Bon took charge of France Telecom a few years ago, privatization of the phone monopoly was the government's *bête noire*. Each time officials made a move, militant unions staged massive strikes, forcing the government into a humiliating retreat. Bon's predecessor quit after just five days, making Bon the third president in three months. Unions struck within weeks of his arrival. Their ominous message to the newcomer: "Don't even think about privatizing." But Bon surprised everyone. Within nine months, the smooth-talking marketer from the retailing industry gained union support and put the privatization plans back on track.

This *Business Week* case study describes how privatization and deregulation are driving France Telecom and other telecommunications companies to change the way they do business. It highlights how Michel Bon not only privatized France Telecom, but is working to make the former government monopoly more competitive. Read through this *Business Week* case study at www.mhhe.com/mcshane1e and prepare for the discussion questions below.

Discussion Questions

1. Use Lewin's force field analysis model to depict the driving and restraining forces for privatization and competitive behavior at France Telecom.

2. What actions did Bon take to minimize resistance to change? Identify these strategies in terms of the options described in Figure 14-3.

Source: G. Edmondson, "The Taming of France Telecom," *Business Week,* January 27, 1997.

VIDEO CASE

Harley-Davidson

Harley-Davidson is the only company currently making motorcycles in the United States. There once were more than 100 manufacturers. However, just over a decade ago, Harley was hemorrhaging. Poorly-built bikes and a customer-be-damned attitude had its share of the motorcycle market going down faster than the Titanic. It was literally hours away from declaring bankruptcy. Fourteen men, including now president and CEO Jeffrey Bluestein, bought the company when it was on its deathbed. Perhaps the most important thing he did was begin listening to what loyal Harley owners wanted. A bike that didn't leak, and a bike that didn't fall apart. And today they are still listening. Bluestein said, "We try to adapt the best of the new with the best of the old. And of course our customers are experts at doing that themselves."

The results of the new Harley have been well documented, but the phenomenal success of Harley continues to build. It has almost reached cult proportions. Harley currently holds 65 percent of the big bike market, and has experienced an 80 percent increase in revenue. All Harley's bikes are sold before they are even built. And in the last year or so everything that has a Harley name on it has worked.

The face lift also had a profound effect on the faces of the people riding the big machine. Dick Knight and his wife Anita certainly don't fit the stereotypical greaser image, but they are part of the new breed. Sometimes they are called Rubs—Rich Urban Bikers. But to the Knights riding is a family affair, and their daughter Lisa, who just bought her first Harley, represents the newest change for Harley: one in four is a woman buyer. The Knights are certainly well-to-do, but when they get on their bikes that all goes away. The motorcycle is an equalizer of both rich and poor. Dick Knight said, "Harley riders have something in common and it doesn't make any difference what kind of an economic background you come from. If you ride a Harley you've got a brother out there that rides a Harley also." About 100,000 Harley riders traveled to Milwaukee for the company's 95th birthday celebration in June of 1998.

Several thousand bikers traveled to Milwaukee from both coasts. They were on the road for about a week, and while much of the time is a lot of fun and games, there is a serious side to it. Harley is a big supporter of Muscular Dystrophy, and by the end of a week they will have raised more than a million dollars for MD.

Discussion Questions

1. What role does the customer play in the turnaround at Harley-Davidson?

2. How does the Harley "image" affect its internal operations?

3. How can a company like Harley-Davidson include employees in the change process?

TEAM EXERCISE

Applying Lewin's force field analysis

Purpose

This exercise is designed to help you understand how to diagnose situations using force field analysis and to identify strategies to facilitate organizational change.

Instructions

This exercise involves diagnosing the situation described below, identifying the forces for and against change, and recommending strategies to reduce resistance to change. The exercise is described as a team activity, although the instructor may choose to have it completed individually. Also, the instructor may choose a situation other than the one presented here.

*Step1:*Students will form teams of four or five people and everyone will read the following situation. (Note: If your school currently has a full trimester system, then imagine the situation as though your school currently has a two-semester system):

Your college has two semesters (beginning in September and January) as well as a six-week "summer school" from early May to mid-June. Instructors typically teach their regular load of courses during the two semesters. Summer school is mainly taught by part-time contract faculty, although some full-time faculty teach for extra pay. After carefully reviewing costs, student demand, and competition from other institutions, senior administration has decided that your college should switch to a trimester curriculum. In a trimester system, courses are taught in three equal semesters—September to December, January to April, and May to early August. Faculty with research obligations must teach any two semesters in which their courses are offered; teaching-only faculty teach courses in all three semesters. Senior administration has determined that this change will make more efficient use of college resources, particularly because it will allow the institution to admit more students without building additional classrooms or other facilities. Moreover, market surveys indicate that over 50 percent of current students would continue their studies in the revised summer semester (i.e., second trimester) and the institution would attract more full-fee students from other countries. The Faculty Association has not yet had time to state its position on this proposed change.

*Step2:*Using Lewin's force field analysis mode (below), identify the forces that seem to support the change and the forces that are likely to oppose the change to a trimester system. Team members should consider all possible sources of support and resistance, not just those stated in the situation above.

*Step3:*For each source of resistance, identify one or more strategies that would manage change most effectively. Recall from the textbook that the change management strategies include communication, training, employee involvement, stress management, negotiation, and coercion.

*Step4:*The class will discuss each team's results.

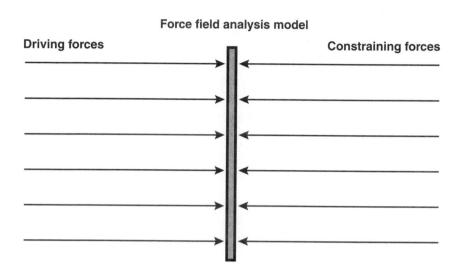

Force field analysis model

Driving forces   **Constraining forces**

NOTES

1   R.T. Pascale, "Leading from a Different Place," in J.A. Conger, G.M. Spreitzer, and E.E. Lawler III, eds., *The Leader's Change Handbook* (San Francisco: Jossey-Bass, 1999), pp.301-20; D.J. Knight, "Strategy in Practice: Making it Happen," *Strategy & Leadership* 26 (July-August 1998), pp. 29-33; R.T. Pascale, "The Agenda—Grassroots Leadership," *Fast Company*, no. 14 (April-May 1998), pp. 110-20; J.Guyon, "Why Is the World's Most Profitable Company Turning Itself Inside Out?" *Fortune*, August 4, 1997, pp. 120-25.

2   D. Hoewes, "Future Hinges on Global Teams," *Detroit News*, December 21, 1998; T.E. Backer, "Managing the Human Side of Change in VA's Transformation," *Hospital & Health Services Administration*, 42 (September 1997), p. 433.

3   N. Byrnes, "The Best Performers," *Business Week*, March 29, 1999, pp. 98-100.

4   J.S. Brown, "Seeing Differently: A Role for Pioneering Research," *Research Technology Management* 41 (May-June 1998), pp.24-33; in particular, see comments by George Gilder, who is credited with developing the law of telecosm, in "Is Bigger Better?" *Fast Company* no. 17 (September 1998). For a general discussion of computer technology and organizational change, see C.Meyer and S. Davis, *Blur: The Speed of Change in the Connected Economy* (Reading, MA: Addison-Wesley, 1998). For an excellent discussion of computer networks, see K. Kelly, "New Rules for the New Economy," *Wired*, September 1997.

5   D. Tapscott and A. Laston, *Paradigm Shift* (New York: McGraw-Hill, 1993); W.H. Davidow and M.S. Malone, *The Virtual Corporation* (New York: Harper Business, 1992).

6   D. Tapscott, A. Lowry, and D. Tocoll, eds., *Blueprint to the Digital Economy: Wealth Creation in the Era of E-Business* (New York: McGraw-Hill, 1998).

7   J.W. Gurley, "A Dell for Every Industry," *Fortune*, October 12, 1998, pp. 167-72.

8   R. Bettis and M. Hitt, "The New Competitive Landscape," *Strategic Management Journal* 16 (1995), pp.7-19.

9   R.L. Brandt, "John Chambers—On the Future of Communications and the Failure of Deregulation," *Upside* 10 (October 1998), pp. 122-33; S. Ellis, "A New Role for the Post Office: An Investigation into Issues behind Strategic Change at Royal Mail," *Total Quality Management* 9 (May 1998), pp. 223-34; S.L. Paulson, "Training for Change," *American Gas* 79 (December-January 1998), pp. 26-29.

10 J. Muller, "Raytheon's Job Cuts Will Total 14,000; 1200 Slots in State Targeted as Defense Firm Streamlines," *Boston Globe*, October8, 1998, p.A1; Gillette to Cut 4,700 Jobs, Shut Factories," *Reuters*, September 28, 1998.

11 "Similar Goals May Smooth Differences in Netscape-AOL Merger," *Dow Jones Newswires*, March 17, 1999.

12 K. Lewin Field, *Theory in Social Science* (New York: Harper & Row, 1951).

13 M. Moravec, O.J. Johannessen, and T.A. Hjelmas, "Thumbs Up for Self-Managed Teams," *Management Review* 86 (July-August 1997), pp. 42-47.

14 D. A. Nadler, *Champions of Change* (San Francisco: Jossey-Bass, 1998), chap 5; P. Strebel, "Why Do Employees Resist Change?" *Harvard Business Review* 74 (May-June 1996), pp. 86-92; R.Maurer, *Beyond the Wall of Resistance: Unconventional Strategies to Build Support for Change* (Austin, TX: Bard Books, 1996); C. Hardy, *Strategies for Retrenchment and Turnaround: The Politics of Survival* (Berlin: Walter de Gruyter, 1990) chap. 13.

15 C.O. Longenecker, D.J. Dwyer, and T.C. Stansfield, "Barriers and Gateways to Workforce Productivity," *Industrial Management* 40 (March-April 1998), pp.21-28.

16 J.P. Kotter, "Leading Change: Why Transformation Efforts Fail," *Harvard Business Review* 73 (March-April 1995), pp. 59-67.

17 E.B. Dent and S.G. Goldberg, "Challenging 'Resistance to Change,'" *Journal of Applied Behavioral Science* 35 (March 1999), pp. 25-41.

18 D.A. Nadler, "The Effective Management of Organizational Change," in *Handbook of Organizational Behavior*, J.W. Lorsch, ed. (Englewood Cliffs, NJ: Prentice Hall, 1987), pp. 358-69; D. Katz and R.L. Kahn, *The Social Psychology of Organizations*, 2nd ed. (New York: John Wiley, 1978).

19 "Making Change Work for You—Not Against You," *Agency Sales Magazine* (June 1998), pp. 24-27.

20 M.E. McGill and J.W. Slocum, Jr., "Unlearn the Organization," *Organizational Dynamics* 22 no.2 (1993), pp. 67-79.

21 R. Katz, "Time and Work: Toward an Integrative Perspective," *Research in Organizational Behavior* 2 (1980), pp. 81-127.

22 D. Nicolini and M.B. Meznar, "The Social Construction of Organizational Learning: Conceptual and Practical Issues in the Field," *Human Relations* 48 (1995), pp. 727-46.

23 D. Miller, "What Happens after Success: The Perils of Excellence," *Journal of Management Studies* 31 (1994), pp. 325-58.

24 T.G. Cummings, "The Role and Limits of Change Leadership," in Conger, Spreitzer, and Lawler, eds., *The Leader's Change Handbook*, pp. 301-20.

25 J.P. Donlon et al., "In Search of the New Change Leader," *Chief Executive*, November 1997, pp. 64-75.

26 L.D. Goodstein and H.R. Butz, "Customer Value: The Linchpin of Organizational Change," *Organizational Dynamics* 27 (Summer 1998), pp. 21-34.

27 G. Brenneman, "Right Away and All at Once: How We Saved Continental," *Harvard Business Review* 76 (September-October 1998), pp. 162-79.

28 A. Gore, "Joel Kocher: Power COO Says It's Time to Evolve," *MacUser*, April 1997.

29 J.P.Kotter and L.A. Schlesinger, "Choosing Strategies for Change," *Harvard Business Review* 57 (March-April 1979), pp. 106-14.

30 V.D. Miller and J.R. Johnson, "Antecedents to Willingness to Participate in a Planned Organizational Change," *Journal of Applied Communication Research* 22 (1994) pp. 59-80; L.C. Caywood and R.P. Ewing, *The Handbook of Communications in Corporate Restructuring and Takeovers* (Englewood Cliffs, NJ: Prentice Hall, 1992).

31 J. Moad, "DuPont's People Deal," *PC Week*, September 29, 1997, p.75.

32 J.P. Walsh and S-F. Tseng, "The Effects of Job Characteristics on Active Effort at Work," *Work & Occupations* 25 (February 1998), pp. 74-96; K.T. Dirks, L.L. Cummings and J.L. Pierce, "Psychological Ownership in Organizations: Conditions Under Which Individuals Promote and Resist Change," *Research in Organizational Change and Development* 9 (1996), pp. 1-23.

33 B.B. Bunker and B.T. Alban, *Large Group Interventions: Engaging the Whole System for Rapid Change* (San Francisco: Jossey-Bass, 1996),; M. Emery and R.E. Purser, *The Search Conference: A Powerful Method for Planning Organizational Change and Community Action* (San Francisco: Jossey-Bass, 1996).

34 R. Dubey, "The CEO Who Walked Away," *Business Today* (India), May 22, 1998.

35 "Making Organizational Changes Effective and Sustainable," *Educating for Employment*, August 7, 1998; D. Coghlan, "The Process of Change Through Interlevel Dynamics in a Large-Group Intervention for a Religious Organization," *Journal of Applied Behavioral Science* 34 (March 1998), pp. 105-19; R. Larson, "Forester Defends 'Feel Good' Meeting," *Washington Times*, November 28, 1997, p. A9.

36 P.H. Mirvis and M.L. Marks, *Managing the Merger* (Englewood Cliffs, NJ: Prentice Hall, 1992).

37 D.K. Cassal, "Taking Over 164 Stores, Kerr Drug Quickly Sets Up Shop," *Drug Topics*, December 8, 1997, pp.106-7.

38 R. Greenwood and C.R. Hinings, "Understanding Radical Organizational Change: Bringing Together the Old and the New Institutionalism," *Academy of Management Review* 21 (1996), p.1022-54.

39 J. Dibbs, "Organizing for Empowerment," *Business Quarterly* 58 (Autumn 1993), pp. 97-102.

40 G. Brenneman, "Right Away and All at Once." G.Flynn, "A Flight Plan for Success," *Workforce* 76 (July 1997), p. 72.

41 J. Lublin, "Curing Sick Companies Better Done Fast," *Globe and Mail* (Toronto), July 25, 1995, p.B18.

42 Nicolini and Meznar, "The Social Construction of Organizational Learning."

43 T.G. Cummings and E.F.Huse, *Organizational Development and Change*, 4th ed. (St. Paul, MN: West Publishing 1989), pp.477-85; P.Goodman and J. Dean, "Creating Long-Term Organizational Change," in *Change Organizations*, P. Goodman and Associates, eds. (San Francisco: Jossey-Bass, 1982), pp. 226-79; W. W. Burke, *Organizational Development: A Normative View* (Reading, MA: Addison-Wesley, 1987), pp. 124-25.

44 R. H. Miles, "Leading Corporate Transformation: Are You Up to the Task?" in Conger, Spreitzer, and Lawler, eds., *The Leader's Change Handbook*, pp. 221-67; L.D. Goodstein and H.R. Butz, "Customer Value: The Linchpin of Organizational Change," *Organizational Dynamics* 27 (Summer 1998), pp. 21-34.

45   Brenneman, "Right Away and All At Once: How We Saved Continental."

46   B. McDermott and G. Sexton, "Sowing the Seeds of Corporate Innovation," *Journal for Quality and Participation* 21 (November-December 1998), pp. 18-23.

47   D.A. Nadler, "Implementing Organizational Changes," in D.A. Nadler, M.L. Tushman, and N.G. Hatvany, eds. *Managing Organizations: Readings and Cases* (Bostone: Little, Brown, 1982), pp. 440-59.

48   J.P. Kotter, "Leading Change: The Eight Steps to Transformation," in Conger, Spreitzer, and Lawler, eds., *The Leaders Change Handbook*, pp. 221-67; J.P. Kotter, "Leading Change: Why Transformation Efforts Fail," *Harvard Business Review* 73 (March-April 1995), pp. 59-67.

49   S. Wetlaufer, "Driving Change: An Interview with Ford Motor Company's Jacques Nasser," *Harvard Business Review* 77 (March-April 1999), pp. 76-88; S. Zesiger, "Jac Nasser is Car Crazy," *Fortune*, June 22, 1998, pp. 79-82.

50   M. Beer, R.A. Eisenstat and B. Spector, *The Critical Path to Corporate Renewal* (Boston: Harvard Business School Press, 1990).

51   R.E. Walton, *Innovating to Compete: Lessons for Diffusing and Managing Change in the Workplace* (San Francisco: Jossey-Bass, 1987); Beer et al., *The Critical Path to Corporate Renewal*, chap 5; and R.E. Walton, "Successful Strategies for Diffusing Work Innovations," *Journal of Contemporary Business*, Spring 1977, pp. 1-22.

52   R. Beckhard, *Organization Development: Strategies and Models* (Reading, MA: Addison-Wesley, 1969), chap.2. See also Cummings and Huse, *Organization Development and Change*, pp. 1-3.

53   Burke, *Organization Development*, pp. 12-14.

54   W.L. French and C.H. Bell, Jr., *Organization Development: Behavioral Science Interventions for Organization Improvement*, 4th ed. (Engelwood, Cliffs, NJ: Prentice Hall, 1990), chap 8. For a recent discussion of action research model, see J.B. Cunningham, Action Research and Organization Development (Westport, CT: Praeger, 1993).

55   A.B. Shani and G.R. Bushe, "Visionary Action Research: A Consultation Process Perspective," *Consultation: An International Journal* 6, no. 1 (1987), pp. 3-19.

56   M.L. Brown, "Five Symbolic Roles of the Organizational Development Consultant: Integrating Power, Change, and Symbolism," *Proceedings of the Annual ASAC Conference, Organizational Behavior Division* 14, pt. 5 (1993), pp. 71-81; D. A.Buchanan and D. Boddy, *The Expertise of the Change Agent: Public Performance and Backstage Activity* (New York: Prentice Hall, 1992); L.E. Greiner and V.E. Schein, *Power and Organization Development: Mobilizing Power to Implement Change* (Reading, MA: Addison-Wesley, 1988).

57   D.F. Harvey and D. R. Brown, *An Experiential Approach to Organization Development*, 5th ed. (Upper Saddle River, NJ: Prentice Hall, 1996), chap. 4.

58   M. Beer and E. Walton, "Developing the Competitive Organization: Interventions and Strategies," *American Psychologist* 45 (February 1990), pp. 154-61.

59   E.H. Schein, *Process Consultation: Its Role in Organization Development* (Reading, MA: Addison-Wesley, 1969).

60   For a case study of poor diagnosis, see M. Popper, "The Glorious Failure," *Journal of Applied Behavioral Science* 33 (March 1997), pp.27-45.

61   Beer, *Organization Change and Development*, pp. 101-2.

62   D.A. Nadler, "Organizational Frame Bending: Types of Change in the Complex Organization," in R.H. Kilmann, T.J. Covin, and Associates, eds., *Corporate Transformation: Revitalizing Organizations for a Competitive World* (San Francisco: Jossey-Bass, 1988), pp. 66-83.

63   T.Y. Choi, M. Rungtusanatham, and J.S. Kim, "Continuous Improvement on the Shop Floor: Lessons from Small to Midsize Firms," *Business Horizons* 40 (November-December 1997), pp.45-50; J.M. Kouzes and B.Z. Posner, *The Leadership Challenge* (San Francisco: Jossey-Bass, 1988), chap. 10; and C. Lindbolm, "The Science of Muddling Through," *Public Administration Review* 19 (1959), pp. 79-88.

64   C.R.Hinings and R. Greenwood, *The Dynamics of Strategic Change* (Oxford, England: Basil Blackwell, 1988), chap. 6; D. Miller and P.H. Friesen, "Structural Change and Performance: Quantum versus Piecemeal-Incremental Approaches," *Academy of Management Journal* 25 (1982), pp. 867-92.

65   M. Meyerson, "Everything I Thought I Knew About Leadership is Wrong," *Fast Company*, Issue #2 (1996).

66   P. A. Strassmann, "The Hocus-Pocus of Reengineering," *Across the Board* 31 (June 1994), pp. 35-38.

67   S.R. Olberding, "Turnaround Drama Instills Leadership," *Journal for Quality & Participation* 21 (January-February 1998), pp. 52-55.

68   Cummings and Huse, *Organization Development and Change*, pp. 158-61.

69   A.H. Church and W.W. Burke, "Practitioner Attitudes about the Field of Organization Development," *Research in Organizational Change and Development*, 8 (1995), pp.1-46.

70   A.H. Church, W.W. Burke, and D.F. Van Eynde, "Values, Motives and Interventions of Organization Development Practitioners," *Group and Organization Management* 19 (1994), pp. 5-50.

71   R.T. Pascale, "Europcar's 'Greenway' Reengineering Project," *Planning Review*, (May-June 1994), pp. 18-19.

72   E.M. Van Aken, D.J. Monetta, and D.S. Sink, "Affinity Groups: The Missing Link in Employee Involvement," *Organizational Dynamics* 22 (Spring 1994), pp. 38-54; G.R. Bushe and A.B. Shani, *Parellel Learning Structures* (Reading,MA: Addison-Wesley, 1991).

73   D. Whitney and D.L. Cooperrider, "The Appreciative Inquiry Summit: Overview and Applications," *Employment Relations Today* 25 (Summer 1998), pp. 17-28.

74   D. Whitney and C. Schau, "Appreciative Inquiry: An Innovative Process for Organization Change," *Employment Relations Today* 25 (Spring 1998), pp. 11-21; F.J. Barrett and D.L. Cooperrider, "Generative Metaphor Intervention: A New Approach for Working with Systems Divided by Conflict and Caught in Defensive Perception," *Journal of Applied Behavioral Science* 26 (1990), pp. 219-39.

75   G.R. Bushe and G. Coetzer, "Appreciative Inquiry as a Team-Development Intervention: A Controlled Experiment," *Journal of Applied Behavioral Science* 31 (1995), pp. 13-30; L. Levine, "Listening with Spirit and the Art of Team Dialogue," *Journal of Organizational Change Management* 7 (1994), pp. 61-73.

76   E. Ransdell, "Lou Bainbridge Builds Teams," *Fast Company*, Issue 20 (December 1998), p. 228.

77   G.A. Neuman, J.E. Edwards, and N.S. Raju, "Organizational Development Interventions: A Meta-Analysis of Their Effects on Satisfaction and Other Attitudes," *Personnel Psychology* 42 (1989), pp. 461-89; R.A. Guzzo, R.D. Jette, and R.A. Katzell, "The Effects of Psychologically Based Intervention Programs on Worker Productivity: A Meta-Analysis," *Personnel Psychology* 28 (1985), pp. 275-91.

78   R.J. Long, "The Effects of Various Workplace Innovations on Productivity: A Quasi-Experimental Study," *Proceedings of the Annual ASAC Conference, Personnel and Human Resources Division* 11, pt. 9 (1990), pp. 98-107.

79   C.M. Lau, "A Culture-Based Perspective of Organization Development Implementation," Research in Organizational Change and Development 9 (1996), pp. 49-79.

80   T.C. Head and P.F. Sorenson, "Cultural Values and Organizational Development: A Seven-Country Study," *Leadership and Organization Development Journal* 14 (1993), pp. 3-7; J.M. Putti, "Organization Development Scene in Asia: The Case of Singapore," *Group and Organization Studies* 14 (1989), pp. 262-70; A.M. Jaeger, "Organization Development and National Culture: Where's the Fit?" *Academy of Management Review* 11 (1986), pp. 178-90.

81   R.J.Marshak, "Lewin Meets Confucius: A Review of the OD Model of Change," *Journal of Applied Behavioral Science* 29 (1993), pp. 395-415.

82   C.M.D. Deaner, "A Model of Organization Development Ethics," *Public Administration Quarterly* 17 (1994), pp. 435-36; M.McKendall, "The Tyranny of Change: Organizational Development Revisited," *Journal of Business Ethics* 12 (February 1993), pp. 93-104.

83   G.A. Walter, "Organization Development and Individual Rights," *Journal of Applied Behavioral Science* 20 (1984), PP. 423-39.

84   "How I Dressed Up as a Sheep and Learned to Love My Boss (and Workmates)," *Evening Standard* (London), July 29, 1997, p.19.

85   Burke, *Organization Development*, pp. 149-51; Beer, *Organization Change and Development*, pp. 223-24.

Chapter 15

Managing Across Cultures

SOURCE: Robert Kreitner and Angelo Kinicki, *Organizational Behavior*, 5th ed., Chapter 4, © McGraw-Hill, 2001, 1998, 1995, 1992, 1989.

Learning Objectives

After reading this chapter, you should be able to:

- Explain how societal culture and organizational culture combine to influence on-the-job behavior.

- Define *ethnocentrism,* and distinguish between high-context and low-context cultures.

- Draw a distinction between individualistic cultures and collectivist cultures.

- Explain the difference between monochronic and polychronic cultures.

- Discuss the cultural implications of interpersonal space, language, and religion.

- Describe the practical lessons from the Hofstede–Bond cross-cultural studies.

- Explain what cross-cultural studies have found about leadership styles.

- Specify why US managers have a comparatively high failure rate in foreign assignments, and identify skills needed by today's global managers.

- Discuss the importance of cross-cultural training relative to the foreign assignment cycle.

www.chryslercars.com

Even the best-kept corporate secrets eventually break into the open. For Stefan Buchner, a 39-year-old purchasing director at Daimler-Benz headquarters in Stuttgart, the news came during an afternoon strategy meeting last May. That's when a colleague rushed in to say German radio had just reported that Daimler was on the verge of a $38 billion merger with Chrysler, America's third largest car-maker. Six time zones away at Chrysler headquarters, Louise Linder's phone rang. Her contacts at Chrysler's suppliers had heard the same news and wanted the inside scoop. "Hey, I know as much as you do," she told them. Late that afternoon Linder's vice president called her into his office. Assemble your staff in the auditorium, he said. Prepare for a big announcement.

Mergers are traditionally tallied in dollars, and the sum hit a record last year: corporate couplings totaled $2.5 trillion. But beneath those piles of money are several million people whose lives are often upended when two companies put themselves together. For top executives, mergers can bring incredible riches; for bottom-rung workers toiling in plants or behind counters, changes may be imperceptible. The folks in the middle face the biggest challenges. Midlevel managers are often axed to cut costs after deals; those who remain are taxed to find savings, work through culture clashes, and integrate two companies into one.

While chairmen Robert Eaton and Jürgen Schrempp make grand plans for the new DaimlerChrysler, it's up to managers like Buchner and Linder, who perform identical tasks on different sides of the Atlantic, to make the deal work. As the anniversary of their merger nears, *Newsweek* asked them to reconstruct their first year in the trenches together.

. . . for Linder and Buchner, there are reasons for optimism. They have big responsibilities. Each ranks one rung below vice president, and together they oversee 140 employees who buy seats, steering wheels and other interior components. But unlike top officers, they haven't had to battle to preserve power or joust for the upper hand as jobs consolidate. Says Linder: "I haven't felt any stress or anxiety about whether they're going to choose between Stefan or I." They also work in purchasing, an area where the companies share similar philosophies and are led by an American, limiting concerns—at least on the US side—of too much German control. Most important, their careers are still on the upswing, and both believe the merger puts their performance in the spotlight. "It's a huge chance to develop my career," Buchner says. Even if they're tempted to complain, they're probably too busy. Mergers breed countless committee assignments and brutally long days. Says Linder: "It almost feels like a second job". . . .

In the last year their teams have gotten well acquainted. The process began at a distance. Linder spent the early summer reading up on Daimler and quizzing suppliers who'd been through mergers. In August Buchner's team traveled to Detroit, where they discussed big-picture issues: how their departments are organized, how they work with suppliers to reduce prices. Until the deal was sealed in November, "the really interesting questions were taboo," Buchner says. "For example, what does an airbag cost here, what does it cost there?" Since then they've begun comparing and brainstorming ways to consolidate and save. Linder and her American colleagues praise their German counterparts' skill with English (though they try to cut out slang to simplify speech when the Germans are in town). To reciprocate, many Americans are taking German lessons. They can also tick off cultural eccentricities: the Germans eat hamburgers with knives and forks and call their cell phones "handies." At a Detroit piano bar one night last summer, Linder's team got its biggest surprise: the Germans know all the lyrics to rock-and-roll oldies.

Back in Stuttgart, the Germans have been experimenting with business casual dress. They've taken classes on cultural awareness (key points: Americans shake hands less and aren't allowed to compliment women). As they've begun meeting with Americans more often, they're learning to understand their different decision-making style. Americans favor fast-paced trial-and-error experimentation; Germans lay painstaking plans, and implement them precisely. The potential result: "The Americans think the Germans are stubborn militarists, and the Germans think the Americans are totally chaotic," says Edith Meissner, an executive at the Sindelfingen plant. To foster compromise, Americans are encouraged to make more specific plans, and Germans are urged to begin experimenting more quickly. Both sides surround workers with their sister culture. When DaimlerChrysler stock began trading on Nov. 17, German workers celebrated with American-style cheerleaders, a country-Western band called The Hillbillies, doughnuts, and corn on the cob.[1]

Globalization of the economy challenges virtually all employees to become more internationally aware and cross-culturally adept. The path to the top typically winds through one or more foreign assignments today. A prime example is Samir F Gibara, chief executive officer of Goodyear Tire & Rubber, who spent 27 of his 30 years with the company on foreign assignments in Canada, France, Morocco, and Belgium.[2] Even managers and employees who stay in their native country will find it hard to escape today's global economy. Many will be thrust into international relationships by working for foreign-owned companies or by dealing with foreign suppliers, customers, and co-workers. *Management Review* recently offered this helpful perspective:

> It's easy to think that people who have lived abroad or who are multilingual have global brains, while those who still live in their hometowns are parochial. But both notions are fallacies. Managers who have never left their home states can have global brains if they are interested in the greater world around them, make an effort to learn about other people's perspectives, and integrate those perspectives into their own way of thinking.[3]

The global economy is a rich mix of cultures, and the time to prepare to work in it is now.[4] Accordingly, the purpose of this chapter is to help you take a step in that direction by exploring the impacts of culture in today's increasingly internationalized organization. This chapter draws upon the area of cultural anthropology. We begin with a model that shows how societal culture and organizational culture combine to influence work behavior, followed by a fundamental cultural distinction. Next, we examine key dimensions of international OB with the goal of enhancing cross-cultural awareness. Practical lessons from cross-cultural management research are then reviewed. The chapter concludes by exploring the challenge of accepting a foreign assignment.

CULTURE AND ORGANIZATIONAL BEHAVIOR

How would you, as a manager, interpret the following situations?

> An Asian executive for a multinational company, transferred from Taiwan to the Midwest, appears aloof and autocratic to his peers.
>
> A West Coast bank embarks on a "friendly teller" campaign, but its Filipino female tellers won't cooperate.
>
> A white manager criticizes a black male employee's work. Instead of getting an explanation, the manager is met with silence and a firm stare.[5]

If you attribute the behavior in these situations to personalities, three descriptions come to mind: arrogant, unfriendly, and hostile. These are reasonable conclusions. Unfortunately, they are probably wrong, being based more on prejudice and stereotypes than on actual fact. However, if you attribute the behavioral outcomes to *cultural* differences, you stand a better chance of making the following more valid interpretations: "As it turns out, Asian culture encourages a more distant managing style, Filipinos associate overly friendly behavior in women with prostitution, and blacks as a group act more deliberately, studying visual cues, than most white men."[6] One cannot afford to overlook relevant cultural contexts when trying to understand and manage organizational behavior.

Culture Is Complex and Multilayered

While noting that cultures exist in social units of all sizes (from civilizations to countries to ethnic groups to organizations to work groups), Edgar Schein defined **culture** as follows:

> A pattern of basic assumptions—invented, discovered, or developed by a given group as it learns to cope with its problems of external adaptation and internal integration—that has worked well enough to be considered valid and, therefore, to be taught to new members as the correct way to perceive, think, and feel in relation to those problems.[7]

The word *taught* needs to be interpreted carefully because it implies formal education or training. While cultural lessons may indeed be taught in schools, religious settings, and on the job, formal inculcation is secondary. Most cultural lessons are learned by observing and imitating role models as they go about their daily affairs or as observed in the media.[8]

Culture is difficult to grasp because it is multilayered. International management experts Fons Trompenaars (from the Netherlands) and Charles Hampden-Turner (from Britain) offer this instructive analogy in their landmark book, *Riding the Waves of Culture:*

> Culture comes in layers, like an onion. To understand it you have to unpeel it layer by layer.
>
> On the outer layer are the products of culture, like the soaring skyscrapers of Manhattan, pillars of private power, with congested public streets between them. These are expressions of deeper values and norms in a society that are not directly visible (values such as upward mobility, "the more-the-better," status, material success). The layers of values and norms are deeper within the "onion," and are more difficult to identify.[9]

Culture Is a Subtle but Pervasive Force

Culture generally remains below the threshold of conscious awareness because it involves *taken-for-granted assumptions* about how one should perceive, think, act, and feel. Cultural anthropologist Edward T Hall put it this way:

> Since much of culture operates outside our awareness, frequently we don't even know what we know. We pick . . . [expectations and assumptions] up in the cradle. We unconsciously learn what to notice and what not to notice, how to divide time and space, how to walk and talk and use our bodies, how to behave as men or women, how to relate to other people, how to handle responsibility, whether experience is seen as whole or fragmented. This applies to all people. The Chinese or the Japanese or the Arabs are as unaware of their assumptions as we are of our own. We each assume that they're part of human nature. What we think of as "mind" is really internalized culture.[10]

In sum, it has been said: "you are your culture, and your culture is you." As part of the growing sophistication of marketing practices in the global economy, companies are hiring anthropologists to decipher the cultural roots of customer needs and preferences (see the International OB 15-1).

A Model of Societal and Organizational Cultures

As illustrated in Figure 15–1, culture influences organizational behavior in two ways. Employees bring their societal culture to work with them in the form of customs and language. Organizational culture, a by-product of societal culture, in turn affects the individual's values/ethics, attitudes, assumptions, and expectations.[11] The term *societal* culture is used here instead of national culture because the boundaries of many modern nation-states were not drawn along cultural lines. The former Soviet Union, for example, included 15 republics and more than 100 ethnic nationalities, many with their own distinct language.[12] Meanwhile, English-speaking Canadians in Vancouver are culturally closer to Americans in Seattle than to their French-speaking compatriots in Quebec. Societal culture is shaped by the various environmental factors listed in the left-hand side of Figure 15–1.

Once inside the organization's sphere of influence, the individual is further affected by the *organization's* culture. Mixing of societal and organizational cultures can produce interesting dynamics in multinational companies. For example, with French and American employees working side by side at General Electric's medical imaging production facility in Waukesha, Wisconsin, unit head Claude Benchimol has witnessed some culture shock:

Figure 15–1   **Cultural Influences on Organizational Behavior**

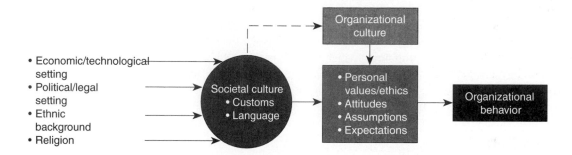

SOURCE: Adapted in part from B J Punnett and S Withane, "Hofstede's Value Survey Module: To Embrace or Abandon?" in *Advances in International Comparative Management,* vol 5, ed S B Prasad (Greenwich, CT: JAI Press, 1990), pp 69–89.

> The French are surprised the American parking lots empty out as early as 5 PM; the Americans are surprised the French don't start work at 8 AM. Benchimol feels the French are more talkative and candid. Americans have more of a sense of hierarchy and are less likely to criticize. But they may be growing closer to the French. Says Benchimol: "It's taken a year to get across the idea that we are all entitled to say what we don't like to become more productive and work better."[13]

Same company, same company culture, yet GE's French and American co-workers have different attitudes about time, hierarchy, and communication. They are the products of different societal cultures.[14]

When managing people at work, the individual's societal culture, the organizational culture, and any interaction between the two need to be taken into consideration. For example, American workers' cultural orientation toward quality improvement differs significantly from the Japanese cultural pattern.

> Unlike Japanese workers, Americans aren't interested in making small step-by-step improvements to increase quality. They want to achieve the breakthrough, the impossible dream. The way to motivate them: Ask for the big leap, rather than for tiny steps.[15]

INTERNATIONAL OB 15-1

Anthropologists Help Adapt Products to World's Cultures

A year ago in a hot, dusty outdoor market in Baku, Azerbaijan, anthropologist Jean Canavan made her discovery.

She was watching vendors display their wares to discerning customers and praise their value and durability. But it was the customers' ability to read intricate origination codes on the merchandise that was the surprise.

"They'd flip the cell phone over, take the battery out and actually read the bar code on it to see where the phone was built," Canavan says.

She and two colleagues were doing fieldwork for their employer, Motorola, investigating how the company could best enter the emerging markets of Azerbaijan, Kazakhstan, and Uzbekistan.

They found that people in the Caspian Sea area have learned to read the numbers on bar codes to see where products were manufactured. The buyers believe that products from American companies are better if they were built in America.

"It created an awareness on the part of Motorola that this is an important purchasing criterion for people," Canavan says.

Think anthropologists spend their days hanging out in Pago Pago studying the local culture? Think again. Like everyone else, anthropologists and ethnographers increasingly are finding jobs with high-tech companies, using their highly developed skills as observers to study how people live, work, and use technology.

"This is not *Raiders of the Lost Ark*," says Susan Squires, incoming president of the 1,000-member National Association for the Practice of Anthropology, which has a Web site at www.ameranthassn.org/napa.htm.

"Anthropology developed methods to understand people who were so different from Europeans that you couldn't just go up and ask questions, so we came up with methods such as participant observation and fieldwork," says Squires, who also works at GVO Inc., a product development company in Palo Alto, California. . . .

The point of hiring anthropologists is to help companies understand their users and find new products and markets the engineers and marketers never dreamed of—such as Intel looking into designing a computer chip that can withstand a blast from a deck hose. . . .

That particular idea came from John Sherry, a member of the end user research group at Intel's Hillsboro offices. Sherry's undergraduate degree was in computer science, not an uncommon combination for techno-anthropologists. He did his doctoral anthropological fieldwork with Navajos, has worked for Microsoft's usability group and has been with Intel for 21/2 years.

Sherry set out to find computers being used in extreme environments. He ended up on an Alaskan salmon boat.

The tender, who picks up the catch from the fisherman and carries it back to the cannery, has to keep a lot of records, from tickets issued for payments to reports filed for the fisheries board, all on a deck slippery with scales and blood. This particular tender, Sherry says, had duct-taped a notebook computer to the entryway of his cabin. "He told me, 'I need a computer that's so durable I can blast it with a deck hose and it will still work.' "

Back in his offices in Oregon, Sherry doesn't regret leaving the halls of academia. "This is a fantastic job," he says. "In my wildest dreams in graduate school I couldn't have imagined a job this great."

Colleague [Genevieve] Bell, in obvious agreement, just returned from a fact-finding mission to look into ways high-speed data communications could work in northern Italy. After weeks of eating, drinking, and spending hours at the dining room table with her Italian hosts, the answer was "not very well."

"It's hard to imagine how technology could improve that life," she says.

She found close-knit communities revolving around family and the table. Dinners are hours-long affairs, husbands come home for lunch, and the kitchen is the center of life. "In the United States, we talk about the computer competing with television," Bell says. "In Italy, it would be food."

But technology in other forms holds possibilities. In households where shoe boxes full of photos were pulled out to show Bell the family history and tell family stories, digital cameras proved interesting.

SOURCE: Excerpted from E Weise, "Companies Learn Value of Grass Roots," *USA Today*, May 26, 1999, p 4D. Copyright © 1999. *USA Today*. Reprinted with permission.

Ethnocentrism: A Cultural Roadblock in the Global Economy

Ethnocentrism, the belief that one's native country, culture, language, and modes of behavior are superior to all others, has its roots in the dawn of civilization. First identified as a behavioral science concept in 1906, involving the tendency of groups to reject outsiders,[16] the term *ethnocentrism* generally has a more encompassing (national or societal) meaning today. Worldwide evidence of ethnocentrism is plentiful. For example, when a congressman said, "It is the English language which unites us,"[17] during a 1996 debate on an English-only bill for US federal agencies, charges of ethnocentrism were made by civil rights groups worried about the loss of bilingual ballots for non-English-speaking citizens. Meanwhile, ethnocentrism led to deadly "ethnic cleansing" in Bosnia and Kosovo and genocide in the African nations of Rwanda and Burundi.

Less dramatic, but still troublesome, is ethnocentrism within managerial and organizational contexts. Experts on the subject framed the problem this way:

> [Ethnocentric managers have] a preference for putting home-country people in key positions everywhere in the world and rewarding them more handsomely for work, along with a tendency to feel that this group is more intelligent, more capable, or more reliable. . . . Ethnocentrism is often not attributable to prejudice as much as to inexperience or lack of knowledge about foreign persons and situations. This is not too surprising, since most executives know far more about employees in their home environments. As one executive put it, "At least I understand why our own managers make mistakes. With our foreigners, I never know. The foreign managers may be better. But if I can't trust a person, should I hire him or her just to prove we're multinational?"[18]

Recent research suggests ethnocentrism is bad for business. A survey of 918 companies with home offices in the United States (272 companies), Japan (309), and Europe (337) found ethnocentric staffing and human resource policies to be associated with increased personnel problems. Those problems included recruiting difficulties, high turnover rates, and lawsuits over personnel policies. Among the three regional samples, Japanese companies had the most ethnocentric human resource practices and the most international human resource problems.[19]

Current and future managers can effectively deal with ethnocentrism through education, greater cross-cultural awareness, international experience, and a conscious effort to value cultural diversity.

High-Context and Low-Context Societal Cultures

Cultural anthropologists believe interesting and valuable lessons can be learned by comparing one culture with another. Many models have been proposed for distinguishing among the world's rich variety of cultures. One general distinction contrasts high-context and low-context cultures[20] (see Figure 15–2). Managers in multicultural settings need to know the difference if they are to communicate and interact effectively.

Ethics at Work

Anyone interested in doing business in Russia should clearly understand that the ethical rules and traditions are going to be different. For instance, what Americans often consider to be small bribes may be seen in Russia as a means of establishing a relationship. In fact, they may be the only way to establish a successful business relationship. To adapt, Westerners essentially have three choices: (1) choose not to do business in Russia at this time; (2) choose to have someone else conduct the transactions; or (3) decide that "while in Russia, do as the Russians do." If one chooses the latter course, it is important to consult current US law. Although outright bribery is illegal for American firms, tokens of friendship usually are not. Typically, such tokens are more important than monetary "gifts," although some "transaction fees" may be necessary to persuade bureaucrats to move paperwork forward.

SOURCE: Excerpted from W B Snavely, S Miassoedov, and K McNeilly, "Cross-Cultural Peculiarities of the Russian Entrepreneur: Adapting to the New Russia," *Business Horizons*, March–April 1998, p 10. For background reading, see D A Andelman, "Bribery: The New Global Outlaw," *Management Review*, April 1998, pp 49–51.

You Decide . . .

Which of the three choices would you make? Why? Is it ethnocentric to impose your ethical values on your hosts when doing business in a foreign country? Explain.

Reading between the Lines in High-Context Cultures

People from **high-context cultures** rely heavily on situational cues for meaning when perceiving and communicating with another person. Nonverbal cues such as one's official position or status convey messages more powerfully than do spoken words. Thus, we come to better understand the ritual of exchanging *and reading* business cards in Japan. Japanese culture is relatively high-context. One's business card, listing employer and official position, conveys vital silent messages to members of Japan's homogeneous society. An intercultural communications authority explains:

> Nearly all communication in Japan takes place within an elaborate and vertically organized social structure. Everyone has a distinct place within this framework. Rarely do people converse without knowing, or determining, who is above and who is below them. Associates are always older or younger, male or female, subordinate or superior. And these distinctions all carry implications for the form of address, choice of words, physical distance, and demeanor. As a result, conversation tends to reflect this formal hierarchy.[21]

Verbal and written communication in high-context cultures such as China, Korea, and Japan are secondary to taken-for-granted cultural assumptions about other people.[22]

Reading the Fine Print in Low-Context Cultures

In **low-context cultures,** written and spoken words carry the burden of shared meaning. True, people in low-context cultures read nonverbal messages from body language, dress, status, and belongings. However, they tend to double-check their perceptions and assumptions verbally. To do so in China or Japan would be to gravely insult the other person, thus causing them to *lose face.*[23] Their positions on the continuum in Figure 15–2 indicate the German preoccupation with written rules for even the finest details of behavior and the North American preoccupation with precise legal documents.[24] In high-context cultures, agreements tend to be made on the basis of someone's word or a handshake, after a rather prolonged trust-building period. European-Americans, who have been taught from birth not to take anything for granted, see the handshake as a prelude to demanding a signature on a detailed, lawyer-approved, iron-clad contract.

Figure 15–2   **Contrasting High-Context and Low-Context Cultures**

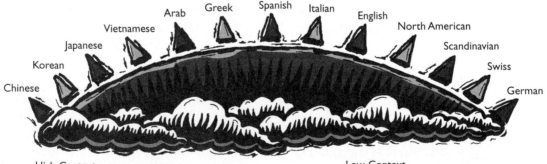

High-Context
- Establish social trust first
- Value personal relations and goodwill
- Agreement by general trust
- Negotiations slow and ritualistic

Low-Context
- Get down to business first
- Value expertise and performance
- Agreement by specific, legalistic contract
- Negotiations as efficient as possible

SOURCE: M Munter, "Cross-Cultural Communication for Managers." Reprinted with permission from *Business Horizons,* May–June 1993, Figure 3, p 72. Copyright © 1993 by the Board of Trustees at Indiana University, Kelley School of Business.

Implications for a Diverse Workforce

High- and low-context cultural differences can be found in countries with heterogeneous populations such as the United States, Australia, and Canada. African-Americans, Asian-Americans, and Native Americans tend to be higher-context than Americans of European descent. This helps explain our earlier example of the white manager's frustration with the African-American employee's nonverbal response. Culture dictates how people communicate. The white manager's ignorance of (or insensitivity to) the African-American employee's cultural context blocked effective communication.

TOWARD GREATER CROSS-CULTURAL AWARENESS AND COMPETENCE

Aside from being high- or low-context, cultures stand apart in other ways as well.[25] Let us briefly review the following basic factors that vary from culture to culture: individualism, time, interpersonal space, language and communication, and religion.[26] This list is intended to be indicative rather than exhaustive. Separately or together these factors can foster huge cross-cultural gaps. Effective multicultural management often depends on whether or not these gaps can be bridged.

A qualification needs to be offered at this juncture. It is important to view all of the cultural differences in this chapter and elsewhere as *tendencies* and *patterns,* rather than as absolutes. As soon as one falls into the trap of assuming *all* Germans are this, *all* British are that, and so on, potentially instructive generalizations become mindless stereotypes.[27] Well-founded cultural generalizations are fundamental to successfully doing business in other cultures. But one needs to be constantly alert to *individuals* who are exceptions to the local cultural rule.

For instance, it is possible to encounter talkative and aggressive Japanese and quiet and deferential Americans who simply do not fit their respective cultural molds. Also, tipping the scale against clear cultural differences are space age transportation; global telecommunications, television, and computer networks; tourism; global marketing; and music and entertainment. These areas are homogenizing the peoples of the world. The result, according to experts on the subject, is an emerging "world culture" in which, someday, people may be more alike than different.[28]

Individualism versus Collectivism

Have you ever been torn between what you personally wanted and what the group, organization, or society expected of you? If so, you have firsthand experience with a fundamental and important cultural distinction: individualism versus collectivism. Awareness of this distinction, as we will soon see, can spell the difference between success and failure in cross-cultural business dealings.

Individualistic cultures, characterized as "I" and "me" cultures, give priority to individual freedom and choice. **Collectivist cultures,** oppositely called "we" and "us" cultures, rank shared goals higher than individual desires and goals. People in collectivist cultures are expected to subordinate their own wishes and goals to those of the relevant social unit. A worldwide survey of 30,000 managers by Trompenaars and Hampden-Turner, who prefer the term *communitarianism* to collectivism, found the highest degree of individualism in Israel, Romania, Nigeria, Canada, and the United States. Countries ranking lowest in individualism—thus qualifying as collectivist cultures—were Egypt, Nepal, Mexico, India, and Japan. Brazil, China, and France also ended up toward the collectivist end of the scale.[29]

A Business Success Factor

Of course, one can expect to encounter both individualists and collectivists in culturally diverse countries such as the United States. For example, imagine the frustration of Dave Murphy, a Boston-based mutual fund salesperson, when he recently tried to get Navajo Indians in Arizona interested in saving money for their retirement. After several fruitless meetings with groups of Navajo employees, he was given this cultural insight by a local official: "If you come to this environment, you have to understand that money is different. It's there to be spent. If you have some, you help your family."[30] To traditional Navajos, enculturated as collectivists, saving money is an unworthy act of selfishness. Subsequently, the sales pitch was tailored to emphasize the *family* benefits of individual retirement savings plans.

Allegiance to Whom?

The Navajo example brings up an important point about collectivist cultures. Specifically, which unit of society predominates? For the Navajos, family is the key reference group. But, as Trompenaars and Hampden-Turner observe, important differences exist among collectivist (or communitarian) cultures:

> For each single society, it is necessary to determine the group with which individuals have the closest identification. They could be keen to identify with their trade union, their family, their corporation, their religion, their profession, their nation, or the state apparatus. The French tend to identify with *la France, la famille, le cadre;* the Japanese with the corporation; the former eastern bloc with the Communist Party; and Ireland with the Roman Catholic Church. Communitarian goals may be good or bad for industry depending on the community concerned, its attitude and relevance to business development.[31]

Cultural Perceptions of Time

In North American and Northern European cultures, time seems to be a simple matter. It is linear, relentlessly marching forward, never backward, in standardized chunks. To the American who received a watch for his or her third birthday, time is like money. It is spent, saved, or wasted.[32] Americans are taught to show up 10 minutes early for appointments. When working across cultures, however, time becomes a very complex matter.[33]

Imagine a New Yorker's chagrin when left in a waiting room for 45 minutes, only to find a Latin American government official dealing with three other people at once. The North American resents the lack of prompt and undivided attention. The Latin American official resents the North American's impatience and apparent self-centeredness.[34] This vicious cycle of resentment can be explained by the distinction between **monochronic time** and **polychronic time:**

> The former is revealed in the ordered, precise, schedule-driven use of public time that typifies and even caricatures efficient Northern Europeans and North Americans. The latter is seen in the multiple and cyclical activities and concurrent involvement with different people in Mediterranean, Latin American, and especially Arab cultures.[35]

A Matter of Degree

Monochronic and polychronic are relative rather than absolute concepts. Generally, the more things a person tends to do at once, the more polychronic that person is.[36] Thanks to computers and advanced telecommunications systems, highly polychronic managers can engage in "multitasking."[37] For instance, it is possible to talk on the telephone, read and respond to computer E-mail messages, print a report, check a pager message, *and* eat a stale sandwich all at the same time. Unfortunately, this extreme polychronic behavior too often is not as efficient as hoped and can be very stressful.

Monochronic people prefer to do one thing at a time. What is your attitude toward time? (You can find out by completing the Polychronic Attitude Index in the OB Exercise).

Practical Implications

Low-context cultures, such as that of the United States, tend to run on monochronic time while high-context cultures, such as that of Mexico, tend to run on polychronic time. People in polychronic cultures view time as flexible, fluid, and multidimensional. The Germans and Swiss have made an exact science of monochronic time. In fact, a new radio-controlled watch made by a German company, Junghans, is "guaranteed to lose no more than one second in 1 million years."[38] Many a visitor has been a minute late for a Swiss train, only to see its taillights leaving the station. Time is more elastic in polychronic cultures. During the Islamic holy month of Ramadan in Middle Eastern nations, for example, the faithful fast during daylight hours, and the general pace of things markedly slows. Managers need to reset their mental clocks when doing business across cultures.

OB Exercise   The Polychronic Attitude Index

Please consider how you feel about the following statements. Circle your choice on the scale provided: strongly agree, agree, neutral, disagree, or strongly disagree.

	Strongly Disagree	Disagree	Neutral	Agree	Strongly Agree
I do not like to juggle several activities at the same time.	5	4	3	2	1
People should not try to do many things at once.	5	4	3	2	1
When I sit down at my desk, I work on one project at a time.	5	4	3	2	1
I am comfortable doing several things at the same time.	1	2	3	4	5

Add up your points, and divide the total by 4. Then plot your score on the scale below.

1.0	1.5	2.0	2.5	3.0	3.5	4.0	4.5	5.0
Monochronic								Polychronic

The lower your score (below 3.0), the more monochronic your orientation; and the higher your score (above 3.0), the more polychronic.

SOURCE: A C Bluedorn, C F Kaufman, and P M Lane, "How Many Things Do You Like to Do at Once? An Introduction to Monochronic and Polychronic Time," *Academy of Management Executive,* November 1992, Exhibit 2, p 20.

Interpersonal Space

Anthropologist Edward T Hall noticed a connection between culture and preferred interpersonal distance. People from high-context cultures were observed standing close when talking to someone. Low-context cultures appeared to dictate a greater amount of interpersonal space. Hall applied the term **proxemics** to the study of cultural expectations about interpersonal space.[39] He specified four interpersonal distance zones. Some call them space bubbles. They are *intimate* distance, *personal* distance, *social* distance, and *public* distance. Ranges for the four interpersonal distance zones are illustrated in Figure 15–3, along with selected cultural differences.

North American business conversations normally are conducted at about a three- to four-foot range, within the personal zone in Figure 15–3. A range of approximately one foot is common in Latin American and Asian cultures, uncomfortably close for Northern Europeans and North Americans. Arabs like to get even closer. Mismatches in culturally dictated interpersonal space zones can prove very distracting for the unprepared. Hall explains:

> Arabs tend to get very close and breathe on you. It's part of the high sensory involvement of a high-context culture. . .
>
> The American on the receiving end can't identify all the sources of his discomfort but feels that the Arab is pushy. The Arab comes close, the American backs up. The Arab follows, because he can only interact at certain distances. Once the American learns that Arabs handle space differently and that breathing on people is a form of communication, the situation can sometimes be redefined so the American relaxes.[40]

Asian and Middle-Eastern hosts grow weary of having to seemingly chase their low-context guests around at social gatherings to maintain what they feel is proper conversational range. Backing up all evening to keep conversational partners at a proper distance is an awkward experience as well. Awareness of cultural differences, along with skillful accommodation, are essential to productive intercultural business dealings.

Figure 15–3   **Interpersonal Distance Zones for Business Conversations**
                          Vary from Culture to Culture

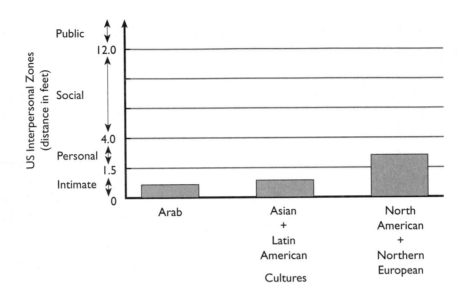

Language and Cross-Cultural Communication

More than 3,000 different languages are spoken worldwide. What is the connection between these languages and information processing and behavior? There is an ongoing debate among anthropologists concerning the extent to which language influences perception and behavior. On one side of the argument, the *relativists* claim each language fosters unique perceptions. On the other side, *universalists* state that all languages share common elements and thus foster common thought processes and perceptions. A study involving subjects from eight countries attempted to resolve this debate. Subjects from the United States, Britain, Italy, Greece, former Yugoslavia, Pakistan, Hong Kong, and Vietnam were shown 15 flash cards, each printed with three pairs of words. Language experts certified the various translations as accurate. The idea was to see if adults from different cultures, speaking different languages, would perceive the same semantic elements in the paired words. Illustrative semantic elements, or basic language building blocks, are as follows: opposite 5 alive/dead; similar 5 furniture/bed. The researchers found "considerable cross-cultural agreement on the meaning and use of semantic relations."[41] Greatest agreement was found for semantic opposites (e.g., alive/dead). These findings tip the scale in favor of the universalists. We await additional research evidence for a definitive answer.

Three Cross-Cultural Communication Options

Those attempting to communicate across cultures have three options: (1) stick to their own language, (2) rely on translators, or (3) learn the local language. The first option, preferred by those who insist English has become the language of global business, are at a serious competitive disadvantage. Ignorance of the local language means missing subtle yet crucial meanings, risking unintended insult, and jeopardizing the business transaction. For example, according to one well-traveled business writer, "In Asia, a 'yes' answer to a question simply means the question is understood. It's the beginning of negotiations. In the Middle East, the response will probably be some version of 'God willing.' "[42] Live translations, translations of written documents and advertisements, and computer E-mail translations are helpful but plagued by accuracy problems.[43] Successful international managers tell us there is no adequate substitute for knowing the local language.[44]

General Guidelines for Effective Cross-Cultural Communication

Regardless of which cross-cultural communication option is used, four guidelines from international management scholars Philip R Harris and Robert T Moran are useful:

- *No matter how hard one tries, one cannot avoid communicating.* All behavior in human interaction has a message and communicates something. Body language communicates as well as our activity or inactivity, the color of our skin, the color of our clothes, or the gift we give. All behavior is communication because all behavior contains a message, whether intended or not.

- *Communication does not necessarily mean understanding.* Even when two individuals agree that they are communicating or talking to each other, it does not mean that they have understood each other. Understanding occurs when the two individuals have the same interpretation of the symbols being used in the communication process whether the symbols be words or gestures.

- *Communication is irreversible.* One cannot take back one's communication (although sometimes one wishes that he or she could). However, one can explain, clarify, or restate one's message. Once one has communicated, it is part of his or her experience, and it influences present and future meanings. Disagreeing with a Saudi Arabian in the presence of others is an "impoliteness" in the Arab world and may be difficult to remedy.

- *Communication occurs in a context.* One cannot ignore the context of communication that occurs at a certain time, in some place, using certain media. Such factors have message value and give meaning to the communicators. For example, a business conversation with a French manager in France during an evening meal may be inappropriate.[45]

Training magazine offers this blunt advice to American managers: "The lesson for those plying foreign markets or hosting business visitors is: *Slow down. Shut up. Listen.*"[46]

Religion

Religious beliefs and practices can have a profound effect on cross-cultural relations. A comprehensive treatment of different religions is beyond the scope of our current discussion. However, we can examine the relationship between religious affiliation and work-related values. A study of 484 international students at a midwestern US university uncovered wide variability. The following list gives the most important work-related value for each of five religious affiliations:

> *Catholic*—Consideration ("Concern that employees be taken seriously, be kept informed, and that their judgments be used.")
>
> *Protestant*—Employer effectiveness ("Desire to work for a company that is efficient, successful, and a technological leader.")
>
> *Buddhist*—Social responsibility ("Concern that the employer be a responsible part of society.")
>
> *Muslim*—Continuity ("Desire for stable environment, job longevity, reduction of uncertainty.")
>
> *No religious preference*—Professional challenge ("Concern with having a job that provides learning opportunities and opportunities to use skills well.")[47]

Thus, there was virtually *no agreement* across religions about the primary work value. This led the researchers to conclude: "Employers might be wise to consider the impact that religious differences (and more broadly, cultural factors) appear to have on the values of employee groups."[48] Of course, in the United States and other selected countries, equal employment opportunity laws forbid managers from basing employment-related decisions on an applicant's religious preference.

PRACTICAL INSIGHTS FROM CROSS-CULTURAL MANAGEMENT RESEARCH

Nancy Adler, an international OB specialist at Canada's McGill University, has offered the following introductory definition. "**Cross-cultural management** studies the behavior of people in organizations around the world and trains people to work in organizations with employee and client populations from several cultures."[49] Inherent in this definition are three steps: (1) understand cultural differences, (2) identify culturally appropriate management practices, and (3) teach cross-cultural management lessons. The cross-cultural studies discussed in this section contribute to all three.

The Hofstede–Bond Stream of Research

Instructive insights surfaced in the mid-1980s when the results of two very different cross-cultural management studies were merged. The first study was conducted under the guidance of Dutch researcher Geert Hofstede. Canadian Michael Harris Bond, at the Chinese University of Hong Kong, was a key researcher in the second study. What follows is a brief overview of each study, a discussion of the combined results, and a summary of important practical implications.

The Two Studies

Hofstede's study is a classic in the annals of cross-cultural management research.[50] He drew his data for that study from a collection of 116,000 attitude surveys administered to IBM employees worldwide between 1967 and 1973. Respondents to the attitude survey, which also asked questions on cultural values and beliefs, included IBM employees from 72 countries. Fifty-three cultures eventually were analyzed and contrasted according to four cultural dimensions. Hofstede's database was unique, not only because of its large size, but also because it allowed him to isolate cultural effects. If his subjects had not performed *similar jobs* in *different countries* for the *same company,* no such control would have been possible. Cross-cultural comparisons were made along the first four dimensions listed in Table 15–1, power distance, individualism–collectivism, masculinity–femininity, and uncertainty avoidance.

Bond's study was much smaller, involving a survey of 100 (50% women) students from 22 countries and 5 continents. The survey instrument was the Chinese Value Survey (CVS), based on the Rokeach Value Survey.[51] The CVS also tapped four cultural dimensions. Three corresponded to Hofstede's first three in Table 15–1. Hofstede's fourth cultural dimension, uncertainty avoidance, was not measured by the CVS. Instead, Bond's study isolated the fifth cultural dimension in Table 15–1. It eventually was renamed *long-term versus short-term orientation* to reflect how strongly a person believes in the long-term thinking promoted by the teachings

---

Table 15–1   **Key Cultural Dimensions in the Hofstede–Bond Studies**

Power distance: How much do people expect inequality in social institutions (e.g., family, work organizations, government)?

Individualism–collectivism: How loose or tight is the bond between individuals and societal groups?

Masculinity–femininity: To what extent do people embrace competitive masculine traits (e.g., success, assertiveness and performance) or nurturing feminine traits (e.g., solidarity, personal relationships, service, quality of life)?

Uncertainty avoidance: To what extent do people prefer structured versus unstructured situations?

Long-term versus short-term orientation (Confucian values): To what extent are people oriented toward the future by saving and being persistent versus being oriented toward the present and past by respecting tradition and meeting social obligations?

SOURCE: Adapted from discussion in G Hofstede, "Cultural Constraints in Management Theories," *Academy of Management Executive,* February 1993, pp 81–94.

Table 15–2		Countries Scoring the Highest in the Hofstede–Bond Studies		
High Power Distance	**High Individualism**	**High Masculinity**	**High Uncertainty Avoidance**	**High Long-Term Orientation***
Philippines	United States	Japan	Japan	Hong Kong***
India	Australia		Korea	Taiwan
Singapore	Great Britain		Brazil	Japan
Brazil	Netherlands		Pakistan	Korea
Hong Kong***	Canada		Taiwan	
	New Zealand			
	Sweden			
	Germany**			

*Originally called Confucian Dynamism.
**Former West Germany.
***Reunited with China.

SOURCE: Adapted from Exhibit 2 in G Hofstede and M H Bond, "The Confucius Connection: From Cultural Roots to Economic Growth," *Organizational Dynamics,* Spring 1988, pp 12–13.

of the Chinese philosopher Confucius (551–479 BC). According to an update by Hofstede: "On the long-term side one finds values oriented towards the future, like thrift (saving) and persistence. On the short-term side one finds values rather oriented towards the past and present, like respect for tradition and fulfilling social obligations."[52] Importantly, one may embrace Confucian long-term values without knowing a thing about Confucius.[53]

East Meets West

By merging the two studies, a serious flaw in each was corrected. Namely, Hofstede's study had an inherent Anglo-European bias, and Bond's study had a built-in Asian bias. How would cultures compare if viewed through the overlapping lenses of the two studies? Hofstede and Bond were able to answer that question because 18 countries in Bond's study overlapped the 53 countries in Hofstede's sample.[54] Table 15–2 lists the countries scoring highest on each of the five cultural dimensions. (Countries earning between 67 and 100 points on a 0 to 100 relative ranking scale qualified as "high" for Table 15–2.) The United States scored the highest in individualism, moderate in power distance, masculinity, and uncertainty avoidance, and low in long-term orientation.

Practical Lessons

Individually, and together, the Hofstede and Bond studies yielded the following useful lessons for international managers:

1. Due to varying cultural values, management theories and practices need to be adapted to the local culture. This is particularly true for made-in-America management theories (e.g., Maslow's need hierarchy theory) and Japanese management practices.[55] *There is no one best way to manage across cultures.*

2. High long-term orientation was the only one of the five cultural dimensions to correlate positively with national economic growth. (Note how the four Asian countries listed under high long-term orientation in Table 15–2 have been among the world's economic growth leaders over the past 25 years, with the exception of the Asian currency crisis in 1997–1998.) In the long term, this correlation may not bode well for countries scoring lowest on this dimension: Pakistan, Philippines, Canada, Great Britain, and the United States.

3. Industrious cultural values are a necessary but insufficient condition for economic growth. Markets and a supportive political climate also are required to create the right mix.[56] (It remains to be seen if Hong Kong can achieve long-term economic vitality following the 1997 takeover by China and if Japan can pull out of its long recession.)

4. Cultural arrogance is a luxury individuals and nations can no longer afford in a global economy.

A Contingency Model for Cross-Cultural Leadership

If a manager has a favorite leadership style in his or her own culture, will that style be equally appropriate in another culture? According to a model that built upon Hofstede's work, the answer is "not necessarily."[57] Four leadership styles—directive, supportive, participative, and achievement—were matched with variations of three of Hofstede's cultural dimensions. The dimensions used were power distance, individualism–collectivism, and uncertainty avoidance.

Table 15–3   A Contingency Model for Cross-Cultural Leadership

Country	Most Culturally Appropriate Leadership Behaviors			
	Directive	Supportive	Participative	Achievement
Australia		X	X	X
Brazil	X		X	
Canada		X	X	X
France	X		X	
Germany*		X	X	X
Great Britain		X	X	X
Hong Kong**	X	X	X	X
India	X		X	X
Italy	X	X	X	
Japan	X	X	X	
Korea	X	X	X	
Netherlands		X	X	X
New Zealand			X	X
Pakistan	X	X	X	
Philippines	X	X	X	X
Sweden			X	X
Taiwan	X	X	X	
United States		X	X	X

*Former West Germany.
**Reunited with China.

SOURCES: Adapted in part from C A Rodrigues, "The Situation and National Culture as Contingencies for Leadership Behavior: Two Conceptual Models," in *Advances in International Comparative Management* vol. 5, ed S B Prasad (Greenwich, CT: JAI Press, 1990), pp 51–68; and G Hofstede and M H Bond, "The Confucius Connection: From Cultural Roots to Economic Growth," *Organizational Dynamics,* Spring 1988, pp 4–21.

By combining this model with Hofstede's and Bond's findings, we derived the useful contingency model for cross-cultural leadership in Table 15–3. Participative leadership turned out to be culturally appropriate for all 18 countries. Importantly, this does *not* mean that the participative style is necessarily the *best* style of leadership in cross-cultural management. It simply has broad applicability. One exception surfaced in a more recent study in Russia's largest textile mill. The researchers found that both rewarding good performance with American-made goods and motivating performance with feedback and positive reinforcement improved output. But an employee participation program actually made performance *worse*. This may have been due to the Russians' lack of faith in participative schemes, which were found to be untrustworthy in the past.[58]

Also of note, with the exception of France, the directive style appears to be culturally *inappropriate* in North America, Northern Europe, Australia, and New Zealand. Some locations, such as Hong Kong and the Philippines, require great leadership versatility. Leadership needs to be matched to the prevailing cultural climate.

PREPARING EMPLOYEES FOR SUCCESSFUL FOREIGN ASSIGNMENTS

As the reach of global companies continues to grow, many opportunities for living and working in foreign countries will arise. Imagine, for example, the opportunities for foreign duty and cross-cultural experiences at Gillette, the maker of razors and other personal-care products. According to company calculations, an estimated 1.2 billion members of the world's population use a Gillette product on any given day.[59] Foreign business accounts for 70% of Gillette's annual sales of more than $10 billion. As discussed a bit later, Gillette and other global players need a vibrant and growing cadre of employees who are willing and able to do business across cultures. Thus, the purpose of this final section is to help you prepare yourself and others to work successfully in foreign countries.

Why Do US Expatriates Fail On Foreign Assignments?

As we use the term here, **expatriate** refers to anyone living and/or working outside their home country. Hence, they are said to be *expatriated* when transferred to another country and *repatriated* when transferred back home. US expatriate managers usually are characterized as culturally inept and prone to failure on international assignments. Sadly, research supports this view. A pair of international management experts recently offered this assessment:

> Over the past decade, we have studied the management of expatriates at about 750 US, European, and Japanese companies. We asked both the expatriates themselves and the executives who sent them abroad to evaluate their experiences. In addition, we looked at what happened after expatriates returned home. . . .
>
> Overall, the results of our research were alarming. We found that between 10% and 20% of all US managers sent abroad returned early because of job dissatisfaction or difficulties in adjusting to a foreign country. Of those who stayed for the duration, nearly one-third did not perform up to the expectations of their superiors. And perhaps most problematic, one-fourth of those who completed an assignment left their company, often to join a competitor, within one year after repatriation. That's a turnover rate double that of managers who did not go abroad.[60]

Because of the high cost of sending employees and their families to foreign countries for extended periods, significant improvement is needed.

Research has uncovered specific reasons for the failure of US expatriate managers. Listed in decreasing order of frequency, the seven most common reasons are as follows:

1. The manager's spouse cannot adjust to new physical or cultural surroundings.

2. The manager cannot adapt to new physical or cultural surroundings.

3. Family problems.

4. The manager is emotionally immature.

5. The manager cannot cope with foreign duties.

6. The manager is not technically competent.

7. The manager lacks the proper motivation for a foreign assignment.[61]

Collectively, *family and personal adjustment problems,* not technical competence, are the main stumbling block for American managers working in foreign countries.

This conclusion is reinforced by the results of a survey that asked 72 human resource managers at multinational corporations to identify the most important success factor in a foreign assignment. "Nearly 35% said cultural adaptability: patience, flexibility, and tolerance for others' beliefs. Only 22% of them listed technical and management skills."[62] US multinational companies clearly need to do a better job of preparing employees and their families for foreign assignments.

A Bright Spot: North American Women on Foreign Assignments

Historically, a woman from the United States or Canada on a foreign assignment was a rarity. Things are changing, albeit slowly. A review of research evidence and anecdotal accounts uncovered these insights:

- The proportion of corporate women from North America on foreign assignments grew from about 3% in the early 1980s to between 11% and 15% in the late 1990s.

- Self-disqualification and management's assumption that women would not be welcome in foreign cultures— not foreign prejudice, itself—are the primary barriers for potential female expatriates.

- Expatriate North American women are viewed first and foremost by their hosts as being foreigners, and only secondarily as being female.

- North American women have a very high success rate on foreign assignments.[63]

Considering the rapidly growing demand for global managers today, self-disqualification by women and management's prejudicial policies are counterproductive.

The Global Manager

On any given day in today's global economy, a manager can interact with colleagues from several different countries or cultures. For instance, at PolyGram, the British music company, the top 33 managers are from 15 different countries.[64] If they are to be effective, managers in such multicultural situations need to develop *global* skills (see Table 15–4). Developing skilled managers who move comfortably from culture to culture takes time. Consider, for example, this comment by the head of Gillette, who wants twice as many global managers on the payroll. "We could try to hire the best and the brightest, but it's the experience with Gillette that we need. About half of our [expatriates] are now on their fourth country—that kind of experience. It takes 10 years to make the kind of Gillette manager I'm talking about."[65]

Importantly, these global skills will help managers in culturally diverse countries such as the United States and Canada do a more effective job on a day-to-day basis (See the International OB 15-2).

Avoiding OB Trouble Spots in Foreign Assignments

Finding the right person (often along with a supportive and adventurous family) for a foreign position is a complex, time-consuming, and costly process.[66] For our purposes, it is sufficient to narrow the focus to common OB trouble spots in the foreign assignment cycle. As illustrated in Figure 15–4, the first and last stages of the cycle occur at home. The middle two stages occur in the foreign or host country. Each stage hides an OB-related trouble spot that needs to be anticipated and neutralized. Otherwise, the bill for another failed foreign assignment will grow.

Table 15–4   **Global Skills for Global Managers**

Skill	Description
Global perspective	Broaden focus from one or two countries to a global business perspective.
Cultural responsiveness	Become familiar with many cultures.
Appreciate cultural synergies	Learn the dynamics of multicultural situations.
Cultural adaptability	Be able to live and work effectively in many different cultures.
Cross-cultural communication	Engage in cross-cultural interaction every day, whether at home or in a foreign country.
Cross-cultural collaboration	Work effectively in multicultural teams where everyone is equal.
Acquire broad foreign experience	Move up the career ladder by going from one foreign country to another, instead of taking frequent home-country assignments.

SOURCE: Adapted from N J Adler and S Bartholomew, "Managing Globally Competent People," *Academy of Management Executive,* August 1992, Table 1, pp 52–65.

Figure 15–4   **The Foreign Assignment Cycle (with OB Trouble Spots)**

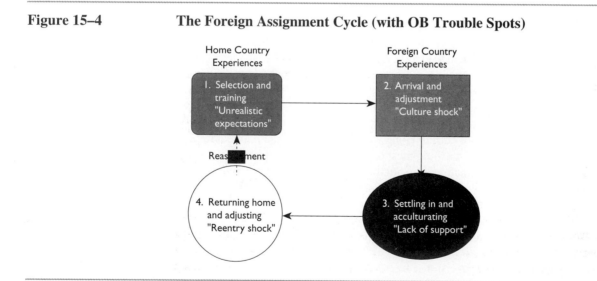

Avoiding Unrealistic Expectations with Cross-Cultural Training

Realistic job previews (RJPs) have proven effective at bringing people's unrealistic expectations about a pending job assignment down to earth by providing a realistic balance of good and bad news. People with realistic expectations tend to quit less often and be more satisfied than those with unrealistic expectations. RJPs are a must for future expatriates. In addition, cross-cultural training is required.

Cross-cultural training is any type of structured experience designed to help departing employees adjust to a foreign culture. As documented in the case at the end of the chapter, the trend is toward more such training. Although costly, companies believe cross-cultural training is less expensive than failed foreign assignments.

International OB 15-2

The Melting Pot Still Has a Few Lumps

Sunwook Kong was a little anxious when he showed up at Purdue University's Krannert Graduate School of Management from Seoul, South Korea, last fall. A media planner with little business experience, he was uncomfortable with his English and desperately feared speaking out in class—a hallmark of the US B-school. "Koreans are accustomed to the kind of education that forces students to learn by heart," says Kong.

Thanks to his study team, he didn't have much of a choice. Kong's group—African-American Jevon Gordon; Jatuphat Tangkaravakoon, a Thai national; Chinese-American Steven H. Tsang; and Shawn A. Vij, an American born in India—forced Kong to do the writing and presentation part of a statistics project. The experience got Kong over his fear and helped galvanize the group. Now, they're not only effective study buddies, they're close pals. This Christmas, they're planning a trip to Asia to visit the homes of Tangkaravakoon and Kong. "They were friends outside of class," says Kong. "They showed me kindness."

"Abrasive." If only all foreign B-school students could say their experience had such a happy ending. Sure, nearly every B-school has gone global, hanging flags for each country represented, offering sushi and couscous nights, Latin dance parties, and study trips to Africa and China. But even as most have embraced classroom diversity as the best way to teach global management, deans at many B-schools have been negligent in making the reality live up to the promise for many students. Foreign students often still find themselves isolated academically and socially. Many also have trouble finding a job. And some domestic students, too, aren't getting the global interaction and deep cultural understanding they thought they paid for.

Start with the most obvious difficulty: The culture of most US business schools remains strongly American, both in the classroom and out. Many foreign students aren't used to a system that requires class participation and direct communication. "At the beginning, I found the more outgoing nature of people in the US abrasive," says Eammonn T. O'Sullivan, an Irish member of the class of 1998 at Dartmouth's Amos Tuck B-school. "I was uncomfortable being very up-front, saying, for example, I want to work with you in your study group." With team-based projects an increasingly important part of coursework—and of each student's grade—this reticence can be a problem.

Moreover, B-school places a huge premium on keg parties and ski trips to provide students the opportunity to make connections that will endure in the workplace. That's a very different idea of school than most non-Americans have. And it's not always clear that it's important to show up for happy hour; even if you're a teetotaler. Because many of the international students are married, any free moment is likely to be spent at home with one's spouse, particularly if that person is new to the country and doesn't have his or her own social network. "It wasn't impressed on [international students] that much of the MBA experience was a social aspect," says Sheung L Li, a recent graduate of Stanford University's B-school born in Hong Kong but raised in the [United States]. "There is a very aggressive social schedule here, and that's something most of the East Asian crowd stays out of." . . .

There's a flip side to the international equation—the unmet expectations and growing frustration felt by American students. When students from abroad aren't encouraged to become active members of the class, Americans, too, are robbed of the window into other cultures that they've been told will be a key element of their education. "Domestic students made all the contributions to class discussion," says Tessa J Jackson, a recent graduate of the University of California, Berkeley's Haas School. "So you don't know how business is conducted in Europe or the Pacific Rim."

SOURCE: Excerpted from J Reingold, "The Melting Pot Still Has a Few Lumps," *Business Week*, October 19, 1998, pp 104, 108.

Programs vary widely in type and also in rigor.[67] Of course, the greater the difficulty, the greater the time and expense:

- *Easiest.* Predeparture training is limited to informational materials, including books, lectures, films, videos, and internet searches.
- *Moderately difficult.* Experiential training is conducted through case studies, role playing, assimilators (simulated intercultural incidents), and introductory language instruction.
- *Most difficult.* Departing employees are given some combination of the preceding methods plus comprehensive language instruction and field experience in the target culture. As an example of the latter, PepsiCo Inc. transfers "about 25 young foreign managers a year to the US for one-year assignments in bottling plants."[68]

Which approach is the best? Research to date does not offer a final answer. One study involving US employees in South Korea led the researcher to recommend a *combination* of informational and experiential predeparture training.[69] As a general rule of thumb, the more rigorous the cross-cultural training, the better. Our personal experience with teaching OB to foreign students both in the United States and abroad reminds us that there really is no substitute for an intimate knowledge of the local language and culture.[70]

Avoiding Culture Shock

Have you ever been in a totally unfamiliar situation and felt disoriented and perhaps a bit frightened? If so, you already know something about culture shock. According to anthropologists, **culture shock** involves anxiety and doubt caused by an overload of unfamiliar expectations and social cues.[71] College freshmen often experience a variation of culture shock. An expatriate manager, or family member, may be thrown off balance by an avalanche of strange sights, sounds, and behaviors. Among them may be unreadable road signs, strange-tasting food, inability to use your left hand for social activities (in Islamic countries, the left hand is the toilet hand), or failure to get a laugh with your sure-fire joke. For the expatriate manager trying to concentrate on the fine details of a business negotiation, culture shock is more than an embarrassing inconvenience. It is a disaster! Like the confused college freshman who quits and goes home, culture-shocked employees often panic and go home early.

The best defense against culture shock is comprehensive cross-cultural training, including intensive language study. Once again, the only way to pick up subtle—yet important—social cues is via the local language. Quantum, the Milpitas, California, maker of computer hard-disk drives has close ties to its manufacturing partner in Japan, Matsushita-Kotobuki Electronics (MKE):

> MKE is constantly proposing changes in design that make new disk drives easier to manufacture. When the product is ready for production, 8 to 10 Quantum engineers descend on MKE's plant in western Japan for at least a month. To smooth teamwork, Quantum is offering courses in Japanese language and culture, down to mastering etiquette at a tea ceremony.[72]

This type of program reduces culture shock by taking the anxiety-producing mystery out of an unfamiliar culture.[73]

Support During the Foreign Assignment

Especially during the first six months, when everything is so new to the expatriate, a support system needs to be in place.[74] *Host-country sponsors,* assigned to individual managers or families, are recommended because they serve as "cultural seeing-eye dogs." In a foreign country, where even the smallest errand can turn into an utterly exhausting production, sponsors can get things done quickly because they know the cultural and geographical territory. Honda's Ohio employees, for example, enjoyed the help of family sponsors when training in Japan:

> Honda smoothed the way with Japanese wives who once lived in the US. They handled emergencies such as when Diana Jett's daughter Ashley needed stitches in her chin. When Task Force Senior Manager Kim Smalley's daughter, desperate to fit in at elementary school, had to have a precisely shaped bag for her harmonica, a Japanese volunteer stayed up late to make it.[75]

Avoiding Reentry Shock

Strange as it may seem, many otherwise successful expatriate managers encounter their first major difficulty only after their foreign assignment is over. Why? Returning to one's native culture is taken for granted because it seems so routine and ordinary. But having adjusted to another country's way of doing things for an extended period of time can put one's own culture and surroundings in a strange new light. Three areas for potential reentry shock are work, social activities, and general environment (e.g., politics, climate, transportation, food). Ira Caplan's return to New York City exemplifies reentry shock:

> During the past 12 years, living mostly in Japan, he and his wife had spent their vacations cruising the Nile or trekking in Nepal. They hadn't seen much of the US. They are getting an eyeful now. . .
> Prices astonish him. The obsession with crime unnerves him. What unsettles Mr. Caplan more, though, is how much of himself he has left behind.

> In a syndrome of return no less stressful than that of departure, he feels displaced, disregarded, and diminished. . .
> In an Italian restaurant, crowded at lunchtime, the waiter sets a bowl of linguine in front of him. Mr. Caplan stares at it. "In Asia, we have smaller portions and smaller people," he says.
> Asia is on his mind. He has spent years cultivating an expertise in a region of huge importance. So what? This is New York.[76]

Work-related adjustments were found to be a major problem for samples of repatriated Finnish, Japanese, and American employees.[77] Upon being repatriated, a 12-year veteran of one US company said: "Our organizational culture was turned upside down. We now have a different strategic focus, different 'tools' to get the job done, and different buzzwords to make it happen. I had to learn a whole new corporate 'language.' "[78] Reentry shock can be reduced through employee career counseling and home-country sponsors. Simply being aware of the problem of reentry shock is a big step toward effectively dealing with it.[79]

Overall, the key to a successful foreign assignment is making it a well-integrated link in a career chain rather than treating it as an isolated adventure.

SUMMARY

1. *Explain how societal culture and organizational culture combine to influence on-the-job behavior.* Culture involves the taken-for-granted assumptions collections of people have about how they should think, act, and feel. Key aspects of societal culture, such as customs and language, are brought to work by the individual. Working together, societal and organizational culture influence the person's values, ethics, attitudes, and expectations.

2. *Define* ethnocentrism, *and distinguish between high-context and low-context cultures.* Ethnocentrism is the belief that one's native culture, language, and ways of doing things are superior to all others. People from low-context cultures infer relatively less from situational cues and extract more meaning from spoken and written words. In high-context cultures such as China and Japan, managers prefer slow negotiations and trust-building meetings, which tends to frustrate low-context Northern Europeans and North Americans who prefer to get right down to business.

3. *Draw a distinction between individualistic cultures and collectivist cultures.* People in individualistic cultures think primarily in terms of "I" and "me" and place a high value on freedom and personal choice. Collectivist cultures teach people to be "we" and "us" oriented and to subordinate personal wishes and goals to the interests of the relevant social unit (such as family, group, organization, or society).

4. *Explain the difference between monochronic and polychronic cultures.* People in monochronic cultures are schedule driven and prefer to do one thing at a time. To them, time is like money; it is spent wisely or wasted. In polychronic cultures, there is a tendency to do many things at once and to perceive time as flexible and multidimensional. Polychronic people view monochronic people as being too preoccupied with time.

5. *Discuss the cultural implications of interpersonal space, language, and religion.* Anthropologist Edward Hall coined the term *proxemics* to refer to the study of cultural expectations about interpersonal space. Asians and Latin Americans like to stand close (6 inches to 1 foot) during business conversations, while North Americans and Northern Europeans prefer a larger interpersonal distance (3 to 4 feet). Conflicting expectations about proper interpersonal distance can create awkward cross-cultural situations. Research uncovered a high degree of agreement about semantic elements across eight cultures. Another study found no agreement about the primary work value across five different religious preference groups.

6. *Describe the practical lessons from the Hofstede–Bond cross-cultural studies.* According to the Hofstede–Bond cross-cultural management studies, caution needs to be exercised when transplanting management theories and practices from one culture to another. Also, long-term orientation was the only one of five cultural dimensions in the Hofstede–Bond studies to correlate positively with national economic growth.

7. *Explain what cross-cultural studies have found about leadership styles.* One cross-cultural management study suggests the need to vary leadership styles from one culture to another. The participative style turned out to be the only leadership style applicable in all 18 countries studied. Still, the participative style has its limitations and is not universally effective.

8. *Specify why US managers have a comparatively high failure rate in foreign assignments, and identify skills needed by today's global managers.* American expatriates are troubled by family and personal adjustment problems. Experts say global managers need the following skills: global perspective, cultural responsiveness, appreciation of cultural synergies, cultural adaptability, cross-cultural communication, cross-cultural collaboration, and broad foreign experience.

9. *Discuss the importance of cross-cultural training relative to the foreign assignment cycle.* The foreign assignment cycle has four stages: selection and training, arrival and adjustment, settling in and acculturating, and returning home and adjusting. Cross-cultural training, preferably combining informational and experiential predeparture sessions, can help expatriates avoid two OB trouble spots: unrealistic expectations and culture shock. There are no adequate substitutes for knowing the local language and culture.

DISCUSSION QUESTIONS

1. Regarding your cultural awareness, how would you describe the prevailing culture in your country to a stranger from another land?

2. What are your personal experiences with ethnocentrism and cross-cultural dealings? What lessons have you learned?

3. Why are people from high-context cultures such as China and Japan likely to be misunderstood by low-context Westerners?

4. Culturally speaking, are you individualistic or collectivist? How does that cultural orientation affect how you run your personal and/or business affairs?

5. Based on your score on the Polychronic Attitude Index, are you relatively monochronic or polychronic? What difficulties do you encounter because of this cultural tendency?

6. In your view, what is the most important lesson for global managers from the Hofstede–Bond studies? Explain.

7. Based on your personal experience with one or more of the countries listed in Table 15–3, do you agree or disagree with the leadership profiles? Explain.

8. What needs to be done to improve the success rate of US managers in foreign assignments?

9. Which of the global manager skills in Table 15–4 do you need to develop? Explain.

10. What is your personal experience with culture shock? Which of the OB trouble spots in Figure 15–4 do you believe is the greatest threat to expatriate employee success? Explain.

INTERNET EXERCISE

www.lonelyplanet.com

Thanks to the power of the Internet, you can take a trip to a far-flung corner of the world without ever leaving your chair. The purpose of this exercise is to enhance your cross-cultural awareness by using the Internet to learn about a foreign country of your choice. Our primary resource is the Internet site www.lonelyplanet.com based on the popular, highly readable, and somewhat off-beat Lonely Planet travel guides available in bookstores. (This is our favorite, but if you prefer another online travel guide, use it and tell others.) At the Lonely Planet Online home page, select "destinations" from the main menu. Use the geographic menus on the Destinations page to *select a foreign country where your native language is not the primary language.* Explore the map of your selected country and then read the material in the "Facts at a Glance" and "Culture" sections. If you have the time and interest, read some of the other relevant sections such as "History," "Economy," and "Facts for the Traveler."

A second important stop on your Internet trip is www.travlang.com to start building your language skills for your selected country. At the home page, follow steps 1 and 2. Next, select "Basic Words" from the language page you picked in step 2. Practice essential words such as "Hello," "Yes," "No," "Thank you," and any others you deem necessary. Take the language *quiz* if you have time.

Questions

1. How strong is your interest in taking a foreign assignment in your selected country? Explain.

2. Culturally, does your focus country seem to be high-context or low-context, individualistic or collectivist, and monochronic or polychronic? Cite specific clues from your Internet research.

3. How do you say "Hello" and "Thank you" in the primary language of your chosen country? (Perhaps you have a classmate who can help you with your pronunciation.)

4. What is the likelihood of experiencing "culture shock" in this country? How could you avoid or minimize it?

OB IN ACTION CASE STUDY

Pack Your Bags, You've Been Transferred to Kenya [80]

Dale Pilger, General Motors Corp.'s new managing director for Kenya, wonders if he can keep his Kenyan employees from interrupting his paperwork by raising his index finger.

"The finger itself will offend," warns Noah Midamba, a Kenyan. He urges that Mr. Pilger instead greet a worker with an effusive welcome, offer a chair, and request that he wait. It can be even trickier to fire a Kenyan, Mr. Midamba says. The government asked one German auto executive to leave Kenya after he dismissed a man—whose brother was the East African country's vice president.

Mr. Pilger, his adventurous wife, and their two teenagers, miserable about moving, have come to this Rocky Mountain college town [Boulder, Colorado] for three days of cross-cultural training. The Cortland, Ohio, family learns to cope with being strangers in a strange land as consultants Moran, Stahl & Boyer International give them a crash immersion in African political history, business practices, social customs, and nonverbal gestures. The training enables managers to grasp cultural differences and handle culture-shock symptoms such as self-pity.

Cross-cultural training is on the rise everywhere because more global-minded corporations moving fast-track executives overseas want to curb the cost of failed expatriate stints. . .

But as cross-cultural training gains popularity, it attracts growing criticism. A lot of the training is garbage, argues Robert Bontempo, assistant professor of international business at Columbia University. Even customized family training offered by companies like Prudential Insurance Co. of America's Moran Stahl—which typically costs $6,000 for three days—hasn't been scientifically tested. "They charge a huge amount of money, and there's no evidence that these firms do any good" in lowering foreign-transfer flops, Prof. Bontempo contends.

"You don't need research" to prove that cross-cultural training works because so much money has been wasted on failed overseas assignments, counters Gary Wederspahn, director of design and development at Moran Stahl.

General Motors agrees. Despite massive cost cutting lately, the auto giant still spends nearly $500,000 a year on cross-cultural training for about 150 Americans and their families headed abroad. "We think this substantially contributes to the low [premature] return rate" of less than 1% among GM expatriates, says Richard Rachner, GM general director of international personnel. That compares with a 25% rate at concerns that don't properly select and coach expatriates, he adds.

The Pilgers' experience reveals the benefits and drawbacks of such training. Mr. Pilger, a 38-year-old engineer employed by GM for 20 years, sought an overseas post but never lived abroad before. He finds the sessions "worthwhile" in readying him to run a vehicle-assembly plant that is 51% owned by Kenya's government. But he finds the training "horribly empty . . . in helping us prepare for the personal side of the move."

Dale and Nancy Pilger have just spent a week in Nairobi. But the executive's scant knowledge of Africa becomes clear when trainer Jackson Wolfe, a former Peace Corps official, mentions Nigeria. "Is that where Idi Amin was from?" Mr. Pilger asks. The dictator ruled Uganda. With a sheepish smile, Mr. Pilger admits: "We don't know a lot about the world."

The couple's instructors don't always know everything about preparing expatriates for Kenyan culture, either. Mr. Midamba, an adjunct international-relations professor at Kent State University and son of a Kenyan political leader, concedes that he neglected to caution Mr. Pilger's predecessor against holding business dinners at Nairobi restaurants.

As a result, the American manager "got his key people to the restaurant and expected their wives to be there," Mr. Midamba recalls. But "the wives didn't show up." Married women in Kenya view restaurants "as places where you find prostitutes and loose morals," notes Mungai Kimani, another Kenyan trainer.

The blunder partly explains why Mr. Midamba goes to great lengths to teach the Pilgers the art of entertaining at home. Among his tips: Don't be surprised if guests arrive an hour early, an hour late, or announce their departure four times.

The Moran Stahl program also zeros in on the family's adjustment (though not to Mr. Pilger's satisfaction). A family's poor adjustment causes more foreign-transfer failures than a manager's work performance. That is the Pilger's greatest fear because 14-year-old Christy and 16-year-old Eric bitterly oppose the move. The lanky, boyish-looking Mr. Pilger remembers Eric's tearful reaction as: " 'You'll have to arrest me if you think you're going to take me to Africa.' "

While distressed by his children's hostility, Mr. Pilger still believes living abroad will be a great growth experience for them. But he says he promised Eric that if "he's miserable" in Kenya, he can return to Ohio for his last year of high school next year.

To ease their adjustment, Christy and Eric receive separate training from their parents. The teens' activities include sampling Indian food (popular in Kenya) as well as learning how to ride Nairobi public buses, speak a little Swahili, and juggle, of all things.

By the training's last day, both youngsters grudgingly accept being uprooted from friends, her swim team, and his brand-new car. Going to Kenya "no longer seems like a death sentence," Christy says. Eric mumbles that he may volunteer at a wild-game reserve.

But their usually upbeat mother has become increasingly upset as she hears more about a country troubled by drought, poverty, and political unrest—where foreigners live behind walled fortresses. Now, at an international parenting session, she clashes with youth trainer Amy Kaplan over whether her offspring can safely ride Nairobi's public buses, even with Mrs. Pilger initially accompanying them.

"All the advice we've gotten is that it's deadly" to ride buses there, Mrs. Pilger frets. Ms. Kaplan retorts: "It's going to be hard" to let teenagers do their own thing in Kenya, but then they'll be less likely to rebel. The remark fails to quell Mrs. Pilger's fears that she can't handle life abroad. "I'm going to let a lot of people down if I blow this," she adds, her voice quavering with emotion.

Questions for Discussion

1. What would you like to tell General Motors' employees in Kenya about working effectively with Americans?

2. Has General Motors done a good job of preparing the Pilger family for an assignment in Kenya? Explain.

3. If you were a cross-cultural consultant, what advice would you give General Motors about preparing employees and their families for foreign assignments?

4. Putting yourself in Dale Pilger's place, would you accept the transfer to Kenya? Explain. Putting yourself in Nancy Pilger's place, would you agree to moving the family to Kenya? Explain.

PERSONAL AWARENESS AND GROWTH EXERCISE

How Do Your Work Goals Compare Internationally?

Objectives
1. To increase your cross-cultural awareness.
2. To see how your own work goals compare internationally.

Introduction
In today's multicultural global economy, it is a mistake to assume everyone wants the same things from the job as you do. This exercise provides a "window" on the world of work goals.

Instructions
Below is a list of 11 goals potentially attainable in the workplace. In terms of your own personal preferences, rank the goals from 1 to 11 (1 5 Most important; 11 5 Least important). After you have ranked all 11 work goals, compare your list with the national samples under the heading *Survey Results*. These national samples represent cross sections of employees from all levels and all major occupational groups. (Please complete your ranking now, before looking at the national samples.)

How important are the following in your work life?

Rank   Work Goals

_____   A lot of opportunity to *learn* new things

_____   Good *interpersonal relations* (supervisors, co-workers)

_____   Good opportunity for upgrading or *promotion*

_____   *Convenient* work *hours*

_____   A lot of *variety*

_____   *Interesting* work (work that you really like)

_____   Good *job security*

_____   A good *match* between your job requirements and your abilities and experience

_____   Good *pay*

_____   Good physical working *conditions* (such as light, temperature, cleanliness, low noise level)

_____   A lot of *autonomy* (you decide how to do your work)[81]

Questions for Discussion

1. Which national profile of work goals most closely matches your own? Is this what you expected, or not?

2. Are you surprised by any of the rankings in the four national samples? Explain.

3. What sorts of motivational/leadership adjustments would a manager have to make when moving among the four countries?

Survey Results [82]

Ranking of Work Goals by Country
(1 = Most important; 11 = Least important)

Work Goals	United States	Britain	Germany*	Japan
Interesting work	1	1	3	2
Pay	2	2	1	5
Job security	3	3	2	4
Match between person and job	4	6	5	1
Opportunity to learn	5	8	9	7
Variety	6	7	6**	9
Interpersonal relations	7	4	4	6
Autonomy	8	10	8	3
Convenient work hours	9	5	6**	8
Opportunity for promotion	10	11	10	11
Working conditions	11	9	11	10

*Former West Germany.

**Tie.

GROUP EXERCISE

Looking into a Cultural Mirror

Objectives

1. To generate group discussion about the impact of societal culture on managerial style.

2. To increase your cultural awareness.

3. To discuss the idea of a distinct American style of management.

4. To explore the pros and cons of the American style of management.

Introduction

A time-tested creativity technique involves "taking something familiar and making it strange." This technique can yield useful insights by forcing us to take a close look at things we tend to take for granted. In the case of this group exercise, the focus of your attention will be mainstream cultural tendencies in the United States (or any other country you or your instructor may select) and management. A 15-minute, small-group session will be followed by brief oral presentations and a general class discussion. Total time required is about 35 to 45 minutes.

Instructions

Your instructor will divide your class randomly into small groups of five to eight. Half of the teams will be designated "red" teams, and half will be "green" teams. Each team will assign someone the role of recorder/ presenter, examine the cultural traits listed below, and develop a cultural profile of the "American management style." Members of each red team will explain the *positive* implications of each trait in their cultural profile. Green team members will explain the *negative* implications of the traits in their profiles.

During the brief oral presentations by the various teams, the instructor may jot down on the board or flip chart a composite cultural profile of American managers. A general class discussion of positive and negative implications will follow. Note: Special effort should be made to solicit comments and observations from foreign students and students who have traveled and/or worked in other countries. Discussion needs to focus on the appropriateness or inappropriateness of the American cultural style of management in other countries and cultures.

As "seed" for group discussion, here is a list of American cultural traits identified by researchers[83] (feel free to supplement this short list):

- Individualistic.

- Independent.

- Aggressive/assertive/blunt.

- Competitive.

- Informal.

- Pragmatic/practical.

- Impatient.

- Materialistic.

- Unemotional/rational/objective.

- Hard working.

Questions for Discussion

1. Are you surprised by anything you have just heard? Explain.

2. Is there a distinct American management style? Explain.

3. Can the American management style be exported easily? If it needs to be modified, how?

4. What do American managers need to do to be more effective at home and in foreign countries?

NOTES

1 Excerpted from D McGinn and S Theil, "Hands on the Wheel," *Newsweek,* April 12, 1999, pp 49–52. For more, see B Vlasic, "The First Global Car Colossus," *Business Week,* May 18, 1998, pp 40–43; K Lowry, "The Auto Baron," *Business Week,* November 16, 1998, pp 82–90; M Maynard, "Merger of Two Equals Appears To Be Unequal," *USA Today,* March 26, 1999, pp 1B–2B; and M Maynard, "Daimler Chrysler Rides High," *USA Today,* April 28, 1999, p 3B.

2 Based on J S Lublin, "An Overseas Stint Can Be a Ticket to the Top," *The Wall Street Journal,* January 29, 1996, pp B1, B5.

3 G Dutton, "Building a Global Brain," *Management Review,* May 1999, p 35.

4 For helpful practical advice, see Table 1 in N J Adler and S Bartholomew, "Managing Globally Competent People," *Academy of Management Executive,* August 1992, pp 52–65. Also see A J Marsella, "Toward a 'Global-Community Psychology,'" *American Psychologist,* December 1998, pp 1282–91; and B Kogut, "What Makes a Company Global?" *Harvard Business Review,* January–February 1999, pp 165–70.

5 M Mabry, "Pin a Label on a Manager—And Watch What Happens," *Newsweek,* May 14, 1990, p 43.

6 Ibid.

7 E H Schein, *Organizational Culture and Leadership* (San Francisco: Jossey-Bass, 1985), p 9. Also see H H Baligh, "Components of Culture: Nature, Interconnections, and Relevance to the Decisions on the Organization Structure," *Management Science,* January 1994, pp 14–27.

8 For instructive discussion, see J S Black, H B Gregersen, and M F. Mendenhall, *Global Assignments: Successfully Expatriating and Repatriating International Managers* (San Francisco: Jossey-Bass, 1992), Ch. 2.

9 F Trompenaars and C Hampden-Turner, *Riding the Waves of Culture: Understanding Cultural Diversity in Global Business,* 2nd ed (New York: McGraw-Hill, 1998), pp 6–7.

10 "How Cultures Collide," *Psychology Today,* July 1976, p 69.

11 See M Mendenhall, "A Painless Approach to Integrating 'International' into OB, HRM, and Management Courses," *Organizational Behavior Teaching Review,* no. 3 (1988–89), pp 23–27.

12 See C L Sharma, "Ethnicity, National Integration, and Education in the Union of Soviet Socialist Republics," *The Journal of East and West Studies,* October 1989, pp 75–93; and R Brady and P Galuszka, "Shattered Dreams," *Business Week,* February 11, 1991, pp 38–42.

13 J Main, "How to Go Global—And Why," *Fortune,* August 28, 1989, p 73.

14 An excellent contrast between French and American values can be found in C Gouttefarde, "American Values in the French Workplace," *Business Horizons,* March–April 1996, pp 60–69.

15 W D Marbach, "Quality: What Motivates American Workers?" *Business Week,* April 12, 1993, p 93.

16 See G A Sumner, *Folkways* (New York: Ginn, 1906). Also see J G Weber, "The Nature of Ethnocentric Attribution Bias: Ingroup Protection or Enhancement?" *Journal of Experimental Social Psychology,* September 1994, pp 482–504.

17 "House English-only Bill Aims at Federal Agencies," *USA Today,* July 25, 1996, p 3A. For another example of ethnocentric behavior, see J Cox, "Summers Has Slightly Tense Relationship with Japanese," *USA Today,* May 13, 1999, p 2B.

18 D A Heenan and H V Perlmutter, *Multinational Organization Development* (Reading, MA: Addison-Wesley, 1979), p 17.

19 Data from R Kopp, "International Human Resource Policies and Practices in Japanese, European, and United States Multinationals," *Human Resource Management,* Winter 1994, pp 581–99.

20 See "How Cultures Collide," pp 66–74, 97; and M Munter, "Cross-Cultural Communication for Managers," *Business Horizons,* May–June 1993, pp 69–78.

21 D C Barnlund, "Public and Private Self in Communicating with Japan," *Business Horizons,* March–April 1989, p 38.

22 See E W K Tsang, "Can *Guanxi* Be a Source of Sustained Competitive Advantage for Doing Business in China?" *Academy of Management Executive,* May 1998, pp 64–73.

23 The concept of "face" and good tips on saving face in Far East Asia are presented in J A Reeder, "When West Meets East: Cultural Aspects of Doing Business in Asia," *Business Horizons,* January–February 1987, pp 69–74. Also see B Stout, "Interviewing in Japan," *HR Magazine,* June 1998, pp 71–77; and J A Quelch and C M Dinh-Tan, "Country Managers in Transitional Economies: The Case of Vietnam," *Business Horizons,* July–August 1998, pp 34–40.

24 The German management style is discussed in R Stewart, "German Management: A Challenge to Anglo-American Managerial Assumptions," *Business Horizons,* May–June 1996, pp 52–54.

25 See D Stauffer, "No Need for Inter-American Culture Clash," *Management Review,* January 1998, p 8; J Scarborough, "Comparing Chinese and Western Cultural Roots: Why 'East Is East and . . . ,' " *Business Horizons,* November–December 1998, pp 15–24; and C B Meek, "*Ganbatte:* Understanding the Japanese Employee," *Business Horizons,* January–February 1999, pp 27–36.

26 This list is based on E T Hall, "The Silent Language in Overseas Business," *Harvard Business Review,* May–June 1960, pp 87–96; and R Knotts, "Cross-Cultural Management: Transformations and Adaptations," *Business Horizons,* January–February 1989, pp 29–33; and Trompenaars and Hampden-Turner, *Riding the Waves of Culture: Understanding Cultural Diversity in Global Business.*

27 A discussion of Japanese stereotypes in America can be found in L Smith, "Fear and Loathing of Japan," *Fortune,* February 26, 1990, pp 50–57. Diversity in so-called Eastern Bloc countries in Central and Eastern Europe is discussed in F Luthans, R R Patrick, and B C Luthans, "Doing Business in Central and Eastern Europe: Political, Economic, and Cultural Diversity," *Business Horizons,* September–October 1995, pp 9–16.

28 Based on discussion in P R Harris and R T Moran, *Managing Cultural Differences,* 3rd ed (Houston: Gulf Publishing, 1991) p 12. Also see "Workers' Attitudes Similar Worldwide," *HRMagazine,* December 1998, pp 28–30; and C Comeau-Kirschner, "It's a Small World," *Management Review,* March 1999, p 8.

29 Data from Trompenaars and Hampden-Turner, *Riding the Waves of Culture: Understanding Cultural Diversity in Global Business,* Ch 5. For relevant research evidence, see Y A Fijneman, M E Willemsen, and Y H Poortinga, "Individualism–Collectivism: An Empirical Study of a Conceptual Issue," *Journal of Cross-Cultural Psychology,* July 1996, pp 381–402; D I Jung and B J Avolio, "Effects of Leadership Style and Followers' Cultural Orientation on Performance in Groups and Individual Task Conditions," *Academy of Management Journal,* April 1999, pp 208–18; T M Singelis, M H Bond, W F Sharkey, and C S Y Lai, "Unpacking Culture's Influence on Self-Esteem and Embarrassability: The Role of Self-Construals," *Journal of Cross-Cultural Psychology,* May 1999, pp 315–41; and M J Bresnahan, R Ohashi, W Y Liu, R Nebashi, and C Liao, "A Comparison of Response Styles in Singapore and Taiwan," *Journal of Cross-Cultural Psychology,* May 1999, pp 342–58.

30 As quoted in E E Schultz, "Scudder Brings Lessons to Navajo, Gets Some of Its Own," *The Wall Street Journal,* April 29, 1999, p C12.

31 Trompenaars and Hampden-Turner, *Riding the Waves of Culture: Understanding Cultural Diversity in Global Business,* p 56.

32 See, for example, N R Mack, "Taking Apart the Ticking of Time," *The Christian Science Monitor,* August 29, 1991, p 17.

33 For a comprehensive treatment of time, see J E McGrath and J R Kelly, *Time and Human Interaction: Toward a Social Psychology of Time* (New York: The Guilford Press, 1986). Also see L A Manrai and A K Manrai, "Effects of Cultural-Context, Gender, and Acculturation on Perceptions of Work versus Social/Leisure Time Usage," *Journal of Business Research,* February 1995, pp 115–28.

34 A good discussion of doing business in Mexico is G K Stephens and C R Greer, "Doing Business in Mexico: Understanding Cultural Differences," *Organizational Dynamics,* Summer 1995, pp 39–55.

35 R W Moore, "Time, Culture, and Comparative Management: A Review and Future Direction," in *Advances in International Comparative Management,* vol. 5, ed S B Prasad (Greenwich, CT: JAI Press, 1990), pp 7–8.

36 See A C Bluedorn, C F Kaufman, and P M Lane, "How Many Things Do You Like to Do at Once? An Introduction to Monochronic and Polychronic Time," *Academy of Management Executive,* November 1992, pp 17–26.

37 "Multitasking" term drawn from S McCartney, "The Breaking Point: Multitasking Technology Can Raise Stress and Cripple Productivity," *The Arizona Republic,* May 21, 1995, p D10.

38 O Port, "You May Have To Reset This Watch—In a Million Years," *Business Week,* August 30, 1993, p 65.

39 See E T Hall, *The Hidden Dimension* (Garden City, NY: Doubleday, 1966).

40 "How Cultures Collide," p 72.

41 D Raybeck and D Herrmann, "A Cross-Cultural Examination of Semantic Relations," *Journal of Cross-Cultural Psychology,* December 1990, p 470.

42 G A Michaelson, "Global Gold," *Success,* March 1996, p 16.

43 Translation services are discussed in D Pianko, "Smooth Translations," *Management Review,* July 1996, p 10; and R Ganzel, "Universal Translator? Not Quite," *Training,* April 1999, pp 22–24.

44 For example, see "When in Rio. . . ," *Training,* December 1998, p 25.

45 From *Managing Cultural Differences,* 4th ed, p 23. Phillip R Harris and Robert T Moran. Copyright 1996 © by Gulf Publishing Company. Used with permission. All rights reserved.

46 "Going Global? Stifle Yourself!" *Training,* August 1995, p 14. (Italics added.)

47 Results adapted from and value definitions quoted from S R Safranski and I-W Kwon, "Religious Groups and Management Value Systems," in *Advances in International Comparative Management,* vol. 3, eds R N Farner and E G McGoun (Greenwich, CT: JAI Press, 1988), pp 171–83.

48 Ibid., p 180.

49 N J Adler, *International Dimensions of Organizational Behavior,* 2nd ed (Boston: PWS–Kent, 1991), p 10. Also see P C Earley and H Singh, "International and Intercultural Management Research: What's Next?" *Academy of Management Journal,* April 1995, pp 327–40; M B Teagarden et al., "Toward a Theory of Comparative Management Research: An Idiographic Case Study of the Best International Human Resources Management Project," *Academy of Management Journal,* October 1995, pp 1261–87; M H Segall, W J Lonner, and J W Berry, "Cross-Cultural Psychology as a Scholarly Discipline: On the Flowering of Culture in Behavioral Research," *American Psychologist,* October 1998, pp 1101–10; and M Easterby-Smith and D Malina, "Cross-Cultural Collaborative Research: Toward Reflexivity," *Academy of Management Journal,* February 1999, pp 76–86.

50 For complete details, see G Hofstede, *Culture's Consequences: International Differences in Work-Related Values,* abridged ed (Newbury Park, CA: Sage Publications, 1984); G Hofstede, "The Interaction between National and Organizational Value Systems," *Journal of Management Studies,* July 1985, pp 347–57; and G Hofstede, "Management Scientists Are Human," *Management Science,* January 1994, pp 4–13. Also see V J Shackleton and A H Ali, "Work-Related Values of Managers: A Test of the Hofstede Model," *Journal of Cross-Cultural Psychology,* March 1990, pp 109–18; R Hodgetts, "A Conversation with Geert Hofstede," *Organizational Dynamics,* Spring 1993, pp 53–61; and P B Smith, S Dugan, and F Trompenaars, "National Culture and the Values of Organizational Employees: A Dimensional Analysis Across 43 Nations," *Journal of Cross-Cultural Psychology,* March 1996, pp 231–64.

51 See G Hofstede and M H Bond, "Hofstede's Culture Dimensions: An Independent Validation Using Rokeach's Value Survey," *Journal of Cross-Cultural Psychology,* December 1984, pp 417–33. A recent study using the Chinese Value Survey (CVS) is reported in D A Ralston, D J Gustafson, P M Elsass, F Cheung, and R H Terpstra, "Eastern Values: A Comparison of Managers in the United States, Hong Kong, and the People's Republic of China," *Journal of Applied Psychology,* October 1992, pp 664–71.

52 G Hofstede, "Cultural Constraints in Management Theories," *Academy of Management Executive,* February 1993, p 90.

53 See Y Paik and J H D Sohn, "Confucius in Mexico: Korean MNCs and the Maquiladoras," *Business Horizons,* November–December 1998, pp 25–33.

54 For complete details, see G Hofstede and M H Bond, "The Confucius Connection: From Cultural Roots to Economic Growth," *Organizational Dynamics,* Spring 1988, pp 4–21.

55 See P M Rosenzweig, "When Can Management Science Research Be Generalized Internationally?" *Management Science,* January 1994, pp 28–39.

56 A follow-up study is J P Johnson and T Lenartowicz, "Culture, Freedom and Economic Growth: Do Cultural Values Explain Economic Growth?" *Journal of World Business,* Winter 1998, pp 332–56.

57 See C A Rodrigues, "The Situation and National Culture as Contingencies for Leadership Behavior: Two Conceptual Models," in *Advances in International Comparative Management,* vol. 5, ed S B Prasad (Greenwich, CT: JAI Press, 1990), pp 51–68. For a study that found consistent perception of six leadership styles across four countries (Norway, United States, Sweden, and Australia), see C B Gibson and G A Marcoulides, "The Invariance of Leadership Styles across Four Countries," *Journal of Managerial Issues,* Summer 1995, pp 176–93.

58 For details, see D H B Welsh, F Luthans, and S M Sommer, "Managing Russian Factory Workers: The Impact of US-Based Behavioral and Participative Techniques," *Academy of Management Journal,* February 1993, pp 58–79. Also see F Luthans, S J Peterson, and E Ibrayeva, "The Potential for the 'Dark Side' of Leadership in Post-Communist Countries," *Journal of World Business,* Summer 1998, pp 185–201.

59 Data from J Kahn, "The World's Most Admired Companies," *Fortune,* October 26, 1998, pp 206–26.

60 J S Black and H B Gregersen, "The Right Way to Manage Expats," *Harvard Business Review,* March–April 1999, p 53. A more optimistic picture is presented in R L Tung, "American Expatriates Abroad: From Neophytes to Cosmopolitans," *Journal of World Business,* Summer 1998, pp 125–44.

61 Adapted from R L Tung, "Expatriate Assignments: Enhancing Success and Minimizing Failure," *Academy of Management Executive,* May 1987, pp 117–26.

62 S Dallas, "Rule No. 1: Don't Diss the Locals," *Business Week,* May 15, 1995, p 8.

63   These insights come from Tung, "American Expatriates Abroad: From Neophytes to Cosmopolitans"; P M Caligiuri and W F Cascio, "*Can We Send Her There?* Maximizing the Success of Western Women on Global Assignments," *Journal of World Business,* Winter 1998, pp 394–416; and T L Speer, "Gender Barriers Crumbling, Traveling Business Women Report," *USA Today,* March 16, 1999, p 5E.

64   Data from B Hagerty, "Trainers Help Expatriate Employees Build Bridges to Different Cultures," *The Wall Street Journal,* June 14, 1993, pp B1, B3. Also see A Weiss, "Global Doesn't Mean 'Foreign' Anymore," *Training,* July 1998, pp 50–55; and G Dutton, "Do You Think Globally?" *Management Review,* February 1999, p 6.

65   C M Farkas and P De Backer, "There Are Only Five Ways to Lead," *Fortune,* January 15, 1996, p 111. The shortage of global managers is discussed in L K Stroh and P M Caligiuri, "Increasing Global Competitiveness through Effective People Management," *Journal of World Business,* Spring 1998, pp 1–16.

66   An excellent reference book in this area is Black, Gregersen, and Mendenhall, *Global Assignments: Successfully Expatriating and Repatriating International Managers.* Also see K Roberts, E E Kossek, and C Ozeki, "Managing the Global Workforce: Challenges and Strategies," *Academy of Management Executive,* November 1998, pp 93–106.

67   Ibid., p 97.

68   J S Lublin, "Younger Managers Learn Global Skills," *The Wall Street Journal,* March 31, 1992, p B1.

69   See P C Earley, "Intercultural Training for Managers: A Comparison of Documentary and Interpersonal Methods," *Academy of Management Journal,* December 1987, pp 685–98; and J S Black and M Mendenhall, "Cross-Cultural Training Effectiveness: A Review and a Theoretical Framework for Future Research," *Academy of Management Review,* January 1990, pp 113–36. Also see M R Hammer and J N Martin, "The Effects of Cross-Cultural Training on American Managers in a Japanese-American Joint Venture," *Journal of Applied Communication Research,* May 1992, pp 161–81; and J K Harrison, "Individual and Combined Effects of Behavior Modeling and the Cultural Assimilator in Cross-Cultural Management Training," *Journal of Applied Psychology,* December 1992, pp 952–62.

70   See G P Ferraro, "The Need for Linguistic Proficiency in Global Business," *Business Horizons,* May–June 1996, pp 39–46. For a study demonstrating that employees tend to prefer foreign assignments in culturally similar locations, see S Aryee, Y W Chay, and J Chew, "An Investigation of the Willingness of Managerial Employees to Accept an Expatriate Assignment," *Journal of Organizational Behavior,* May 1996, pp 267–83.

71   See Harris and Moran, *Managing Cultural Differences,* pp 223–28; M Shilling, "Avoid Expatriate Culture Shock," *HR Magazine,* July 1993, pp 58–63; and D Stamps, "Welcome to America: Watch Out for Culture Shock," *Training,* November 1996, pp 22–30.

72   S Tully, "The Modular Corporation," *Fortune,* February 8, 1993, pp 108, 112.

73   Additional instructive resources on the expatriate cycle are M Solomon, "One Assignment, Two Lives," *Personnel Journal,* May 1996, pp 36–47; L A Collins Allard, "Managing Globe-Trotting Expats," *Management Review,* May 1996, pp 39–43; J S Lublin, "Is Transfer to Native Land a Passport to Trouble?" *The Wall Street Journal,* June 3, 1996, pp B1, B4; and M Richey, "Global Families: Surviving an Overseas Move," *Management Review,* June 1996, pp 57–61.

74   See H H Nguyen, L A Messe, and G E Stollak, "Toward a More Complex Understanding of Acculturation and Adjustment," *Journal of Cross-Cultural Psychology,* January 1999, pp 5–31.

75   K L Miller, "How a Team of Buckeyes Helped Honda Save a Bundle," *Business Week,* September 13, 1993, p 68.

76   B Newman, "For Ira Caplan, Re-Entry Has Been Strange," *The Wall Street Journal,* December 12, 1995, p A12.

77   See Black, Gregersen, and Mendenhall, *Global Assignments: Successfully Expatriating and Repatriating International Managers,* p 227. Also see H B Gregersen, "Commitments to a Parent Company and a Local Work Unit During Repatriation," *Personnel Psychology,* Spring 1992, pp 29–54; and H B Gregersen and J S Black, "Multiple Commitments upon Repatriation: The Japanese Experience," *Journal of Management,* no. 2, 1996, pp 209–29.

78   Ibid., pp 226–27.

79   See J R Engen, "Coming Home," *Training,* March 1995, pp 37–40; and L K Stroh, H B Gregersen, and J S Black, "Closing the Gap: Expectations versus Reality among Repatriates," *Journal of World Business,* Summer 1998, pp 111–24.

80   Excerpted from J S Lublin, "Companies Use Cross-Cultural Training to Help Their Employees Adjust Abroad," *The Wall Street Journal,* August 4, 1992, pp B1, B6.

81   This list of work goals is quoted from I Harpaz, "The Importance of Work Goals: An International Perspective," *Journal of International Business Studies,* First Quarter 1990, p 79.

82   Adapted from a seven-country summary in Ibid., Table 2, p 81.

83   See A Nimgade, "American Management as Viewed by International Professionals," *Business Horizons,* November–December 1989, pp 98–105; R Calori and B Dufour, "Management European Style," *Academy of Management Executive,* August 1995, pp 61–71; and W A Hubiak and S J O'Donnell, "Do Americans Have Their Minds Set Against TQM?" *National Productivity Review,* Summer 1996, pp 19–32.

Chapter 16

Managing Stress

SOURCE: John M. Ivancevich and Michael T. Matteson, *Organizational Behavior and Management*, 5th ed., Chapter 7, McGraw-Hill, 2002, 1999.

Learning Objectives:

After completing this chapter, you should be able to:

- Define what is meant by the term *stress.*

- Describe the various components of the organizational stress model.

- Distinguish between four different categories of stressors.

- Discuss major individual and organizational consequences of stress.

- Identify some of the variables which moderate the stress process.

- Describe several different organizational and individual approaches to stress prevention and management.

- Define the following key terms:

 burnout
 qualitative overload
 quantitative overload
 stress
 stressor

The experience of stress is certainly not new. Our cave-dwelling ancestors faced stress every time they left their caves and encountered their enemy, the sabertoothed tigers.[1] The tigers of yesteryear are gone, but they have been replaced by other predators—work overload, a nagging boss, time deadlines, lack of job security, poorly designed jobs, marital disharmony, financial crises, accelerating rates of change. These work and nonwork predators interact and create stress for individuals on and off the job.

This chapter focuses primarily on the individual at work in organizations and on the stress created in this setting. Much of the stress experienced by people in our industrialized society originates in organizations; much of the stress that originates elsewhere affects our behavior and performance in these same organizations. In the article "Who Beats Stress—and How," which is part of this chapter, the author points out that what we do not understand about stress would fill volumes. His point is well taken. One of the complicating issues in understanding stress is the fact that it has been defined in many ways. We begin this chapter with our definition of stress.

WHAT IS STRESS?

Stress means different things to different people. From a layperson's perspective, stress can be described as feeling tense, anxious, or worried. Scientifically, these feelings are all manifestations of the stress experience, a complex programmed response to perceived threat that can have both positive and negative results. The term stress itself has been defined in literally hundreds of ways in the literature. Virtually all of the definitions can be placed into one of two categories, however; stress can be defined as either a *stimulus* or a *response.*

A stimulus definition treats stress as some characteristic or event that may result in a disruptive consequence. It is, in that respect, an engineering definition of stress, borrowed from the physical sciences. In physics, stress refers to the external force applied to an object, for example a bridge girder. The response is "strain," which is the impact the force has on the girder.

In a response definition, stress is seen partially as a response to some stimulus, called a **stressor.** A stressor is a *potentially harmful or threatening external event or situation.* Stress is more than simply a response to a stressor, however. In a response definition, stress is the consequence of the interaction between an environmental stimulus (a stressor) and the individual's response. That is, stress is the result of a unique interaction between stimulus conditions in the environment and the individual's predisposition to respond in a particular way. Using a response definition, we will define **stress** as:

> An adaptive response, moderated by individual differences, that is a consequence of any action, situation, or event that places special demands on a person.

We think it is useful to view stress as the response a person makes and to identify stimulus conditions (actions, situations, events) as stressors. This allows us to focus attention on aspects of the organizational environment that are potential stress producers. Whether stress is actually felt or experienced by a particular individual will depend on that individual's unique characteristics. Furthermore, note that this definition emphasizes that stress is an adaptive response. Since the great majority of stimuli in the work environment do not require adaptation, they are not really potential stress sources.

In the context of our definition of stress, it is important to understand that stress is the result of dealing with something placing "special" demands on us. *Special* here means unusual, physically or psychologically threatening, or outside our usual set of experiences. Starting a new job assignment, changing bosses, having a flat tire, missing a plane, making a mistake at work, having a performance evaluation meeting with the boss—all of these are actions, situations, or events that may place special demand on you. In that sense, they are *potential* stressors. We say potential, because not all stressors will always place the same demands on people. For example, having a performance appraisal meeting with the boss may be extremely stressful for Lynn and not the least stressful for her co-worker, Sabrina. Such a meeting makes special demands of Lynn, for Sabrina it does not. For Lynn the meeting is a stressor; for Sabrina it is not.[2]

In order for an action, situation, or event to result in stress, it must be perceived by the individual to be a source of threat, challenge, or harm. If there are no perceived consequences—good or bad—there is no potential for stress. Three key factors determine whether an experience is likely to result in stress. These factors are importance, uncertainty, and duration. *Importance* relates to how significant the event is to the individual. For example, let us suppose that you are facing a job layoff. The more significant that layoff is to you, the more likely you are to find it stressful. If you expect the layoff to be followed by a period of prolonged unemployment, you will probably view it as a more important event than if immediate reemployment is assured.

Uncertainty refers to a lack of clarity about what will happen. Rumors of an impending layoff may be more stressful to some people than knowing for certain they will be laid off. At least in the latter case, they can make plans for dealing with the situation. Frequently, "not knowing" places more demands on people than does knowing, even if the known result is perceived as negative.

Finally, *duration* is a significant factor. Generally speaking, the longer special demands are placed on us, the more stressful the situation. Being given a distasteful job assignment that only lasts a day or two may be mildly upsetting, while the same assignment lasting for six months may be excruciating. Most people can endure short periods of strenuous physical activity without tiring; prolong the duration, however, and even the most fit among us will become exhausted. The same holds true for stressors. Stress of short duration is sometimes referred to as acute stress. It may last a few seconds, a few hours, even a few days. Long duration stress, on the other hand, is sometimes referred to as chronic stress. Chronic stress may last for months and years. It is the ongoing tension experienced by the people in the Middle East or the turmoil that ethnic rivalries have brought to the people of Chechnya and Russia. It may also be the unrelenting pressure of a job one finds no satisfaction in performing, the constant demands made by an unreasonable boss, or the never-ending struggle to advance in one's chosen career.

ORGANIZATIONAL STRESS: A MODEL

For most employed people, work and work-related activities and preparation time represent much more than a 40-hour-a-week commitment. Work is a major part of our lives, and work and nonwork activities are highly interdependent. The distinction between stress at work and stress at home has always been an artificial one at best. With the explosive increase of dual-career couples in the latter part of the twentieth century, even this artificial distinction has become blurred. Our primary concern here, however, is with direct work-related stressors.

The model shown in Figure 16-1 is designed to help illustrate the link between organizational stressors, stress, and outcomes. Recall from our earlier definition that stress is a response to an action, situation, or event that places special demands on an individual. These occurrences are represented in Figure 16-1 as *work stressors*. We have divided these stressors into main categories: individual, group, organizational and extra organizational. The first three stressor categories are work-related.

The experience of work-related and extraorganizational stress produces outcomes behavioral, cognitive, and physiological. The model suggests that the relationship between stress and outcomes (individual and organizational) is not necessarily direct; similarly, neither is the relationship between the stressors and stress. These relationships may be influenced by *stress moderators*. Individual differences such as age, social support mechanisms, and personality are introduced as potential moderators. A moderator is a valuable attribute that affects the nature of a relationship. While numerous moderators are extremely important, we focus our attention on three representative ones: personality, Type A behavior, and social support.

This provides managers with a framework for thinking about stress in the workplace. Consequently, it suggests that interventions may be needed and can be effective in improving negative stress consequences. Stress prevention and management can be initiated by individuals or the organization. The intention of most preventive programs is to reduce the occurrence, intensity, and negative impact of stress. The management of stress attempts to eliminate or minimize negative consequences of stress. Prevention and the management of stress are difficult as will be illustrated later in this chapter.

IS THE ORGANIZATION RESPONSIBLE FOR AN EMPLOYEE'S STRESS?

The text refers to stress as an adaptive response that is a result of a situation that places special demands on a person. If those special demands are related to an employee's job, should the employer be responsible? One employee thought so. Here's what happened.

James Carter was an automobile assembly-line worker employed by General Motors Corporation. The problem was, he was having a difficult time keeping up with the speed of the production line. The line moved past his work station faster than he was sometimes able to perform the operations for which he was responsible. Making the situation even more stressful for James was the fact that his supervisor frequently criticized him for his failure to keep up with line speed. Eventually the stress became more than he could cope with and he suffered a psychological breakdown. He wanted to be compensated for his "mental injury" and receive worker's disability payments. GM argued that it wasn't the job that caused the problem; thousands of workers perform essentially the same job in assembly plants without problems; it was Carter's reaction to the job, they said, and thus they were not responsible.

Was Carter's stress an injury? Was GM liable? You be the judge!

WORK STRESSORS: INDIVIDUAL, GROUP, AND ORGANIZATIONAL

Stressors are those actions, situations, or events that place special demands on a person. Since, in the right circumstances, virtually any occurrence can place special demands on a person, the list of potential stressors is infinite. We will limit our examination to a small number of stressors that are relatively common in each of our model's three work-specific categories.

FIGURE 16–1   **A MODEL OF STRESSORS, STRESS AND OUTCOMES**

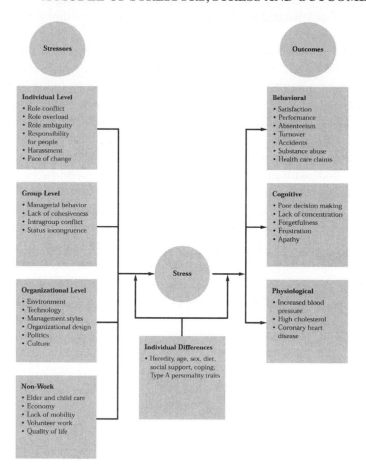

Individual Stressors

Stressors at the individual level have been studied more than any other category presented in Figure 16-1. Role conflict is perhaps the most widely examined individual stressor.[3] Role conflict is present whenever compliance by an individual to one set of expectations about the job is in conflict with compliance to another set of expectations. Facets of role conflict include being torn by conflicting demands from a supervisor about the job and being pressured to get along with people with whom you are not compatible. Regardless of whether role conflict results from organizational policies or from other persons, it can be a significant stressor for some individuals. For example, a study at Goddard Space Flight Center determined that about 67 percent of employees reported some degree of role conflict. The study further found that Goddard employees who experienced more role conflict also experienced lower job satisfaction and higher job-related tension.[4] It is interesting to note that the researchers also found that the greater the power or authority of the people sending the conflicting messages, the greater was the job dissatisfaction produced by role conflict.

An increasingly prevalent type of role conflict occurs when work and nonwork roles interfere with one another. The most common nonwork roles involved in this form of conflict are those of spouse and parent. Balancing the demands of work and family roles is a significant daily task for a growing number of employed adults.[5] Pressure to work late, to take work home, to spend more time traveling, and to frequently relocate in order to advance are a few examples of potential sources of conflict between work and family. When both spouses are employed, added conflict potential exists when one partner's career progress may be negatively impacted by the career progression of the other.

Virtually everyone has experienced work overload at one time or another, and the incident rate is increasing.[6] Overload may be of two types: qualitative or quantitative. Qualitative overload occurs when people feel they lack the ability needed to complete their jobs or that performance standards have been set too high. Quantitative overload, on the other hand, results from having too many things to do or insufficient time to complete a job. As organizations attempt to increase productivity, while decreasing workforce size, quantitative overload increases (as does stress). The New York law firm of Cleary, Gottlieb, Steen, & Hamilton was sued by the father of an associate at the firm. The associate, unable to cope with the workload, committed suicide by jumping off the roof of the firm's building.[7]

From a health standpoint, numerous studies have established that quantitative overload might cause biochemical changes, specifically elevations in blood cholesterol levels. One study examined the relationship of overload, underload, and stress among 1,540 executives. Those executives in the low and high ends of the stress ranges reported more significant medical problems. This study suggests that the relationships among stressors, stress, and disease may be curvilinear. That is, those who are underloaded and those who are overloaded represent two ends of a continuum, each with a significantly elevated number of medical problems.[8] The underload-overload continuum is presented in Figure 16-2. The optimal stress level provides the best balance of challenge, responsibility, and reward. The potential negative effects of overload can be increased when overload is coupled with low ability to control the work demand.[9] Research suggests that when individuals experience high work demands with little or no control over these demands, the physiological changes that occur persist even after the individual has left work.[10]

Perhaps the most pervasive individual stressor of all is the unrelenting pace of change that is part of life today. At no other point in the history of industrialized society have we experienced such rapid change in the world around us. The last third of the 20th century included the advent of such wonders as communications satellites, moon landings, organ transplants, laser technology, nuclear power plants, intercontinental ballistic missiles, supersonic transportation, artificial hearts, and many other space-age developments. The pace of change within organizations has been no less remarkable at the start of the 21st century. Radical restructuring, new technologies, the stunning emergence of dot-com firms, new organizational firms, mergers, acquisitions, downsizings, and renewed emphasis on teams support this commonsense conclusion. On the other hand, many people who experience a great deal of change show absolutely no subsequent health problems. For some reason, these people are strong enough to withstand the negative consequences of large doses of change that others do not.

Why this is so is an intriguing question. One organizational researcher, Suzanne Kobassa, has proposed that individuals who experience high rates of change without consequently suffering health problems might differ in terms of personality from those who do. She refers to the personality characteristic as "hardiness."[11] People with the hardiness personality trait seem to possess three important characteristics. First, they believe that they can control the events they encounter. Second, they are extremely committed to the activities in their lives. Third, they treat change in their lives as a challenge. In a longitudinal study to test the three-characteristic theory of hardiness, managers were studied over a two-year period. It was found that the more managers possessed hardiness characteristics, the smaller the impact of life changes on their personal health. Hardiness appeared to offset, or buffer, the negative impact of change.

Hardiness is proposed as a factor to reduce stress by changing the way stressors are perceived. The hardy person is able to work through and around stressors, while the less hardy person becomes overwhelmed and unable to cope. The hardy respond by coping, attempting to control, and taking on the stressors as a challenge. This type of response typically results in better behavioral, cognitive, and physiological consequences.[12]

Individual stressors abound. Not only can they cause stress but a number of negative consequences as well. As we will see later in the chapter, stress consequences can affect not only health, but a variety of job performance variables as well. Ethics Encounter 16-1 suggests stress may even be related to unethical behavior.

Group and Organizational Stressors

The list of potential group and organizational stressors is a long one. These include group norms, leadership, and the status hierarchy. Each of these can be a stressor for some group members, as can the different types of group conflict. One problem in discussing group and organizational stressors is identifying which are the most important ones. In the paragraphs that follow we will briefly highlight what we feel are the more significant stressors.

FIGURE 16–2   The Underload/Overload Continuum

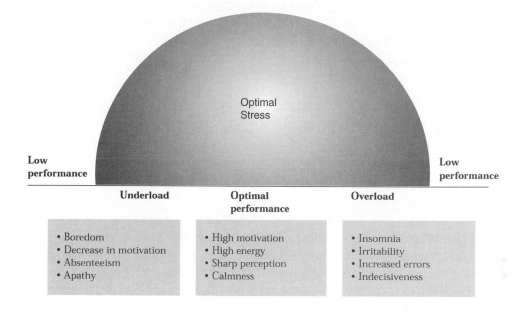

Source: Based in part on an April 5, 1997, Associated Press wire release.

ETHICS ENCOUNTER 16–1

Are Some Unethical Behaviors Stress Related?

Have you ever:

- Called in sick, when you really weren't?

- Lied to a boss, underling, or customer?

- Taken more time for a break or lunch than you should?

- Taken credit for someone else's idea?

- Overstated how much time you spent on a work assignment?

If you answered yes to one or more of these questions, well that makes you like a whole lot of other people. Despite renewed interest in employee and employer ethics in the last several years, dishonesty in the workplace is becoming as common as casual Friday. Nearly half of workers engaged in unethical and/or illegal acts in a recent year, according to a survey completed by the Ethics Officer Association and the Chartered Life Underwriters and Chartered Financial Consultants.

According to the survey results, the high stress atmosphere in many organizations may be to blame. Faced with demands of overtime, balancing work and family, and downsizing-related job insecurity, workers said they feel more stress than they did five years ago, as well as more pressure to act unethically. "Daily pressures are extreme, and it's those pressures that may be driving unethical practices," according to John Driskill, vice president of the society of underwriters and financial consultants.

Participation

Participation refers to the extent that a person's knowledge, opinions, and ideas are included in the decision-making process. It is an important part of working in organizations for some people. Groups and organizations that do not encourage or allow participation will be a source of frustration to those who value it. Likewise, others will be frustrated by the delays often associated with participative decision making. Others may view shared decision making as a threat to the traditional right of a manager to have the final say. Participation will act as a stressor for these people.

Intra and Intergroup Relationships

Poor relationships within and between groups can be a source of stress. Poor relationships may include low trust, lack of cohesion, low supportiveness, and lack of interest in listening to and dealing with the problems that confront a group or group member. Problem relationships can lead to communication breakdowns and low job satisfaction, further increasing the likelihood of stress.

Organizational Politics

High levels of political behavior in organizations can be a source of stress for many employees. Office politics are consistently cited as a primary stressor in organizations. Political activity, game playing, and power struggles can create friction, heighten dysfunctional competition between individuals and groups, and increase stress.

Friction, stress, and a hard-driving style are exemplified by the actions of Al Dunlap, a designated turnaround chief executive officer. Dunlap was given credit for turning around troubled American Can, Crown Zellenbach, and Scott Paper. On the other hand, he was a failure at Sunbeam and was eventually fired.[13] He had a reputation of being political, gruff, and demeaning. One of the first meetings at Sunbeam was described as follows: "It was like a dog barking at you for hours. He just yelled, ranted, and raved. He was condescending, belligerent, and disrespectful."[14] Many managers left Sunbeam because it became a highly politicized and stressful place to work. Al Dunlap was himself a stressor for many of the managers who wouldn't tolerate his behavior and style.

Organizational Culture

Like individuals, organizations have distinct personalities. The personality of an organization is shaped largely by its top executives. A tyrannical and autocratic executive team is able to create a culture that is filled with fear. Ernest Gallo is credited with being the stress producer at Gallo Winery because of the culture he has established with his hard-driving style, unrelenting insistence on superior performance, and low tolerance for failure.[15]

Lack of Performance Feedback

Most people want to know how they are doing, and how management views their work. All too often, however, meaningful performance evaluation information is lacking. Or, the information is provided in a highly authoritarian or critical manner. Performance feedback information must be provided, and if it is to be provided in a way that minimizes stress, it must take place in an open two-way communication system.

Inadequate Career Development Opportunities

Career development opportunity stressors are those aspects of the organizational environment that influence a person's perception of the quality of his or her career progress. Career variables may serve as stressors when they become sources of concern, anxiety, or frustration. This can happen if an employee is concerned about real or imagined obsolescence, feels that promotion progress is inadequate, or is generally dissatisfied with the match between career aspirations and the current position.

Downsizing

Downsizing is primarily associated with the reduction of human resources by layoffs, attrition, redeployment, or early retirement.[16] As some organizations strive to become "lean and mean," increasing numbers of employees are either downsized or fear being downsized. In either case, it is a potent stressor. It can have negative effects for both individuals and organizations. Studies have shown, for example, that disability claims can increase as much as 70 percent in companies that have recently downsized.[17] This increase comes both from employees who have been dismissed as well as from those who remained. That is probably why many companies have followed the lead of ReliaStar Bankers Security Life Insurance Co., who established a program to help employees cope with the stress of reorganizations and layoffs.

Nonwork stressors are those caused by factors outside the organization. Although, the emphasis in the chapter is on work, nonwork stressors should not be ignored. Raising children, caring for elders, volunteering in the community, taking college courses, and balancing family and work life are stressful situations for numerous people. The stress produced outside of work is likely to impact a person's work, behavior in general, and performance. The distinction between work and nonwork is blurred, overlaps, and is significant in any discussion or analysis of stress.

MANAGEMENT POINTER 16–1

Recognizing the Warning Signs of Stress in Employees

As a manager you should be alert to warning signs of stress in your subordinates. One indicator is change in behavior. Some of the more common changes include:

1. A normally punctual employee develops a pattern of tardiness (or a pattern of absences in a usually reliable worker).
2. A normally gregarious employee becomes withdrawn (or, less typically, a loner suddenly becomes a social butterfly).
3. An employee whose work is normally neat and demonstrates attention to detail submits messy, incomplete, or sloppy work.
4. A good decision maker suddenly starts making bad decisions (or seems to be unable to make decisions).
5. An easygoing employee who gets along well with others becomes irritable and discourteous.
6. A normally well groomed employee neglects his or her appearance.

Stress Outcomes

The effects of stress are many and varied. Some effects, of course, are positive, such as self-motivation and stimulation to satisfy individual goals and objectives. Nonetheless, many stress consequences are disruptive, counterproductive, and even potentially dangerous. Additionally, as was discussed earlier (see Figure 16-2), there are consequences associated with too little stress as well as too much.

Not all individuals will experience the same outcomes. Research suggests, for example, that one of many factors influencing stress outcomes is type of employment. In one study, conducted at the Institute for Social Research at the University of Michigan, a sample of 2,010 employees was chosen from 23 occupations to examine the relationship between stress and stress consequences. The occupations were combined into four specific groups—blue-collar workers (skilled and unskilled) and white-collar workers (professional and nonprofessional).

Blue-collar workers reported the highest subjective effects, including job dissatisfaction; white-collar workers, the lowest. The unskilled workers reported the most boredom and apathy with their job conditions. They specifically identified a number of major stressors that created their psychological state: underutilization of skills and abilities, poor fit of the job with respect to desired amounts of responsibility, lack of participation, and ambiguity about the future. Skilled blue-collar workers shared some of these stressors and consequences with their unskilled counterparts, but not all; they reported above-average utilization of their skills and abilities but had less responsibility and more ambiguity. White-collar professionals reported the fewest negative consequences. In all groups, however, there were indications that job performance was affected.[18]

In examining stress consequences, the distinction in our model between organizational and individual consequences is somewhat arbitrary. For example, a decrement in job performance due to stress is clearly an individual consequence; it is the individual's performance that is being affected. Just as clearly, however, the organization experiences important consequences from stress-related performance decrements.

Individual Outcomes

The emergence or evolution of stress outcomes takes time to identify or pinpoint. Eventually, evidence is available upon which to reach a number of conclusions. For example, a promoted employee develops an uncharacteristic pattern of Friday and Monday absence. A salesperson begins to lose repeat business; nonrenewing customers complain that he has become inattentive and curt in his dealings with them. A formerly conscientious nurse forgets to administer medications, with potentially serious patient consequences. An assembly worker experiences a significant increase in the percentage of her production rejected by the quality-control unit. A software designer displays sudden, apparently unprovoked outbursts of anger. Each of these individuals is experiencing the effects, or consequences, of excessive stress.

Stress can produce psychological consequences. These would include anxiety, frustration, apathy, lowered self-esteem, aggression, and depression. With respect to depression, a comprehensive survey of American workers concluded that a third of them experienced job stress-related depression.[19] Nor are such consequences restricted to American workers, as International Encounter 16-1 demonstrates.

There is a stigma associated with depression.[20] Part of the stigma is that most people lack an understanding of depression and its frequency. Unfortunately most managers are not aware of these facts:

- According to the National Mental Health Association, the cost of depression is $43 billion a year in medical bills, lost productivity, and absenteeism.[21]

- Depression is the seventh most common cause of adult deaths.[22]

- Depression is difficult to detect, especially within the present health care system.[23]

The Diagnostic and Statistical Manual of Mental Disorders (DSM-IV) is the diagnostic tool used to detect depression. The DSM-IV indicates that the diagnosis of depression requires the presence of either a depressed mood or diminished interest in all or most activities, marked psychomotor retardation, significant appetite or weight change, changes in sleep, fatigue, or loss of energy, problems thinking or concentrating, feelings of worthlessness, excessive feelings of guilt, or thoughts of suicide or death. These signs must be persistent over the course of two weeks.

Managerial understanding of these symptoms can help the organization especially when the manager requests professional counselors to intervene. Managers are not skilled enough to intervene. Mild and moderate cases of depression can be treated over a period of time. It would be unwise for managers to ignore depression or to attempt to counsel workers suspected of being depressed. Being aware of depression symptoms and the situations that precipitate it is the first line of intervention. Unfortunately, the stigma of depression results in a lack of understanding of its pervasiveness, costs, and treatment possibilities.[24]

Some outcomes may be cognitive. Cognitive outcomes would include poor concentration, inability to make sound decisions or any decisions at all, mental blocks, and decreased attention spans. Other effects may be behavioral. Such manifestations as accident proneness, impulsive behavior, alcohol and drug abuse, and explosive temper are examples. Finally, physiological consequences could include increased heart rate, elevated blood pressure, sweating, hot and cold flashes, increased blood glucose levels, and elevated stomach acid production.

Among the individual outcomes of stress, those classified as physiological are perhaps the most dysfunctional because they can in turn contribute to physical illness. One of the more significant of the physiological consequences and illness relationships is that of coronary heart disease (CHD). Although virtually unknown in the industrialized world a century ago, CHD now accounts for almost two out of every five deaths in the United States. Traditional risk factors such as obesity, smoking, heredity, and high cholesterol can account for no more than about 25 percent of the incidence of CHD. There is growing medical opinion that job and life stress may be a major contributor to the remaining 75 percent.[25] Several studies have found, for example, a relationship between changes in blood pressure and job stress.[26]

INTERNATIONAL ENCOUNTER 16–1

Stress and Death in Japan

Have you ever felt, or heard someone else express the feeling, "This job is going to kill me!" Chances are you—or the person you heard—didn't literally believe that. If you were a Japanese worker, however, you might be very serious. Polls indicate that over 40 percent of Japanese workers aged 30 to 60 believe they will die from the stress of overwork, what the Japanese call Karoshi. The victims of Karoshi are known in their companies as moretsu shain (fanatical workers) and yoi kigyo senshi (good corporate soldiers).

In spite of recent revisions of the Japanese labor standard law that reduced the length of the average work week, Japanese workers spend on average about six weeks (or about 250 hours per year) more on the job than most Americans. A Japanese Health Ministry report called Karoshi the second leading cause of death among workers (the first is cancer). Fierce competition among employees, as well as a strong sense of responsibility to their companies, lead many workers to stay at the office well into the night. When they do go home they are tense and anxious because they feel that they should really be back at work. Some workers deal with the pressure by disappearing. As many as 10,000 men disappear each year, choosing to drop out rather than face the pressure of their jobs.

There are signs, however, that things are changing. The government has funded a multimillion dollar study of Karoshi. Some of Japan's leading firms, such as Sony Corporation, have begun to require employees to take vacations whether they want to or not. Also, more companies are closing on Saturday, part of a national drive toward a five-day work week. Traditions die hard in Japan, however, and no one believes fear of Karoshi will disappear any time soon.

Some stress outcomes combine effects from several of the categories of consequences described above. Consider, for example, the following two scenarios:

> Bob is a teacher in an inner-city high school. He barely remembers the time when he could not wait for the start of each school day; now he cannot wait until each day ends. As much as he could use the money, he quit teaching optional summer school three summers ago. He needs that break to recharge his batteries, which seem to run down earlier with each passing school year. Many of his students are moody, turned off to society, and abusive to others. Bob is beginning to realize that he himself is becoming moody, turned off to society, and abusive to others.

> Paula works as an air traffic controller in the second-busiest airport in the country. Every day, the lives of literally thousands of people depend on how well she does her job. Near misses are an everyday occurrence; avoiding disasters requires quick thinking and a cool head. At 31 years of age, Paula is the third oldest controller in the tower. She knows there are few controllers over the age of 40, and she is certain she will never be one. To make matters worse, she is in the final stages of a divorce. Paula was told after her last physical that she had developed a stomach ulcer. She is thinking of going into the nursery business with her sister; having responsibility for the well-being of shrubs and trees, rather than people, is very attractive to her.

Bob and Paula are both experiencing job burnout. Burnout is a psychological process, brought about by unrelieved work stress, that results in emotional exhaustion, depersonalization, and feelings of decreased accomplishment.[27] Figure 16-3 displays some of the indicators of these three burnout outcomes. Burnout tends to be a particular problem among people whose jobs require extensive contact with and/or responsibility for other people. Indeed, much of the research that has been conducted on burnout has centered on the so-called helping professions: teachers, nurses, physicians, social workers, therapists, police, and parole officers.[28] Organizational Encounter 16-1 presents some of the myths that surround the burnout concept.

FIGURE 16–3   **BURNOUT INDICATORS**

Emotional Exhaustion	Depersonalization	Low Personal Accomplishment
Feel drained by work	Have become calloused by job	Cannot deal with problems effectively
Feel fatigued in the morning	Treat others like objects	Do not have a positive influence on others
Frustrated	Do not care what happens to other people	Cannot understand others' problems or identify with them
Do not want to work with other people	Feel other people blame you	No longer feel exhilarated by your job

A very important idea implicit in this conceptualization of burnout relates to job involvement. A high degree of involvement in, identification with, or commitment to one's job or profession is a necessary prerequisite for burnout. It is unlikely that one would become exhausted without putting forth a great deal of effort. Thus, the irony of burnout is that those most susceptible are those most committed to their work; all else being equal, lower job commitment equals lower likelihood of burnout. Various individual variables also affect the likelihood of developing burnout. For example, women are more likely to burn out than men, younger employees are more susceptible than older ones (particularly beyond age 50), and unmarried workers are more likely to burn out than married ones.

Organizations contribute to employee job burnout in a variety of ways. Researchers identify four factors that are particularly important contributors to burnout: high levels of work overload, dead-end jobs, excessive red tape and paperwork, and poor communication and feedback, particularly regarding job performance. In addition, factors that have been identified in at least one research study as contributing to burnout include role conflict and ambiguity, difficult interpersonal relationships, and reward systems that are not contingent upon performance.[29]

Organizational Consequences

As illustrated in Figure 16-1 a number of the behavioral, cognitive, and physiological outcomes that are individually linked also have organizational consequences. While the organizational consequences of stress are many and varied, they share one common feature: stress costs organizations money. Although precise figures are lacking, based on a variety of estimates and projections from government, industry, and health groups, we place the costs of stress at approximately $150 billion annually. This estimate, which probably is conservative (some estimates are as high as $300 billion annually),[30] attempts to take into account the dollar effects of reductions in operating effectiveness resulting from stress. The effects include poorer decision making and decreases in creativity. The huge figure also reflects the costs associated with mental and physical health problems arising from stress conditions, including hospital and medical costs, lost work time, turnover, sabotage, and a host of other variables that may contribute to stress costs. When you consider that employers pay approximately 80 percent of all private health insurance premiums, and that workers' compensation laws increasingly include provisions for awarding benefits for injuries stemming from stress in the workplace, it is clear that organizational consequences are significant.

Excessive stress increases job dissatisfaction. Job dissatisfaction can be associated with a number of dysfunctional outcomes, including increased turnover and absenteeism, and reduced job performance. If productivity is reduced just three percent, for example, an organization employing 1,000 people would need to hire an additional 30 employees to compensate for that lost productivity. If annual employee costs are $40,000

ORGANIZATIONAL ENCOUNTER 16-1

Myths and Burnout

A study reported in the Wall Street Journal involved interviewing dozens of managers in an attempt to understand managerial behavior that seems to push employees over the edge into job burnout. In the process, three myths were uncovered that organizations need to dispel if they are to reduce incidents of burnout amoung their staff.

Myth One: When a client says jump, the only answer is "How high?"

Lawyers, accountants, and management consultants are particularly vulnerable to believing this myth even when it appears to result in high levels of burnout and turnover within their staffs. However, the study reported that a few professional firms are taking steps to integrate personal needs and concerns with the work lives of their employees. For example, Deloitte & Touche has implemented a policy that limits their employees' travel time. It is no longer company policy to for employees to spend all five working days of the week at clients' offices. At a maximum, employees are to spend only three nights (four working days) away from home and work the fifth day in their own offices each week, even when on lengthy assignments. A Deloitte managing director stated, "Most clients recognize that this policy is a good thing." Among other things, it also limits the amount of time clients' employees have to be involved with the work Deloitte is doing for them, thus allowing better control of their own schedules.

Myth Two: Reining in employee's workloads will turn them into slackers.

Managers often behave as though a reduction in work overload will cause productivity to drop. Yet, studies often show the opposite result. Ernst & Young has a committee that monitors its staff accountants' workloads to head off burnout situations. The company says that its policies are raising retention rates and improving client service. A senior manager at Ernst, observed that employees typically won't admit to burning out; thus having some compassionate, objective overview is useful. "About the only time we would find out that someone was suffering from job burnout was during the exit interview, and then it was too late."

Myth Three: If employees are working themselves into the ground, it's their own fault.

Although this attribution may sometimes be true for some people, it is far from true for most. At the International Food Policy Research Institute, a nonprofit research organization in Washington D.C., consultants discovered that 'crisis mentality' was driving scientists and support staff to work incredibly long hours. Management of the institute assumed that either 1) employees wanted to work these hours or 2) employees were managing their time poorly. Neither of these assumptions was valid. Rather a shift in research focus coupled with an increased emphasis on using research teams allied with groups from other agencies and organizations had created an inefficient pattern of work for many people. Meetings, phone calls, and other forms of coordinated activity were eating up the workday, driving more productive research and writing into the evening hours. Once the institute's management became aware of the inefficient patterns of work behavior, major changes were made in workplace routine. The redesign of activities reduced the amount of time people were having to work, which in turn reduced stress and increased productivity. In this case, management initially viewed the time problems as failures of individuals when, the fact, it was a failure of the organization.

SOURCE: Adapted from Sue Schellenberger, "The Myths That Make Managers Push Staff to the Edge of Burnout," *Wall Street Journal*, March 17, 1999. B1.

per employee including wages and benefits, stress is costing the company $1.2 million just to replace lost productivity. This doesn't include costs associated with recruitment and training. Nor does it consider that decreases in quality of performance may be more costly for an organization than quantity decreases. Customer dissatisfaction with lower-quality goods or services can have significant effects on an organization's growth and profitability.

Further examples of organizational costs associated with stress include:

- 60 to 80 percent of worksite accidents are the result of stress.[31]

- Stressed workers smoke more, eat less well, have more problems with alcohol and drugs, have more family problems, and have more problems with co-workers.[32]

- As many as 75 to 90 percent of visits to physicians are stress related, costing industry over $200 billion a year.[33]

- Costs associated with stress may reduce U.S. industry profits by 10 percent.[34]

- Stress explains over 20 percent of the total number of health care claims and 16 percent of the costs.[35]

Estimates and projections such as these (including our own estimate of annual stress-related costs) should be treated cautiously. There are simply too many variables to measure costs precisely. There is no doubt however, that the consequences of excessive stress are significant in both individual and organizational terms.

STRESS MODERATORS

Stressors evoke different responses from different people. Some people are better able to cope with a stressor than others. They can adapt their behavior in such a way as to meet the stressor head-on. On the other hand, some people are predisposed to stress; that is, they are not able to adapt to the stressor.

The model presented in Figure 16-1 suggests that various factors can moderate the relationship between stressor, stress, and consequences. A moderator is a condition, behavior, or characteristic that qualifies the relationship between two variables. The effect may be to intensify or weaken the relationship. The relationship between the number of gallons of gasoline used and total miles driven, for example, is moderated by driving speed. At very low and very high speeds, gas mileage declines; at intermediate speeds, mileage increases. Thus, driving speed affects the relationship between gasoline used and miles driven.

Many conditions, behaviors, and characteristics may act as **stress moderators**, including such variables as age, gender, and the hardiness construct discussed earlier in the chapter. In this section, we will briefly examine three representative types of moderators: (1) personality, (2) Type A behavior, and (3) social support.

Personality

The term personality refers to a relatively stable set of characteristics, temperaments, and tendencies that shape the similarities and differences in people's behavior. The number of aspects of personality that could serve as stress moderators is quite large. We will confine our attention to these aspects of personality: the Big Five Model, locus of control, and self-efficacy.

The Big Five Model of personality is made up of five dimensions: extroversion, emotional stability, agreeableness, conscientiousness, and openness to experience. Of these, emotional stability is most clearly related to stress. Those high on this dimension are most likely to experience positive moods and feel good about themselves and their jobs. While they certainly experience stress, they are less likely to be overwhelmed by it and are in a better position to recover from it. To a somewhat lesser degree, those high on extroversion are also more predisposed to experience positive emotional states. Because they are sociable and friendly, they are more likely to have a wider network of friends than their introverted counterparts; consequently, they have more resources to draw upon in times of distress.

If you are low on agreeableness you have a tendency to be antagonistic, unsympathetic, even rude, toward others. You are also probably somewhat mistrusting of others. These attributes increase the likelihood you will find other people to be a source of stress, and since others are more likely to find interacting with you stressful as well, an interpersonal relationship environment full of stressful situations is created. Conscientiousness is the big five dimension most consistently related to job performance and success. To the extent that good performance leads to satisfaction and other rewards, those high on conscientiousness are less likely to experience stress with respect to these aspects of their jobs. Those low on this dimension, however, are more likely to be poorer performers, receive fewer rewards and generally be less successful in their careers, not a recipe for low stress levels! Finally, those high on openness to experience are better prepared to deal with stressors associated with change because they are more likely to view change as a challenge, rather than a threat.

Beliefs people have about where control over their lives resides relates to locus of control. "Internals" perceive themselves to be in control of the events that shape their lives to a greater extent than "externals," who feel that control is external to them. The traditional assumption is that if people feel they have control in a situation, they will be less likely to assess the situation as threatening or stress causing.

While this assumption may be valid in a general sense, the relationship between locus of control and stress is not always that straightforward. A more inclusive depiction suggests that internals are more likely to experience stress when they are unable to exercise the control they believe they should, while externals will be threatened (and consequently stressed) in situations where they can exercise some degree of control over what is happening. Viewed from this perspective, the locus of control-stress relationship is a function of personal beliefs and environmental realities: when a person's beliefs about where control resides are congruent with the actual locus of control in a given situation, there is less likelihood stress will result. When beliefs and reality are not the same, the likelihood of experiencing stress increases.

Self-efficacy is another personality attribute that is an important moderator variable. Individuals with high levels of self-efficacy feel confident in their abilities and in their job performance. They are more likely to perceive potential stressors as challenges and opportunities, rather than threats and problems. Those with low levels of self-efficacy, on the other hand, are less confident in their abilities and more likely to assume they will fail. Since they believe they will fail, they will likely exert less effort, and thereby ensuring their assessment of their abilities is correct! Even when a situation is perceived as threatening, those with high self-efficacy are more likely to deal with the threat quickly, effectively, and with fewer negative outcomes.

The relationship between self-efficacy and stress is not confined to one part of the stress process. Self-efficacy may moderate the process from the perception of stressors (workers with low self-efficacy are more likely to experience work overload, for example) to consequences (low self-efficacy has been associated with increased incidence of coronary heart disease risk, for example). Thus, as a moderator, self-efficacy plays a rather pervasive role.

Type A Behavior Pattern

In the 1950s, two medical cardiologists and researchers, Meyer Friedman and Ray Rosenman, discovered what they called the Type A behavior pattern (TABP).[36] They searched the medical literature and found that traditional coronary risk factors such as dietary cholesterol, blood pressure, and heredity could not totally explain or predict coronary heart disease (CHD). Coronary heart disease is the term given to cardiovascular diseases that are characterized by an inadequate supply of oxygen to the heart. Other factors seemed to the two researchers to be playing a major role in CHD. Through interviews with and observation of patients, they began to uncover a pattern of behavior or traits. They eventually called this the Type A behavior pattern (TABP).

The person with TABP has these characteristics:

- Chronically struggles to get as many things done as possible in the shortest time period.

- Is aggressive, ambitious, competitive, and forceful.

- Speaks explosively, rushes others to finish what they are saying.

- Is impatient, hates to wait, considers waiting a waste of precious time.

- Is preoccupied with deadlines and is work-oriented.

- Is always in a struggle with people, things, events.

The converse, Type B individual, mainly is free of the TABP characteristics and generally feels no pressing conflict with either time or persons. The Type B may have considerable drive, wants to accomplish things, and works hard, but the Type B has a confident style that allows him or her to work at a steady pace and not to race against the clock. The Type A has been likened to a racehorse; the Type B, to a turtle.

More recent research into TABP suggests that not all aspects of the behavior pattern are equally associated with negative consequences. Specifically, hostility has been identified as being the TABP subcomponent most predictive of the development of coronary heart disease among Type As.[37] Nor is CHD the only negative outcome. TABP has been associated with a number of health related consequences including, ulcers, insomnia, and depression.[38] As researchers learn more about the individual components that comprise Type A behavior, further refinements in our understanding of this moderator can be expected.

Social Support

Both the quantity and quality of the social relationships individuals have with others appear to have a potentially important effect on the amount of stress they experience and on the likelihood that stress will have adverse effects on their mental and physical health. Social support can be defined as the comfort, assistance, or information one receives through formal or informal contacts with individuals or groups. A number of studies have linked social support with aspects of health, illness, and stress.[39]

Social support may take the form of emotional support (expressing concern, indicating trust, boosting esteem, listening); appraisal support (providing feedback and affirmation); or informational support (giving advice, making suggestions, providing direction). People who can serve as sources of social support at work include supervisors, co-workers, subordinates, and customers or other nonorganizational members with whom an employee might have contact. Nonwork support sources include family members (immediate and extended), friends, neighbors, care-givers (ministers, for example), health professionals (physicians, psychologists, counselors), and self-help groups (Alcoholics Anonymous, Weight Watchers).

A co-worker listening to a friend who failed to receive a desired promotion, a group of recently laid-off workers helping each other find new employment, or an experienced employee helping a trainee learn a job are all examples of providing support. Social support is effective as a stress moderator because it buffers the negative impact of stressors by providing a degree of predictability, purpose, and hope in upsetting and threatening situations. Most everyone has experienced feeling "better" (calmer, less anxious, or concerned) after having talked about a problem with a spouse, friend, or co-worker. Similarly, most everyone has provided support to someone else that has had positive effects for that person. Thus, virtually all of us know from first-hand experience the moderating role support can play.

A number of studies reinforce what we know to be true for our own experiences. Social support has been shown to reduce stress among employed individuals ranging from unskilled workers to highly trained professionals; it is consistently cited as an effective stress coping technique, and it has been associated with fewer health complaints experienced during periods of high stress.[40]

MANAGEMENT POINTER 16-2

Social support

Developing Social Support
As a manager, there are actions you can take to help create a supportive work environment. These include:
1.   Set an example by being a source of support for others, particularly subordinates.
2.   Encourage open communication and maximum exchange of information.
3.   Make certain you provide subordinates with timely performance feedback, presented in an encouraging, nonthreatening manner.
4.   Provide for mentoring of the less experienced by more senior members of the work group.
5.   Work to maintain and increase work group cohesion this).

STRESS PREVENTION AND MANAGEMENT

An astute manager never ignores a turnover or absenteeism problem, workplace drug abuse, a decline in performance, hostile and belligerent employees, reduced quality of production, or any other sign that the organization's performance goals are not being met. The effective manager, in fact, views these occurrences as symptoms and looks beyond them to identify and correct the underlying causes. Yet most managers today likely will search for traditional causes such as poor training, defective equipment, or inadequate instructions regarding what needs to be done. In all likelihood, stress will not be on the list of possible problems. Thus, the very first step in any attempt to deal with stress so that it remains within tolerable limits is recognition that it exists. Once that is accomplished, a variety of approaches and programs for preventing and managing organizational stress are available.

Figure 16-4 presents how organizational stress management programs can be targeted. Programs are targeted to (1) identify and modify work stressors, (2) engage employees in modifying and understanding of stress and its impact, and (3) provide employees support to cope with the negative impact of stress. In a rapidly changing work environment this type of targeting is difficult to accomplish. However a trained, educated, and knowledgeable workforce can make modifications with the help of management in how work is performed. Some of the targeted, corrective programs include:

- Training programs for managing and coping with stress

- Redesigning work to minimize stressors

- Changes in management style to one of more support and coaching to help workers achieve their goals

- More flexible work hours and attention paid to work/life balance with regard to child and elder care

- Better communication and team-building practices

- Better feedback on worker performance and management expectation

These and other efforts are targeted to prevent and/or manage stress. The potential for success of any prevention or management of stress program is good if there is a true commitment to understanding how stressors, stress, and outcomes are linked.

There is a very important distinction between preventing stress and managing it. Stress prevention focuses on controlling or eliminating stressors that might provoke the stress response. Stress management suggests procedures for helping people cope effectively with or reduce stress already being experienced. In this concluding section of the chapter we will examine organizational programs and individual approaches to stress prevention and management, with the emphasis on management. First, however, we will look at a way of thinking about organizational stress prevention.

Maximizing Person–Environment Fit

In defining stress earlier in the chapter, we emphasized that stress is the consequence of the interaction between an environmental stimulus (a stressor) and the individual's response. From this perspective, stress may be viewed as a consequence of the relationship between the individual and the work environment. While there are many ways of thinking about individual–organizational relationships and stress, the concept of person–environment fit is the most widely used.[41]

A person–environment fit (P–E fit) approach generally focuses on two dimensions of fit.[42] One is the extent to which work provides formal and informal rewards that meet or match (fit) the person's needs. Misfit on this dimension results in stress. For example, a job may provide too little job security, insufficient compensation and reward for the effort expended, or inadequate recognition to meet the individual's needs or preferences. The second type of fit deals with the extent to which the employee's skills, abilities, and experience match the demands and requirements of the employer. To the extent that the individual's talents are insufficient for or underutilized by job requirements, stress results. By improving the quality of, or maximizing, the fit between the employee and the organizational environment, potential stressors are eliminated and stress is prevented. Violations of the psychological contract represent breakdowns in P–E fit.

Figure 16–4   **Organizational Stress Management Program Targets**

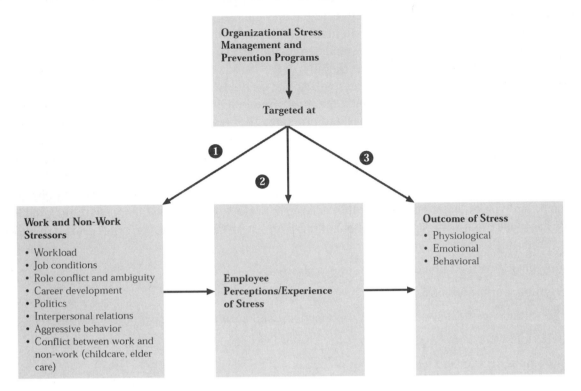

There are numerous strategies for maximizing P–E fit. Ideally, the process begins before an individual even joins the organization. Employee recruitment programs which provide realistic job previews help potential employees determine whether the reality of the job matches their needs and expectations. Selection programs that are effective in ensuring that potential employees possess the requisite skills, knowledge, experience, and abilities for the job are key elements in maximizing fit.

Job skills and knowledge are not the only important factors to consider in employee selection, however. Fit can be maximized by closely linking personal predispositions to relevant aspects of the work environment as well. For example, as was suggested earlier, individuals with a low tolerance for ambiguity who find themselves in jobs or organizational environments in which there is little structure will very likely experience stress. There are many other examples: an individual who is by nature authoritarian will experience stress in a participative organization; those who value intrinsic satisfaction will be frustrated by an environment that provides only extrinsic rewards; those wishing autonomy will be distressed by tight controls; individuals with a high need for performance feedback will be stressed by supervisors who never communicate performance information.

Once in the organization, a critical variable in maximizing fit and preventing stress is effective socialization. Socialization is the process by which the individual learns and internalizes the values, expected behaviors, and social knowledge that are important for becoming an effective organizational member.

A number of other organizational activities and programs can be helpful in maintaining good fit. For example, effective job design and ongoing redesign efforts have a critical role to play in maximizing fit. So do organizational reward systems, communication processes, effective leadership, and a variety of other variables addressed in previous or coming chapters. All of these activities can serve to eliminate or defuse potential stressors, and thus serve to prevent organizational stress.

Organizational Stress Prevention and Management Programs

In addition to the variety of activities that may be undertaken to improve person–environment fit, an increasing number of organizations have developed very specific stress prevention and/or management programs. Some of these programs focus on a specific issue or problem, such as alcohol or drug abuse, career counseling, job relocation, or burnout. The United States Postal Service, for example, has developed a workplace violence prevention program. This program, the most comprehensive one in existence, represents an attempt to reduce the employee-initiated violence that characterized the service in the past.[43]

Still other programs may target a specific group within the organization. An example is the Resident Assistance Program in place at Baylor College of Medicine. This program was designed to help medical residents cope successfully with the multitude of stressors they encounter.[44] Some programs may focus on a particular technique, such as developing relaxation skills. (For an example of a somewhat unusual focus, see Encounter 16-3). Others are more general in nature, using a variety of approaches and geared to a cross-section of employees, such as the Employee Assistance Program at B.F. Goodrich, the Coors Brewing Company Wellness Program, and the Emotional Health Program at Equitable Life. Two specific types of organizational programs have become particularly popular during the last two decades: employee assistance programs and wellness programs.

Employee Assistance Programs (EAPs)

Originally conceived as alcohol abuse programs, most current **employee assistance programs** (EAPs) are *designed to deal with a wide range of stress-related problems, both work and nonwork related, including behavioral and emotional difficulties, substance abuse, family and marital discord, and other personal problems.* B.F. Goodrich, IBM, Xerox, and Caterpillar are examples of companies with such programs. EAPs tend to be based on the traditional medical approach to treatment. General program elements include:

- **Diagnosis**: Employee with a problem asks for help; EAP staff attempts to diagnose the problem.

- **Treatment**: Counseling or supportive therapy is provided. If in-house EAP staff are unable to help, employee may be referred to appropriate community-based professionals.

- **Screening**: Periodic examination of employees in highly stressful jobs is provided to detect early indications of problems.

- **Prevention**: Education and persuasion are used to convince employees at high risk that something must be done to assist them in effectively coping with stress.

An increasing number of employers believe that good health among employees is good for the organization. Blue Cross/Blue Shield determined that every dollar spent on the psychological care of employees with breast cancer saved $2.50 to $5.10 in overall medical expenses. The public school system of Orange County, Florida, found that the cost of medical claims dropped by 66 percent over five years for employees who used the EAP. At the end of five years, the same employees were taking 36 percent fewer sick leaves. At McDonnell-Douglas (now called Boeing) workers treated for alcohol and drug problems missed 44 percent fewer days of work after the EAP was set up.[45]

EAPs may be internal company-run programs or external efforts in which the organization contracts with a private firm to provide services to company employees. The previously cited Emotional Health Program at Equitable Life is typical of such programs. It is concerned with prevention, treatment, and referral of employees. Staffed with a clinical psychologist, a physician, a psychology intern, and a counselor, it focuses on individual intervention. Offered are biofeedback, relaxation training, and counseling. When appropriate, referrals are made to external health practitioners and hospitals.

Crucial to the success of any EAP is trust. Employees must trust that (1) the program can and will provide real help, (2) confidentiality will be maintained, and (3) use of the program carries no negative implications for job security or future advancement. If employees do not trust the program or company management, they will not participate. EAPs with no customers cannot have a positive effect on stress prevention and management.

Wellness Programs

Wellness programs, sometimes called Health Promotion Programs, *focus on the employee's overall physical and mental health.* Simply stated, any activity an organization engages in that is designed to identify and assist in preventing or correcting specific health problems, health hazards, or negative health habits can be thought of as wellness-related. This includes not only disease identification but lifestyle modification as well. Among the most prevalent examples of such programs are those emphasizing hypertension identification and control, smoking cessation, physical fitness and exercise, nutrition and diet control, and job and personal stress management.

It might appear strange that we would include wellness programs in a discussion of stress management. There are several reasons we do. First, stress prevention and management is a vital part of wellness, and, as we have already noted, it is frequently a component of wellness programs. Second, many of the concerns of wellness programs are at least partially stress related. Stress has been cited as the greatest cause of poor health habits,[46] and poor health habits are what wellness programs attempt to change. Third, a major reason organizations are interested in stress management is that it contributes to healthier, more productive, and more effective employees, and consequently to healthier, more productive, and more effective organizations. Corporate wellness programs simply extend these payoffs. Fourth, it is impossible to divorce the topic of stress from health. In a sense, wellness programs represent a broad-based, contemporary extension of stress programs; their focus is concern for employee health and quality-of-life issues.

Examples of well-established wellness programs (all of which include a stress reduction component) include Mass Mutual's Wellness Partnership, 3M's Lifestyle 2000 program, Warner-Lambert's LifeWise program, and Control Data's StayWell program. StayWell has been so successful that it is now marketed to other companies. Wellness programs, however, are not restricted to large companies like those just cited. Over 60 percent of firms with fewer than 250 employees provide some form of wellness program for their workers.[47]

Roche Pharmaceutical of Nutley, New Jersey, found that it spent only 3 percent of medical benefit dollars on preventive health measures. This small expenditure was in spite of the fact that 39 percent of the health claims submitted were the result of preventable conditions. Roche management concluded that focusing on prevention would mean healthier, more productive, less stressed, more creative, and less absent employees. Roche named its wellness program "Choosing Health."[48]

Choosing Health starts at the individual level by assessing employee health risks via a 76-item survey. The form takes 15 minutes to complete. A health profile is provided and sent directly to the employee's home. All employee responses and profiles are confidential and not released to a third party. The company also provides on-site screening for such ailments as high blood pressure, high cholesterol, and breast and skin cancers. Roche's Human Resource Management (HRM) group receives only aggregated data showing risks within the general population. HRM then patterns preventive health programs after the health risks and education needs of employees as a group. Almost 100 percent of Roche employees participate in Choosing Health.

The Roche program provides a $100 incentive for completing 100 sessions at a fitness facility or in a group exercise program. In the second year of the program, 23 percent of Choosing Health participants have reduced their health risks.

A part of Choosing Health is an evaluation process to evaluate the impact of the program. In two years, the average lifestyle score has increased from 63 to 68 (100 is the optimal score). Roche is constantly working to align prevention, intervention, employee health, and productivity.

Simply offering an EAP or wellness program does not guarantee positive results for either employers or the sponsoring organization. While many factors determine how successful any particular program will be, a number of recommendations, if followed, will increase the likelihood of achieving beneficial outcomes. Among the more important are:

1. Top-management support, including both philosophical support and support in terms of staff and facilities, is necessary.

2. Unions should support the program and participate in it where appropriate. This can be particularly difficult to accomplish. Many unions take the position that instead of helping employees deal with stress, management should focus on eliminating those conditions that contribute to the stress in the first place.

3. The greatest payoff from stress prevention and management comes not from one-shot activities, but from ongoing and sustained effort; thus, long-term commitment is essential.

4. Extensive and continuing employee involvement would include involvement not only in the initial planning but in implementation and maintenance as well. This is one of the most critical factors for ensuring representative employee participation.

5. Clearly stated objectives lay a solid foundation for the program. Programs with no or poorly defined objectives are not likely to be effective or to achieve sufficient participation to make them worthwhile.

6. Employees must be able to participate freely, without either pressure or stigma.

7. Confidentiality must be strictly adhered to. Employees must have no concerns that participation will in any way affect their standing in the organization.

ORGANIZATIONAL ENCOUNTER 16-2
Dealing with Stress Can Be a Laughing Matter

While passengers were preparing to board a Southwest Airlines flight, a Southwest customer service agent came over the public address system to announce, "Southwest Airlines would like to congratulate one of our first-time fliers who is celebrating his eighty-ninth birthday. As you board, be sure to stick your head into the cockpit and say happy birthday to your pilot, Captain John Smith."

The above true anecdote typifies the culture at Southwest Airlines, where they firmly believe that if employees are having fun they are going to do their jobs better and be less likely to experience dissatisfaction, stress, and burnout. Increasingly, companies are turning to humor as a way of improving employee morale and combating stress. A growing number of "humor consultants" are being hired by companies nationwide to lighten up an overworked and anxious workforce. Research supports the conclusion that humor boosts the human immune system, reduces stress, and helps keep people well. Other research shows decreases in production of stress hormones while people are laughing.

One group of humor consultants is developing a program called Subjective Multidimensional Interactive Laughter Evaluation (SMILE) which will survey humor preferences, coping styles, and help tailor a personalized humor approach to stress reduction. What kind of organization would use such a program, or hire a humor consultant? The answer seems to be companies suffering from low morale, cutbacks, or buyouts. Corporations undergoing downsizing are a major user.

The rationale for these programs is that humor is a set of skills that some people have developed better than others. For those in need of skill development, humor programs can help people increase the tools they have to combat stress.

Source: Based in part on "Firms Use Laughter To Aid Workers," Maggie Jackson, Houston Chronicle, April 23, 1977, pp. 1C, 3C.

Du Pont Corporation has for years been dedicated to health promotion.[49] Cost effectiveness studies at Du Pont indicate that fitness programs work. Du Pont estimates that for every dollar invested in the health promotion program, at least two dollars is received in return. One analysis at Du Pont indicates that the annual company costs per person at risk are as follows:

Smokers	$960
Overweight	$401
Excess alcohol use	$389
High cholesterol	$370
High blood pressure	$343

Du Pont also determined that reducing absenteeism annually by about 6.8 percent would pay for the firm's entire health promotion effort.

Individual Approaches to Stress Prevention and Management

Organization members do not have to—nor should they—rely on formal organizational programs to assist in stress prevention and management. There are many individual approaches to dealing with stressors and stress. To see this, all you have to do is visit any bookstore on-site or online (www.amazon.com, www.fatbrain.com) and look at the self-improvement section. It will be stocked with numerous how-to books for reducing stress. Below, we will briefly examine a few of the more popularly cited and frequently used approaches for individual stress prevention and management. It is not unusual for any of these approaches to be included in the range of options available within an organizational stress management or wellness program. It should also be noted that there is a great deal of variation in the effectiveness of these techniques. What one person finds useful, another may not. There is still a great deal we do not know regarding the effects of individual differences on stress management outcomes.[50]

Cognitive Techniques

The basic rationale for some individual approaches to stress management, known collectively as cognitive techniques, is that a person's response to stressors is mediated by cognitive processes, or thoughts. The underlying assumption of these techniques is that people's thoughts, in the form of expectations, beliefs, and assumptions, are labels they apply to situations, and these labels elicit emotional responses to the situation. Thus, for example, if an individual labels the loss of a promotion a catastrophe, the stress response is to the label, not to the situation.

Cognitive techniques of stress management focus on changing labels or cognitions so that people appraise situations differently. This reappraisal typically centers on removing cognitive distortions such as magnifying (not getting the promotion is the end of the world for me), overgeneralizing (not getting promoted means my career is over; I'll never be promoted in any job, anywhere), and personalization (since I didn't get the promotion it's clear I'm a terrible person). All cognitive techniques have a similar objective: to help people gain more control over their reactions to stressors by modifying their cognitions.

Evaluative research of cognitive techniques to stress management is not extensive, although the studies reported are generally positive. Representative occupational groups where research has indicated positive outcomes with the use of cognitive approaches include nurses, teachers, athletes, and air traffic controllers.[51] The positive research, coupled with the wide range and scope of situations and stressors amenable to such an approach, make cognitive techniques particularly attractive as an individual stress management strategy.

Relaxation Training

The purpose of this approach is to reduce a person's arousal level and bring about a calmer state of affairs, both psychologically and physiologically. Psychologically, successful relaxation results in enhanced feelings of well-being, peacefulness and calm, a clear sense of being in control, and a reduction in tension and anxiety; physiologically, decreases in blood pressure, respiration, and heart rate should take place. Relaxation techniques include breathing exercises; muscle relaxation; autogenic training, which combines elements of muscle relaxation and meditation; and a variety of mental relaxation strategies, including imagery and visualization.

Conditions conducive to achieving relaxed states include a quiet environment, a comfortable physical position, and closed eyes. Simply taking a few moments of "mental rest" from job activities can be an effective relaxation activity. Short, more frequent breaks of this sort are more relaxing than fewer, longer breaks.[52]

Meditation

Many of the meditative forms that have achieved some degree of popularity in this country are derivatives of Eastern philosophies. Included in this category are Zen Meditation and Nam Sumran, or Sikh meditation. Perhaps the most widely practiced in the United States is transcendental meditation, or TM. Its originator, Maharishi Mahesh Yogi, defines TM as turning the attention toward the subtler levels of thought until the mind transcends the experience of the subtlest state of thought and arrives at the source of thought.[53] The basic procedure used in TM is simple, but the effects claimed for it are extensive. One simply sits comfortably with closed eyes and engages in the repetition of a special sound (a mantra) for about 20 minutes twice a day. Studies indicate that TM practices are associated with reduced heart rate, lowered oxygen consumption, and decreased blood pressure.[54]

Not everyone who mediates experiences positive payoffs. A sufficiently large number of people report meditation to be effective in managing stress, however, that a number of organizations have started, supported, or approved of meditation programs for employees. They include Coors Brewing, Monsanto Chemicals, Xerox, Connecticut General Life Insurance Company, and the U.S. Army.

Biofeedback

Individuals can be taught to control a variety of internal body processes by using a technique called biofeedback. In biofeedback, small changes occurring in the body or brain are detected, amplified, and displayed to the person. Sophisticated recording and computer technology make it possible for a person to attend to subtle changes in heart rate, blood pressure, temperature, and brain-wave patterns that normally would be unobservable. Most of these processes are affected by stress.

The potential role of biofeedback as an individual stress management technique can be seen from the bodily functions that can, to some degree, be brought under voluntary control. These include brain waves, heart rates, muscle tension, body temperature, stomach acidity, and blood pressure. Most if not all of these processes are affected by stress. The potential of biofeedback is its ability to help induce a state of relaxation and restore bodily functions to a nonstressed state. One advantage of biofeedback over nonfeedback techniques is that it gives precise data about bodily functions. By interpreting the feedback, individuals know how high their blood pressure is, for example, and discover, through practice, means of lowering it. When they are successful, the feedback provides instantaneous information to that effect.

Biofeedback training has been useful in reducing anxiety, lowering stomach acidity (and thus reducing the likelihood of ulcer formation), controlling tension and migraine headaches, and, in general, reducing negative physiological manifestations of stress. Despite these positive results, people looking to biofeedback for stress control should understand that success requires training and the use of equipment that may be very expensive.

SUMMARY OF KEY CONCEPTS

1. Stress may be viewed as either a stimulus or a response. We view it as an adaptive response moderated by individual differences, that is, a consequence of any action, situation, or event that places special demands on a person.

2. Major variables in the model of organizational stress presented in this chapter are: (1) work stressors (work environment, individual, and group and organizational); (2) stress itself; (3) stress consequences (organizational and individual); (4) stress moderators (personality, Type A behavior, and social support); and (5) stress prevention and management (maximizing person–environment fit, organizational programs, and individual approaches).

3. Stressors are actions, situations, or events that place special demands on a person. Three important categories of stressors are: (1) work environment (e.g., chemicals, radiation, temperature); (2) individual stressors (e.g., role conflict, work overload, change); and (3) group and organizational stressors (e.g., politics, culture, interpersonal relationships, downsizing).

4. While some consequences of stress are positive, many are dysfunctional. Negative individual consequences include accident proneness, poor concentration, drug and alcohol abuse, and burnout. Organizational consequences may include absenteeism, turnover, increased health and medical costs, and quantitative and qualitative decrements in productivity.

5. Some factors affect the nature of the stress response. These are called stress moderators. Three important moderators are personality (e.g., locus of control and self-esteem), Type A behavior, and social support.

6. Stress prevention and management strategies include (1) maximizing person–environment fit, (2) organizational programs such as employee assistance and wellness, and (3) individual approaches such as cognitive techniques, relaxation training, meditation, and biofeedback.

KEY TERMS

burnout
qualitative overload
quantitative overload
stress
stressor

DISCUSSION QUESTIONS

1. It has been suggested that "stress is in the eyes of the beholder." What does this mean? Do you agree?

2. Why should managers not even attempt to counsel or provide advice to any employee suspected of being depressed?

3. The issue of who should be responsible for dealing with work stress—the individual or the organization— is an important one. What do you think? What are the arguments for and against each position?

4. Do you think some types of jobs or organizations attract Type A individuals? Do some attract Type B individuals? Why?

5. What is the relationship between work stress and work motivation? If we could eliminate all stress, what effect would this have on motivation?

6. Work underload may be every bit as dysfunctional as work overload. Can you think of other work variables where "too little" may be as counterproductive as "too much?"

7. What kinds of things could an organization do to better maximize employee–environment fit?

8. What is the relationship between stress and personality? What aspects of personality might tend to increase stress? Decrease it?

9. Why are people in certain occupations more susceptible to burnout? What kinds of things might organizations do to reduce the likelihood their members will experience burnout?

10. Increasingly, American workers are being sent on overseas assignments. What stressors might be unique to such assignments? What might organizations do to minimize their impact?

READING 16.1 WHO BEATS STRESS BEST—AND HOW

In a faster-spinning world, managers are finding new ways to ease stress in workers and themselves. Wisdom comes from surprising sources—like the Army—and pays off.

What we don't understand about stress could fill volumes. And it does. Some books say stress is an invigorating tonic; others, that it's lethal. Stress stands implicated in practically every complaint of modern life, from equipment downtime to premature ejaculation, from absenteeism to sudden death. Some workers in high-stress occupations— bomb deactivators, for example—suffer its effects hardly at all. Yet a man who tastes port for a living lies awake some nights worried that "the whole business is riding on my palate." There's enough apparently contradictory information about stress to make any honest seeker after truth, well, anxious.

Isn't there more stress today than ever before? There might be. There might be more love. But neither condition is quantifiable. Diseases to which stress contributes—hypertension, heart attack, ulcers, the common cold—are quantifiable, but since stress isn't their only cause, an increase in them doesn't necessarily signal an increase in stress.

Ask people if they feel more stressed, and, of course, they say yes. Who would admit, even if it were true, that he feels less stressed than he did a year ago? Inner peace is seen to be the prerogative of dweebs. It's hip to be stressed. Earlier this year, Northwestern National Life Insurance questioned a random sample of 600 U.S. workers. Almost half (46 percent) said their jobs were highly stressful; 34 percent said they felt so much stress they were thinking of quitting.

Some of them were telling the truth. Commutes really are growing longer, highways more congested. In more families, both husbands and wives have jobs. And with upsizings, downsizings, rightsizings, takeovers, and mergers, the corporate world in recent years has turned upside down more times than James Dean's roadster.

The number of stress-related workers' compensation claims has ballooned in states such as California that compensate for so-called mental-mental injuries. In these, an intangible (mental) injury results from an intangible (mental) cause, such as stress. California courts have awarded compensation to workers who just say they feel hurt. Judith Bradley, a former cake decorator with Albertson's, a supermarket chain, won compensation in part because she said her supervisor had been "very curt" with her. He had told her to "get the lead out" and to "get your butt in high gear," and had reprimanded her for leaving cakes out of the freezer. She was distressed, sued, and won.

Though recently the number of stress-related claims has begun to decline in California, dollar costs nationally continue to rise. Donna Dell, manager of employee relations for Wells Fargo Bank, says workers suffering from stress "typically are out a long, long time, and they need lots of rehabilitation," including costly visits to psychiatrists. In medical treatment and time lost, stress cases cost, on average, twice as much as other workplace injuries: more than $15,000 each.

Perhaps the most telling sign of stress's apparent rise: strong business for purveyors of relief. Psychologist Stanley Fisher, a Manhattan hypnotist, says the demise of New York's boom-boom real estate market has sent many relief-seeking former brokers and developers his way. Gene Cooper, a partner at Corporate Counseling Associates (a supplier of corporate employee assistance programs), says, "It used to be, 3 percent to 5 percent of our calls for counseling were stress related. Now, more like 8 percent to 14 percent." They come from all levels, clerks to VPs.

There are stress-fighting tapes, goggles that send pulses of white light into your head, vibrating music beds ("not quite like the first time you had sex," says one manufacturer, "but maybe the second"). Morgan Fairchild has a video out (Morgan Fairchild Stress Management, $19.95).

Whenever the status quo gets a good shaking—even where that shaking eventually results in greater opportunity and freedom of choice—stress goes up as people scramble to adapt. Yet if change is a constant, and if everyone is susceptible to stress, why doesn't everyone suffer from it equally? Why do some maddeningly healthy people appear not to suffer from it at all?

Not everyone finds the same event stressful. Drop a scorpion into a box of puppies, and you get stressed puppies. But drop it into a box of elf owls, which eat scorpions, and you get satisfaction. If a tree falls in the rain forest and nobody from Ben & Jerry's hears it, is there stress? No. Perhaps you think drinking port is fun. Peter Ficklin, wine master of Ficklin Vineyards, a California portmaker, says, "Sure, it's a pleasure to taste port. But the fortified wine category is down. There's increased competition. In the busy season, sometimes, I have trouble sleeping. The whole business is riding on my palate."

Some people are protected from stress by buffers. For example, the more mastery or control a person feels he has over circumstances, the less stress he's apt to feel, even if his control extends no further than the power to decide how he's going to feel about change. A surefire recipe for creating stress is to put someone in a job that affords him little decision-making power but carries great responsibility or imposes heavy psychological demands.

Rare is the job where an employee has complete control. Wally Goelzer, a flight attendant for Alaska Airlines, has plenty of control over his schedule—he's got 11 years' seniority. But the workplace limits his freedom: "Probably the worst incident in the last six months was an alcohol situation. The plane was full of a mixture of tourists and commercial fishermen. I had to tell this guy, one of the fishermen, that we wouldn't serve him any more alcohol. Now these fisherman are out on their boat sometimes six or eight weeks. He wasn't pleased. Yelling. Profanities. People around him were not having an ideal travel experience. 'What you're doing,' I told him, 'is you're being loud now.' I didn't want to stir him up too much, since we're all trapped in a tube at 29,000 feet."

The most potent buffer against stress may well be membership in a stable, close-knit group or community. Example: the town of Roseto, Pennsylvania. Stress researcher Dr. Stewart Wolf wondered 25 years ago why Roseto's residents, though they smoked, drank, ate fat, and otherwise courted doom, lived free from heart disease and other stress-related ills. He suspected their protection sprang from the town's uncommon social cohesion and stability: It was inhabited almost entirely by descendants of Italians who had moved there 100 years previously from Roseto, Italy. Few married outside the community; the firstborn was always named after a grandparent; ostentation or any display of superiority was avoided, since that would invite "the evil eye" from one's neighbor.

Wolf predicted Rosetians would start dying like flies if the modern world intruded. It did. They did. By the mid-1970s, Rosetians had Cadillacs, ranch-style homes, mixed marriages, new names, and a rate of coronary heart disease the same as any other town's.

The U.S. Army tries to instill a Rosetian cohesion prophylactically. Says Dr. David Marlowe, chief of the department of military psychiatry at the Walter Reed Army Institute of Research: "If a bond trader feels stress, he can go meditate for 20 minutes. A soldier facing enemy fire can't. So we have to give him the maximum protection ahead of time." Marlowe says that where stress is concerned, Army research shows the primary issues are organizational. "You want to build cohesion into a group, by making sure soldiers have good information, that they aren't faced with ambiguity, that they have solid relationships with leaders. If a man feels his squad is listening to him, if he can talk to it about his hopes, fears, anxieties, he's not likely to experience stress." The Army's No. 1 psychological discovery from World War II, he says, was "the strength imparted by the small, primary work group."

Keeping group cohesion strong after battle is crucial, too, since members, by collectively reliving their experience and trying to put it in perspective, get emotions off their chests that otherwise might leave them stressed out for months or years. The process is called debriefing. Squad members, for example, are encouraged to use travel time en route home from a war zone to talk about their battlefield experience. "It helps them detoxify," says Marlowe. "That's why we brought them back in groups from Desert Storm. Epidemiologically, we know it works." Thus, the group emerges both as the primary protection against stress and as the means for relief after a stressful event.

In light of the Army's approach, much of what passes for stress management in U.S. industry looks superficial. Most Fortune 500 companies offer employees either an employee assistance program (EAP), a wellness promotion program, or both. Some of these emphasize stress management. At Liz Claiborne, for example, well-attended lunchtime seminars explain how workers can relax by using mental imagery, muscle relaxation, and a variety of other proven techniques. Why the big turnout? "Misery loves company," says Sharon Quilter, Claiborne's director of benefits. Honeywell has offered a 45-minute program called Wellness and Your Funny Bone, taught by Sister Mary Christelle Macaluso, R. S. M. (Religious Sister of Mercy), Ph.D., "a lecturer/humorist with a Ph.D. in anatomy."

Ted Barash, president of a company that provides wellness programs, dismisses such approaches to stress reduction as "Band-Aid happy hours and traveling humor shows." Professor Paul Roman, a University of Georgia expert on behavioral health who has surveyed EAP programs, says most "never address the source of the stress. They blame the victim. Our studies at Southwestern Bell and other companies show the single biggest source of stress is poorly trained and inept supervisors."

External suppliers of EAP programs, such as Corporate Counseling Associates, purveyors of counseling to Time Warner, Digital Equipment, Liz Claiborne, and others, are understandably reluctant to tell clients how to run their own businesses. Says CCA partner Gene Cooper: "We help employees develop coping mechanisms. We don't reduce the stress itself." One of Cooper's counselors, asked if she ever suggests stress-relieving organizational changes to employers, says no, "that would be presumptuous."

Stress experts who advocate a more interventionist approach ask how it can possibly make sense for a company to soothe employees with one hand—teaching them relaxation through rhythmic breathing—while whipping them like egg whites with the other, moving up deadlines, increasing overtime, or withholding information about job security. Any company serious about stress management should consider the following steps:

Audit stress

Dr. Paul J. Rosch, president of the American Institute of Stress, thinks any intelligent program must begin and end with a stress audit. Questionnaires typically ask workers and managers to list conditions they find most stressful. Answers can illuminate areas where workers are stressed by boredom, as well as those where they are stressed by overwork. (Rustout, stressmeisters are fond of saying, can be as anxious-making as burnout.) Rosch says, "An audit may show a need for programs not generally thought of as stress reducing, though they serve that function." Examples: child care and flextime. Follow-up audits show results.

Use EAPs aggressively

Try to catch stress before it blooms. At McDonnell Douglas, EAP director Daniel Smith uses a program called Transitions to prepare workers for potentially traumatic organizational changes. "You tell people what they're going to feel before they feel it," he says. "It prevents more significant problems downstream."

Case in point: Pete Juliano, head of McDonnell Douglas's 2,000-person facilities management operation, knew he would have to flatten and streamline his division to make it more responsive. Specifically, he would have to strip five levels of management with 260 managers down to three levels with 170.

"Nobody was going out the door," he says, "and nobody was getting a pay cut. They'd all be staying on, though not all as managers. Still, that's a tough nut to crack: One day you're a manager. The next, you're carrying tools. How do you tell your wife and kids? How do you go to work each day and face not being a manager?"

Juliano called in the Transitions team, whose members made a two-hour presentation to the department. They covered such topics as how to face your spouse and peers if you don't continue as a manager, how to recognize denial, how to cope with anger. The counselors also told listeners about career options if they decided to leave the division or McDonnell Douglas. "It gave them a chance to vent," says Juliano. "There have been cases of guys committing suicide when they had to go back to carrying tools. But we didn't have any serious problems."

Examine EAP usage

If you've got an EAP program, study the usage data that counselors collect: How many employees from what departments are requesting help, and for what? For example, if you know that (1) in the past five years nobody from your tax department has ever used the EAP program, (2) half the accountants signed up for stress counseling last week, and (3) it's not mid-April, then you might be seeing evidence of a problem.

Give employees information

They can't feel in control of circumstances if they lack it. When Donna Dell became manager of employee relations at Wells Fargo Bank last November, she saw there were about 3,000 workers' compensation cases outstanding. Accidents accounted for 80 percent; another 10 percent were from workers claiming various injuries from working at video display terminals; and 10 percent were from stress. She wanted to know where the stress claims came from. Were they, for instance, from employees who had been laid off or who had just been through a performance review? There was no correlation to either event. "I was surprised," says Dell. "Vengeance, apparently, was not the issue."

Asbestos was. "We don't have any claims for asbestosis per se," she says, "but we get stress claims from people who fear they may have been exposed. You don't have to prove you were exposed to get workers' comp. The fear is enough. Now we provide instruction at sites where toxic material construction has been scheduled. We go in, in advance, with trainers and explain to the employees what's going to happen. Since we implemented this program about a year and a half ago, we haven't had any more such claims."

Match employees with jobs they can master

In his bestselling book, _Flow_, Mihaly Csikszentmihalyi, a psychology professor at the University of Chicago, points out that the least-stressed people often are those who are working flat out on some task that they have selected—something they really love to do. They give themselves so completely that they achieve a kind of precision and grace—what the author calls "flow." The chance of your getting such performance from workers goes up, and their stress down, the more choice you give them over assignments.

Be prepared for trauma

It's easy to forget that stress isn't always the result of a thousand tiny cuts. "Having a gun put to your head can be upsetting," says Chris Dunning, a trauma expert at the University of Wisconsin at Milwaukee. She ought to know. Her business is de-stressing shot cops, crews of crashed airliners, and, at this writing, the forensic examiners in the Jeffrey Dahmer case ("they're having trouble eating meat").

Abrupt and upsetting things happen in offices. Homicide and suicide—not accidents—now account for 14 percent of male on-the-job deaths and 46 percent of female, reports psychologist James Turner, an expert on workplace mayhem. At the emergency department of Oakland's Highland Hospital, says chief resident Linda Jenks, mounting stress—with no end in sight—precipitated two suicides. "A young intern got into her car, numbed up her neck with lidocaine, took out a scalpel, and dissected herself in her rearview mirror. Within a week, a night nurse started an I.V. on herself—injected potassium, which stopped her heart immediately. After that, the hospital said, 'Okay, we're ignoring a problem here.' It's as if to admit it is a sign of failure." A suicide, an industrial accident, or any other traumatic event, says Dunning, leaves a lingering psychological strain on survivors: "It usually takes a good three months to get an organization back on track."

But, says Mark Braverman, president of Crisis Management Group, a Massachusetts consulting firm, these traumas present management with opportunities as well as problems. "Management sometimes won't talk about the event or face up to it directly," he says. "We try to tell them that if they do face up to it and answer workers' questions, they can build a bond that lasts longer afterward." Even if you can't talk, he says, talk: "If you can't tell them much because OSHA is still completing an investigation, tell them that."

Braverman cites an example of trauma handled right: "A computer company had had a helicopter crash. They'd also had a work site shooting. So they decided, within the structure of their EAP, to create a protocol for dealing with traumatic stress. Later a safety system failed in a plant with 2,000 people, killing one. Every work group got together. The international manager of facilities was flown in to answer questions, including the ones on everybody's minds: Why did the system fail? Could it happen again? EAP counselors were available, but it was the information itself that was most stress-relieving."

Traumatic stress tends to be infectious. Since large numbers of employees are involved, clusters of stress-based workers' comp suits can result. In court, the cases are much harder to defend against than less-dramatic stress cases. Says Jim Turner: "It behooves you greatly to go in early with counselors, since this will reduce your overall long-term cost."

At Wells Fargo, where bank robberies rose 37 percent in this year's first quarter, tellers have been traumatized. "We do get stress claims from robbery incidents, and we don't dispute them," says Donna Dell. Instead, the bank dispatches EAP counselors to affected branches, where they conduct group debriefings, much the way the Army does.

Bryan Lawton, head of Wells Fargo's debriefing program, explains how it works: "The professional asks them things like, where were you when the incident happened, how did you respond, how did the others act? When the employees start to talk, they find out they're not alone, not the only ones who feel the way they do. Everybody else feels guilty or angry over the event. They're told these are normal emotions." The professional then tells them how they can expect to feel weeks later.

Nobody is sure why debriefings work, but they do. And they are cost-effective. "All it takes," says Lawton, "is one case to lead to a significant expense. One person's trauma can wind up costing the bank $100,000." The figure includes lost time, medical treatment, and retraining cost.

O'Dell Williams, with the bank 16 years, has survived ten robbery situations, the most recent one as a branch manager in Vallejo, California, on May 20. The robbery attempt scared more than 20 of his employees. "I was afraid we'd lose some afterward," he says. But EAP counselors intervened quickly, and so far nobody has quit. And nobody has filed a workers' comp. claim.

Don't forget the obvious

Managers who want to reduce stress should make sure workers have the tools and training they need to get job done. Says John Murray, a police bomb deactivator in Florida: "I'm lucky. I've got the best equipment and the best training. There are departments where all they used to give you was a mattress and a fishhook." Managers should set realistic deadlines and go out of their way not to change deadlines, once set. What works well for the Army works just as well in the office: Build cohesion through communication. Straighten out managers who like to play the Charles Boyer part from Gaslight—who hold sway over subordinates by keeping them confused, by withholding information, or by keeping roles and responsibilities ill-defined.

Do all these things, behave flawlessly, and your exposure to stress-based lawsuits still remains almost unimaginably broad. Chris Dunning cites a case where an employee, as part of some lunchroom high jinks, got silly and taped a co-worker's arm to a chair—very lightly, not so it restrained her. She started screaming. Other workers looked at each other in disbelief: What was the woman's problem? It turned out that, as a child, she had been forcibly restrained and raped. The taping of the arm caused her to reexperience the trauma of that, and her subsequent disability was judged to be 100 percent the employer's responsibility. At least this worker's distress was real. Some employees undoubtedly abuse the system, and there are lawyers and doctors eager to help them. Listen to Joseph Alibrandi, chairman of Whittaker Corp., an aerospace manufacturer: "We try to minimize the problems in the physical workplace, to do all we can to reduce true stress. But a lot of that seems frustratingly irrelevant. There's always an epidemic of 'sore back' after a layoff. Or they say they can't perform sexually. How the hell are you going to defend against that?"

It's almost impossible, of course, but you can try to flag potential claimants early on. New hires can be asked, as part of their medical evaluation, "Have you ever been off work due to a stress-related illness?" A "yes" may indicate to the doctor that the employee's assignment should be changed.

Performing a periodic stress audit, or making stress management part of your EAP or wellness program, can pay off in court. Says John M. Ivancevich, dean of the business school at the University of Houston: "Even a sloppy attempt at stress management can be a legal defense."

Finally: you. Feeling stressed? Not sure what to do? The first rule, says Dr. James Turner, is, Don't quit your job. "They build these fantasies," he says of stressed-out executives. "They'll go sailing. They'll open a copy center. Lately, for some reason, they all want to open copy centers." But sooner or later everyone wants to come back.

Instead of quitting, learn the techniques of coping. You'll find plenty of experts willing to teach them to you for a price, but they're not too complex, and many stressed workers have discovered them without help. Flight attendant Wally Goelzer and plenty of other people use them daily without knowing it. "Sometimes I put my hands out like a scale," he says. "I ask myself: How much does this problem matter? I think of a friend of mine who was killed in a plane crash. 'Life is too short,' I can hear her say. She used to say that, and I can see her face."

Emergency room resident Jenks and bomb deactivator Murray know the stress-relieving power of humor, even when it's of the gallows type. Says Murray: "Yeah, I get a certain amount of kidding. I've got three daughters, and when Father's Day comes around they give me a card with a fuse in it." Says Jenks: "We use black humor at work so much that it's gotten so I have to remember to clean up my act when I'm around normal people."

Then again, you might want to put aside the tricks and strategies, since these change like frocks. You might think about your life. Is it the way you wanted? If not, all the perspective and joking in the world will get you only so far. Mihaly Csikszentmihalyi, who lectures occasionally to 40-ish managers, notes that those who insist on regaining control of their lives, even at what temporarily may seem the peril of their careers, often see an unexpected payoff down the line. "There comes a point where they're working 70 hours a week, and they're not sure why. Their family lives are suffering. Maybe they've never given any thought to setting priorities. Some decide they can't do everything—that they have to step off the fast track to get back their family life or take better care of their health. And then a most interesting thing happens: The ones who do it, most of them, in a year or two, they get promoted." Dare to be second-rate, if that's how you have to think of it. It may not be what you imagine.

EXERCISE 16-2   BEHAVIOR ACTIVITY PROFILE—A TYPE A MEASURE

Each of us displays certain kinds of behaviors, thought patterns of personal characteristics. For each of the 21 sets of descriptions below, circle the number which you feel best describes where you are between each pair. The best answer for each set of descriptions is the response that most nearly describes the way you feel, behave, or think. Answer these in terms of your regular or typical behavior, thoughts, or characteristics.

1. I'm always on time for appointments.   7 6 5 4 3 2 1   I'm never quite on time.

2. When someone is talking to me, chances are I'll anticipate what they are going to say, by nodding, interrupting, or finishing sentences for them.   7 6 5 4 3 2 1   I listen quietly without showing any impatience.

3. I frequently try to do several things at once.   7 6 5 4 3 2 1   I tend to take things one at a time.

4. When it comes to waiting in line (at banks, theaters, etc.), I really get impatient and frustrated.   7 6 5 4 3 2 1   It simply doesn't bother me.

5. I always feel rushed.   7 6 5 4 3 2 1   I never feel rushed.

6. When it comes to my temper, I find it hard to control at times.   7 6 5 4 3 2 1   I just don't seem to have one.

7. I tend to do most things like eating, walking, and talking rapidly.   7 6 5 4 3 2 1   Slowly.

TOTAL SCORE 1–7 _____ = S

8. Quite honestly, the things I enjoy most are job-related activities.   7 6 5 4 3 2 1   Leisure-time activities.

9. At the end of a typical work day, I usually feel like I needed to get more done than I did.   7 6 5 4 3 2 1   I accomplished everything I needed to.

10. Someone who knows me very well would say that I would rather work than play.   7 6 5 4 3 2 1   I would rather play than work.

11. When it comes to getting ahead at work, nothing is more important.   7 6 5 4 3 2 1   Many things are more important.

12. My primary source of satisfaction comes from my job.   7 6 5 4 3 2 1   I regularly find satisfaction in non-job pursuits, such as hobbies, friends, and family.

13. Most of my friends and social acquaintances are people I know from work.   7 6 5 4 3 2 1   Not connected with my work.

14. I'd rather stay at work than take a vacation.   7 6 5 4 3 2 1   Nothing at work is important enough to interfere with my vacation.

TOTAL SCORE 8–14 _____ = J

15. People who know me well would describe me as hard driving and competitive. <u>7 6 5 4 3 2 1</u> Relaxed and easygoing.

16. In general, my behavior is governed by a desire for recognition and achievement. <u>7 6 5 4 3 2 1</u> What I want to do—not by trying to satisfy others.

17. In trying to complete a project or solve a problem, I tend to wear myself out before I'll give up on it. <u>7 6 5 4 3 2 1</u> I tend to take a break or quit if I'm feeling fatigued.

18. When I play a game (tennis, cards, etc.) my enjoyment comes from winning. <u>7 6 5 4 3 2 1</u> The social interaction.

19. I like to associate with people who are dedicated to getting ahead. <u>7 6 5 4 3 2 1</u> Easygoing and take life as it comes.

20. I'm not happy unless I'm always doing something. <u>7 6 5 4 3 2 1</u> Frequently, "doing nothing" can be quite enjoyable.

21. What I enjoy doing most are competitive activities. <u>7 6 5 4 3 2 1</u> Noncompetitive pursuits.

TOTAL SCORE 15–21 _____ = H

Impatience (S)	Job Involvement (J)	Hard Driving and Competitive (H)	Total Score (A) - S + J + H

The Behavior Activity Profile attempts to assess the three Type A coronary-prone behavior patterns, as well as provide a total score. The three a priori types of Type A coronary-prone behavior patterns are shown:		
Items	Behavior Pattern	Characteristics
1-7	Impatience (S)	Anxious to interrupt. Fails to listen attentively. Frustrated by waiting (e.g., in line, for others to complete a job).
8-14	Job Involvement (J)	Focal point of attention is the job. Lives for the job. Relishes being on the job. Immersed in job activities.
15-21	Hard driving/ (H) Competitive	Hardworking, highly competitive. Competitive in most aspects of life, sports, work etc. Racing against the clock.
1-21	Total score (A)	Total of S + J + H represents your global Type A behavior

Score ranges for total score are:

Score	Behavior Type
122 and above	Hard-core Type A
99-121	Moderate Type A
90-98	Low Type A
80-89	Type X
70-79	Low Type B
50-69	Moderate Type B
40 and below	Hard-core Type B

Percentile Scores

Now you can compare your score to a sample of over 1,200 respondents.

Percentile Score Percent of Individuals Scoring Lower	**Raw Score**	
	Males	Females
99%	____140	____132
95%	____135	____126
90%	____130	____120
85%	____124	____112

Percentile Score Percent of Individuals Scoring Lower	**Raw Score**	
	Males	Females
80%	____118	____106
75%	____113	____101
70%	____108	____95
65%	____102	____90
60%	____97	____85
55%	____92	____80
50%	____87	____74
45%	____81	____69
40%	____75	____63
35%	____70	____58
30%	____63	____53
25%	____58	____48
20%	____51	____42
15%	____45	____36
10%	____38	____31
5%	____29	____26
1%	____21	____21

EXERCISE 16-2 HEALTH RISK APPRAISAL

The Health Risk Appraisal form was developed by the Department of Health and Welfare of the Canadian government. Their initial testing program indicated that approximately one person out of every three who completed the form would modify some unhealthy aspects of lifestyle for at least a while. Figuring the potential payoff was worth it, the government mailed out over 3 million copies of the questionnaire to Canadians who were on social security. Subsequent checking indicated that their initial projections of the number of recipients altering their behavior was correct. Perhaps you will be among the one-third.

Choose from the three answers for each question the one answer which most nearly applies to you. The plus and minus signs next to some numbers indicate more than (1) and less than (2). Note that a few items have only two alternatives.

Exercise

_____ 1. Physical effort expended during the workday: mostly?
    a. heavy labor, walking, or housework
    b. —
    c. deskwork

_____ 2. Participation in physical activities—skiing, golf, swimming, etc., or lawn mowing, gardening, etc.?
    a. daily   b. weekly   c. seldom

_____ 3. Participation in vigorous exercise program?
    a. three time weekly
    b. weekly
    c. seldom

_____ 4. Average miles walked or jogged per day?
    a. one or more
    b. less than one
    c. none

_____ 5. Flights of stairs climbed per day?
    a. 101   b. 102   c. —

Nutrition

_____ 6. Are you overweight?
    a. no   b. 5 to 19 lbs   c. 201 lbs.

_____ 7. Do you eat a wide variety of foods, something from each of the following five food groups: (1) meat, fish, poultry, dried legumes, eggs, or nuts; (2) milk or milk products; (3) bread or cereals; (4) fruits; (5) vegetables?
    a. each day   b. three times weekly   c. —

Alcohol

_____ 8. Average number of bottles (12 oz.) of beer per week?
    a. 0 to 7   b. 8 to 15   c. 161

_____ 9. Average number of hard liquor (1 1/2 oz.) drinks per week?
    a. 0 to 7   b. 8 to 15   c. 161

_____ 10. Average number of glasses (5 oz.) of wine or cider per week?
    a. 0 to 7   b. 8 to 15   c. 161

_____ 11. Total number of drinks per week including beer, liquor, or wine?
    a. 0 to 7   b 8 to 15   c. 161

Drugs

_____ 12. Do you take drugs illegally?
    a. no   b. —   c. yes

_____ 13. Do you consume alcoholic beverages together with certain drugs (tranquilizers, barbiturates, illegal drugs)?
    a. no   b. —   c. yes

_____ 14. Do you use painkillers improperly or excessively?
    a. no   b. —   c. yes

Tobacco

_____ 15 Cigarettes smoked per day?

        a. none   b. 10 —   c. 10+

_____ 16. Cigars smoked per day?

        a. none   b. 5 —   c. 5+

_____ 17. Pipe tobacco pouches per week?

        a. none   b. 2 —   c. 2+

Personal Health

_____ 18. Do you experience periods of depression?

        a. seldom   b. occasionally   c. frequently

_____ 19. Does anxiety interfere with your daily activities?

        a. seldom   b. occasionally   c. frequently

_____ 20. Do you get enough satisfying sleep?

        a. yes   b. no   c. —

_____ 21. Are you aware of the causes and danger of VD?

        a. yes   b. no   c. —

_____ 22. Breast self-examination? (if not applicable, do not score)

        a. monthly   b. occasionally   c. —

Road and Water Safety

_____ 23. Mileage per year as driver or passenger?

        a. 10,000-   b. 10,000+   c. —

_____ 24. Do you often exceed the speed limit?

        a. no   b. by 10 mph+   c. by 20 mph+

_____ 25. Do you wear a seat belt?

        a. always   b. occasionally   c. never

_____ 26. Do you drive a motorcycle, moped, or snowmobile?

        a. no   b. yes   c. —

_____ 27. If yes to the above, do you always wear a regulation safety helmet?

        a. yes   b.—   c. no

_____ 28. Do you ever drive under the influence of alcohol?

        a. never   b. —   c. occasionally

_____ 29. Do you ever drive when your ability may be affected by drugs?

        a. never   b. —   c. occasionally

_____ 30. Are you aware of water safety rules?

        a. yes   b. no   c. —

_____ 31. If you participate in water sports or boating, do you wear a life jacket?

        a. yes   b. no   c. —

General

_____ 32. Average time watching TV per day (in hours)?

    a. 0 to 1   b. 1 to 4   c. 4+

_____ 33. Are you familiar with first-aid procedures?

    a. yes   b. no   c. —

_____ 34. Do you ever smoke in bed?

    a. no   b. occasionally   c. regularly

_____ 35. Do you always make use of equipment provided for your safety at work?

    a. yes   b. occasionally   c. no

To Score: Give yourself 1 point for each a answer; 3 points for each b answer; 5 points for each c answer.

Total Score:

—A total score of 35–45 is *excellent*. You have a commendable lifestyle based on sensible habits and a lively awareness of personal health.

—A total score of 45–55 is *good*. With some minor change, you can develop an excellent lifestyle.

—A total score of 56–65 is *risky*. You are taking unnecessary risks with your health. Several of your habits should be changed if potential health problems are to be avoided.

—A total score of 66 and over is *hazardous*. Either you have little personal awareness of good health habits or you are choosing to ignore them. This is a danger zone.

CASE 16.1   NO RESPONSE FROM MONITOR 23

Loudspeaker: Ignition minus 45 minutes

Paul Keller tripped the sequence switches at control monitor 23 in accordance with the countdown instruction book just to his left. All hydraulic systems were functioning normally in the second stage of the spacecraft booster at checkpoint 1 minus 45. Keller automatically snapped his master control switch to GREEN and knew that his electronic impulse along with hundreds of others from similar consoles within the Cape Canaveral complex signaled continuation of the countdown.

Free momentarily from data input, Keller leaned back in his chair, stretched his arms above his head, and then rubbed the back of his neck. The monitor lights on console 23 glowed routinely.

It used to be an incredible challenge, fantastically interesting work at the very fringe of man's knowledge about himself and his universe. Keller recalled his first day in Brevard County, Florida, with his wife and young daughter. How happy they were that day. Here was the future, the good life . . . forever. And Keller was going to be part of that fantastic, utopian future.

Loudspeaker: Ignition minus 35 minutes.

Keller panicked! His mind had wandered momentarily, and he lost his place in the countdown instructions. Seconds later he found the correct place and tripped the proper sequence of switches for checkpoint 1 minus 35. No problem. Keller snapped master control to GREEN and wiped his brow. He knew he was late reporting and would hear about it later.

Damn!, he thought, I used to know countdown cold for seven systems monitors without countdown instructions. But now . . . you're slipping Keller . . . you're slipping, he thought. Shaking his head, Keller reassured himself that he was overly tired today . . . just tired.

Loudspeaker: Ignition minus 30 minutes.

Keller completed the reporting sequence for checkpoint I minus 30, took one long last drag on his cigarette, and squashed it out in the crowded ashtray. Utopia? Hell: It was one big rat race and getting bigger all the time. Keller recalled how he once naively felt that his problems with Naomi would disappear after they left Minneapolis and came to the Cape with the space program. Now, 10,000 arguments later, Keller knew there was no escape.

Only one can of beer left, Naomi? One stinking lousy can of beer, cold lunchmeat, and potato salad? Is that all a man gets after 12 hours of mental exhaustion?

Oh, shut up, Paul! I'm so sick of you playing Mr. Important. You get leftovers because I never know when you're coming home . . . your daughter hardly knows you . . . and you treat us like nobodies . . . incidental to your great personal contribution to the Space Age.

Don't knock it, Naomi. That job is plenty important to me, to the Team, and it gets you everything you've ever wanted . . . more! Between this house and the boat, we're up to our ears in debt.

Now don't try to pin our money problems on me, Paul Keller. You're the one who has to have all the same goodies as the scientists earning twice your salary. Face it, Paul. You're just a button-pushing technician regardless of how fancy a title they give you. You can be replaced, Paul. You can be replaced by any S.O.B. who can read and punch buttons.

Loudspeaker: Ignition minus 25 minutes.

A red light blinked ominously indicating a potential hydraulic fluid leak in subsystem seven of stage two. Keller felt his heartbeat and pulse rate increase. Rule 1 . . . report malfunction immediately and stop the count. Keller punched POTENTIAL ABORT on the master control.

Loudspeaker: The count is stopped at ignition minus 24 minutes 17 seconds.

Keller fumbled with the countdown instructions. Any POTENTIAL ABORT required a cross-check to separate an actual malfunction from sporadic signal error. Keller began to perspire nervously as he initiated standard cross-check procedures.

"Monitor 23, this is Control. Have you got an actual abort, Paul?" The voice in the headset was cool, but impatient, "Decision required in 30 seconds."

"I know, I know," Keller mumbled, "I'm cross-checking right now."

Keller felt the silence closing in around him. Cross-check one proved inconclusive. Keller automatically followed detailed instructions for cross-check two.

"Do you need help, Keller?" asked the voice in the headset.

"No, I'm O.K."

"Decision required," demanded the voice in the headset. "Dependent systems must be deactivated in 15 seconds."

Keller read and reread the console data. It looked like a sporadic error signal . . . the system appeared to be in order.

"Decision required," demanded the voice in the headset.

"Continue count," blurted Keller at last. "Subsystem seven fully operational." Keller slumped back in his chair.

Loudspeaker: The count is resumed at ignition minus 24 minutes 17 seconds.

Keller knew that within an hour after lift off, Barksdale would call him in for a personal conference. "What's wrong lately, Paul?" he would say. "Is there anything I can help with? You seem so tense lately." But he wouldn't really want to listen. Barksdale was the kind of person who read weakness into any personal problems and demanded that they be purged from the mind the moment his men checked out their consoles.

More likely Barksdale would demand that Keller make endless practice runs on cross-check procedures while he stood nearby . . . watching and noting any errors . . . while the pressure grew and grew.

Today's performance was surely the kiss of death for any wage increase too. That was another of Barksdale's methods of obtaining flawless performance . . . which would surely lead to another scene with Naomi . . . and another sleepless night . . . and more of those nagging stomach pains . . . and yet another imperfect performance for Barksdale.

Loudspeaker: Ignition minus 20 minutes.

The monitor lights at console 23 blinked routinely.

"Keller," said the voice in the earphone. "Report, please."

"Control, this is Wallace at monitor 24. I don't believe Keller is feeling well. Better send someone to cover fast!"

Loudspeaker: The count is stopped at 19 minutes 33 seconds

"This is Control, Wallace. Assistance has been dispatched and the count is on temporary hold. What seems to be wrong with Keller?"

"Control, this is Wallace, I don't know. His eyes are open and fixed on the monitor, but he won't respond to my questions. It could be a seizure or . . . a stroke."

Case Questions

1. Is there any way of avoiding the more serious manifestations (as with Paul Keller) of pressure on the job? Explain.

2. Are there any early warning signs given by employees under stress? If so, what are they?

3. What is the proper role of the supervisor here? Should he attempt counseling?

VIDEO CASE

Job Sharing, Rhino Foods, and Job Pressure and Ethics

The videos "Job Sharing at Rhino Foods" and "Job Pressure and Ethics" illustrate the positive power of distributive and procedural justice and the negative consequences when managers fail to treat employees fairly. Rhino Foods, the Burlington, Vermont, maker of cheesecakes and cookies that employs 60 people, faced a serious challenge. A sales slump left the company with the need to temporarily downsize its workforce by laying off 11 workers.

Rhino President Ted Castle communicated the problem to his employees and asked them for possible solutions. The employees themselves proposed the solution: find temporary jobs for these 11 workers. It also was proposed that employees be allowed to volunteer for the temporary jobs. Castle agreed and placed five workers at Ben and Jerry's Ice Cream, four workers at a mail-order gardening supply business, and two workers in community service. From the beginning, employees had strong perceptions of procedural justice. They thought that Rhino management valued their input, and they perceived the decision-making process to be a fair one.

The displaced Rhino Foods employees were paid the same wages at their temporary jobs as they received at Rhino, and Rhino provided them with uninterrupted health benefits. Rhino Foods employees therefore also had strong perceptions of distributive justice. In other words, the employees felt that the distribution of salary and benefits was fair. No employee, whether temporarily displaced or not, lost or gained anything relative to any other employee.

Rhino employees' strong sense of equity ultimately paid off for Rhino Foods. As Ted Castle says,"What we gained out of this is an incredible trust from our employees, I feel. They know that we're willing to do whatever it takes before we lay them off."

"Job Pressure and Ethics" shows what can happen when employees do not perceive fairness in procedures and outcomes. Ed Petrie, member of the Ethics Officers Association, reported the results of a survey that found that almost half of the respondents admitted to illegal or unethical actions in the past year. As Petrie says, "Even good people can be tempted to cut a few corners, misrepresent some data, lie about what they've done and do everything they can to cover it up."

What is the cause of this behavior? One cause is unrelenting job pressure, which has increased in the workplace. According to the survey, top contributors to workplace pressure include poor leadership, poor internal communication, too much work, and lack of management support. These factors represent some of the organizational influences that determine unethical behavior, particularly poor role models and perceived pressure for results. This type of organizational climate can lead employees to feel inequity: Their inputs are too great relative to the outputs received. If workers feel they are being overworked, one solution may be to engage in unethical activity to strike a balance between their own needs and those of the employer.

In addition, employees feel that poor communication is one of the leading causes of pressure. If employees do not feel that managers are communicating all information concerning their roles in the organization and they do not perceive they have a voice in organizational outcomes, they may perceive that decision-making procedures are unfair. This can lead to lower satisfaction, low organizational commitment, and decreased trust in management, ultimately resulting in unethical behavior. Solutions to this problem, according to survey respondents, include better organizational communication, more commitment by management, and greater job security.

These two examples show the positive results when employees perceive outcomes and procedures to be fair, and the negative consequences when employees do not believe they are treated fairly. Managers should make every effort to communicate with their employees and attempt to manage perceptions of fairness.

Discussion Questions

1. According to Adams's Equity Theory, what inputs and outcomes were important to Rhino Foods employees when making equity comparisons?

2. How might perceptions of inequity lead employees to commit illegal and unethical acts?

3. What can managers do to improve the organization's ethical climate and reduce the likelihood that their employees will engage in unethical activity?

4. How does providing employees a "voice" in organizational procedures and outcomes lead to perceptions of equity?

VIDEO CASE

Workplace Perks and More companies Provide Fitness

Have you ever considered bringing your laundry to work or taking home dinner prepared by the company chef? These are just a few workplace perks offered by today's companies. Until recently, most organizations rewarded their employees in the traditional way: with paychecks, overtime pay, and standard benefits such as medical coverage and retirement programs. However, with workers today working longer, harder, and with less job security, managers are seeing the benefit of creative perks to keep their employees satisfied and motivated.

At CIGNA, employees can place take home orders with the company chef; at Salamon Brothers, employees are able to see their own physician and even get prescription drugs delivered at the office! Anderson Consulting subsidizes a concierge to run any type of errand for employees, and still other companies provide on-site dry-cleaning and laundry services so that employees can enjoy more of their off-work time for leisure activities.

Are all of these perks purely for the benefit of the employees? Not at all, according to one manager who says, "Treat people as if they are human beings with needs and concerns and you'll get back loyalty and good work." In other words, providing these services to workers is just good business. This is evidenced by one worker at a Charlotte, North Carolina, packaging plant with subsidized day care who refers to her boss: "We try to make him happy in every way we can because he's been very good to us?" Though these perks have a short-term cost for companies, ultimately managers believe that they will get a long-term return on their investment from happier, more productive workers.

Another way organizations save money in the long run is by making their employees healthier. Many corporations, including Home Depot, Coca-Cola, and the Centers for Disease Control and Prevention, understand that by providing on-site fitness centers for employees, their long-term health costs can be drastically reduced because employees are more fit. Coco-Cola estimates that participants in its fitness center have over $500 less in health care costs per year. This results in a total savings at corporate headquarters of $1.2 million each year. In addition to savings due to reduced health costs, corporate fitness centers are also thought to reduce stress and absence and lead to greater productivity.

Though American workers will likely never give up traditional extrinsic rewards such as bonuses and vacation time, companies are proving that a little creativity in providing employee perks can achieve long-term benefits for both employees and companies.

Discussion Questions

1. Explain how providing such perks as day care and fitness centers can lead to increased organizational productivity.

2. Is it best to offer workplace perks to all employees, or just those that are good performers? Why or why not?

3. What are some potential negative effects of workplace perks?

VIDEO CASE

Fighting Stress

According to one survey, 46 percent of American workers suffer some form of work-related stress. The causes include too much work, uncertainty, monotony, and too little control over things that impact them at work. Unfortunately, corporate America as a whole does not seem to be willing to address the problems of workplace stress.

Stress can lead to indirect costs to organizations such as absenteeism, turnover, lower productivity, and quality problems. Employee stress can also cause direct costs to organizations. Kemper Insurance had to pay $300,000 to Francis Dunlavey, an insurance claims adjuster, who sued the company arguing that workplace stress caused his depression. Managers should be aware of the causes and effects of stress for these reasons, as well as for the sake of employees' physical and mental health.

Some companies understand that work-related stress impacts employees and organizational productivity and thus have developed creative ways to tackle stress. CIGNACorporation helps its employes cope with stress by providing employees access to an exercise physiologist, who provides massages and teaches stress-management techniques. Employees in the customer service department at S. C. Johnson in Racine, Wisconsin, are allowed to engage in squirt gun fights in the office to reduce job-induced stress. Both of these techniques are symptom-management strategies—targeting the consequences of stress after it occurs. These work environments just make good business sense by helping reduce stress, says one executive. However, managers should remember that it is always best to address organizational sources of stress, such as role overload, before symptom management becomes necessary.

When one must deal with stress symptoms, it is important to remember that coping with stress is an individual matter. Shooting one's supervisor with a water pistol may not be effective for every employee or appropriate in every office. Coping effectively with stress must take into account both situational and personal factors.

Discussion Questions

1. Relatively few companies employ stress-management programs despite the high costs of stress. Why do you think this is the case?

2. Are there potential negative consequences of allowing workers to cope with stress in such ways as having water pistol fights?

3. How can organizations help workers combat stress by enabling them to use the control strategy of stress reduction?

NOTES

1   Richard S. DeFrank and John M. Ivancevich, "Stress on the Job: An Executive Update," *Academy of Management Executive*, August 1998, pp.55-56.

2   Michael T. Matteson and John M. Ivancevich, *Controlling Work Stress* (San Francisco: Jossey-Bass, 1987).

3   Cary Cooper, "Future Research in Occupational Stress," *Stress Medicine*, March 2000, pp. 63-65.

4   R.L. Kahan, D.M. Wolfe, R.P. Quinn, J. D. Snoek, and R.A. Rosenthal, *Organizational Stress: Studies in Role Conflict and Ambiguity* (New York: John Wiley & Sons, 1964), p. 94.

5   Stewart D. Friedman and Jeffrey H. Greenhaus, *Work and Family-Allies or Enemies?* (London, Oxford University Press, 2000).

6   P. Cramer, "Defense Mechanisms in Psychology Today: Further Processes for Adaptation," *American Psychologist*, June 2000.

7   A. Stevens, "Suit Over Suicide Raises Issue: Do Associates Work Too Hard?" *Wall Street Journal*, April 15, 1994, pp. B1, B7.

8   Clinton Weiman, "A Study of Occupation Stressors and the Incidence of Disease/Risk," *Journal of Occupational Medicine*, February 1977, pp. 119-22.

9   Toby Wall, Paul Jackson, Sean Mullarkey, and Sharon K. Parker, "The Demands-Control Model of Job Strain: A More Specific Test," *Journal of Occupational & Organizational Psychology*, June 1996, pp. 153-66.

10 Einar M. DeCroon, Allard J. VanDerBeek, Roland W.B. Blonk, and Monique H.W. Frings-Dresen, "Job Stress and Psychosomatic Health Complaints among Dutch Truck Drivers: A Re-Evaluation of Karasik's Interactive Job Demand-Control Model," *Stress Medicine*, March 2000, pp. 101-107.

11 S.R. Maddi and S.C. Kobasa, *The Hardy Executive: Heath Under Stress* (Homewood, IL: Dow Jones-Irwin, 1984).

12 R.Frank, "Coping: The Psychology of What Works," in C.R. Snyder (ed.), *Coping* (New York: Oxford University Press), pp. vii-ix.

13 Pamela L. Perrewe, Gerald R. Ferris, Dwight D. Frink, and William P. Anthony," Political Skill: An Antidote for Workplace Stressors," *Academy of Management Executive*, August 2000, pp. 115-23.

14 J.A.Byrne, "Chainsaw: The Notorious Career of Al Dunlap," (New York: Harper Collins, 1999).

15 M.T. Matteson and J.M. Ivancevich, *Controlling Work Stress*, p. 48.

16 James B. Shaw, "A Conceptual Framework for Assessing Organization, Work Group and Individual Effectiveness During and After Downsizing," *Human Relations*, February 1997, pp. 109-27.

17 Martha H. Peak, "Cuttting Jobs? Watch Your Disability Expenses Grow," *Management Review*, March 1997, p.9.

18 J. French, W. Rogers and S. Cobb, "A Model of Person-Environment Fit," in G. Coelho, D. Hamburgh, and J. Adams (eds.), *Coping and Adaptation* (New York: Basic Books, 1974).

19 C.L. Park and S. Folkman, "The Role of Meaning in the Context of Stress and Coping," *General Review of Psychology*, Spring 1997, pp.115-44.

20 Josph Kline, Jr. and Lyle Sussman, "An Executive Guide to Workplace Depression," *Academy of Management Review*, August 2000, pp. 103-14.

21 Sharon Johnson, "Depression: Dragging Millons Down," *The New York Times Magazine*, October 29, 2000, pp. 39-47.

22 Ibid.

23 K.B. Wells, R. Sturm, C.D. Sherbourne, & L.S. Meredith, *Caring for Depression: A Rand Study* (Cambridge, MA: Harvard University Press, 1996)

24 M. Dewan, "Are Psychiatrists Cost-Effective? An Analysis of Integrated versus Split Treatment," *The American Journal of Psychiatry*, Summer 1999.

25 D.C. Schwebel and J. Seels, "Cardiovascular Reactivity and Neuroticism: Results from a Laboratory and Controlled Ambulatory Stress Protocol," *Journal of Personality*, January 1999, pp. 67-92.

26 C.Aldwin, *Stress, Coping, and Development* (New York: Guilford Press, 1994).

27   R.J. Burke, "Workalcoholism in Organizations: Psychological and Physical Well-Being Consequences," *Stress Medicine*, January 2000, pp. 11-16.

28   Ibid.

29   Cynthia L. Cordes and Thomas W. Dougherty, "A Review and an Integration of Research on JobBurnout," *Academy of Management Review*, October 1993, pp. 621-56.

30   Cooper, "Future Research," p. 63.

31   P.J. Rosch, "Job Stress: America's Leading Health Problem," *USA Today*, May 1991, pp. 42-45.

32   Janet Cahill, Paul Landsbergis, and Peter L. Schnall, "Reducing Occupational Stress," *Presented at Work Stress and Health Conference*, Washington D.C., September 12, 1995.

33   Joseph A. Dear, "Creating Healthier Workplace," *Presented at Work Stress and Health Conference*, Washington DC, September 14, 1995.

34   Richard S. Lazarus, *Stress and Emotion: A New Synthesis* (New York: Spring 1999).

35   Ibid.

36   Meyer Friedman and Diane Ulmer, *Treating Type A Behavior and Your Heart* (New York: Alfred A. Knopf, 1984).

37   K. Orth-Gomer and N. Schneiderman (eds.), *Behavioral Medicine Approaches to Cardiovascular Disease Prevention* (Mahwah, NJ: Erlbaum, 1996).

38   Ibid.

39   See, for example, Fran H. Norris and Krzysztof Kaniasty, "Received and Perceived Social Support in Times of Stress: A Test of the Social Support Deterioration Deterrence Model," *Journal of Personality & Social Psychology*, September 1996, pp. 498-511.

40   C.R. Snyder, "Coping: Where Are You Going?" in C.R. Snyder (ed.), *Copy* (New York: Oxford University Press, 1999), pp. 324-33.

41   See, for example, Jeffrey R. Edwards, "An Examination of Competing Versions of the Person-Environment Fit Approach to Stress," *Academy of Management Journal*, April 1996, pp. 292-339.

42   Jeffrey R. Edwards, "An Examination of Competing Versions of the Person-Environment Fit Approach to Stress," *Academy of Management Journal*, April 1996, pp. 292-330.

43   "How the Postal Service Plans to Stop 'Going Postal'," *Government Executive*, December 1996, p. 14.

44   Iris C. Mushin, Michael T. Matteson, and Edward C. Lynch, "Developing a Resident Assistance Program," *Archives of Internal Medicine*, March 1993, pp. 729-34.

45   Vijai P. Shaimi, "Take Advantiage of Employee Assistance Programs," *Mindpub*, October 2000, p. 225.

46   Ernesto A. Randolfi, "Stressed Out about Stress Management Program Evaluation?" *Presented at Outcome of Preventative Health Programs Conference* (Atlanta, GA), December 12, 1996.

47   Laura M. Litvan, "Preventative Medicine," *Nation's Business*, September 1995, pp. 32-36.

48   Kelly Dunn, "Rocke Choses Health by Promoting Prevention," *Workforce*, April 2000, pp. 82-84.

49   Discussion with DuPont Health and Wellness Services Manager on October 16, 18, and 20, 2000.

50   David Bunce, "What Factors Are Associated with the Outcome of Individual-Focused Worksite Stress Management Interventions?" *Journal of Occupational and Organizational Psychology*, March 1997, pp. 1-17.

51   Donald Meichenbaum, *Stress Inoculation Training* (New York: Pergamon Press, 1985).

52   Julia Von Onciul, "Stress at Work," *British Medical Journal*, September 1996, pp. 745-48.

53   E.E. Solberg, R. Halrorsen, and H.H. Holen, "Effect of Meditation on Immune Cells," *Stress Medicine*, April 2000, pp. 185-200.

54   Ibid.

Index

M

N